THE LETTERS OF RUPERT BROOKE

THE LETTERS OF

RUPERT BROOKE

chosen and edited

by

GEOFFREY KEYNES

Harcourt, Brace & World, Inc., New York

RECIPIENTS OF LETTERS

The page numbers will be found in the index

ILLUSTRATIONS

(Between pages 176 and 177)

(Between pages 432 and 433)

PREFACE

RUPERT BROOKE died in April 1915. Thereafter his friend Eddie (later Sir Edward) Marsh acted as his literary executor and, with a view to writing a memoir (not published until 1918), set about collecting Brooke's letters. He had no difficulty in obtaining many of these, in particular those written to the friends whom he had himself introduced to Brooke during the last two years of his life. Those to a number of other friends were inaccessible owing to war conditions. Marsh quoted extracts from those he was able to gather, yet without achieving a balanced illumination of Brooke's life—through no fault of his own. His published *Memoir* was brief and unavoidably somewhat misleading, as Brooke's mother was well aware. In her short Introduction she deplored the lack of collaboration from so many of her son's friends who had known 'the largest part of him'. Circumstances had made this impossible and so she had ultimately consented to the publication of the *Memoir*, though it was 'of necessity incomplete'. Nevertheless, this account of Brooke, prefixed to the first edition of his *Collected Poems*, met with the approval of the public who had not known him. It touched in, somewhat superficially, the more obviously attractive characteristics of the handsome youth, whose premature death and burial in romantic surroundings in the Aegean Islands had started a wave of rather sentimental posthumous adulation. The 'War Sonnets' had been immensely popular and often quoted. Winston Churchill's solemn requiem pronounced in *The Times* at the time of Brooke's death had prepared the ground for elevating him to the position of a twentieth-century Sir Philip Sidney. So 'the Rupert Brooke legend' flourished until, as the years passed, it became a fixed image, repelling some, attracting the majority, and obscuring the human being, who had lived, enjoyed and suffered through a mere eight years of adult life. The 'young Apollo, golden-haired' figure of Frances Cornford's epigram[1] provided an attractive visual image around which fancy could play to fashion an imaginary creature of shining, though rather inhuman, qualities. The resulting figure could inspire love or dislike for all the wrong reasons and could detract from a proper appreciation of his poetry. His gift was genuine, though, having been silenced prematurely, it was deprived of the opportunity to unfold its true worth.

[1] 'Youth', in *Poems by Frances Cornford*, Cambridge, 1910.

Many of Brooke's friends appeared to acquiesce in the valuation set by the 'legend'. To me, who had known him intimately from the age of fourteen until his death at twenty-seven, it seemed unjust. His reputation, that of an ineffectual aesthete and sexless minor poet, suffered, I thought, far more from the 'legend' than it could ever do from the truth. In 1931 I became by the terms of Mrs Brooke's will one of four literary trustees, whose names did not include that of Sir Edward Marsh. This exclusion from any share in the administration of the trusteeship was a cruel blow to Marsh, though it was with friendly grace that he surrendered all the letters and *memorabilia* that he had accumulated. As time passed it appeared that I was the only trustee likely to take any active steps towards the protection of Brooke's reputation, and I resolved to try to form a more credible public image by the collection and printing of a considerable body of his letters. These would surely fill in the details of a more human figure than had come through from the abnormal conditions of the First World War. Marsh, acting as literary executor up to 1931, had gone far towards making the collection representative and during the next twenty years I had managed to fill many gaps. It was soon apparent that few people who had ever received letters from Brooke had destroyed them. They were sufficiently individual and lively to preserve in their pages much of the writer's personality. Nearly all of those owners who were still alive were willing to let them be printed, and the representatives of others no longer alive did not put any obstacle in my way.

By 1955 I had made what seemed to me a satisfying selection—for there were far more letters than could ever be printed *in extenso*. Brooke was not a major poet, a 'great' letter writer, or a mature personality revealing himself through his letters after a life of achievement and renown. He was nevertheless a young man of exceptional personal attractions, informed by an intellect of rare quality, and possessing for his friends perceptive sensibilities such as they would not willingly allow to be extinguished for ever either by silence or through a legend imposed by circumstances which no longer obtained. A contract for publication by Messrs Faber and Faber was accordingly signed and the letters were set up in galley proofs by the Cambridge University Press. My co-trustees had given me such letters as they possessed and had agreed that they should be printed. I therefore thought it unnecessary to burden them with reading of typescripts. I was frankly astounded when reading the proofs led to disagreement as to their suitability for publication, the opinion being expressed that the letters seriously misrepresented their writer. No agreement could be reached and so I reluctantly abandoned the project. The publishers were mystified, being like myself unable to understand how so large a body of letters written to a variety of friends could seriously misrepresent the author. They acquiesced, however, in allowing me to withdraw in view of my difficult situation, though they believed that publication must one day be possible and, in spite of the expense, kept the type standing. The chief dissentient trustee died a few months later. After much discussion it was agreed by the remaining trustees that Christopher Hassall should be invited to write a full-scale biography of Brooke, with use of the printed letters and permission to quote such passages as he thought would illuminate the narrative. Hassall was already familiar with the subject through being Sir Edward Marsh's literary executor. He completed his task in April 1963, but unfortunately died soon after and saw no part of his book in print. It fell to me to see his book through the press and it was published in April 1964.

Thus twelve years have passed since the original project to publish the letters was abandoned. I have seen no reason to alter my opinion that Brooke's reputation would be enhanced rather than harmed by their publication and my resolution has been fortified by the wish expressed by reviewers and by many readers of the *Life* to be allowed to read a selection of the letters in their original form. The episode has taught me that a man's whole character is not always apparent even to his nearest friends. An image may be formed early in a friendship which is not changed, either because loyalty will not allow it, or because few people reveal every facet of their personalities to any single friend. Brooke's personality was not a simple one, and isolated letters may easily convey a false impression because of his tendency to write in a variety of poses according to whatever assumed character he thought would amuse each correspondent. He had a precocious intellect, as he was well aware, and would sometimes assume, even as a schoolboy, an attitude of elder and instructor, as in some of his letters to his cousin, Erica Cotterill, and, with every justification, occasionally to myself. He did indeed make serious attempts to inculcate in those of us who developed more slowly, appreciation of all poetry and art deemed worthy of our adolescent attention. Another favourite pose during his earlier years was that of pessimist and decadent, but this could be overdone and some of the attitudinizing has been eliminated. To his other school friend, Hugh Russell-Smith, he chose to write in a vein of light-hearted nonsense and facetiousness. These private jokes have less value for outsiders fifty years later and much of this correspondence has been omitted.

In spite of his precocity Brooke, as a schoolboy at Rugby, did not at first shine as an intellectual prodigy. He was recognized as clever, but never showed any trace of priggishness, yet to me he appeared quite different from any other boy in our house. He possessed a quality of understanding friendliness and sympathy to which I was responsive, though without fully realizing at the moment the exceptional quality of the personality that lay behind it. Partly it was disguised by the high spirits and sense of fun that coloured so much of our schoolboy exchanges. During his years at Cambridge Brooke acquired a magnetic quality felt by everyone who came into contact with him, a quality so difficult to communicate to those coming after. He took himself more seriously than before as a poet, though few of his friends would have put this faculty first as a claim to notice. It was rather his general intellectual grasp coupled with unusual aesthetic sensibilities that compelled our admiration. His conscience was guiding him to become a Fabian socialist and to feel contempt for luxury and conventional comforts. There was a strong puritan strain in his character and this, blended with an impulse to break out of his Victorian middle-class bondage, produced an attractive originality without spoiling his essential goodness. Sometimes this resulted in a degree of ribaldry and coarseness in his letters not really typical of him—another feature tending to suggest misrepresentation.

Usually Brooke was the gayest and most entertaining companion imaginable, but he was no egoist and never tried to force his personality on to others. With his male friends he combined much delightful nonsense with a serious desire to discuss the affairs of the world and to put them to rights. With young women he could achieve an equally easy companionship, though inevitably emotional entanglements would sometimes arise. His rather slow achievement of a completely adult mentality made these abnormally agonizing, his sensitivity and the underlying puritanism already mentioned contributing to his difficulties. Not many of his friends realized, when he was about twenty-five, how seriously emotional strain had affected his mental and physical balance. This led to an outpouring of letters which would be tedious if too many appeared in print. Enough are included to set the scene. After this episode Brooke decided to try to recover his normal balance by spending a long period abroad, and so the years 1913–14 saw him growing in mental stature with the help of new experiences in North America and the South Seas. These furnished material for the *Letters from America*, published in *The Westminster Gazette* 1913–14 and in 1916 as a book, thus providing letters written in a more finished literary style than were those to his friends. When he returned to London in June 1914 he was toughened in spirit, if not in body, without any loss of the extraordinary attraction exercised by his physical presence and his mental gifts. In addition there still remained much of the youthful idealist, and this combined with the utter ignorance, from which we all suffered, of what war really meant, tricked him into accepting it with the lyrical enthusiasm of the War Sonnets composed in the last months of 1914. It was the mood of the moment and it would have turned into disillusionment and revulsion had he lived.

When Brooke died it was not primarily the poet that his friends mourned. It was rather the sense that an outstanding personality and intellect had been extinguished. His poetic faculties might have increased in power or perhaps they would have waned with the growth of more critical and scholarly perceptions. His creativeness might have taken quite other turns, but we believed he would have left his mark in some unexpected way on the life of England. Nevertheless Brooke's poetry has been so widely and consistently read until the present time that it has reached the status of a national heritage, even though the artificially segregated period of 'Georgian poetry' is now out of favour with the critics. It is therefore likely to be for some little time of real interest to a great many present and future readers, who will want to know something of the background of the writer. Every poet's work can be better understood, apart from purely critical and literary 'evaluation', if his circumstances in time and space can be appreciated. There can surely be no more direct way of finding this context than by reading the poet's letters written in a variety of moods to a number of friends, some deliberately and self-consciously posed, others unself-consciously poured out in a state of enthusiasm, excitement, depression, or emotional conflict. All these states of mind will be found in this selection of Brooke's letters, but judgement must be based on general impression rather than on isolated passages. His love affairs sometimes led to much unhappiness, this being reflected in artless letters, which, by their very artlessness, show how false the 'legend' was. Brooke was far from perfect, but the human imperfections, the goodness, the weaknesses and the strength composing the whole man make a more interesting and credible personality than the lay figure created by the myth.

In a letter written not long before his death he himself expressed the wish that the truth about his life should be made known if it were thought to be of interest. It is this wish that I have tried to carry into effect. The chosen letters have been divided into sections determined, after the first, by the year in which they were written. The main facts of Brooke's life have been given in the brief notes prefixed to each section.

*   *   *

Portions of letters omitted are indicated by three asterisks. These elisions have usually been made because the material was of small interest at the present time or in order to omit repetitions. Occasionally a name has been suppressed to avoid giving offence. Brooke's letters were not written as literary compositions and have not been submitted to scholarly editing such as a complete or definitive edition might have demanded. On this principle his occasional lapses in spelling or other minor mistakes have been silently corrected. He so frequently omitted to date his letters that many guesses have had to be made in fixing the sequence, and some errors may have resulted. The reader will have no difficulty in appreciating where these uncertainties occur.

ACKNOWLEDGEMENTS

My debt to the late Sir Edward Marsh for his preliminary work on the letters has already been recorded. Much further work of sorting, cataloguing and dating them was done after 1945 by Robin Skelton, now Professor in the English Faculty at the University of Victoria, B.C. More recently I have profited by the advice and help of my co-trustee, Jon Stallworthy. Letters have been withheld by Dr Noel Olivier Richards and by one or two others of Brooke's friends for personal reasons. I am grateful to all the other owners who have lent them for publication or have deposited them in the custody of the trustees. All of the second category will ultimately be added to the Rupert Brooke archive already housed in the library of King's College, Cambridge. I am indebted to the Lady Pansy Lamb for permission to reproduce the drawing of Katharine Cox by Henry Lamb, and to Messrs. Heinemann for allowing me to use the drawing of Edward Marsh published in his book, *A Number of People*, 1939. The remainder of the illustrations have been made from prints in the custody of the trustees.

GEOFFREY KEYNES

1967

BIOGRAPHICAL PREFACE 1887–1905

RUPERT CHAWNER BROOKE was born at Rugby on 3 August 1887, the second of three sons of William Parker Brooke and his wife, Mary Ruth Cotterill. W. P. Brooke, known as 'Tooler Brooke' to the boys of Rugby School, was then a form master in the school and in 1892 became housemaster of School Field, the only Rugby house besides the School House which abuts on the Close. The three Brooke boys, Dick, Rupert and Alfred, were all sent to a neighbouring preparatory school at Hillbrow, and Rupert entered his father's House at Rugby soon after his fourteenth birthday in September 1901 during the Headmastership of the Rev. H. A. James, known to the school as 'the Bodger'. I was a few months older than Rupert and entered the school at the same time, though my first term was spent in a smaller House (Dewar's), so that I did not make his acquaintance until I entered School Field in January 1902. We soon became friends, both of us being especially attached to a third boy, Hugh Russell-Smith, whose younger brother, Denham, also came to School Field two years later. Many of Brooke's early letters were addressed to Russell-Smith and myself, though the earliest letter that has survived was written to a Hillbrow friend, Owen (now Sir Owen) O'Malley, afterwards Ambassador to Hungary and other countries. As will be seen, Russell-Smith came up to Cambridge in the same term as ourselves, but lost his life, as did so many of our generation, in the First World War. Denham Russell-Smith also died soon after leaving Rugby.

Others of Brooke's early letters were written to his first cousin, Erica Cotterill, daughter of Mrs Brooke's brother, C. C. Cotterill, and to an older friend, St John Welles Lucas Lucas. Rugby town had given Brooke two friends much older than himself with literary interests, Lucas and Arthur Eckersley. Lucas, though born in Rugby, was schooled at Haileybury and went up to University College, Oxford, in 1896. He was afterwards ostensibly a barrister practising in London, but his chief interests lay in poetry and contemporary literature, especially of the 'decadent' kind. He was author of numerous novels and volumes of poetry from 1903 to 1922, published anonymously a facetious work, *Bluff's Guide to the Bar*, and edited the Oxford Books of French and Italian Verse. He died in 1934. Eckersley was a playwright and a contributor to *Punch* and other magazines, and lived in Rugby until his death.

These two men naturally attracted Brooke as older practitioners of the art of writing, to which by 1904 he was consciously directing his attention, when the main series of his surviving letters begins. To Lucas in particular he entrusted many of his early poems, and he sought to entertain both of them by adopting the pose of a disillusioned decadent belonging to their own youth of ten or fifteen years before. Something of the same pose entered into his letters to Erica Cotterill and to myself, and he and I fostered an adolescent taste for the drawings of Aubrey Beardsley and the poetry of Wilde and Dowson.

Little record remains of Brooke's life before he entered Rugby School. At the beginning of 1902 he was a lively, good-looking boy with cropped fair hair, who was always popular with his fellows, for he soon lived down the slight suspicion with which he was bound at first to be regarded through his being the housemaster's son. He was a voracious reader of English poetry, but gave himself no airs and entered wholeheartedly into all the noisy fun which delights schoolboys of fifteen and sixteen. Though often succumbing to minor complaints, he was muscular, and could excel at any game to which he chose to give his mind, getting his School Colours for both football and cricket. He also took the School Cadet Corps seriously enough to become a cadet officer in his last year at school.

Brooke's first major effort at writing poetry was in 1904 when he entered for the school poetry prize, gaining a *proxime accessit* for a poem on *The Pyramids*. He was more successful in the next year when he was awarded the prize for a long poem on *The Bastille*, part of which he recited in New Big School on Speech Day. Meanwhile he was contributing facetious doggerel and prose pieces to school magazines, with an occasional more serious poem. In December 1905 we three, Brooke, Russell-Smith and myself, came up to Cambridge to sit for University scholarships. Brooke was awarded a classical scholarship at King's, Russell-Smith another at St John's, and I obtained an exhibition for natural science at Pembroke.

In the October term of 1905 Brooke became Head of the House at School Field. Before this he had grown his hair to an unseemly length—as a poet it was his duty to do so—but his athletic prowess together with his lively and intelligent mind so dazzled his schoolfellows that they forgave his minor eccentricities and regarded him with affectionate amusement.

During the school holidays Brooke often left Rugby with his family and sometimes stayed abroad longer for the sake of his

health, as when he spent some weeks in Italy at the beginning of
1905. He frequently enlarged in his letters on the horrors of family
life, though this was only one of his many poses. He was in fact
devoted to his family, and regarded his mother in particular with
much affection and respect. She was a person of strong character,
though without much sense of humour, and she watched over
Rupert's moral and physical welfare with an affectionate, but
critical eye. She could not really approve of her son's friendship
with people whom she regarded as dilettanti *littérateurs* such as
St John Lucas, and Rupert did not confide to her his more intimate
thoughts. Relatively few of his letters to her have been included
here, as they are not usually of much interest.

To OWEN O'MALLEY   *School Field, Rugby*
                                                     [*1901*]

From Ye Oyster to Ye Bug Greeting

Child,

Wherefore sendest thou strange manuscripts adorned with divers devices which bring back to the mind thoughts of a time which is past? Also, the manner in which thou inscribest the word 'exeat' (which thou hast spelt exiat, O friend) sheweth clearly that thou art of one race with the strange people who inhabit the country (known to some as 'the Isle of Emerald hue') across the sea: for this people have many strange habits, such as flourishing shillelaghs and other divers things. But I have somewhat whereof I would tell thee. On the 9th day of May the Sports for Athletes were held, and I did win many heats, and when I had finished running 3600 inches (in a heat) a boy by name B. Foote was about 70 inches behind. And on the next day I was ill and unable to compete wherefore my temper was exceeding warm. And the aforesaid Foote did win the 3600 inches Final amidst divers other things in the which perchance I might have gained honour and prizes; wherefore my temper's temperature did increase. And I lay on my bed many days—more or less—and finally I was unable to compete in the Examination of Scholars, wherein one Russell[1] was successful. Wherefore an irritability of marvellous size possessed me—and still possesses me. Also, I have partaken of but 4 games of cricket this century—woe is me.

Forgive my letter being strange in manner. The reason is that much trouble hath unhinged my brain; wherein I resemble Hamlet. And if you gaze closely on my portrait which I have sent you, you will see a wild look in my eyes; denoting insanity.

                                                       Farewell

To AN AUNT   *School Field, Rugby*
                                     Sunday, 27 December 1903

My dear Aunt,

Thank you very much for the 'Lowell' which you sent me. I am getting quite a large library now.

We have quite a large party here for Christmas, & on Thursday

---

[1] A. L. N. Russell, who entered Whitelaw's house at Rugby with a scholarship; afterwards an architect.

& Saturday they, Dick & Harry Hoare, have been playing hockey with a friend of theirs from London. I am very doleful at present because I am not allowed to play hockey on account of a finger which I had dislocated at football last term. 'Podge'[1] has been playing a good deal and is turning out quite a good hockey player. I am going to have quite a gay time this week—progressive whist, fancy dress-balls etc.for 4 nights running! I am going to the Fancy Dress Ball as Sir Walter Raleigh, & a most gorgeous yellow & purple dress has been procured for me, the envy of the whole house, especially 'Podge'.

We have found only one draw back to Christmas, & that is that Boots Library is closed for three days, & therefore we have to subsist for three whole days with only 6 books to read—or rather 5 because one of them is chosen by Mother and therefore not worth reading! Dick, Podge & I finished these 5 books on Saturday & for a day & a half have had nothing to read.

Thanking you again for your present,

I remain,

Your affectionate nephew

RUPERT C. BROOKE

[*Rugby*]
[*May 1904*]

My dear Erica,

Excuse the paper I am using. Ostensibly & to the eagle eye of Mr Wynne-Willson[2] I am preparing Thucydides for an exam., but I know it quite well enough, and therefore I employ my time more profitably. (N.B. Compliment.) But breathe not a word of it, lest the tale comes to ears of the Powers, and evil falls upon me. I am delighted to hear about the Italian gentleman—a most romantic and short-story-esque episode. I pray you, let me know the latest developments; a duel of course, and, I suppose, suicide. Or hasn't that arrived yet? Some day, I hope, you will publish a volume 'Letters I have received', commencing with the aforesaid Roman bravo's polyglot attempt. I might contribute a few—for a consideration. (But then, of course, mine would all be serious, like this.) It's no use asking *me* about that poem,[3] I have nothing to do

[1] His younger brother, Alfred.
[2] Form master of the Lower Bench of the VIth, afterwards headmaster of Haileybury.
[3] *The Pyramids*, the MS. of which is now in the Temple Library at Rugby.

with it. Mother took it from me & stowed it away in the family archives, & I have no control over it. If you don't see it first you must clamour for it on your next visit to Rugby. As a matter of fact *I*'ve disowned it long ago. It was a failure, an irredeemable & gigantic failure—nay more, it was a tragedy. I will explain. As you know, Confucius & many after him have divided tragedies into two classes, when anything intended to be humorous is taken seriously, & when a would-be serious thing is received as witty. My tragedy belongs to the first & more fatal class. I perpetrated a screaming joke. I entered for the Prize Poem a parody on William Watson[1] in his less inspired moments, an ultra-classical, ultra-academic, ultra-frigid caricature; and behold! it fell into the hands of the Philistines, & they thought it was meant serious, & they dug latent & unexpected excellencies out of it, & viewed it on every side, & found it good, & awarded it second prize. Such is always my fate. When I say what I mean, people tell me 'O *Rupert*, what delightful nonsense you talk!' & when I venture on the humorous, I am taken seriously & very promptly & thoroughly squashed for 'saying such strange things'. In fact I often remind myself of the hero of Miss Florence Montgomery's delightful book 'Misunderstood'—if you haven't read it, do; it is Elevating, Instructive, & generally amusing, I wept oceans of salt tears over it. He was *never* valued at his true worth by *anybody*. Everyone looked on him as a Common Boy, while in reality he was a poorly-disguised angel. Nor does the likeness end here. He also had washy blue eyes, tow-coloured hair, a habit of doing the wrong thing unintentionally, and a propensity for dying young. The Resemblance however cannot be pushed further. He expired from compound pneumonia & a broken leg: I am slowly dying of simple lassitude & a broken heart.

In accordance with the common prejudice for news in letters, I may inform you that the family are uniformly well, that the School XI is nearly as bad as it pretends to be, & that the weather is alternately absurd & unspeakable. To return to higher things, I have fulfilled one of the ambitions of my life; I have met a real live poet,[2] who has presented me with a copy of one of his books signed with his own hand. Of course, like all poets worth counting nowadays, he is Celtic & very melancholy. Last but not least he knows George Meredith quite intimately! A most enchanting man. And—quite incidentally—his poems are often readable.

There is nothing else worth the writing for me to tell you.

[1] Sir William Watson, 1858–1935.   [2] St John Lucas.

Therefore I will bring these wild & whirling words to an end. If ever I think of anything sensible to tell you I will write, but till that long distant day, farewell.   Yours ever

RUPERT C. BROOKE

To ST JOHN LUCAS   *Villa Molfino, Rapallo*
                                                  nr Genoa
                                  Saturday, 4 February 1905

Dear St John,

Is that better? I am sorry for the 'blatant diminutive'. It slipped off my pen, because (I don't know if you are aware of it) in that part of the 'great centre of unintellectuality' called Rugby you are still spoken of as Jack Lucas—I hope you don't object to being reminded of it—so you must attribute my slip to the Rugby atmosphere. I have a kind of circular return ticket which limits me to 60 days in Italy and 15 more in France; so that I shall stay in Italy till March 20 (possibly, by an extension, a week longer) and cannot be in France after April 4th. I fear this will be too early for you; but if not your suggestion would delight me vastly. I have a great desire to see Paris, and I am far too ignorant to do so without some very patient and omniscient person—such as I conceive you to be—to drag me round. I should only burden you a couple of days and I should learn many things. I might even find out something about the Bastille: for I have come away without looking it up; and my knowledge of it is a little vague at present. I have only a suspicion that it was a prison, and fell in the French Revolution: and there is no English Encyclo-pedia in Rapallo. However facts don't really matter, I suppose.

I have been very lazy since I've come here, too lazy to go any-where or see anything. I have confined myself to sitting in the garden and watching the sunset. Genoa is 18 miles away and so we rarely go there. After a little however I hope to go to some of the places you mention. I shall probably stay for the first fortnight in March with some cousins in Florence. Especially I wish to see Siena because Maurice Hewlett I think describes it as 'swooning like a great tiger-moth on the rock:' which makes me rather curious. Apropos of that gentleman I have been spending the intervals between meals and sunsets lately in reading his 'Queen's Quair' which is rather pleasing although I bark my shins about once a page on some adjectives or verbs of his. Hitherto I have been carrying out a beautiful plan. I promised my family to let them hear from me frequently; so every other day I send off a picture postcard of Rapallo with my initials in the corner and a remark to the effect that the weather is fine; which is all there is room for. Lately however they have struck and demanded (of course!) my 'impressions of Italy'. I find it a vast trouble to be impressed to order; but a local guide-book has proved invaluable. One or two things however I *have* discovered which interested me. E.g. When a very ugly or deformed baby is born to an Italian, the proper exclamation is 'O dear, how terribly English he is!' Much as we might say 'Its just like a little Jap!' Even thus one gathers experience.

I don't remember the 'cry of "Dijon" at two o' the morning' you refer to. It may have come during the 10 minutes' sleep I got that night; more probably it was drowned by the snoring of a Frenchman in the bunk above me, who snored all night a Gallic snore, falsetto, intermittent, and wildly exasperating. The same villain had a slimy hatred of fresh air; and thereby I got my revenge. For I opened the window by stealth in the chill early hours of the morning, when it was snowing, and froze him out. Almost the only writing I have done here has been for my deserted 'Phoenix'.[1] I have spent many hours sitting pen in hand *trying* to be very, very, funny in a high satirical line, scourging School follies with a stinging lash! But the result is not hopeful.

Your last request caused me much deep thought and ended in the production and restudy of a green note-book which I treasure. It was a rash demand, as made to one avid for criticism and help. You know not how nearly it brought on you a parcel of MSS. many feet square and weighing innumerable ounces. (I am talking—if you have forgotten what you wrote—about your mandate 'Send some golden words from Italy—and some verse!') You have had some four pages of words, gilt to the best of my power. Follows the other half which you have brought on yourself. I intend the first two for the Phoenix if my fellow Editor submits! But the third I daren't show him for fear of what he might say.

But I should like a full-grown live critic's opinion of where they are worst.

Hence these,[2] with all proper apologies.

[1] A Rugby School magazine.
[2] The three poems following were all printed in *The Poetical Works*, ed. Keynes, 1946.

The Path of Dreams

Go, heart, and pluck beside the Path of Dreams,
Where moans the wind along the shadowy streams,
  Sad garlands wreathed of the red mournful Roses
  And Lilies o' moonbeams.

Strange blossoms faint upon that odorous air,
Vision, and wistful Memory; and there
  Love twofold with the purple bloom of Triumph
  And the wan leaf of Despair.

Go, heart; go quickly; pluck and weave thereof
Dim garlands, scattering pallid dew above,
  And far across the sighing tides of darkness
  Lay them beside my Love.

The Return

Long had I dwelt in dreams and loneliness
 Until thy sad voice sighed through the dusk to me,
 Hinting of joy, of better things to be,
Laughter and light beyond my dim distress.
Then I arose. Amid the fevered press
 Of hot-eyed men, across the desolate sea,
 Hoping a dreamer's hope I sought for thee.
Wisdom at last I found, and weariness.

Nay, I was foolish, weak: I shall return
 Back to the Night and Silence that I love,
 Back to my dreams. It may be even yet
The old fires on the old grey altars burn,
 The old gods throng their shadowy haunted grove,
 Where I can sleep, and rest me, and—forget.

'Afterwards'

O brother, dost thou know what this thing means, to dread
 The cold inevitable dawn, the sickly light,
 The hours' slow passage marked by tolling bells, that smite,[1]
Madness and swift blind pangs within the aching head?

[1] Altered in *Poems*, 1911, to read:
  The hours long passing, and the bells that toll and smite.

Knowst thou this too, brother, when the day is fled
   How to the sleepless eyes the strange fears of the Night
Come mocking, and the bitter thoughts of old delight
Mix with the unforgiving faces of the Dead?

Ah, if thou know'st this sorrow, thou art even as I;
   As one who has long outlived his joy, and would forget;
   Who nurses in his festered soul a slave's dull hate
For this interminable Hell of Life; and yet
   Shrinketh from ending it, in fear of what may wait
Behind the pitiless Silence of Eternity.

Yours ever

RUPERT C. BROOKE

To ERICA COTTERILL   *Villa Molfino, Rapallo*

[*February 1905*]

Dear Erica,

*   *   *

How is London getting on? I hope there is a Spring in England this year. I never noticed the Spring before, until I came to a place where there wasn't any.

*   *   *

Have you ever lived in a house with a mad butler? We are doing so now. He is a butler-cook really, but we call him the Butler....I will give you an example. A lamp leaked. A plate was put to catch the paraffin, & then laid aside to be cleaned. Next day dear old Butler forgets all about it & puts the cake for tea on this plate. The cake of course soaks up all the paraffin. Mrs G. took a large mouthful of the cake. Her face was amusing. This was two days ago & she still swears that she can taste paraffin in everything she eats....We have a gardener, Italian of the Italian. If he sees a plant looking unwell, he folds his arms, looks picturesque if possible, & gazes at it for an hour. Then he goes home to déjeuner....Buona sera.

RUPERT C. BROOKE

To ST JOHN LUCAS   *Villa Molfino, Rapallo*
                                        [*January or February 1905*]

Dear St John,

Many thanks for the much-needed criticism and the encouragement. By a coincidence your letter came by the same post as a number of the Spectator which contained one of your 'rustic ballads'—
that of the 'Ridgeway'. This helped to fill me with an unwonted
desire for walking; insomuch that yesterday I went up and down the
highest of the innumerable hills round here; and am to-day in consequence stiff and somnolent. Nevertheless I have enough mental
energy to discuss a point or two in connexion with your letter. Of
course I recognize the truth of most of your criticism; but as 'there
are nine and sixty ways. . .' I should like to attempt an apologia for
the one I have chosen. As to the first sonnet on the whole—though
a little doubtful—I think a 'sad voice' could 'hint of joy', and 'better
things to be'; at least in this case. Also I cannot find a substitute,
except perhaps 'low'; which would preserve most of my meaning;
yet seems to spoil the sound in some inexplicable way. However
I still waver on that point. In the second sonnet I think you have
mistaken my intent. Regarding the normal line of the usual sonnet
as made of 5 iambi, I have tried to build a sonnet on a line of 6 iambi,
adding in short $\cup$ – to the ordinary line, not $\cup$ $\cup$. But of course as
the line is longer, the average of the syllables has to be rather lighter
than in a decasyllabic line, in order to make the thing fairly readable.
In the second place they aren't my own rules that I substitute.
I know nothing about French poetry, but I fancied that this form is
fairly common therein: but the actual idea of using it was suggested
by a delightful sonnet, 'To one in Bedlam', by the late Ernest
Dowson, built on the same plan, apparently. I expect you know it:
I saw it quoted in A. Symon's 'Studies in Prose and Verse'. I certainly think that it is a complete justification of the method!

Anyhow because the first man had a decasyllabic bent, and all
others have followed him without thinking, I don't see that *that*
constitutes a law. It is merely a precedent. And precedents are only
made for fools and old men, I take it. The ear, I suppose, is the only
judge of what is right and wrong; and I think that a dodecasyllabic-
lined sonnet can give sound effects that a decasyllabic ditto can't. At
least I meant by the longer line to give a feeling of weariness (don't
interpret this in the wrong sense!) and dullness which I could not
reach with the ordinary line.

I admit that one could not write Greek *hexameters* with an additional spondee (I got *200* lines for doing so once in Latin hexameters!); but I see no reason why Greek *heptameters* should not be a *legitimate* and quite melodious form of poetry.

These were my ideas, rather presumptuous I fear; for I really have very vague notions about technique. I generally trust to luck and put down anything that sounds all right. But the Italian winds though they may whisper many beautiful ideas in my ear, will not, I fear, teach me much about the structure of a sonnet. My faith in the 'impulse from a vernal wood' (forgive me if I have quoted wrong)[1] does not extend to that.

I am labouring to reduce the overheavy onomatopeia in the third line.

For the rest I bow in repeated gratitude.

I have a large amount of leisure; but I too find it difficult to write here. I have only evolved about 40 lines of verse and as much of prose. As a matter of fact I can always write better when I am very busy. More than half of all I have written has been in form, jerkily, in the intervals of other languages.

Now I am out here I am finding what a mistake I made in omitting to read beforehand some author like Symonds. In a public school we are not allowed to know anything about Italy after Hadrian at the latest—generally after J. Caesar: and anyhow we are told nothing more interesting than dates. Hence I feel equally and abysmally ignorant about both the history and art of Italy.

In more interesting matters—has O. Wilde's 'De Profundis' yet appeared? I fancy it was announced for the spring and I am rather eager to hear about it.

How is your evening cultivation of the 'asparagus bed' you spoke of progressing? Encouraged by your demand, I offer three more victims. I don't think you would appreciate receiving 'the whole green note book'. Not that it's very full; but I frequently and seriously consider tearing about 8 pages out and burning the rest. For it is by now becoming outgrown. Someday soon I shall demolish it.

However, here are three, the first a year and a half old, and the other two not quite a week and a half—all, naturally I suppose something in the nature of experiments. About the second I alternate, sometimes thinking it passable (if a little tame), sometimes thinking it mere rot. I should like to be fixed one way or the other.

---

[1] 'one impulse from a vernal wood', from Wordsworth's 'The Tables Turned'.

The first and the third are quite hopelessly contradictory ideas. But that doesn't matter, does it?

I find it difficult—in prose—to express any thanks for your letter—except the postscript.

I fear I cannot get to Venice or Verona as things are at present.

Yours ever

RUPERT C. BROOKE

I have tried to make the verses more legible than the letter.[1]

I

It is Well

Nay, love, I weep not, but laugh o'er my dead,
My dreams long perish'd; though I forfeited,
To save thee sorrow, joy unutterable—
I would not have it otherwise; 'twas well.

Well is it that I bear thy load of sin,
And fall defeated so *thou* mayest win;
And cast my heart before thee in the mire
To help thee upward to *thy* heart's desire.

And, when our Death dawns pale, and we must go,
Though infinite space may part us, *this* I know;
If, looking upward through the bars of Hell,
I see *that* face in Heaven, it will be well.

II

In January

What shall I tell thee of?
Of the new sad memories one name can move?
Of the Heaven that Love brings? or of the Hell
That followeth such Love?
Of these shall I tell?

I have not forgotten yet
The mist that shrouded all things, cold and wet;
The dripping bough; the sad smell of the rotten
Leaves. How should I forget?
—Hast *thou* forgotten?

---

[1] Of the three poems following the first two were printed in the *Poetical Works*, ed. Keynes, 1946.

Dost thou remember now
How our eyes met; and all things changed; and how
A glorious light thrilled all that dim December;
And a bird sang on the bough?
Dost thou remember?

III

(Nameless at present)[1]

Lo! in the end the pure clean-hearted innocent throng
Will climb the spacious star-lit road and enter Heaven;
And I shall watch far off and desolate there, among
Those that have dared the sins that cannot be forgiven.

With bitter hearts and silent lips we shall line the way,
Foul with the mire we chose and hopeless to forget,
Envying them who never learnt to hate the Day,
Nor knew the strange wrong loves we knew, nor found regret.

Yet shall I stand, defiant, glorying in my sin,
Though conquered, still unconquerable;—only this,
What if my sullen gaze should see one entering in,
—One with the sorrowful lips I once had died to kiss,

One with the fluttering eyelids and grey wistful eyes
The long chin dying in the neck's pale loveliness,
The low voice heavy with a thousand nameless sighs,
And delicate pleading mouth that droops in weariness?

Ah! my strong pride, as once my heart, will break and die,
Hungrily I shall watch till that sad face be gone
Then turn me, knowing at last my black foul misery,
And face the dreary night, remembering, alone.

R. C. B.

To GEOFFREY KEYNES   *Villa Molfino, Rapallo*
[February 1905]

*   *   *

I liked that last touch—the postscript—very fine and pathetic.... I
scarcely knew whether to laugh or weep. In the event I became
a little hysterical. Your story of Boxer[2] & the Bodger is very

---

[1] 'In the end.'   [2] W. H. G. Saunt of School Field.

pleasing, save that a faint thought entered my mind that it must have been exaggerated ere it reached me. For your last question—No, you won't see me back ere the end of the term—as far as I know. Endeavour to bear up. Ere May comes I shall probably be dead and mouldering. The verdict no doubt will be 'corfragium'. . . .

I am thinking out a really humorous method of dying. One might do it quite wittily. It is an opportunity not to be lost. News takes two days to reach England from Rapallo: so you will probably hear of my decease on April 3rd. You express a very polite (and probably entirely fictitious) desire to hear what I am doing and undergoing. I don't know why. It probably won't interest you in the least. However it *can't* interest you less than it interests me so I will weary you by the account of what I do this afternoon, as an example. You can build up the other 59 days of my visit from this. I hope you find it very exciting. (It is now 6 p.m.)

(Roughly) 1–2. Lunch.

          2–3. Lie down on a sofa & read.

          3–4. Walk up & down garden trying to compose tail end of sonnet.

          4–4.30. Tea.

          4.30–5.30. Walk up & down garden throwing lemons at the cats and. . .thinking. . . .

          5.30–6.30. . . .Letters.

And so on. About 9 I retire to bed with the cheerful prospect of another happy, happy day when I wake. Half the night perhaps I lie awake thinking. . .all the time I am profoundly bored. At intervals they drag me up to Genoa & round a picture-gallery; which is wasted on me. I say, 'How beautiful!' at every fourth picture, and yawn.

I have been here 3½ weeks: and shall stay 5 more.

Your wide erudition has no doubt made you acquainted with R. Browning's

          'It's Oh to be in England

          Now the Spring is here

          And whoever. . .' etc.

I have probably quoted it very wrong & spoilt it. But it approximately expresses my opinions. If you don't know it, *read* it. It's worth it. Quite short.

I fear I am a little unreasonable however. . .

Here there is no spring. Only the hot sun grows hotter, and the long day longer. I am sodden with that stickiest of sentiments, self-pity: forgive my wearisome drivelling.

*   *   *

Yours scientifically
RUPERT C. BROOKE

To ST JOHN LUCAS   *3 Via Bonifazio Lupi, Firenze*
Friday, 10 February 1904
[mistake for 1905]

Dear St John,

*   *   *

While I am in London I intend to break in upon your 'disgustful labours' and thank you, in speech for the 'De Profundis'. So beware! I cannot fix a date, but I shall be rushing about to Whistler Exhibitions and such like, and so if I try often enough I shall probably find you in. I am counting on 'De Profundis' as going far to alleviate the nerve-racking horrors of a railway journey by day and night. But—I fear I have not the self-restraint to keep myself from reading it for 5 days, until Thursday. I shall probably have finished it at least once before then. I have seen three or four reviews of it. One, very irritating and patronizing in the 'Times'; and another, quite sympathetic, it seemed to me, in the Saturday Review. However I shall be in more of a position to discuss it when I have read it. Here I am enjoying myself more than I thought I should. I have been spending much time in the galleries, trying to cultivate the Artistic Eye. But hitherto I have failed signally. I have achieved nothing except a certain admiration for Botticelli; and even that I am bitterly disappointed to find fashionable.

On Tuesday night we went out into the streets to watch the Carnival rejoicings. It was a peculiar sight full of colour and noise, and very Italian. In the distance the scene had a certain fantastic charm; but when one saw the figures at close quarters they became merely vulgar; much like a circus clown. The Piazza del Duomo was full of rather pathetic incongruity. Giotto's Tower swung upward grimly into the darkness, the summit invisible, the base surrounded by coloured lights and gay quick-moving figures and clouds of confetti. Florence attracts me rather; it has an indefinable quiet sadness;

I like it best in the late afternoon. But I shall be glad to get home. I am looking forward—though I fear this is profoundly Philistine— to leaving Italy as though I were being freed from prison. A nice prison, of course, almost equal to the best American ones—yet a prison. However there are better moments. I am filled with a cruel desire to torture you by describing at length an expedition we made yesterday to Fiesole. How we had tea on the hillside and squabbled over Browning and others. How the sun began to set across the plain and beyond Florence; and the world was very quiet; and we stopped talking and watched: And how the Arno in the distance was a writhing dragon of molten gold, and the sky the most wistful of pale greens.

*   *   *

Yours ever
RUPERT C. BROOKE

To GEOFFREY KEYNES   *Villa Molfino, Rapallo*
                             Sunday night
                             12 March 1905

My returned Shade, my revenant spook, O Traveller come back from 'the bourn' of 'that indiscovered country', O shadowy friend! Dost howl around the house o' nights, or clank weird chains adown the dusty corridors, or moan an unearthly 'Boo!' to some belated fag? Tell me I prithee why hast thou left Lethe stream to revisit the moil of human things? Nevertheless your spectral fingers still can wield an unsubstantial pen with the old skill. Witness your letter lately with gratitude received. However these things may be, I can only quote two lines from 'The Shropshire Lad' you have often heard upon my lips—a little altered this time.

> 'So dead or living, drunk or dry,
>   Keyney, I wish you well!'...

And with that endeth the exordium, and—be you in the body or out of it—I begin the letter proper.

*   *   *

I am delighted to hear of Ross' Oxford exploit.[1] It shows that the dear fellow's spirits are up to their usual high level. So like him to

[1] J. E. C. Ross of School Field, Rugby.

try his tumbling tricks in a public street! Funny dog he is! à propos of Ross (I am not trying to be sarcastic) your news of the Corps interests me. I suppose the various heroes are now sitting round on pedestals and admiring one another. How true it is that acts of real heroism are frequently found to be committed by people whom you would *never* suspect of it! Such brave souls can be content with the admiration of one another, and of the new boys.... So easy too to defy the Powers when you know you won't be punished for it!....

I hope poor old Ross isn't taking it to heart too much. The luckless devil is cursed with a weak will and a strong conscience. I know him of old. Now *I* have a weak will and a weak conscience; and I am proportionally happier. I was—for a moment—almost cheerful at your warm presage of the reunion next May. It made me remember that Life is not all grey—a thing I have frequently forgotten of late. I hope that evening will be a God-sent one, purple with the dying sunset and odorous with young spring: that all things in fine will be symbols...but I wonder. You must forgive my wild style of writing, I have been in prison for two months, warded by two Philistines. I am very tired of being grown-up: I want to laugh again, and be irresponsible and childish again, and be at School again. Have you ever been treated as an adult for 8 weeks in succession? It is a dreary experience.

Never mind. Next term I shall surpass myself. I shall be quite intolerably foolish.... And then we shall pull the world to pieces again. You may think me impatient. But you see that is a thing one can only do while one is quite young, I take it. I have made an epigram upon it. Before the age of 25 you pull the World to pieces: after 25 the World pulls you to pieces. And we are getting on for 18, you know!... I sometimes think I am getting a little bald, Keynes.

* * *

You should have pity on the woes of an exile, on this my πόθος τῶν ἀπόντων.[1] Some jests, you know (all this to your private ear), are not all jest. Nay, dear Keynaanite, think of the innumerable benefits I have conferred upon you. Have I not introduced you to G. K. Chesterton? Did I not once lend you an H. G. Wells? Have I not often made you laugh? Have I not occasionally even made you *think*?

Ponder all these things, and requite me as I would wish, prithee.

---

[1] i.e. my longing for absent people.

As for other matters (though really there are no other matters) you observe that I am more than a little doubtful about your assertions of life. Still if you *say* so, of course... ! Yet you figure me coldly, but quite politely, incredulous....

I think there is nothing else.

I fear you will curse me for ingratitude in replying thus wearisomely. It is my nature. I am always either grumbling or trying to be funny. Which bores my hearers most I can't decide.

So, I will cease; and blow out the candle, entrusting this letter to its hideous envelope, my body to fair Sleep, and my mind to Dreams...of Botticelli...etc. An exile prefers the Night to the Day.

RUPERT C. BROOKE

To GEOFFREY KEYNES   *London*
                                                                      25 March 1905
                               *   *   *

I am conscious that this illiterate scrawl is a very poor attempt at a 'birthday present', but I console myself with the thought that on Wednesday you will have a much more worthy one. I refer, of course, to the great event of the term, the appearance of the Phoenix. May I repeat my former words? If you (& other—more or less— illuminati) recognize, as in many places you will, a touch, a trick of thought or phrase, that you have laughed at of old, chuckle over it an you will but don't publish that it is mine. I am of a painfully retiring nature (as you know); & sudden notoriety is very abhorrent to me. Besides there are one or two things which look as if they might be from my august pen: but aren't. It's not a bad number, a bit uneven of course; but then you can't expect the other men to ascend to my level. One or two things are immensely squiffy, and another decidedly skippy.... I have just realized that this letter probably will not reach you in time. It may. But what does it matter? Time is a delusion. Let us not be deluded.

Yesternight I was vastly happy. I saw Peter Pan. It was perfect. It is merely & completely the incarnation of all one's childish dreams —the best dreams, almost, that one has. Red Indians, A Pirate Captain, Faeries, & all mixed up with Home...did you see it? If not, you must, next Christmas. It is wonderfully refreshing and never silly. And it brings out people's natures so—shows, I mean, if they are real children or no. For instance: a little way from me there was a 'grown-up' of perhaps, 10 summers, male, very blasé, and greatly bored. He obviously thought the whole thing too unutterably childish for him. Next him was a child, a white haired child of 90, his grandmother I expect. It must have been the happiest evening of her life. She chuckled and laughed all the time, with that sweetest of laughs, through which the tears shine.

Gerald du Maurier as the Pirate-Captain was perfect. You remember him at 'The Admirable Crichton' I expect—wasn't it there we chanced one afternoon on each other?...

There's nothing else. Greeting to all. 'Watchman, what of the night?' Here the watches of the night are long: but I think it will soon be morning. If this finds you between earth and heaven, may the blessing of the Black Pig be upon you.

'Who's there?'

'Friend!'

'Pass, friend—and

ALL'S WELL!'   RUPERT C. BROOKE

To GEOFFREY KEYNES   [*Bournemouth*]
Towards the end of March 1905
or thereabouts. R. C. B.

Incipit

I am answering with this great—and inartistic—promptitude, because I wish to know from you, as being a (fairly) unprejudiced and (comparatively) intelligent observer, (*a*) what is the prevalent opinion about the Phoenix, (*b*) what is the opinion of the intelligent, (*c*) what is your opinion. This differentiation is *not* an insult: on the contrary I rate your views very highly—when they coincide with mine. But I appeal to you for some truth. I feel so awkward in my complete isolation. For other matters—I duly admire your device for proving yourself unconventional; but really, you know...! That is to say, I am staying with two faded but religious aunts. They happened to be in when the post came, and one of them, chancing on your letter, received a quite severe shock.... It's not as if she were young, either.... You really must be careful...!

I laud as I say your desire to be unusual. You are. But you must be thorough. I have a faint fear that still perhaps you read Dickens or even Tennyson on the sly when no one is looking.

*   *   *

I haven't, as you surmise, much to do here. However it is, I think, less like Hell than Italy is. Hell is a place where there are no English books. I fill a spare hour or so in trifling with a supernaturally vacuous speech of M. T. C[icero] pro Murena.

I bow humbly before your wrath at my omitting to date my letter. In a business correspondence it is, I admit, a low habit. But my letter was scarcely, I thought a business one. However.... But if you are so concerned at the difficulty which will arise when that letter is included in the 'Life and Letters', you *might* obviate it by dating the letters when you receive them. It would be, I imagine, approximately correct.

I suppose you never thought of that. Again if you are extremely curious as to the day on which I sent it, you might examine the post-mark.

I suppose you never thought of that either.

I hope Honest John has succeeded in his Little going.

After all he always was a *little gone*, wasn't he? Ha! Ha!

Don't forget my request. RUPERT C. BROOKE

To ARTHUR ECKERSLEY *Southsea*
[*1905*]

I don't think they were 'wild(e)ly subtle' as you put it: though they were meant to combine Oscarian neatness with Shakespearian profundity—'A little more than Will, and less than Wilde' in fact.

However if you go on trying you may succeed in fathoming them.

I haven't.

The sun is about to undergo a partial eclipse on Wednesday, which appeals to my symbolical soul so much that I am thinking of writing a sonnet on it. It is, by the way, a terribly decadent act for the usually staid and conventional sun. Otherwise there is no news.

I have finally given up all kinds of writing (except letters). There are only ten beautiful words and I have used them all many times— there is only one subject I can write upon, and I have written on that too often. So I have abandoned letters, and shall devote the rest of my life to being a parish-beadle, a pork-butcher, a suicide, or an M.P., or something equally thrilling. I am already cultivating whiskers and a taste for sport.

* * *

I have, much to my surprise, discovered that I am going to Heaven. The qualification, I believe, is to have done one's duty in the eyes of God. Now God, I take it, is the Supreme Artist. Therefore He prefers tragedy to comedy, and artistic tragedy to all things. There are two kinds of tragedy, the stage-kind, and the other. In the stage-kind the hero dies in the last scene to slow music: in the other there is no music—and he lives. I am qualified under the second heading, and feel assured that I have pleased (and shall to the end of this play) the Supreme Artist. Wherefore I am certain of Heaven.

In addition to the whiskers etc., I am cultivating a halo (much less difficult). Fired by your example I have begun a school novel. It sticks to truth about as much as most, but takes rather a different view. But I have got stuck. Can you help me to finish it?

Chap. I

Chrysophase Tiberius Amaranth sat in his study, a small pale green room, reading. From one hand an opium-flavoured cigarette circled wreathes of odorous pallid smoke among the shadows. There was a knock at the door, and the Headmaster entered. 'Ah!' he exclaimed genially, 'Studying the classics, Amaranth?'

Chrysophase laid down his book. It was French, bound in dark green, and strangely scented.

'Scarcely!', he replied, 'the exact opposite, in fact. A classic is read by nobody, and quoted by everybody. This book, on the contrary, is read by everybody—in secret; and quite unquoteable.'

'Thank you,' said the Headmaster prettily: 'I see that you have learnt one of the two duties of the modern youth.'

'?'

'To embrace the world in one sentence.'

'And the other?'

'To embrace the world in one person,' answered the Headmaster with a musical sigh.

'My dear James,' exclaimed Chrysophase, 'you are magnificent tonight! May I offer you a cigarette?'

'Thank you. I never smoke them. Their shape is so banal. But if you have some absinthe...Yes, just a little. Thanks. Have you heard what has happened?'

'No. I never hear what has happened. It is so common. It is only the things that haven't happened that really matter, just as it is only what a man doesn't say that you need listen to; only the things he doesn't imagine that you can judge his soul by. An epigrammatic silence is the most crushing form of rejoinder. Silence is older and more terrible than speech. Man speaks. God is silent. Sooner or later we shall all yield to silence...'

It is not very difficult; but I haven't thought of a plot yet. However there are great possibilities.

Did you ever hear of S[imeon] Solomon, painter? He died the other day, and I read an article on him in the 'Westminster'. He was a delightful painter of 1850–1870—about; but he succumbed to drink, etc., and became 'impossible'. He spent his last twenty years selling matches, etc. He died in the gutter. Swinburne wrote 'Erotion', and others of the 'poems and ballads' to some of his pictures. Engravings of his were very popular at Oxford for sometime previous to '95. Titles of some are—Amor Sacramentum—Sappho—Antinous. Why haven't I ever heard of him? Have you ever seen any?

Yours

RUPERT BROOKE

To GEOFFREY KEYNES   *The Palace Hotel, Hastings*
                              14 April 1905

*   *   *

For the rest I have been leading the tranquil yet beautiful existence of a vegetable—eating much (query, does a cabbage dine?) sleeping much, thinking—*not* much.

Tomorrow my eyes will be soothed by the sight of Rugby's ivied towers once more. As a matter of fact I have roused myself sufficiently to write this merely that I may express in delicately chosen polysyllables my deep gratitude for your so kind criticisms & reports on the feelings of the populace....

I think (but don't let this make you too conceited) that I almost agree with your criticisms. 'Ah! ha! ha!', though of some literary merit, was rather too long, at least for *our* public: 'a contrast' to the comparatively uneducated portion of the readers (snff! snff!) must have been quite unintelligible: while the triolets were of course quite unspeakably vulgar.

Your guesses at my handiwork[1] (though you hedged a little afterwards) were astonishingly accurate. I scent witchcraft. You got a bull every time. Weren't they silly, too!...

---

[1] In the *Phoenix*.

Which (the dots, I mean) reminds me—you have noticed the appearance in book-form of the Modern Utopia?[1] It is very amusing to read reviews. The poor people really don't understand it a bit. But they are very serious and profound; & after all they mean well. It appears that there are some fantastic illustrations by J. F. Sullivan.... And isn't that last chapter exquisite?

The only tolerable things in Hastings are dinners at this Hotel. They are noble. I had some soup tonight that was tremulous with the tenseness of suppressed passion; and the entrées were odorous with the pale mystery of starlight.... I write after dinner, by the way. The real reason of this absurd epistle is this. I wish to warn you. Be prepared. It is this: I am writing a Book. There will only be one copy. It will be inscribed in crimson ink on green paper. It will consist of thirteen small poems; each as beautiful, as perfect, & as meaningless as a rose-petal, or a dew-drop. (These are not yet written, however.) When the book is prepared; I shall read it once a day for seven days.

Then I shall burn the book: and die.

RUPERT BROOKE

To ST JOHN LUCAS   [*Rugby*]
24 April [*1905*]

Dear St John,

My days (and nights) are now divided between Aeschylus and the Bastille. What time do you suppose I have for spontaneous verse? As a matter of fact I *have* evolved twelve lines, which I enclose; but they are, I know, of a sort it is merely ridiculous for me to write. Perhaps they are produced by too much thinking about such gloomy things as the Bastille—and Aeschylus. However it is written, so I send it. Having forgotten what of mine you have seen, I am rather confused, but I have happened on this 'Dedication' and I fancy I never showed it to you. I wrote it long ago. If you *have* seen it I apologize—or, better perhaps, I apologize anyhow.

Are you still in the aged ghost-thronged house, with Eckersley and Dagon (I think you said Dagon)? I am directing this there, on that supposition. Eckersley has sent me a series of postcards purporting to be views of the house from different sides; but as he has

---

[1] By H. G. Wells.

marked a different house each time (the church once, but *that* I refuse to believe!) I am entirely confused.

There is no Rugby news—not that I should inflict it on you if there was. It is Good Friday or Easter Monday or something and vast crowds—Rugbeian and rustic—of vacuous people in their ugliest clothes are proceeding past the window to see a polo match. Other vast crowds are listening to a brass band contest in the distance!— though it does not sound distant. I believe the worst band is going to be roasted whole in the close tonight. Thousands of youths are running up and down the streets, screaming hoarsely. As for me— my brain is a Bastilian prosy paste. I have fought the Muse for a week without the faintest success. Like Mary of Scots I have defied all laws of God, man and metre. The week's result is fifty lines. Fifteen I have had to delete as being likely to shock the lofty moral standard of the Rugby School authorities. The remaining thirty-five are the worst I have ever written. They have no ideas. They don't scan. And with the exception of two lines they are as dull and vulgar as a Bank-holiday.

There's only a fortnight more for it: I'm in despair. I think the result will be on a par with the historical Holy Roman Empire. My English Poem on the Bastille will be neither English, nor a poem, nor on the Bastille.

Yours ever

RUPERT BROOKE

Two days ago I found your delightful Demeter in Longman's (I think). I am going to show it to every master who teaches Greek plays at Rugby, that they may learn more wisdom, and we less grammar!

R. C. B.

> Only the slow rain falling
> Sobs through the silence of this bitter place.
> (*And in my heart returns one pale lost face*
> *And the old voice calling, calling,...*)
>
> Only the grey dawn breaking
> Makes visible the long despair of rain.
> (*And from weariness of sleep I turn again*
> *To the weariness of waking...,*
>
> Only the dark wave crying
> Mocks ever the loneliness of hearts that yearn.
> (*Till from the weariness of Life at last I turn*
> *To the weariness of dying....*)

R. C. B.

Dedication

When I have laid my head upon the breast,
  Of kindly Earth, and infinite Night above
Weighs heavy on mine eyes, and brings me rest
  From all my sins and sorrows, and my love;

Then it may be that thou, O Heart's Desire,
  Wilt chance upon these broken rhymes that I
Fashioned and forged in the fierce hidden fire
  Of this my love, the love wherein I die.

Will not a sudden gleam to thee make plain,
  In one great moment what thou had'st not seen?
Wilt thou not weep for great love given in vain,
  And sigh to think of all that might have been?[1]

R. C. B.

To ST JOHN LUCAS   *Rugby*
                                                    [*July 1905*]
Dear St John,

*   *   *

The Speeches[2] were rather amusing. I am informed that my effort
was one of the only two audible; and as the other was in a foreign
tongue, I carry off the honours. I am also told—by a cricketer and
friend of mine—that half the audience were moved to laughter, the
other half to tears. Which I regard as a compliment, though I can
understand the feelings of neither half. My friend added that he was
in the former division; but that was probably merely an amenity.
Anyhow I got a Browning and a Rossetti out of it, which is something, tho' they *are* in prize binding. The Bell for prayers.

Yours ever

RUPERT BROOKE

[1] Printed in the *Poetical Works*, ed. Keynes, 1946.
[2] In New Big School when he received the prize for *The Bastille*.

To HUGH RUSSELL-SMITH   *School Field, Rugby*
                                  Monday [*25 September 1905*]

So you happened twentily on the Sabbath. Did it hurt much? or did you take gas for it, as I did? With advancing years I find one's thoughts turn increasingly towards the Hereafter and the Serious Things of Life. In this small pamphlet (from which I have quoted often?) you will find many helpful thoughts; notably in the merry verses that recommend the habits of Drinking, Chronic Lugubrious-ness, and Suicide. À propos I go to Cambridge on Friday. I may see the fair Geoffrey before he has the happiness to be with all of you at B[rocken]hurst. I think I shall kill him out of jealousy. Here I am old and stuffy: more than ever. From 8 to 10 p.m. I read Roman History: But you are in black woods.

*   *   *

Last night it was fine. The stars are inconceivably further and sleepier at Rugby in the holidays than at B'rst. Even Casabianca sits and snores in the elms. Sometimes she mutters in her sleep: but I shan't tell you what. I am too antique and stuffy in Rugby to write a sensible letter. I shall probably disguise myself as Pimpo and visit you at B'hurst again. Alfred B. is well. Pa (sh! don't tell Mrs S.) is fairly well. Ma behaves as though she were well, but certainly isn't. I am very badly treated here, and made to wear a collar at dinner. In such matters you (plural) are very sensible though you pretend to be conventional. I see through you. My love to your mother (to whom I precipitately and presently write) (but don't tell her: it will be a delightful surprise).   RUPERT

To THE REV. ST J. B. WYNNE-WILLSON   [*Rugby*]
                                  10 October 1905

Dear Mr Wynne-Willson,

As I promised you somewhere in Marylebone last August, I am writing to you; though of course there is little School news to tell. Yet you may like to hear the School view of what news there is, as opposed to the Master's view, which you must have heard many times by now.

The Calendar—just out and unusually early—promises an un-exciting term.

It is the common opinion that the preachers this term are a poor lot, being mostly drawn from the staff, and not the most popular part of it at that: but this is irreverence.

There is to be no Shakesperian play in the Town Hall this term as of former years. I hope this is not caused by Benson's A Company being indignant at the Meteor[1] review of last year; I looked forward to reviewing it again.

The lectures this term are even worse than of late, being on 'The Thibet Expedition' and 'The Siege of Port Arthur, as I saw it'. However there is only one New-Big-School Sunday night address fixed, as yet.

In other lines, the 'Phoenix' is no more, and I rather believe the 'Vulture' has been forbidden. But a new attempt, 'The Venture', has been brought out under the editorship of Hugh-Jones and Butler. Its aims are literary (and in that it is rather successful); but, as no school magazine can exist by literature alone, it contains also a long article on School Football by Mr C. P. Evers, the idea being that the illiterate are by this to be tempted into buying the 'Venture', & so will be educated unawares.

Almost all the 'Eranistae'[2] are new this term, and therefore a little timid. Tonight however a paper by Mr Hardy on 'Classical Metres in English Poetry' was followed by a heated discussion on many more or less relevant subjects. Later in the term Duke is reading on 'Calverley', I on [Swinburne's] 'Atalanta in Calydon'.

I hope you are as kind to the Haileybury VI as you were to us one term in the Lower Bench; I mean, by reading some English Literature to them one hour in the week; I feel certain they would benefit more from that than from Greek Grammar.

Yours ever

RUPERT BROOKE

I am sending you, in thanks, a signed copy of the 'Bastille'.[3] You have done more with it than ever I could.[4]

[1] The Rugby School magazine.
[2] Eranos, a sixth-form discussion society (from ἔρανος, a meal, to which each contributed his share).
[3] Now, with this letter, in the Temple Library, Rugby School.
[4] Wynne Willson had quoted the concluding lines of the poem in his farewell sermon in Rugby School Chapel when he was leaving to become headmaster of Haileybury.

To ST JOHN LUCAS [*Rugby*]
[*Beginning of autumn term,*
1905]

Dear St John,

The latest and final decree (as I think I forgot to tell you) is that in December I am to try for a scholarship at King's *Cambridge*, and go there whether I get one or no. So that Oxford will not know me. In consequence of this project I am plagued all the time with 'extra work' and have scarcely any time for writing verse, or for reading (as opposed to perusing grammars). This course of extra work however has its advantages. It introduces me to many authors whom the usual course neglects as 'unclassical'. Of these, Pindar I do not appreciate. Propertius I like a little (and should do more, no doubt, if the dullest poems were not chosen). Lucan I find pleasing, but a little above me yet; Theocritus I adore. The hour a week which is reserved for Theocritus almost compensates to me for all the interminable dullness of Demosthenes and the grammars on other days. And that is very high praise. I have never read Theocritus before. I am wildly madly enchanted by him.

Another thing which occupies my waking hours at present is the composition of a paper on 'Atalanta' for our Sixth [Form] Literary Society. It is to be read in about three weeks, and at present I have barely started it. Can you, out of your wisdom, enlighten me on one point—who are the Chorus? They speak like old men, but then all Choruses (or Chori?) do. I think they must be elders, but it does not describe them in my edition, so I should like to be certain. When I found that I had to read, I decided that Swinburne would be a great aesthetic blessing to the starved Upper Sixth, but after reflexion I reluctantly concluded that our president, being a master, might veto the 'Poems and Ballads', so I chose 'Atalanta'. The difficulty is to find any part not to quote. The choric odes of course are essential; and how could I omit the messenger speeches? and who would pass over that perfect κόμμος[1] at the end?...If ever I finish anything more this term, I will send it you. But I doubt it. At present I have only one short attempt, which I thought too feeble to send last time I wrote. Nevertheless in default of anything better I send it. Some photos are coming in soon. You may expect one in a few days, if I don't go mad ere that with excess of Classics. At present I am rather weary of Football and Work. The masters who

---

[1] A lament sung by the Chorus.

teach me this term are very terrible. Wynne-Willson has gone and left me to the mercy of several soulless dull automata; who make Beauty tedious and Life an affair of Syntax. I would I were Rhadamanthus to devise new tortures for them, the mummies!

Yours

from an abyss of loneliness and dreariness

RUPERT BROOKE

' *Vanitas* ' ¹

Laugh now and live! our blood is young: our hearts are high:
Fragrant of life, aflame with roses, all the Spring
Thrills in our windy souls and woos to wayfaring.
And the glad sun goes laughing up the eastern sky.

Laugh now! the immortal Gods are with us: death and tears
Are dreams we know not. Life, mysterious, divine,
Lifts to our scarlet mouths her young immortal wine,
And wreathes with roses all our passionate laughing years.

Only—remember: the day passeth: not for long
Stays the mad joyance of our golden revelry.
The young eyes darken: the rose-petals fade and die;
Sleep ends and crowns our carnival, silence our song.

Too soon the pale hour calls us! Suddenly cold and chill
Dies on our lips the jest, the joy within our heart:
From the loved comrades, the warm feast, we steal apart,
The lonely night before us. Pitifully still

Lie the young limbs, the feet that delicately trod
Life's fluted measure, the red lips that sang, the whole
White beauty of our body: and the startled soul
Flutters and fails before the darkness that is God.

RUPERT BROOKE

To ST JOHN LUCAS   [*Rugby*]
                                [*Autumn term, 1905*]
Dear St John,

I think I remember seeing an article on G. B. S. in a quarterly some time since; and it must be the one to which you refer. I was

¹ Printed in the *Poetical Works*, ed. Keynes, 1946.

rather curious about G. B. S. at the time, and so started the article, but left it in the middle, with a vague conviction that G. B. S. must be very dull and foolish. I do not know quite how far Shaw is sincere, but I can accept him even if he means all he says. I find that at present (whether owing to my nature of mind or my state of education I know not) all my sympathies are intensely liberal—wide as the grave. I can enjoy and appreciate in part—or so I have the audacity to think—every kind of doctrine. I have an extreme sympathy with all fanatics, and yet am an ardent admirer of law and order! I see what I take to be the truth in the Bible, Socrates, Wilde and Shaw. No doubt I shall grow up into a rabid partisan of some extreme view; but at present I enjoy a position of great impartiality. I enjoy even Kipling.

Just now my days are passing very happily, and many beautiful things occur. I am so joyful that I fear lest the Greek idea may be true, and Nemesis fall blackly and suddenly. At present however I am plucking flowers in the sun, with this additional advantage (is it an advantage?) over my companions that I am aware of it.

Last Sunday I read a little paper on Atalanta and was mightily pleased. The usual papers we have are on such subjects as *Hood* or *Calverley*—'something to make you laugh'. Imagine the dismay of the rest of the society at being compelled to listen for three-quarters of an hour to a paper on an obscure play by an author of whom they had scarcely heard. Never a laugh from beginning to end! I saw my opportunity and took it. 'Have I not', I said, 'many a time and oft been bored past endurance by such Philistines? Now my revenge comes; I shall be merciless.' So I prepared a very long and profound paper full of beautiful quotations and read it to them for a very long time and they were greatly bored. They sat round in chairs and slumbered uneasily, moaning a little; while I in the centre ranted fragments of choruses, and hurled epithets upon them. So they were bored for 45 minutes: and at length I ended with Meleager's last speech, quoted almost entire; and my voice was almost husky with tears: so that they awoke and wondered greatly, and sat up, and yawned, and entered into a discussion on *Tragedy*, wherein I advanced the most wild and heterodox and antinomian theories and was very properly squashed. So, you see, even in Rugby the Philistines do not get it their own way always.

I send you a sonnet I have just made: which seems to me to have some nice lines but to be quite incomplete as a whole. I have just discovered a recent book 'the Gods of Pegana' by *Lord Dunsany*

which pleases me greatly. And the illustrations are absurdly delightful and wonderful—by *S. H. Sime*. Do you know either of them?

Yours

RUPERT BROOKE

'*The Dawn*'[1]

When on my night of life the Dawn shall break,
    Scatt'ring the mist of dreams, the old sad gloom,
    Before the terrible sunrise of the Tomb;
Shall I forget the dull memorial ache?
Shall not my tired heart, as a child, awake,
    Filling the morn with music? nor retain
    Aught of the sad notes of my former strain
But through that splendid dayspring rise, and make
Beauty more beautiful, the dawn more fair?
    Only—I fear me that I may not find
That brave smile that once lit my sunless air,
    The bright swift eyes with purity there-behind,
Nor see the pale cloud of her tossing hair
    Laugh and leap out along the desolate wind!

R. C. B.

To GEOFFREY KEYNES   *School Field, Rugby*
31 December 1905

Dear Geoffrey,

Many congratulations on the Savoys;[2] I am filled with a wild envy.
However we have one vast triumph to set beside yours. I am an
invalid confined to the house, & today I was seized by a sudden wild
desire to read Malory's *Morte D'Arthur* through; so I sent my brother
off to the T[emple] R[eading] R[oom] to get one. He couldn't get
the small one, so he returned with a large aged-looking one in three
vols. It was illustrated by A. Beardsley. I never respected the
T.R.R. so much in my life. Yet I was insulted. I thought I knew the
Library by heart: and this treasure had lurked there for such ages
unobserved of me. How strange is Fate!

You I believe were one of those who scoffed, saying, 'Classics!
forsooth! he got it on his Essay!'[3]...But we have received my

---

[1] Printed in the *Poetical Works*, ed. Keynes, 1946.
[2] Seven parts of the magazine, illustrated by Beardsley and others.
[3] He had been awarded a scholarship at King's College, Cambridge.

marks, together with those of the next man, and they enable me totally to refute your last calumny. I was about 40 marks ahead of him altogether, and of these I gained but 3 on the essay. Essay, quotha! It was my classics, my grammar, my history, my Cole-like[1] memory, that did it. Pray thank your brother for his letter of congratulation & for the news it contained, which was at least exciting. On the 9th prox.(!) I am going to London for 5 days—if my incipient consumption is by then departed—to witness anew the ever-wonderful-and-delightful *Peter Pan*, & whatever else happens. Shall I find you there as usual?

I have read the whole of the Elizabethan Dramatists through in 3 days.   Yours enigmatically,

RUPERT BROOKE

[1] E. L. D. Cole, form-master of the Lower Bench of the VIth Form.

In January 1906 Brooke had only two more terms to spend at Rugby. I had already left school and gone to live for several months with a family in Germany, where his letters formed my chief remaining link with Rugby. Early in the term he was highly amused to find himself the object of worship by a boy in another house, and he reported the development of this 'affair' with great gusto, though the letters that he wrote to his admiring friend have not been preserved. Before long, romance was shattered by a very troublesome attack of inflammation of the eyes, which kept him in confinement for several weeks of the term.

In April Brooke went with his family to Italy, staying in Venice and Padua, and soon after his return to England he was taken by Arthur Eckersley for his first visit to Oxford. During his last term at Rugby Brooke realized that his boyhood was ending and sensed acutely the happiness of being at school. He repeatedly expressed this in his letters in exaggerated literary terms, so that it sounded like another pose, but there can be no doubt that his regrets at leaving school were genuine. In a letter written to St John Lucas in May comes the first mention of William Denis Browne, whose friendship was later to become an important feature in Brooke's life. Denis Browne was a precocious and expert musician both as performer and composer, and was often called upon by Basil Johnson, the Rugby music master, to play the organ for the services in the school chapel. His request, however, for an 'Easter Day Song' to be written by Brooke for his music was not taken very seriously and the 'Hymn in Praise of Cremation' was the result. Denis Browne remained a close friend as an undergraduate at Clare College, and was with Brooke, as will be seen, at the end of his life, being himself killed in Gallipoli soon afterwards.

The last term at Rugby ended with July, and a walking-tour with Hugh Russell-Smith was tentatively planned, but was abandoned. Instead, Brooke went to stay with the Russell-Smith family at Brockenhurst in the New Forest and then made a short visit to the Rugby School Mission Camp. The remainder of August was spent with his own family at Eastbourne and at Rugby. In September he visited the Stracheys and made his first contacts with the so-called 'Bloomsbury set'. Although he had been a friend of Lytton Strachey's younger brother, James, at his preparatory school, Brooke was never included in this circle, and, indeed, came to dislike intensely some of the attitudes of mind that they professed. At the beginning of September he was at Bournemouth, and was soon afterwards installed at King's College, Cambridge. He did not write many letters during his first term at Cambridge, partly, perhaps, because he had not thrown off the depression that followed his leaving school. He was slow to make new friends in the University and spent much of his time with the Rugbeians who had come up to Cambridge in the same term. The Greek play—on this occasion the *Eumenides* of Aeschylus—provided a distraction in November, and Brooke's handsome person suggested his being cast for the part of a herald. He was never a good actor, although afterwards associated with the Marlowe Dramatic Society and the Amateur Dramatic Club, so that the unexacting character of a herald, who neither moved nor spoke, was well suited to his genius. The University term ended earlier than the school term, so that he was able to return to Rugby before the boys had dispersed and to indulge again for a short space his nostalgia for lost youth.

To ST JOHN LUCAS   *The Liberal Publication Department*
Rugby
[*January 1906*]

Dear St John,

Many thanks for your patience in displaying to me the wonders of the wicked city. I found my headmasters[1] flourishing exceedingly. By themselves they are shy, frightened individuals; but when they foregather in large numbers they become very rowdy. Most of the day they spent in discordant religion in the Chapel; but I managed to chat with a few for some quiet minutes: I was very patient and gentle. I told them many things they did not know before. They went away a little dazed. I am now hopelessly involved in politics. Every night I go down to the Liberal Club and cheer, from 10 to 12 p.m., at the results of the polls. I am even editing an election paper, '*The Rugby Elector*', which appears on alternate days in the Liberal interest. It is full of cheap and low gibes at Steel-Maitland, which proceed from my middle-class imagination. The whole thing is ridiculously English.

The Rugby masters are beginning to return. I meet them at intervals. They ask me what I have been doing. I mention Simeon Solomon and G. B. S. Some of them look vacant and smile in a blissful ignorance of either name. Others, illuminated by a kind of twilight knowledge, look shocked, blush, and go away. And these are the people who have the charge of my unconscious tender youth, and who bid me read Pater!... There are two classes of Rugby schoolmaster; those who insult Beauty by ignoring it, and those who insult Beauty by praising it.

To guard against the noxious influence of politics I shut myself up for an hour each evening, put a green shade over the light, and chant The Sphinx[2] in a jewelled monotone.

Thus I contrive to keep the *mens insana in corpore sano* which is all the English decadent may hope for.

Yours radically
RUPERT BROOKE

[1] A Headmasters' Conference held at Rugby.   [2] By Oscar Wilde.

To GEOFFREY KEYNES   *South-Eastern or*
                                 Rugby Division of Warwickshire
                                      Mr Corrie Grant's
                                      Committee Rooms
                                      10 January [*1906*]

Dear Geoffrey,

Isn't this absurd & delightful? We are having a ferocious fight down here; in which I am taking a great part. I edit a paper which is produced every other day in the Liberal interest. It is full of cheap scores against Protection, which my fertile brain evolves in thousands. In an interval of waiting for proofs for the next (& last) number I scrawl this ridiculous note. *Peter Pan* was good still, but less wholly beautiful than last year. Shaw's play was highly amusing & interesting, & very brutal. I suppose you have seen it? Shaw is a terrible example of the effect of commercial socialism on genius:...brilliant brute. He is like a public school career, amusing but utterly soul-destroying. There was one sentence in *Major Barbara*, a virulent attack on the ordinary public-school master, at which I applauded very loudly & suddenly from a prominent part of the house. They nearly turned me out.

You figure me, covered with Liberal rosettes, rushing about the town & discussing the political situation with M[orris]-Davies, H. A. J[ames], and all the other most rabid Tories in the town. I have made 37 mortal enemies in 4 days. And the immense joke of the matter is that I really take no interest in politics at all.

The heat is most oppressing in Rugby: shall we get *no* snow before summer? To-morrow little boys with black clothes & white collars come back in great numbers to this necropolis: and you will soon be going to far-off & more guttural lands.[1] I wonder if you are as angry as I was a year ago. It is terrible to feel that one is exchanging the cynicism of youth for the bright optimism of manhood; it is very sad to outgrow one's disillusions. I shall write at rare intervals & send you news of the great play I am writing, in imitation of Shaw's latest, entitled ' *Major Mojah* '.

But in October we twain will paint Cambridge green.

Ha! ha! the printer's devil....Farewell.

RUPERT BROOKE

Congratters on Cambridge's political enlightenment.[2]

[1] I had left Rugby and was about to go to Germany for several months.
[2] A Liberal Member had been elected.

To GEOFFREY KEYNES   *Rugby*
                                                  3 February 1906
Dear Geoffrey,

Innumerable thanks for the second work of art I have received within a fortnight from you, each in its way delightful. Of course I should have preferred you à la A[ubrey] B[eardsley] as the first[1]—a black mass and a white mass for your face, and dotted lines for your raiment—yet, for the subterfuge of photography, it is not inartistic. I like the autumnal browns of it: the greys of Dean's[2] atrocities show cold and bleak against it. This term, as you may have heard, has been enlivened by a scandal. The unsuspected [. . .] has been discovered (a) showing up proses done for him by a wee & terrified Sixth, (b) writing love letters to a small child in another house. For these offences his XV has been taken away, and he has been requested:[3] reason (b), however, has not been published. Otherwise things are quiet. There will very soon, however, be a tremendous fight during Chapel, in the upper Bench seat. . .

The Calendar has appeared. There are about eight foreigns;[4] to which I look forward with a dumb, patient, resignation. (One was fought today, & we lost—especially myself—heavily.) The intellectual side of the School is also considered. [Lord] Roberts is coming down to teach us to be patriotic: a person talked last week about *Natural Life at the South Pole*: and later on the Rev. Somebody will kindly tell us how he saw Jerusalem. An enlightened land, England! Last week I dined with H. A. J. & sat next to Crutwell. We conversed (C. R. M. F. and I—*not* James) amicably about A. Beardsley, whom Crutters disliked. I said that I adored Beardsley, because he caricatured Humanity, & I was amused by caricatures of Humanity. As I spoke I beamed on him, but he did not grasp the insult: he was merely impressed, & bit his nails in wonder & perplexity. The Old Dame[5] enjoys her customary & wonderful health. She is a little bored with me just now, because I have affected several new creeds, including the worship of Moloch and Bi-metallism. I have converted half the House to Socialism, & the rest to Mormonism. I was almost lynched the other day for saying that at the age of eight I deserted the Church of England for Christianity: at the age of eighteen I am deserting 'Christianity' for the teaching of Christ.

[1] A photograph of a drawing by Aubrey Beardsley.
[2] A Rugby photographer.   [3] i.e. requested to leave the school.
[4] Football matches against outside teams.   [5] Hugh Russell-Smith.

The pale ululation of a bell reminds me of supper, of a Cole-prose & of other barbaric survivals.

The Dawn has not yet come. Farewell.

RUPERT BROOKE

To GEOFFREY KEYNES   *Rugby*
                                              23 February 1906
Dear Geoffrey,

You are wonderful! I did not realize that photography could be used to perpetuate beauty in that way. I shall have to acknowledge that there is something in science if it can copy Aubrey so perfectly.

You display the depravity of the aesthetic conscience in hankering after scandalous details. Of course The Aged Dame told you not—how could she? Besides she knew only what all knew—a very little; whereas I have heard more. But I am bound to secrecy about the names; and there is little else to add to the tale. It was the usual romantic comedy, which the Schoolmaster delights to nip in the bud—perhaps wisely, for most boys are beasts.

Grandeur et Décadence de G. B. S. is quite clever and convincing. It attacks the gentleman for lack of moral courage in his latter plays, and, to my paltry brain, seems to prove a tendency to shirk the issue. It is probably written by one Whibley. À propos, the delectable Fabian himself in a recent speech at some lewd Socialist gathering, expressed the political situation neatly: 'The difference between Campbell-Bannerman and Chamberlain is that C. B. tells lies which the country believes, Chamberlain tells lies which it doesn't.'

They say you are vaguely anxious to spend £7 on books[1] (of course you didn't credit the sceptical vapourings of our moonish aged dame). (What a place Rugby is! The Bastille got £3, and a farrago of pseudo-archaeological haverings about Roman(?) rubbish fetched a pound more! Oh, ha! ha! ha! I am not angry, only bitterly amused. Ha! ha!) I know a man who was in a similar position at Oxford. He bought seven volumes, all French: 1 Baudelaire, 2 Verlaine, 2 Huysmans, 2 Catulle Mendés; and had them bound in a pale distant green. When the College authorities saw them, they turned a complementary red, and refused to allow the College crest to be printed on them. However my friend kept the books, which was the

[1] I had been awarded a special prize for an essay on some excavations on a Romano-British site carried out during the holidays in Cambridgeshire.

chief thing, and has studied them ever since. The story must be true, for I had it from his own lips. He comes out of prison again in March.

If this is too unRugbeian, perhaps the complete edition of A. C. Swinburne would suit you? Yet you would get very much chaff for the grain. But I enclose a list ranged in order from decency downwards to....

A purple and terrific scandal has arisen around me. It is tremendously intricate, and even I know only three-quarters of it. No one else knows more than a quarter. Also don't ask Russell-Smith, who combines feminine curiosity with the ignorance of age. It began by Dean catching me one day & informing me that 'a gentleman' in another House, had been trying to buy a photo of me: Dean was willing, but my leave was necessary. My enormous conceit was swelled even more—and I gave leave. Dean unluckily mentioned the name of the House. And there were who overheard. Whence rose a scandal; which I yet nipped in the festering bud. (Forgive my archaic style—it is beautifully reasonless.) Sundry however heard of it, and theorized—to my much discomfort. H. F. R[ussell] S[mith] for instance has an unfounded yet stubborn faith that it was the Anarchist!![1] But I secretly made inquiries and found it was one I knew of old—one with the form of a Greek God, the face of Hyacinthus, the mouth of Antinous, eyes like a sunset, a smile like dawn....It appears that the madman worships me at a pale distance: which is embarrassing but purple....So I wander around, taking a huge aesthetic delight in the whole mad situation.

There's scandal for your non-moral artistic nature.

But don't tell Mrs Grundy-Smith.   RUPERT

P.S. Of Wells's new tale anon.

R. C. B.

Atalanta in Calydon. A. C. S.

Browning.

Poems and Ballads. 2 Series. A. C. S.

Marlowe.

Webster.

Sir Thomas Browne. (Ought to be higher up, quite pure.)

Collected Poems. R. C. B. (42s. net. Printed in France. Very scarce.)

---

[1] A boy in another house.

To GEOFFREY KEYNES   [*Rugby*]
                                                 7 March 1906

Dear Geoffrey,

   Whenever I am out of school I am too lazy to write the letter
I wish to send. Therefore I take the advantage of twenty spare
minutes in school to do so. My unseen is finished; Kitter's[1] eagle
eye—I hope—is elsewhere; so I shall do what I can at this favourable
moment.

   As you surmised I gave the permission. What else could my soul
have let me do under the circumstances? Very little further has
happened outwardly. I catch his eye occasionally in Chapel: it is
rather difficult to avoid it! But this weather is so intoxicating that
something must soon flash forth. Such events ripen so swiftly in the
Spring; and four days ago, the Spring, violet crowned & with
laughter in her eyes, danced into England. Before that we had
execrable rain & snow: but since the whole world has been a miracle
of Spring, warm and radiant. The English pale blue sky, the warm
wind, laden with fragrances of immortal youth, the joy in the heart,
have filled me with divine rapture. I am maddened & inspired to do
anything. It is such an English Spring as I wept for in the arid heat
of Italy, a year ago. I feel on the brink of vast dramatic situations.
Yet I hesitate. You see, the present position is (to me) so exquisite,
so delicately appealing to my aesthetic heart, that I fear to move
forward. Knowledge is so disillusioning. He may be one of those
who have expended their faculties on their faces. The idyll might
become a tragedy. On the other hand in real Life the situation cannot be left hanging as it might in a novel or a prose-poem. And to
retire would be inartistic. I can only advance, in the hope that the
event may be happy if possible, anyhow beautiful.... Do not be
surprised to hear that I am found dead some day in the Close, a self-
thrust dagger in my heart, and a volume of Swinburne pallidly open
before me. It may be the only way.

   A week ago that vile game football ceased; and we have since
played hockey; which is at least faintly enjoyable.

   Otherwise all things are respectably dull.

   In my note-book is appearing a life of H. A. James by E. L. D.
Cole which is rather amusing.

   I can tell you nothing so I send some lines I wrote for that
eminently respectable old woman the Venture.[2] The editor refused
it plaintively. 'It didn't suit their public. Could I do something

_____
[1] H. F. Kittermaster.   [2] A school magazine.

funny?' I smiled dangerously, & told them that *this* was meant to be funny. They believed, gulped twice, and expired. The lie was a good one—better than the very Wild(e) verses.[1]

*   *   *

RUPERT BROOKE

To GEOFFREY KEYNES   *Rugby*
                                    23 March 1906

Dear Geoffrey,

The prophecy in your last letter displayed an astounding insight into the ways of man and of fate, and was immediately and remarkably justified. A little more than a week ago our friend developed a disease (rose-rash, I presume) and so left the paths of men. Our romantic comedy pauses. There is more from the hand of Fate. A week after this calamity there is another greater one. On Tuesday last I awoke with ophthalmia. This ties me up for about a week; and just before the end of that week is my time to rush into rose-rash, which I must have caught from the Lady who started it a fortnight ago. Therefore I fear the entr'acte will be lengthened to some eight weeks.

This will allay your fear of my 'doing something rash' during this term. But next term you must be prepared for the worst. An English Summer (and my last term) really invites one to all that is 'rash'—except the rose-variety! Moreover I feel it incumbent on me to make some actual material protest against the conventional hypocrisy of the public school. It is my obvious duty to live the aesthetic life I preach, and break the laws I loathe.

(Besides, how else can I contrive an effective 'curtain' to the comedy? (. . .and think what a sonnet I shall make from it!))

But I trifle on a too serious subject.

I am so glad you recognized the 'influence of Spring' in those verses. They were of course, written last December. At present, the Spring is in abeyance, probably till May. The other ophthalmaniacs are Sinclair & the Dame, who started ophthalmia as soon as she had completed rose-rash. Her wee pig-eyes ooze yellow *pus*—a feline subject for my *un*feelin' laughter. She is however the life and soul— and most of the body—of the party. Sinclair has stopped out four weeks now, and is very bored: I am, of course, in one of my

---

[1] 'Vanitas', already quoted in a letter to St John Lucas, p. 30.

occasional weeks of depression: but she is bubbling over with the high spirits of second childhood: she sits between us and plays the utter, utter fool to her own intense satisfaction. I look very glum but really enjoy it tremendously. The old wretch has already dragged me out four walks, averaging 6 miles, in two days!

This letter by the way is probably not infectious. H. G. Wells's serial in the Chronicle has a delightful main idea & very pleasing disquisitions: but the 'love-interest' does not quite please: yet it is hard to judge from daily scraps. We shall probably be in Florence for 10 days from about April 8th. You'd better warn your brother!

RUPERT BROOKE

To ST JOHN LUCAS   *The City of Dreadful Night*
                                      [*Rugby*]
                                      26 March [*1906*]

Dear St John,

I assure you that I am no hallucination—except in so far as I, like you and all the world, am 'part of the Red King's dream'. I am very real and corporeal, especially my eyes, which are painfully present. It is an evil thing, this ophthalmia. Not to read is a great trouble to me. The disease comes of gazing too often upon Butterfield's architecture.[1] They treat me—very unsuccessfully—with Boracic Lotions; but the only real cure would be to see things beautiful. If for five minutes I might see my Botticellis I should be healed in an instant. Meanwhile I grow gradually worse. The real reason of my frailty, which I dare not tell to the School Doctor, is as follows. At Rugby School there are 573 other children. Of these 500 are ugly, 70 moderate, and three beautiful. The latter three were seized by diverse plagues and departed for a time; therefore my eyes inconsolable, languished thus...the others, who are still physically healthy, are in these days occupied with what are called 'Athletic Sports'. These take place within view of my window, and give me something to see. The runners and jumpers are clad in ugly clothes; many are ungainly and clumsy in motion; and they run for cups of precious metal, instead of laurel and parsley crowns. Yet they are young, eager, and very alive; so that, even under these grey skies, there is something that recalls Hellas, giving to that dream a moment's reality.

[1] Rugby School Chapel.

We are having read to us Belloc's new book.[1] I had expected something like 'The Path to Rome', and was therefore disappointed. So far as we have got—about half-way—it is historical, descriptive, quite interesting, the expression of an unusual view. But it is not Belloc. I miss that grave and fantastic irresponsibility; it is a clever book which might have been written by any of several men; I wanted one that only one could have made.

As my eyes grow slowly worse, the idea of Italy gradually recedes. Moreover the 'Beardsley brother'[2] may develop mumps (a fit subject for a Beardsley picture). Also, I cannot promise to come to London by the 7th—unless it be to see an oculist! If however you are here in the holidays, you may meet in one of Rugby's unlovely ways a muffled form with haggard face and bloodshot filthy eyes (a symptom of the disease is to drop into blank verse): you will sketch it and entitle the picture 'The Fate of the Decadent' and publish it as a companion picture to Beardsley's 'Débris d'un Poète'.

RUPERT BROOKE

To GEOFFREY KEYNES   *Rugby School*
                                        W. P. Brooke's Esq.
                                        31 March 1906

Dear Geoffrey,

A joint pilgrimage to worship Holbein at Bâle is a delightful idea, but, I fear, not feasible. For I have only persuaded my insular family to go to Italy on the terms of my being interpreter & general courier, and therefore I dare not desert them. I have indeed sworn that I speak French & Italian like a native (with the mental reservation 'of England'), although I know neither to any extent. Therefore I feel bound to comfort & reassure by my presence the others; they will refuse to part with me. Owing to this my ophthalmia our start has been postponed a few days, and we are to attempt Venice alone, with a few days halt in Paris on the way back. (Besides what a fall there would be, from the Italians to your lumpy raw German painters!)

I am now deserted. The Dame has gone home to recover her sight in the pure breezes of the sea-girt Thanet. I therefore stay, to lead my solitary bookless life—meals, sleep, & lonely rambles. Thrown on my own resources I do nothing but evolve doggerel. In

---

[1] *Hills and the Sea*. Methuen, London, 1906.   [2] Alfred Brooke.

two days I have composed 109 poems (4 religious epics, 2 satires, 9 ballads, an episode, a question, 33 love sonnets, & 59 lyrics) all too bad to be worth writing down....

But I have one recreation. Having nothing else to do I have developed the romance of which I told you. I have obtained Antinous's photograph from him; and I employ my spare time in sending & receiving letters. We scorn subterfuges and openly employ the post. It is highly interesting and very amusing. How much I am in earnest—or how much he is—I really can't say. But it is spring. What he thinks of my epistles I cannot imagine. They are perfectly frank and highly improbable. They are written in very good and musical English with a tendency to over-elaboration. In parts they recall the Song of Solomon—indeed they are often in imitation of that wonderful purple ecstasy. I usually address him as Hyacinth, Apollo, or Antinous, and end with a quotation from Swinburne or Catullus. I bring in odorous & jewelled phrases 'The Greek gods lived that you might be likened to them: the world was created that you might be made of gold and ivory: the fragrance of your face is myrrh & incense before the pale altar of Beauty.' I frequently add a postscript containing fifty adjectives and an exclamation mark. I don't know what he thinks of such communications; but if he has any literary sense, they must do him a lot of good. His letters are very quaint and a little sad. They are filled with little halting sentences, faintly expressive. 'Sunday is very dull now that you are not in Chapel'....'X said he met you going out a walk. *I* never seem to be able to do so for all my efforts'...at the close he suddenly flares out into sentimentalism: 'yours *ad astra*'....It is all rather sweet and rather unusual: and he really looks very nice.

Your strange reference to a 'German publication' mystified me. I await something eagerly.

Farewell. I am still a lonely leper: but men say I shall some day be well. RUPERT BROOKE

To ERICA COTTERILL
Rugby
Sunday, 1 April [1906]

Dear Erica,

I should have liked immensely to go with you to see the Hippolytus, but my eyes are not well enough yet, and I dare not risk not going to Italy by getting them worse. Hippolytus is a great play in

Greek and I suppose Gilbert Murray is good. I grieve for your nerves, but I am glad you have recovered again. I practically never suffer from them except when I listen to one of the Headmaster's sermons. By the way, there is one going on as I write, but I escape it. The ophthalmia is really gone, but my eyes are a bit weak, & the doctor considers that I am still infectious, which is foolish of him. I started this disease, together with another lad in the house, rather badly, and as the San. was full, we were put into a room in the house. Our cases were obstinate, & for a week we never improved. So Father got annoyed, & one day when Dukes,[1] the school doctor, was paying us his hurried visit, rushed in & accused him, practically, of being a fool, and a careless ass, and many such things. Dukes replied in suitable terms, and the pair almost came to blows at the door. The other lad & I sat up in bed & cheered. It was a very inspiriting sight, and really did our eyes a lot of good. The consequence is that now the other fellow has gone home, & I am alone, they have deserted Dukes & have Simpson in instead. As a matter of fact their treatment is practically the same, but Simpson always stays a few minutes to gossip with Mother about other people's diseases (we get a résumé with symptoms at the next meal!) & is therefore preferred.

A great dispute has arisen lately between myself and the family over my term's report. It has come in, & is very bad. Result: the family are shocked, I am cheerful. I told them last holidays that having got a much better scholarship than was expected, I considered I had done my duty, & that I was not going to be bothered any longer to work at useless subjects in the wrong manner under a set of Philistine, soulless, dull, ugly, unintelligent, bat-eyed idiots like my present masters. I have kept my word: hence the report. However I have determined to be a martyr to my principles; as they will find out again when they see my next report. Anyhow my present methods are quite satisfactory. While the other idiots are laboriously learning an hour's dull Greek Grammar, I read Swinburne or Shaw or something really worth reading, & then go into School & invent beautiful answers out of my head. They are of course generally wrong, but I am quite happy, the others get more marks than I, & so are satisfied (the silly rabbits); in fact it's only the masters who aren't satisfied. And they don't count. About a year ago I got, for my sins, into the top form of the school, & found it was the meeting-place of the dullest fools in the school, who know everything & understand

[1] Dr Clement Dukes, F.R.C.P.

nothing. The noticeable thing is that they're all like myself the sons of schoolmasters. Who can say that crime is not hereditary?

If on Monday Ap. 9th you go to the entrance of Victoria you may soon see passing (at about 11 a.m.) a cab. On the top will be 9 large boxes labelled Venice belonging to Mother & Father, & a small parcel with my things & Podge's. Inside will be Father very irritated & excited, Mother trying to put me tidy, Podge *very* nervous at the thought of the Channel, & last, with a broad smile of vast delight, Your patient cousin

RUPERT BROOKE

To ST JOHN LUCAS [*Rugby*]
Thursday [*3 April 1906*]

Dear St John,

We have decided to go to Venice after all, and I am saved from utter despondency. My eyes are now practically well, but an evil philistine who insults me with drugs, still forbids me to read. In consequence I have to read stealthily and in distant dusty rooms, a practice akin to that of secret drug-taking. It gives a flavour even to history, of which I consume vast quantities. The reasons for this last step, so alien to my taste and inclination, are two. I wish to know something of the tales men believe about Venice; and I have undertaken to write an essay for a prize. If I win this I shall stand up next speech day and recite weird 'historical' platitudes to a vast slumbrous audience. This idea is so pleasingly incongruous that I desire to realize it. To live a paradox is better even than to say one; and almost as hard as to live an epigram. Moreover I once airily told a pedantic and aged man that, if I liked, I could understand even History, and he, scoffing, stirred my pride to try to prove it. Therefore I am going to write an essay on 'The Influence of William III on England'. Of William III I know very little. He was a king or something, they say, of the time of Congreve and Wycherley. Of England I know nothing. But being aware of your omniscience in French poetry and Greek sculpture I thought you might aid me in a little matter like this. If ever you have written an epic, a monograph, an anthology, or a lyric on William III please send it to me that I may quote it in full.

*   *   *

RUPERT BROOKE

To GEOFFREY KEYNES
Margate, Italy
15 April 1906

My dear Geoffrey,

Venice is an American colony, chiefly peopled by Germans. There is also a small Italian element in the population. It is still a little out of date, but the steamers and hotels are rapidly supplanting the old-fashioned gondolas and palaces. It promises soon to be a First-Class Popular Holiday Resort.... I am really very grieved. They told me that I was going to a city of dreams, 'an opal betwixt sky & sea', and with my young-eyed simplicity, I believed them. We arrived at midnight and were rowed to our hotel by strong moonlight between sleeping palaces. That was very lovely, and five days ago. Since then I have persuaded myself with more difficulty every day, that I am enjoying myself. Today I have finally abandoned the attempt, and confess that I hate it. It is hot and malodorous. The Venetian painters are mostly shams, more or less gorgeous. Their palaces have been turned into first-class hotels, or over-decorated. And the place is befouled by a mob of shrieking tourists. Moreover my family are extremely obnoxious people to travel with. (This evil English is brought on by an even more evil Italian brass band hard by.) I wonder if the country of your adoption is adequately represented by the specimens of it one meets here. If so, I pity you very deeply. They are very oily and guttural. But what can you expect of a country that calls this place Venedig when it might say Venezia?

You wonder how much of my affaire is true. So do I. (So, no doubt, does he!) It does not do to inquire too closely. It is now very pleasant. Some day perhaps we shall grow old and 'wise', and forget. But now we are young, and he is very beautiful. And it is spring. Even if it were only a romantic comedy, a fiction, who cares? Youth is stranger than fiction. At present he—the adorable, rose-crowned —is at Rome: and I receive affectionate pale letters from him whenever the Gods, and the Italian posts, permit. As for me, I shut myself up in a little room, and try to forget that I am in Venice, and divide my time between an historical essay and the composition of exotic little litanies in mediaeval Latin to Antinous.

I am glad to hear that you are content again. I like to figure you, subtly foreign and green-clad, relentlessly pursuing white butterflies in a Black Forest, a type of Science demolishing the Arts. It isn't a nice thing to be a type of (!again!), but that does not reflect discredit on you. I once knew a man whose uncle kept a baptistery.

I just exist here (till Saturday, by the way), irritably and feebly. I am never really happy except at Rugby in the Summer Term. So I look for May. Next term will, I hope, be superb, and it must end appropriately—even if it has to do so before July 30th!

RUPERT BROOKE

To ST JOHN LUCAS *Padua*
Saturday night [*April 1906*]

Dear St John,

Venice is a little disappointing in April. Germans and Americans rather obscure the view. Also I hate the brawling ugly steamers that disturb the Grand Canal. There were moments when the world seemed fine—when, after Mestre (although we came in by train) the lights of Venice started out of the sea: and again, when from the heat of the train and the bustle and noise of the station we rushed into a white silent city, and slid down the Grand Canal in a quiet gondola under a full Italian moon. To enter Venice at night is fit and proper. But it is disheartening to wake next morning to electric launches and cosmopolitan hotels and Americans and all the other evils that our civilized age gives. Some day when I have been driven away from Cambridge for being too young, I shall go and live in Venice in December or July, when the tourists have returned to their proper hells; till then I shall tell myself that I have never been to Venezia, only to Venice at Earl's Court. Yet though the whole was a failure there were times when I was happy. Sometimes I sat in the vaporous gloom of St Mark and gazing on the mosaics, mused of all my religions, till everything became confused, the grand pulpit changed to an altar of Moloch, the figure of Mary grew like Isis, and the fair Byzantine Christ was lost in the delicate troubled form of Antinous. Also, when the ancient night made Venice ancient again, and the Teutons slept stertorously after their dinners, I escaped and stole in a gondola up lost little waterways till I forgot what the stars were like. But I was really miserable, being modern and decadent, in an ancient eternal city. And I hated almost all the Venetian painters, who are of the flesh and yet do not know that the most lovely flesh is that through which the soul shines. The stolid but respectable damsels of Bellini developed into the ponderous carnalities of Titian and Paolo—and I longed for my Botticellis. The Venetians were never purely young and never beautifully decadent, but always in a tawdry and sensual middle-age. But tomorrow I shall delight in the Giottos here; and they may prove a remedy. We spend Monday in Verona and then proceed to Paris, where I shall worship in turn the lovely classics at the Louvre and the wicked moderns in the Salons. And in a fortnight I return to taint the righteous atmosphere of Rugby School for one last purple term.

Yours

RUPERT BROOKE

To GEOFFREY KEYNES *School Field, Rugby*
[*10 May 1906*]

Dear Geoffrey,

I shall hurry to get the book you recommend. I am evil not to have written to you before: but I spent the last five days of the holidays in a feverish attempt to write an English Historical Essay. This effort has incapacitated me so much & worked such havoc in my carefully elaborated prose-style, that I dared not write a letter sooner. Even now some lingering harshness and cacophonies betray me...

The Summer Term has dawned. It is my last, and I weep. The same fantastic things happen, there is that strange throng of young beings, unconscious of all their youth & wonder. Another Spring dies odorously in Summer....But I am quite happy. To be here is wonderful, and suffices. I live in a mist of golden dreams. Afterwards life will come, cold and terrible. At present I am a child.

Antinous has got—the mumps! This is so horribly incongruous that it sounds like a line from one of Heine's most bitter lyrics. He will be back in a week or two. I am a little sorry. For though I love to look upon him—as a supreme work of art—yet he is something of a *tertium quid*—the note of tragedy in my romantic comedy....

Some day, when I am 180 and very wise and very tired, I shall explain to you these things.

I liked your postcard this morning. Receiving it at breakfast, I laughed suddenly & wildly. People thought I was very mad, and poured milk over me to soothe me.

I am writing nothing, not even a Hymn to Antinous. I am content to exist. I know now whither the Greek Gods have vanished now-a-days. They are to be found in public schools. Always, in the sunshine, and the Spring, I see them, thinly disguised, rushing over the grass, supple of limb & keen-eyed, young and beautiful. Here is Olympus, and now. I feed on the nectar of Life, from Ganymede's hands, and from amidst my young unconscious gods, write to you now, ecstatically.   RUPERT BROOKE

To ST JOHN LUCAS   ˪*Rugby*]
                                        May 17 [*1906*]

...you see, there was a vast quarrel among us in Paris. After we had been there two days, and I had sent you that postcard, my people were scared by newspaper reports of labour risings and revolutions. Knowing my anarchical tendencies, and being perplexed by visions of my dying fantastically upon some street-barricade, they hurried the party at very short notice to more moral and safer places of England. So all my plans fell wrong, and I was very wroth, and I could not see you in London. At present I am infinitely happy. I am writing nothing. I am content to live. After this term is over the world awaits. But I do not now care what will come then. Only, my present happiness is so great that I fear the jealous gods will requite me afterwards with some terrible punishment, death, perhaps —or life. I have discovered whither the Greek gods went, when they left Olympus. Heine was wrong, beautifully wrong, in sup- posing that they took up subordinate positions in the new religion. They came to the English public schools. I have seen them often, young unconscious deities in flannel, running swiftly over the grass. Apollo is here, divinely cruel, and Dionysus, who maddens by his presence. Even Jove, lewd and bearded as of old, is not absent....

The School musician,[1] a youth of 18 who knows Arthur Eckersley and composes fluently, sent me a request that I should give him a song to set to music. The idea irritated me so much that I complied. With much labour I hammered out a 'song'. It is unlike other songs. It is called 'A song in praise of Cremation, written to my lady on Easter Day'. It treats, in a laboured cunning metre, of the dis- comforts of being buried in a grave. It is closely modelled on Baude- laire's 'The Corpse'. How he received it I have not heard; but I think it will satisfy him. I am eager to hear the music.

When will you be in London, next holidays?

                                        RUPERT BROOKE

        [1] W. Denis Browne.

An Easter-Day Song[1]

in Praise of Cremation written to my Lady Coesyra

Suddenly, at the pale death-whisper, I
    Must go
Down to the cruel dark, and lie
Remembering thy lips, and know
Upon, around, within my helpless form
    The feeding worm.

I loathe the obscene darkness of the tomb;
    —To lie
Through the slow hours of stifling gloom
In shameful, helpless agony,
Changed by the worms' unnatural cold lust
    To slime and dust!

Far in the lonely night, the rain and cold
    To sleep
Till through the gloomy, putrid mould
The blind, lewd things that mouth and creep
Fondle and foully kiss these lips anew,
    Once kissed by you.

Rather for me the sudden flame's embrace
    Which clings
Once..., and therewith the perfect face
Shall fade, the last of mortal things
So for all time I'll quench my hot desire
    In that clean fire.

                              R. C. B.

To GEOFFREY KEYNES

Rugby
4 June 1906

Your alliterative appeal stirs me to activity. I seat myself at my green table in one of those Monday 'early thirds' once so sweet to me. Before me lie, picturesquely scattered, your letter, a Latin prose, five bottles of diverse-hued ink, books (Baudelaire, Latin Dictionary, Theocritus, Sterne, Pater...) and a framed picture of the Roman

[1] There are two versions of the Easter-Day Song, of which this, written in the hand of Denis Browne, seems to be the final one.

Antinous (the prototype, of course. The reincarnation's likeness is within a cupboard). There are also flowers, a bowl of warmly-odorous wallflowers, and a little hyaline Venetian vase holding forget-me-nots....I wonder what I shall say to you. That mundane affair of the King's Medal[1] passed off with success after all; for my people, for once intelligent, laid money down and said 'Buy books!' So I am now, with prayer & much fasting, considering what to purchase with three guineas. But there was a tragedy in the affair. As a motto I made up a little epigram 'History repeats itself; Historians repeat one another'. But James, the dotard, read out only the first half: and the world considers that instead of so witty a remark I chose that hideous platitude to represent me.... One point to James!

Did I tell you Antinous had the mumps? He has now returned, radiant as ever. I took him a walk yesterday. We were both highly amused, and spoke of irrelevant topics, such as cricket, all the time, with great gusto. Only rarely a tinge of poetry flickered & faded through my mundane words: and he laughed. But he is very Greek to see, and quite intelligent—a thing so rare in the beautiful! He said drily humorous things rather swiftly in a delightfully inappropriate voice—a rather distant, almost cracked voice, but laugh-ful. Being young and divine he is restless, ever moving, full of life....

The Gods are dealing very kindly with me. My days are filled with the sound of failing lutes and falling rose-leaves. I am beginning to value the things around me more every day, the good and the bad in them. This school-life, with its pathetic transience and immense vitality, calls to me with a charm all the more insistent that I am soon to lose it. In the gigantic game I play my part with zest, alternately 'siding' and ragging, yet always inwardly laughing, not in malice. The others are so beautifully unconscious: I am both actor and spectator.

From heaven

Your

RUPERT

To ST JOHN LUCAS

[*Rugby*]

17 [*c. 4 June 1906*]

Dear St John,

This morning I sent off the Sphinx I have kept so indecently long. Many thanks. Why is it not quite satisfactory? I think he was writing too much for his actual readers. A poet should write, for himself,

[1] Given for the prize historical essay on 'England's debt to William III'.

for God, and for one reader—probably ideal. The poems written in the last way always seem to me the best. Is that heresy?

The *Miscellaneous Studies* [by Pater] fill me with happiness. Apollo in Picardy, Emerald Uthwart, and the Child in the House —oh! especially The Child in the House—are wonderful.

I am just now—despite variable health—seated on the topmost pinnacle of the Temple of Joy. Wonderful things are happening all around me. Some day when all the characters are dead—they are sure to die young—I shall put it all into a book. I am in the midst of a beautiful comedy—with a sense of latent tears—and the dramatic situations work out delightfully. The rest are only actors; I am actor and spectator as well; and I delight in contriving effective exits. The world is of gold and ivory.

I am finishing my paper on James Thomson. I have cut out all the wicked parts, but I still fear for the reception. Last week we had a paper on T. Gray. The stupendous ass who wrote and read it, after referring to The Elegy as 'a fine *lyric*', ended with the following incomparable words: 'In conclusion then, we may give Gray a place among the greatest poets, above all, except perhaps Shakspere, Milton, and Tennyson.'

This lewd remark roused me from the carefully studied pose of irritating and sublime nonchalance which I assume on such occasions. I arose and made acid and quite unfair criticisms of Gray and Tennyson, to the concealed delight of all the avowed Philistines there, and the open disgust of the professing 'lovers of literature'.

I was nearly slain.

*   *   *

Who wrote *Grandeur et Décadence de Bernard Shaw* in Blackwood's? To my undramatic mind it seemed clever. How is London? Here the slushy roads, grey skies, and epidemic mumps, cannot conceal a wonderful beauty in the air which makes even New Big School almost bearable.   RUPERT BROOKE

To ST JOHN LUCAS   [*Rugby*]
                                      [*June? 1906*]
Dear St John,

There was a wild rumour in Rugby that you were coming hither in a few days; so I waited. But now the rumour is authoritatively contradicted; so I hasten to write, as I should have done long since, to thank you for those delicate immortal books. I have scarce begun to read them, through stress of mundane work; but even now my Greek Proses are becoming tinged with a plaintive beauty, at once the secret envy and the professed scorn of my masters.

Have you seen the *Nero*? I suppose it is as terrible as the other Tree-Phillippic combinations. I am so glad I can't see it. The sight of my beloved Nero daubed with golden sugar to please the British Public, would give me intolerable pain.

I am enjoying everything immensely at present. To be among five hundred people all young and laughing, is intensely delightful and interesting. I take the whole thing as an enormous fantastic game wherein the other players think it is all in earnest. My present pose is as a Socialist and as most of the present Rugbeians hail from that 'upper-middle-class' of England which regards Socialists as demons only one degree in the ranks of the Pit less wicked than Artists, I have quaint and pleasant arguments. Tomorrow I am leading the defence of the Labour Party, in a School Debate!

I enclose that little poem[1] I made for our School magazine. The Editors read it, frowned, blushed, and excused themselves.

Yours ever
RUPERT BROOKE

To GEOFFREY KEYNES   [*Rugby*]
22 June 1906

I don't expect this will get to you in time. I have deferred it till the last instant, typically. Yet if it does, I should rather like Félicien Rops. I know him little, but should like to know him more. He is, I suppose, one of those strange souls that hunger after perversity, and find it in paradox; that form terrible harmonies out of discord, and discover in ugliness a nocturnal, disquieting beauty. Is he, too, I wonder, among those who have looked into their own souls, and tried to escape them by art? In that, at least, he is like me. Anyhow the brutalities of Rops would suit my humour just now. The world, for me, is full of greyness and the sound of great cries falling discordantly. Beauty and light have fled on tumultuous wings, and walk in lonely unlit places beyond the stars. Rugby is full of the dreary ghosts of dead hopes and remembered joys. At the beginning of this mad term I crowned myself and my harp with roses and walked singing along the foolish ways of κουφόνοων ἔρωτων (you'll have

[1] No longer found with the letter.

to guess it!).[1] But now I have come to a place where the roads part, and I have sat down to weep, because, I think, either way ends in darkness. The bitter Gods gave me nearly everything, and then have mocked me by showing me what they have not given. That gay witch, the Summer, who charmed me three weeks ago! I have looked into her face, and seen behind the rouge & the smile, the old, mocking visage of an harlot.

Oh! damn prose-poetry   and everything else.

from Hell

RUPERT

To ST JOHN LUCAS   *A bed of pain*
[Rugby]
Sunday [July 1906]

My dear St John,

As a reward for my infamous negligence and supineness in not writing to you the gods have sent a visitation on me, an influenza-cold and an hay-fever-ophthalmia. Neither are severe and I shall soon return from this inkless sick-room to Life; meanwhile I propitiate the gods and you. A month since I began a pale little letter to you and Theocritus (address—The Nenuphars, The Thames) but ere I could finish it my life was blighted, or I trod on my soul, or some other cataclysmic event happened, and I left it unfinished. I have been living during this term with great determination and thoroughness. As a consequence I have thus relapsed—for a time; my eyes have gazed overlong upon great beauty, and are blinded.

Did I tell you that I am to read to some of the Rugby Sixth a paper on 'Modern Poetry'? The deed is due in a fortnight. I have written them a rhapsody in prose modelled on Pater's 'Leonardo' and interspersed with such sentences as 'Beauty cannot be moral or immoral: it is white or coloured: that is all'. I end with a convincing proof that all future English poetry will be written in tribrachs.

For myself I have elaborated a novel and overwhelming way of writing poetry. It shall henceforth be my only method. It is very simple, and in three stages:

(a) Get an idea (opium, or any of the conventional methods).

(b) Write in as luscious, intricate, scarlet, exotic, decadent, hothouse, polyphonous, verse as possible (perfectly easy).

(c) *Then* translate the result of (b) into rough, simple verse, and

_____

[1] i.e. of thoughtless desires.

simple, rough language, making the whole as rural, balladic, mediaeval, and unaffected as you can (a trivial task).

The result combines all the virtues of all the styles ever known.
I enclose you my first attempt.

A week ago I went to the Warwick Pageant. Did you see it? The
performers, being simple country folk, were very theatrical and
artificial. Arthur Eckersley as Edward II was very (His) Majestical.
About half-way through the show I saw the man, as Tree, stalking
across the vast lawn which was a stage. He started two scenes
before, because it takes a quarter of an hour to stalk regally over
300 yards of grass; but he arrived at the right time and hurled
Marlowe at us in a voice borrowed for the occasion from some
sonorous parson-friend, and quite unrecognizable.

They are coming to put into my eyes a remedy which blinds one
with exceeding pain for the space of two hours. This they do twice
a day.   Weep for me,

                                        RUPERT BROOKE

    Some day I shall rise and leave my friends[1]
    And seek you again through the world's far ends,
    You whom I found so fair,
    (Touch of your hands and smell of your hair!)
    My only God in the days that were!
    My eager feet will find you again,
    Though the ugly years and the mark of pain
    Have changed you wholly; yet I shall know,
    (How could I forget, having loved you so?)
    In the sad half-light of evening
    The face that was all my sunrising.
    So then at the end of the earth I'll stand,
    And grasp you fiercely by either hand;
    And, seeing your age and ashen hair,
    I'll curse the thing that once you were,
    Because you are changed and sad and old,
    (Lips that were scarlet, hair that was gold!)
    And I loved you before you were grey and wise,
    When the flame of youth was strong in your eyes,
    —And my heart is sick with memories.

                                        R. C. B.

[1] Printed as 'English Minnesong' in the *Westminster Gazette*, 16 February 1907,
and as 'The Beginning' in *Poems*, 1911.

To GEOFFREY KEYNES   *School Field, Rugby*
5 August 1906

As we don't reach Cambridge yet and I cannot explain in person, I write an apologetic letter. I am a little grieved that my conduct at the end of last term was strange. You must have found me absent & very frigid, at Rugby and at Lords. I suppose I seemed, as I felt, to be existing rather perfunctorily, my attention fixed upon things many millions of miles away. I had warned you so of course you understood, in part. You realized that I considered myself *in profundis*; that, to my puerile imagination, my heart was being slightly fractured, or at least strained. It is, you know, merely one of those delusions to which very young & uncontrolled natures are so liable. As my wiser friends comfort me, I shall recover in a few weeks. Sometimes I fear their words are true; at others I hope so. I go on Tuesday to be ordinary and, I hope, merry, with the merry, ordinary, Russell-Smith. After that I shall write letters less obviously tr-r-r-agic. And by October you will find me as raucously hilarious as ever, remoulding the Universe as of old. Only, in future, my Scheme of Things will never be quite as real and homelike as in recent, dead days when I, with one other, imagined heaven, and found it real, for a time.... But my self-pity must be as nauseous to you as it is to me. It is not fashionable to feel these things deeply. But this deserted Rugby is Hell, and I am a pale ghost who has lived, and can now only dream.

Pah!   RUPERT BROOKE

To MRS RUSSELL-SMITH   *School Field, Rugby*
Sunday [*August 1906*]

Dear Mrs Russell-Smith,

Since I left you I have been away from civilization, in a place where were neither ink nor stamps; so I have been unable to write to you. But now I do write, more than the conventional letter of thanks. I can truthfully say that I never enjoyed a visit more in my life (with the possible exception of one to my aunt, when I was nine, and discovered there for the first time Browning's poems). I never was in an home where everyone was so affectionate towards one another and the world at large. It made me very envious. I now understand the secret of Hugh and Denham's unfailing cheerfulness during the term—a constant enigma. I was vastly sorry to go; I should like to have stayed five months. As it was, I was almost sociable for ten days—a rare thing in me. Many thanks for tolerating me so long. I shall soon write to one of the boys. I loved it all—even the excessive physical exercise, in a way—and especially one of the hammocks—the one further from the house. Please give my love to it—a delightful hammock!   Yours ever

RUPERT BROOKE

To GEOFFREY KEYNES   *School Field, Rugby*
                                        19 August 1906

I have returned from the place Brockenhurst, and from a wild three days at the Mission Camp. Soon we are going away again to Eastbourne, but in this interval, a lull between two storms, I write to you. Your letter found me at Brockenhurst, where I did in truth enjoy myself more than I thought I ever could. I forgot my weariness for a time in assuming the part of cheerful imbecility. I played it so well that for a time I deceived myself too. Among that unconscious mad lovable family I was irresponsible again and very infantile. Now I am back in this melancholy Rugby & my melancholy family, and I find August a thing of mist and chill, existence an habit once more, rather dreary. Within three weeks I may be in Cambridge. I hope I shall see you. You will come with me and help to curb my fantastic family's taste for suburban furniture and puce wall-papers. Meanwhile I intend to write hard at something—anything. It may be that in Art I can forget Life, and in dreams of God escape from my own dreams. So, perhaps, I shall rediscover the waters of Youth, which are beyond all price. Even, now, at times, I find myself slipping a little into the old folly—an epigram or a fairy-tale. There are yet roses in the Garden. Next term, perhaps, with your cunning aid, o decadent, I shall pluck some; and devil take the thorns!

RUPERT

To GEOFFREY KEYNES   *School Field, Rugby*
                                        Sunday, September [*1906*]

If your venerable brother is at Great Oakley Hall with the Strachey's, kindly transmit to him the following pieces of advice. (a) Let him not be tempted into playing croquet there: they play a mean & wildly exasperating game. (b) If he is in want of anything to read, do not let him attempt (as I did) 'The Sorrows of Satan' by M. Corelli. It is the richest work of humour in the English (?) language: but the effects it produces on the unwary reader...! I am now a positive wreck.

Do not make a joke.

Lytton Strachey I found most amusing, especially his voice...

I am glad you like 'Love & Mr L[ewisham]'. There are moments when you seem almost intelligent. But to rank it with Kipps...! My poor child! You must have the soul and perceptions of an undeveloped weasel. I am not surprised, only loftily sorrowful and a little annoyed....

You really are very blatant.

Murderer & vandal! To spend your holidays in massacre—blood & sudden death! Ugh!...

'Avenge, O Lord, thy slaughtered saints, whose bones
Lie scattered on the Alpine mountains cold!'[1]

(Do butterflies have bones?)

[1] Milton's *Sonnet* xv, 'On the late Massacre in Piedmont'.

Monday

Your ridiculous postcard has just arrived. I am delighted to hear you are going to ' J[ohn] B[ull]'s other Island'. It is unspeakably delightful. The average of acting all round at the Court [Theatre] is exactly four times as high as at any other theatre in London. Each character is perfect. And the play itself is exquisite, wonderful, terrific, an unapproachable satire on everything. The man[1] who acts Broadbent is a genius. The only weak point in the whole thing is the first ten minutes of the first act. I envy you having it before you.

How amusing of dear old Ross. Pray do not forget to bring the photos to School with you. I wrote the villain the most charming & witty letter possible about a month ago and he has not answered a word.

I spent two or three days in London between Liberty's, an art furnisher, & old bookshops. At both, & especially the former I got wonderful & beautiful things. With the results I am busy draping my study which will be the 8th wonder next term.

It will be covered with rugs & draperys of various shades of green, pale & very sorrowful, & all the bookshelves are full of minor poetry...Altogether highly effective...Farewell till next term, which will no doubt prove as amusing as ever, in spite of the absence of Tubby[2] and Ross.　　　　Yours ever

RUPERT BROOKE

To ST JOHN LUCAS　　　　　　　*Bournemouth*
　　　　　　　　　　　　　　　　3 October [1906]

Dear Tiresias,[3]

Your eyeless letter found me in this strange place, which is full of moaning pines, and impressionist but quite gentlemanly sunsets. With other decrepit and grey-haired invalids I drift wanly along the cliffs. I shall be in Rugby by Saturday, probably, to stay till Tuesday. It may be, too, that Dick will be there. He is expected. Shall we seize the Racquet Court and play furiously on Saturday or Monday morning? It is a little irritating of you to tell me to write and say how happy I am. Happy! Ugh! at present, in this interstellar limbo I have forgotten what happiness is. Here I have nothing to do except moan and write whining sonnets. I wish I could get even to Cambridge, a 'weary empty house...', and have something to do.

[1] Louis Calvert.　　　[2] L. R. D. Anderson of School Field.
[3] A prophet in Greek mythology struck blind by the goddess Athena.

Meanwhile I linger here and read Sordello and Baudelaire altern-ately: and the weather is very fine. I am very busy with an enormous romance of which I have written 5 chapters. It is really a medieval paraphrase of the 'Marble Sphinx'.[1] It begins with my famous simile about the moon, but soon gets much more lewd. One of the chief characters is a dropsical leper whose limbs and features have been absorbed in one vast soft paunch. He looks like a great human slug, and he croaks infamous songs from a wee round mouth with yellow lips. The others are less respectable.

I suppose you'll have to leave England again about October 16th?

How did you find the Darkness? Did you see enormous visions of Hell and Heaven upon the night? I too am going blind and shall soon join you in the dim places of twilight. I have seen everything there is to see and my eyes are tired. The moon is an empty jest in autumnal skies, and the sun is a stellar body of incandescent gases.

ἐπιλελήσμεθ᾽ ἡδονῆς
γέροντες ὄντες . . .[2]

Or do I insult you?   RUPERT

To GEOFFREY KEYNES

Bournemouth
4 October 1906

Long ago I had a letter from you which I have been too bored to answer. But now being too bored to do anything else, I reply. I shall see you within a week. I expect to turn up early on Tuesday morning, if I have not, ere that, killed myself in the train that bears me from Rugby. I have been in this quiet place of invalids and gentlemanly sunsets for about an hundred years, ever since yesterday week. But tomorrow I return to Rugby for a few glorious ghastly days. I shall be wonderful there, laughing wonderfully all day, & through the night wonderfully weeping. Then—leaving the people I have hated and loved I shall throw off, too, the Rupert Brooke I have hated and loved for so long, and go to a new place and a new individuality. I shall live in Cambridge very silently, in a dark corner of a great room, clad perhaps in cowl and scapular. I shall never speak, but I shall read all day & all night—philosophy or science—nothing beautiful any more. Indeed I have forsworn art and things beautiful; they are but chance manifestations of Life. All

[1] By St John Lucas.
[2] i.e. In old age we forget what pleasure was like.

art rests on the sexual emotions which are merely the instruments of the Life-force—of Nature—for the propagation of life. That is all we live for, to further Nature's purpose. Sentiment, poetry, romance, religion are but mists of our own fancies, too weak for the great nature-forces of individuality and sexual emotion. They only obscure the issue. Our duty is but to propagate the species successfully and then to wait quietly for the disintegration of our bodies, brains, and 'souls', in the grave; heeding as little as possible the selfish and foolish greed for personal immortality, or the incomplete love for an individual, which is but a diseased warping of our generative instincts. This is the teaching of all our highest & clearest thinkers, Shaw, Meredith, Wells, Nietzsche....It is rather grey, but quite logical & scientific....Science! (Only—don't tell any one, but there is one little disquieting doubt. It is rather well expressed in a dialogue of a play of a French poet.

'...We have Science, which is a torch, dear mystic. We will analyse your sun if the planet does not burst to pieces sooner than it has any right to!'

'Science will not suffice. Sooner or later you will end by coming to your knees.'

'Before what?'

'Before the darkness!' V. de L. A.)[1]

Moi, je ne sais pas! It is a vague game, guessing this riddle, life. Once I knew it, in that I didn't care, but lived. Now, being dead, I play with philosophy.

> 'Not till the fire is dying in the grate
> Look we for any kinship with the stars!'[2]

I am glad you liked that quaint afternoon we had in London, once—oh! very long ago! when I was barely middle-aged.

RUPERT BROOKE

To ST JOHN LUCAS   *King's College, Cambridge*
                           Saturday [October 1906]

Dear St John,

This place is rather funny to watch; and a little wearying. It is full of very young people, and my blear eyes look dolefully at them from the lofty window where I sit and moan. Innumerous people I knew

---

[1] Villiers de Lisle-Adam, 1840–1889.   [2] Meredith's *Modern Love*, iv.

on the other side of the Styx come in to see me. They talk vivaciously for three minutes and I stare at them with a dumb politeness, and then they go away. My room is a gaunt yellow wilderness with a few wicked little pictures scattered here and there. The book-shelves are enormous and half empty: but it was rash in you to inquire about books I needed. I had thoughts of sending you a list of all the evil books I really should like. I want, for instance, to complete my set of the three great decadent writers (Oscar Wilde, St John Lucas, and Rupert Brooke.) Of the last and most infamous of the three I possess most of the works but of the other two I have less. But perhaps these would have a too bad influence on me. I have none of Belloc's ridiculous works; the madder Elizabethans would please me; and if you dare find some of your evil Frenchmen of the more decadent sort they would delight my wicked mind. A complete set of the most infamous of Beardsley's drawings might be purchased for about 50 guineas in Paris and would certainly bring a gleam of faint interest into my wan eye. Of particular authors I might welcome any of Fiona Macleod's poems, or Maeterlinck's, or any fair book illustrated by one of these infamous moderns in whom I delight—such as 'Time and the Gods' by Dunsany and Sime—the new one. But you know my disgusting mind. There is a wide field open—if you have time before leaving England. Anyhow, I shouldn't advise you to get anything for me. I have given up reading or writing nice things now. I only read Shaw and write clever verse. It's very easy; and hurts less than writing poetry.

I go to my frugal lunch.   RUPERT

To ST JOHN LUCAS   *Cambridge*
                           Monday [*November 1906*]
My dear St John,

Many thanks for Dunsany's book; which is very wonderful. The illustrations are more terrible than beauty, and as beautiful. Dunsany is obviously the greatest prose writer alive, after you; even as Sime is the greatest artist, except me. In spite of your unkindness I have read and wept over your infamous novel.[1] I have written a review of it for the Times Literary supplement in which I prove that it is (a) immoral, (b) a thinly-veiled attack on Campbell-Bannerman, (c) unscientific. I recognized a life-like portrait of myself in the

---

[1] *Quicksilver and Flame*, London, Duckworth, 1906.

Italian nobleman; and Arthur Eckersley is firmly convinced that you made Gerald a physical and moral double of him. Therefore he is very irritated that no hint of Gerald's fate is given. Has Belloc yet slain you for making him recant on his death-bed?

You see to what a condition of watery incompetence I am reduced, to write to you of nothing but your own book. At certain moments I perceive a pleasant kind of peace in the grey ancient walls and green lawns among which I live; a quietude that does not recompense for the things I loved and have left, but at times softens their outlines a little. If only I were a poet I should love such a life very greatly, remembering moments of passion in tranquillity; but being first and chiefly only a boy I am restless and unable to read or write.

At the end of last week I went down for two days to Rugby (to play football!) and found that already I am very far away from them. So I have returned with a little disappointment to the hermit-life I live here. These people are often clever and always wearying. The only two persons I ever make any effort to see are those who were in my house at Rugby and have come up with me this term. Here across the Styx we wander about together and talk of the upper world, and sometimes pretend we are children again, a little pitifully. If you come to Cambridge at the end of the month you will see a performance of the Eumenides, in which an aged and grey haired person called Rupert Brooke is wearily taking the part of the Herald. I put a long horn to my lips and pretend to blow and a villain in the orchestra simultaneously wantons on the cornet. It is very symbolical.

RUPERT

To MRS BROOKE   *Cambridge*
                                              9 November [*1906*]

Dear Mother,

I have just realized that I have neither written to nor heard from home since I was there. I was very glad to hear of the victory over Uppingham, which I always prophesied. I hope we beat W.G.M.,[1] whom I am told we have to play, but I fear.

The idea of my playing Hermes fell through, but they have given me the equally large part of the Herald. I stand in the middle of the stage and pretend to blow a trumpet, while somebody in the wings makes a sudden noise. The part is not difficult. The rehearsals are very amusing.

[1] Mitchell's House at Rugby.

I am going to see the South Africans, if they play, to-morrow. As it has been raining for a week they will probably have a wet ball and be handicapped considerably, but I suppose we shan't beat them. I have an atrocious but cheap seat right behind the goal-posts. Great things are expected for tomorrow evening, after the game.

I went to lunch with the 'O. B.'[1] on Sunday. He was rather quaint to watch, but I did not much like him. He was so very egotistical, and a little dull. I got Lucas' novel from the library and enjoyed it. I have seen no other reviews of it yet. The people, like all his characters, are very amusing, but I am not sure that I like them so well when they become serious and dramatic. I am now reading G. K. Chesterton's Dickens. Has a second Meteor been out this term yet? If so I should like to see it.

Has Dick said anything about coming down here this term?

Your loving son

RUPERT BROOKE

[1] Oscar Browning, 1837–1923, schoolmaster, historian, and Fellow of King's.

The opening of the year 1907 found Brooke in bed at Rugby suffering from a sharp attack of influenza. He went up to Cambridge a few days late for term, but before his return the family had been stricken with grief by the sudden death from pneumonia of his elder brother, Dick. In a letter to Francis MacCunn, a boy still at School Field, but afterwards at Oxford, he gave some indication of how much this unexpected loss had affected him. He was still without many friends at Cambridge (though this was soon to be changed), but his 'literary life' was developing. He was beginning to contribute poems and reviews to the *Cambridge Review* and other periodicals and to take more part in the competitions in the *Westminster Gazette*, where he had already won a prize in September 1905. When the Lent term was over he went for short visits to the south of England with Hugh Russell-Smith and, after returning to Rugby, set off with Alfred to Italy, visiting Genoa, Florence and Milan.

One of the chief features of the following May term was a series of encounters with Hilaire Belloc, following a meeting of a Pembroke Society to which I had invited him; but there had also been meetings with some of the many friends who were soon to form the familiar circle in which he chiefly moved, and their names begin to appear in his letters. Andrew Gow of Trinity had been in the School House at Rugby two years senior to ourselves. Justin Brooke of Emmanuel College had come up from Bedales School in our year, already with a reputation as an actor, and had taken part in the Greek play of the previous November. He was not related to Rupert, but some confusion has often been caused by their having the same surname, accentuated by the fact that Justin had an elder brother called Rupert, who was not, however, at Cambridge. During the Lent term Justin was the moving spirit in the foundation of the now well-known Marlowe Dramatic Society. Founded with the object of performing Elizabethan plays in Cambridge, the Society began with a trial performance of Marlowe's *Faustus* in November, Justin taking the part of Faustus and Rupert acting Mephistophilis. The Society was not formally constituted until the beginning of the following year, with Justin as Producer, Rupert as President, Francis Cornford of Trinity as Treasurer, and myself as Secretary. The preliminary Committee had consisted of Justin Brooke, Francis Cornford, Andrew Gow and Miss Jane Harrison of Newnham.

Through Justin had come a friendship with Jacques Raverat, an advanced student reading mathematics at Emmanuel. Though a Frenchman, Raverat had also been educated at Bedales. After a trial of printing at the Ashendene Press, he married Gwen Darwin and practised as a painter. He contracted a slowly progressive form of disseminated sclerosis and died after prolonged suffering at Vence in the Alpes Maritimes in 1925. I had also introduced Brooke to Charles Sayle, an under-librarian at the University Library. Sayle was a bachelor and his house in Trumpington Street was a meeting-place for many young dons and undergraduates, among these being George Leigh Mallory of Magdalene, the famous mountain climber, and Hugh Wilson of King's. Sayle had been at Oxford in the nineties, but had returned to Cambridge, his native town, and lived there until his death in 1928. Gerald Shove, an economist, and Geoffrey Fry, afterwards a distinguished civil servant and later Sir Geoffrey Fry, Bt., were contemporaries of Brooke at King's, where he had also made many older friends among the Fellows; some of these were J. T. Sheppard, afterwards Provost of the College, A. F. Scholfield, later University Librarian, and my brother, Maynard Keynes. Another very close friend met in this year was Dudley Ward, who was reading economics at St John's, and there were the beginnings of many friendships with the young women of Newnham College, as will presently appear. Nevertheless, during the vacations Brooke still turned to his older friends from Rugby and the summer vacation was spent in a hilarious 'reading party' with Hugh Russell-Smith at Lulworth Cove in Dorset and after-wards at Brockenhurst. In September he went on a sightseeing expedition to Belgium with his brother, Alfred.

During the Michaelmas term at Cambridge Brooke began to take an active part in the affairs of the University Branch of the Fabian Society. He had been brought up by his mother in stern Liberal principles, and his uncle, Clement Cotterill, was an advanced Socialist. Brooke, aided and abetted by Dudley Ward, now turned naturally from Liberalism to the next stage of political thinking as represented by the tenets of the Fabian Society, and came into contact with enthusiastic spirits, such as Hugh Dalton, afterwards Minister of State in Socialist governments. Brooke later followed Dalton as President of the Cambridge University Fabian Society. He was also associated with Dalton in founding a discussion society in King's, called the Carbonari. This flourished until their third year, when it was allowed to die.

During the Christmas vacation Brooke was a member of a large party going to Switzerland for winter sports. It was organized by Margery Leon of Newnham and her mother. The year closed, therefore, with a very much larger circle of friends and acquaintances than Brooke had possessed at the beginning. He nevertheless still pretended that he disliked his life in Cambridge and preferred a misanthropic solitude.

To GEOFFREY KEYNES   [*Rugby*]
                                      [*8 January 1907*]

It is half past one and I have just 'lunched' off a milk pudding,
which contained all the delicate perfection of a rose-petal or a dew-
drop, and about as much sustenance. Since 9 o'clock this morning
I have read for four hours and a half. . . '*If you have nothing else to do,
write.*' sez'e; so I write. But—'immortal drivel'! My unworthy
Geoffrey, you should know that I can only write drivel to children.
I write absolute bosh to the Old Thing[1] and others, but to you . . . !
You have reached man's estate (poor fool!); you are 'grown-up';
to you I write as a man, I think as a man. . . Perhaps, in the excitement of the moment, I misled you. I find, on reflection, I have not
really got the influenza. I am merely victim to a bad cold, which is
strong enough to confine me to bed. I lie here amid white sheets,
against which my face is almost invisible, defined only by a short,
healthy beard of strong red hair, in patches. I have a headache now
and then, principally then. I am suffering from constipation, but my
pulse is fairly steady, thank-you. The last time they took my temperature it was ninety-eight by tricks, with simple honours and a
hundred for the rubber.

I rather envy you in London. You will see all the Rodins at the
International; but there will be none so good as the Baisée. I
wonder if you will be in that great city on Monday & Tuesday when
I shall be there. If ever you are near *Goldsmith Building*, The
Temple, drop in & see the Lucas and give him my dying messages.

Arthur Eckersley was tremendously excited about you. He said
you had the most decadent face he had ever seen; but then he writes
for Punch. I told him that you were a notorious evil liver and that your
distinguishing feature was your sincerity, and he was very pleased.

I shall not tell the Aged Inconsequence[1] of my disease. She wrote
and said that at 11 on Thursday morning she will come round to my
rooms & pull me from bed. I know what will happen. She will
turn up duly, find my doors shut, think I am doing it to keep her
out, & yammer on my bedroom door until the O.B. comes out to
shoot her. So will the Antique Irrelevancy[1] be gathered to her
mothers . . .
                    *   *   *

I don't feel especially 'genuinely' depressed, just now. It's not
very enlivening to lie here in bed; but it would be quite as 'dull' if

[1] Hugh Russell-Smith.

I were 'well' and up. Anyhow I escape some languid exams and put off Cambridge for another week.

I have thought over your idea of my at length giving up the pose of discontent and taking to optimism in my old age. I think not. The change might be refreshing, but I scrape along very well as I am; and the pessimistic insincerity pleases *me* at any rate, which is the main thing.

And a week today I return to Cambridge! And there I shall find all the witty and clever people running one another down again. And I shall be rather witty and rather clever & I shall spend my time pretending to admire what I think it humorous or impressive in me to admire. Even more than yourself I attempt to be 'all things to all men'; rather 'cultured' among the cultured, faintly athletic among athletes, a little blasphemous among blasphemers, slightly insincere to myself. . .

However, there are advantages in being a hypocrite, aren't there? One becomes God-like in this at least, that one laughs at all the other hypocrites.

The perennial gaiety of my nature, which you so cunningly discern beneath the mask, enables me to take delight in the great *Influenza* sonnet. It is, as you know, probably the work of Oscar Wilde—at least of his school; its gracile imagery and suave diction ensure it a place in any anthology. . .

Sonnet. *To my Lady Influenza*

As rode along the paven ways of Rome
   Isis, and smiled imperturbably,
While monstrous eunuchs yapped in obscene glee;
   Or perhaps rather as thou us'd'st to come,
Phoibos, in all thy pale pink nudity;
   Or *she* (wearing a fillet on her brow
And absolutely nought else) from the sea
   Rising, an argent dawn! so cometh now

My Lady *Influenza*, like a star,
   Inebriously wan; and in her train
   Fever, the haggard soul's white nenuphar,
And lily-fingered *Death*, and grisly *Pain*,
And *Constipation*, who makes all things vain,
   Pneumonyer, Cancer, and Nasal Catarrh.

Par les dieux jumeaux tous les monstres ne sont pas en Cambridge!

RUPERT

To ERICA COTTERILL   [*Rugby*]
                                Wednesday [*January 1907*]

I am not writing, this time, to provoke either of your Wonderful
Secrets, nor in any special hope or desire of an answer, nor because
I want to write. It is merely because I am in bed with a cold & am
too bored to go on reading & must do something. There's can-
dour! The fact that I am in bed also serves to explain my handwriting.

I don't feel a bit in a mood for writing. I don't know why I began.
Mother has the 'flu', & a trained nurse therefore, who attends me,
too. She is young & Colonial & very businesslike. I have long
conversations with her, slightly smiling all the time, because I mock
her, & she never understands.

She is quite fond of me, because I am a good patient; but she
cannot understand my permanent look of resigned melancholy. I tell
her it's my broken heart, & sigh.

I was to have returned to Cambridge for exams yesterday; as it is
I shall go next Tuesday. I am neither glad nor sorry in the least to
miss Cambridge. On Monday I hope to go to London & see the
Doctor's Dilemma, before proceeding to King's; but ταῦτα θεῶν
ἐπὶ γούνασι κεῖται.[1]

I hope that your education has made progress; at least that your
health is better. I have just read through *Plays Pleasant* again, &
feel more certain than ever that *Candida* is the greatest play in the
world. These holidays have been paltry & pottering as usual. The
only thing of interest—a profound secret—is that Gertrude Lindsay[2]
has been drawing me. I sat on a chair in her studio several afternoons
& wrangled with her while she caricatured me. She has taken the
thing away with her to London to 'finish'; but when I saw it last it
represented me as of a round fat youthful chubby & utterly contented face, instead of the gaunt sallow aged haggard thin expression
at which I always aim. Pah! how one is misunderstood!...

I hope you have been in no more difficulties lately. Last time, if
you remember, I settled the little matter of Socialism for you. I distinctly remember killing it. And now I suppose Wells & Co. are out
of work. Tut! Tut!

All the holidays I have been idle. They are offering a medal to any
fool at Cambridge who writes a good poem on Edward I. I tried
feebly to drivel about him, but failed. I find I know nothing about

[1] i.e. All things lie on the knees of the gods.
[2] Daughter of the drawing master at Rugby School.

him. I tried putting 'Little Arthur's Kings of England' on that period into verse:

> (Edward One
> Had a son
> Who
> Was Edward Two...
> Edward Third
> Was a bird...)

but it didn't seem good enough.

How delightful it is knowing no facts. I flee knowledge as others seek it. The more one knows the less likely one is to find the Light. In consequence I shall take a bad degree.

I think when I have lost all the vain knowledge I ever had I shall go to London or Paris & live for one year a life like a great red flame. As I know nothing, I shall fear nothing. As I seek for nothing, all things will flock to me. I shall wreathe scarlet roses of passion round my smooth brow & drink the purple wine of beauty from the polished skull of some dead Archbishop. I shall write subtle tribrachs & strange anapaests that shall have more delicate melody than all the lilies swaying in the wind of Dawn. I shall never have a cold in my head.

I once dreamt I was in the Gardens of Heaven walking between great odorous beds of helichrys & asphodel. Turning a corner I met the present Headmaster of Rugby School in his shirt-sleeves. He was digging up all the beautiful flowers. I hit him severely on the nose, & asked what he was doing. He said he was uprooting the useless flowers & planting vegetables for food instead. I told him that in Heaven one subsisted entirely on beautiful thoughts. He replied that he would starve; & continued to dig, muttering. He began to swell as I gazed, &, still grunting 'Cabbages & Onions', grew so big that he blotted out all the sky....

To make up for all this bosh, I shall copy out for you the wonderfullest sonnet[1] of the Century. But if you show it to respectable people they'll kill you.   RUPERT

---

[1] The Vision of the Archangels (*Poems*, 1911).

To FRANCIS MACCUNN   *Thursday* [*17 January 1907*]

My dear Francis,

Thinking I should see you today or tomorrow, I did not write. But now it is decided that I 'go up' this afternoon.

You have heard of our trouble,[1] or at any rate this paper explains itself. I am very glad to get away before you all return. This sounds rude. But I am feeling terribly despondent and sad, and I feel that I could not face everybody. The only thing was if I could help Father and Mother by staying, but they say not, and I do not think so. And if I stayed I know I should break down.

There is an instinct to hide in sorrow, and at Cambridge where I know no one properly I can be alone. Therefore I am running away from all you whom I like so much, and one especially. I should only make you unhappy.

I hope you'll all be gentle to my pater at first. He has had a terrible time, and is very tired and broken by it.

*   *   *

Yours ever
RUPERT BROOKE

To ST JOHN LUCAS   *King's* [*Cambridge*]
22 January 1907

Dear St John,

It seems so strange that you haven't heard. I had thought that all the world must know. I suppose I ought to have written and told you: but there were so many letters to write: and I had to try to comfort Mother a little....

Dick died on Sunday the 13th, nine days ago, after a week's illness. Father was with him—but I don't think details matter much. Mother was very weak after influenza when all the trouble came; and directly afterwards the Rugby term began; so she and Father have had a bad time altogether. But I have just heard they are both seeming better.

On the day Dick died, the Head of the firm for which he had been working, who had not even heard of his illness, was writing to Mother. We got the letter the next morning. He praised Dick very

---

[1] The death of his elder brother, Dick.

much, and ended 'Your son has *just finished at* Pembroke [Dock], where he has done very well...we have found another job for him...'. It's the sort of ironical coincidence one reads in a book and winces at.

I came up here on Thursday, partly to escape my Rugby School friends who were coming back that day, and whom I daren't face, and partly that I might be alone. Another thing has happened that hurts a great deal, too; but that affects only me so I suppose it doesn't matter. So that on the whole I am in a state alternating between carelessness and vain resentment.

I don't feel in a mood for writing much.

Yours ever

RUPERT BROOKE

To ST JOHN LUCAS   *King's [Cambridge]*
                                        Thursday [24 January 1907]

My dear St John,

I feel quite certain that this will cross with a letter from you. Did you realize how our last letters got mixed? On Tuesday I wrote to you under the impression you had not heard the bad news. Next day I received a letter, not in answer, dated Saturday, 4 days before; your legal office-boy must have carried it about in his pocket for a few days.

Mother, as far as I can gather from her letters, is getting a little better.

I've met a man who is very anxious to know about *Basil de Sélincourt*, who is writing, art-reviewing etc. nowadays. He thinks him 'the art-critic of the future', and rather bad. I hazarded a theory that he was a younger brother of *Hugh de S.* and that you knew him. Is that so? Tell me of him. We agreed that he was 'very Oxford'.

When is Newnes going to destroy his good name by publishing your marble monstrosity?[1] The 'literary notes' in the papers preserve an ominous silence about it. Is it to burst upon the world one green Spring morning with thunder and flame?

I am rather wretched and ill. In my 'literary life' I have taken the last step of infamy, and become—a reviewer! I have undertaken to 'do' great slabs of minor poetry for *The Cambridge Review*. I have read volumes of them, all the same, and all exactly the stuff I write.

[1] Lucas's *Marble Sphinx*, published in October, 1907.

I frequently wonder whether I have not written several of them myself under a pseudonym, and forgotten about it.

I had once thought of rushing out to Italy this spring, but now, of course, I shan't. Are you now vacillating between London and Paris? I suppose you will be going to spend golden days in the South soon; among flowers and sunshine. Cambridge is terrible, slushy and full of un-Whistlerian mists.   Yours

RUPERT

To GEOFFREY KEYNES   [*Cambridge*]
Sunday, 1.30 a.m.
[*27 January 1907*]

For two hours I have been trying the translation.[1] This is all I have produced: & I fear it's not very literal.   R. C. B.

A Comment

God gives us, in earth's loveliness,
    His own great song-book, it is stated.
We stumble through, (and have to guess
    To whom or what it's dedicated!)

On first perusing, how we yearn to
    Mark every song! but soon, my friend,
The only page we want to turn to
    Holds two best words of all, 'The End'.

But, since we've got to read it through,
    Let us, as true philosophers,
Sit down, and critically review
    God's *very* minor book of verse.

One poem I've underlined—the best—
    (There's all sorts in God's poetry-book!):
But of the lot I most detest
    God's vulgar lyric 'Rupert Brooke'.

.   .   .

[1] I had translated for him a verse of 'Liederbuch der Gottheit' by Christian Wagner, which had been set as a competition in the *Westminster Gazette*. My translation was in prose. His verse rendering was awarded the prize and printed in the *Westminster Gazette*, 2 February 1907.

> And, if you're lenient, and declare
> The faults and merits pretty equal,
> At least you'll join my hearty prayer
> 'Dear Author, *please* don't write a sequel!'

To GEOFFREY KEYNES   [*Cambridge*]
                                        30 January 1907

Dear G.

Come to tea

Yours ever,

R. C. B.

P.S. This refers to tomorrow (Thursday) not today, but it was too much trouble to work it into the rhyme.

I shall ask no one else except an old acquaintance of yours who is so changed since you used to know him that you won't recognize him—one Rupert Brooke. He wants to read you his latest verses. They are very amusing *verse*.

Of course, if I meet any old things about, I might bring them in as chaperones. You can come this afternoon if you like but if you do you'll have to go away again at 5.15. Or tomorrow evening.

R. C. B.

Comment. Attempts at the epistolary style of one's childhood fail. verb. sap.

To ST JOHN LUCAS   *Tomorrow at*
                                        The Green Dragon
                                        Market Lavington
                                        The Good Friday [*1907*]

My dear St John,
                    *   *   *

I was ill with age at Rugby. Then my sad heart sang over Kent and Sussex, with the ridiculous and gross Russell-Smith. We slew a million dragons and wandered on unknown hills. We met many knights and I made indelicate songs about them. We passed Amberley and Arundel, and Dunton and 'Petworth, a little town' as Belloc somewhere finely says. But now I am rather sick and sorry again. I am terribly Fabian; which in our family is synonymous with 'atheistical', 'Roman Catholic', 'vulgar', 'conceited' and 'unpractical'. I try to write Fabian hymns; but ah! my uncles weep. . . .

It's a sad and damnable state when one used to be able to write tinkly verse of a pretty kind and now can't, for the life of one. Will it ever come back? or shall I have to confine myself to discussing up-to-date aesthetics with damned Cambridge fools all my life, and reading other people's verses? Did you ever have aphasia for years? I think I shall take a pass degree this term and go to Japan or Samoa for fifteen years. *Coelum* would be something. . . .

But I may see you on Wednesday.   RUPERT

To JACQUES RAVERAT   *School Field, Rugby*
                                         Easter Sunday [*1907*]
My dear Raverat,

I am so sorry to hear that you sickened again, and cannot attain Greece. I expect you would have found it intolerably and drearily modern, and full of provoking ghosts of dreams that died. Our family party for Paris also is disposed by Fate. My father has been very ill and cannot get abroad. He and my mother are going to some quiet and healthy place in England, while my young brother and I dash out to Italy. We go to Florence and Siena and other places where we shall lose a few of our remaining illusions. I fear we shall not be in your sacrilegious city at all. I am very grieved. *Mona Lisa* will have to languish in her comparative obscurity for yet another year: we go to the tedious Primitives of Italy, whom I pretend to like. We shall quaff great draughts of *Botticelli* wine, and worship before the pale masterpieces of *Chianti* and *Vermicelli*.

England is full of the shade of dead Springs and the mockery of a living one.   RUPERT BROOKE

To MRS BROOKE   *Pension White*
                        Piazza Cavallegieri 2, Florence
                                (till Sat. perhaps)
                        Sunday morning [*7 April 1907*]
Dear Mother,

I expect you got our postcard from Genoa. I hope you and Father are resting and enjoying Bournemouth, and getting as nice weather as we are now. As I said, we had an excellent journey.

Podge thought he didn't feel perfectly well between Calais and Paris; beyond that he was quite right all the way, and slept like a top, using me as a pillow. We had rain for a very hurried glimpse of Pisa (the train was 3/4 of an hour late) but since we came here the weather has been warm and delicious.

Rather luckily, I think, we secured a cheap room in this Pension. It is kept by rather a dear English lady, and is quite the resort of the English middle classes! There are about five males and forty or fifty females. The latter are mostly middle-aged, and all quite serious. All the sitting-rooms are so full of them that Podge and I are terrified of going in. They are, of course, all English. I'll wager Miss Mclure comes here. They are all just like her—pleasant, if only one dare speak to them. At dinner last night I sat next to the widow of an Army Chaplain who is also aunt of the Chaplain of King's, whom I know pretty well. When she discovered this she told all the other widdies (this is quite like Lincoln) that we were utterly respectable. So we are safe. She is rather a discerning old person. She asked me if I came from a public school. I said 'yes'. She gazed at me for a minute, and said, 'Rugby'. I was terrified at her wisdom!

I hate writing on foreign paper. We were busy yesterday. I showed Podge round Florence; then we separated and 'did' Churches and things. He seems quite happy. He has a slight cold in the nose, for which we have procured ammoniated quinine. It is quite trivial, and in no way interferes with our happiness—except that he snores like a pig! To-day, being Sunday, all galleries are free, and Podge and I, who are provident fellows, are going to spend the day in them, so saving some *four* francs! Yesterday, we both separately met Eckhard (once of R.W.)[1] the ugly friend of the Simpson's, who won a prize at our bridge last winter. A person called *White*, in father's form, travelled as far as Dijon in our train, bound for Mentone. I got talking to him, and reproved him for his place in the term's order!

*   *   *

Love to the aunts. Tell them we are revelling in *Botticelli*. I wish you were here; I think you'd both like it.

Your loving son
RUPERT

---

[1] Oscar Eckhard from Whitelaw's House at Rugby.

To MRS BROOKE   *Pension White, Florence*
                                               Thursday
                                  [*Postmark: 12 April 1907*]

Dear Mother,

I don't know if this is going to find you at Bournemouth. I am
sorry no one wrote yesterday. On Saturday we go to Siena but the
address is yet unknown. Today I went for the afternoon to Prato,
about ten miles away, a pretty little town with certain paintings
I wanted to see, in the Church. Podge is frightfully busy all day (in
the intervals of Florentine cakes) with seeing pictures. He has
a vastly greater appetite for both than I. After four strenuous days
I had an indigestion (only metaphorically) and took things more
easily. Podge has shaken off his cold completely I think.

                    *   *   *

At the present moment Podge is being very pleasant about pictures
to a lady (aged 50 or so) a few yards off. He has picked up a good
deal, and very cleverly pretends to about three times as much knowledge. I recognize one or two second-hand remarks of mine! The
lady is frightfully impressed. My book on Florence (which I think
the aunts gave me) is very useful indeed. Weather today glorious,
yesterday rather poor and rainy. Today I went in state with an
armful of flowers which I placed on Landor's and Clough's graves.
I felt I represented Rugby, and ought to! I also spared one rose for
E. B. Browning.

A propos, fancy roses! There are lots of them about, especially in
the Flower-Market, which is held on Thursdays.

                                        Love to all
                                        RUPERT

To ST JOHN LUCAS   *King's* [*Cambridge*]
                                      Tuesday [*May 1907*]

I have tied up and posted to you lately a thing I promised you
a long time since, and we have both forgotten, and now I remember.
I hope it will arrive with this letter. It is the photograph of the
Herald in the late Greek play; an evil photograph; but you may find
it good to put in your legal room and frighten delicate barristers
withal.

I have persuaded the L.N.E. to run a cheap excursion to London
on Saturday. Will you be there, and vacant? I shall get in about

11 a.m. and go to Max's show, and to a matinée. (1) I shall *probably* come up alone, in which case you *must* come, *at the least* to lunch and *Patience* and dinner. Or (2) *Possibly* I may bring two other people with me—Geoffrey Keynes, whom you met before, and another elderly person, quite delightful, called Wilson.[1] I warn you of them, but you'd like them both. There are only seven possible people in Cambridge; and they are two. If they come you had better join us at lunch and a matinée and anyhow I shall bring them to sit in your rooms from 5.30 to 7—an otherwise empty and evil time. And then you could interpret for us at the *Petit Riche*. Is any or all of this possible? Write instantly, and say if you will be in London and free then; I will write when I can find out if the others are coming.

Do be in. I want to talk of next September. I am thinking of taking you to the Touraine or Bohemia (somewhere on the coast) or some such delectable place. Will you come? Why are there no matinées at the Court on Saturday? I suppose *Patience* is the best thing: or would you like *The Palace of Puck* or G. du Maurier?

Scrawl a postcard.

I must go and continue Ridgeway's 'Early Age of Greece': do you know it? It is my favourite reading.   RUPERT

To ERICA COTTERILL   [*Cambridge*]
                                                     21 May [*1907*]

Owing to your quaint regularity in not dating the letters, I can't make out if it's your last or your last but one that I'm answering. Perhaps it doesn't matter. Anyhow you display your customary ineptness in saying I 'extract unreasonable misery from art'; which is all bosh. Art isn't the thing that makes one happy or miserable: it's Life. Art is only a Shadow, a Second-rate Substitute, a Refuge after Life—real Life. I don't extract misery from Art: if anything I occasionally am fortunate enough to find forgetfulness & a watery reflexion of content in it. Pah!

*   *   *

I live on a landing opposite Oscar Browning; a man of bad character & European fame. Your last letter got mixed with *his* morning's post by mistake; & he opened it, naturally. As there was no ordinary beginning, he may have got some way before discovering his error. I still laugh to think of him trying to grasp your highly

[1] Hugh Wilson of King's College, afterwards a master at Rugby School.

ethical & valuable advice. I wonder when I'm going to see you again. I feel it's some time since I saw you last. I met you once, a thousand years ago—nearly a year. Or was it someone else? I forget. Anyhow I am wholly changed; & infinitely old & wise. I have given up writing poetry, or believing in God, or in myself, or any such youthful things. How great is wisdom—I am sorry: I am desponding again. But when you last saw me, I wrote & talked very smartly of death & separation & such things. Now I have known them; & it hurts; & I'm puzzled & tired, & there's nothing to be done. But I'm not really always miserable, or thinking I am. I mislead you. But you see when I'm with Father & Mother, or writing to them, I have to be cheerful & happy. They're so unhappy already, I don't want to add to it. So when I turn to others, I work off my accumulated gloom on them. Selfish, perhaps, but in some ways it is better than storing it up! Anyhow, I'll soon be all right again—mentally, as you physically.   RUPERT

To FRANCIS MACCUNN   [*Cambridge*]
                                    Saturday night [*May 1907*]

Yes, I am afraid I owe you an apology, My dear Francis!

I *could* make the excuse of 'no news', but it's one that I never accept. It would be true, but no excuse. And yet—I'm rather a doleful person, and I hardly know what to say. I have been observing in the Sportsman the career of the Rugby School Cricket XI, with some interest. If I were there this year my batting average of 2· something would bring me out quite high in the list. However, I noticed they reached double figures the other day. I fear that they have been neglecting the left-hand bowling talent in the school.

I am in the middle of exams. They begin at 9 every morning! I believe myself to be doing phenomenally badly. For the history (Greek –404 B.C. Roman 133 B.C.–120 A.D.) we had a year to prepare. I read 300 pages of Bury on the last two days and no Roman History at all. It quite reminded me of old times.

                    *   *   *

Last night I went to a private small society in Pembroke where Hilaire *Belloc* came and read a paper and talked and drank beer—all in great measure. He was vastly entertaining. Afterwards Gow and I walked home with him about a mile. He was wonderfully drunk and talked all the way. I *may* be going to meet him at lunch tomorrow. Tell this to my little brother, who is in the same house as you: you can tell Ma if you see her; but for God's sake don't say he was drunk, or she'll never read him again.

What else is there to say? The world is infamously dull. I shall see you perhaps in a fortnight or so. My plans are typically vague. Next week is '*May week*' here—dances and things. I shall shut myself up for it. The place will be full of giggling females, who are even worse than Dons.   Yours always

RUPERT BROOKE

To MRS BROOKE   [*Cambridge*]
Sunday [*2 June 1907*]

Dear Mother,

I write feeling a little depressed. The Chapel Clerk has just been in to tell me I'm reading in Chapel this week—8 a.m. every morning, and just when I was looking forward to taking things easy after the 'Mays'! I am in the middle of those wretched exams now. I don't know how I'm doing: Yesterday I must have been bad. For all day exams on Friday and the excitement of hearing *Belloc* in the evening, or something, prevented me sleeping much that night, and so yesterday I was frightfully tired. However, today's a welcome rest.

Today I have been mingling with the great! R. S. Durnford gave the annual 'landing' breakfast—i.e. for all on this landing of this staircase, the two Durnfords, myself, and the 'O. B.'. The last was in great form, talking of what he was going to do when his 'old friends', 'Curzon and Campbell-Bannerman', came up to receive honorary degrees this week, and so on. And at lunch I met Belloc. For him I must begin at the beginning. On Friday I went and heard him read his paper on History in Pembroke. Gow was also there: I had introduced Belloc's works to him and he is very keen on them. Belloc (in the intervals of discussion) drank beer all the evening: his paper and replying was all magnificent to hear. Afterwards Gow who is a person of consummate conceit and 'unabashedness' got into conversation with Belloc, and invited him to lunch for today. Hence my lunch: for of course I went, too. After the paper on Friday, Gow and I were coming away when I remembered that Belloc was not staying in Pembroke, so we turned back to see if we could escort him home. We met him coming out of Pembroke and discovered he was staying about a mile away, and had no notion where it was. There was no cab to be found, so we showed him the way, and walked there with him. He was excited after the discussion on his paper and talked absurdly—rather in the *Path to Rome* style— all the way. And at 4 p.m. today I met him again in the street and, finding he was still hazy as to the best way to his house walked there with him again. So altogether I feel rather pleased with myself!

*   *   *

Your loving son
RUPERT

To HUGH RUSSELL-SMITH   *BMTH* [*Bournemouth*]
[*June 1907*]

(Δηρύ)¹
(Bolly Boll)

Mrs* Chaffey, of the Post Office, W. Lulworth thanks me for my card, and will reserve rooms, 'as agreeded'. (She thinks my name is Brooks, and ∴ she is P.P.*) She is no Woman of Business: for she doesn't say what is agreeded (Doric for 'agreed') and *I* don't know. The only thing I have any idea of is that I *think* I said we'd go on the 14th; which turns out to be Sunday. Perhaps we'll go on the 15th. The effort of conducting a correspondence in the Arcadian variety of the Doric dialect, with Mrs Chaffey, P.P., is exhausting.

Tell me what sort of books you are going to take.

. . .So you 'don't think much of Δηρύ'? I'm sorry. I think of it a good deal myself. You must *try* to think more of it, Hugh. It's the only way. Try a cold bath in the morning, followed by a brisk rub down with a *rough* towel; and then think of it for ten minutes before breakfast—a *light* breakfast. I don't know if *prayer* would help you. I once knew a young man who *became a successful man of business* merely by thinking of the word 'biddle' for an hour a day. And now he wears four studs, and his second daughter's name is Yvaille. There are indeed many devious difficulties which may be tided over by a bright face and I always, like you do too, I hope, trust in Provi- dence although these things may not always be.

You know I always like to keep you *au fait* (as our Gallic neigh- bours would have it) with my latest literary activity. This *came to me*

* Or Mr   * P.P. =Puce Pig.

¹ A fictitious word.

as I was sitting by the sea the other day. I don't know what it was—
perhaps it was the rhythm of the waves. But I felt *I must sing.* So
I sang:

> 'I love a *scrabbly* epithet,
> The sort you can't ever forget,
> That blooms, a lonely violet
> In the eleventh line of a sonnet.
>
> I know one such; I'm proud to know him.
> I'll put him in my next GREAT POIM.
> He plays the psack-butt very well:
> And his Aunt was a Polysyllable.'

The night is purple with a weariness that is older than the stars;
and there is a sound of ineventual tears.   R.

To HUGH RUSSELL-SMITH   *Grantchester Dene*
                                      Littledown Road
                                      Bournemouth
                                      27 June [1907]
                                      Thursday evening anyhow

δήρῦ

Weather's execrable.

Tomorrow (or day after) I shall dare the rain and the wind; and
win through to Lulworth to charter that Palace. The station to
Lulworth is called Wool; $4\frac{1}{2}$ miles from Lulworth. I find Lul'th
must be that achievable locality and place, which we shall bless. Why?
Because half a mile therefrom are the *Mupe* rocks.

Mupe....

Have even *we* made a better name?

The books I have here are:

Philoctetes⎫
          ⎬ Jebb.   Theocritus   Cholmely.
Electra   ⎭

                     Dignity: Liddell and S[cott].

                     (So don't you bring him: unless we want
                     two.)

Pelham's Roman History
Bury's Greek History   (*History*!)
Plato.   Phaedo ⎫ Archer-Hind.
         Phaedrus⎭ Thompson.

(You said you were going to Read Plato. You had better read these: at any rate the *Phaedrus*; *and* the Symposium? in which case I'll get a copy. I think so.)
Demosthenes   De Falsa Legatione.   Mithter Thilleto.
Kit Marlowe
Percy B. Shelley
John Donne
Walt Whitman
? Spenser
John Keats
Alighieri Dante Inferno (!)

And all these will be subservient and apt to your usage if you admit need of them.

You note that I'll be reading all and only Greek. Admirable forethought! And with *you* (that so Hellenic figure!)...

*   *   *

Lulworth, you would know, is 'a favourite resort of the cycling confraternity'. It is also 'Prankt in a sapphire sea', 'Sun-facing, with a vista of rathe waves' and Museous, with 'growth of slow, low, flowery Hours'. Population 723.

If you have not read 'Tess of the D'Urbervilles' do so, ere you come. This is Wessex; and she lived near P. P.[1]

My Opes for Enley. I ave done seven hrs. Sophokles today and shall do another, ere I rest.

We shall edit a P. P. Journal. *I* will do a leader and the book-reviews. *You* will do the fashion-notes, and Society Jottings. *We* shall do a Short Story. I will conduct an antiquarian correspondence on the First Countess Pimpinella. You shall adumbrate a *Causerie* on the Artistic Temperament....

'V' eard from me Tutor. 'Got a bad second* in me Mays.' Examiners held a special meeting 'to decide what steps to take in consequence of my "flippant remarks" in my History Papers'.

I feel almost youthful again.   RUPERT

* Explain difference between Bad Second and Bad 2th (*tooth*). See! He! he! R.

[1] i.e. Pimpinella Palace, his name for the lodgings at Lulworth.

To ANDREW GOW   *South of England*
                                             [*Bournemouth*]
                                        Sunday [*July 1907*]

Thank you for your condolences about my 'Mays'. It is a subject
on which many views can be, and are, held; some, I regret to say,
with partisan fervour.

It must have been very delightful for William Yeats, Miss Horniman, & Synge being introduced to you. I did not see anything about
it in the papers. I, about that time, was spreading the Gospel of
Cambridge Intellect in yet another place, Oxford. I was staying with
two popular novelists, who were, at that time, Bacon & Shakespere,
for Pageant Purposes. At Cambridge, once, I lunched with two
Greek deities and a matricide. But that was nothing to dining every
day with Bacon & Shakespere. In connexion with the Pageant
(whose fair dress-rehearsal I saw) I met various amusing people; an
undergraduate who was taking the part of Mr W. H.—an incident
that was altered before the real performance, also Frank Lascelles,
master of the Pageant; Laurence Housman, who wrote an episode;
and a nice man called Dion Clayton Calthrop, who was arranging
the dresses. The last is an Amusing Artist, a friend of Belloc &
G. K. C., and the author of a fascinating book called 'a guide to
Fairyland'. Read it. It will do you good.

The book of the Horace Club is amusing; good for Oxford. Shall
we get up a rival at Cambridge? In Belloc's Sussex poem I remember
taking keen pleasure. A great friend of mine, St John Lucas, was
a member of the H.C., and tells delectable tales of Belloc; who would
attend a meeting, declare he'd forgotten to write anything, &, retiring
into the corner with pencil & an old envelope, produce a 'song'
swiftly.

Tomorrow I'm going to the most beautiful place in England to
work. It is called West Lulworth. I have made seven poems on it,
some very fine, and all resting on the fact that Lulworth Cove
rhymes with love: a very notable discovery. As this is Sunday,
however, I will leave such secular subjects, and tell you a very
beautiful poem of the Doleful kind, which I have made. It is called:

A song, Explanatory of Strange Sense of Incompatibility
        between Self and Universe,
            and,
                In Praise of Decease.
                        Written to a Fellow Sufferer

I . 'Things are a brute,
       And I am sad and sick;
       Oh! you are a Spondee in the Fourth Foot,
       And I am a final Cretíc.'
                         (I hope the technical terms are right.)

II. 'Things are beasts:
       Alas! and Alack!
       If Life is a succession of Choreic Anapaests,
       When, O When, shall we arrive at the Paroemiac?'

                                             R. C. B.

To GEOFFREY FRY   [Postcard]
                                        South of England
                                          July [*1907*]

I'm working 13 hours a day in a House where they do not have
Sir T. Browne. So I forget which the xliv section is.[1] Perhaps it is of
the *Iniquity of Time blindly scattering*[2] ... My edition of the City of
Dreadful Night is Mosher's, that beneficent pirate. I got it 2nd
hand. 1st hand it costs many dollars & other Western coin. It is
more delectable, but no more complete, than a small volume issued,
for 3 shillings perhaps, by Bertram Dobell of Charing Cross Road.
Either contains all of J[ames] T[homson] that one wants. In a week
I am going to the most beautiful place in England, Lulworth Cove.
Tess came from those parts and I have seen her there. I met Laurence
Housman the other day. His brother is the only poet in England.

                                             R. C. B.

To ST JOHN LUCAS   *Bournemouth: South of France*
                                       [*July 1907*]

Dear Memmius,[3]

I can prove you are an Accident, a Superb Accident. Its all in
a book, such a good book, I'm reading here; a book called '*Things*',
by T. Lucretius Carus, an author whom Arthur declared yesterday,
with an high strange laugh, to be *dear* at any price. From which you
may know that Arthur is in excellent health; in spite of the fact that
they played '*Gentlemen Boarders: A Farce*'[4] in the Theatre Royal,
Bournemouth, three weeks ago, and he was nearly lynched. I look

---

[1] *Religio Medici*, pt. 1.   [2] From *Hydriotaphia*.
[3] A Roman orator and tribune.   [4] By Arthur Eckersley.

at him for twenty minutes a day, and go back to my work refreshed. As for Lucretius, who could write like an Hebrew prophet when he wished, and then takes half a book to prove that all atoms are infinitely small, and some smaller!...I'm making a theory by which he wrote all the Ecclesiastes bits and the Primavera beginning and so on; and the rest is by a thirteenth century schoolman called Euhemerus Spencer. (Why has your Gilbert Murray proved Homer a syndicate again?) All great minds go astray; Lowes Dickinson, Lucretius, and myself, through too much love of philosophy; you through a perverted and miserable sense of irony which leads you to print superb, soul-kindling, things like the *Ship of Fools*, in the Spectator. Do do it again; and leave the Law. It was more glorious than bugles at night.

Here, in the South, it is hot. In the mornings I bathe, in the afternoons lie out in an hammock among the rose-beds, and watch them playing croquet (pronounced krōky).

Are you skating yet?

A week ago was a great oasis in a dull life. Whenever I drink port and eat *pâté de foie gras* I think of it. I hope you liked my Wyckhamist. I'm vexed to miss you at Rugby. You may walk through our garden to the Courts, and play water-polo on the lawn, or do anything else with it.

My Evangelical aunts always talk at meals like people in Ibsen. They make vast Symbolical remarks about Doors and Houses and Food. My one aim is to keep the conversation on Foreign Missions, lest I scream suddenly. At lunch no one spoke for ten minutes! Then the First Aunt said '...The Sea?...The Sea!...' And an Old Lady Visitor replied: 'Ah?'

A merry Christmas (or Xmas as they say in America).

RUPERT

P.S. Lucretius loved children. So much is forgiven him.

To DUDLEY WARD [*Bournemouth*]
[*July 1907*]
Honble & dr Mr,

In reply to your favour of 7th inst. I beg to enclose map.

*   *   *

From Wool one bicycles 4 miles to Lulth Cove. Does the road wind up hill all the way?[1] No, not quite to the very end; in spite of

[1] From Christina Rossetti's 'Uphill'.

Miss Rossetti. But its a stiff bit. Natheless, as you say, we'll do it. If it rains—. But you won't travel in your best clothes.

(How the luggage comes from Wool, I don't know.)

I shall *probably* bring Jowett's Plato, Vol. I, containing Phaedrus and Symposium, Englished. It *might* take the luggage from Wool to Lulth Cove. (See?)

Our address will be just* Post Office. West Lulworth, Dorset.

The Mrs Chaffey, the lady who will land us, wanted to know what food to get in. I told her, porridge, jam, coffee, marmalade, and ordered a fruit tart and rice and some meat for Munnay evening. Amn't I business man?

I don't know what
quinquequitous means.

*   *   *

I can blow smoke-rings.

Write if you will be having the midday meal here. Oh! I think you will   RUPERT

* Not in the address: adverb qualifying be.

To MRS BROOKE   *Post Office, West Lulworth*
                                               Sunday [*21 July 1907*]

Dear Mother,

Many thanks for the various commissions. Laurence's have sent 'Tess', but not 'Symposium' yet.

I do a fair amount of work here: less than at Bournemouth, a little; but I take more exercise. This is the seventh day we have been here and we have not had a drop of rain, scarcely a cloud. Every morning we bathe. The drawers you sent were too old and I have got some more. Sometimes we go in a boat in the Cove, or outside, for exercise, and sometimes walk on the downs or ramble about the cliffs and rocks. This last pastime is extremely destructive to shoes. Where we are is really Lulworth Cove, West Lulworth being half a mile further up from the sea, East Lulworth three miles to the N.E. There are very few people, whether visitors or inhabitants, and they peaceful. The sea is always different colours, and sometimes there are good sunsets. The place suits us very excellently; but I do not think it would quite do for you. You would find difficulty in getting a carriage, and one cannot walk more than 100 yards without having to go up a place at this angle _/ . The lodgings are quite nice, but rather free and easy. Many things of surpassing interest have happened. On Monday when our boxes appeared, I found I had lost or left my keys, and my box had to be broken open with a pick-axe. On Wednesday evening I was very ill for about two hours; because I had eaten too much, or something that disagreed with me, or because I had been lying about in the sun too much, or because I had been reading History all the morning. But I soon recovered, and am now very well, and last night I had Lobster and it did me no hurt.

*   *   *

With love
RUPERT

To GEOFFREY KEYNES   *Post Office, Lulworth*
21 July 1907

In response to yours I started a letter which told the truth incisively. It commented very veraciously upon your decaying & spangled style. But I will not complete it. Why should you be puzzled & irritated for a little? You probably mean well.

But you shouldn't ask for a 'real letter', as of old. Aren't we a little too wise for the nonsense that once amused us?

And you are unintelligible about a photograph. You have one of two years ago which is good enough; if you want a much worse one of one year ago (XI) I will send you one when I get home.

Lulworth is a tiresomely backward & old-fashioned place. There are no promenades, nor lifts, nor piers, nor a band; only downs & rocks & green waters; & we sit & bathe & read dead & decaying languages. Very Dull. Hugh is becoming very rustic & Varmer-loike. His language is quaintly rural, being composed of such words as 'Dod rot'un!' 'Iss, fay' 'Gormed' etc. His conversation is almost exclusively on Turmuts. Our few moments of intense & quiet joy are when we think we might be in Cambridge now.

My death is not yet announced, as you say. It almost occurred yesterday; when I ate what should not have been (some-when and -how) and evil fell. I was violently sick four times; throwing up, indeed, all I had eaten for weeks and also my immortal soul, and several political convictions. Even then Stomach was unsatisfied & attempted to repeat its performance 16 times. I lay groaning. Hugh was frightened. Today I am weak but cheerful. I can sit up & take a little weak Plato.

On Tuesday we sat on seagirt rocks & read J. Keats. When I leapt from rock to rock J. K. fell from pocket into swirling flood beneath; &, ere aught could be done, was borne from reach on swift current. We rushed to the harbour, chartered a boat, & rowed frantically along the rocky coast in search of it. The sea was ∿∿. At length we spied it close in, by treacherous rocks, in a boat we could not get to it alive. We beached our barque (at vast risk) half a mile down the coast & leapt lightly over vast boulders to the spot. At first we re-saw it not. Then Hugh's small but acute left eye saw it in the midst of a roaring vortex. There was a Pause.

With a hurried misquotation from Diodorus Siculus I cast off my garb, & plunged wholly naked, into that 'fury of black waters & white foam'—Enough. J. K. was rescued, in a damaged condition. All (except my Stomach) is well.

Hugh salutes you.   RUPERT

[Enclosed with the foregoing letter from Lulworth]

THE PIMPINELLA PALACE POST

THEY COME!

B. and The OLD THING. Enthusiastic Scenes

SPECIAL INTERVIEW

Monday, 15th inst. was indeed a red letter day in the *fasti* of our humble homestead. The day dawned, long before the rest of the world was astir, with full presage of a summer day. Everything looked blue, except the sky; which was of a burnt umber hue, with occasional pink spots in the East. The rain was mainly in two sharp showers from 6 a.m. to noon & from noon to 6 p.m. The ardour of the crowd was undamped, and about 4 p.m. the cry went up 'They are on the point of effecting their ingress into the station!' Lightly as boys The Pair leapt from the train, The Old Thing being slightly in front and a good deal behind. With a repeated and affable smile they bowed their acknowledgements to the general acclamation. Our representative managed to get in a few words with the veteran *poseurs*. In response to his questions The Old Thing said: 'Yes (he! he!) yes, of course (te! he! he!)...or, rather, I suppose perhaps...', but at that point was prevented by ill-mannered mirth from saying any more. B. looked elderly & said nothing.

Outside, the massed clergymen of the diocese sang Hymn No. 499; followed by the undenominational school-children's rendering of their special anthem, 'Huzza! Huzza!' With repeated acclamation

'We welcome Them as They issue from the station...
   ...This is, as far as we can see
       B.
  ...With the thunder of trumpets & the blare of drums,
             SHE comes!'

NOTES ON DRESS

by our Lady Correspondent

The Old Thing was looking very chic and a little piqué in a plain pink travelling dress with bodice to match. The chiffon cut-away was neatly worked in with trimmings of fleur-de-lys rosettes down the side, the whole being smartly taken up by valanced double-couplings of mouse-coloured mousseline. The skirt was cut low & full & got clear away over the hips, but was caught up by a neat flounce of cream plush. A small bunch of imitation cherries on the left shoulder completed the *ensemble*, which, though quite *tout fait* for July, must be held a little hard on the tonal values.

B. was wearing his *coiffure* full, but rather low, and a little to windward.

POETICAL CORNER

Drinking Song,
           against Teetotal Habits.

'I'd rather be a gorm'd twoad,
  In a mucky road,
Than soop t'watter all day,
  Iss, fay!'
(Chorus) 'Pass ta moog!'   O. T.

Topographical Sonnet

'Lulworth is one of the most delectable of towns,
  Being pleasantly situated among downs
Some of them hundreds of feet large, and more,
  Such as I never saw
Before.
On the other side of it
Are the billows of the ocean.'

INTERVIEW WITH GAFFER PLUGG

Startling Pronunciamento

Our representative called upon Gaffer Plugg, the notable func-
tionary and prognosticator, at his well-appointed residence in Mupe
Lane. At a request for a statement of his opinion upon the now state
of affairs, Gaffer Plugg was understood to give egress to the
following statement:

Gaffer Plugg: 'Gor brast 'un mucky!'

On being pressed to commit himself further, he said:

Gaffer Plugg: 'Dang'ee.'

The company then sat down to a sumptuous repast; and a very
enjoyable evening was terminated by the singing of the National
Anthem.

POITICLE ADRES

WROT BI ME AND UGH

×   HOUR MARX

×

Verse I

Oh give our love to Lulworth Cove,
    And Lulworth Cliffs and Sea!
Oh Lulworth Down! Oh Lulworth Town!
    (The name appeals to me.)
If we were with you today in Lulworth,
    How happy we should be!

Verse II

The Lulworth downs are large and high
    And honourable things.
There we would lie (old Hugh and I!)
    On the tombs of the old sad kings:
If you lie up there, with your face in the grass
    You can hear their whisperings.

Verse III

And each will sigh for the good day light
    And for all his ancient bliss.
Red wine, and the fight, and song by night,
    Are the things they chiefly miss.
And one, I know, (for he told me so)
    Is sick for a dead lad's kiss.

Verse IV

Ah! they're fain to be back for a many things
    But mainly (they whisper) these:
England and April (the poor dead kings!)
    And the purple touch on the trees,
And the women of England, And English springs
    And the scent of English seas.

Verse V

But a lad like you, what has he to do
    With the Dead, be they living or dead,
And their whims and tears for what can't be theirs?
    Live you in their silly stead,
With a smile and a song for the live and strong
    And a sigh for the poor old Dead.

Verses VI to LX

Still simmering.   B. & S.

To MRS BROOKE   *Lulworth*
                  [Postmark: 30 July 1907]

Dear Mother,

      *   *   *

I forgot I hadn't given you my present Westminster pseudonym which is *S. E. N.*; I think I told you I had gone in for a competition. I didn't contribute anything: only won a guinea about ten days ago. I changed my name because my last one became too well-known! and all the stuffy people at Cambridge used to talk to me about it. I hope *S. E. N.* will not spread too far. How did you hear I won anything?

I suppose you are very glad holidays have begun again. I am rather busy finishing up odds and ends of packing and work.

                      Your loving son
                         RUPERT

To ST JOHN LUCAS   *at Watersgreen House*
                           Brockenhurst
                          4 August [1907]

My dear St John,

The Russell-Smith and I were full of woe that you would not come.   *   *   *

Now I am staying with this foolish family again till about next Saturday. They are delightful, and exactly as they were last year. But I, I have a year of 'University Life' between then and now; and I am older than the hills. A few days ago they found I was exactly—20: and congratulated me on my birthday, giving me a birthday cake, and such things. I hated them, and lost my temper. I am now in the depths of despondency because of my age. I am filled with a hysterical despair to think of fifty dull years more. I hate myself and everyone. I have written almost no verse for ages; I shall never write any more. I have forgotten all rhythm and metre. The words *Anapaestic dimeter acatalectics* that fired me once, now leave me cold. The sunset or a child's face no longer remind me of a bucolic caesural. But I still read plaintively (to pass the time); and I keep a daily look out in the Times for your *Funeral March of a Mad Poet*. I shall be in Rugby at the end of this week for some months. Shall I play tennis with you there? You will find the lurid Philip Coles with us; and you can discuss decadent French literature with him and Alfred. But I shall leave the room.

Life is a burden. There are too many questions I can't find an answer to. The rest are coming back from church. They want to tell me what the sermon was about. RUPERT

To CHARLES SAYLE *at Watersgreen House*
Brockenhurst
[*August 1907*]

My dear Sayle,

Is a person with illiterate handwriting who signs himself S. Gaselee,[1] & claims to be editor of the Cambridge Review, the one I have heard you speak of? Do I gather he is 'in residence' for next year? And is he a stuffy man (as Editor) who will expunge acrimonious attacks and unfair abuse on other minor poets as his clerical predecessor did? Yours ever

RUPERT BROOKE

[1] Stephen Gaselee of King's, afterwards Sir Stephen, Librarian to the House of Lords.

To GEOFFREY KEYNES *School Field, Rugby*
12 August 1907

My dear Geoffrey,

I had just formulated a letter of wildly ironical thanks for your answer to P[impinella] P[alace] Post—when—

Your letter came: just as I had finished a postcard to Sayle. It was opportune. S. & I had reached what my great-aunt used to call an *impasse*. I had written 'Am coming with relations to stay with you.' He replied 'Will tolerate you: refuse relations.' I answered 'Many thanks. Self & relations appear on Friday.' Then your letter appeared. It is very noble & sweet of you—& your mother; if she was consulted. We gratefully accept: *unless* Sayle has produced an extra bed meanwhile. It will only be for Friday night. Denham [Russell-Smith] was the last person you thrust on your people. If they're looking forward to another Denham, they'll be disappointed in Alfred. But I'll warn him not to say too frightful things in public. M'uncle is changing his house or face or wife or something: or we would not burden you. I've rather a fancy for Peter P[an] & Patience. *Perhaps I* may stay at Sayle's over Sunday to avoid visitors here, & if I can't get things finished. But don't tell Sayle. I shall be very prettily mannered this time: though my clothes are indescribable. I should love to go to the Orchard[1] (time permitting): but (a) I can't swim 100 yards, (b) *In Chapel* has found no successor. I shan't dream of letting you 'look after' Alfred at all. I have too much regard for that youthful innocence which lies so purely on your face.

Also you would give him but a prejudiced idea of Hell. By the way, you scoff at my entering Cambridge. It is merely a business visit: *in re* my rooms. And though Cambridge is loathsome (less in the absence of 'undergrads') yet (don't you know, yet?) what I chiefly loathe & try to escape is not Cambridge nor Rugby nor London, but—Rupert Brooke. And I can only do this by rushing suddenly to places for a few days. He soon overtakes me. If you desire to break your loco-motor-bicycle journey to B'hurst, Rugby is a central place to spend a night in. It is not very lively; but there is always Arthur Eckersley to laugh at. A ludicrous (if scarcely decent) exhibition. He is more impossibly ridiculous than ever. But you will probably be dead by then. I loathe you with a deadly jealousy because you have B'hurst to look forward to. I shall probably kill you on Saturday morning. I have just returned from the dear Smiths. I was

[1] At Grantchester.

asked for a week & stayed two and had to be thrust out. Half the time I was impossibly rude. Don't corrupt them with your modern decadence! Denham is more fascinating & bewildering than ever. I am afraid he found me, generally, too old. Be very young to them. To watch Denham's behaviour towards the rest of the family turns to sweetness (for a moment) even the dour pessimism of

Yours

RUPERT

To CHARLES SAYLE   *School Field, Rugby*
23 August [*1907*]

My dear Sayle,

Many thanks for enduring me for three days. How more pleasant is Cambridge in the absence of University regulations, 'college life', and hordes of people of the intolerable age! Even the allophonic barbarians scarcely blotted its serenity.

You have quite determined the particular branch of failure my brother [Alfred] is going to adopt in life. He has been searching in secret and rarely opened cupboards of the T[emple] R[eading] R[oom] for *incunabula* and carburettors and such technical objects. I believe he caught some. I was with him for a bit; a little carelessly, but on my own quests. I discovered an old *Pericles & Aspasia*, with the bookplate of one Frederick Leighton—the notable oleographist, I take it? At any rate, it was infinitely the most desirable bookplate in the world.

Your *carillon* words o' Sunday have borne fruit. Hungry for summer, we have abandoned Scotland. Alfred has taken over the arrangements, proposed (& carried) three weeks in Belgium— Brussels, Bruges, & Ghent. If you have in these places any especial advice or not-to-be-missed antiquity, pray tell one of us on a post-card. It may be I shall have fallen for those gross painters when I see you next. At least I shall be looking at them when you & Arthur Watts are staring at picture-postcard skies & snow. To him my salutations. Oh yes, & tell him (& yourself) that Yeats' Deidre is out today or yesterday (of course he *knows*). A good play, his best. Never say I did not tell you.

The modern Geoffrey is going to snort over here & break our old-world serenity this week-end. While he sleeps I shall steal out

& prick his automobile-bicycle all over & remove many screws & ungum the best bits. Then he will mount it on Monday; & die.

With all thanks (mine & Alfred's) & wishes for Switzerland.

Ever

RUPERT BROOKE

To DUDLEY WARD   *Belgium* (*a flat country*)
[*9 September 1907*]

Which is the more intolerable, you who write two letters to anotha fella's one, or Denham who answers long letters by return of post? In either case you (or he) have the perennial advantage of me, being *e superiore loco* as it were—so.

Flemish is an amusing language. *Rechtstreeks* = directly: and the place where trams stop is called *tramstilstand*. They spell beer *byrrhe*. Brussels is rather a sickening place. Perhaps Bruges will be less sickening a place than Brussels, which (for a place) is rather sickening. Oh, it will *do*, of course. Not like England. But one wouldn't expect it. (No downs; and the children laugh differently.)

*   *   *

The ocean, as we crossed, was monstrous. It steamed, and slid into wrinkles, and heaved with obscene regularity, like the great paunch of some German sea-god, overfed and stertorous. Things were livid; and one's soul slimed. Once on *terrus firmae*, however, one's *joie du vivre* began to rapidly recover.

*   *   *

To think of discovering Menander! They'll be discovering *us* soon. My great Poem: 'Le Pedant ivre' is not yet published. My Home thoughts from Abroad is already out, however.

> By George! I do not like a foreigner
> He is green and grey as sea water
> Unfascinating is the face of him (or her)
> (Chorus.) By George
> (Minor Chorus.) Bibble.
> Nebuchadnezzar and Asshur-banipal
> Kosh, Lushoo, & John K. Billings, were
> foreigners all,
> and now of them what memorial?
> but you know it.

I am sleepy.   RUPERT

To GEOFFREY KEYNES   *De Boeck's Hotel, Place Louise*
                                              Brussels
                              Sabbath, 10 September 1907

I am sorry Raverat has poisoned you. It is however perhaps some excuse for your temporary vileness in talking of that thing as a sonnet. Do ask someone. Even Raverat would tell you what a sonnet is.

I do not climb.

I will send a postcard to Mallory at the improbable address to say so: that your combined plans may be facilitated. I will send it this evening.

I don't know what a rücksac is.

If you are passing through Rugby on the 13th do drop in at School Field. We shall none of us be there.

Much as I should enjoy...old Cambridge friends...pleasant out-door life...delightful reunions...intellectual conversations ...good, hard mountaineering...

As I don't return to England till the 20th & then must work hard to make up time, I fear I must reluctantly, very reluctantly, I may say, decline[1]... Middle-aged & lewd Dutch painters are really more my mark. Though, of course you need some elderly & common sense person like me to restrain your (plur.) boyish ardour.

If you are returning through Rugby between Sept. 21 & Oct. 6 do bring yourself & Wilson & Mallory, or any of them, in to see the place for a day or two or three. You may happen on Hugh Smith or Saunt also.

*   *   *

My compliments to Jacques. And remember me, as they say in England, to Wilson & Mallory. Thanks.

                                        RUPERT
Belgium has no hills.

To ERICA COTTERILL   *Café Maritime*
                         Boulevard Anspach, Brussels
                                  Friday 6 p.m.
                         [*10–12 September 1907*]

Today I meant to do millions of things; but at lunch developed intolerable neuralgia. I slept all afternoon; & now, slightly better, have wandered down to the busiest café in the busiest street. I called

[1] Rock-climbing in Wales with George Leigh Mallory, Hugh Wilson and myself.

majestically for pen, ink, paper & coffee, in French. The waiter (who insists on speaking to me in English) has brought two vessels of black liquid. I have tasted both; & neither is coffee. However, I am writing with the nastier, & drinking the other. It is, of course, an usual outdoor café. A yard in front, thousands of cosmopolitan beasts walk swiftly by. They are all misshapen, & some day God will burn them. A nosy Jew at the little table next me sips *absinthe*. (When I drink *absinthe* I have to go to out-of-the way cafés lest my English parents see me.) But for my superb self-restraint I should occupy the whole letter in describing the fantastic people & things that happen just before me. As for the forgotten things of England —I am sorry that Life is not as fair as the chryselephantine Athene to you.

I am a little cheered by the unwonted foreign pictures & people. We stay here a few weeks & then I go to Rugby to work frightfully hard (as I have been doing) till my Cambridge term. I am afraid my world-stained & white feet will not lead me to the faint hills of Godalming. (An example of my new prose style.) We may meet in London some time, any time for the Savoy: I from Rugby or Cambridge. When does Granville Barker's play *Waste* happen? In November I fancy. I have not been in London (except for two hours on the way here) since June. As for play-writing, or writing of any kind—I have been too busy with dead & decaying languages to dream of such things. I am afraid you, in common with the rest of the impatient world, will have to wait, at least for some years, for the divine products of my inspired pen. I am sorry for the world.

There is in the hotel we stay at (De Boeck's Hotel, Place Louise) a man who would madden you. Even the placid me he sometimes infuriates rather than amuses. He has a truculent little moustache & the beefy face of a brute. He is English, of an unpleasant accent, & utterly intolerant. Some day I shall put him in a book. He talks in a most ignorant & offensive way about things he detests—working-people, Socialism, etc. Socialism is a name he applies to any kind of reform. He is the most coarse & little-minded man in the world; & I despair of England.

There is little to say. I am going out to study Flemish painters whom I really loathe. They are too much like Life; & I loathe Life.

RUPERT

To GEOFFREY FRY   *De Boeck's Family Hotel*
                                     54 Avenue de la Toison d'Or
                                     (*Place Louise*) *Brussels*
                                     for a very few days
                                     [*10–12 September 1907*]

*   *   *

The other night I went to an opera of Berlioz—Les Troyens
à Carthage; a very notably funny dramatization of Aen. IV (it was
meant serious). The names of the characters moved me from the
beginning to an asbestos laughter. Didon (pronounce them with
the fully clipped French accent to get the full flavour)—Didon was
played by an elderly woman in an advanced state of pregnancy, who
wroth wearily on a steaming pyre. Enée (!) was a puny Jew, with
speckled stockings who was more fantastic in odd corners of the
stage than any one I have ever seen. Other characters were *spectre
d'Achille* and—Ascagne! They all sang well: I am told. But I do not
understand noise music.

Hence to Antwerp where I may die preposterously upon a street
barricade: if not, on to Bruges. Have you ever seen Brussels? The
newest building is the *Palais de Justice* (1876), quite good, in the old
Assyrian style. I have written a great poem of a madman who
monologizes on it for a thousand lines under the impression it is
really 40,000 years old, and on being undeceived, puts his head under
a passing tram. It is full of vast lines made of names got from the
appendix to my Bible: 'What of the East? who stands where Sargon
stood?' and 'The grey dust that was Asshur-bani-pal.' And so on

Yours ever

RUPERT BROOKE

To GEOFFREY KEYNES   *De Boeck's Family Hotel,*
                                     54 Avenue de la Toison d'Or
                                     Brussels
                                     12 September 1907

I am too old to be anything but weary. Try reading it again; with
the other eye. The letter (which I quite forget) was probably as much
in 'good faith' (whatever that may mean) as your kind offer. Perhaps
it seemed different and cold without the courteous smile I wore in
writing it. I remember no single point of '*nastiness*' '*peevishness*' or

'*sarcastic irony*' in what I wrote. '*Childish*' I always try to be. Of '*bad taste*' I am no judge.

I expect I was too allusive: almost, I fear, flippant. I will try to be simple.

During this Belgian visit I can't leave my family; who probably like my company more than I like theirs. All the hotel rooms are taken on ahead; & plans made. We return to England Sat. Sept. 21st. My travelling capacity after a Channel crossing is limited: my desire to live less than usual. Limited too is travelling on Sunday in England. I *might* discover the improbable name by Monday: & be with you during what hours of your visit still remained.

But: at that time I should be more boorish than ever, worn out by the excessive & insincere geniality of my conduct towards my people: for whom I feel great pity, if nothing else. I require a fortnight's private sulking before I face the ordeal of Cambridge. (This is a secondary & personal reason.)

*   *   *

I have written the lines fairly straight & close; that you may not strain your eyes in trying to read between them. There is nothing there.

My bare statement is, of course, of no value; except for decoration. I can refer you to my father, my mother, my brother, & H. H. Sills Esq.: King's, for corroboration.

The Sonnet was borrowed from the Italians in the 16th century. It is almost always (purists say always) of 14 lines, each an iambic pentameter. According to some it can be of 16 lines (c.f. G. Meredith's *Modern Love*) & in Alexandrines (as always in French) or tetrameters. There are two distinct varieties: (1) The Shakesperian; of three quatrains & a clenching couplet. (2) The ordinary; formed of two rhyme-groups—an octave & a sestet, of 8 & 6 lines respectively as their names indicate. Considerable latitude in the arrangement of rhymes is allowed in the latter variety.

The Spenserian & other types are really only variations of these. All verses in these forms are sonnets.

All in others, from *Ozymandias* downwards, are not.

This rule applies to invalids & scientists.

'Herr' de Boeck (M. de Boeck *he* would have said) died 20 years ago. I hope you will have a good time. This is not meant to be 'nasty'. I am only nasty to my friends, you should know, behind their backs.

RUPERT
poseur & hermit

To ANDREW GOW   *Hotel de la Paix, Antwerp*
    Thursday [September 1907]

I am here with a little brother for a day or two. In the morning I see placid pictures & in the afternoons fight magnificently on the street barricades for the sacred cause of Trade Unionism. This evening I have sat in a café sipping an exquisite pale green liquor that tasted like an half-ripe hyacinth & smelt like an Italian cesspool & looked like the waves that murmur about Lesbos. The city was white with innumerous lamps, more startling & brilliant than many of my best jokes. They hid the iron laughter of the stars: & my soul rotated wearily like the unmeaning sails of some vast windmill.

As a matter of fact things have been quieter today, & there was little or no shooting. The strikers hung in heavy clouds about the streets, staring at one with strange thin eyes. One day they will set fire to the whole city. We have been in Brussels; a city swept & garnished. Have you ever been to a French opera about Roman things? I heard *Les Troyens à Carthage* by Berlioz.

*   *   *

I howled with mirth; but those around me loved it. They were convex Germans, who leant forward, resting each his many little chins on his one enormous paunch; &, when the stickly love-passages came, they wobbled & sweated & stank with obscene glee.

Today a man rushed up to me in the street & said 'The world is roast beef & I am the mustard. God will eat us both.' He was a thin man with blue eyes; & it is a portent of many ineluctable dawns & sombre autumns.   à toi

    RUPERT BROOKE

To CHARLES SAYLE   *Anvers, Thursday, Friday*
    [September 1907]

My dear Sayle,

I am here for two days with my little brother, leaving my people at Brussels. We all meet at Bruges on Saturday—Zatterdag as we say in Belgium. If you knew my habitual mood at home you would not have regarded my condition in those three days as melancholy. This ink is essence of charcoal, filled with the decomposing bodies of Flemish flies & German waiters. All evening we have been sitting at an evil café sipping thunder-coloured coffee from glasses. In the afternoon I had an hour or two's fighting at a street barricade (you know my Socialist tendencies). Few deaths. Things are becoming disgustingly quiet. Your various hints & directions have been exceedingly valuable. The Palace d$_u^e$ Cinquante something, for instance, I should wholly have missed, otherwise. That white hall of all the statues that ever were was a sudden inspiration (such as Dutch painting does *not* often bring). Your baby head, I confess, left me as cold as a classical don, but the J- de Barbaris had points. Your tobacconist read my guileless nature & deceived me terribly: unless, indeed (as it may well be), the cigars only achieve that perfection of taste in one room in the world.

I thought the Bibliothèque would be beyond my scope & left it but a few minutes at the end. I'll confess I was rather sorry; though I but looked with the round large eyes of the unappreciative & ignorant.

I went to Louvain.

I did *not* go to Waterloo.

As for the state of my prejudices about pictures: I think I have attained greater affection for the early, comprehension of the late, Flemish old masters. I'm wholly Italist; but Roger van der Weyden's Pietà & one or two more I quite enjoy. (This is only of Brussels: on Antwerp & Bruges later.) The late moderns gave me great pleasure. Meunier & Rodin I adore. Why did no one ever tell me the Penseur was in Brussels? It is worth more than all the stolid daubs of the Flemings & Walloons.

(Continued, Bruges.)

*   *   *

Last night I had a room overlooking the square. At night I do not agree with Browning's Italian friend;[1] and the bells are less ethereal. When I sank at length into an evil & broken doze, about 3 a.m., the lights in the square were still on, filling my room with moon-radiance & the bells alternated with shouting Belgians. Antwerp was fairly good, but so steaming & airless that I felt ill & tired all the time. I rather loved some of the pictures there: a Vandyck or two especially & a Franz Hals. The modern pictures were enormously less good than those at Brussels. I cannot write on tissue paper with a borrowed fountain-pen; though the result fully stands for the condition of my mind. I am fond of Bruges after the hard ways & mirthless laughter of the great cities: or should be if I were not

[1] In Browning's poem, 'Up at a Villa—down in the City'.

infinitely weary. This hotel is solemnly adjudged to be insanitary by my people; so we are going to move on to another tomorrow. Sorry for the late Chief Librarian.[1] Today I sat beneath trees by an old green-black canal & saw the great tower in the afternoon light, beyond lime-trees. Suddenly, round the corner, slid a real Venetian gondola! Spiritually I was in Venice for a moment—and it is a better place, or am I an heretic? This evening I sit opposite the Belfry in the window of the Panier d'Or room. The bells have just chimed & round the corner opposite crawls a long black dragon of a street-steam-tram. Tomorrow I go to the Toison d'Or exhibition, opportunely here—Memlings and things. I don't know where you are, but this will reach you sometime. If you are in Cambridge when Geoffrey Keynes is about do not heed all he says about me. It is probably true, but nothing to the things I should have said about him had I been a little younger.

When I get back I am going to a matinée of Attila, &, later to one of Galsworthy's new plays at the Savoy (née Court [Theatre]) I hope you both $\begin{cases} \text{are finding} \\ \text{have found} \end{cases}$ Switzerland all you could dream. I shall write to Arthur Watts very soon I hope. As my former headmaster with his sermons, so I with my correspondence scraps, end with a quotation: Swinburne do you like?

> From too much love of Memling,
>   From John van Eyck set free,
> I swear, without dissembling,
>   They don't appeal to me.
>   Rubens is far too clever
>   Vandyck & Teniers never
>   Could captivate
>
>   Yours ever
>   Profoundly   R. C. B.

Exigencies of metre & rhyme dictate the frigid haughtiness of the close.
                                                            RUPERT

---

[1] Francis Jenkinson.

To GEOFFREY KEYNES School Field, Rugby
26 September 1907

My dear Geoffrey,

'The middle of next week' is a proverbially vague date. It would be admirable of you two to dawn strangely upon my tenebrous twilight. I am more morose than ever, among my intolerable family, but if I prove too sullen you can drag Mallory off & display before him the barbaric splendour of Rugby architecture. I have had a furious quarrel with my insufferable mother, & we are not on speaking terms; but I brought myself to remark that you were coming, & she growled an uncivil assent. When? 'The middle of next week'...Wednesday, Thursday...what? You won't be able to stand it for more than one day & night. If you object to having meals at the same table as a Liberal M.P. & his wife, let it be Wed. night (Oct. 2nd). Or will you be too bored to do more than remain for the 'inside' of a day; appearing at cockcrow & fading at sundown, the opposite to ghosts? In any case it will be amusing for you to glow exquisitely against the scrofulous wall-papers & autumnal curtains of this lazar house. I fear there are no mountains here (save, perhaps, a large dung heap in our garden, where I sit, Job-like, scratching). The Devil will not be able to take you up into exceeding high places *here*—not physically, at least. Even spiritually the district is mostly swamps. ' *You*' is plural—dual rather—throughout. Say when: it doesn't matter to us. This (like everywhere else) is Hell.

RUPERT

To HUGH RUSSELL-SMITH School Field, Rugby
September the so & so [1907]

THE INTRODUCTION

I wanted to answer your letter but I can't remember where I put it. Can you? Well, well, I suppose we must do without it—

THE LETTER

Dr. (=dear) Mister
or dear Mystery, *libentius audis?*[1] (Humph! we've not forgotten our classics, eh, old cock?)

* * *

[1] i.e. you hear with more pleasure.

As for the Church of England Young Lady, I wasn't cynical. I used to be cynical about the C. of E. when I went every Sunday, but didn't care (or think) twopence. (And that's, I gather, the position the Y. L.'s now in.) Now I'm no longer cynical about it. I hate it; and work against it; because I think it teaches untrue things; and that it is bad for people to believe untrue things. It leads to misery; on the whole. Also I think it has a bad influence. A very small part of this may be seen, very clearly, if you and the other Liberal members of your family will get a book and see exactly how the Bishops in the House of Lords have voted for the last twenty years. It's amusing reading: but indignation-stirring in a quite serious minded person without any sense of humour like

RUPERT

Love to Mrs S. and all.

If Denham ever wants to come to Cambridge next term: I've a spare room in my rustic Mansion.

To GEOFFREY KEYNES   *School Field, Rugby*
29 September 1907

Your plan sounds feasible. I don't like my mother's pen. On Thursday afternoon I shall be playing football if it is cold, tennis if it is as it is. So I *may* not be anywhere to greet you.

It depends what time you come. You needn't wear dress clothes at meals or at any other time. Saunt is coming on Saturday. Your literary style is still crude. The School is said to have reassembled. School life is still very fascinating & more infinitely remote than ever. There are about two who pretend to remember me. On such I inflict myself & my sorrows occasionally. They are polite. But they yawn: heavens, how they yawn! Such is Denham (who is younger) I sat in his study tonight & was violently morbid all over the sofa. He smiled a charming smile outwardly: but loathed it and

Yours
RUPERT

To ST JOHN LUCAS   *School Field, Rugby*
[Early October, 1907]

My dear St John,

When you see this parcel, you will think it is either a present of surpassing value for your twenty-first birthday, or your Sphinx returned in disgust and abhorrence. You are disappointed. It is only the French Book which you rashly lent me. I kept it till I wrote. Many thanks.

The Sphinx herself[1] has just come, viâ *King's*. In plain brown paper and light mauve tape it looked quite innocent from without— and most legal. But within. . . .

Geoffrey Keynes has been here for two days, and read it. He was enormously impressed. Corrie Grant also read it yesterday. He said he could find no ulterior motive and purpose in it; and was puzzled. He is taking steps to have you turned out of the Temple.

Mother dislikes it. . . .

It has coloured my dreams for nights. I love and loathe it more than ever. Your treatment of the Olympians is revolting and un-gentlemanly. I am all for Thanatos and thought the dryads' replies exhibited a puerile lack of logic: barely atoned for by the perfumed rhythm of the sentences.

Why didn't you meet me outside the Savoy that Tuesday? I did not know you were about. I go to Cambridge on Tuesday: not through London. When is it you are coming to Cambridge? If you tell me, I will find some rooms. Attila was admirable. Don't see 'Joy'. I scrawl from a sofa; where I lie with a stiff leg. I played football on Thursday with yellow haired people half my size and a quarter my age: who knocked me down and kicked my left knee. It is as swollen and strangely green and black as your prose style: but not nearly so pleasant. I only walk when Mother has gone out and cannot catch me on my feet. Then I rush up and down to relieve my feelings. Rugby is full of the next generation. It is raining.

Many thanks
RUPERT

To ST JOHN LUCAS   *King's College, Cambridge*
Wednesday [*23 October 1907*]

My dear St John,

Cambridge is less tolerable than ever. Therefore in a week today I shall come up to London and see Sarah Bernhardt acting in Phèdre —if, as I understand, she is going to do so on that day. I write now to give you warning that you had better be in London then and come and see it. Also, and anyhow, we will find you in your rooms

---

[1] Lucas's *The Marble Sphinx.*

at 5, and you will lunch and dine with us. I use the plural because I shall probably come up with another person: called Sayle. He is 'quite pleasant': being a kind of Librarian here; an Oxford man of enormous age (42); both of which facts he tries to conceal, however. Write *by return*, as I desire soon to write for tickets. I pant for London. Cambridge is a bog. I have new and more nauseous rooms. *When* are you coming to see them? You promised to do so sometime, and refused to fix a date. Like all lawyers you are hopelessly unpractical. But the first point is more immediate. Be in London on Wednesday.   RUPERT

To JACQUES RAVERAT   *King's College, Cambridge*
                                                      Monday [*October 1907*]

My dear Jacques,

I am, indeed, villainous not to have written. Only when I returned to this miasma did I know you were not to be up this term. And since then this tinselled booth we call life has been filled with flaring torches and shouting and the scarlet of trumpets and squeaking of the puppet-show. I spend my hours in seeing vain and shadowy people; and even so I can never flee myself. And my soul is an eremite; and rebels.

And you—why should you wish to be in this swamp, pilgrim? Where are you? A man ran swiftly, like a sudden flame, at midnight, and cried that you were at Venice. Then there was silence. Do you indeed glide in sombre silence down fantastic wriggling canals, where the gloomy houses on either side spring into the night sky, and from invisible windows overhead strange voices whisper to one another hot, wild endearments, or wail out once, and no more? And thence do you swing out and round into a wide moonlit glory of silence, called the Grand Canal?

Or are you in Florence, climbing the steep way between cypresses to Fiesole, or lolling in cool galleries, before that sorrowful Venus of Sandro's, or Lippo Lippi's girl-Madonna's, with the maladive sensuality of their tired faces?

But I drivel. Only know that in Cambridge the hard streets are paven with brass and glass, and tired, wounded feet of pilgrims flutter aimlessly upon them. Two and two pass the damned, with blank yellow faces, and great spectacles hiding the wide eye in which no soul gleams. The strange great paunch that is O. B. crawls pen-

dulously down K[ing's] P[arade] once a day; and weekly Geoffrey
hurries along on a smell-machine, killing children. By the way, I am
writing a great novel, called 'The Stomach'. The hero, eponymous,
is Oscar Browning's Paunch. The plot is that it grows and grows and
develops a separate individuality by degrees. It begins by waking at
nights when the O. B. is asleep, and twittering like a bird. It gradually
learns a kind of broken English, and has long quarrels with him. All
the time it becomes more and more detached, till at length the
Paunch and the O. B. are only connected by a thin thread of skin.
And one night, when they are undressing, this breaks and the
separation is complete. Then, both naked, they have an immense
fight. Finally the Stomach wins and pursues O. B. round his rooms,
rolling and flopping, and at length comes and suffocates him. I think
it is very beautiful.

Faustus[1] progresses: in spite of your absence and an inefficient
Mephistophilis. Justin is excellent: Geoffrey and Mallory both bad.
Are you going to join the Leon's party at Adelboden in December?
All my family are going to be there: and I.

If you are in Florence, and using Vieseux' library: find.if they
have Yeats latest play *Deirdre*, and read it. Quite excellent.

The Saints that are in God salute you.

Yours ever

RUPERT BROOKE

To MRS BROOKE   *King's College, Cambridge*
                                   Tuesday [29 October 1907]

Dear Mother,

If you and Mrs Leon motor over on these days (v. bill, enclosed),
you will be able to see Justin Brooke as Faustus, and myself as
Mephistophilis.

Today Mrs, Margaret, and Rose Macaulay, are coming to tea, and
bringing a friend! So I am busy tidying up. This afternoon there is
a game against John's. King's are weak this year and need my services.

*   *   *

I have talked to Justin about Switzerland. Some of his family are
going—the other Rupert among them! What confusion! Justin

[1] Marlowe's *Faustus* was being rehearsed for the first performance by the Marlowe
Dramatic Society on 11 November 1907. R.B. acted Mephistophilis.

himself is not going: a pity. Perhaps the Raverats will be there: and people called Beveridge. But you probably know all this already from Mrs Leon. I re-enclose her letter.

*   *   *

With love
RUPERT

To CHARLES SAYLE   [Postcard]
[*6 November 1907*]

I read them through: but gave up jotting down comments. I think he should read Browning, St Francis & Herbert Spencer's Auto-Biography.

The Dream is not so bad.

He should wait a little while: & not only read Swinburne & J. Thomson (B.V.).

Just occasionally it's got merits.   R. C. B.

[Criticism of Victor Newburg's *Wild Honey* in proof at the request of Charles Sayle]

To FRANCIS MACCUNN   *Cambridge*
Tuesday [*11 November 1907*]

My dear Francis,

A fortnight today I shall be in *Oxford*; by God's help.

Why?

I dare hardly tell you—I am coming with an indecorous atheistical, obscene set of ruffians called the Fabians. We are coming to chat with a similar set of ruffians in your University. (*I* shan't speak!) I insist on seeing you. I come over on Tuesday 25th, afternoon, and go away again next noon, and I fear my hosts will be dragging me round most of the time. But I shall steal away and look at you. It will make me feel young again and just now I am dreadfully old and ill. You will not recognize me. I look just like a Socialist. I don't suppose you will be coming to the meeting; you are too young for such vices, and far too beautiful. But tell me when you will be in next morning and I will find you.

Your questions and demands of last letter are a little out of date now. I expect you have already startled an impatient world with your Stevenson paper. If not I can't tell you much. I can only refer you to a description of him by his friend the late W. E. Henley. It is in the form of a sonnet entitled *Apparition*. It occurs in Henley's *Book of Verses*, or in his collected *Poems* (1897), in the section, *In Hospital*, p. 39. It is as good a criticism and portrait of him as you will find anywhere. If you work from that you won't be far wrong. But, of course, there's books an' books on him.

As for other questions: I never write nowadays: I am too old. If your morbid desire still holds for a copy of the *Bastille*; you had better remind me before I go home next time. They are stored in a barn there.

I must sleep.   Yours ever

                                 RUPERT BROOKE

To ERICA COTTERILL   *King's* [*Cambridge*]
                                         28 November 1907

[Erasure by the recipient] a speech by Bernard Shaw. It was the same speech as he made the night before, in London, & the night after, somewhere. Mostly about the formation of a 'middle-class party' in Parliament: which didn't interest me much. I preferred the funny bits. A lot of people asked questions—mostly the stock arguments against Socialism—afterwards: & he answered very well & quickly—all except one, on Capital leaving the country, which he didn't make clear to ordinary minds—probably through lack of time. He's been writing on it lately in that amusing paper the *New Age*. The Chairman (a don) told a very good story of Shaw's first appearance in Cambridge (circa '85), which I'll sometime repeat to you.

Granville B[arker] was utterly divine. His lecture was not very original: but wholly sensible. Being on Socialism & the Drama, it appealed to me more than discussions on economic points, like Shaw's. I had lunch & dinner with him (G. B.). At dinner (a short early one. He had to get off.) I sat next him!! I neither spoke nor ate, but sat still watching his face. The profile is one of the nicest things in the world. And his voice!...

I have been elected by an enormous majority to the committee of the Fabians here. And that though I am only an Associate, *not* a Member, i.e. I've not signed the Basis. Most of the committee are Newnhamites, strange wild people, whom I shall infuriate by being utterly incompetent. I am greatly looking forward to it.

The Switzerland party of the Leons (whom you met) is *28* in number. Mostly young, heady, strange, Females. I am terrified. I doubt if I'll have courage to go. But Mrs L. is a good woman. I was *very* good as Mephistophilis, in our play. I am now taking a small part in an A.D.C. performance. I've just returned from one. Love to Uncle Clem & Aunt Maud.   RUPERT

To C. C. COTTERILL   *Grantchester Dene*
Littledown Road
Bournemouth
12 December 1907

Dear Uncle Clem,

When I got home last Saturday, I found, and read, your book,[1] which Mother had just finished. She wanted to write to you and thank you (and will), but at the end of last week she got rather worse, and hadn't the strength to write. So she asked me to do so, in her place, at present. I haven't the book by me now—though I shall have tomorrow—so I cannot be accurate in facts.

I am an Associate (not an actual Member) of the Cambridge Fabian Society, and have lately been coming across there a good many Socialists, both of the University and from without, as well as unattached sympathisers like Lowes Dickinson. I wish I could get more of these, especially among the Fabians, to accept your definition of Socialism. Most of them, I fear, would define it as 'Economic Equality', or, the 'Nationalization of Land and Food Production' or some such thing. In a private way I have some influence among some of them, and have been trying to urge on them a more human view of things; I shall be able to do so a good deal better and more clearly now. Socialism is making great advances at Oxford and Cambridge just now; but its upholders are too apt to make it seem, to others and to themselves, a selfish scheme of economics. They confound the means with the end; and think that a compulsory Living Wage is the end, instead of a good beginning. Bernard Shaw came down last term, and made a speech that was enthusiastically received, in which he advised a state of things in which each 'class' had its own party in Parliament fighting for its own hand. The whole thing was based on selfishness. It was not inspiring.

Of course they're really sincere, energetic, useful people, and they do a lot of good work. But, as I've said, they seem rather hard.

[1] *Human Justice for Those at the Bottom*, London, 1907.

Must every cause lose part of its ideal, as it becomes successful? And also they are rather intolerant, especially towards the old order. They sometimes seem to take it for granted that all rich men, and all Conservatives (and most ordinary Liberals) are heartless villains. I have already, thanks, in part, to various words of yours, got some faith in the real, sometimes over-grown, goodness of all men; and that is why I have found your book so good, as a confirmation rather than a revelation. And this faith I have tried to hammer into those Socialists of my generation I have come across. But it's sometimes hard. The prejudices of the clever are harder to kill than those of the dull. Also I sometimes wonder whether this Commercialism or Competition or whatever the filthy infection is, hasn't spread almost too far, and that the best hope isn't in some kind of upheaval.

Anyhow I hope your book will find its way into the hands of ordinary Socialists, besides those for whom it is especially intended, and teach the spirit of Socialism to those who only know the dogma.

I'm afraid I've written rather wildly on what is more or less a side-issue. But I thought you'd like to know one part of the thoughts that came to me most forcibly when I read the book. Many thanks.

Love to Aunt Maud, and Erica,

Your affectionate nephew
RUPERT BROOKE

To ERICA COTTERILL

Danioth's Grand Hotel
Andermatt
Boxing Day 1907

You would scarcely recognize me if you saw me leading the extraordinarily healthy life which plagues me at present. I spend nearly all the day ski-ing & tobogganing. I am fat & red & my nose has no skin. I am completely healthy.

(I forgot to say: A Happy New Year & A Merry Christmas.)

It is very strange spending Christmas Day in this manner. I miss 'Hark the Herald Angels'. My outdoor life has taken from me all ability to write coherently. The Party I am with is rather nice. They are nearly all Socialists, & 'interested' in things: but fairly pleasant all the same. They are all great personal friends of H. G. Wells. Even the Newnhamites & others of their sex & age are less terrible than they might be. Several are no duller to talk to than males.

There is One!...oh there is One....aged twenty, *very* beautiful & nice & everything.... My pen is dragging at its bit to run away with me about her. I adore her, for a week. Every evening we rehearse the *Importance of being Earnest* (you know it?). I am Algy & she Cecily, & I have to make love to her all the time. But for the fact that I am very old & that she hates me, it is very pleasant.

In a week we return, & I go up to Cambridge for exams. I shall never see you in London for a million years. Perhaps I shall find you at a matinée of *Arms & the Man* in January? I don't know where your last letter is. I suppose I left it at Rugby. I seem to remember your talking a lot of bosh in it. You not infrequently suffer from the delusion that I do too much work. You are quite wrong. I may fall ill of a broken heart or of perpetual misanthropy or, certainly, of the Cambridge climate...but of overwork, never!

* * *

I'm a bad person to be of a party, of merry people like these. I'm too dull & sulky. I shall be glad when I can retire to a hut in a desert: out of the way. I shall be more in my element

RUPERT

BIOGRAPHICAL PREFACE 1908

Among the new friends whom Brooke had met in 1907 were the Oliviers, and the name begins to appear in his letters of 1908. Sir Sydney Olivier (afterwards Lord Olivier) had been Governor of Jamaica and in England moved in Socialist circles; it was probably after a Fabian meeting that Brooke first met Sir Sydney and his four daughters, Margery, Brynhilde, Daphne and Noel. Margery was at Newnham, Noel at Bedales. Meetings with these four girls, all of whom were much admired for their unconventional charm and their beauty, became frequent, though none of the letters that Brooke wrote to them is at present available. It may be assumed that many were written, and his affection for Noel in particular was for a period very deep. Their names will often appear in his letters to others, but their importance in his life will not be fully appreciated until all his letters are accessible.

Early in the year he was greatly excited by meeting H. G. Wells, who, like Belloc, had been addressing a Pembroke Society, Brooke being again my guest. We had both for some time felt much interest in Wells's writings, mine being chiefly in the scientific romances, his more in the political works. He was, indeed, throughout this year becoming more and more interested in politics and increasingly involved in the affairs of the Fabian Society. The influence of Hugh Dalton was making itself evident and in April he expressed a wish to sign the 'Fabian Basis' and to become a full member of the Society. He was soon elected a member of the Cambridge Committee, and made many other friends of the same persuasion, among them Michael Pease, Ben Keeling (killed in France in 1916), Bill Hubback (who later married Eva Spielmann), and Godwin Baynes, a rowing 'blue', who, after qualifying as a doctor at St Bartholomew's Hospital, practised as a Jungian psychologist.

Apart from a brief walking-tour with Russell-Smith in the spring and a few days at Torquay, Brooke stayed more constantly than usual in Cambridge and Rugby. The two important factors limiting his tendency to wander were the performance of *Comus* given by a company of University amateurs as part of a Milton tercentenary celebration organized by Christ's College, and the necessity to do more serious reading than hitherto in preparation for the Tripos examination in the following year. He also became conscious that he was really enjoying life in Cambridge. His part in the cast of *Comus* was that of the Attendant Spirit, which his striking appearance enabled him to sustain with great effect, but he was also deeply involved in the production of the play and at one time was left virtually in sole charge, Francis Cornford, who acted Comus, and Albert Rothenstein, who was designing the sets, having departed. *Comus* was successfully performed at the beginning of July, but Brooke himself collapsed from exhaustion immediately afterwards and was carried off by his mother to Rugby to recuperate. A new and important friendship resulting from the production of *Comus* was that with Frances Darwin, daughter of Sir Francis (Frank) Darwin. She did much work behind the scenes and later in the year became engaged to marry Francis Cornford. Brooke also grew better acquainted with Professor E. J. Dent of King's, and Clive Carey of Clare, afterwards a professional singer.

Brooke's twenty-first birthday occurred on 4 August and at the end of the month, feeling that he had really attained manhood, he went off to a Socialist gathering in Wales. Towards Christmas he again joined a party for winter sports in Switzerland. During their stay he and Helen Verrall composed a burlesque melodrama, which was performed in the hotel. He returned to Rugby before the New Year.

To GEOFFREY FRY
King's [*Cambridge*]
8 January 1908

My dear Fry,

I am in this morass again: as you shortly will be. I do exams all day; indifferently; seated next to the famous Butler,[1] whom I had never seen before. He looks so wise all the time that he gets on my nerves. Your letter came to me in Switzerland, at Andermatt. The pamphlets I found at home when I got back, a few days since. So many thanks. They are delectable. Andermatt is on the Gotthard: a nice place in a Christmas-card sort of way—but ah! to be so near Italy and yet not to go! But I was of an enormous party of people, mostly young and frivolous; and nearly all rather nice. So I was rather happy in my elderly way; leading a morbidly healthy life on snow and ice, and eating—ah! how we ate! But no matter-r-r---. I have since seen the delectable Peter Pan, and laughed and wept. All things were rose for three hours. Now I am regrown up.

How hateful are the feet of the middle-aged. If you have not seen the Albany for January, do so; and read *The Celestial Omnibus* by E. M. Forster. Excellent.

James Strachey has been in. He has come up early—to work! He has sojourned at Mentone of late and was sorry. He tried to get into the gaming-rooms at Monte Carlo but was turned out because he was too young! So does tragedy border upon farce.

Yours ever
RUPERT BROOKE

To ST JOHN LUCAS
[Two postcards]
King's College, Cambridge
[*13 February 1908*]

Infamous mute!

Since you will not come, I, Hermes-like, am coming to fetch you psychopompically to Hell. On Saturday. I arrive at 10 as usual. I shall proceed to you with a thousand things to tell you. I shall have a Retinue (of Geoffrey Keynes) which may be sent on to picture galleries.

I shall not lunch with you, but you may lunch with us—at

[1] J. R. M. Butler, son of the Master of Trinity, afterwards Sir James and himself Vice-Master.

Eustace Miles! And go with us to the pit of *Rosmersholm* and return
to you for tea. I shall be bound to return early again. I pine to be
out of Cambridge which I *loathe*. A postcard!

RUPERT

To JACQUES RAVERAT   *King's* [*Cambridge*]
                                        Tuesday, February [*1908*]

My dear Jacques,

   I am sorry I have been so evil about writing. Many a time I have
all but done so, and at the last moment dull people or things have
intervened. And the term is so full of busy-ness. I never possess
what soul I have. I am glad to hear you are, like Europe, progressing
towards health. I wish I could have stayed longer at that strange
Swiss place to witness the process: but duty called. And I am glad to
hear, moreover, that you are coming (or have come?) to the only
land in the world; as I increasingly affirm. 'England! my England!'
in the superb words of the late W. E. Henley; the home of Freedom,
of Blank Verse, of The Best People, of Brynhild Olivier (whom you
met), of a Greater Yet.... As Mr Belloc says 'She (England, I mean)
is to remain'. I am persuaded she is to remain.

   Now, however, it is not from Real England that I write. It is from
the Hinder Parts, the *faeces* or *crassamentum* or dregs, the Eastern
Counties; a low swamp, a confluence of mist and mire, a gathering-
place of Dankness, and Mud, and Fever; where men's minds rot in
the mirk like a leper's flesh, and their bodies grow white and soft
and malodorous and suppurating and fungoid, and so melt in slime.

   I have a cold.

   Today I have been to a Fabian Committee Meeting for hours, and
worked, and read, and worked. And soon I have to go out to dinner
miles away with the egregious Dent[1] (whom perhaps you don't
know). I shall go to London on Saturday; and so evade this godless
Marsh for a day or two. There is no news. Only foul figures slink
o' nights through the sweating gloom, and the air is insistent with
lazars' whines. On Thursday the Marlowe D.S. will read *Comus*.
On Wednesday week [H. G.] Wells comes to Pembroke and the
good Geoffrey takes me as a guest. In a fortnight I go to Oxford
to tell them what I think of Socialism. Very good for them.

   I suppurate on the face of existence. Soon God will burn me.

Yours   RUPERT

[1] Prof. E. J. Dent of King's College.

To MRS BROOKE [*Cambridge*]
Monday [*March 1908*]

Dear Mother,

I am so sorry about the Boots token. I quite failed to realize until I re-read the letter some days later that it was wanted at once. Tomorrow I am probably going to Oxford for a day with a Fabian party to have a debate with their Fabians. Wells is going to be there, I expect to see MacCunn, who's asked me to tea.

On Wednesday last Wells addressed a Pembroke Society on *Socialism* and I was taken by Geoffrey Keynes; it was very interesting. On Saturday the *Carbonari* (our literary King's Society) had a debate on '*The Family*', in these rooms. Wells came and spoke, very well; also Lowes Dickinson, Selwyn, Keeling, Father Bull of Mirfield (or some name like that) and others; so that we had an interesting lot of points of view. Wells is a very pleasant little man, insignificant in appearance, and with a thin voice (he has only one lung) and slight Cockney accent ('thet' for 'that'). He is rather shy.

* * *

With love
RUPERT

To ST JOHN LUCAS [*Cambridge*]
[*Early 1908*]

[First part missing]
On the other side of this I write the sort of stuff one is driven to write by a cold in the head—un ancien vaudeville. Que je fausse inperturbablement!

Pity me! RUPERT

Failure[1]

Because God put his adamantine fate,
    Between my sullen heart and its desire,
I swore that I would burst the Iron Gate,
    Rise up, and curse Him on His Throne of fire.
Earth shuddered at my crown of blasphemy,
    But Love was as a flame about my feet.
Proud up the Golden Stair I strode; and beat
    Thrice on the Gate; and entered, with a cry.

[1] Printed in *Poems*, 1911.

... All the great courts were quiet in the sun,
And full of vacant echoes: moss had grown
Over the glassy pavement, and begun
To creep within the dusty council halls;
An idle wind blew round an empty throne
And stirred the heavy curtains on the walls.

RUPERT BROOKE

To HUGH DALTON [Postcard]
3 Beacon Terrace, Torquay(!)
8 April 1908
(and for 10 days)

Under the influence of

(a) Talks with the wee, fantastic, *Wells*.
(b) His books.
(c) Fabian tracts.
(d) Private meditation and prayer.
(e) Arguments on the other side.
(f–z) Anything...etc....

I have decided to sign even the present Fabian Basis, and to become a member (if possible) of the central Fabian Society.

The former part, I suppose, may wait till next term; as I have no Basis with me. Spiritually, the thing is done (not without blood and tears). But the latter—is it possible, and what steps can I take, even now? Where write? What say?...Tell me....I am eager as a neophyte always is, for action RUPERT BROOKE

To ERICA COTTERILL [Postcard]
[*Postmark: Torquay*]
[*15 April 1908*]

Thanks for the play. Its market value would be higher if you had written 'from the Authoress, to her adorable cousin', or words to that effect, inside. I carry it about with me, & sit on it at intervals, so that it often lies quite flat, now. But generally, entering the room, I find it waving an appealing arm to me....Mother doesn't like it, Father (to his surprise!), rather does!...The idea about the 12th is rather alluring. You are strangely practical. I shall be frightfully full of work, & ought not to stir, but I shall come. (Mother will swoon if she hears.) Only you are to behave and *not* 'clutch my arm at thrilling moments'. If you do, I shan't lose my head, but I shall lose my temper. Bring an umbrella & clutch that, if you *must* clutch. I shall need all my wits & attention for understanding the line of thought in a new Shaw play.[1] It's not so easy, for an outsider & dullard like me. So if I'm going to be very kind, & look after you & put you in the wrong bus & all, you must be very good & patient, & only speak when you explain the jokes to me.

G[ranville] Barker will be superbly hypocritical as a Bishop. You seem to have had an ecstatic day in London. It was very nice of him. Has he subdued the avaricious——& brought him to your feet? Thanks.

RUPERT

To HUGH DALTON   [Postcard]

Torquay even yet
The Good Friday
17 April 1908

Many thanks. The first strange fever flickered and died, and I am content to sit quietly till next term. So I have left Pease in peace. 'Pease, perfect Pease': as the hymn says. My high young heart is withered and scarred by Aristotle and this popular resort: but I am convalescing. By next term I shall be able to sit up and take a little Webb-and-milk. I am quite brave and cheery. But ah! my uncles weep.

So Masterman has—what has he? Spread his wings for a great flight? or taken the second step down to the Mire? Anyhow, it is all very exciting.

* * *

Your remarks about the Licensing Bill are strangely like a passage of Ibsen. They haunt me.   R. B.

---

[1] *Getting Married*, produced at the Haymarket Theatre, 12 May 1908.

To GEOFFREY KEYNES *3 Beacon Terrace, Torquay*
17 April 1908

This to catch the post.

I hope you're still there [Lulworth Cove]. Give my love to the whole lot, downs and all, and specially the Left-handed Boy, who dwells in the coast-guards cottages, & the Village Idiot, & all the Williamses, and...but no! Our walk was goodish for a wawk. I am too old to rhapsodize. But I will deliver lectures on it next term. I agree with you about Belloc, but oh! amazingly about New Worlds[1]...

It has made ME sign the Basis (B. sign the B. as ME would say...) Shall you be through London on Thursday or Wednesday? I am at my club.* Last time I was at it I met Wells and talked with him— a month ago. Did I tell you ? If not, you're a bright, bright green. More anon.

As a Socialist you should be careful about facts, even in a peroration. I am not a poet: I was, that's all. And I never, ah! never, was a Superman. God forbid.

May I quote from my next novel but two? 'Your only fault, my dear X, is that you are part of the Universe; a fault that you can hardly remedy! You share it with many others, including myself.'

I am not really, you know, high & proud & hard or anything out of a popular novel. I am only small & shy and tired and old. Really. I have always been *very* precocious. This is the penalty.

Ever

RUPERT

* A sniff.

To JACQUES RAVERAT *King's [Cambridge]*
4 May? [1908]
Monday anyhow

My dear Jacques,

My affairs are just beginning to grow simpler. At last I know vaguely what I am going to do in the summer.

And that is...work.

Work for ever. I swoon at the idea. But it must be. I shall not go abroad, for three months, as I had meant to do, to learn your fair language. I may not. I shall linger with my unlovely family for an

[1] *New Worlds for Old*, by H. G. Wells.

eternity, reading. So I fear that I cannot accept your pleasant proposal—much as I long to. In any case I should have had to persuade my parents to pay my passage out!—though I *might* have succeeded in that. (I have for ever ruined myself buying many books.) So I am *almost* certain I shall not be able to see you at Prunoy[1]—nor in the Alps. It is very kind of you to ask me. If—and it's just possible—it is discovered that I need 10 days holiday, I will surely write and find out if the invitation is still open... But I fear.

Till October then?

Cambridge is as ever; but now speciously arrayed in a pretence of heat and light green buds. Really, of course, it is a swollen corpse, and we buzz on it like flies. And yet...and yet—there has been a stirring. My long dead life thrills strangely and opens its eyes. The golden age may yet return—or has a letter cheated me?—Pah! I riddle. The night awaits me—and this letter.

Comus goes ahead—about as much as a crab. My work rather less. And my Muse—but she died long ago, the poor lady; of sheer boredom, *I* think.

Here's rosemary—   Thine
                                                                  RUPERT

To MRS BROOKE   [*Cambridge*]
                                                  Monday [*11 May 1908*]
Dear Mother,
                          *   *   *

Things have been pretty quiet for some time, until these two days. Yesterday there was a dinner in Keeling's rooms—a very Socialist dinner of one course and fruit and twenty-five persons—in honour, more or less, of Sir Sydney Olivier. Wells also was there, Lady Olivier, and the two youngest Olivier girls. Brynhilde Olivier is left behind to run Jamaica! It was great fun. Amber Reeves[2] (your friend!) and Wells were perched up behind on a window-sill. They came in late and couldn't find a seat. I found myself between Margery Olivier and a rather nice bright person, who turned out, I think, to be Dorothy Osmaston;[3] who (again I'm not sure) is the person Uncle Clem and Aunt Maud know. (Give them my love,

---

[1] J.R.'s home, the Château de Vienne, Prunoy, Yonne, France.
[2] A Newnham student, afterwards Mrs Blanco White.
[3] Also of Newnham, afterwards married to Walter (later Lord) Layton, economist.

when they come.) Afterwards we went on to Cornford's rooms and smoked there. The females cleared off about ten, Olivier with them, and we all assaulted Wells (you'll be sorry to hear) about his Manchester letter. He argued in his thin little voice for a long time, in a very delightful manner. Tonight Lawson Dodd is giving a lecture about the Medical Profession and Socialism. Keeling is away, so Dalton is entertaining Dodd in King's; and after the lecture they are going to adjourn to my rooms to talk, etc.

It's been very warm and nice in the last few days here. Today I had my first game of tennis and found myself quite bad.

With all love

RUPERT

To FRANCES DARWIN
King's

[*May 1908*]

Dear Miss Darwin,

I should love to meet Max Beerbohm. I shall certainly come. Many thanks.

Justin Brooke has a power of consecutive speech and of organization that I lack. But I have more leisure. Therefore I am doing some of the things he arranged yesterday. I am going to London on Saturday, on all business. Today I saw Redfern[1]—couldn't get him last night. Almost all the days this week and next are *filled* by this opera company and by Benson. All the dates we arranged are impossible.

*   *   *

There is no scene-painter in Cambridge. To hire one would cost about £5—paint etc. £2 or 3 more. I took (to pacify him—he was very pleasant) the address of a London scene-painter called Jones! which, if ever you want, you can have.

Yours

RUPERT BROOKE

To MRS BROOKE
Monday morning

25 May [*1908*]

Dear Mother,

*   *   *

The C[ambridge] Review article on Hensley Henson was by the High Church editor himself! I believe it is no secret! There was

[1] The Manager of the New Theatre, Cambridge, where *Comus* was to be performed.

some annoyance about it: but more excitement generally, through-out Cambridge, at the letter on the Math. Trip. and Trinity and John's methods. Did you read it? It was very hard hitting and, *I* thought, rather amusing. It was, Gaselee says, done by some rather important Math. Don, whose name no one knows for certain. But Trinity and John's were very angry. At the last Review Committee meeting Henry Jackson and Glover (John's) made a bitter attack on Gaselee for printing it.

Yesterday, for the week-end, there were forty people from the Working-Men's College—nr St Pancras—in Cambridge; Cornford was receiving them. He made me give them supper—four of them I mean!—last night. I had Geoffrey Keynes in to help. They were very nice people, quite intelligent (we wrangled about Kipling, Chesterton's poems, Gothic Architecture, etc.), and pleasant to talk with. They were all much against the observance of Empire Day!

Milton was born 1608. Christ's here are getting up a tercen-tenary festival, on *July 10th*. They have asked some of us to get up a performance of *Comus*. It will take some of my time (after the 'Mays' are over!), and I think I shall stay up till then.

* * *

Comus will only take two or three hours a day; there will be hardly anyone in Cambridge; so I shall get through quite as much reading here as I could at home. So that my work will not suffer; only my pocket! On July 11th I shall come home, I suppose, till August 27th (about). Then a week at the Fabian Summer School —three days walking there. Then more work for a month. So that I shall have 11 weeks for reading at home; besides what I do at Cambridge. Which ought to be abundant!

Those are my arrangements, as far as I can see. By 'home', of course, I mean wherever you all are at the time.

If you, or Father, or anyone, would like to see *Comus*, I can make Christ's invite you—it is entirely an invitation affair.

* * *

It will be rather a swell show. Christ's will be giving a dinner to their big people beforehand; peers, politicians, judges, poets, etc. All of the literary publicists in England have been invited. Alfred Austin has accepted already, by the earliest post! and Robert Bridges; and various titles—I daresay you've noticed puff paragraphs about it in the papers.

Yesterday I went out to lunch with the Frank Darwins here; Jane Harrison was there, the two *Rothensteins*—big painters—and. . . Max Beerbohm! who is a quaint little person.

With much love

RUPERT

To MRS BROOKE

Monday [*1 June 1908*]

Dear Mother,

I enclose the document[1] you wanted. I believe everything in it is absolutely true. The people who wrote and circulate it are anonymous. I may say however that they are prominent Fabians!—*not,* unfortunately, myself. I wish I'd been able to correct one or two things. . .

*   *   *

I'm glad you'll be able to come to Comus. It will be great fun doing it. The dancing people have begun their rehearsing—or rather learning their dances. Any edition will do—they're all practically the same, and nothing will be left out. Justin Brooke is not acting. I hoped I should be able merely to stage-manage; but they wanted me to take a part and made such a fuss that I've had to give in. I am rather sorry: Because one can't stage-manage much properly unless one is off the stage entirely. However. . .

The Newnham garden-party—my sole one this year!—was rather fun. All the Comus people were there; and so it was practically a committee-meeting for me.

My Mays begin this week, and I am reading in Chapel at 8: also it is very hot and I am rather tired.   With all love

RUPERT

To FRANCES DARWIN

King's College, Cambridge
24 June 1908

Dear Miss Darwin,

I hope you have had occasional news from Cambridge. I ought to have been compassionate before, and answered your letter. But when one's thoughts are tied to the offensive business details that have enveloped me for a month, it is impossible to direct them across a continent. A thousand insuperable difficulties have appeared before

---

[1] A printed leaflet giving an account of the ragging of certain members of Trinity Hall on political grounds.

us; and over each in turn we have laboured painfully. Redfern was more wicked than words can say. First Miss Harrison, then Cornford, & last Justin Brooke, retired from Cambridge to recuperate. So I was left to bear all burdens alone, and shall be, for some days more—a most unwilling and incompetent Atlas. The first Burden was that Albert Rothenstein who should have come on Monday, fell ill, & has only just appeared. He is deplorably vague. I wish you were here to define him. This evening, however, I sent him round to interview your cousin Gwen [Darwin], so tomorrow morning he may be better. I lie awake at night thinking what the scenery *may* turn out like. Albert is staying in King's tonight: but tomorrow must turn out, into Justin's rooms. Justin is down.

Tomorrow we daub from 9 to 5. The King's porters are going to pull Albert out & make him breakfast at 8.

We are probably going to have a matinée on the Saturday—for money.

This letter may depress you, I realize. Actually, things have gone well, so far. And I am only a little doubtful through weariness and much grappling with Practical Problems. I frequently tell my friends nowadays that an Actor-Manager's life is a dog's life, & advise them not to take it up. It irritates them. I am going to compose a threnody on Redfern (whom I poisoned this morning) & then to bed.   Yours sincerely

                                        RUPERT BROOKE

To ALBERT ROTHENSTEIN   *King's* [*Cambridge*]
                                Thursday [*June 1908*]

Dear Rothenstein,

Many thanks for your letters and the design. It will be quite splendid if you can get effects like that on the stage. Only, don't you think the forest ought to be a lot darker and more forest-y? The first scene, of course, takes place right in the centre of a thick pine-forest; and they keep referring to it every few lines—'The nodding horror of whose shady brows'—'here, in thick shelter of black shades embowered', 'the perplexed paths of this drear wood', and so on. Do you think you could get more of that spirit in it— more of the closeness and darkness and mystery, with trees all round? The second scene, I suppose, will have to be very like the first, only with a throne, a dining-table, and—if we're allowed—some torches...

Redfern was so obstinate and difficult that the Christ's people ultimately decided to *hire* the theatre from him. At present he is considering—and I don't want to ask him any questions about ground-rows etc. till we get him securely—but I think he is pretty certain to accept. Almost certainly, therefore, you will have the painting loft from June 22 for a week (when Miss Frances Darwin will be here I think) and the whole theatre will be ours from July 3 to July 10 for alterations, light, etc. I will let you know again when everything is *finally* settled. But I think all this is fairly certain. Of course it is costing Christ's money, so we must be as parsimonious about scenery as we can! But we *couldn't* make shift with the Theatre stuff, however the light worked!

With thanks   Yours sincerely
                                        RUPERT BROOKE

To MRS BROOKE   *King's College, Cambridge*
                                        Sunday [28 June 1908]
Dear Mother,
                    *   *   *

I suppose you heard of the dreadful tragedy that happened last Saturday week—Headlam's[1] death? It was terribly sudden. He was about in King's all the week—kept the procession for the Chancellor's installation on Wednesday waiting for half an hour by being late—in his usual way! On Friday he was in King's, about, as usual. Friday evening he went up to town, had a slight operation (by some accounts), and died on Saturday morning—of strangulation of the bowels, they say. We heard on Saturday evening. Did I tell you in my last letter? It was a terrible shock. It made me feel quite miserable and ill for some days. One gets so *angry* at that sort of thing. I didn't know him *very* well. But he was the one classic I really admired and liked: and I had done a good deal of work with him. The papers made very little of it—it's odd to compare the fuss they made when Jebb died, and Headlam was a far greater man than Jebb. He published so little that outside people didn't know much of him. But his friends and we who were his pupils, knew his great genius. I don't know how much of him they will be able to rake together from his papers. But all the great, ripe, splendid works we all proudly looked forward to him achieving—which we knew he might consummate any time he gave himself a few months have died

---

[1] Walter Headlam of King's College.

with him; can never be made. That's the terrible thing. Even in Cambridge many people knew of him most as a brilliant 'scholar', i.e. emender of Greek texts. But he was also about the best writer of Greek there has been since the Greeks. And what I loved so in him was his extraordinary and living appreciation of all English poetry, modern and ancient. To hear him repeat it was a delight. He was an excellent poet himself; and had perfect taste. He first inspired me with a desire to get *Comus* done, a term or two ago, and has often talked about it since. I had made up, in my mind, a little list of things about which I was going to ask him, large and small points, in Comus, to make certain that we should interpret and understand it in the best way possible; but I put it off till too late...the whole thing makes one so rebellious; to think what the world has lost....

For other things—I'll see Jane H[arrison] and get her to a meal or something with you. There will be plenty of time.

With love
RUPERT

To FRANCES DARWIN *School Field, Rugby*
18 July 1908

Dear Miss Darwin,

It's not really fair, you know. There's no rhyme to Darwin (as the Press will discover next year), and anyhow I couldn't keep it up for a whole letter. Thanks for the returned Deirdre.[1] I hope you found it a good play—or at least good poetry. I'm sorry I can't come to lunch on Sunday: but I am glad to find that my desertion is not yet known. The fun being over I sneaked away on Monday, & left you all to clear up the mess—the dresses for all of you, the accounts for poor Comus, and so on....I felt very mean, even, in the midst of my depression that all was temporarily over. I went off without

[1] 1909 was the year of the Charles Darwin centenary. F.D. had returned the *Deirdre* with the note:

Dear Mr Brooke,

I send back the book,
 I fear not so clean
As it ought to have been,
 But I read in the train
(I confess it with pain)
 And a very large smut
(Oh Fie and tut tut)
 Blew in with a whack
And dirtied the back
 It *was* careless of me.

Yours sincerely,
F.D.

saying good-bye and thank-you to people. My mother (I can plead) packed me up and snatched me here to sleep & recover. I am now convalescent, & can sit up & take a little warm milk-and-Tennyson. I feel a deserter: but I can always adduce the week when the committee went to the seaside and I faced the World & Albert's Artistic Temperament, alone.

But it is terrible to relapse into Reality & private life. I take a solitary tea, now—or, sometimes with a Kitten—I reading Aristotle; and sigh for the Confusion of a Committee Tea at the Grange.[1] I apologize to everyone concerned for (symbolically) leaving my robes, sky- and earth-, at the Grange last Saturday. I did not know what to do with them.

* * *

I begin to think the weekly journals quite enlightened. Have you seen the Spectator & the Athenaeum?

Comus [F. M. Cornford] writes two business postcards a day, always with a p.s. suggesting a fresh play to do next summer.

RUPERT BROOKE

P.S. The best poem in English (before 1908) is called *Pearl* of 1350.

To DUDLEY WARD *Rugby*
Monday [end of July 1908?]

Attendez!

Hubback's coming. Margery [Olivier] was overpowered by my eloquence, has said nothing to me, but suddenly accepted to my mother, not, however, saying who she will bring.

My mother has a mad characteristic idea (Oh, Lord!, *I* never suggested it!) that you're afflicted with an uneasy passion for some or all of those people, and she coldly fears you will become engaged to some of them on the spot; which she would hate. 'Of course' (she stares at me with hard, tired eyes, chattering thus) 'of course I *like* Dudley Ward.... Perhaps he'd better not come at the same time as those Oliviers...?'—as who should say, behind the eyes, '—*I* know about Country House Flirtations'. ('Spooning' they call it. I'm sorry!) Oh, well! I'm working continuously and insidiously and I think it'll be all right. I am very adamantine and cruel at times. Only I thought you'd better know. It may open your poor pedantic gravel-blind eyes to the World—to what *I* see, my boy. (Consider-

[1] Newnham Grange, the home of Sir George Darwin.

ing that I am quite uninterested, a little bored, over the whole party, of course—my vast exertions in organizing have something fine.) To continue. There is a Young Person at present in Rugby (I've not seen her) who hails from Jamaica—is, indeed, a friend of the Oliviers—is going soon to stay at Limpsfield. Mother met her; said 'Oh yes we're going to have two of the Oliviers to stay with us, do you know them?' 'My, yes!' the Person shrilled, 'the Oliviers! they'd do *any*thing, those girls!' Mother (whose '*any*thing' is at once vastly ominous and most limited) is, and will be for two months, ill with foreboding. She pictures, I think, Margery climbing the roof at night, or throwing bread about at table, or kissing the rural milkman.

I asked Donald Robertson, and forget if he answered, do you know if he's coming?

And would he, does he, know Hubback, and like him, or would they hate each other? Are they compatible? do tell me.

Another kindred question. A. Y. Campbell has written infinitely vaguely, full of quotations from the poets, to say he doesn't know what he is going to do in the vacation; but ends by being (for a poet) fairly certain he *will* come... some time! But he ends 'If I should coincide with Dalton I hope you will defend me from him'. Now consider! A. Y. C. *doesn't* (seriously) dislike poor Hugh [Dalton], does he? They'd get on all right, *half* coinciding, wouldn't they?

I asked Hugh if he knew and liked A. Y. C. 'Aeou yéés!' he yawned 'Iye expect hé admires me! Letimocoem! Letimcoem!' So the emotions from that side are all right.

*   *   *

Albert Rothenstein sends you his regards (by a letter). Answer!

RUPERT

To JACQUES RAVERAT   *School Field, Rugby, pah!*
4 August 1908 hélas!

Dear my Jacques,

How I am a villain, a shameless Beast! I cry when I think I have not written to you for months and shall not see you for years! The young and credulous Geoffrey was here a week or two ago. He was ingenuous all over the tennis-court. I shall send him this letter to address to you. He is sure to know your address. I don't. Are you still camping out on the lower slopes of Parnassus?—

Now—all my news is stale. *Comus* was a success, or a failure, I forget which. But you must have heard of it. It was all rather an exciting time: and I met Thomas Hardy at breakfast. He was quite incredibly shrivelled and ordinary, and said faintly pessimistic things in a flat voice about the toast.

As for English Books—up to a few weeks ago I had forgotten they existed. Since then I have been living here with my godless and accursed family and reading. By night I sleep out among the rose-beds: but by day I sit here in my private room and read—*classics, they* think, but no, ha! ha!—but *no* ho! ho! *Really* I have been reading

William Morris	Yes!
Milton	*Yes!*
Jefferies	Ho! Ho!
Campanella	Ha! Ha!
Doughty	(?!)
Coleridge	Eh?
Stacpoole	(!!?)
and *lots* more ;	all GOOD

and some DAMGOOD.

There's a poem called *Pearl* (of A.D. 1350) which is like sugar-fairies, and distant sleigh-bells, and dog-roses.

Abercrombie's[1] really got the promise of great things, and the performance of not small things. He is a Metrical Motor Bicyclist, a mumbly Wump, but often splendid. He lives.

I stay here and work till October: with the exception of 7 days flight to Wales, to the Fabian Summer School! Life is too dreary for words. As a man said to me 'Life's so flat, that you can see your own tombstone the other end'.....All my dreams are dead. Ghosts of old hopes get into the ink and make it blotchy. At night I would tell my silly fancies to the roses: but oh! they're deaf. They turn their shapely heads the other way, and mouth and mutter to the prim stars.

By God I'll write to you somewhen soonish.

Always

RUPERT

---

[1] Lascelles Abercrombie, the Georgian poet, afterwards one of the three 'heirs' to whom R.B.'s royalties were bequeathed.

To GEOFFREY KEYNES   *Schoo. Field, Rugby*
                                         4 August 1908

They say I'm taking it very well!!¹—Your compassion was my
stay all through the worst. There were times—There Were Times—
when I nearly—Nearly—wept.

*   *   *

Or, dreadful thought, have I already forgotten the language of
Childhood? But will you address this, & stamp it, and once I will
pay you! I loathe, & am loathesome. Always I groan. The family
shrilly gossip: my temper is 'all to ruffled & sometimes impaired'.
Often I sit, reading Mr Sampson's Prose Works (with quotations
from Blake) & think of you.² And anon Arthur E. comes to tea.
My mild regards to the world: and an Old Man's affection to the
Youth of 8 Trumpington St. [Charles Sayle]. Continue instant in
prayer. Fear God. Love the brotherhood (C.U.F.S.?). Honour
King's.   R.

To CHARLES SAYLE   *Rugby = Askra*
                                         11 August 1908

My dear Sayle,

It is really very good of you to remember my birthday. In that,
you were one of a select band of seven (not counting relatives)!
I eagerly expect the bowl of roses when autumn sends them. And
what a delightful present to think of! How it doubles the value of
a gift (as of a prose style) when it is 'exquisite' and fetched from far,
with pains! For the gift that my people will give me I am going to
get a *John* drawing. Ha! Ha! Cambridge culture will be vindicated.
Nowadays I do nothing. I live in Tea & Tennis. I am of the family.
To read, alone; and not to be taking part in a Dramatic Renaissance
in company with all the most splendid enthusiasts there are!

I lead a meagre life. Saunt & Russell-Smith are in France. Lucas
in Italy. 'And I am here in Kent and cristendome' as old Wyatt³ said
—& not even Kent, alas! I read degrading works by Teutonic
pedants on Hesiod & sich-like all day. I am faint for want of food,
occasionally, though, I fare better. Dryden I read steadily, and
generally love. What a thing style is, to meet in this age! But he

¹ He reached the age of 21 on August 4.
² I had given him a copy of *Blake's Poetical Works*, edited by John Sampson,
1905.
³ Sir Thomas Wyatt in 'Of the Courtier's Life', *Poems*, London, 1831, p. 194.

seems to me hollow, often. I have discovered a superb & unparalleled poem called *Pearl*, of the 13th or 14th century. Do you know it? But you know everything. Isn't it nice? A lad called Ward of your adopted College[1] is here, teaching Alfred history. He is a Fabian of honourable mind & body. Economics. Patiently he reads (and has read) everything. I lent him Mr Arthur Symons on the French Symbolists & Decadents. He read it, very earnestly. 'Do you know', he confided to me as we sat reading in the garden, 'I can't help thinking these fellows are rather *dangerous*. You know when a man begins seeing things that aren't *there*...well I mean, he may see *anything*, one feels!' He beamed at me patiently through his spectacles. I did not know what to say; so turned the conversation onto fluctuations in unemployment; and his storm-tossed spirit was at ease. But what does one say?

But Ward is an excellent person. He, Alfred and I read *Sigurd* aloud at nights, round & round till our brains sleep, & we only hear the great plash of the wave-like verses. And in the mornings I read T. E. B[rown] or Swinburne. A quiet life has its advantages.

I cease. What it is not to be able to write a letter! My warm & distant greeting to all that are of the Elect—the Comus crew, I mean—Comus, Dent, the Lord Brackley[2] (do you see him?) and all—to Geoffrey & the youth [Arthur] Watts...to all, & most to you.   RUPERT

To ERICA COTTERILL   *Rugby*
                                                  14 August 1908

The cushion arrived today—at least, the other day. It is superb & splendid, sybaritish indeed (*sibberitish*, as you prefer it). What am I to say to persuade you of my bursting heart? Shall I say 'My gratitude, my dear cousin, is inexpressible—& ah! how deep': or shall I drop, as always when deepest moved, into poetry: saying

                        ...I do
                        Thank you....

I love the flaming roses or violets or whatever they be. They fill me with strange emotions. I am writing a sonnet to them.

*   *   *

[1] St John's.
[2] A. Y. Campbell, who had acted the elder brother, originally played by Lord Brackley, in *Comus*.

Aug. 17th. We get to the School on August 30th perhaps; staying a night *en route* with the Sidney Webbs; & walking & sleeping out for four days. I am becoming a wild rough elementalist. Walt Whitman is nothing to me. Will you be at the camp then? I hope to listen to lectures for an hour a day, & for 15 hours a day read, read, read. A Cambridge Fabian called Ward is here teaching Alfred History. He is coming to Wales. A good sound fellow. Very short-sighted & unintelligent. Has read everything, & likes to lead a sensible life. Yesterday (Sunday) he & I went off to Stratford-on-Avon, & lay in a punt from 11 to 5, drinking beer & reading Meredith. The rest stayed here, & went to church, & were shocked at us. But we, in our old clothes & new ideas, were at ease.

I do a lot of work here, reading dull dead books of classics. I look forward to the Fabian School enormously, open air & talk—the only good things—though I shall hate most of them, the prigs. But one can hate in a loving hearty way. So I hate intellectual prigs, God bless 'em. O the Fabians, I would to God they'd laugh & be charitable.

I return from the exalted heights of (mentally) contemplating you, to the putrescent marsh of Greek. Farewell.

My thanks & love
RUPERT

To HUGH DALTON   *School Field, Rugby*
18 August [*1908*]

My dear Dalton,

Your letter is admirably precise and leaves me utterly undecided. I should love to sleep out with nothing but a few extra socks on—and yet—and yet.... The Weather is Very Mild. It has taken a turn for the worse of late—You in your close, low-lying Cambridge may not realize how cold it is o'nights: but I have felt and know, I on these bleak uplands of Rugby, where the snows lie all the year long and one is very near to the stars and to God. I feel that Wales may be like this. I don't know what to do. I shall do what the majority do. Tell me what the majority will do.

If you and Ben [Keeling] are passing through this city on Wednesday, you'd better drop in and take lunch here, play tennis if you like, and take me on. Ward will follow the next day, and meet us at Llanfairfechan. The invitation holds good to all Fabians who pass through, Walesward, on that or the previous day.

I don't know Mr Service[1] or his works. I don't think I should like them. I mistrust *Sourdoughs*—What *is* a Sourdough? Pronounced Sour dô or Sour duff?

The sad [Dudley] Ward is here, and quacks patiently to my little brother for six hours a day. We have little talks, he and I, sometimes about Economics, sometimes about Dancing (oh! the superb Titterton!).[2] His round honourable spectacles beam in a decided yet cultivated manner upon me. He has the Main Scheme fixed and decided already; and now only fits things into their places as he meets them; fits them in swiftly and surely, quite relentlessly and certainly perceiving their places. A little incautiously I said to him 'Why is metre such fun?' For a moment the world rocked.... Then he reached stability. 'Damit, man', he replied, 'because it's so decent...'. Human conversations are ever inconclusive. I told my Mother that the chief end of Life was Pleasure, and she burst into tears. I await your Epiphany, your bright and glorious coming, with many attendant daemons, to snatch me from my drab household. My Uncle the Dean will be here. No matter. It will add to the Comedy....But Ben must be not-blasphemous. I told the family a lot of people would be lunching here that day—'Who and what kind of?' they said. 'Oh! All right' I vaguely smiled at them 'practically Liberals—there's Dalton, son of a Canon, rather a Sourdô, you know...A Sourduff, I mean.' 'What's A Sourdoff?' said my Mother menacingly. 'A colonial sentimentalist' I said; and drifted through Explanation for four meals. Do bring them all. My soul is too diffuse to write ought but mush: it lies mistily over seven acres. The rumour about my age was quite true. I did it a fortnight ago. Leaving my unprofitable youth and its fancies, I stepped across the Threshold of Manhood, jauntily, manfully; leaving a company of dancing children behind. I stumbled a little on the step, which I did not perceive. Taking to me the Sword of Cheerfulness, the Helm of Quack, the Targe of Abstraction, the whole Armour of Self-righteousness,[3] of Impracticability (which is called Polytics) I strode forward, saying in a thin flat voice 'Ha! ha! talkin' of the Joy of Life, the Board of Trade Returns for Exp—' and then I found a black square room, and sitting all round, their faces to the walls, staring at me with the backs of their bald heads—rows of—

Adults—

[1] R. W. Service, a Canadian poet, author of *Songs of a Sourdough*.
[2] W. R. Titterton, a writer in the Socialist press.
[3] cf. *Ephesians*, VI, 13–17.

Goodbye oh Goodbye. Tell us on a card what to get for Wales-walk, that we may be of the best—   RUPERT BROOKE

P.S. Beatrice Webb's eye. . . . *Can* such things be? No, No, I am too old—Hush—

To HUGH DALTON   [Postcard]
                                          School Field, Rugby
                                                Sunday
                              [*Postmark: 24 August 1908*]

I shall debouch at Leominster or some of those neighbouring places about 5 or 4 or so on Wed. I shall expect to find that you have secured a place for me to sleep in for a night without darkness and the death-hour rounding it. Leave your address at all stations and places within ten miles. I am sorry you are so old. I bring a blanket, chocolate and 19 books, all in a bag.   R. B.

To FRANCIS CORNFORD[1]   *Rugby* (= *Hell*)
                                          2 October [*1908*]

My dear Comus,

How simply splendid!! I was aroused from a month's languor to incessant screams. I never had known before—they never told me—that quite consummate and perfect things happened in this world: 'such a sacred and homefelt delight. . .'.

But I shall hold a meeting of the *Comus* people and pass a vote of censure on you both. (I feel that Brierley will second it.) You are really very disgraceful. I'm glad you're ashamed. I think the beasts will tearrr you both to pieces. That their leader should forsake the palace & the *absinthe* in the flower-vase, for an assistant dresser—something less than a stage-hand—one to whose bullying & cozening in the matter of changing the *caste* Justin [Brooke] too can witness, one who (I fear you must have forgotten) *wanted to cut out part of the text!*

Yet as Stage-Manager, as Patriarch and Head of that Body of the Elect who were concerned in Comus, I can almost forgive the infamy. It would be so dreadful to think of any of the Elect breaking away outside—

---

[1] Who had become engaged to marry Frances Darwin.

But oh! I wish I'd all of them here now that we could add our joy at the news, & rejoice. I go about alone in this desert, in the most absurd state of elation about it, as if I'd done something splendid myself! I felt, when the great time of Comus was over, that somehow the glory was incomplete, a thirteen-line sonnet. And now comes the perfect crown of a perfect summer. You observe I regard the whole thing from the point of view of the joy it gives *me*! Seven million congratulations to both!

> 'Noble Lord & Lady bright,
> *You* have brought me new delight!'[1]

It was awfully kind of you to tell me.   Hilariously ever
                                          RUPERT

My mother (who once met you) heard me yell & inquired. She sends her congratulations.

Don't worry to decipher or answer this mess. I go to London for a week. I shall see you in ten days, & then howl & laugh the joy I can't write.

To DUDLEY WARD   *Hell* [*Rugby*]
                                          2 October [*1908*]

Dear Dudley,

Splendid! I thought it a superb vision that should never be, and wept to think of that gay company, and I not of it. But I so mentioned the matter to my parents, so wove a tissue of strange falsehood, and so much are they weary of my boorishness, that they accepted the notion. So, in sum, I come. Many thanks. I shall stay nineteen months. But I must sit and write a strange triumphant essay of vast size all the day on Monday. May I stay two nights or so? I shall reach the wilderness that is Marylebone on *Sunday* at 2.30, and burrow through London. So I shall get to you at 3, or 4, or whatever time it takes; hung round with bags and garlands I shall arrive. But don't be there to welcome me. I would not prevent you preaching in Hyde Park all afternoon. I will sit on the doorstep and read Kant in the original Hebrew till you return.

I am in a wanton, a bloody mood. That purulent ulcer of *hysterica passio* that ran in me through the summer, and, most, at Llanbedr, is clean now and dry. But it has left me weak, ah! weak. Foul slug!

---
[1] Altered from *Comus*.

injurious sneerer! why do you say '*If you don't want the meeting you needn't go, but the meal is the great thing?*'? I know what you think, that I am a classic, knowing and caring nothing of politics...you foul-minded 'practical' addle-pated, economic, snobly-business, arrogant gourd. But I am full of knowledge and skill and economic interest know you, and will certainly sude-come[1]. The names of the gallant company enchant and inveigle me. You and Ben [Keeling] are the centres of all that is young and debonair. How splendid to meet the golden Bryn again; I had thought to have parted with Dafne (as they spelt it when *words were words*) for a whole year, with tears through a railway-carriage door, you remember. But ah! why not *Noël*, why? Can't she be kidnapped from Bedales?

It is most noble of Ben to endure for a meal Margery O. with whom I shall have a Word about a Book.

And I shall tell them (unless it's old news?) the superb and splendid tidings—are they all over London?—about Cornford. The ridiculous eld!

Oh! shall I bring your bicycle and leave it at Marylebone; or send it; or what?   Ever

                                    RUPERT BROOKE

P.S. I hope you're better.
I shall bring a tennis ball.

To HUGH DALTON   *National Liberal Club*
                                    Whitehall Place, S.W.
                    Tra! la!   *Wednesday, 7 October 1908*
Dear Hugh,

I stay here now.
I meant to say—
But you slid away—

at that thing on Sunday—this:

That on *Monday* next, *Masterman* is going to speak at Rugby and dine and sleep at our house. I'll be there, and return to Cambridge on Tuesday. If you think it worth while to come across, and stay Monday night, and meet the Man, and hear him, do! I can't promise that you'll be able to talk a lot with him because there may be a lot of filthy Liberal provincial politicians hanging about. But at least we'll have him more lonely at breakfast next morning. He leaves early.   *   *   *

                    [1] Perhaps *South* is meant.

Dr Ede's Endowment of Motherhood is a very choice work, full of anecdotes—you might tell the Secretary that I'm coming up to London to hear him eugenicate on Thursday; and returning that night.   RUPERT BROOKE

To FRANCES DARWIN   *King's College, Cambridge*
                                       Friday [*c. 10 November 1908*]
Dear Frances,

I am very sorry to say that I can't come on Sunday. An incidental reason is that I am giving a feast to our Dent and a number of philosophers that night. The real cause is that I have pawned all my boots. Why?—TO BUY JOHNS. This does not refer to the college; but to the drawings of Augustus John; of which I purchased an enormous number[1] in London on Wednesday afternoon. I am for ever a pauper; and shall not even be able to go to London to see Mrs P. Campbell in *Deirdre*. But I spent two superb days in London with Albert R. But the *Bacchae* was not good. *We* shall do it much better.

When the Johns arrive I am going to give a great party of the Artistic of Cambridge to see them. But one day, it may be, I shall suddenly appear to you at tea—it is, they say, a custom—and relate, among other things, the wonderful and unfinished episode of Miss Stocker—(Miss) M. I. Stocker, as she mysteriously prefers to call herself. I am working it into an epic: or a Henry James story.

                                       Yours ever
                                       RUPERT BROOKE

To MRS BROOKE   *King's* [*Cambridge*]
                                       Sunday [*November 1908*]
Dear Mother,

It is a dreadful thing I send you, made by a young female artist in Wales in September, who drew us all, and has just sent it. She is a nice person, a good artist, perhaps, but oh! she cannot make a likeness! My large and splendid nose she has reduced to a button! However, it may amuse you. You might present it to the Art Museum, or to Alfred.   *   *   *

Very many thanks for the cheque—I had an amusing two days in London. The prices of the drawings fitted in awkwardly, I

[1] He purchased two, one of which was given to me by his mother after his death.

found. And so, though I had meant not to go above 10 guineas for them, I found it was much more convenient to do so, a little, and get *two* drawings. Anyhow I did not spend quite so much at Headlam's sale as you think! The bookseller in charge was very good and priced the books very low. Very many thanks. The drawings are splendid ones. Even the critical Albert Rothenstein admitted that, and confessed jealousy. They are being framed, and photographed (for John) in London; and will appear here shortly. I am going to have a tea-party to celebrate it, and invite the Artistic —Frances Darwin, etc.!

Clive Carey is up for the week-end, ebullient as ever. I forgot to tell you (but you probably know) that a Westminster Problems Book (1904–1907) is out.[1] It consists of all the worst things that have been sent in for prizes in recent years; many therefore of mine. Most, but not all, of things under my name, were written by me. Most too, I should like to disavow. It is horrible to find forgotten things knocked off in a hurry, solemnly resuscitated in cold blood! I hate it: in spite of the pleasant fact that the book is almost entirely by Rose Macaulay, Lord Curzon, and myself!

RUPERT

Please tell Alfred gently, in reference to his last letter or card, that the Fabian Society has been part of the Labour Party since 1900— since the Labour Party was born, in fact.   R.

To EDWARD MARSH   *King's College, Cambridge*
    Friday [November 1908]

Dear Marsh,

The meeting will be in [Maynard] Keynes' rooms, Bodley's Buildings. The Verralls invited me to lunch on Sunday, but I had already promised to go elsewhere, unfortunately. You will meet the delightful little [Francis] Birrell at the Verralls' at lunch on Sunday. He may, some day be an *embryo*![2]

Yours fraternally
RUPERT BROOKE

[1] This anthology included six pieces attributed to R.B., one of which was not by him. See Keynes, *Bibliography of R.B.*, 1964, p. 59.

[2] i.e. admitted to the Apostles Society of which R.B. was a member.

To MRS BROOKE *King's College, Cambridge*
Wednesday
25 November [*1908*]

Dear Mother,

If Aunt Frances fulfilled her promise, you have received the *Granta*, and in it another picture of me.[1] I am sorry about it if you hate it: but you may be amused to see what sort of impression your son makes on people of other colleges!

I am really writing about the Swiss trip. I am feeling rather down, as I have been hard at something or other, I find, ever since last Swiss trip, a year ago; except for a week's walking with Hugh R. S. in the spring. I am rather low, and I want a change of some sort. Also, you remember, we agreed I shouldn't be at Rugby for the house-supper, not, therefore, till the 23rd. Well, the Swiss trip is only for 11 days, eighteenth to twenty-eighth of December, and only costs 11 guineas, including railway. I was wondering if it might be a good thing for me to go? It would be only for ten days, of which I should be away for *five* anyhow. The only thing is, that I should be away from you for Christmas.... Term here ends on the 11th. So if I went, I should have a week between times, at Rugby (or Bourne-mouth): and 2½ weeks with you, wherever we are, afterwards, until the 15th January when term begins.

Carey and Scholfield are probably going, Dudley Ward and [Godwin] Baynes and various other people. What do you think about it? In some ways I should rather like to go for the ten days; though it is no great matter. The only thing is that I find one has to tell them by *Dec. 1st*, if one goes. Therefore I write in this hurry. Please send me a line about it.

I went to tea with Frances Darwin last night....

Did I tell you I made my first public speech on Friday, to two hundred Liberals and Socialists, advocating 'union among re-formers'? It *was* bad: and I frightened.   Your loving son,

RUPERT

[1] A portrait with an article on R.B. in the series 'Those in Authority'.

To JACQUES RAVERAT   *King's!*
                                           Wednesday 25 November
                                                    [?*1908*]

My dear Jacques,

   The book is beyond speaking admirable. A thousand thanks!
I am an infamous fellow not to have said so before. Ah! if you could
conceive the degradation, the busy-ness, the σπουδαιότης* [serious-
ness] of me!...I am filled with a thousand woes and carking petty
sores and cares, that have eaten away my great romantic soul and left
a hollow hollow vacuum, a place of darkness, where the grey
thoughts of mundane life rattle like little pebbles rolling down an
infinite hill. I am delighted to hear that London greeted you
superbly. I rushed wildly to it for the *Bacchae*, a week agone. But
oh! it was bad—*the Bacchae* I mean, not London, mistress of my
soul, city of smoky glory, no! I am wild tonight. I have conceived
a passion, a lithe amber-coloured passion, for a stiff strange little
figure in one of the pictures in the admirable book of St Francis. It
is a wonderful destiny to die of love for a person who died hundreds
of years ago, and then was probably nothing like her portrait.

   Did you see the admirable noble pictures of London? The Goupil
Gallery?—what a name! I saw Ka [Cox] yesterday and she spoke of
a recent sweet letter from you and of your fair health. I am rejoiced.
But you must hardly think of coming to this den of the hollow,
hatchet-faced old and the meagre middle-aged, yet awhile. Complete your romance first, your French thing in English, and read it to
us in the Guildhall in May, when the lilac blooms. I will wreathe
you in it.

   I think of Italy. A splendid hope on the horizon; but hardly more.
For my abominable family will tie me at home, I know, in the Spring.
Yet if I could slink away!... What have I with Italy? If ever I am
free from these intolerable toils I will write to you a *letter*, not such
balderdash as this.   Ever grateful
                                              and ever
                                           RUPERT

---

* I meant πολυπραγμοσύνη [officiousness].

To MRS BROOKE *King's College, Cambridge*
Sunday [*29 November 1908*]

Dear Mother,

Very many thanks for the leave and the cheque. I did not mean to ask you for the whole eleven guineas. I expected to have to pay part myself. It is very good of you, to have sent the two things so immediately.

I am afraid I may have written rather dismally. What I meant about the holidays is this. It is quite true that I have plenty of opportunities of resting. But I always feel that I oughtn't to, and I can't, do nothing. There are so many things I must learn and do; and there is not too much time. My brain *must* be working. And so the only way (I find) I have a real holiday from *my* work, is on a walking-tour, or in Switzerland; times and places where it is impossible to think or read for more than five minutes. In a way such things are a waste of time. And I can't imagine anything I should hate more than a long holiday like that, of more than a week or ten days. It would be intolerable. But, I think, just a week's mental rest strengthens a mind for some time. This sounds rather priggish; but I'm really very much in earnest about reading and writing.

The place is Klosters, in the Engadine, 4000 ft. We leave London at 11 on the Friday. And reach there at 1 on Saturday.

The Eleven Guineas really covers everything, thanks. From London to London again. Except little incidents like Milk Chocolate. I am a rich man. My income is £2555 a year, and a little more— £7 a day, that is, judging by yesterday, when I got £5 from the College for the First Prize for the Essay: and £2. 2s. 0d. from the Westminster[1]—I suppose you saw The Saturday Westminster?

I met Arthur Benson at tea today. He is rather odd: and of course I didn't get to know him much. But I don't think I like him. The egoism seemed to be part of his character; and to make him hard and morbid. But perhaps it's some nervous disease that's responsible.

I don't know the full names of the people going to Switzerland: when I do I will tell you of them. Carey and Scholfield, perhaps, Ward, the Oliviers, Spielmans, a Trinity man called Pinsent, Hugh Morgan and Dolly Rose, as last year—Mrs Rose is in charge of the party—some Thornycrofts (whoever they be), Baynes, the rowing blue. I don't know who else.

[1] A prize for a poem, 'The Jolly Company' (*Poems*, 1911).

Alfred will be all right. I will see he goes to bed early, and gets up. I have written to him to wear comfortable untidy clothes. He will want very little—no dress clothes or any nonsense. I see, from the list, Henderson[1] comes also.

*   *   *

With many thanks and much love

RUPERT

To ERICA COTTERILL   *King's*
                                            30 November 1908

I have a letter of yours which *may* be your last—you never date them!—I have been reading & learning & writing so many things in the last few weeks that anything that happened more than ten days ago seems years old. But I will answer part of this letter.

I sent you a postcard a week ago to say that I wasn't writing. I suppose your debate is long past by now, & all the valuable advice I might have given, from the depths of a twenty-one years' experience of the world, useless, for that occasion at least. I wonder what you did. I don't think anything I say is much good, for I often think I don't know how the mind of anybody else works—certainly of you. My own point of view is this. How one says things is very important. For, I often find, when I have something in me I want to tell people, I fail through being unable to find the right words, and so *I* give people the wrong impression. The great thing is to *make other people understand what one means.* So merely to blurt it out and understand it oneself, does not do, I find. So, for myself, I always go very slowly and carefully; telling a little every now and then, picking my time. And this is because I have to feel my way. I know neither how other people think, nor how to express my own thoughts, at all well: so I go slowly. This, of course, won't suit you in the same way. You instinctively think it rather dull and crawly. But it is a point of view worth considering. This is the difficulty which makes me very rarely speak to a lot of people at once, &, when I do, say almost nothing important; because, as crowds are stupider than individuals, & I am bad at public speaking, I cannot feel I make them understand. I prefer talking to one or two people, or, better still, writing, as one

---

[1] Hubert (afterwards Sir Hubert) Henderson, who had been at School Field. He became a distinguished economist and was Warden-Elect of All Souls College, Oxford, when he died in 1952.

can think & stop & change words, then. I think it is good to shock people a little, & speak out to them, but one must be careful to do it gradually, as a rule, so as to get them accustomed by degrees. Only, I think, if one really feels 'inspired'—feels it *absolutely necessary* to tell out some burning thing—if one is sure of this feeling, to speak out is right at all costs. It is a matter to settle with one's own conscience, I think. And I am rather ignorant about it.

*　　*　　*

Brooke was in Rugby during January 1909 until the Cambridge term began. The Marlowe Society had chosen Ben Jonson's *Epicoene* for its February performance, and he had some part in arranging this, though he was not in the cast. Justin Brooke had gone down in the previous year, and the chief responsibility for the production of *Epicoene* fell upon Reginald Pole, nephew of William Poël, the well-known producer of Elizabethan plays. Pole had had a minor part in *Faustus*, but afterwards came to the fore as one of the best of the Marlowe Society actors. Cosmo Gordon of King's and William Foss of Emmanuel also gave much help in the new production. In February Brooke went to see a performance of *The Frogs* by Aristophanes at Oxford, and returned to Rugby at the end of the Lent term. He tried to plan a vacation tour with Dudley Ward, but this broke down. In the end he went to Manaton in Devon with Russell-Smith, whom he deserted, however, in the middle of the period to spend four days with Ward in the New Forest, partly because the Oliviers were staying in the neighbourhood. From Manaton he went to join his family at Sidmouth.

Already in the previous year the name of Katharine Cox, known to her friends as Kā, had appeared in Brooke's letters. She, with Dorothy Osmaston, Dorothy Lamb and Helen Gardner, was a Newnham student, and during 1909 her friendship with Brooke and his circle became more intimate. Two or three years later her relations with him had grown complex, as will be seen, and the source of great distress to both of them, but during 1909 there were no signs of any clouds on the horizon.

In January 1907 Brooke had first met Eddie (afterwards Sir Edward) Marsh, a civil servant, who was for many years private secretary to Winston Churchill. By the summer of 1909 they knew each other 'pretty well', as Marsh recorded in his *Memoir*, and in April Brooke was writing from Sidmouth to arrange a stay with Marsh in Gray's Inn before going on to Cambridge. From this time onwards Marsh's friendship and guidance were important elements in Brooke's life and his labours for Brooke's posthumous fame are well known. Brooke frequently stayed in Marsh's chambers in Gray's Inn, looked after by his housekeeper, Mrs Elgy.

At the end of the May term Brooke took the Classical Tripos, gaining only a second class. He had not anticipated a higher class, having decided that English literature was of far more importance to him than any dead language. Soon afterwards he determined not to live any longer in College, but to move out to the neighbouring village of Grantchester, where he found lodgings in the house attached to the tea-gardens by the river, known as the Orchard. At the end of June he was for a short time in Rugby, but returned to the Orchard as soon as possible. In August he joined his family at Clevedon in Somerset, where he tried the experiment of inviting his Cambridge friends to stay, but found that few of them met with his mother's approval. From Clevedon some of his letters were concerned with the arrangements for a Fabian Society meeting to discuss the Poor Law Report, which was complicated by consisting of two parts—the Majority and the Minority Reports.

In September Brooke was back at Rugby and on the 19th was writing to Lytton Strachey about his coming to live in the Old Vicarage at Grantchester, but nothing came of this, Brooke himself migrating there in 1911. He had paid a short visit to a camping party in Wales, but soon settled down for the Michaelmas term at the Orchard and from there wrote a long letter to Jacques Raverat outlining a plan for the reunion of a number of chosen friends at Basle railway station on 1 May 1933 in order to escape the deadening effect of middle age. In December Raverat was working at St John Hornby's Ashendene Press and Gwen Darwin at the Slade School of Art in London, while Brooke, from Rugby, was making arrangements to attend the Slade fancy-dress ball in the character of the West Wind. At the end of the month he went, as usual, with a party to Switzerland.

In June of this year Brooke had first met Henry James, who was staying for three days in Cambridge as the guest of Charles Sayle, A. T. Bartholomew (also of the University Library), and myself. A memorable incident was an expedition on the river in a punt with James, Sayle and Bartholomew, but this is not mentioned in the letters. An account of the whole episode with many of James's letters will be found in *Henry James in Cambridge* by Geoffrey Keynes (Cambridge: Heffer, 1967).

To E. J. DENT   *School Field, Rugby*
                                                          1 January 1909

And the usual feelings of the day to you!

Dear Dent,

I'd not *Epicoene* with me. And you know what health-resorts are—out all day, and, in the evening, snatched pens, foreign ink, and no paper. Moreover we were doing a melodrametta[1]—but of that later. I hope Cosmo [Gordon] and Pole have not been worrying you. I of course went away wholly vague about the music. ἄμουσος οὖν[2] you know, I left it all to Pole. I feel that if he and the ingenious Denis [Browne] (a Marlovian) cannot make a decision about music, I shall not try.

Only (in my diffident way) I agree with you and firmly and finally decide there is to be no music between the acts, and that without consulting Pole or Cosmo or any of them.

I feel they will agree.

I am rather helpless, because I don't know if Pole has got, or is going to be able to get, anyone who can sing for the song in Act I. The band is more in my line! It will be good fun, but not, I should think, requiring a lot of labour from anyone? But I write to Pole.

Switzerland was good fun! I am now feeling ridiculously healthy. It will last four or five days. Then I shall be at ease again. Clive was immensely entertaining. He, I, Miss Verrall, and another wrote this melodrama, which we all acted. He was the villain, I the hero. So much I need not tell you: nor indeed the rest. It was all exactly what it should be; and we all very pleased with ourselves. I parodied my Comus gestures and voice: no difficult matter. Clive was Scholfieldian and intense. '*I lôf her! C—Curse her!*' and so on.

                    *   *   *

                                                          RUPERT

To HUGH DALTON   *School Field, Rugby*
                                                          2 January 1909

My dear Hugh,

On the first day of this new and superb year came from you to me a letter and a postcard in splendid companionship, but contradicting one another. By a subtle process I discovered that the postcard was

---

[1] In the Swiss hotel.   [2] i.e. unmusical therefore.

more recent, and therefore more 'reliable' as the politicians say. And so was angry. For the 14th is the one evening I shall and can be in London, and the 9th, 10th and 11th are wholly and utterly impossible, and yet I want to dine with the Cambridge Fabians, for I love them. Dear! Dear! what's to be done? I must suffer in silence. In spirit I shall be with them. (Even yet God may be good and change the hearts of them, and the date.)

*   *   *

Switzerland was an amusing change. A Doddish party appeared in our hotel: but not Dodd, alas! If he asks me to address '*a number of earnest people*' I shall do it. Then he'll be sorry. I shall talk about Art and Metre. Yes! yes! Herbert Samuel (Bertie, we call him) is a Socialist. S. D. P. We Fabians were rather shocked at him. He used to sing *The Red Flag* after dinner every night instead of grace.

*   *   *

Of the rest—all were jolly. Hubback turns out to be a good sentimentalist: Pinsent less noxious than might be believed: Noel Olivier the Coming Messiah: and the Treasurer more kindly. I put them all straight about things: persuaded them that Gerald [Shove] was human and wise, if young: you and I distinguished and omniscient: Jenkins adorable: Schloss well-meaning but...(they all thought him *so* clever!! But I told them about Lloyd-George). I even succeeded in explaining to the Treasurer how it was that I had received £2 for Fabian Literature, and yet possessed only 11*d*. But oh! her conscience!

Would God I were with you, and away from my family!

RUPERT

To GEOFFREY FRY   *Rugby*
[*January 1909*]

Dear Geoffrey,

Many thanks. The letters are great. I think it's hardly fair, though. But I think perhaps Barrie wrote the *whole* thing—including preface. The illustrations are indeed our Halbert's[1]! Those strange realistic criminaloids...crawling round the edges of a baby-book! New English Art and Old Scotch Sentiment! My, what a mixture! Ha! but How Like Life!...

----

[1] Albert Rothenstein.

No. I'm too poor, old, sad and busy ever to look at London again. Actually, I'm going to tear a moment on Thursday as I go through to our filthy Academy in the Fens, and look...at Perchance Pan; I don't know; but in any case (by a month-old engagement) with a pack of women, Swiss women (Swiss refers not to their nationality but to their...atmosphere). Pinkie[1] (Pynquy, *I* call it) I suppose I shall never see.

I am at home with my *abominable* family: and very bad-tempered. In Switzerland things were fair: if only because we had escaped from English home life. We made a mellowdrama, and played it.

The Senior Dean on Art is always amusing. He cannot love the Academy: and they've put a Clause in the 37th Article that he mayn't love the International. So where is he—where can he be?...I do not work or write. I read Socialist books for me country's good. Ha! ha!   RUPERT

To GEOFFREY KEYNES   [Postcard]
School Field, Rugby
[*Postmark: 7 January 1909*]

Thanks, but I can't come to parties for Twelfth Night. I! No!...When is Twelfth Night? Today? Nor London. I am old & poor. Though I may pass through on Thursday.

Nor Blake. I've given up writing. I tried to do you a sonnet, something about things you'd *understand*, but it wasn't much good. One began something like this—

> Poor dear Mr Punnett[2]
> *Has* gone & done it.
> They say he's a Fabian
> Or very likely *may* be one....

And there was another, about—

> Prof. Weissman
> Can *hardly* be a nice man,
> If he thinks that to be a Blakian mystic
> Is merely a recessive Mendelian characteristic.

But oh! I'm weary: sick of me family. Switzerland fair (I morose). Noel Olivier superb.   RUPERT

[1] Graham Robertson's play, *Pinkie and the Fairies*.
[2] R. C. Punnett, afterwards Professor of Genetics at Cambridge.

To HUGH DALTON   *Rugby*
10 January [1909]

My dear Hugh,

I hope the Feast went off admirably. Did you all sing The Red Flag, and get turned out? And did you notice, in a corner, my subliminal self, a cheery comrade and visitor to the dinner, drinking *crème de menthe?* I'm extraordinarily pleased to hear about Dickinson. (Not that I'd have read, anyhow.) I learnt of it from you and also from the latest of a series of tender and witty little notes, passionately typewritten, all of which begin 'Dear Madam' that Gerald has been sending me.

Here I only read Fabian Tracts and write the Carbonari an illustrious paper on The Real America or something. (I met an American.)...

I shouldn't say anything to your female friend, if I were you. I like her mind better than her metre: and her present title *A Question* better than her former one. But it's rather a damsilly Question, isn't it?

(A) Perhaps she is Mr Whitman, or Gerald, or someone, who meant not to scan. (B) Perhaps she wanted to write blank verse. If the latter is true she is very bold. There's the dear old rule that you begin de dúm de dúm or dum de de dum. A few (myself and Mr Philipps), beginning rather hurriedly dúm de dúm, always put in a little 'de' later, somewhere, in the line. If we remember. But merely dúm de dúm de dúm de dúm de dúm (de). Oh! but its unusual! Chaucer a few times, Beaumont & Fletcher five times a play, Keats once

'Thea, Thea, Thea! Where is Saturn?' (pretty!)

Shakespeare once anyhow (in Lear)

'Never, never, never, never, never!'

(a good and original line)...

And she does it 12 times in 52 lines, perhaps twice more, and uses three lines a foot too short, and one a foot too long. Just one line in three wrong. What can you say? But at least you have learnt about Blank Verse!

On Friday night I *may* come and see you.

                           RUPERT

To MRS BROOKE   [*Cambridge*]
                               Tuesday, 2 March [*1909*]

Dear Mother,

I am so sorry to hear you developed a cold after Bournemouth. I hope it has gone again by now. Were you surprised to hear from me at Oxford? *The Frogs* was quite extraordinarily bad. I don't hold with Greek plays anyhow—certainly not farces. But to do them with very dull by-play with a pantomime donkey! I had bad luck all through. (Perhaps you've heard of it?) Next me in the theatre came in—Hilda, Arthur, and Christina D——!!! with a lot of dreary rowing men. Hilda sat next me and almost drove me mad by talking to me all through the music, which I wanted to listen to. She kept asking me if I liked Keats! When I was going to publish 'a little volume of my own'! what the Greek words meant! and so on! At one point I almost left the theatre.

*   *   *

I do not think there is much exciting news since I returned from Oxford. Ramsay Macdonald came down to give a speech. Some people tried to break up the meeting; but failed. Macdonald seemed a nice simple sort of person. On Saturday I went out to dine with the Horace Darwins (the family includes Nora, whom you thought so pretty). I had refused one or two invitations from them before; and I thought I might accept for once, as they're pleasant people. Though I think dining-out a waste of time in nearly all cases. On Sunday I met Virginia and Adrian Stephen at tea. They vaguely remembered about St Ives. At supper with Maynard Keynes I met Geoffrey Scott (O.R., R.W.)[1] who is spending a week-end with him. On Friday I am going to supper with Frances Darwin, Cornford, and Will Rothenstein, the painter, and on, afterwards, to a lecture delivered by Rothenstein on Art. I am in the middle of one of my periods of seclusion. Since Sunday night I have seen nobody but the bed-maker; and shall not till tomorrow tea. At such times I get through a great deal of reading, writing and clearing-up, and feel much more contented than at others. If only I had a room on the second floor, instead of the ground!

Is there any truth in the rumour that you are going to be let in for a by-election?   With love
                                 RUPERT

[1] i.e. of Robert Whitelaw's house at Rugby.

To DUDLEY WARD   [Postcard]
                                        Rrrugby
                            Saturday, 12 March [*1909*]

My dear Dudley,

For some days I have been struggling with a party of philosophers I was engaged to in Cornwall. That, though, I hear this morning is off—for me. They can't manage my time. So, rather suddenly, I'm without plans for my few days' holiday.

Well, I'm quite vague. I have not a thought. I thought of going, disguised in purple whiskers, to a hut hard by in Wales. Then I thought of tramping through Devonshire. You see, the devil of it is that everyone I know is going (by an odd coincidence) to *Wales*! So I can find no companion. Then your proposals flashed across me. Well, Italy's the most dim and forgotten of dreams. It was never very real—never real at all, I think. It sounded well. But as a matter of fact I had pledged myself to Cornwall since November. Also, we have damned little money. I am living on £150 a year: and that doesn't leave much for Italian trips. (As it is I owe you £3 for the National Debt, and untold gold for the Constitutional Crisis at the beginning of January.) But you say 'any part' of Europe. Well, I discover I can get a return ticket to Belgium or Holland (or Hamburg) cheaper than I can to Cornwall. The only thing is, they're rather far for you. But I can't afford an inch further. I shall very likely do it even if you don't. Brussels (I've measured) isn't really further from Munich than Florence is. I can get from London to Rotterdam for 13*s*. We could walk through Belgium or Holland or both: or bicycle; and anyhow use trains a certain amount, for the land is FLAT. But Bruges is quite a good place: and Brussels is amusing. And both have some pictures which would help me to educate you. So, they say, has Holland. Ostend won't be so funny as it is in the summer, when the French bathe. I have a Belgium Baedeker, and we can get a Netherlands one. The Distances are quite short. I don't know if it's hot or cold in those places: or if one wants a mere rucksack + walking tour or a combined civilization and barbarity (rucksack + bag). If we don't settle by April 6th, I shall go off; so write. If I don't hear, and better things appear, I shall take them. You know German and I know Latin, so we can manage Dutch between us.

George Meredith's *Early Poems* contains a long one called *Daphne*. I am coming up to Grantchester next term. What a devil

you are! How shall I bathe? And think of the early summer in those
woods! Come back as soon as possible. I don't see why we shouldn't
caravan after June. Those bloody people (I hear) are going to
Switzerland in August: to place the sea and several ranges of mountains between Noel and my sinister self. Jacques, by the way, was
here last Sunday, when your letter came. I read him extracts and he
rolled his vulturine neck with joy. About once every ten minutes for
two days he pressed me to come to Wales. By the end of the second
day I became unjustly morose. Politics—my God! The worst I ever
said of Asquith is ludicrously too little. And Tory money! It flows
in great oily waves over the country. I suppose your German-
worshipped Pole is Stanislaw Wyspianski, who looked like a cross
between Augustus John and Jesus, and died recently of syphilis.
Learn the Lute, by God! You shall play it along the endless plains
of Belgium, and I my pipe. I can reach the upper upper Z on it, and
my tone is super Marsyan. Would it be impossible to do it in a donkey cart through Holland? I will write a better letter soon: after
a card from you perhaps. I send this to catch whatever posts may be.
Bring back books full of old French and German songs. I write
nothing, and think less. But in April I shall be a God let loose. By
Heaven, I will storm through Belgium. But I'm rather tired here.
I wish we'd got the New Forest trip before us again. There's no
spring, this year, without it.   Exsul exsuli

                                                        RUPERT

To ERICA COTTERILL   *25 March 1909*
                                          c/o Mer Hern
                                          Beckey Falls
                                 near Manaton, Devonshire

   My view from the window before me includes a lawn, flower-beds
with many flowers, a waterfall, rocks & trees, forests, mountains, &
the sky. It covers some twenty miles of country & no houses. It is
(indeed) raining; & has been for the two days I have been here. Yet
it is very pleasant. I am leading the healthy life. I rise early, twist
myself about on a kind of pulley that is supposed to make my chest
immense (but doesn't), eat no meat, wear very little, do not part my
hair, take frequent cold baths, work ten hours a day, and rush madly
about the mountains in flannels & rainstorms for hours. I am sur-
prisingly cheerful about it—it is all part of my scheme of returning
to nature. Also, I try to write a story. But I can't while I am working

The family imagine I am working for my tripos. But I am not....

I want to see your play, & should rather like to listen to you again. (It's ages since I've seen you, & I was rather obnoxious then.) But this month or two the family are keeping a very tight hand on my doings. After May, perhaps, when my exams are over & I am as nominally free from classics as I am actually now—then indeed I may come, perhaps to Godalming for a week-end?...

RUPERT

To DUDLEY WARD

Place: England
Time: Spring A.D.
[*March 1909*]

'To Manor Street from Manaton
Th' obedient missive flies'

—as the old song has it. But how the devil was I to know that you lived in Manor Street? How am I to remember the bloody name? *Manor*! MANOR? MANOR? *Hovel* Street would be better. But perhaps its only a manor of speaking. Eh? Ha! Ha!

Well, damn you, all seems to be well. Yes, I did mean G. Friday eve to Tuesday noon. So that's settled and you can't back out of it. Choose a nice journey through a romantic country, and portioned out in small stages; with lots of little mounds by the roads where I can sit and sing. I heard from poor old Margery [Olivier](a fool, but honourable about once a week). And she said that they were going to try for a hut in the New Forest after the 7th; but, if unsuccessful, were going to stay in Studland and (in her own classical English) 'lump the crowd'. This, it seems, must be; for the she-Radford is working; and therefore they cannot walk for a week. Well! if they're in the New Forest, good, I'll go. If not, I'm doubtful if I can stand it. I must consider. But, for various reasons, I leave it to you to learn of their arrangements, discover all, and break to them that we shall be passing their door. I do so because (a) I've been writing to Margery about once a week since January, and she'll be about sick of me, (b) I daren't do it, (c) I have no time: and you have plenty. So you must settle. But oh! be tactful, be gentle, be gently tactful! Perhaps they will hate us? Horrible thought! Do not intrude! apologize! apologize!

I must think of other things; and be calm. One thing is that all must be settled by tomorrow (Monday) week—all, I mean, about the place of meeting and starting. Another is this: very important. *You must not breathe a word!* Nobody must know where I am in those four days. It must be a profound, a profound secret. I am cleverly deceiving my family about it all. I have been obliged to tell Hugh R-Smith that there *will* be this *lacuna* of half a week. But he knows not why. I have told him I am going to 'seek Romance'! He believes I am going to wander through Surrey disguised in an Italian *sombrero*, with a guitar, singing old English ballads for pence! Ho! ho! But remember, a profound secret. It adds *so* much to the pleasure of it all. To vanish utterly for four days, and on *such* an errand. Be wholly discreet! If you have told any, deny it. Be mysterious!

Here it rains infinitely. But I—I dance through the rain, singing musically snatches of old Greek roundelays. Have you ever seen me in flannels and my mackintosh walking-cape, dancing seventeen miles in the rain? Like this?

[drawing]

H. F. R. S. accompanies me, uncomplainingly

I call him by many pet-names: 'Guts' 'Little Grub' and (sometimes) 'The Liberal Party'. He addresses me only as 'Uncle Rupert'. So we progress.

If you're in Bournemouth: *do* go to 5 Crowther Terrace (West Cliff) and dig out Arthur Eckersley. The poor thing's very lonely there. I may be going to B'm'th meself after Our Walk....I am dreadfully excited and shall go and write a sonnet. Remember exactly all I have said. Farewell. Tell me where.

RUPERT

To DUDLEY WARD *Devon*
Friday [*2 April 1909*]

Your noble but breathless letter arrived this morning. Since then we have walked twenty-seven miles in 6½ hours. I am alert and fresh, but a little ashamed. We met the Keynes family and Katharine Cox halfway across Dartmoor, for—a picnic! Lunch in the open and the rest.

Well! (as you and Mr W. Pater write)—well! I will tell you all that I shall do. I shall leave this place at 10.30 next Tuesday, the 6th. That evening I reach Penmenner House
The Lizard

and stay there till *Friday* morning. Then I come wherever you wire or write. If you write to the Lizard, do so in good time: for the house is 12 miles from a station and the posts are said to be irregular. You will have gathered, if you have read the foregoing carefully, that it will be little use (for the immediate purpose of meeting me) for you to bicycle, in disguise or not, through Manaton that day. But, if you let me know some place I can not hardly reach from the Lizard in one day, and if you appoint a time that will fit in as well as possible with the nominal times of these trains, and if you will bring a good deal of money, we may yet meet: a week today. But, as I said in a card yesterday, you must arrange, and *let me know*, in Cornwall or here, some place we can be in, on Monday, 12th, evening or Tuesday, 13th, morning. So that my letters may be forwarded. For, as I am going to join my people at Sidmouth (the bloody latest!) on Tuesday morning, pretending to have arrived from Cornwall that moment, I must be up in their last few letters to me. That you may understand how everything stands, I will draw out programmes of my movements as various people believe them.

	April	Family & rest of England (with following exceptions) believe me at	H. F. R. Smith & the Cornish	You, I, and the Almighty
Tuesday	6	Beckey Falls	Cornwall	Cornwall
Wed.	7	,,	,,	,,
Thurs.	8	,,	,,	,,
G. Friday	9	Cornwall	the Unknown	— X —
Sat.	10	,,	,,	Arcady
East. Sunday	11	,,	,,	,,
B.H. Monday	12	,,	,,	,,
Tuesday	13	Sidmouth	Sidmouth	Sidmouth

So you see, I must be careful.

If you like to start from here, I could get back here on Friday evening, and we could start hence on Saturday, at dawn, having slept here. It is a pleasant place: and that would obviate difficulties about letters.

I shall be in disguise on Friday: and you will fail to recognize me. Look out for one in a black beard, and an eyeglass: with a pink rose in his button-hole, and waving a scarlet handkerchief. By these signs you will know me.   RUPERT

P.S. *Do* advise them a farmhouse near Sidmouth. (A beastly place.)

To JACQUES RAVERAT
                                                    Devon (for a day)
                                                    and Cambridge
                                                    April [1909]

My dear Jacques,

I have been so ignoble that I have not written to you for a thousand years; and I am so laborious that I am losing all hopes of ever
seeing you more. Are you going to attempt Cambridge again, now
when the little trees are green and white, and the Socialists are
singing all down the backs?

Now here's the devil of a mess! I have your last letter by me—one
dated 25. i. 09—and I can't for the life of me remember whether
I answered it. *A priori,* no. And yet—

O, your letter came from the South, and was full of the South and
the sun and the sea and flowers, smelling of them as a rose smells of
wine! (That means nothing.) It was headed 'Corsica'. I've never
heard of Corsica; but a wise man at Cambridge told me it was near
the Sun. Are you still there and laughing in the light?

My history for the past five months is as uneventful and perfect as
a bird's. I went to Switzerland and felt a magnificent creature.
I returned to Cambridge and read poetry, laughed, and argued, all
day and all night, for a term. I have done no 'work' for ages: and
my tripos is in a few weeks. All the old and dreary who control me
are infinitely sick. And I am wholly radiant. This holidays I fled my
family for long. Part of the while I walked through Devon. Always
it rained and always I sang. Then in a hut by a waterfall on Dartmoor,
a strange fat Johnian and I 'worked' for three weeks. He read—oh!
Aristotle, I think! And I read the Minority Report of the Poor Law
Commission; and books on Metre (I'm a poet, you know!); and
Shakespere! It was a great time. We walked for hours a day. On
one side were woods strangely coloured with green and purple by
Spring: and on the other great purple moors. The Sunsets were
yellow wine. And the Wind!—oh! there was never such a wind to
take you and shake you and roll you over and set you shouting with
laughter!

Thence went I, always luggageless, and strange, and free, to the
Lizard; and stayed some days. Cornwall was full of heat and tropical
flowers: and all day I bathed in great creamy breakers of surf, or lay
out in the sun to dry (in April!); and all night argued with a Philosopher, an Economist, and a Writer. Ho, we put the world to
rights!

But then, after the Lizard, oh! then came the Best! And none knows of it. For I was lost for four days—I went clean out of the knowledge of anyone in England but two or three—I turned, and turned, and covered my trail; and for three–four days, I was, for the first time in my life, a free man, and my own master! Oh! the joy of it! Only three know, but you shall, that you may from your far islands, picture to yourself what a strange place was our England for four days about Eastertide. For I went dancing and leaping through the New Forest, with £3 and a satchel full of books, talking to everyone I met, mocking and laughing at them, sleeping and eating anywhere, singing to the birds, tumbling about in the flowers, bathing in the rivers, and, in general, behaving naturally. And all in England, at Eastertide! And so I walked and laughed and met a many people and made a thousand songs—all very good—and, in the end of the days, came to a Woman who was more glorious than the Sun and stronger than the sea, and kinder than the earth, who is a flower made out of fire, a star that laughs all day, whose brain is clean and clear like a man's and her heart is full of courage and kindness; and whom I love. I told her that the Earth was crowned with windflowers and dancing down the violet ways of Spring: that Christ had died and Pan was risen: that her mouth was like the sunlight on a gull's wings. As a matter of fact I believe I said Hullo! isn't it rippin' weather?

As for your request for a letter about me, 'my doings, feelings, dreams', etc.—what am I to write? Some doings, and feelings, I have told you. I am not unlike the R. B. you used to find, as you say, learning Ernest Dowson by heart. And yet different. From being sad I have travelled far; to the same goal as you, that of laughing, at times—often—for the joy of life; and by how different a route! I find all things—the sum of things, at least—admirable. Splendour is everywhere. I have come out of the Night; and out of the Past. There are many great poems and paintings in the world, and I love them; also there are the sun on the sea, and flowers, and people's faces. I am intensely happy; and not with that *Maeterlinckian* happiness that always fears the gods' jealousy. For I feel certain that the happiness is abiding. At least, I have had it, and known. Nothing can take that. So I dwell, smiling. The world is full of tremendous hopes. I am going to be a 'failure' in my Tripos. And they all curse me for wasting my career. I smile at them. Never was my conscience so serene. I know more than they.

And having found the mountain-tops, I try to be hard and forgetful, as happy people sometimes are, to those who still wail in the valley-mist. I love them and know them. In the sunlight I have not forgotten the songs of the moon—oh! never! My mountain-top has room for all. My joy embraces sorrow. In my pure happy light I know and love all those broken, perverse loves. I have been among them. They are a part of me.

To explain all this stammering: To show how it is not selfish, but wide and clear (that's Socialism!)—there is no room. By mouth some day I will tell you: and you shall sing of the Sun to me. In the μακάραι νῆσοι,¹ or before.　　　Till then
　　　　　　　　　　　　　　　　　Yours
　　　　　　　　　　　　　　　　　RUPERT

To GEOFFREY FRY　　　　　*Gloucester House*
　　　　　　　　　　　　The Esplanade, Sidmouth
　　　　　　　　　　　Saturday [*15–20 April 1909*]

My dear Geoffrey,

Your postcards pursued me madly round this land of ours,* and, in the end, hot and breathless, ran me to earth here. A hot postcard, terrible thought!

I envy you your Italy. My heart is sick for the high staccato smells of Florence. Yet England ('my England' [Henley]), is to use an old-fashioned word, nice. I have walked, oh! madly and raggedly, over it for a long time; resting sometimes in towns for a few days, but never for long. 'A bird of passage' is what I like to call myself. 'O, the call...of...the...road!' as one of Dalton's poor young men sings. And on my walks I have made a thousand new ballads and slain a Dragon, and met deities, and not read any Greek or Latin. I am infinitely happy about a million things and furiously angry about two. One, that some devil read a funeral service over Swinburne, against Swinburne's wish: and the other, that that bloody man the Czar is probably coming to this cowardly country.

I may be in London for a short space on Friday: but I am not sure. And anyhow, if I am, I shall be staying with a man called Marsh, so I don't know what meals (if any) I shall be free for. So I can scarcely arrange any rencounter (an English word). Though I'd love to meet Aubrey Herbert. Can't you bring him to Cambridge?

There is a grey sea like this...and a grey sky like this...and I have just read Cymbeline.　　　　　　　　R. B.

* England.

¹ i.e. the blessed isles.

To EDWARD MARSH   *Gloucester House*
                                      Esplanade, Sidmouth
                                      15 April [*1909*]

My dear Eddie,

Returning on reluctant and bare feet from a long period of fantastic roaming, to the bosom of my sad family in their present seaside resort, I have found documents from King's that passionately demand my presence earlier than I had thought.

I have to go from here to London on Thursday, the 22nd, and I rather ought to be in Cambridge on Friday; but that is not so important.

I write, therefore, not at all imperatively, to know if I may substitute the 22nd for the 23rd, Thursday for Friday? This is only if it exactly doesn't matter to you, a person of intricate life, which night I stay. It is a matter not at all worth bothering about.

But, *if* you are busy on Thursday night, could you yet give me a room for that night as well as Friday, to save me from the unhealthy Socialist resort in Walworth, which I otherwise frequent.

This, too, is a slight matter. I wish I had the adverbs of Henry James, to indicate precisely the degree of mignificance of my requests.

I have been to the Lizard to look for Mrs Davidson, & to the New Forest, where I killed a Dragon. But now I am in mourning for Mr Swinburne and the Independent Labour Party. I said '*poor* Professor Saintsbury'[1] partly because he is a Professor: partly because he will die of swallowing his false feet. He has a passion for feet. It sounds horrible.

I hope you secured your John.[2]   Yours

                                      RUPERT BROOKE

To HUGH DALTON   *Gloucester House*
                                      The Esplanade, Sidmouth
                                      16 April [*1909*]

My dear Hugh,

You will wonder why the Simple Life ends in a Seaside Resort and lined paper. It looks a little like Second Childhood, doesn't it? I think it is merely the first, revenant. But it is all too difficult to explain. I play a great deal on the beach.

On reluctant and naked feet I turned from the violet wilderness to

---

[1] Professor George Saintsbury (1845–1933), literary critic and historian, was an authority on English prosody and prose rhythm.
[2] A picture by Augustus John.

the sad breast of my family in their present seaside resort. For the first time for three weeks I wear a tie; almost, a collar. This is a bloody place. And in this house Mr Joseph Hocking was staying a week ago; and, last year, Mr Beerbohm Tree and family! I move, as ever, you see, among the tinsel Stars. I did not go to Cut Hill; it appeared to be not in my direction. At Dartmeet, however, I met the Keynes family and Katharine Cox (C.U.F.S.C.). Maynard Keynes described to me how he read a Fellowship formula to them in Chapel, pausing, impressively, for a long time at the part where he promised to do his best to uphold the religion of the College.

I *may* pay you x shillings for the F.S. dinner, y shillings for your purchases of 'Literature', next term. I have just won a great sum from the Westminster Gazette; so I am rich. But I must refund my current peculations, also—perhaps first—to the pessimistic Treasurer. I wish she would pay some of the Literature Bills, though. Also, Gerald still owes me 8s. 7d.

Is the position clear?

Minnie Bodkin is magnificent. But would her Poor Law meeting *draw* next term? or shouldn't it happen the term after? Perhaps that would be too late. You might tell Minnie Bedlam that for £10 *I* will deliver the lecture. Say I'm *very* notable. And I hope you suggested to Minnie Bullfinch other ways of spending for the Cause. She might give the Committee an expensive dinner, once a fortnight.... Shall we elect her to the Committee? I shall canvas for her. 'Bodmin and Free Breakfasts' would be a good electioneering cry. Or 'Your Bidcup will cost you less'. (For she might pay every one's subscription.)

Let's have a committee meeting *very* early: that I may know Marchand by sight. And to discuss Thursday meetings for the Minority Report. It seems rather impossible merely to argue about the M.R., in a circle. Would you have a series of two or three papers, followed by discussions? One on each part, perhaps, and one on the Majority Report? (which, at least, James Strachey has read: and, I suppose, you?). Or one on the 2nd part; and two on the first, one on the destructive chapters, one on the constructive proposals. And the papers to be, I figure it, almost entirely explanatory *résumés*? Mr Nightingale could be turned on to do one.

And then what about Associates? Oh, there's a many things. Here I still dally with the Minority Report, and Sonnets. (Did you see my superb Love-Poem 'To a Voice'[1] in the Saturday West-

---

[1] Printed in the *Saturday Westminster*, 10 April 1909, and included in *Poems*, 1911.

minster?) I stay till Thursday. But reach Cambridge only, perhaps on Saturday. My family are subdued by the death of an Aunt. But unmoved by Swinburne's extinction. As he couldn't die twenty years earlier, he might, one feels, have survived another twenty. Did you see that, against his desire, the bloody parson mouthed Anglicanisms of blasphemous and untrue meaning and filthy sentimentality over him? God burn him! Do you know Bonchurch? I twice dwelt there for months. Once, we will go to the grave, and put flowers there, and spit at the Rector, bathe, and weep.

My brother is still impudently argumentative and young. But my massive silence and sudden bitter sneers at the Middle Classes rather awe him. He turns, slowly. He may yet, in Cambridge, be an influence for the good; a Fabian, even, if he will not (as I fear), come under the Jesuitical and dark-browed influence of that sinister and bewildering intellect, Mr Harold Wright.[1]

Oh, yes! he may read *John Rump*.[2] I don't much approve: for when people have great difficulty in making out that sort of thing, they lose part of it, and judge it too low. And I am vain. Yet, let him read it. It may do him good; and the crudities will evade him.

I cannot tell, for a long time, about Mochras Island. I should like to come: though I fear that insidiously hysterical atmosphere. But poverty, and the family, may indeed detain me. And next year is too immensely distant. I may, indeed, not come up: or, for a term, or two terms, only. Or I may even stay in College, under pressure, and amid a generation that knows me not. But, if I followed that alluring plan of solitarily reading Ben Jonson in a far hovel, you, in another part of the hovel, would, I think, find me hideously unsociable. You have no conception of the disagreeableness of me towards those who dwell under the same roof. I am a hermit, by disposition. And when the poetic fury takes me, I knock my head, like poor Mr Horace, for hours against the wall; a disturbing noise. Yet Time will decide.

The Labouring Classes have no sense of Humour. Don't you think Mr Keir Hardie and his three friends rather babyish?

All, I suppose, will be well in the end. My clerical and Socialist cousin writes many of the second leaders in the Morning Post. There is no other news.   RUPERT

I have made a *very* good Anti-Nature Poem to Railway Lines on

[1] Of Pembroke College and President of the Union Society, regarded by R.B. as a reactionary influence.

[2] A burlesque novel, part of which was printed by Sir Edward Marsh in his book, *A Number of People*, 1939, p. 315.

Which I Suddenly Came When Walking on the Edge of Dartmoor;
Being Tired of Irregular Things. It begins

> 'O straight and true! straight and true!...'

and further on there's a verse

> 'For no Laws there be in Sky and Sea,
>   And no Will in the wayward Wood;
> Nor no States of Mind in the Gypsy Wind,
>   —The which alone are good.'

It halts a little, perhaps.   R.

To GWEN DARWIN

The Orchard, Grantchester
[*May 1909*]

Dear Gwen,

I don't know if you're going to be in Cambridge this week end,
or at the *matinée*, but, in case there's hope, will you come to tea on
Saturday—if you'd like exercise and have time? I'm giving a party
to meet some distinguished friends who are making up my house-
party for the week-end—their names are Justin and Jacques (you
know Jacques?). I also believe Miss K. Cox is coming, bringing
Miss D. Lamb and a sister of Miss D. Lamb (as a chaperone: Ka is
Senior Student and has a conscience). At least so she seemed to
think. Also I've written to tell Geoffrey. One can't exactly May[1]
here: but you might all sit on the floor and have tea. There is not
room for chairs.

So can you come, and Margaret [Darwin], about 4.30? (You needn't
answer.)   Yours

RUPERT

[Recipient not identified]

Guildhall [*Cambridge*]
10.30. 18 May 1909

Splendid, by God! Your card made me leap from bed half an
hour too early; to dance and sing. My enormous felicitations to
both. I shall come through London sometime within a month, and

---

[1] A carefully chosen May Day party was to be formed to go 'Maying' in the
country. On this occasion it took place very successfully on 10 May in the meadows
near St Ives.

shall certainly appear in the ecclesiastical Abort. Your tidings make
even this grey place, in which I sit, bright. For I am a prisoner
beneath the picture of the late Queen Victoria, in a room where
a hundred and eight damned fools are writing Greek verses for the
classical Trip. And I am writing an ode to spring and a letter to you.
Also there is a bald invigilating don, asleep. I saw that devil Dudley
[Ward] yesterday, and he was obviously gleaming and bubbling
with suppressed excitement and secrets, but he was silent as to the
cause. I merely supposed he had seen a lot more women he loved.
I saw Cornford on Saturday, and again on Sunday. He's terribly
relapsing into that old weariness of his. The thought of meeting
'odd' people at the Fabian Summer School appals him. It would do
him immense good. I think he'll not come this year; but will next.
His woman, Frances Darwin (a superb woman), is very keen on it.
I shall try to see her alone and put pressure on so. But I *think* he
won't. Jane Harrison, of course, is ill. George Trevelyan is a good
idea. Has Gilbert Murray been approached? We have a secretary of
the C.U.F.S. who does not know how to spell Graham Wallas'
name.

I shall be in London for the inside of a day, anyhow, on June 4th,
seeing Shaw's new play, with *Foss*:[1] I expect you'ld like to meet him.

What a damned good month May is to get married in! When I am
ninety I shall get married in May.

If you could get G. M. Trevelyan to go to Wales at a certain time
and make him write to Cornford to join him, it *might* be done.

Joy!

R. B.

To DUDLEY WARD

Coombe Field, Godalming
Sunday [June 1909]

This bloody but magnificent world necessitates (as it needs)
rearrangement. I am returning to Cambridge late on FRIDAY. I may
not (the Tutor says) stay till Sat.

Therefore(∴) I am going to be in London on *Thursday* night:
sleeping, I hope, at Ben's: seeing *What the Public Wants*.[2] Will you
come to it, then? and all they? (I am writing to Eva). And on Friday
morning (anyhow, perhaps) I could explain pictures to you, at the
New English.

[1] William Foss of Emmanuel, a member of the Marlowe Society.
[2] A play by Arnold Bennett.

I don't know when this will reach you.

About Wednesday week. Will next Saturday be too late to hire carriages? *If so, you can engage a couple if you like.* For I've not yet done so.

There's something else, and I can't think what.

The Westminster is a devil.

Don't you let on I know I'm going to see Noel. It will be (if it is, at all, ever) purely accidental. So don't frighten the stupid, starched, stuffy, slick, Margery—the dear!

Oh ho! the South! The Lakes of Surrey! They call me! And I shall possibly see Noel in the distance! The air and sky is full of noise about it! Tremendous sensation in the heavens! The earth wildly enthusiastic! Life is splendid. I am king of infinite glories. Tra! la!

And then to have to pack a bag! And even that is a ritual of infinite joy and calm splendour. All things are romantic as means. This piece of paper has come to an end. R.

To A. F. SCHOLFIELD *King's College, Cambridge*
Saturday [June 1909]

Dear Scholfield,

I was in other lands all this week and only returned yesterday.

In many ways I should like nothing better than to come into rooms with you next term: but I think I must refuse the offer. I shall, obediently 'studying the truth', explain.

There are various reasons. I am passionately enamoured of solitude; and as a housemate I cannot imagine myself as anything but wildly irritating. I am still uncertain, a little, whether I may not continue in King's and achieve complete solitude here. If not, I am going to try to get rooms in Grantchester, or further, even. I passionately long to shut myself wholly up and read only and always. Also, I promised Dalton, last holidays, that if I *did* share rooms with anyone, I would with him. (But I shan't.)

Blame my misanthropy: disregard my manners: applaud my truthfulness: and believe me to be

Yours very sincerely
RUPERT BROOKE

To DUDLEY WARD   *Orchard*
                                          Thursday [*Summer, 1909*]

[E. M.] Forster's staying out with the Merediths,[1] and refuses to
come into any meal in Cambridge. So there's no chance, almost. But
he's in London every Wednesday. Meet him then *chez* Hilton [Young].

I'm getting up a tea party here again on Saturday. Is that right?
I think so. Ask Jacques. I've written to Margery and Gwen.

My poetry is paid for at two shillings a line—more than twopence
a word.

As it's a pair of dribbly dotards I'm writing to, I won't again
bespatter the page with merriment that's above their heads. Globules!
puh! Slime-bellies! Snots! I am one with the Seven. I smile, and
remain,   from beyond the moon
                          RUPERT (sed adhuc barbatus)

To KATHARINE COX   *The Orchard*
                                          Friday [? *June 1909*]

You ought to be here tonight. Keeling is reading on Labour
Exchanges. I hope I shall see you. Are you busy? Could we go
a walk? I have Keeling on my hands, so I don't yet know when I'm
free. As soon as I know I'll communicate with you. I shall be in
to Raleigh's lecture, tomorrow. I do want to see you.

I doubt if I ever go to London again.

Or anywhere else.

I am extremely harassed with trying to write a paper on a minimum
wage for Poets.   Yours in the mud
(a worm)   Job xxx. 29–31 (R.V.)

To ERICA COTTERILL   *The Orchard, Grantchester*
                                          near Cambridge
                                          Sunday [*July 1909*]

Well, I've been frightfully busy with work, & that's why I've not
written about books. Also it takes such a frightful lot of thinking
about. I've been at home for ten days & came here on Friday. It is
a lovely village on the river above Cambridge. I'm in a small house,
a sort of cottage, with a dear plump weather-beaten kindly old lady

---

[1] H. O. Meredith, economist and Fellow of King's; published *Week End Poems*,
1911.

in control. I have a perfectly glorious time, seeing nobody I know day after day. The room I have opens straight out onto a stone verandah covered with creepers, & a little old garden full of old-fashioned flowers & *crammed* with roses. I work at Shakespere, read, write all day, & now & then wander in the woods or by the river. I bathe every morning & sometimes by moonlight, have all my meals (chiefly fruit) brought to me out of doors, & am as happy as the day's long. I am chiefly sorry for all you people in the world. Every now & then dull bald spectacled people from Cambridge come out & take tea here. I mock them & pour the cream down their necks or roll them in the rose-beds or push them in the river, & they hate me & go away. The world smells of roses. Books? pah!—however—

Read: *G. E. Moore's Principia Ethica* very slowly & carefully, as you want to think.

Samuel Butler.

The best story ever written is in the July *English Review*, called *Other Kingdom*, by E. M. Forster.

E. M. Forster's novel *A Room with a View*, is very good : lighter than the other things I recommend.

W. H. Hudson's *Green Mansions* ditto.

You've read Yeats' *Ideas of Good & Evil*, I think.

McDougall's *Social Psychology*.

Havelock Ellis, *The New Spirit*, a *little* book. What about *Meredith?*

Shakespeare's *Anthony & Cleopatra* is very good.

Do be careful about Wells' *First & Last Things*. It is nice: but it *does* encourage inaccurate thinking so.

If you're reading the New Quarterly, as you say, don't miss *Roger Fry* in the April number.

Have you read any Lowes Dickinson? such as *Justice & Liberty: Modern Symposium: Letters from John Chinaman?*

Arnold Bennett's *The Old Wives' Tale* is good: I believe I told you.

I suppose it would do you good to read Congreve's *The Way of the World*.

Rossetti & Browning I hope you will enjoy. Browning's not a very good poet. *Blake* is.

As for people in love with people of the same sex as themselves, I know all about it, & will tell you some time.

RUPERT

To HUGH RUSSELL-SMITH   [Postcard]
Clevedon
[*Postmark: 21 August 1909*]

Love to Denham, Alan, Mrs S., Elsie etc.. . . .

A Limerick

This is to remind you I have got yr Bradley
(Lectures on Shakespearian Tragedy)
I read it very readily
For he writes not at all badly
Though he has the usual Oxford malady.*

This is a bad place. But I play tennis well. Will you be there
(Brock[enhurst]) after Sept. 6th? I fear not. Dudley Ward will be:
Boxer has been: here. Boxer's in Luv. I don't like my family. Can
you dive better? It rained yesterday.

In Clevedon me Barber will not cut hair on Saturday, only shave.
Last night I dreamt of Mrs Hern.   RUPERT

* Muzzy Mind.

To EDWARD MARSH   (*The Vicarage, Clevedon*)
The Sabbath [*August 1909*]

O yes, Tuesday to Saturday will be admirably suitable. You will
find Francis Birrell, & Dalton, a leader of the *Demi-monde*, whom
you may have met, & you may find the silent Gerald Shove. And
later the songful Clive Carey. Have you ever seen him? He is
rather a dear.

This is a quite dreadful place. One cannot stir outside the garden.
And my family are too detestable for words. There is a book of
Lord Avebury's here, about Life, which I read aloud at tea. And
when we laugh they think us irreverent.

Balliol? But perhaps you have softened him. Do bring him in to
tea or any meal. I cannot read the name, Horner or Homer? Not *the*
Homer, dare I hope, the writer? But I have forgotten those things.

The Johns stayed a long time at Grantchester.[1] I fell deeply in
love with all the children, some of them with me.   R.

The rose-bed if you like. But there will even be the second-best
clerical bedroom.

[1] Augustus John and his family were living in a caravan.

To DUDLEY WARD   *The Vicarage, Clevedon*
Somerset
done by me
with a hand-stamp
[*August 1909*]
God's bloody day

Clevedon is insufferable. I have followed up all the Rivers for miles round and they are all ditches. But I persévér. I mayn't invite God Baynes because Mother doesn't want the House too full. But we shall get along all right with you, them, and Hubback. I've lost your letter, so can't answer. The family disliked Foss and suspect Shove and Hugh. Occasionally one hires a boat, goes out and bathes in the sea. But its not the same thing. And I have no practice, diving. I have forgotten it, I expect. I envy you at Cambridge. I told Margery (she asked) they *were* to bring bicycles. Don't you agree? One (or rather you : I shall work) can get out of this damned suburb easier so. And that's the chief thing. Round, it looks nice country, in a mild, oozy way. But its damned hot.

I hear Ben's up. My love to him.

I have been ill for a fortnight, sleeping in. So my only way of keeping in touch with 'life' is playing tennis barefoot. It's not so effective as living in a tent and a river with three Oliviers: but it annoys the family. I am becoming eminent (no thanks to them) but detestable. The family atmosphere is too paralysing. I am sinking. Save me, or I die!

O for ten minutes with the John family! But all is vain. I shall be a schoolmaster.   X R.[1]

Come as soon as you can.

To DUDLEY WARD   [Postcard]
The Vicarage, Coleridge Road
Clevedon, Somerset
Wednesday
[*Postmark: 25 August 1909*]

I daresay you're coming tomorrow. If so, you may find those people at Paddington at 1.

Campbell and I want to read a play, all together. We don't know what. What do you think? Bring any volumes of Synge you can lay

[1] i.e. ex-Rupert.

hands on, also Yeats, and Atalanta in Calydon. You can ransack my rooms, and Dalton's. Use your discretion which to bring. We can always fall back on Shakespeare. Synge can be bought as well as brought. There is a strong feeling for *The Playboy*. Also *if* you're getting G. Barker's plays have them sent to you here. They appear on Friday. You're a devil not to come sooner.

R.

To A. F. SCHOLFIELD   *The Vicarage, Clevedon*
                                              Somerset
                                        4 September 1909

My dear Scho.,

Every day for—is it a month?—I have buttoned your cheque determinedly into my pocket, and sallied forth into the City, nigh at hand, murmuring to myself 'Yes, yes...I must purchase a little tooth-paste, and some sardines, and the Boys' Own Paper, and another handkerchief; and Cash the Cheque!' And always I have come back blowing my nose, brushing my teeth, nibbling sardines, reading the B.O.P., but oh! not bearing a pocket-full of cash. Until today. Today I have done it. I cashed the cheque: gave the maid 7 *d.* for the parcel, the vicar ½*d.* for the matchbox. And now my pocket is thronged with the rest. What can one do with 4½*d.*? My mother wanted me to return it to you. But I objected that the sudden regain of so much might turn your head. Shall we, one day, steal to some place of entertainment near Cambridge and carouse on it? Or shall we buy some expensive antique book as a '*memento*'? I cannot decide. The impossibility is killing me.

A number of the Epigins[1] have come here since you faded in a chariot, with a pleasant selection of your luggage, to the station. Lately the little Birrell was observed about. And even today the women called Olivier have gracefully departed. They sighed for you, once.

Oh, I don't suppose you're still in Cambridge. You can't be. But I just address it thither. I return about the 24th to my hut; and after I've floored Bill Shakespeare, I shall try to proceed to London for a few days. The Follies, then! And you'll be there?

The wicked Clive [Carey], did you hear? was ensnared by a Duchess, and didn't come here at all. Ah! these butterflies!

Yours ever

RUPERT BROOKE

---

[1] i.e. ἐπίγονοι, successors.

RUGBY SCHOOL RIFLE CORPS
School Field Group 1904
Front row: J. H. Pillman, L. R. D. Anderson, R. C. Brooke,
J. E. C. Ross, F. B. A. Fargus
Second row: F. J. MacCunn, D. B. Burt-Marshall, J. Harvey,
G. Brooke, H. Macdonell, H. H. Ridsdale
Top row: J. W. Cardew, H. C. H. Eden, G. L. Keynes,
J. L. D. Ridsdale

Rupert Brooke, Rugby, 1905

Rupert Brooke as Cadet Officer
Rugby School, 1906

Geoffrey Keynes, 1906

Rupert Brooke, Rugby, 1906

Frances Cornford about 1909

Katharine Cox, 1911

Noel Olivier in camp, 1911

Margery Olivier,
Dudley Ward
and Rupert Brooke,
New Forest, 1911

Brynhilde Olivier
and Justin Brooke
in camp, 1911

To KATHARINE COX   *The Vicarage, Clevedon*
                                              Somerset
                                        4 September [*1909*]

Dear Ka,

Oh, this won't get you in time! It will pursue, and pursue, you,
and then catch you in France weeks ahead. . . . I always procrastinate
just too long.

However—

Well, its now quite moderately firmly fixed like this.

    I. Preliminary and Children.   Dalton
   II. Old Age, loonies, Sick.   H. Gardner
  III. Unemployed etc.   Toulmin
   IV. Machinery and Majority.   You.

Won't that do? Because if, as you say, you're reading the Majority,[1]
you'd better describe it us. I think you could manage IV.

Eva [Spielmann] and Dorothy O[smaston] might be in the background. But I think its a good thing for people up to read, if
possible. A Principle. . . .

Dear Jacques sent me the beautifullest postcard the other day.
I shall shortly write to him. But I never remember his horrible
French address. If you're accepting, thence, no. IV, you might send
it me.

O yes, I've *enormously* meant to tell you, talk to you, about that
present. Writing, I've always forgotten. I told Justin to tell you.
What can we give that superb pair?[2] Nothing worthy, but what?
and who will give it? Justin and you and I. Dorothy Lamb? Who
else? Don't you think six of us (the roughest guess at a number)
should or might be found? Do think of some others. What of
Geoffrey? But perhaps he doesn't quite well know them. . . . And
we'll plot the object (a Piktcher, or Books . . .) next term.

Oh, poor Mother's Experiment of having Some of my Acquaintances in a House in the Country this Summer! They've come and
gone, singly and in batches. And the Elder Generation couldn't
stand *any* of them! O Ka it was quite dreadful, and most harassing
to my tactful organization of the day, how they strongly didn't like
Dalton, Foss—*anybody*! Most painful: and a little amusing. Mother
also frightenedly persuaded Margery [Olivier] and Bryn to come.

[1] The Majority Report on the Poor Law.
[2] Frances Darwin and Francis Cornford.

(They've been delightfully here till today.) Would you believe that the not human Bryn could fail to please? She did, just! Oh, well, not when she was shiningly, bubblingly, there: but in her absence. She (very innocently) preferred to be, and *did* be, alone or with anybody, in the garden, rather than in the drawing-room with Mother: and plunged up mountains all day. In 1870 it was quite invariable to be in the drawing-room.... And so they're both quite right and wrong—should be the verdict. But what *does* one do with Nymphs, with quite inexplicable Sparkling people?...

Today is Saturday. But this evening we all couldn't help thinking it Sunday—all of us (4) *under* 30. And at length we discovered why. It was the sudden absence of Bryn.... The blood of the admirable Sir Syd. produces strange effects. Did I ever tell you why Mother didn't *at all* like Noel? She met her, a year ago, at a picnic. There was some mouldy cake. Noel waved it, and, revolving, chanted:

> 'Bury it deep!
> It won't keep.
> Bury it well!
> It *will* smell!'

Mother thought it tasteless in the youngest of the party.... I ramble.

RUPERT

To HUGH DALTON   *School Field, Rugby*
                                    8 September 1909

*   *   *

I suppose you know that Stewart Headlam won't come. So we can with quite clear conscience toss to Maynard his one chance of really feverish LIFE. Another cause of excitement is that Sir William Chance is organizing a Poor Law Conference in Cambridge on Nov. 19, 20, & 21. I am in touch with it. Mrs Keynes wrote to me 'Sir William Chance *hopes* you will be kind enough to arrange the date of Mr Webb's meeting, so that it doesn't clash, or come anywhere *near*...'. I almost telegraphed to assuage the poor old thing's anxiety.

*   *   *

O *yes*, I made it intensely vivid about the absence of expenditure and Presence of Prestige to Geoffrey Toulmin. I am a very competent letter writer. Perhaps he ain't enthusiastic by nature. But I think we'll get 'em.   *   *   *

We will give Webb the time of his life: but who's to meet him? Maynard, indeed: but not, surely, that tall, fair, stupid man? Do you want Fay?[1] . . . There *are* no economists.

* * *

I'm sorry Dudley's epigram didn't take you. Me it tickled. I admire his wit. Departing, he waved a careless hand and bade me tell you that Politics was a game for clever children, women, and fools. He vanished, lit up by the flash.

I am sorry if everyone is turning against that good poet, that gaunt, sorrow-stricken zany (his own description), my friend James Flecker.[2] I love him yet. He has seen Life.

* * *

Your account of Snowdon is invigorating; to one, who, amid the *bourgeoisie*, and flatness, but exists, not lives. But who was the third on the summit, together with the two eloping lovers you found? He must have been extremely *quid*. He fascinates me; a silent, unobtrusive, haunting figure.

Alfred said to me, shyly, 'Can *Associates* of the Cambridge Fabian Society go to meetings, and soon?' 'O yes,' I was cheerily off-hand 'they can do everything, almost. . . . The only thing is they are all Conservatives. The Liberals are all full members.' Had him there!

I am conducting, through the dear Treasurer, an acrimonious controversy with Eva Spielmann, a capable person who has lately been doing and organizing, a lot of Minority Report meetings. She has a great phrase about 'dividing up horizontally' instead of perpendicularly: a plan she professes to find, empirically and theoretically, best. She means what I expressed to you by an *a priori* division: I think I agree with her. I agreed all along. Only she doesn't know what she means. She suggests

I. Non able-bodied ⎰ Description of *status quo* (and perhaps
II. (of all kinds) ⎱ history)
                     ⎰ Scheme of Reform.
III. Able Bodied   *Status quo* and scheme of Reform
IV. Comparison with Majority.

(Notes by R. B.) (1) To sociologists children are not able-bodied.

[1] C. R. Fay, an economist of King's.
[2] James Elroy Flecker of Caius College, author of *The Golden Journey to Samarkand* and other volumes of verse; he died in 1915.

(2) In sociological language you say *status quo* where an Englishman would say 'Present Position'.

Well: you see, that's precisely what we've got. Only that they've left out machinery: and we're even more horizontal. But I agree with them that 'we are not much interested in the treatment of the aged and infirm. Except as part of the whole system—we don't want to study *them*—we want to find out what's wrong with the whole damned Poor Law'.... (That sentence, I grieve to say, fell from the Treasurer's lady-like pen.) In our List, Children should fall to 2, I agree.

Helen [Gardner] has just written to me, to refuse the paper. She is giving up all her time to 'Suffrage Propaganda'. She wants to resign the Committee: or, if that would cause another election, and fuss—to lapse at the end of the term. Which, I guess, would be easier, unless there's anybody whom we want to get onto the Committee immediately. Damn her soft soul! I'm writing to Nightingale.

Swanage! but even Clevedon is less refined....

οὐκ ἐν τοιούτοις ἐστὶν εἰρήνη τόποις[1]

RUPERT

To DUDLEY WARD
Rugby
Saturday
[8–21 September 1909]

I got your letter this evening at dinner. I was very sick: because I was waiting for another: on TENTERHOOKS. I answer yours now: because I'm a trifle lonely, to tell the truth; and I've had a damn bad week: but just now my irrepressible thoughts of SPLENDOUR have bubbled up again, and in spite of my people, my work, and my troubles, I am defiantly, sincerely and vastly hilarious. Not my meagre mother's nightly anti-Olivier lectures do more than momentarily inflame to wrath my bumptious joy. Therefore I may do you good. And tomorrow's post may depress me. So, as I say, I am writing now. * * *

I talked, you know, with Margery at Clevedon. Then she wrote to me about (1) Minority Report, (2) Scheme, (3) Me and Music, (4) Noel...saying '...do be sensible!...she is so young...you are so young...'. Damn her for a fool! but dear and good. I wrote

[1] i.e. there is no peace in such places.

to damn her: a very long, long, good letter. Full of logic and passion. Quoting Shakespeare. And ending on a mystical note; but a true one. I smashed her (less than I thought, though, it turned out...). But Fate was against me. For she answered, that Lady O. was going to take Noel to Lear, herself (as if *she* knew about Lear!!!), that I (not as an individual, but as a Young Man) was to be shut out of Noel's existence (except at Limpsfield). Lady O.'s New Educational Scheme. Then Margery added seven pages of damn plain speaking of her own. All about my 'wild writing', 'looking ahead' and a thousand things. A great fierce blazing kind sermon. But my God! she said some dreadful things, about women, that made me hate her. I *won't* believe them. Love, for a woman, she said, destroyed everything else. It filled her whole life, stopped her developing, absorbed her. 'You'll see what I mean if you look at women who married young', she grimly adds. 'No woman should marry before 26 or 27' (why *then*? if it kills them). And later 'if you bring this great, terrible, all absorbing thing into Noel's life now...it will stop her intellectual development', etc. It's a bloody theory, isn't it? The Logical outcome is that one must only marry the quite poor, unimportant, people, who don't matter being spoilt. The dream of any combined and increased splendour of the splendid you, or the splendid I, with the splendid X—that's gone. We can't marry X. At the best we can, if we try to marry X, marry her corpse.

It's very cheering, isn't it? One pictures Margery sitting in that dining-room, in front of the Motto 'Love is enough'...: and commenting on it, from a woman's point of view. It's funny.

But I'll not believe it of Noel. All the same, I was torn by mistrust of myself, fear, perplexity, and despair, all that night. I didn't get to sleep till 6; having gone to bed at 11. The next night three a.m. saw me awake, thinking. My dear, I've had an *awful* time. I don't know what to do. 'Wait!' was the burden of her letter. 'Go away if you like! But don't tell her! Wait! for her sake!' And I'm still perplexed; as to what is best for Noel. There were other upsetting things in the letter: of all kinds. I quote. 'Are you sure this is final?...If it were not, and you went on now so that she came to love you, have you thought how it would be with her? (I think I would find a way to kill you).' I loved her, then. Lord, how they love each other, that family! They make me feel rather mean and solitary. Then, in another place there was a sentence: 'She is so reasonable about you now. Let her remain so!...'. That was painful. I didn't imagine she *wasn't*. But to have it rubbed in! Oh! of course, I am delighted! I wave my hat with pallid enthusiasm: And say in a high voice 'Hurray, hurray! Just what she should be— reasonable about me! Excellent, excellent!' *Reasonable*—Lord, what a word!

Sunday

You'll have had enough of my letters and woes. One thing, though; she ended up by asking me to Limpsfield. At first I was so sick I decided not to go. But by the time I replied to her : I accepted. (Well?...) The plan is, of course, that I leave Rugby for Cambridge, as usual; and, as usual, get into the wrong train, and get carried, this time, to Limpsfield. ('On your way to Cambridge' said Margery.) One night's absence will be never detected by the family. I might have gone two nights, Monday and Tuesday; but can't. And may not be able to go the only other day I can, Wednesday. 'May not'— I'll tell you why; and why I'm this morning in the worst temper I've ever been in. (Lord! I've had a scene with Mother! She *crept* out of the room, at the end—which was brought on by my choking with rage, and being therefore unable to continue.) It begins 16 days ago: when you and I and admirable people were charging ridiculously down a far hill in the dark. You with the gay childish *abandon*, which is indeed your most lovable characteristic, ran up behind me and kicked my left ankle with your heavy boot, laughing the while with high hysterical delight. The hole you made was poisoned by a sock, and, they say, inflamed by tennis: and changed into a sore that grew wider and deeper with incredible rapidity. When I got home the doctor examined it. And I have been on a sofa with my left leg in bandages ever since. The wound slowly diminishes. But if I 'go about on it' before it's well, the elderly, shifty, fraud who is my doctor, says it will turn to an abscess and eat the bone of my leg. *Then* I shall be a bit of a fool at wooing dryads.

Well, the creature, damn him!, stopped my going to 'Cambridge' tomorrow. But I thought Wednesday would be all right. And when a letter from Margery came this morning, suggesting Wednesday, I sang Easter Hymns in bed for half an hour, till Mother came in to dress my foot. She was a bit startled. But she was more startled, when, at my careless mention of Wednesday, she pooh-poohed the idea, and I broke into invective. I made such a good speech of concentrated fury, that she was brought to admit that Wednesday would probably be all right. But I've still the doctor to face. If he flatly forbids, they've got me in bandages, moneyless, and without luggage: so I'm pretty helpless. But if he *does*, when he comes on Tuesday—this house, from then till I *do* go, will be laden with an inspissated gloom to which the Egyptian darkness was a positive *glare*.

So there's the situation. I *may* be through on Wednesday: but I can't tell till Tuesday. I'll let you know on Tuesday. I expect I'll be up by lunch-time. I hope you'll be there. I'll let you know when and where, in case. I suppose the flat's no good at midday? I shall be a bit shabby for the N.L.C.[1]—or for anywhere smart (I can't set out for *Cambridge* in London clothes!). We might sigh at a matinée (any except the one I *want* to see, Lear. That'll be filled with Lady O., Margery, and—Noel!). If lunch, lets go to some *very* obscure place, where they won't be. I'm to catch the 5.50 down with them. If I *do* appear in London I shall be flaringly tearingly radiant: so I hope to cheer you. I've worked out all the chances, and I've decided that if going to Limpsfield *does* dish my ankle badly, (a) the abscess'll be right again by January; (b) January's the next important, the next real, date; (c) its therefore worth it: but that's an axiom! So the doctor'll have to give in.

So you see, I'll probably see you: you equally see, I must refuse Ben's invitation to the flat. Shall I see him anywhere at midday, or in the afternoon? I've not seen him for ages: and I want to. I've got a spare room in that hut at Cambridge if ever he, or Ashley Dukes, wants a semi-rustic few days.

I don't see that there can be two theories as to the meaning of the *Beasts* poem.[2] The others are rather muddled. But that's clear enough.

The English Review is mentioned every time anyone comes to a meal here. 'Do you ever see the English Review, Mr X?' leading gracefully up to 'Rupert had a lot of poems in it the other day!' (That's Mother.) Then the family all cheer. Alfred tries to look solemn and giggles: the servant does a step-dance in the background: I turn brick-red: the visitor gives a start, says 'Really? how interesting! Let me see, what name did you say? English Review? for September? yes! I must get one immediately!' and jots down something on his shirt-cuff. (He thinks it'll be 6*d.* or 1*s.* But it's half a crown.) And I make some ghastly jape about mentioning my name to the publishers. Then it's over till next time.

The English Review sent me £3 this morning. (Good post, this morning.)

And yesterday the Westminster promised me two guineas for half

[1] National Liberal Club.
[2] 'The Song of the Beasts', *English Review*, September 1909, and *Poems*, 1911.

an hour's despicable work. (Which reminds me of Sherborne Station, one Saturday before Easter. When we look back on our lives, you and I, they're none so bad!)

I never thought Ben would accept:[1] or should: either. But it was so clearly worth while telling him. I told Margery in my first letter that he wouldn't, and why he wouldn't. You and they, I told them, were wicked and selfish. Ben, and such as I, were good and noble. *I* am lucky because 1933 won't harm the way in which my goodness works. But any good people we ask whose goodness happens to lie in other ways—they probably won't come.

Godwin'll have accepted by now. He's at Limpsfield as I write: the lucky man. So is Bunny G.[2] I'm glad about Godwin and Bryn. Though what, do you know, are Bryn's feelings? I suppose she'll refuse, however much she accepts, to marry for very many years. They'd be a great pair! But I doubt....

Tell me more of your new scheme of Life. Will you be able to fit in occasional pilgrimages, with me? as indeed, of old. January and April next are dates not to be forgotten. And in February I will again have lunch with you at the Union, and explain to you about Spring. Are you going to Bathe at Grantchester next term? Or shall we take the Leys [School] baths?

I've not yet *organized* my *Vita Nuova*. But next term I'm going to learn to,

DIVE

SING

BOX

RIDE

JU-JITSU[1]

FENCE[2]

WRITE PROSE[3]

CLIMB

and

LIVE[4]

Notes: (1) I don't know the verb.
        (2) I learnt once. It will be easy to pick up again.
        (3) This won't interest you.
        (4) This will.

Also, will you Caravan with me in the Spring, or Summer? We can arrange our route...satisfactorily...in a way!

[1] This and the next paragraph probably refer to the re-union of 1933. See p. 194.
[2] David Garnett.

For the rest: I don't know if Daphne'll be at their Wednesday *matinée*. Margery never mentioned her name. If you want accidentally to join them on Wednesday: do so. I'll be happy elsewhere. But remember Lady O. will be there: and may turn you off; for Noel's sake.   RUPERT

To EDWARD MARSH   *School Field, Rugby*
                                                                  [*September 1909*]

You said

'For men have marble, women waxen minds'[1]

came from POPE!   R. B.

To G. L. STRACHEY   *Rugby*
                                                  Sunday, 19 [*September 1909*]

Dear Lytton,

My knowledge of the house at Grantchester is oddly fragmentary; and I'm doubtful which part you'll want. But I'll lay it before you.

My landlady told me about it, recommended it for a place to stay in, and gave me the address: which I decipher as

                          Mrs Neeve,
                                The Old Vicarage,
                                      Grantchester.

The Neeves are 'working-people' who have 'taken the house and want lodgers'. (Beware of that plural.) So far they have been singularly unsatisfied. Mr Neeve is a refined creature, with an accent above his class, who sits out near the beehives with a handkerchief over his head and reads advanced newspapers. He knows a lot about botany. They keep babies and chickens: and I rather think I have seen both classes entering the house. But you could be firm. The garden is the great glory. There is a soft lawn with a sundial and tangled, antique flowers abundantly; and a sham ruin, quite in a corner; built fifty years ago by Mr Shuckburgh[2], historian and rector of Grantchester; and *most* attractive. He used to feast there nightly, with...I don't know whom. But they still do, spectrally, in the evenings; with faint lights and odd noises. We of the village

---

[1] E.M. had probably thought the line was from Pope's 'Epistle II, to a Lady'. It is, in fact, from Shakespeare's 'Rape of Lucrece', l. 1240. Not in the *Oxford Dictionary of Quotations*.

[2] In fact built by Samuel Widnall, eccentric author and printer.

hate passing. Oh, I greatly recommend all the outside of The Old Vicarage. In the autumn it will be very Ussher-like.[1] There are trees rather too closely all round; and a mist. It's right on the river. I nearly went there: but I could find no reason for deserting my present place. Its only the inside of the house I don't know about. I put Jacques there for a week (James will tell you who Jacques is) and he seemed happy. But he's very wild. The cooking mightn't be *good*. But I think they're cleanish and docile. I go to Grantchester on Thursday: so if you'd like me to talk to them, I will. Or I can give you a bed at my Orchard, for you to reconnoitre.

Yours ever

RUPERT BROOKE

To HUGH DALTON   *Rugby*

21 September 1909

I don't much admire *the* new epistolary style—by numbered paragraphs. But I am always at least up-to-date.

1. Yes.
2. I will ask Blinks.
3. No, oh! *no!* ...
4. Goddam.
5. Well, well, boys *will* be boys...!
6. ...—in *bed*, too?...and such a *square* young man!...But of course, in *that* part of the country!...

Now I will write in the old style: for I want to convey things.
I hope you are still enjoying your romantic habitat.
(My style is *ruined* by a recent reading of The Condition of England.[2] Do you know that 'undistinguished' occurs 137 times in the first 200 pages? But he's rather a dear. I welcome his gift for extracting the best out of recent books. Mr Tom Smallways and Progress, for example, the child in *The Yellow Van*, and—oh! *do* you remember the bit from *Love and Mr Lewisham?*—'"Male an Female created 'E them" said Mr Lewisham's friend to Mr Lewisham' —which was damn rough luck on assistant-masters.)
Mrs Keynes, the Protectress and Procuress (I use the word quite *cleanly*) of Nunn, so worried me that on my own authority I replied

---

[1] i.e. like Edgar Allan Poe's 'Fall of the House of Ussher'.
[2] By C. F. G. Masterman.

to her, in very much the terms you communicate from Sid and Bice [Webb]. So that's well: no doubt.

(*Bice*, my good man, is the amorous diminutive of Beatrice, in Italian. It was used by Dante; and the sound of it is not unlike Beechy: but nicer.)

Terence [Hickman] has written me from Putney. He and the S[ocial]. D[iscussion]. S[ociety]. come *trotting* in. (Hancock Nunn is going to address *them* next term!) His handwriting is boyish.

Rev. Selwyn put me into communicaggers with the Beauty of Oliness:[1] who says he runs the Church Society. *He'll* come in, too: but 'subject to my assurance that the poster makes clear that the meeting is not ostensibly in favour of the Minority Report, but to discuss it'!!—I think we can satisfy his Oiliness. It may be worth while to keep my hand on him (he loves me a little): for he says the *other* Bootys of Holiness number 450. ('We will put it on our card, which will go round to 450 members'...is his proud own way of putting it.) It is, in a *way*, 'not ostensibly in favour of the Minority Report', but 'to discuss it', isn't it? I'm writing to point out that Sid himself is not going to pretend that he's not in favour of the M.R.! But can you sugggest a poster? You've done them before. I don't know how they go. Something without 'In support of...' if possible. And shall we have a resolution?

Then, about the Secretary. I now write to Jerry Pinsent, to tell him, I suppose that so unconstitutional a step is forgivable. Or *is* it unconstitutional?

Watkins also, I must consider how he's to be got there.

Grief[2] can't find an old Freshers' prospectus: so in an idle moment, I'll think of what they should be told.

Keep on at your other Liberal and Christian bodies.

The Economists' meal. My God! what a sight! Dear Maynard and even the tall man[3]—and Layton of course—but *Claffam*![4] Can't you see him *bulging* with fear?

And are you going to include [Lowes] Dickinson? Well, well.

I remember noting something in your letter about Dodd and Flecker marrying each other. I suppose it's all for the best....

I'm sorry about Dudley. I told him. He admitted it: 'but after all', he rapped out, 'isn't originality only unconscious plagiarism?' He may be right.

---

[1] — Reynolds of Sidney Sussex College.
[2] A Cambridge printing office.   [3] A.C. Pigou of King's College.
[4] J. H. Clapham of King's College.

'The Poet Laureate frequently paraphrases whole leaders of the Standard Newspaper, while large chunks of Mr Kipling's "Stow it!" are taken from the Police Gazette' (H. B[elloc].) while G. B. S. and Wilde's epigrams is a well-known case.

'Appreciate my wit?' said Dudley, a little later, 'appreciate wit?...No. The adder is not *appreciated* by the Giraffe. It only kills him!' He was pleased. He went on with 'The Book of Life begins with a Man and a Woman in a Garden. It ends with Revelations!'[1] But I left him at that.

What about Arnold Bennett and the Carbonari. Shall I write?

RUPERT

To A. F. SCHOLFIELD   *24 Bilton Road, Rugby*
                                              [*September 1909*]
Dear Scho,

I had qualms about spoiling Geoffrey Fry's evening—though my stern resolve to see you would probably have crushed them. But he has telegraphed from his Somerset vicarage in peremptory and ecstatic terms. So I replied 'Yes!'.

(By the way the Post Office think your name is 'Shop'. There is something occult in that, and sinister.)

I hope they'll get Clive [Carey] in for the Greek play.

I expect I shall hear about times and places from Geoffrey. I enquired of him, should we dress? For I knew that Empire-builders and lawyers and such were apt to the higher civilization. I can always hire evening clothes from some cheap East End place—

Yours

RUPERT

P.S. I am *not* going to be a resident fellow of Kings, nor a lecturer in Leeds, I am going to be a

Bloody

Yah!   POET

[1] From Oscar Wilde's *A Woman of No Importance*.

To GEOFFREY FRY   *School Field, Rugby*
                                            25 September? [1909]

My dear Geoffrey Fry,

For the Sharp-book,[1] the gift of a thousand ages ago, I thank you.
Almost at the moment it came I was reading a long account of
a Jacobean Morris-dance in Two Noble Kinsmen. It had several
features unexplained even in Sharp's book—which is charming. The
subject wants investigation still. You had better write a fellowship
thesis on the subject.

Wales was well, fairly well. There were three thousand females,
and some mountains, and William Archer. A superb figure this
last—do you know him? Whiskers, and no brains; but infinite
mid-Victorian kindliness. The walking party started together and
ascended a steep slope ceaselessly for four hours. The stronger part
went over great snowy hills to Llanbedr. But we—

((We went by train))

At camp a mad crew—James Strachey, Jolly, several Reitlingers,
and so forth. Now I am at peace again; with books and solitude:
the only real life. Yet I lust for the mad folk at Cambridge.

I have lately read Gilbert Murray's *Greek Epic* and love it ex-
ceedingly—all the nice vague bits about the Greek Spirit, anyhow.
Did you ever see Wilamovitz' verses on Headlam in the Spectator?
James Strachey and I are starting a Marie Corelli reading society in
Cambridge. You must join; unless, as is probable, it is run as a rival
to the Meredith Society.

Macbeth is to be done at His Majesty's by Tree and—*Gordon
Craig!*
and I owe you 3s.

Otherwise the world is blank.

                                    Yours
                              RUPERT BROOKE

To EDWARD MARSH   *The Orchard*
                                            The Sabbath
                                      26 September [1909]

I find I shall be in London sometime between Monday Oct. 11th
& the next Thursday. Will you be there then? or still in...is it
Russia this time? I want to see Lear, if they keep on at it.

---

[1] *The Country Dance Book,* by Cecil Sharp, pt. 1, 1909.

The orchard is golden & melancholy and sleepy & enchanted.
I sit neck-deep in dead red leaves.   RUPERT

To E. M. FORSTER[1]   *The Orchard, Grantchester*
                                                    Cambridge
                                                    16 October [*1909*]

Dear Forster,

As a matter of fact I did open it quite gently with a tea-spoon.
The tattered corpse of your first letter, which was in the same form,
rose up and warned me. It is marvellous to have written a paper
a fortnight beforehand. They are generally composed after dinner
on Saturday evening. As you put forward such a choice of dates,
I have thought it might be finest if you came out on the Monday
the 31st isn't it?—For two reasons:

(1) that a city man (Brewing Interest) will then come & stay
here over the weekend. City Men cannot manage other times.

(2) Only people who don't mind sleeping out under hedges in
October are wise to try to come from the Society hither at 1.30 a.m.
on Sundays. And you *might* turn out to mind. And it is a question
that doesn't arise with the city-man.

Would that Monday do, then? Perhaps if you don't come to
Cambridge till the Friday or Saturday, you might stay on till the
Monday? Will you—oh, I suppose so—be able to find places on
Saturday & Sunday & before? The Merediths, or King's no doubt.
King's is full of the *queerest* people, Mondays.

                                        Yours fervently
                                        RUPERT BROOKE

To A. F. SCHOLFIELD   [Postcard]
                                        Arcady
                                [Postmark: 19 October 1909]

I suppose you simply can't stand my writing on whitish paper,
unscented, with a really quite inexpensive ink? I'd love to come to
lunch. But on Thursday I have an Eminent Politician, and his
business, on my hands nearly all the day; and I am *almost* certain to

---

[1] *Endorsed on the letter by Charles Sayle:* Found in the London Library by me,
Sitzungsberichte der Wien. akad. der Wissenschaften. Bd. 61 1869–70 (Phil. hist.)
24 Sept. 1912.
But how the blazes did I come to be reading that volume? 26 Feb. 1922 C.S.

be obliged to attend on him at lunch. So I must say no. But as I munch my little midday bean, I shall think of you all amid your fer-lesh-pots.

'Almighty God, that thy spawn should be such ephemera!' as the most modern of modern poets,[1] whom I am just reviewing, says.

Many thanks
RUPERT

To JACQUES RAVERAT   *Arcady*
3 November [*1909*]
(and I just bathing!)

My dear Jacques,

Why do you compose Vergil?[2] I thought it was done these two thousand years ago very adequately.... But let me not discourage your young ambitions.

I tear out and enclose my Review criticism.[3] I had to write it in a great hurry: and so I fell into that unexquisite use of words you notice, especially at the end—though there I fancy misprinting *may* be also guilty. It is rather a fiddly little article—more about Henry Ibsen than about all of you—but then wasn't that what you wanted?

What nonsense to pretend I have your lute of jade![4] I have mislaid even my own lute—and that's but of cheap wood and cat-gut, a tinkly little affair. But yours—I have never seen it. Sometimes, roaming in my meadows, I have thought to hear a little tinkling and a sad little voice quaintly uplifted in foreign song, away in the dark somewhere. But it was not French! that was not you, I'll swear! I felt it must be—I looked everywhere for—some flowery-gowned little Mandarin with ivory thin pellucid tiny hands and wrists brushing some delicate curved lute, little slanting eyes obliquely pathetic in some fantastic sorrow, and little mouth exquisitely rounded into a funny red O. But I never could quite hit on him. There is no jade lute round here.

As a recompense I enclose a little book you left with me once.

---

[1] Referring to Ezra Pound's *Personae*, 'Revolt against the crepuscular spirit in modern poetry'; reviewed in the *Cambridge Review*, 2 December 1909.

[2] As a printer, J.R. was then learning composition of type with St John Hornby.

[3] Notice of a performance of Ibsen's *Love's Comedy* in the *Cambridge Review*, 28 October 1909. J.R. was in the cast with a party of Bedalians.

[4] *PIH YUH SHE SHOO. Le livre de jade; Poésies traduites du Chinois par Judith Gautier*, Paris, 1902.

Your offer is splendid and noble. I fall upon your neck. I love
seeing my little things in print. And I can torture people I know
with them more easily so. But when? You say 'immediately'.
But I've several rather admirable things (to *me*) half done. In three
weeks or a month I expect to have them finished, or most of them.
I could make a better, and more generally hated, show, then, I feel.
Do you feel inclined to wait till then? I'm afraid my illustrations
won't do: nor my explanatory notes, good as they are. Just the
text....

I mean to 'make an offer'—or rather propound a scheme to you.
But there were always so many people....I will do so now. But it
is, whatever your answer, *a secret*.

It is difficult. I begin thus.

The world is, in certain ways, rather bloody, at present. It is
a good world, but imperfectly organized. One fault, one great
fault, in it, is that its inhabitants grow old.

Examine this. I don't mean in *years*—that's inevitable, and not
necessarily bad—but in *spirit*. Now, there are two classes, I am
certain, of people; and very splendid people in both. The first
naturally get old in spirit, as they get old in years. They are quite
happy in it—it's not necessarily a blemish—only a shortcoming,
a pity. Many good splendid people are such. Geoffrey,[1] I should
think, might be one. There are many.

The other class doesn't *naturally* grow old. It does so, in this
present world, because of the bloodiness of arrangements. But it
needn't. And if people of that class *don't* grow old they are—my
God how splendid! Just sometimes they don't. You are of this
second class. So am I. So are many people I know and you know.
At this point you object 'But, Rupert, *we* shan't grow old!'. My
dear Jacques, we're very admirable and we youthfully lead splendid
lives—with Art and Friendship and the great blusterous beautiful
world about us—now. We are twenty-something. In 1920 we shall
be thirty something. In 1930 we shall be forty something. Still
running to and fro—London, Petersfield, Cambridge. Still in a
country where one *has* to know so many dull stupid grey-lived
sleepers. Still going to the last play, reading the last book; passing
through places we've been in for twenty years; talking to rather fat,
rather prosperous, rather heavy, married, conservative, suspicious
people who were once young with us; having tea with each other's

[1] Probably myself, not Geoffrey Fry.

wives; 'working' 10–5; taking a carefully organized holiday, twice a year, with Ruskin, luggage, and a family, to Florence, disapproving of rather wild young people. . . .

My dear Jacques, think of 1940, 50!. . . We *shall* become middle aged, tied with more and more ties, busier and busier, fussier and fussier; we *shall* become old, disinterested, peevishly or placidly old men; the world will fade to us, fade, grow tasteless, habitual, dull; and at xy years, in a stuffy room, with *all* our relatives, wife's relatives, friends, servants, and medical attendants, around, we shall swollenly stupidly and uninterestedly—*die!*

There've been other people in other generations who swore not to get old, who found Life as good as we do, and vowed to keep it so, to stay young and clean-eyed.

Where are they now? Dead. You meet their bodies walking the streets of London, fat, dead, top-hatted, ghosts, haunting the civilization that was their ruin. . . .

O, never fear, we'll get old, you and I and the rest, and dull, as all the others did. It is certain.

You'll say you've had these thoughts, as all of us have. We who *could* keep young to the end, will grow old. It is the age's fault.

Suppose that a band of the splendid young people in the past had formed a scheme to escape the great destroyer, to continue young, and suppose they had succeeded—wouldn't *that* have been a *wonderful*, and unequalled triumph? a splendid example for the world? and a glory for themselves?

So far theory: stale, you may think. But poignant enough to me. Be patient: and hear now History.

In the beginning of September I was walking on a cliff top with four splendid people, Dudley Ward and Margery and Bryn Olivier and Hubback. The world was before us, sun, rain, wind, the road, and each other. We were filled with joy and youth and ecstasy. We talked as we ran and swung along, of Davidson—quoted (you know it?)

> Out of time and out of all
> While others sing through sun and rain
> 'Heel and toe, from dawn to dusk,
> Round the world and home again.'[1]

We were the 'others' then. We should die, as he had died; and there'd be others. . . and others. . . .

---

[1] From a poem by John Davidson, who had drowned himself.

Had he died? we wondered (the body'd not been found then). I drew a picture of the poet, married, with grown up sons, hampered, driven to write, poor, worried, fettered, walking out one day from it all, changing his name and appearance and facing the world anew, reborn, tasting every drop of life with the keen sense of youth and freshness and the added relish of experience. It couldn't last long perhaps, twenty years or so; but twenty years of that is worth an immortality of—the other. It wasn't true: but it might have been.

The idea, the splendour of this escape back into youth, fascinated us. We imagined a number of young people, splendidly young together, vowing to *live* such an idea, parting to do their 'work in the world' for a time and then, twenty years later, meeting on some windy road, one prearranged spring morning, reborn to find and make a new world together, vanishing from the knowledge of men and things they knew before, resurgent in sun and rain—

We determined to be those people.

Will you join us? Will you, in twenty years, fling away your dingy wrappings of stale existence, and plunge into the unknown to taste Life anew? There'll be many, I hope—not too many, though! We choose people we all agree on. Some people are obviously right; some not. We're going to ask Ka. You'll suggest others. It's the greatest grandest offer of your life, or of ours. You'll accept! I'll explain the conditions.

On the 1st of May, 1933, at breakfast-time, we will meet on Basle Station. Did you ever hear of so splendid a place of meeting? We may have parted, lost sight of one another for years. But on that spring morning, in that mad place, whiskered and absurd and unrecognizable, we'll turn up. And then?...

Then, Life! What else matters? Details elsewhen.

In *April* 1933 R. B. will be a greying literary hack, mumbling along in some London suburb.

In *May* 1933 the offices, muddy drawing-rooms, hatchet-faced middle-aged fools, and snivelling newspapers that knew R. B. will be dully wondering what the devil.... The newspapers will talk about suicide... one or two people, left in England, in the know, will smile and be silent.

And R. B. will be fishing for tunnies off Sicily or exploring Constantinople or roaring with laughter in some Spanish Inn or fitting up a farmhouse or two, with some friends, in America, or rushing wild-haired through Tokio pursuing butterflies, or very sick on an Atlantic tramp. What does it matter? Only—we'll be *living*.

This is an offer. A damn serious and splendid offer. Take your time and consider. The Oliviers, Ward, Hubback and I are going: also Baynes and one or two more : and others we're going to ask. All splendid people. We'll select, all of us, people—the right people— slowly and surely. If, at the last moment, any person daren't do it, he stays at home, holds his tongue, and only he is the worse. Details later. All can slowly be worked out. Some are in favour of going once and for all; some want there to be an option of returning to the old things at the end of...three? five? ten? years. It is possible. Few would return: and those returning would never be as if they'd never gone. They'd have changed everything. They'd have taken the Step: made the Choice. Consider all these things: you'll find reasons for them. Supply details. They may all be altered or filled in. The great essential thing is the Organized Chance of Living Again: The SCHEME.

It has made me wholly happy about Life. Life is beyond words *good*. And now, by this, it *will be*: always to the end. We shan't have to murk and spoil this flaming gift of God—these few years out of Eternity—this great chance that is Life. We'll take and live it to its full extent—be glorious at fifty!! We'll be children seventy- years, instead of seven. We'll *live* Romance, not *talk* of it. We'll show the grey unbelieving age, we'll teach the whole damn World, that there's a better Heaven than the pale serene Anglican windless harmonium-buzzing Eternity of the Christians, a Heaven in Time, now and for ever, ending for each, staying for all, a Heaven of Laughter and Bodies and Flowers and Love and People and Sun and Wind, in the only place we know or care for, ON EARTH.

RUPERT

Postscript

I'm still *thinking* of Petersfield in December. I want to tour the South   (a) delivering lectures on Shakespeare,
   or   (b) disguised as a pedlar selling broadsides.
Will there be a market for broadsides or for Shakespeare lectures in Petersfield?   R.

To A. F. SCHOLFIELD   [Postcard]
Arcady [*Cambridge*]
[*Postmark: 4 November 1909*]

Many thanks. I shall certainly come: undeterred by any amount of sneers and smirks and bitter mirth that will proceed, I have no doubt, from you, whenever I begin to lay before you all the great Terewths of Science, POSITIVISM & PATRIPASSIANISM. When had a prophet honour in his own country? I suppose when I'm gawn you'll all be sorry, and think what you've lost—Verrall, on Fridays, sometimes keeps us till 1.10 or 1.15. But I will speed on wings of fire and Hunger.   R. B.

To A. F. SCHOLFIELD   [Postcard]

[*Postmark: 6 November 1909*]

Well! well!

(And I hear you've been ragging the Proviss[1] *too*!)

I was sorry to miss the lady.   R. B.

P.S. It's not as if I *wanted* yer cooked flesh....

P.P.S. Have you seen the Gownsman[2] this week? It tries to quote poor Lord Tennyson's famous line:

'Faultily faultless, icily regular, splendidly null.'[3]

It comes out as

'Faultily faultless, icily regular, splendidly *well*'!!

To FRANCES CORNFORD   *The Orchard* [*Grantchester*]

Friday [*November 1909*]

Dear Frances,

Between 7 and 7.30 last night I copied out—for practice, partly—two colloquial sonnets. I meant to show them you: but then the Merediths came, and I daredn't. So they lay in my pocket; and now I send them to you—mostly out of egotism. Read them and hurl them away.

It struck me later (about Blank Verse) that—even for the feeling and atmosphere you want to get—it mustn't be taken too much for granted that simple verse is right and complicated verse always wrong, for your purposes. I mean that simplicity is not always expressed by simple lines, or complexity by elaborate blank verse harmonics: that you needn't think yourself *a priori always* bound to a series of lines that end at their own ends, and have few breaks or madnesses—though you would be *nearly always* bound to it,

---

[1] The Provost of King's.   [2] A Cambridge magazine.   [3] *Maud*, Pt. 1, 2.

I imagine. For instance, all Marlowe, pretty well, is in simple lines, *metrically*; but most of them wouldn't do in your play! While in *The Tempest* Shakespeare had left all that *miles* behind him, and was writing immensely varied and complicated and suggestive and built-up verse; but some of it is far more in your atmosphere: e.g.

> 'This music crept by me upon the waters...'

Or,

> 'Be not afeard; this isle is full of noises,
> Sounds and sweet airs, that give delight, and hurt not.
> Sometimes a thousand twangling instruments
> Will hum about mine ears: and sometime voices
> That, if I then had waked after long sleep
> Will make me sleep again; and then, in dreaming,
> The clouds methought would open, and show riches
> Ready to drop upon me; when I waked,
> I cried to dream again.'

And Fletcher, too—

> 'Oh, but thou dost not know
> What 'tis to die.'
> 'Yes, I do know, my lord:
> 'Tis less than to be born; a lasting sleep;
> A quiet resting from all jealousy,
> A thing we all pursue; I know, besides,
> It is but giving over of a game
> That must be lost.'

—But all this, and especially what I said last night, is so perilously off the point. For if you did change one line for what was, abstractly, the better, you might do it at the expense of the whole atmosphere. And then, Oh—! It's the individual atmosphere—feeling—of the *whole* thing that's so important. If you hadn't anything particular in that way, I mightn't feel clumsy and intrusive in making blank verse generalizations. But you have.   RUPERT

To MRS BROOKE   *Grantchester*
                                   Saturday [27 November 1909]
Dear Mother,
                        *   *   *

*　　*　　*

It hasn't really been at all cold here. I have been quite warm and happy. It has frozen occasionally: but today's really rather hot. I bathe—in and out again—in the afternoon, still. I should like to have met Mrs Nutt—I haven't the vaguest remembrance of her. I am now (I find it is Monday that I am finishing this letter!) tired and extraordinarily bad-tempered, and out of sympathy with things in general. I think it is the number of people I have seen and fed with in two days and a half—Jacques Raverat, Justin, H. F. Garrett (once S[chool] H[ouse]), Bob Trevelyan, Eddie Marsh, E. M. Forster, Margery and Bryn Olivier (who sent their love), A. Y. Campbell, and a thousand other people between 20 and 80 and of all conditions.

*　　*　　*

Last night I dined with a lot of Oxford people from the Board of Trade and elsewhere, who were supposed to be very brilliant. But Oxford brilliance is very odd.

I don't think I told you that I wrote once to the Westminster saying I should like to review for them. They answered recently, that their 'reviewing-staff was overfull at present' but they 'hoped to give me a chance soon and wanted to'. So I expect they will send me books one day.

By the way did you see the dreadful puff, in Saturday's Westminster, of the 2nd problem book and especially on my things?[1] It makes me quite red all over to meet anybody who read it. 'Did you see the attack on you in Saturday night's Westminster?' one of the Oxford men asked me.

I saw Scholfield today. He is dreadfully depressed. After the way the Brit. Mus. treated him, he suffered in exactly the same way just now from an Italian family (titled!) who had engaged him for some months to tutor a boy. They have thrown him over. Also a letter about another job from the Appointments Board was never posted. And to crown all he finds he cannot finish his Fellowship thesis in time—not for want of work either. He has been a hermit for months.

They don't show any signs of giving me Scholarship money: so perhaps I may want Father to advance it.

I'll be in Rugby again some time in the first half of January for a bit, I expect.

RUPERT

[1] *The Second Problems Book*, 1909, contained three poems by R.B.

To JACQUES RAVERAT
School Field, Rugby
Saturday [*November 1909*]

Do not be misled. I am not at Rugby. I am at the Orchard. And I have no telephone.

Your great letter was like an April day in the Autumn. We shout hilariously of youth to each other across the skies—while the little grey people mumble down to death. It is splendid to meet or hear from other people who are Going. They have an halo round them. We smile to each other. Margery Olivier writes, it may be, that she has had three weeks rain in Surrey, 'but it will be fine on Basel platform in 1933.'

Or one meets Dudley with three legs broken—'but I shall be active enough, that first of May'!

Yes I'll give you lodging next week right enough: and Justin. If your poem, the Aeneid, is selling like hot cakes, and you're rich: I shall make you pay for lodging here or hereabouts: for I'm poor. We will dismiss Justin to his dreadful friends, and talk sometime. We will discuss further people. Everyone going has to approve before anyone's asked—Ka's not been asked. I can't get hold of her. She's going to be—

I am not going to the Wasps on Sat. afternoon. I must work. I shall be out Sat. evening. On the Monday (I think) I'm going to give a vast lunch party—Oliviers, Dudley, all of you, everybody.

I say, I didn't mean my joke about lecturing serious! I'm sorry you bothered that poor man, 'The Chief'.[1] He must loathe me! I admit, I know all about Shakespeare. But I doubt if I could lecture.

*   *   *

But this, and all the world, we will talk of next week, in such moments as I can snatch from working: and you from gallivanting.

RUPERT

But I want to see your divine woman.

To EDWARD MARSH
School Field, Rugby
Friday [*10 December 1909*]

Dear Eddie,

I find I'm going to be in London from the 20th to the 22nd, Monday to Wednesday. May I stay with you the Monday & Tuesday nights? I hope these days'll be all right for you. On the Monday

[1] The Headmaster of Bedales, J. H. Badley.

night, I'm going, I gather, with a vast party to the Blue Bird. Will you be free to take me to gape at any London wonder, in my rustic way, on the Tuesday night? I don't know what'll be on.

I hope you've evaded the Suffragettes so far. What do you do when they fling vitriol at you? Is an umbrella any use? I rushed up to *Blanco Posnet* on Monday. It was very mournful, I thought, to see the beginning of senile decay in that brilliant intellect. 'Gawd, 'E's a sly One! 'E's a low One'...and 'Bully, boys!' & 'There's a Great Game & a Small Game' & so on....The influence of the Rev. R. J. Campbell & Mr Hall Caine has done it, I suppose. Is it true that Mr Shaw has a passion for the Rev. Campbell? I went to the New English & saw the famous picture of James' legs;[1] also a perfectly divine thing by John perhaps the most sheerly beautiful that he has done. It made me quite sick & faint with passion, because it was so beautiful....

I sit here & read the Drama & study the Poor Law. Tomorrow night my father is going out to dinner, & I have to take House Prayers. Imagine it! I am immensely excited. I shall recite the admirable phrases of Edward VIth's Prayer-book to 54 pink & white cherubs. I may perhaps extemporize a notable 'prophesying' —or isn't that Anglican?   Ever

                                                            RUPERT

To GWEN DARWIN   *School Field, Rugby*
                              Saturday [*11 December 1909*]
Dear Gwen,

Your letter reached me here this evening. You'll understand that I can't 'drop in' to borrow anything, unfortunately. I quite agree to your suggestion. In fact I agree to anything—if there's a later one—so long as I know what I'm expected to do. I'd feel very very important, but rather horridly egoistic, if I'm to be a Wind and you each a Dead Leaf.[2] (Jacques'll be a jolly good dead leaf.) Isn't it giving me too good a job? I see that the leaves are 'yellow and black and pale and hectic red', so there's some choice! I may point out though (of course, I'm a very literary person, you know, well-read, etc.) that the West Wind conducts Clouds and Waves as well as Leaves (vide P. B. Shelley). Ka would be a very good wave —she'd have to be blue and large, and lie down and roll up and down

---

[1] A portrait of James Strachey by Duncan Grant, in profile, seated on a chair with legs extended.   [2] At a Slade School ball.

the Slade like this 〰〰〰〰 and then break in foam. Could she break in foam? She might come out all over white frills periodically, and snap and roll her eyes. I'd thought out a lot of *seven* ideas; in case the leaves fall through. We might be the Seven Branched Candlestick, or the Seven Against Thebes (with Baynes as Thebes) or the Seven Deadly Virtues (Honesty, Hypocrisy, Faith, Respectability, Stupidity, Charity, and Monogamy) (I'd be Faith in my blue dress, with a silly smile) or The Seven Seasons (False Spring, Spring, Summer, St Luke's Summer, Autumn, Winter, and Fog) or the Seven Rays of the Spectrum, or the Seven Seas. But we could go as these at the last moment.

Oh! I must say about 40 things very seriously: for I'm dreadfully excited and frightened. I am so helpless here in the provinces among my family. I am going to London on *Thursday* (and I'm going to the Stephens in the evening. Haven't you been heard to go there? Perhaps I shall see you there). So I shall be able to get things in London a bit—sandals etc. Have you got the blue tunic? Does it want patching up? If so send it here, if you don't mind. There's a woman about the house who does such things. Sandals and white cloak came elsewhence, didn't they? I shall have to try to get a white thing. I suppose a sheet wouldn't do. What's the name of the *stuff* I had it of last time? And, do you know if Ka, or any Londoner, would have such a thing, to lend me?

I suppose there's no other way I could embellish my costume,[1] you can suggest? I'm not very good at dress-thinking, perhaps. I foolishly quite forgot, and had my hair cut this morning. However I can fluff it out, and get some man to arrange it with silver—or without. I might have a WAND.

(I don't believe Shelley thought of the W[est] W[ind] as blue and white.)

As for St George's, is a separate room ordered for us? I wonder if I shall dress after; or come in a compromise. Dare I rush about London in the middle of the afternoon with bare legs? My *largest* overcoat only comes down so [to the knee]. My dress is *so* sky-roby, wove by Iris, that it affords special difficulties. (By the way, I hope so much leg won't offend the Slade?) Is there a room at the Slade, where we can all arrange each other's drapery and hair?

I guess my Comus dress isn't very heavy. But if you don't send it here, will you take it to London and deposit it with Jacques, Justin or somebody?

[1] That of the Attendant Spirit in *Comus*.

It's lucky I don't dance. I shall be able to sit out all the time near a stove. Is there any record of what Spirits wore in Winter? I suppose a jolly fur-rug wouldn't be allowed?

What's a Dead Leaf like?   RUPERT

To GWEN DARWIN   *School Field, Rugby*
                                Tuesday [*14 December 1909*]

My dear Gwen,

Many thanks for the dress. I have given it to a woman to sew. And she's going to get hold of a large white thing for me.

I shall have a large brown rug with me. So I shall wear that if I'm cold.

May *non*-dancers dispense with gloves? However proper at a dance—I feel they'd be wrong for a wind. (Moreover I hate them.)

It is very young and impudent of Margaret [Darwin] to be a *green* leaf. Shall I wither her with a look? As a dead leaf one is very nice colours I suppose. Do you have brown paper instead of a face? And all the ends and edges of you ragged?

I'm glad St George's Restaurant is given up. I've never met a Butler; but I'd like to come soon after 5 to 11 Egerton Place.[1] I cannot play the penny whistle. But I have a 13 *s.* pipe on which I can play Moms Off and the PAVANE.

On Thursday I'm going to stay with James Strachey at 67 Belsize Park Gardens, so if anything at the last moment is to be telegraphed to me, I'm there. (It's a pity he can't come as a DEAD TWIG.)

My mother's awfully shocked...   R. B.

Many thanks for taking so much trouble with my wretched dress.

[1] The home of G.D.'s uncle, William Darwin.

BIOGRAPHICAL PREFACE 1910

The New Year, 1910, found Brooke at Rugby where his father's health was causing much anxiety, so much so that he had to leave Cambridge for the time being to help his parents run the House. As it turned out his father died on 24 January just before the boys returned to school, and he remained as deputy Housemaster for the whole of the Lent term. So he had to abandon all thought of taking part in various projects—the Marlowe Society's performance of *Richard II*, which took place in February; a play by W. B. Yeats, *The Land of Heart's Desire*, which Frances Cornford was promoting; the Fabian Society's affairs, and so on. He was thus fixed at Rugby until 6 April, when term ended. Soon afterwards he joined Lytton and James Strachey at Lulworth. He returned to The Orchard for the Cambridge May term and was there continuously until the beginning of July, except for a few days in June, when he camped with me at Overcote, near Huntingdon, on the banks of the Ouse.

About this time discussions began with a view to staging a revival of *Faustus* for the visit of a party of German students to Cambridge in August. Justin Brooke, who had been abroad for several months in Canada and the United States, had just returned and was again able to take charge of the production.

In July Brooke was back at Rugby, but now staying with his mother at 24 Bilton Road, where she lived until her death in 1931. He was planning a caravan tour later in the month with Dudley Ward in the south of England with the object of haranguing the villagers on Socialism, the Poor Law, and general political propaganda. In the early part of August he went camping with a party of friends on Beaulieu River, and later in the month returned for a few days to Grantchester, but stayed at the Old Vicarage instead of in his lodgings at The Orchard, which were occupied. It was probably at some time during the late summer of this year that he was present at a camp in North Devon, when the tea party commemorated in his poem, 'Dining Room Tea', took place in the house of an ex-Bedalian, Pauley Montagu, at Clifford's Bridge. He also attended a Fabian Summer School meeting before returning to Rugby for September. At the beginning of October he went again to The Orchard for the Michaelmas term, after which he was at Rugby until nearly the end of the year, when he stayed with a few friends for a week at Lulworth.

New names that appear in his letters during the year include those of Sybil and Ethel Pye, who lived at Priest Hill, Limpsfield, and came to know all his circle of friends, David Garnett, then a younger member of the 'Bloomsbury' group, Hugh (A. E.) Popham, who later married Bryn Olivier, and A. Y. Campbell (mentioned before, but now more frequently), classical scholar of St John's College, later Professor of Greek at Liverpool University.

To KATHARINE COX   *School Field, Rugby*
Friday [*2 January 1910*]

Dear Ka,

By the time this gets you, I shall be in Cambridge. I am coming up for a week-end (to Grantchester), to collect books and clothes. Then...I am coming down for the term. I've got to live here and help run things: for my father's eyes have temporarily gone—and he has neuralgia. 'Duty to one's family', Ka, that you sometimes, and so solemnly, mention! That is what's dragging me from the place where I am happier than anywhere, (*no*, not Cambridge—Grantchester!) to...*this*! And I'd hoped to see the Spring in Grantchester!...But I'm sorry and sad for my father and mother. I'll be envying you all Richard II, and the Verrall lectures, and so on! I shall talk to that young man Allen[1] about the C.U.F.S. I guess all will be well. I shall tell Dalton to keep an eye on things. And you can, when you meet him, softly restrain him....

I may see you about, or even 'call' on you in that funny dreadful room....

Have you recovered? Are you hardened? Or was it what Mr Kipling calls 'the makings of a bloomin' soul'? Your account of your states of mind amused and terrified—

Gloomily
RUPERT

I feel such a *devil* for deserting all my trusts! What will the Union Library *do*? I am, of course, convinced that *all* things will go to rack and ruin in my absence!

To ERICA COTTERILL   *Rugby*
Sunday–Tuesday
9 January 1910

My dear, I *have* been rather a beast, I think. I so often *nearly* write. But last term, between Fabian & other business & work, I found the hours alarmingly few when I could grasp a pen; & these short times I often tried to give to 'writing' in the technical sense in which it is my profession, & will, when I am sixty or so, give me as much as £100 a year, with luck. The surprise may rather be that I am writing now. That is easily explained. I have lately been to

[1] Clifford Allen, afterwards Lord Allen of Hurtwood.

Switzerland. There—or on the way back—I eat some poisonous food, & also got influenza. I spent about a week on the homeward journey seeing the most admirable pictures & people in Basel, Paris, & London; very ill all the time. And here they have put me to bed.

I had a faintly pleasant time in Switzerland; but mostly I was wishing to be elsewhere, & rather cubbish. Ee—ee! an unpleasant condition. I went with some good & some bad people. Among the former were many who were at the Summer School that year we were there, Daphne & Margery Olivier, Dudley Ward, Godwin Baynes & also Raverat, that youth who came to see me at Godalming in the summer.

I've heard you're all pleased about the Minority Report. I too, in my calm way. I regard it as certain to be taken up, from what I hear in London. I rather wonder what you've been writing. I heard at one time that you weren't allowed to, at another that you had been. With the Haymarket & Mr Frohman, you young dramatists ought to have a good chance of being all very rich & famous. There is also Miss Horniman; whom I talked to for hours the other day.

Dalton is here for a night, making political speeches in the division with Alfred. I don't do these things. I can't talk slow enough. I'm to canvass local Socialists, when I'm well enough. I've been reading your friend Clutton-Brock's book on poor old Shelley. He *is* a silly man—Clutton-Brock not Shelley. Full of stodginess & middle-class sentimentality; & very ignorant of people. Yet he means well.

I hear my tapioca approaching.

*   *   *   RUPERT

To FRANCES CORNFORD

School Field, Rugby
11 January 1910

My dear Frances,

I fancy I never answered your letter—which found me careering round London in preparation for the fancy dress ball. I quite agree it would be much nicer if we had *Dent's* music, unless he *insists* on Carey's. I've not seen Dent since, but if he says anything I will be full of tact and firmness. I saw Carey a moment; but I was dark as the grave.

I have heard from the young men. [J. S.] Wilson accepts with joy, though full of doubt about his Irish accent. Denis Browne is also very keen though he inserts the word 'small' before 'part'—

'I should love to take a—small-part.' But they're all small, aren't they? So that those two are all right.

I'm glad such good & right people have been gathered together for the Land of Heart's Desire. It will make working together so much easier & nicer.

I am most excited about your book of poems. To show you you aren't *everybody*, I may say I'm also having a volume printed in a month or so! Mine however is privately printed, I think; & in Chelsea,[1] a far more respectably artistic, if less up to date, locality than Hampstead. Are you also Tortured by the impossibility of selecting more than about five poems you can still bear? I have lately returned from Switzerland, where Helen Verrall & I & others performed (having written) an opera.

*   *   *

The Slade Ball was great fun. I did go as the West Wind. Justin was a most lovely dead leaf. Will Rothenstein made for himself, impromptu, an astounding costume of laurel leaves & a red cloak.

I hope you've both had a good time & are doing your duty as keen politicians in the Election.

Love to Francis.   Ever

RUPERT BROOKE

To KATHARINE COX   *Rugby*
                                      [*January*] *1910*

          From a Couch of Pain and Fever

Dear Ka,

I need scarcely say the doctor put me here and kept me here ever since I returned. Poisoned Abroad! Yes!

And very queer in the 'ead.

*   *   *

I lie and read the papers. Some of the things in the Liberal papers and *all* the things in the Tory papers make me shout with impotent rage. Dr Clifford was in Rugby last night and made a vastly popular speech for the Liberal cause. His chief point was that Robert Blatch-ford was an ATHEIST. Oh, my country!

---

[1] This was a suggestion that his poems should be printed by Jacques Raverat at the Ashendene Press, Chelsea.

Alfred makes highly successful speeches everywhere. I can't even canvass. Maynard is coming here on Saturday to speak in villages.

Next term I probably shan't be up quite at the beginning. But you can have a committee meeting.

The secretary has secured

Montague Fordham   (a fool they say)
B. L. Hutchins   (a dear)
Raymond Unwin   (topical)

Do you know Miss Hutchins? Would you like to put her up in Newnham? Also little meetings—Cornford at one.

It will be nice to see Bryn. Wouldn't it be fun to see her and Frances meet?

                                        Ever

                                        RUPERT

To JACQUES RAVERAT   [Postcard]
                                School Field, Rugby
                                    Wednesday
                        [*Postmark: 12 January 1910*]

Pounds more, but I shall write. From the tortures of the damned, from the mouth of Sheol.   R.

The Intuitionist's Way Out

If I loved a young Lady called Flossibel
Whose manners were frankly impossible
I should pray to Our Saviour
To implant the Behaviour
Of a Middle Class Lady in Flossibel.

To GEOFFREY KEYNES   *Rugby*
                                      14 January [*1910*]

Strange ulcers like bright sleepy snakes crawl gracefully about my mouth, throat & inside. But I guess I shall be in Cambridge in 8 or 9 days. Then I'll help in anything that's wanted. I've heard nothing of the play,[1] or the cast. Keep an eye on the pale Duchess'[2]

---

[1] Richard II.   [2] Reginald Pole.

extravagance. And make her offer little parts to all old Marlovians. If little parts suddenly fall through, I will take them. But I'd better be understudying the entire cast, taking rehearsals, & teaching them to say blank verse. Has the buffoon cut large lumps to make an 'acting-version'? And is leave obtained from your bloody pal Mason[1] (A Liberal, I see!—God! what a party!)?

Ricketts has pretty taste; but...I don't at all believe that Buckmaster's[2] an admirable fellow. Our candidate is an Irish Lord Clonmell, a baby & a fool. (Corrie Grant's much too ill to stand.)

I think about nothing, much. The Election, Socialism, C.U.F.S., C.U.M.D.S., Shelley, & the little hard harsh poems I write. Were I but well, I would he helping some jolly Labour man. 'But I am old and these same crosses vex me.'

My disease comes from eating too much bad honey at Basle. Honey! it's funny, eh? And Justin left for America forty hours ago. Well, well.

I hope the Sid-let[3] will be masculine. If there's a C.U.F.S. committee ere I return, & you go, keep them cool & calm. I took liquorice this morn: & now me bowels are strangely writhen. I fly.

RUPERT

To GEOFFREY FRY   *School Field, Rugby*
                                     Friday, 14 January 1909 [*1910*]
My dear Geoffrey,
                    *   *   *

Know that I left my Swiss mountain one day in a little mad party of Raverat (the Art Printer, and Bergsonian), the bald Dudley Ward, an entrancing female artist who exhibits bronzes at the International, and myself. We had to go $2\frac{1}{2}$ hours by sledge to get to a railway, and we ran down the valley just ahead of the dawn all the way. By the afternoon we got to Basle, where we had meals with the admirable Hugh Wilson, saw the exquisite Holbeins and went to an opera. But oh, ere leaving Basle by the midnight train, I ate of some dreadful thing—I think it was the green honey in the restaurant. It was poisoned. I spent two days in Paris (the Louvre, my God!) and two in London, in an incredible fever and with astounding things

---

[1] Canon Mason, Master of Pembroke College and Vice-Chancellor.
[2] The Liberal Candidate for Parliament.
[3] i.e. the child of Sir Sydney Cockerell, Director of the Fitzwilliam Museum.

working within me. I crept here to die. I've not died: but I'm still in bed, and very ill. Do you know Wilfred Blunt's sonnets[1]

'. . .the old and bitter cry
I have tasted honey, and, behold! I die!'?

I lie here, my face bright orange. I subsist on Tapioca. My tongue and mouth and throat and stomach are raw where that accursed stuff touched them. The skin peels off like bad paper from a rotten wall. 'Alas! that men decay before they're dead!' So from this bed of purulence and torment I toilfully pen my febrile gratitude. My mother (I gather) has some similar debt. She sat in her drawing-room and there entered corpses twain, by you murdered. She chews them, I am told, ever and anon. Well, well! I read only Max and Prometheus Unbound. And sometimes I write little poems. They are very hard and bitter and contemptuous and short. They have craggy little rhymes, and they leave me with the impression that all human life is the intolerable dream of a very very sick old man. Some of them are love-poems to fat ugly commonplace people, explaining that they are quite bloody, and that it's the sickly joke of an idiot God that such a jolly creature as I should be in love with them. And some say young fellows fall in love, alas! and all human flesh is like the grass. Or again that I am bloody and the other person's rotten, and the other person'll be smug and fat when I'm forgotten—But I maunder in delirium. Have you embarked on some excellent career? Are you yet determined to be a gay Ambassador in Rome, or to embrace the errors of the holy Athanasius, or to represent the Agricultural Labourer in Parliament? And have you heard what is to be the even immediate future of that learned man, the Reverend Scho?[2]

On gruel or gristle,
Ever

RUPERT

To DUDLEY WARD *School Field, Rugby*
Tuesday, 18 January 1910

My gloom has in part increased. As it may relieve me: I shall pour it solemnly out. You may read and ponder. But better leave it all unread.

[1] *The Love Sonnets of Proteus*, 1881. Perhaps a reference to the last line of Sonnet LXIII.
[2] A. F. Scholfield.

How do I begin? I am not coming up to Cambridge this term. And this is why.

But first, be secret as the grave. I will tell you things no one knows. They won't exactly amuse you. But for God's sake hold your tongue.

Well, I'm fairly well again. But a week ago my father was seized with pains in his head. He has been unable to see more than men as trees walking. He's a very pessimistic man, given to brooding, and without much inside to fall back on—in the way of thought. It has been bad to see him tottering about the House, or sitting thinking and brooding over the future for hour on hour, never speaking, and always in pain. The doctor said Neuralgia. Then he said, perhaps neuralgia. Then he said he didn't know. And then there was a time when we all talked of other things and Mother and I kept looking at Father, and at each other, and nobody dared to say the things they thought, and there were words floating in the air and in the brain and in the middle of conversation one suddenly saw them and felt unable to speak. Then we got to saying the word 'brain', and so it went on.... The doctor here admits he thinks it's a clot of blood on the brain—just beginning. Today they went up to London to see the oculist and a nerve specialist. The oculist could find 'nothing wrong with the eyes'. The other man didn't know; wouldn't say; thought something was wrong in the brain.... He's going to see him again in a week.

So that's let in upon us. There's very little doubt. There's just a silly flicker of hope. But, probably, there's a choice of three things, gradual blindness, gradual madness, and death. And the last, I'm afraid, is rather distant.

My father had intended to keep the House till July: then retire, but keep on the form-work for a few years. That would give him £800 a year: besides which he has £600 or a little more, and after this year would have nearly £900. Now, whatever happens he'll almost certainly do no more work. The new headmaster *may* turn us out this term. In that case we all four live on £600 (one an invalid) for a year! Probably we'll stay here till Easter, which'll help a bit. Mother and I are going to run the House, and hire a man to take the form. The money question is, indeed, not frightfully important. But it troubles mother enormously: and as the days pass, and father's sight and head get no better, he slowly begins to wonder about the financial future, if this goes on, and to get unhappier and unhappier. It is terrible and pitiful to watch him groping about. And it is more terrible and pitiful to see Mother's agony. Her hope has been slowly going. She suddenly broke down with me tonight: and prayed he could die quickly. He had left the room. She is rather too despondent: but it's a black look-out. We keep up the Neuralgia theory in front of him; and he gravely debates if he ought to start term on Thursday week on full work or only half...and so on. Which afflicts Mother more than ever.

It's all pretty wretched. We keep it all pretty dark (which for God's sake do you), but the old servants get to suspect, and creep about sniffling; and I am full of self-pity.

Well, I'll go on to other woes. I still grind and write about Easter. I had a scrawl from Noel, thanking me for the book. It ended 'you don't climb at Easter, so good-bye for some time'. That rather cheered me. But it probed the wound. Noel related how she had, on her own responsibility, bought a dog. Which immediately slew 12 sheep, value £22. So that she is in debt for the rest of her life, and dependent on relations and friends for the slightest luxuries. I spent the night in dreaming interminable dreams of Noel's dog, which is sufficiently ignominious. With trouble round, I laugh whenever I think of it. Noel also mentioned her 3 sisters sitting round the fire (last Sunday). Lo, you! they are not gone yet! And that she devil Margery swore the 8th, the 12th at latest. And it's the 18th. By God, I hate and despise her more each day. The meanness! I have planned out—Lord what a letter to her! But I hesitate to send it. I still have a love and pity for her.

* * *

Poor old Cambridge, to do a term without me. Well, well! If Margery returns for the summer, she'll be able to bring Noel on a visit to Cambridge, ere she goes to Bedales for the summer, without fear. So this peculiarly ill wind blows *some* good. The worst Hell of it is—if this goes on through the Summer, for me, what of our Caravan?

These things must be borne.

But I'm sick for mother. I send you a poem or two I've lately written—in fact, when I was in bed. (For three days they thought I had typhoid.) Read and laugh. Ever

RUPERT

I dreamt I was in love again
  With the One Before the Last.
I smiled to greet that pleasant pain
  Of the innocent young past.

But I jumped to feel how sharp the pain
  Had been when it did live,
How the faded dreams of nineteen-ten
  Were Hell in nineteen-five.

The boy's woe was as keen and clear,
  The boy's love just as true;
And the One before the Last, my dear,
  Hurt quite as much as you.

Sickly I pondered how the Lover
  Wrongs the unanswering Tomb,
And sentimentalises over
  What earned a better doom.

Gently he tombs the poor dim last time,
  Strews pinkish dust above,
And sighs 'The dear, dead, boyish pastime!
  But *this*—ah! God! is *Love*!'

Better oblivion hide dead true love,
  Better the night enfold,
Than men, to eke the praise of new love,
  Should lie about the old!

* * *

Oh, bitter thoughts I had a plenty
  But here's the worst of it!—
  I shall believe, in nineteen-twenty,
You never hurt a bit.[1]   R.

[1] Printed as *The One Before the Last* in *Poems*, 1911, with minor variations.

To GEOFFREY KEYNES   *School Field, Rugby*
                                    Thursday [*20 January 1910*]

The worst has happened—for me. That is—I am not coming up
this term—at least, not the first part. Almost certainly not at all.
My father has bad neuralgia in the eyes, and he'll not be able to do
much for some time. So I have to stay here to help with things.

My dear Geoffrey, I am more harassed with woe than I can say.
Richard II, the Land of Heart's Desire, the Fabians...! If you
knew how I hated Rugby! And how solitarily happy I am in my
hut at Grantchester—and with the Spring coming on! Eh! I weep
to think of it.

But I'm dutiful, though I hate my family. I come over to Cambridge this week-end to get books to work with—I shall be over
several times for that purpose during the term. So my life has a ray
of light. Could you give me an egg for lunch on Saturday? Will
you be in? Let me know—or leave a message. And we will talk of
the term. Alfred will do any work that's wanted in connexion with
R. II. My suppurating stomach has healed: but ah! not my ulcerated
heart!
                                    Thine from the deeps
                                    (*de profundis*)
                                    RUPERT

Do you, D O you—C A N you, know of anyone who would like the
most exquisite rural rooms, books & all, *very* cheap, for a term or
any part of it? Keep yours ears open. It would save me infinite
monies, which are needed. R.

To FRANCES CORNFORD   *School Field, Rugby*
                                    Thursday [*January 1910*]

Dear Frances,

I've a difficult task. And I feel rather ashamed. Though the Lord
(a rather unpleasant person, just now) knows I am blameless. It's
this.

Last week my father was seized with an attack of bad neuralgia in
his forehead and eyes. It quite prevents him working, reading, or
seeing anything but large objects. He has been to a doctor in London,
but he can't get cured in time to do his work next term, and he has to
keep very quiet. Well, we can't turn out of a house we've lived in
fifteen years at a few days' notice, and my father's work has to be

done & a house of fifty boys managed *somehow*. The sum of the matter is that I've got to stay here this term and help my mother run things. I shall be able to do a lot of my own work, of course; and I shall come across to Cambridge at intervals for books. An additional reason for my staying here is, that if my father's eyes and health continue bad long, there's financial difficulties ahead; and though that doesn't much bother me, it adds enormously to the worry of elderly people like my father and mother. Please don't say all this to people, if they wonder why I'm not up; we're only saying that as my father has neuralgia in his eyes, I have to stay at home a bit and help. But I feel I owe you a fuller explanation for so scurvily treating you as to back out of The Land of Heart's Desire.[1] That's of course the head of my offence. There *is* a faint chance of my being able to come up in March; but it's the negligible ghost of a possibility. Someone must be got for my part. I am very much disappointed. I was looking forward to it all. I feel it will be very good. I was really keen on it; though I haven't, I'm afraid, that ability to *show* when I'm keen about things that people like Justin so splendidly have. When people suggest schemes to me, I sit still and begin to imagine out the details.

There are other things I'm very sick to miss, the Marlowe play, and Verrall's lectures, and other things—seeing you all—the whole life of it in fact. Also I fear I may have confused the Fabians rather by not coming up. I'm a general nuisance. Oh! and I'm so sad and fierce and miserable not to be in my garden and little house at Grantchester all this term. I love being there so much—more than any place I've ever lived in. I love the place & especially the solitude so much. I'd thought of being there when the spring was coming, every day this winter, and dreamt of seeing all the little brown and green things. And I always hate being at home. It's horrible of me to talk like this when I'm in the house with two other people who are infinitely worse off in happiness than I am, and one of them in pain. But my method is to be vacuously cheery and bland with them all day, and relieve myself by writing very savage, stern letters all the evening!   I apologize.

I meant, after explaining my perfidy, to answer one or two things in your letter. But I seem to have wandered. Many thanks for your letter by the way. You wrought more beautifully than you knew. For besides hurrying on my convalescence, it cheered me greatly at the exact time when I was sitting gloomily waiting for my father's

---

[1] By W. B. Yeats. The plan to perform this play was afterwards abandoned.

return from the London doctor, and wondering what the verdict would be. I had sunk into that abysmal darkness which comes on a convalescent when anything goes wrong. I have shaken off my dreadful disease now. It inspired me with thousands of Hardyesque short poems about people whose affairs went dismally wrong, or frightfully detestable persons I couldn't help falling in love with, or interviews with the Almighty in which he turned out to be an absolute and unimaginative idiot. By the way, I see in today's Review that that devil Gow stole the Hardy poems and puffed out a meaningless notice of them. So I'll scarcely be able to write about them there again, just yet. However, I shall mention it to Butler when I see him, with an offended air. I thought they were very good. They drove me to re-read his earlier volumes, which, I found, can be got in one volume for 2s.—with his very bad interesting wood-cuts. His command of metre is so astounding. I met him at Comus time. He talked of the best manure for turnips, all the time. I'm glad he's so nice. You ought to tell him, when you see him again, that a heterogeneous party of jolly people in Switzerland did nothing but read his poems, this Christmas. We had both volumes. On the way back one person said they were too pessimistic; and I was fired to make a speech that lasted an hour and a quarter, and converted all the people I was with, and startled two Germans at the other end of the carriage.

I'm glad you chose that 'pheasant feathers' one,[1] & like it so much. It attracted me enormously. I shall come & sit in front of it for hours. But perhaps that wouldn't sufficiently 'dispel any atmosphere of distrust in the front hall' as you desire. It might add to it—if old ladies, already grim, called & found me so, Bunthorne-like, silent, & on the floor. But I think your house'll be a good one.

Your dual and portentous warning has overcome me. In truth, I had never thought of people *writing and asking* me for the book.[2] The idea makes me white with terror. I am writing to urge on Jacques Raverat to sell the thing at a low price in all the shops in Chelsea. But they will review us together. The Daily Chronicle, or some such, that reviews verse in lumps, will review thirty-four minor poets in one day, ending with

'Thoughts in Verse on Many Occasions
by a Person of Great Sensibility'

By F. Cornford

[1] An etching by Augustus John.
[2] His poems; but these were not, in the end, printed by Raverat.

and

'Dead Pansy Leaves: & other flowerets'
By R. Brooke

and it will say 'Mr Cornford has some pretty thoughts; but Miss Brooke is always intolerable'. (They always guess the sex wrong.) And then I shall refuse to call on you. Or another paper will say 'Major Cornford and the Widow Brooke are both bad: but Major Cornford is the worst.' And then you will cut me in the street. . . .

But I hope to occupy my exile by composing some work of immortal genius.

Am coming over to Cambridge to collect books, etc., on Saturday, the day after tomorrow, till Monday. I wonder if you people'll be in any time, that I may come round and jog Francis about his Fabian paper & try to suggest to you somebody for the L. [of] H.D.? On Sunday evening? or Monday? If you do happen to be in Cambridge and vacant, a note to King's or Grantchester, where I stay, would find me. If not, I daresay I shall discover Francis about or in Trinity.

In gloom and with abject apologies   RUPERT

To GEOFFREY KEYNES   [Postcard]
                                    School Field, Rugby
                                    24 January [1910]

My dear Geoffrey,

I was summoned suddenly home this morning.[1] Will you apologize for me to Pole, for not coming to the rehearsal, as I had promised, & wanted?

I *am* writing for the Review. You may keep my *Gownsman*. My father is much worse. I may, or may not, be up for the performance.

                                    RUPERT

C.U.F.S. Vote for MacCrae.

To DUDLEY WARD   *School Field, Rugby*
                                    24 January [1910]

This may not get you in time. I hope my telegram found you. I'm sorry. I was fetched from Cambridge this morning by telegram. Father has had a stroke. He is unconscious. We sit with him by

[1] R.B.'s father died on this day, and was buried on the following Thursday.

turns. It is terrible. His face is twisted half out of recognition: and he lies gurgling and choking and fighting for life. He is much weaker now. Probably he will not last the night. I hope not. It is all terrible for mother.

I wish I could have seen you. I'll write. Send me your German address. I shall be here till you've gone: probably long after. There's only worry ahead—all the settling and keeping mother going, and probably mother and I will have to go on managing the House for ten weeks—the world won't stop for a death. And father, who's strong, in a way, *may* fight it out for—a week? And 54 boys come into the House on Thursday!...

My love to Margery and Daphne and so on if you see them—to everyone. I re-read the parts of your letter about Noel. Does it cheer me or make it worse? A death-bed is so infinitely far from her. I think she and all of you are dreams I've had. It's so faint. And there's pain everywhere.   RUPERT

You and Jacques spend the summer in a Caravan! I will take occasional weeks with you.

To JACQUES RAVERAT   [Postcard]
                                                School Field, Rugby
                                                25 January [*1910*]

Your note's just arrived—Many thanks. We got quickly to the end. Now it's the dreary task of sorting papers, and the rest. And the family gathering. And black. Death's horrible. I've never before seen it. But death's kind.   RUPERT

I'll write one day.

To E. J. DENT   *School Field, Rugby*
                                            31 January [*1910*]
My dear Dent,

I had planned to find you last Monday morning, and arrange that you should give me a meal that day or the next. But a telegram brought me back here before I could see you at all. I found my father, who had been slightly ill, had had a kind of stroke. We couldn't do much but watch him die. I expect you've heard by now that he lately died. Then there was the weariness that follows, confusion, relatives, and the rest. And fifty schoolboys arriving in the middle. I was barely convalescent from gastric poisoning (Swiss water!) when it happened. And the day after the funeral influenza, finding me white and sleepless, fell on me: at a most unhappy moment. I'm slowly crawling up from that. I've got to come to Cambridge this week-end to get books to work on. I'm going to work here and manage the House. I wonder if I shall see you any time, and talk? I know nothing of Richard II. I only know that last week there was uncertainty about the *Land of Heart's Desire*. In fact, I promised the Cornfords to tell you that my not coming up had shaken all plans. But I was snatched off into this whirl. I'm sorry I didn't tell you: but I expect you have found out by now. Anyhow my absence and silence are accounted for. Apply to the Cornfords for the latest news. I hope you'll make a stand for it not being put off too long.

Can you give me a meal on Sunday? if not, Monday lunch?

I've just been looking at the new *Mask*.[1] I wish they weren't so bitter with good workers on different lines.

I'm glad to hear about Denis [Arundel].

I feel rather grey and weak.   Yours

RUPERT BROOKE

To E. J. DENT   *School Field, Rugby*
3 February [*1910*]

Dear Dent,

I was going to accept your invitation very gratefully. But unfortunately the doctor has forbidden me to come over to Cambridge this week-end, for I'm not getting sound so fast as he had expected and I had desired. I shall have to come to get books and so on the next— the Marlowe week-end. I had rather hoped to escape it, though I am very keen about it. For I couldn't be much help, and I rather shrink from a multitude, as I feel now. But I expect a week, and the feeling of being in Cambridge, will change all that.

*   *   *

I want to catch this midday post; so that I can't thoughtfully answer what you say. My thoughts are still tangled, and have to be concentrated on the needs of fifty half-fledged youths. There are things—pieces of folly, or bad taste, or wanton cruelty—in the

[1] The magazine edited by Gordon Craig.

Christian, middle-class way of burying the dead that make me ill. I don't—at present—feel in myself, the 'ancestor-worship' you speak of, though I think I can understand it, and it appeals to me— in the general. But I've always felt so especially unlike and separate from my parents—in good and bad qualities alike—I'm wholly an individualist.

I wish I could have come this week-end. But you'll be able to have a spare meal on Sunday week?

Yours ever
RUPERT BROOKE

To GEOFFREY KEYNES   [Postcard]
School Field, Rugby
Thursday
[*Postmark: 10 February 1910*]

Thanks for your letter.[1] It was a relief from the ones about God. Butler tells me he's printing my thing[2]—for I acted on your post-card. But as I was hurried & worried & still ill, it isn't so jewelled & precise as you might desire.

I hope to come up for this week-end. I don't know if I shall see the play. Anyhow I guess I'll see you.   RUPERT

I shall be at Dent's. All luck for tomorrow night.[3]

To JACQUES RAVERAT   *School Field, Rugby*
Thursday, 10 February [*1910*]

My dear Jacques,

I was glad to get your letter. I hear I shall see you this week-end. I'm to be staying with Dent. Then you shall tell me of all the fine doings I have missed, miss, and shall miss in London. And we'll fix some next time when we meet. And I'll talk of the book by me that you yearn to print. I want, indeed, to be, for a day and a night and a morrow, garrulously immersed in the moving world. I shall return to it, as far as the impoverished family exchequer permits, in April—O, I'll see Spring yet in Grantchester! But at present. . . .

I've been ill again since my Father died—influenza of a kind. I'm

[1] About his father's death.
[2] An article on *Richard II* in the *Cambridge Review*.
[3] The first night of *Richard II* by the Marlowe Dramatic Society.

better—all right—now: but full of hard work and minor, sloppy, self-piti-ful emotions. Two illnesses and the rest hang like a veil between me and a month ago. You all, and the things that were, are oddly, appealingly, like a dream. Did I, a million years ago, wallow on a white hill-side? Was Daphne like Diana, and one called Margery a brown woodland goddess? Was there a man called Dudley, more honest than the hills? I have a ridiculous fancy that I once saw two people idiotically dressed, moving through impossible attitudes, and one quavered 'Like will cling to like, ther po-ho-ets tellus!' and the other answered 'Terew!'. . . *Is* there such a person as Ethel Pye? *Weren't* you really printing in London all December?

Bits—quite unreasonably—stand out very clearly—especially a rush through some absurd Swiss town to see a Cathedral. Was it very sunshiny that morning?

My heart is warm, and has been half secure—or confident, rather —throughout this last four centuries (just a month) because of the splendid people I know. Half are scattered abroad now. But you'll all meet in April—I'll find all of you by August.

Ever

RUPERT

To GEOFFREY KEYNES   *School Field, Rugby*
                              Thursday [*17 February 1910*]

If you will send me a prose translation of this, by Saturday or Sunday, I will give you 2*s*. 7*d*. of what prize I get.[1]   R.

To GEOFFREY KEYNES   *Friday* [*25 February 1910*]

By the time this letter reaches you, I suppose we shall both be immensely richer. I will send you a cheque for the amount. My lines were exquisite & slate coloured. Many thanks for the con [translation].

I'm glad Richard [II] was such a financial success. I think I shall be up during the Autumn term this year. I am willing to be President, indeed, for that one term—the important one, after all. I don't think I ought to be, because I'm a little out of sympathy with this younger generation. Steuart Wilson would be better: but then, of course, the Secretary's place would be hard to fill. [Frank] Birch I dont know.   *   *   *

[1] A *Saturday Westminster* competition, but no prize resulted.

To have had *one* performance of the ordinary serious drama in the ordinary style—a rather weak play performed by an actor-manager who hadn't the slightest correct idea of the part—is all right, if only for the sake of the incidental virtues. To prolong this into a series would be as fatal as it would be financially successful. Steuart & Denis [Arundel], on their own lines, might, if they've not been led astray by theatricality, be the life of some very good real play—of any earthly kind—next year. But I suppose the winter performances of the Marlowe won't be a long-lived institution, unless they *do* go on to Edward II, Julius Caesar, & all of it, as managed by Arundel & inspired by Sir Henry Irving. The worst of it is, that it'll never be so good, even in the Tree tradition, without Pole; who has a touch of arboreal genius, & may be destined to become a quite prominent actor-manager in London.

*   *   *

I promised Miss Horniman I would do a thing for her: it's this (she would have no other help from us). She wants a list of all the likely people in Cambridge (University, mostly). To them she will send a detailed card of when each play takes place, & so on. The quickest way to give her what she desires, would be to mark a Residents' List—that shilling thing. Could you get one?—I will pay you 1*s.* later—& mark anyone you know in your damned college. Then sometime get Steuart & Alfred to mark profitable people in King's. I'll write to Alfred about it. Hand him the list. I guess Jim Butler'll do Trinity. I'll command him later. But it must begin *somewhere*— & why not Pembroke?

You're at liberty to mark people at other colleges as much as you like!

Where'll you be at Easter? Dartmugger again? How agile one was, a year ago!   RUPERT

To JACQUES RAVERAT   *School Field, Rugby*
                                                1 March [*1910*]
My dear Jacques,

Yes, yes, I am *Mnemon.*[1] Tra! la! 'Perfectly sincerely' I'd like you to come a 'clergyman's week-end' (if you know what *that* is). I only left it vague to see how my mother was. She is much better than I thought she'd be and quieter. We've an Aunt staying with us

[1] In the *Saturday Westminster* competitions.

to help—but you won't mind her? She's venomous, but you needn't see her more than once a day. She is a Christian Scientist. So we shall sit in this untidy room of mine, while they talk in the drawing-room.

Mother was wanly afraid at first; because she thought you were very rich and deduced that you must be of very exquisite taste in living: and we have to put [you] in an Attic. But I reassured her by saying you were the dirtiest man I knew. (The Attic happens, indeed, to be the only room in the house a human being with an aesthetic soul can live in for an hour.)

The only horror is that I shall have to dine out on Saturday. So you must come by the 8.45 (or the 8.0) from Euston on Saturday evening. Then we will talk and drink cocoa an hour, and so to bed. And I will show you a public-school Sunday. Stay till Monday noon, and bring (or find) a book, for I shall have to work an hour or two on Sunday. Bring *Tristram* and read it to me, and if its perfectly dreadful I will read you some of my notes on the Poor Law at the same time.

*　　*　　*

If you want to be good on Saturday: and have spare time, volunteer. I enclose part of my *Fabian News* to explain (front page). Find the nearest candidate—or even help Progressive in Chelsea—

Always

RUPERT

To GEOFFREY KEYNES *School Field, Rugby* *2 March [1910]*

My dear Geoffrey,

It's the alteration of the little words that makes all the difference between Poetry & piddle. What a devil the Duchess is. Does she know how she has let us in? I suppose her attitude to the M.D.S. is '*after Me, the deluge*'. I sent a guinea—1s. for the Residents' List; as you didn't say you *wouldn't* get it. 20s. to give as much of as you like to the M.D.S. Of course, 5s. from each of the new members will help. We will devote the whole of the next German[1] to it!

We break up April 6th, & shall be 'moving' a fortnight before that. So your 'After Easter' visit plan is no good, I'm afraid. Mother has refused to have anyone the last few weeks of term.

[1] i.e. the next competition in the *Saturday Westminster* needing a German translation.

I hear from James Strachey & others that *Justice*[1] is immense. Shall we see it in April? Will you be in London? For a short time I may be on Dartmoor: Or solitarily vagabond in the South with a rück-sack & a book.   RUPERT

Asquith...is a wicked worm.

Don't forget I (by Jacques) paid you my 5*s.* subscription.

To EDWARD MARSH   *School Field, Rugby*
                                                     3 March 1910
My dear Eddie,

Many thanks for your letter & indeed for the earlier ones to an invalid: though those seem so long ago that I cannot find continuity between that time & this. It is the smallest part of the gulf that I have been ill again. I collapsed, unforgivably, just after the funeral; & again subsisted for days on milk & the pieces I could surreptitiously bite out of the end of my thermometer. Now, & lately, though, I am well, & bursting with activity. I work like a Professor & feel the Spring in my bones. Your rumour of my taking my mother abroad is merely tantalizing. Duty, poverty, & a thousand black barriers keep us here. I am acting Housemaster in my father's place till the end of the term. Then we are to be turned from this place by cold strangers, into a little house with a patch of grass in front, on a road, stiff & ugly. For the gentlemanly equivalent of poverty has seized us....Next term I'll be at the Orchard again. It will be a pink Paradise of blossom. Will you come & have lunch in a bower of apple-blossom there? During the third week in April I shall be in London for a day or two. Will you be there & able to put me up for a day or two? I shall be extraordinarily busy catching Mr Frohman[2] up. I hear frenzied admiration of *Justice*. But I am responsible for the souls & bodies of 50 little boys; & so I may not leave Rugby.

A bare two days at Cambridge to collect absolutely essential books was all the devil of a Headmaster would allow me; & that barely. So I sit & grind my teeth to hear of live things moving in the world beyond my cave. I take no form-work; so I am free to do my own work. Being a Housemaster is in a way pleasant. The boys are delightful; & I find I am an admirable schoolmaster. I have a bluff Christian tone that is wholly pedagogic. Also, they remember I used to play for the School at various violent games, & respect me

---

[1] Galsworthy's play.   [2] The theatrical producer and manager.

accordingly. Every night at 9.20 I take prayers—a few verses of a psalm & one or two short heartfelt prayers. I nearly had to prepare the lads for Confirmation, but I, rather pusillanimously, wriggled out of that. But a certain incisive incredulity in my voice when I mention the word God is, I hope, slowly dropping the poison of the truth into their young souls.

But the society of Schoolmasters is simply bloody. I am going to write a novel about them. But even that barely comforts me.

I read twenty pre-Elizabethan plays a week: all poor.

I suppose you're hanging the Home Office[1] with Cromes & Coxes now. Why won't you let me have my way with the Constitution?

Ever

RUPERT

To GEOFFREY KEYNES *School Field, Rugby*
Monday, 7 March [1910]

A letter from Rupert. (In Prep.)

Why is your epistolary style developing monstrous new growths? Why is it resembling the way in which Granville B. thinks Politicians speak?

I dimly remember you first desired to come at or after Easter. Well, we begin to 'move' precisely then. And though *I* don't see why one sensible man shouldn't stay with another sensible man whether the second sensible man is living in two houses, or one, or none, my mother, who is not unnaturally tired & nervy, thinks it wouldn't do. So I said you couldn't come towards the end of *our* term. March 14 or 12 or 16 or any-teen, however, is quite different. In brief, come any day within the next fortnight. Sooner the better. Hugh Smiff, I may say, is probably coming on the 14th: so you'd have to share a room. Could you stand it? Could he? All I beg is that you let me know when you mean to come. I gather the wee [J. B.] Trend doesn't suit you. Otherwise I might have taken you a Sunday Tramp. But I may take you an Xday tramp, praps. Bring a book to read: for I pretend to work a few minutes a day. Th'old Jacques was with me till this dawn. He is a cunning old foreigner, full of life & heresy. He found—you will find—an efficient schoolmaster, tired & high-voiced & snappish; whose health of soul yet gets better as Spring grows.

*   *   *

[1] Churchill was now Home Secretary.

Thanks for the Blake. Jacques & I agreed that Blake was an hysterical charlatan. Jacques refuses to print me till the autumn. Jacques, by the way, is a mere fool about Galsworthy, etc. *Macbeth* is really, I fancy, due to him & the ghost of Justin. I'd like something done; even that perhaps. But I don't think Shakespeare or any of the Elizabethans wrote stuff that is bearable when acted.

Devonshire—perhaps. Probably Cornwall. And you?

The inky babes are splashing each other. I must rise & cuff them. A postcard, please! My love to Cambridge. I'll contribute another guinea at least to R. II: which is noble, considering that my income is £150 for the whole year.

To FRANCES CORNFORD   *School Field, Rugby*
16 March [1910]

My dear Frances,

For an hour I have tried to put myself into the frame of mind in which a middle-aged maiden would write to a literary Colonel. But it is vain. I am not Mr Henry James. Many thanks for the book. The Prior of Hampstead seems to be a man of pleasant ways. I was very glad to meet *Autumn Evening*[1] again. I once found it in a paper and copied it out. Then I lost the copy & after some weeks of indecisive attempts made another. Later, I lost that. Then, a long while afterwards, I came across one of them when I was 'sorting' papers; but couldn't afterwards remember where. And so on. So it has bound my life together in a way! And I still like it almost best. I rather want to point my pen suddenly and say, in my stern schoolmaster's voice, 'Why do you truncate the sixth line of a triolet?' There are no rules but convenience. But I always want to find out how and why things sound to other people. Personally I always want all the lines in triolets *very* equal. Perhaps it's because I don't really like triolets—or rather, prefer them as means, not ends. I think, I mean, one should write triolets and publish—poems, stanzas, or whatever the opposite is. In *Harvest* & *Dislike of Death* & the *fat lady*, of course, it does come off. But I cling to my generalizations. I especially found that *Dislike of Death* seemed good to me. I generally liked the longer poems best—like *Pre-existence* and *In Dorset* and *The Two Armies* (all except the penultimate verse). But *Dawn's* about the best of all for me. Didn't you find it in a way best?

[1] In *Poems* by Frances Cornford, published March 1910.

I suppose one can't compare one's own poems. It's perfect & exquisite & the sort of thing one of these filthy musicians (who have no sense of rhythm or metre) will set to a damned tune and spoil. Is this a bad sort of letter to write? It reads so damned pontifical. But if one belongs to a craft oneself, one somehow gets a different attitude in talking about it. One wants to hurry on and talk details: & one feels on a level with every other craftsman somehow and therefore perfectly at liberty to feel absolutely & unassailably right on every point. I suppose it's being a 'professional', in a way. In the same way I used to feel at full liberty to argue about cricket with other people in the XI here, when I was in it, & contradict them & feel immensely right, though they were better cricketers than I. I do like the poems. They stir and live in this place where to me sometimes everything seems dead. May forestalls April. It's rather odd that the ones I like the subjects of, & the ones I like the poetry of, are often not the same. But that's a dichotomy Prof. Bradley won't let us make. And I quite agree with him. I felt April 7th would be no good. It is hateful of Rugby to go on so long. And hence till the end of term I shall think of you people streaming in wind & rain & sun in those stony brown high places & hate you. Whereabouts are you to be? My own plans are now even madder & vaguer. My Cornish party said it was off. So I wrote off to a man in Munich to come & walk through Holland with me. Now my Cornish party says it is on again. So I am engaged to both. I shall probably end by staying here. I find one can get a return ticket to Rotterdam for a pound. I don't know where Rotterdam is: but I expect it's very nice. Are you going to be near Two Bridges, Princetown? Dalton's in a farm near there. I wonder if you'll see him. He's a nice old thing.

What about the *precis* or *scenario* or whatever it's called, of the immorality?[1] I'd like to have it in my head if I'm walking anywhere in the middle of April, though I doubt if I could do much with it *before* I get away from Rugby. It's in the same way that I at present refrain from doing anything more than making notes in my brain for my '*View of Life*'.[2] If I wrote it down now it would be astringent and just wrong. So I shall wait till I get more central—April & May, when I shall see Life as unsteadily but more whole. I *wish* I were coming to Dartmoor. It would be perfect to write a View & an Immorality & fly over those brown places by turns. I feel wind about me to think of it. I continually remember Dartmoor last year. I had

[1] i.e. F.C.'s morality play *Death and the Princess*, 1912.
[2] F.C. had youthfully invited some of her friends to write on this subject.

a note from Dalton today and he says 'the smell of peat is the best in the world': & it has made me so jealous and restless I can't do any work this morning. In July or August if Dudley Ward & I go in our caravan will you two come & stay a week-end with us? You will have tents to dwell in & nothing to eat.

Ever

RUPERT

To GWEN DARWIN *School Field, Rugby*
18 March 1910

Dear Gwen,

I forgot in Cambridge—I've forgotten before and since, but slowly the things that happened in the dim past that men call Christmas 1909 come back to me. I owe you money. I send it to you in a document that a servant of the State in a Socialistic institution called the Post Office gave to me. Fill up the blanks in it: for I dare not. It is, by the way, for the Slade ball. Tell me if it is the wrong amount.

At present I am in sole command of an enormous house and the eighty people in it. They are mostly small boys and I prescribe for their physical ailments and beat them for their mental and moral ones. I take prayers in the evening, but am not allowed to prepare them for Confirmation. Occasionally they bring me difficult sentences in dead languages and ask help in translating them. And when I fail they hate me.

I hear dim rumours of Salting pictures and Repertory plays: but these things are not for provincial schoolmasters. Are you going to storm over Devon with Franc-is and -es? Their dates are wrong or I should have been there for a short while. I am very sad, and angry. But I shall be at the Orchard next term. Will you have a meal in the Meadows in May with me—i.e. honey under the Orchard apple-blossom?

RUPERT

To KATHARINE COX *School Field, Rugby*
Friday, 18 March [1910]

Soon, detestable one, you go to Italy. I hope you will have a rough passage. I hate you all.

I have lately gained enormous sums by little prize poems. So I hasten to pay you before I squander it all in chocolates. The exquisitely dressed Geoffrey has lately been here. He said he was going to revel at a theatre with you. Perhaps you are at a theatre now. I hate you more than ever. As for modern plays, I shall know more about them when I have seen these latest. The only thing I'm certain about is that Jacques' taste is irretrievably bad. Give my love to the spot by the *Loggia dei Lanzi* where one Italian stabbed another, and Miss Somebody fainted into George's (was it George's?) arms.[1] And do not omit to buy something at the *Quarantotto* shop: if it's only for the sake of the change they give you. And go to the *Cinematografo*. There are also, I believe, some pictures in Florence, but they do not matter: (except possibly the *Boltraffio* in the Men's room). I am going to Prague. I don't know what country it is in. But it is a better country than Italy: and a lot better than Mid-England.

My dear Ka, we are in the middle of 'business'. Have you ever been? 'Landlord's fixtures' and so on. And every now and then we learn that the Electric Light installation has only been valued at £39, and we expected £61. So we sit all lunch in a cold fury....

Lots happening. Gibson is still in the Sanatorium with swollen glands. Bacon mi has got his *Gym*. XX. House mile on Saturday and Confirmation on Tuesday. No other news—

RUPERT

To HUGH DALTON   *School Field, Rugby*
                                    Wednesday, 23 March 1910

Dear Hugh,

You are a devil to tell me about the smell of peat. I dream of it and wake sobbing. Scholastic trammels are about me till April 6th. Will you still be on the Moor then? I fancy not: or I might drop in....I've not the faintest idea what is to happen then, to me. I may go up and see Ben [Keeling]. Give my love to [Raglan] Somerset. I thought he was in the Bosphorus. Alfred tells me you, Dent, he, and 'Ted Haynes' all went a walk together. Did you all have 'strong instincts of personal affection'?

If you are really careering through England in the second and third weeks in April I might join you for a day or two. I imagine I shall shoulder a pack and tramp about Rural England to note the conditions. I might defy Rural Tyranny and get a medal from the Gladstone League. Who knows?   RUPERT

Or come to Holland and Belgium. It is possible to do so for 10s. each way—£1 in all.

[1] An incident in E. M. Forster's *Where Angels Fear to Tread*.

To DUDLEY WARD   *Rugby*
                                   (*24 Bilton Road for the future*)
                                          [*27 March 1910*]

Easter! the season when One had rebirth
Whom some call Ishtar, some call Mother Earth,
And others Jesus, or Osiris. Now
A certain subtle magic on the bough
And a bright strangeness in the wind (a sort
Not known in Germany or here) has brought,
These hundred centuries past, the bloody rotters
Who lusted, raped, and (knowing not) begot us
—In fact, our Fathers, from remotest times—
To sing in company, make foolish rhymes,
Lust more than ever, dance, drink wine, eat bread,
To greet the jolly spring. And They are Dead.
(And lately—since the Greeks—they've spoilt the feast
With morbid superstitions from the East.
E'en now small boys at chapel down the road
Munch little morsels of a Jewish God.)
Easter, you bloody man! And a full moon!
And so I think of you; and write.

                                   Oh, soon
The little white flowers whose names I never knew
Will wake at Cranborne. They've forgotten you.
Robin, who ran the hedge a year ago,
Runs still, by Shaston. Does he remember? No.
This year the ways of Fordingbridge won't see
So meaty and so swift a poet as me
Mouthing undying lines. Down Lyndhurst way
The woods will rub along without us.

                                   Say,
Do you remember the motors on the down?
The stream we washed our feet in? Cranborne Town
By night? and the two inns? the men we met?
The jolly things we said? the food we ate?
The last high toast in shandy-gaff we drank,
And—certain people, under the trees, at Bank?

By God! no pilgrim ever trudged to Rome,
Nor Christ's Crusaders ever hied them home,

Nor Paris stole to his adulterous joy,
Nor buggering Bishop went to taste his boy,
Nor Pagan martyr to the Christian pyre,
Nor Antony to clip the World's Desire,
Nor did grey Dante to his Bice come,
Nor God to Mary at Capernaum,
So rathe, so riotous, so richly-tended,
So scarlet, and so scornful, and so splendid!
By God! our singing, laughing, leaping, running!
You weren't half bad. And I was simply stunning.
By God! But that was Eastertide last year.
And you're in Germany and I am here.

As for your letter, what can I say to shake you?
Windle-straw! Weather-cock! The devil take you!
The foul pox seize upon you! The French disease
Writhe your slight guts and twist your beastly knees,
Turn all to mud your marrow, rot your toes,
Gum up your ears and eyes, lay flat your nose,
Freeze all your urine and foment your gall,
Burn in your bowels, blister each bloody ball!
Your hair fall out, your teeth run pus, your tongue
Rot at the roots, each separate ★ ★ lung
Suppurate with the scab Neapolitan!
Brute! bald-pate! beastly b...! bloody man!
You will not come with me to Rotterdam.
You've lost a life-time's chance.
                      What's more, *I* am
Planless for April, damn you! I may be
With Lucas, or alone; on land, or sea;
Hampstead with James? Dartmoor with Hugh? with Ben
In Leeds? Perhaps in Paris once again?
Reading—on roads—in motors—under sails—
Home—Hell—or Holland...
                     (anyhow, not Wales...)

For now—the days ebb to a close: and I
Shall soon be no more pedagogue. I fly
On Wednesday hence to London—*Justice!*...
                           yet

I meet my freedom quietly. I get
A certain pleasure from the fifty dam
Young fresh-faced mindless scamps to whom I am
Father, and mother, and all their maiden aunts.
I feed their minds. I satisfy their wants.
I train them, cane them, lie to them (for truth
Is not revealed to impressionable youth).
They are upper-class. They do not know the Light.
They stink. They are no good. And yet. . .in spite
Of the thousand devils that freeze their narrowing views
(Christ, and gentility, and self-abuse)
They are young, direct, and animal. In their eyes
Spite of the dirt, stodge, wrappings, flits and flies
A certain dim nobility. They are MAN,
Still, for a year or two. . .And so they can
—In mind *and* body—not unawkwardly move,
At times. . .in the sun. . .in April. . .

                         So I love
(Partly because to live it, once, I found
All glory, and. . .there are. . .spots of holy ground
—Oh, mildly holy!—about the place!) each line
Of the fine limbs and faces; love, in fine,
(O unisexualist!) with half a heart,
Some fifty boys, together, and apart,
Half-serious and half-sentimentally. . .
—But, by the 6th, all this thing ends for me. . .

And there, too, ends this fragment. My ink & my inspiration run
dry together. Yesterday I went over to Birmingham to see my
dentist. It coincided—I had inquired from her—with the day Noel
passed through Birmingham, for. . .Bethesda. She was due there
at 1.45. So my dentist required me at 1. So I had to take a train that
reached B'ham 12.11. The family quite saw it. Just before I set out,
I got a card from N. to say that she might get to B'ham at 12.10; or,
missing that, at 1.45. I leapt out of the 12.11 directly it touched
B'ham: & saw the extraordinarily inexpressive behind of the 12.10
sliding westward out of the station. Nobody seemed to know if she
had been in it—or, really, to care. I felt if she *had*, she'd have had her
head out of the window. So I waited cheerily for the 1.45. I searched
every carriage in that train. She was not there.

Nothing else *very* funny has happened lately.   R.

To GEOFFREY KEYNES   [*Printed address:*
School Field, Rugby]
Friday 10 April
[*8 April 1910*]
Nevermore
Cove Cottage, West Lulworth
Dorset

Here (ecce iterum!) I roam the cliffs & try to forget my bleeding soul. Tonight some Stracheys join me—James for his journalist's week-end, Lytton for a week or so. After that, i.e. next Saturday or Sunday, (or rather, Sat. or Sun. the 16th or 17th) Jacques & Godwin Baynes *may* be joining me, or I them, somewhere for a day or two's

walk. So if you're wandering then you could join $\left\{ \begin{array}{l} \text{them} \\ \text{me} \\ \text{us} \end{array} \right\}$ —or drop

in here on Friday or Saturday. For we've here a thousand spare rooms.

The Editor of the Nation was so astounded by them [the poems] that he has preserved an awe-struck silence ever since. Of course it's a compliment in its way. But I sometimes wish they'd not been *quite* so good. Then he might have sent me Twenty Pounds quicker.

About wandering—if still your feet itch—you can write to Jacques—if you like. He may be at Ogwen Lake Cottage, Bethesda still—or may not. *I* may refuse to leave this bower after all. And we all *may* meet, *if* we meet, anywhere between here & London, or elsewhere. So it's all Dim.

But oh! what *is* a cretin. You make me feel so queer. I thought it was a Decadent: but is it—as I gather—really, a—oh! a Man-that-is-not-a-Man?...oh!...oh!...

Have you read Mr F. Harris in the [*English Review*] April Number? Paralysis for Dust?[1] I don't admire your taste.   REUP

To EDWARD MARSH   *Cove Cottage, Lulworth Cove*
Dorset
12 April [*1910*]
My dear Eddie,

At length I am escaped from the world's great snare. This is Heaven. —Downs, Hens, Cottages, & the Sun. Did you see the American Colonel's account of Heaven, where he is, in a recent American spiritualist's book (vouched by Prof. James)? I am sorry I have been so vague about my visits. Did you get a postcard?

[1] Both printed in *Poems*, 1911.

I leave here on Saturday, then I walk wildly towards Rugby, which I shall attain (by train) on Monday. On Tuesday, the 19th, I come up to London. Can you put me up for Tuesday & Wednesday nights? And will you be free to see *Trelawny of the Wells*[1] on either evening? But I fear you will have seen it. How dreadfully that theatre seems to be failing. Is there any other admirable play on in London? I suppose the Follies still continue. As there are no papers in this place, I know nothing. Perhaps the Government has resigned. Lulworth goes on its way, & catches its lobsters, undisturbed.

All the morning I souse myself in Elizabethan plays: & every afternoon I walk up perpendicular places alone, for hours. Lytton Strachey is here at present: James has been here over the week-end. I rushed through London on the way here & saw *Justice*; which shattered & refreshed me. Behind me were two men who had come in under the impression it was *Trelawny of the Wells*, & did not discover their mistake for some time. I gather that nothing has been published lately of 'lasting literary merit' except O. B.'s reminiscences & Mr Frank Harris' story in the English Review. In my few hours in London I slipped into the International & saw about a quarter of it, & explained the Principles of Modern Art to poor Professor Bateson,[2] whom I found there. But I shall have to return and complete the survey.

For the rest of Eternity my stabile address is 24 Bilton Road, Rugby. School Field, that palatial building, will know us no more. And henceforth I shall have to play on other people's Tennis lawns. I wept copiously last week in saying good-bye to the three & fifty little boys whose Faith & Morals I had upheld for ten weeks. I found I had fallen in love with them all. So pleasant & fresh-minded as they were. And it filled me with purpureal gloom to know that their plastic souls would harden into the required shapes, & they would go to swell the indistinguishable masses who fill Trinity Hall, Clare, Caius...& at last become members of the English Upper, or Upper Middle, Classes. I am glad I am not going to be a schoolmaster for ever. The Tragedy would be too great.

There are no good plays between 1500 & 1650, except The Faithful Shepherdess.[3] And, perhaps, Antony & Cleopatra.

Ever

RUPERT

Let me know if these days are too impossible.

[1] By Arthur Wing Pinero.
[2] William Bateson, F.R.S., Professor of Genetics at Cambridge.
[3] By John Fletcher.

To MRS BROOKE

National Liberal Club
Whitehall Place, S.W.
Friday, 3 p.m. [April 1910]

Dear Mother,

This place is crammed with smoke and fat people, chattering. I'm in Chelsea, now. I asked E. M. about Alfred. He didn't know much personally. But he promised to talk to the head of the—isn't it called the Whip's Office?—Jesse Herbert: and get him to see Alfred some time, and advise him what to do. It won't be, probably, for some time yet: for J. H. is very busy. But I said any time before the middle of June would do. For it would be worth while Alfred coming up for an afternoon from Cambridge for it: and it pays to be accommodating. I think that is all right. For they'll give Alfred special attention with Eddie Marsh's influence: and it appears to be the central place from which all political activity starts out. Then they'd put whatever various courses there are before Alfred to consider for the next two years, and give him advice, and his name would be on their books.

Did you notice an 'Urgent' letter you sent on to me? It was from the *Nation* about one of two or three poems I sent them. They wanted me to change two or three phrases, which they thought, generally, 'too strong'. I was very angry; and went round to see the miscreant—it was signed 'for the Editor'—and then some initials. It turned out to be Nevinson, who is editing the paper for a fortnight while Massingham's away. He said he liked the poems very much. I convinced him about one or two of the suggested alterations; but there were still two or three more he said the public wouldn't stand—though, he added, if he were sole Editor himself, he'd print them, because he liked them. It's all nonsense. But I said I'd try to think of some alternatives. He said he expected that several of the poems I sent in would come out in the Nation at intervals.[1] So I'll keep my eye on it and let you know. It's not worth while taking it in: because the intervals may be of a month or two. Nevinson asked me if I was a don!

The 'Urgency' was because he wanted to get it in this week. But as it had to come King's—Rugby—Gray's Inn, it was too late.

I can stand these Jews and their liqueurs and whiskies no more.

With love

RUPERT

---

[1] One poem, 'The Goddess in the Wood', was printed on 24 September.

To KATHARINE COX [Postcard]
The Orchard
Friday–Saturday
[*Postmark: 30 April 1910*]

Geoffrey and Gwen are coming.[1] Geoffrey is to bring Margaret K[eynes] and Cosmo [Gordon]. Gwen is to bring Margaret D[arwin] and perhaps Jacques. Will you bring Dorothy Lamb? Justin is inaccessible. Francis and Frances *may* appear. Geoffrey and Gwen were incredibly fresh—7.30 'for 7.45', and breakfast under the blossom in the Orchard! Oh! oh! But I gave in; after breakfast, which will be 'going' for some time, the programme gets vague. But you'll be able to get into Cambridge for lunch. R.

To EDWARD MARSH The Orchard
Monday [*9 May 1910*]

My dear Eddie,

It was very kind of you to offer to take me away. I have spent a day or two in trying to work it in, but I'm afraid there isn't a ghost of a chance. I'm so extraordinarily inextricable and necessary! You think this conceit: but it's not. Various bodies and societies have arranged things in which I am continuously & hopelessly involved. Also my labours & the University Library press most insistently upon me. I wish I could have come. It would have been lovely. Grantchester's lovely, though, too. When are you coming? The apple blossom & the river & the sunsets have combined to make me relapse into a more than Wordsworthian communion with nature, which prevents me from reading more than 100 lines in a day, or thinking at all.

When I mentioned to my mother that you were going to mention Alfred's name to—is it Jesse Herbert?—she became highly excited, and said that he, J. H., owed us a vast debt of gratitude. A few years ago he sneaked down to Rugby on the secret errand of finding out why the Liberal majority there was so small. We fed & sheltered him, gave him infinite information & lent him a false beard. He certainly should appoint Alfred Chief Police Spy.

Ever
R.

[1] For a May Day celebration at Grantchester.

To HUGH DALTON   *The Orchard*
                                              Tuesday [*early 1910*]

My dear Hugh,

   Does your PaPa still pay for your food? Mr Allen and I have
each given distinguished visitors food this term. He is not rich: and
I am very poor. So it would be a very good thing if you would give
a dinner in King's on Thursday. At 7.15. Let me know if you will
by return. If you don't, I suppose I must. Where? Gerald's? or
could we just bag Meredith's rooms?

                      Present

          Three Oxonians
          Me
          You
          Cornford
          Secretary
            and
          x Londoners probably 2.

   I dropped in on Mr Allen today, and into—oh! what a fuss! It
may be rather serious. I am very angry: even, a little, with him.
Though one can't *show* it to the poor little man, in *his* state.... Well
it was the night before last?, at a meeting of the Peterhouse discussion society, which they ever so innocently call 'The Sex Society'.
Mr Allen, 'in private conversation', remarked to his neighbour he
was glad the late King had died now, because George V was a weaker
man, and the monarchy would thus gradually lose some of its power.
Before fainting, the neighbour spread the remark. An uproar grew.
I imagine howls and confusion and the red and white miscreant
refusing to deny. I gather that the meeting broke up. Waves seethed
around Mr Allen's room all night. Next day or so a meeting of 'The
Sex' was held, to hurl him out. He defended himself in a speech
which he, and another Peterhouse man I interrogated, call 'the
speech of his life'. He was (I read his notes) apparently quite discreet about Teddy VII; basing his defence on the 'private conversation' point of view. He made personal attacks on his assailants, which
enraged them. This morning they, with big sticks—they are leading
rowing-men—pulled him out of bed and would beat him.... He
said he had curved spine and might be eternally injured. So they
were frightened and went away. If you can, see him. If anything
more happens, we'll turn on the University and get them sent down.
   Damn you for being out.

To DAVID GARNETT   *The Orchard*
                                  Grantchester, Cambridge
                                  Tuesday, 10 May [*1910*]

My dear David Garnett,

I live here. It is a village two miles from Cambridge. I hear you
are in the neighbourhood—at Letchworth; employed, they tell me,
in Revolutionary Farming. I was told this by Noel Olivier; and the
correspondence columns of my daily paper seemed to confirm her.
I am here till the last days of June. There is a river beyond my
garden; one bathes in it. The whole place is very lovely, with apple-
blossom now, later with roses. Will you come and stay here? I can
promise you bathing and all manner of rustic delight, cheeses, and
fruit, and expeditions into Cambridge to see the people and buildings
there. Certain of both are worth seeing. Suggest any time or times
in the next seven weeks, and we'll see what can be done in the way of
arranging. In fact, whenever you get bored with Letchworth, pack
up your tent (I figure you always bearing a tent with you) and come
and encamp in some field near me & by the river. I do not mean that
a mere room is not ready if you prefer it.

A week-end or week-middle: I cannot distinguish between them.

And sometime we might arrange a party in a tent here (in June)—
Dudley Ward may be back from Germany by then: Godwin might
be lured from his woman: Jacques might come. Perhaps you
don't know Jacques? Is it conceivable anyone does not know
Jacques?...Anyhow answer anything in this letter that you can
grasp.   RUPERT BROOKE

To DUDLEY WARD   [*Grantchester*]
                                          [? *May 1910*]

Dudley,

The room's all right, *but*...

I return at 11 or so. There's no bed for you. Do what you like.
But keep FRIGHTFULLY quiet at *The Orchard*: I've had dreadful
scenes with the Stevensons. The village 'talked' because of bare
feet. So they[1] MUST keep their boots on! Otherwise they mayn't
stay! This is true.   More when we meet,
                                          RUPERT

[1] Annemarie von der Planitz and Clothilde von Derp.

To MRS BROOKE   [*Grantchester*]
                                        Monday [*May 1910*]

Dear Mother,

It is very hot and splendid here today. James Strachey has been here over the week-end, and he and I have been out to bathe. At least, he paddled. When, as today, it is a really hot day, I throw Laddie in. Did I ever tell you how, when I was bathing alone, he jumped in after me one day, being carried away by excitement at seeing me dive. It was the first time he had been in the water: and he found he didn't like it a bit. He sleeps at the foot of my bed nowadays: because he used to howl rather in the shed. He is quite clean (so far). I think it probably keeps him so.

I have seen Tilley, who is the chief person in King's on the Medieval and Modern Language Trip., and also talked to W. H. Macaulay. Apparently my last chance for sending in a dissertation would be in the December of 1912. They think *two* shots is much the best thing. So that probably I had better send in something in 1911. All this gives me a year more than I thought, which is excellent. Tilley said he always read my reviews in the Cambridge Review very carefully and thought they were good, and that I had a very good chance. He advised some subject that would give me an opportunity for 'research' *and* critical writing. He said, as he wasn't an expert, he couldn't advise me what subject to take up: but that I'd better apply to G. C. Macaulay, and then, if necessary, to Walter Raleigh (of Oxford). Which I shall do. He also said I'd better get to know enough German to be able to read and quote the books in that language.   *   *   *

                                              Tuesday
                      *   *   *

Many thanks for your offer of £10 for my holidays. Only, as they won't be any different from my term, in the way of expense, I don't think I ought to have it. In fact in a caravan I live on about £1 a week, all told, and that's a good deal cheaper than my life here. When I said I thought I wanted £150 a year (and this year I'm getting more) to live on I meant all the year round. I don't have 'terms' and 'holidays' really: as if I were still in Cambridge. I live along comfortably on my income, as I have frugal tastes; and, as a matter of fact, I shall save in July, and August or September, and October, by being at home part of the time. So I think that— especially *this* year, when your finances aren't clear yet—you'd better hold up the £10, and, if the annual income's discovered to be all right at the end of the year, I might have some of it to help me to get to Germany.

*   *   *

The Post!
With love
RUPERT

To KATHARINE COX   [Postcard]
[*Postmark:
Cambridge, 8 June 1910*]

I have spent two hours of my (at present) very precious time in writing to Allen. I have seen Francis Cornford. The Licensing Syndicate won't license probably. Even if they do, F. is keen, and so am I, on getting *only* C.U.F.S. *rooms*. Not a House: nor a meeting-room. I think the meeting room in Ram Yard will be stuffy, and unpleasant of access. What *do* Newnham think?—the Authorities I mean. I thought from F's manner some of you, or Jane [Harrison], had been at him. These old people are so transparent. If Newnham *do* object to going to all meetings through a stable tell Allen: in time to deflect his enthusiasm to 'only rooms'.

Don't we see you Friday morning? But before! I'm in that damned U[niversity] L[ibrary] all Thurs. (and Wed.) writing with one hand and eating bread and butter with the other. But Thursday *after* 4 p.m. Even Jacques'll be here about then, mebbe. I'm sick of Puritans and Responsibility.[1]   RUPERT

To MRS BROOKE   *The Orchard*
Saturday [*June 18 1910*]

Dear Mother,

I am sorry I have not written for so long. I meant to write to you from camp, but somehow it never got fitted in. I went into camp (a tent 6 feet each way) with Geoffrey on Monday. He had been there two or three days previously. We had a very good time, with no rain at all. I slept out, and Geoffrey slept inside the tent. We got extraordinarily red and brown. My nose is peeling, whilst Geoffrey's arms and ankles went quite raw the last few days. We bathed a good

---

[1] His essay for the Harness prize on 'Puritanism in the English Drama up to 1642'.

deal. I became quite expert at cooking; especially fried eggs. When I'm at Rugby I want to get Hilda to tell me one or two things. We had one or two visitors in camp—the Batesons among others. But it was too far for many people to come. Overcourt (or, more correctly, Over*cote*) is a lovely place, with nothing but an old inn, and a ferry. There are villages round a mile or two away, but hidden. And there's just the Ouse, a slow stream, and some trees and fields and an immense expanse of sky. There were a lot of wild birds about —wild duck, and snipe, and herons. I sat and wrote my beastly essay most of the day. We rose about 6.30 on Friday yesterday, made breakfast, washed up, packed everything up, and rode off. I had an immense *rück-sack* filled with books on my back, but I did the 13 miles to Grantchester in just over an hour, and worked the rest of the day in the University Library. I have been working and writing the whole of today, and shall do so, *collecting* the references etc., tomorrow and half Monday. Then I am going off to write the stuff out and piece it together on a wherry a man called Rogers (a doctor) has got on the Broads for three or four days. No fixed address: though I may send one address back here when I get there. Then I shall return, and finish off here, bully the typewriters, and send it in on the 30th. I shall sleep all the 1st, go to London on the 2nd for a Fabian Annual meeting, which ends 6 p.m., and catch a 7 p.m. train for Rugby, probably. (This exact and business-like arranging of things is quite a new thing.)

* * *

I have ordered another copy of that photograph from Mottram. I shall bring it when I come, if I can get it out of him.

With love
RUPERT

To REGINALD POLE   *The Orchard, Grantchester*
                        Monday [20 June 1910]

I saw Dent and the Cornfords on Friday, the people 'in charge' of Faustus.[1] We discussed performers, etc. The original idea that as many old performers should take their old parts as possible, I persuaded them to modify. We want to get all the parts acted in one

[1] A second production of *Faustus* by the Marlowe Society was arranged for the Long Vacation during the visit of some German students.

method, and together. I am going to be Chorus, if necessary, &
supply expert knowledge about what the play means. (It mustn't be
sentimentalized.) Will you take Mephistophilis? The performance
will be about the 18th I think. It is a good thing to keep up an idea
of 'Long' plays. Till next year. I hope you'll be able to take Mephistophilis. You'll be able to do all the things I tried to and couldn't.

RUPERT

To CHARLES SAYLE   *24 Bilton Road, Rugby*
                                       3 July [*1910*]
Dear Sayle,

   I didn't get my essay complete: but I sent it in in an incomplete
state which may suffice. I expect not, though. I got bored with the
subject; and I can never do decently when I get bored. However,
it's off my hands. And now I'm going to write perfect things of my
own instead of platitudes about other people's second-rate efforts.

   I wonder, by the way, if you were in London on Friday night, as
I was. I went to *Così Fan Tutte*. All the world was there, including,
just behind me, O. B.

   They've discovered a new painter in the 'Fair Wanton', Grafton
Galleries, called Ricard. French 18th–19th century. Do you know
him?

RUPERT

To DUDLEY WARD   *24 Bilton Road, Rugby*
                                       [*Postmark: 3 July 1910*]

   Let's send all our things to some station
   next beyond Winchester, some quiet place:
   and land up there.

   In the intervals of a most pleasant Fabian Conference I strolled
into the

N
C
P
D
B
U
P
L

Offices. A perky man called Gaunt was there: but I subdued him. He pretended Lloyd was either just writing or had just written to you. I don't fancy they'll really organize us much ahead. They were very dim, and said, couldn't *we* find an advance agent. *No*, said I. But I promised we'd take their poster round. It is much too 'artistic', by the way. I have a thought of getting Gwen Darwin to chalk us off a telling one. Gaunt, and Schlosser, advocated *open*-air meetings very much: and proposed that even if we didn't speak in any village we sailed into, we should display the poster, look wise, and scatter pamphlets. They had *no* special rural information; though they had tried to get some. They *may* have some by the time we start.

Anyway, Lloyd's writing to you: and sending you the *new* Lecture Notes, which they've got out for I.L.P. lectures.

I've written to Bunny [Garnett].

I got to the station the time the train went: leapt off my bicycle and gave it to a porter: and plunged through the window. God knows what happened to the bicycle.

In London I dashed for papers, and ran into Hugh Popham at a junction on the way. So we went together. I explained social Phenomena to him. Lucas and I went to Mozart. The world was there, including Pinsent, Ted Haynes, Evelyn, and Oscar Browning. The latter tried to kiss me. My hat was again a great success in London. But my mother was rather bitter about it this morning. She won't let me go out in Rugby today: and tomorrow I have to buy a straw, first thing.

I have written to Wilson.

I wear shoes, and we have no garden. But the Time approaches!

RUPERT

I hope my bag of poems hasn't too much gone to your head. And that you realize the most recent ones aren't there.

To JACQUES RAVERAT   *24 Bilton Road*
                                                      Monday [*July 1910*]
My dear Jacques,

Will this reach you before you go to Sardinia? In God's name, answer immediately, if it does.

Dudley and I are going to—or want to—go to Petersfield before we start off in our cart: in, that is, about ten days from now. It is enormously unfortunate that you'll not be there. For I, of course,

daren't face Bedales without you. But all, almost, we want to do is
to see the gorgeous Noel and talk with the tired [Edward] Thomas.
Thomas himself has a wife and babes, so we should not bother him
as a host, I suppose. But what of [Geoffrey] Lupton?[1] You know the
world, and him, and us. Would it be possible for me to suggest that
he gave us a bed (or, an outhouse) and, if necessary, had Noel to tea.
(For I understand that there are difficulties in getting hold of her,
nowadays.) Or is he too quiet-loving, and does he hate us quick-
tongued urbane people whom you have brought there, too much?
Tell me these things. For if all would be possible, I should like
Dudley to see Life on a Hill, as well as Thomas. Is, if all's well,
Lupton's address just Froxfield, Petersfield?

Justin! Hooray!

> Is it true that our Justin's appeared?
> Has he come, as we all of us feared,
>   Not the Justin we knew,
>   But Western, but new,
> With an Accent, a Soul, and a BEARD?

Will he be in Petersfield then? or when shall we see him? When
are Dudley and he to meet?   R.

To DUDLEY WARD   [*Rugby*]
                                            Wednesday [*July 1910*]
                        *   *   *

My dear,

I begin this in a Lawyer's Office. My mother started to explain
some of her finance to me last night; and I was (of course) so extraordinarily clear-headed that I found two errors and an omission and
cleared up the whole tangle of my father's affairs. So this morning
she has entrusted me with the task of explaining to the Lawyer.
Ultimately we have to pay the government £30 more. I was adamant
about it.

My letter, which crossed yours, explained some things. The Wilsons rather insist on the 28th. So I have suggested they find us on
the afternoon of the 28th: we all feast and sleep round the caravan
that night, and they drive off on the 29th leaving us at the nearest
railway station. That will at any rate get rid of the horse and cart.

I have written to Noel, and to Jacques, about Lupton. If Jacques

---

[1] Formerly at Bedales with Raverat and Justin Brooke; in 1910 making oak
furniture at Froxfield.

doesn't answer, I must pluck up courage and write to Lupton [my] himself. I rather shrink from hanging about Petersfield with no reason and no *pied-à-terre*. It's *too*...and also Noel wouldn't be allowed to see us. We'll go and *talk* to Thomas (who, Bunny says, will be *there*) but, having met him once, I daren't ask him to put a lot of us up.

'I put it to you' (as Dickinson says) that we meet, in town perhaps, on *Thursday*: and leave Winchester on Saturday, staying Thursday and Friday nights with Lupton.... Or would that be too long?

If we *can't* get put up we might get the Caravan on *Thursday*, gallop to Petersfield, and return after an interview. (If I don't hear from Jacques by tomorrow morning, I shall write straight to Lupton. I *must* see Noel.)

In the package at the Orchard are many things;

> Primus stove
> 6 plates
> knives forks & spoons
> a large kettle
> 4 cups
> I think { a frying pan
> { a saucepan
> Cocoa and salt and one or
> two other foods

and one or two more things. I forget what.

* * *

I want to get Justin to join us for a week-end in the Van.

RUPERT

I hope you got yr MS.: and talked about my razors. Horse £1 a week *maximum* Cart 5*s*.

Horse very quiet.

To DUDLEY WARD *24 B.R., Rugby* *Friday* [*July 1910*]

Hurrah for Mrs Bestwish of Corfe. Will it be an assembly of matrons in a drawing-room? My extensive obstetric knowledge (derived from the Elizabethan drama) will tell. And I've prepared an amazing peroration on Puerperal Fever. *That*'ll fetch 'em.

I'll take your points in order (both letter and card have come).

(1) I think you'd better write postcards about the price of the horse. If we leave it till 16th Wilson *may* hold out for more. And he'd have us. I guess we shan't get it for *less*. I enclose a card J. S. Wilson forwarded. However: that's all right, now, according to you.

(2) Extract an answer from Lloyd. I'm damned if I can: and I'm trying to get notes etc. *here*, to prepare with. He *may* be away. If we can't get a Majority Report, I can borrow James Strachey's.

(3) Corfe: v. above.

(4) I'm writing about Chard. Are you corresponding with L. R. D. Anderson?[1]

(5) *I* believe we could start from Winchester in time to get to Stockbridge: certainly if we leave (ah...h...h!) Petersfield on *Friday*. But anyhow, have you given serious and sufficient consideration to other places (e.g. Shanford—Twyford)?

(6) But I'm rather in favour of getting to Petersfield *latish* on Thursday, and staying till Sat. Still, I'll be able to take any London train on Thurs. that you like. Though I doubt if I, otherwise, spend Wednesday in London.

(7) I've written to Lupton: yesterday. But, you know, he's one of these splendid, dour, natural, stupid men; who hates my dialectical skill and conversational wit, and would not scruple brutally to say so, or kick me in the stomach with his hobnailed boots. Still, I've written him in a winning letter.

(8) Yes.

(9) I don't know what it is, but somehow I feel I don't particularly care about the camp that first week. You talk about 'a short time': but one'll have had quite enough of it by the 11th. Think how long 36 hours were last year. We must be near some station with the caravan on the evening of the 28th, to meet the Wilsons. Therefore, if you like, we'll settle in—on the 29th. What you will.

(10) I'll leisurely consider the List.

I can reach Euston about 9.50 on Thursday morning. We might see a picture, and go away. I don't know what you mean by saying my career's 'simple': damn you.

Your flirtations with Tariff Reform fill me with suspicion. And why do you pretend we're going to leave *Kultur und die Kulturwelt* for a month? *I*'m not.

I'll send a list of Books.   RUPERT

[1] Formerly at School Field, Rugby.

To HUGH DALTON   *24 Bilton Road, Rugby*
                                            5 July 1910

Where are you? I sit here and prepare stirring harangues for the People of South England on Poor Law. I go there at the end of next week. On Saturday Messrs Allen Pinsent Paget and self attended the Fabian Conference. It was great fun. Dear Ensor in the chair. The Northern delegates were superb men. They lashed the women with unconquerable logic and gross words. There were most frightful scenes, and the women gibbered with rage. Mabel was almost beyond herself with purple-faced hatred. They were quieted by Sidney [Webb], with an evasive speech. But they *were* devils, ruining 'The Cause' for all they were worth—against Socialism. The Executive were, I gathered, better than last year: though they still shirked the populace a bit. Old Shaw popped up and down; and a man from Manchester and I conspired democratically in a corner. But vainly.

What I want is *Local Government* (isn't it?): anyhow one of the Webbs' books. Can you let me have it? Or are you beyond? Young men in London kept coming up and telling me that Winston or Lord Wolverhampton were goin' to write a preface to your novel about your parents. I affirmed the report. A postcard from you to my brother was hurled in here the other day. I just rescued it before my mother got hold of it. I shall send it to him sometime. Don't know where he is. I have not seen him since May.

You might let me know sometime *when* it is you are coming to Llanbedr: and I'll try to fit the dates.

I suppose you talk in nominatives absolute now: God help you!

                                            RUPERT

Oh, yes. What I *do* want is the latest Thorpe manifesto. Can you let me have it? I hear you're the repository....

To DUDLEY WARD   *24 Bilton Road*
                                            Sunday [*July 1910*]

Lupton's answered, and will be alone and can manage us. So all is well.

My books will be, perhaps—

                    Marlowe (Mermaid)
                    Congreve („)
        (Probably) Ford III Volumes.

	Keats 1 vol.
little	Spenser ,,
books	Donne ,,
	Swinburne Atalanta
	,, Poems & Ballads I
	Thomas' Pocket Song Book

	Ascending Effort	Bourne
Review	Art & Life	Sturge Moore
	Study of Drama	Matthews
	Prose Remains	Miss Coleridge

perhaps Shakesperian Stage. Allbright

> Bergson *L'Evolution Créatrice*
> History of English Prosody Vol. III Saintsbury
> Have you Webb's Local Government?

We want, besides, *special Local information* about the counties we pass through—about Poor Law, etc. Where can we get it?

RUPERT

To FRANCES CORNFORD *24 Bilton Road, Rugby*
Tuesday [*7 July 1910*]

My dear Frances,

I *was* away. I left Cambridge on Friday, went to *Così Fan Tutte*; spent Saturday at a Fabian Conference, and finished the day by arriving 'home'. (Do you know, it's the first time I have ever lived at a number. I've always been at a house with a name, before. The difference is extraordinary.) I'm sorry I couldn't come to supper.

I am slowly recovering from Work. Henceforth I am going to lead what Dudley Ward calls 'a Life Dedicated to Art'. Hurray!

Oh, how good about Justin. I am thirsty to see him. Do you know his address? I want to write to him. I'm glad he'll be able to manage Faustus. I heard yesterday from Her Grace [Reginald Pole]. The only definite bit of news, almost, was that he was tackling his uncle about the dresses. He accepted, grudgingly, what he calls 'Mephisto'. 'Though I must say I am not at *all* the sort of person *I* should have chosen for the part if *I* had had the choice, out of all those available. *Cornford*, I think, is the *ideal* person for it; it *just* suits...', etc. etc. all underlined and girlish. Faustus he thought should be taken by Birch or himself. There followed a long refutation of the idea (which I suppose I hinted at) of his acting of Faustus being sentimental. . . .

I'm replying to him. I suppose, that in spite of his unsuitability to the part we're glad he has accepted Meph. In fact, I've begun a letter which starts 'Your frankness does you great credit. . .'. Of course, as I'm only to be up for a few days, I'm not saying anything definite: I see you & Francis & Dent & Justin being at the head of it all. But as I, in the name of everybody, offered him the part: I suppose he has got it now.

I hope the whole thing—the casting, I mean—has been laid before Justin: especially as he has to control it. If he has some especial view on the various parts, it is valuable in itself, & especially decisive if he's to manage them.

I hadn't heard much of the Lakes. It seems to have been splendid. I'm glad you found out about Jacques. He's an amazing person. I sat working all day and most of the night at the Orchard, envying you rather.

I'm studying Faustus (among other things) and I shall send along a thought or two about scenery sometime. I wonder if you'll agree that, as we have to have the whole stage put up for us, we might as well take pains to try to make it as *tall* as possible.
If you think of Gordon Craig's things you'll see what I mean.

I daresay much can't be done in either direction. But it's worth thinking of, as a principle. Ever

RUPERT

Did I say—I meant to—the later the play is put the better, from my & some points of view.

To REGINALD POLE   *24 Bilton Road, Rugby*
                                       8 July 1910

I didn't answer at all when I got your letter, two or three days ago, did I? I am rather busy preparing my lectures on Poor Law. I don't start off for another week yet. I've told the Cornfords & Dent & Justin you'll be able to take the part. I'm very glad. I quite see what you mean about Cornford, though I think you underrate his possibilities rather. In any case, if he were quite what you say, he'd scarcely be 'just the man for Mephistophilis'. I don't think Mrs Cornford is in any way obdurate about it. In fact she was rather especially anxious not to decide, but to leave the allotting of any parts

affecting Cornford, as much as possible in other people's hands. Did I tell you Justin had returned from remote parts, and was going to take over the management? As that is so, of course he will have the final decision about making—or attempting to make—any alteration in parts. Perhaps he will deprive me even further, of my last foothold, as Chorus. . . . Who knows what the future may hold? I haven't heard from him at all. I suppose he's in London. If you see him you might explain your view of Cornford. But I expect things are fairly well settled by now: & we must abide by what the people who have the time, money, & opportunity to get these things up, want. Do you know Bridges-Adams of Oxford, who staged *Fidelio*? He's a very competent creature, who's coming across to take a small part. I expect you'll hear from Justin, or Dent, or somebody, about dates. I don't know them; & I'm off into the wilds. Many thanks for your Uncle's address. I *expect* we shall pass through there. Your—is he cousin?—& his mother were in the other day. *She* & I argued about your Career and your Health. I was very solemn, & said the Stage was a Noble (and Healthy and Lucrative) calling: & that you were always much better in health when on the stage. She was immensely impressed—for she regards me with veneration as a successful schoolmaster—especially with that part of my harangue which began
'The Drama, my dear Mrs Sharp, is in a Period of Transition . . .'.

RUPERT

All the same, I wonder how you take it that [that] mad fellow Marlowe meant Mephistophilis. I never felt very sure. We have wandered so far out of sight in three centuries—Perhaps we'd on the whole disagree, as about Richard [II]'s Character.   R.

To FRANCES CORNFORD   *24 Bilton Road, Rugby*
8 July 1910

Cheer up! (I bubble with heartiness)—though I expect my exhortation's unnecessary by now, if you've got the American Justin with you or have heard from him. He'll manage it all right, & fire the Duchess with altruistic & lofty enthusiasm. And anyhow her Grace's high breeding will come to the rescue. You needn't fear a 'grudging' Meph. Nor need you think we all 'dislike acting with him'. I'm the only person who has done it before: & I assure you it's no different from acting with other people. The people one acts with are all always wrong and all pleasant. As for your questions.

(A) I think Pole's fairly well engaged for it: unless Justin takes it on him to do anything in the way of alteration. (Tell Justin that if Pole's deposed, I've discovered an edition of Faustus, in which there's an addition to the 6th scene. It is by another hand, probably *Dekker's*. It contains an extra part, which might suit the Duchess, an Eighth Deadly Sin, called 'The Artistic Temperament'.) (B) If Pole died, & Scholfield couldn't be procured, I *could* come up earlier, out of the wilderness, quite easily. So that—if that's safety! —all's safe.

I wish I knew what you thought in the middle of the night about Menelaus & Helen.[1] It is probably very important, and would entirely alter the whole of all the poems I am just about to write.

I gather you'll be in your new house in August. Will it be a centre of Food, for dramatic workers at odd moments? You had better rail off some square yards of a *parterre* for that purpose. By the way, I think rather more than speaking is wanted for Mephistophilis—acting of a rather unvehement & unordinary kind, but very certain. There were a lot of things I wanted to do, and couldn't, last time.

Oh, this afternoon I invented and performed, by myself, a superb scene, of Justin, with a goatee beard and a high American accent, coaching Francis in Faustus. 'Wáz thís the faíce...' I was performer & audience. The audience screamed with mirth.

Ever

RUPERT

Tell Francis I'm very nearly certain—from other plays of the time—'Ah Pythagoras metempsychosis...' is scanned 'Ah, Pý-thágóras métempsýchŏsís....'.

To FRANCES CORNFORD   *24 Bilton Road, Rugby*
                              Wednesday [July 1910]

My dear Madam,

It's very good of you all, of course; though I'm sorry for her Grace. I still think it would have been right enough. I hope Justin's succeeding. Because the extra bother of it is that if Justin isn't extraordinarily—as far as I can see *impossibly*—successful, it means that one good actor is out of Cambridge performances—*our* Cambridge performances—for ever. Who's *now* to be Macbeth?...But of course I don't know just what is being said to Pole. But I'm sorry he couldn't have been fitted in—as it seems he won't be.

*   *   *

[1] Printed in *Poems*, 1911.

I'll ponder on Helen & Menelaus: pointing out (for what it's worth) to fill up, that the last line of the first sonnet, has a touch of a giggle behind it, perhaps, in some lights—though that probably makes the offence worse. Thanks for what you said about it. Ponder & pardon all this. I wish I were a quite quite good man, like Mr Shaw or Marcus Aurelius. But video meliore proboque Deteriora sequor.[1]

You don't know what that bit means. But Francis will tell you.

Oh! Oh!

Horribly

RUPERT

To ERICA COTTERILL   *Black Bear Hotel, Wareham*
                              [July 1910]

My dear,

I ought to have answered you sooner. I've been fearfully busy; *first* doing a Prize Essay against time: *second* getting up a speech on the Minority Report. The last week (& the next) I have been going round delivering it at towns & villages in the New Forest & round here. We travel in a caravan & live like savages. As a public orator I am a great success. As a caravaner, less. It rains incessantly. I didn't—you'll have discovered—send those books. I was thinking them over when I discovered you'd returned. But for God's sake let me advise you. You know nothing about it, probably. A pound isn't much, if you include, for instance, Henley or Yeats. But it'll cover a good many of these good little shilling books. Don't omit to send Masefield, Hueffer, Stephen, W. H. Davies, Gould...who are about a shilling each. Abercrombie costs 5s. & A. E. two or three. Francis Thompson, & especially Thomas Hardy, are both very modern, & very good. But if you want a good selection, get N. G. Royde-Smith's 'Poets of Today'. Oh, I forgot John Davidson. I also recommend 'Poems' by Frances Cornford (about 1s.); and '36 Poems' by James Flecker (5s.). Also Arthur Symons, Chesterton & Belloc—but his are very hard to get hold of. Lord Alfred Douglas' sonnets are perfect.

I'm glad you've been among people who live for Art. It must be very good for you. I live for Art myself; especially in the evenings. But why are you not a Fabian? Which kind of non-Fabian are you? the feeble-minded, or the emotional?   RUPERT

[1] i.e. I see the better course and I approve it; I follow the worse.

To MRS BROOKE   *The Old Vicarage*
Grantchester
Wednesday [*17 August 1910*]

Dear Mother,

As horrible people were in my house[1] I have settled in here. We are all rather busy with rehearsals etc. Fifty German students who are 'seeing England', and taking Cambridge this week, will be there—it's for them, in a way, the show[2] is being got up. And there'll be such other people as are still left in Cambridge—among them Rose [Macaulay], whom I met in the street yesterday, and Mr Macaulay. The performance will be rather good, I think. Cornford is Faustus, and does most of it well. All sorts of experts are hovering round the place—Carey, Justin, and Scholfield. Albert Rothenstein is coming down for the performance. Rosalind Murray, Gilbert Murray's daughter, is taking a small part. She has just written a novel which has been praised a lot. It is called '*The Leading Note*'. You might order it from Boots if you are passing. Also Felix Wedgwood's *The Shadow of a Titan*.

*   *   *

I had a letter from Brimley Johnson, an ex-publisher whom I know, who lives here, the other day. He had been asked by Dent, the publisher, to find him 'the best young scholarship of all kinds in Cambridge'. So he wanted to know if I had prepared a volume of critical work of any kind. Of course, I haven't. But I may, I suppose, do some sort of work for him. If it is editing or writing introductions it might fit in very usefully with the rest of my work. But I daresay I may hear further, and more particularly. Meanwhile, Brimley Johnson marked the letter 'Confidential'.

A. Y. Campbell is up in John's writing a dissertation for a fellowship. John's are very keen to give him one. But it is doubtful if he has done enough reading for it. Dudley Ward is up, reading up money-matters, and acting as general call-boy behind the scenes in Faustus. After the performance we are all going in a great brake to have supper at the Cornford's, in our dresses: which will be rather fun.

With love

RUPERT

[1] At The Orchard, Grantchester.   [2] Marlowe's *Faustus*.

To SYBIL PYE

24 Bilton Road, Rugby
Friday
[*Postmark: 27 August 1910*]

Dear Sybil,

How horrible. That means I shall never get my money from Bryn. However...I enclose a cheque for £2. 13s. 0d. I have written it very carefully and left no space for you to insert a figure before the 2, and put a line to prevent you adding in any half-pennies—just as my father told me always to do. I consider it extremely unlikely you will ever get more than about three shillings in the pound on it. For I am without money.

I'm glad the successors at the Old Vicarage are aware of their proper position. But next term—oh! I shan't be able to face the loneliness of Grantchester.

After five weeks in the desert, and ten days theatricals I've returned to civilization and solitude with an astounding appetite for books and thoughts. Since Monday I have read 11 plays, 3 novels, a book on Stocks and Shares and [Moore's] *Principia Ethica* besides all the current magazines and papers. How gorgeous it is to work! Ha!

I'm glad you agree about *remove*.[1] I think it's all right. I once went through the Sonnets very carefully, with all the commentators and a huge note book, giving an hour to each. So now I have the tatters of a hideous and pedantic knowledge of them. I have just convinced another expert *littérateur* about 'remove'—James Strachey, who is writing cheques the other side of the room. But then Noel says he's not an expert.

Oh, I wish I could have from Ethel or you the stained-glass names she suggested to me.   RUPERT

I came back to find that my mother had just been knocked down by a horse, her nose dislocated and her mouth cut up. So I felt life rather additionally queer.

To GEOFFREY KEYNES

24 Bilton Road, Rugby
Sunday, 4 September 1910

Silvern Geoff,

I loathe you for bathing in beautiful Grantchester. I splash occasionally in municipal baths made fetid by the middle-classes.

---

[1] Shakespeare's Sonnets, 116, l. 4: 'Or bends with the remover to remove'.

I'm just back from doing my accursed duty at the Fabian Summer School. It was, really, rather fun. A thousand different people from different parts of life. A lady doctor who'd taken up medical inspection of schools & was alone responsible for 8000 children at Colchester. She is interesting; certainly valuable.

I enclose a cheque for your extortionate demands. Dudley can be found by writing to him at The Economist. I shall see him, maybe, on Wednesday when I go to choose papa's stained-glass window.

I'll be in London for a week or so in the beginning of October. You'll be over your work by then? Perhaps I shall have tea with you?...

Oh, I sit & work. I do love it. But what queer fine times we had in Cambridge a few weeks since! Eh? Don't you think Ethel [Pye] is rather fine?   RUPERT

To KATHARINE COX   *24 Bilton Road, Rugby*
                                        Monday, 5 September 1910

I went to Llanbedr. You ought to go one year, to learn a little about Life, and to teach them a little about—what? Anyhow, it's not so bad as you think. There were, of course, a many people I didn't very much *like* to see: but there were a lot of good people, and more interesting ones, and I was acting on my Conscience in going there, instead of reading peacefully. And acting on one's Conscience is always rather fun. The Webbs, too, are very nice; and even better than they're nice. Apart from all of which, they're fine, and funny. *They*, by the way—or, at least, Beatrice—$\frac{are}{is}$ the source for you to get *the* best information about your dear old career. They're good at that. Oh, there were a lot of people—the overworked lady medical inspector from Colchester responsible for 8000 children: the hearty young public-school business-man from Manchester, a millionaire; James Strachey: the expert on Tolstoy: a London journalist who had entirely educated himself, and now knows all about everything, but is a little inclined to sentimental Anarchism: Hugh Dalton: the American Professor of Sociology from Maurka University, Pa.: the admirable woman who had just left Bedales, had a large sensible head, always sat quite still, and replied clearly and satisfactorily to the exact question one put, knew Noel, and is going to study at the Slade for fresco-painting:. . .

Oh, yes! there were a lot.

On Wednesday, I go to London to choose a first selection of Jones' designs for a Window. Otherwise, I'm here for a month. Unless. . .I sneak off to France. I, even yet, just may. For as Alfred is here, and it's a wee house, Prunoy may be as easy to work in as Rugby: (and more stimulating, for my Great Drama!. . .). As for Brynhild Olivier, she is an impertinent busybody, and the last dilettantiest person to talk about 'working' and 'settling down'. Beat her, if you see her. Apart, as a matter of fact, from Bryn's ignorance, and my own benefit, I'm rather anxious (in no gloomy sense) about Prunoy. At least, I've been thinking. I didn't, as a matter of fact, feel sure if you were to be there. I'm glad if you are, especially if I'm not. For it will be splendid for both parties—and

for everyone else—if Brynnoel and Franc$_i^e$s love each other. But

that sort of joining-up is made easier by an extra person who knows and loves both lots and has a calmer, more intriguing and far-seeing mind than the romantic dreamer Jacques. So that I felt, though they of course *would* join, Franc*is*' brooding and Franc*es*' energy and Brynnoel's shyness and partly affected stupidity might *just* possibly make it less complete and happy than it would be under the benign encouragement of one so wise and so competent in *both* the languages and natures as (I was perfectly confident!) myself.

And, you see, I now write, as you.

So, though I *may* yet suddenly appear (but hush!) I feel con-science-blest and noble at having openly entrusted my solemn, almost Jacquesian, strategy to you! (No, I'm not pretending, even to myself, that I imagine you hadn't thought of it just as much as I; having seen, as you did, for instance, the frightened gleaming silence of Bryn and Noel at Faustus' time—in company.)

As for everything else, I am immersed in Elizabethan Literature. I wrote a long letter to Margery at intervals during a month, and sent it off yesterday. I have suddenly realized it will pass her in the Atlantic, and follow her back, and finally reach her, perhaps, in October, at Newnham. It's very funny, I think; and I laughed all night at it: I don't know why.

I hope to come and watch you working under some clergyman you really like.

What are 'the odd things we come out of'? Just everything? But

I agree, we'll be in the *oddest* things. And even now, very now, I think things are just amazing, all round. Things, and people, and ideas, and every second.   By George!
                                                    Yours
                                                    RUPERT

To FREDERIC KEELING   *24 Bilton Road, Rugby*
                                         20–23 September 1910
                                              (Age 23)

Dear Ben,

I've several times started to write you a notable and rhetorical letter. But my life has been too jerky to admit of much connected thought lately. So the letter always fizzled away and was not. I'm sorry I didn't write sooner. But I wanted to be able to write down a great attack on your pessimism, in abundant reasoned language. And such a thing takes time and thought. Also, I may agree with you. What is pessimism? Why do you say you're becoming a pessimist? What does it mean? He may (I say to myself) mean that he thinks that the Universe is bad as a whole, or that it's bad just now, or that, more locally and importantly, things aren't going to get any better in our time and our country, no matter how much we preach Socialism and clean hearts at them. Is it the last two? Are you telling us that the world is, after all, bad and, what's more, horrible, without enough seeds of good in it? I, writing poetry and reading books and living at Grantchester all day, feel rather doubtful and ignorant about 'The world'—about England and men, and what they're like. Still, I see some, besides the University gang. I see all these queer provincials in this town, upper and middle and lower class. And God knows they're sterile enough. But I feel a placid healthy Physician about it all. (Only I don't know what drugs to recommend.) This is because I've such an overflowing (if intermittent) flood of anti-pessimism in me. I'm using the word now in what is, I expect, its most important sense, of a feeling rather than a reasoned belief. The horror is not *believing* the Universe is bad—or even believing the world won't improve—on a reasoned and cool examination of all facts, tendencies and values, so much as in a sort of general *feeling* that there isn't potentiality for good in the world and that anyhow it's a fairly dreary business, an absence of much appreciation and hope and a somehow paralysed will for good. As this is a feeling it *may* be caused by reason and experience, or more often by loneliness or soul-measles or indigestion or age or anything else. And it can equally be cured by other things than reason: by energy or weather or good people, as well as by a wider ethical grasp, at least so I've found in the rather slight temporary fits of depression I've had in exile and otherwise lately—or even in an enormous period of Youthful Tragedy with which I started at Cambridge. I have a remedy. It's a dangerous one, but I think very good on the whole; though it may lead to a sterile but ecstatic content, or even to the asylum. In practice I find it doesn't—or hasn't yet—made me inefficient.

I am addressing an Adult School on Sunday. I have started a group for studying the Minority Report here. I am going to Cambridge in a week to oversee, with the light of pure reason, the powerful energies of those who are setting forth the new Fabian Rooms; and later, to put the rising generations, Fabians and otherwise, on the way of Light, all next term. The remedy is mysticism, or Life, I'm not sure which. Do not leap or turn pale at the word Mysticism. I do not mean any religious thing, or any form of belief. I still burn and torture Christians daily. It is merely the *feeling* —or a kindred one—which underlay the mysticism of the wicked Mystics. Only I refuse to be cheated by the *feeling* into any kind of *belief. They* were convinced by it that the world was very good or that the Universe was one or that God existed. I don't any more believe the world to be good. Only I do get rid of the despair that it isn't, and I certainly seem to see additional possibilities of its getting better. It consists in just looking at people and things as themselves—neither as useful nor moral nor ugly nor anything else, but just as being. At least that's a philosophical description of it. What happens is that I suddenly feel the extraordinary value and importance of everybody I meet, and almost everything I see. In *things* I am moved in this way especially by some things; but in people by almost all people. That is, when the mood is on me. I roam about places—yesterday I did it even in Birmingham!—and sit in trains and see the essential glory and beauty of all the people I meet. I can watch a dirty middle-aged tradesman in a railway-carriage for hours, and love every dirty greasy sulky wrinkle in his weak chin and every button on his spotted unclean waistcoat. I know their states of mind are bad. But I'm so much occupied with their being there at all, that I don't have time to think of that. I tell you that a Birmingham goaty tariff-reform fifth-rate business-man is splendid and desirable.

It's the same about the things of ordinary life. Half an hour's roaming about a street or village or railway station shows so much beauty that it is impossible to be anything but wild with suppressed exhilaration. And it's not only beauty, and beautiful things. In a flicker of sunlight on a blank wall, or a reach of muddy pavement, or smoke from an engine at night there's a sudden significance and importance and inspiration that makes the breath stop with a gulp of certainty and happiness. Its not that the wall or the smoke seem important for anything, or suddenly reveal any general statement, or are rationally seen to be good and beautiful in themselves—only that *for you* they're perfect and unique. It's like being in love with a person. One doesn't (now-a-days, and if one's clean-minded) think the person better or more beautiful or larger than the truth. Only one is extraordinarily excited that the person, exactly as he is, uniquely and splendidly just exists. It is a feeling, not a belief. Only it is a feeling that has amazing results. I suppose my occupation is being in love with the Universe—or (for it is an important difference) with certain spots and moments of it. I wish to God I could express myself. I have a vague notion that this is all very incoherent. But the upshot of it is that one's too happy to *feel* pessimistic; and too much impressed by the immense value and potentialities of *everything* to *believe* in pessimism, for the following reason, and in the following sense.

Every action, one knows (as a good Determinist), has an external effect. And every action, therefore, which leads on the whole to good, is '*frightfully*' important. For the good mystic knows how jolly 'good' is. It is not a question of either getting to Utopia in the year 2,000, or not. There'll be so much good then, and so much evil. And we can affect it. There—from the partly rational point of view —is the beginning and end of the whole matter. It oughtn't to make any difference to our efforts whether the good in 2000 A.D. will be a lot greater than it is now, or a little greater, or less. In any case, the amount of good we can cause by doing something, or can subtract by not doing it, remains about the same. And that is all that ought to matter. Lately, when I've been reading up the Elizabethans, and one or two other periods, I've been amazed more than ever at the way things change. Even in talking to my Uncle of 70 about the Victorians, it comes out astoundingly. The whole machinery of life, and the minds of every class and kind of man, change beyond recognition every generation. I don't know that 'Progress' is certain. All I know is that change is. These solid, solemn, provincials, and old maids, and business men, and all the immovable system of things

I see round me will vanish like smoke. All this present overwhelming reality will be as dead and odd and fantastic as crinolines or 'a dish of *tay*'. Something will be in its place, inevitably. And what that something will be, depends on me. With such superb work to do. and with the wild adventure of it all, and with the other minutes (too many of them) given to the enchantment of being even for a moment alive in a world of real matter (not that imitation, gilt stuff, one gets in Heaven) and actual people—I have no time now to be a pessimist.

I don't know why I have scribbled down these thin insane vapourings. I don't suppose you're still as desperate as you were when you wrote in June. When are you coming to Cambridge? I am going to Germany for the Spring Term. But if you can get over next term, are you coming out to stay at Grantchester? I lead a lovely and dim and rustic life there and have divine food. Hugh [Dalton] is going to be in London, and Gerald [Shove] is old as the hills and withered as a spider, and I am the oldest Fabian left (except Tram,[1] who is senile) and I dodder about and smile with toothless gums on all the gay young sparks of the Fabian Society, to whom I am more than a father. So you might tell me if you are going to shake off for a day or a month the ghastly coils of British Family Life and of Modern Industry that you are wound in, and come to see the bovine existence of a farmer.

In the name of God and the Republic

RUPERT

To EDWARD MARSH

The Orchard
Wednesday, 5 October 1910

Splendid! Yes, I shall be able to go to the Follies next week. I'll be at Gray's Inn at 6.30 tomorrow. As a matter of fact being unmusical I've never seen Tannhauser. But I suppose I'd better wait till I get to Munich in January. I'd like the Coliseum—I *love* Yvette Guilbert, & I'd like to see what happened in La Tosca. I suppose Priscilla Runs Away is flimsy stuff? I don't really know about the plays. Except that McKinnel is a 'Northern Literary man'. What is a Northern Literary Man? Bluff & rustic like me? Hawtrey doesn't attract me. But I could watch McKinnel for a year, & Du Maurier for ever. Unless their plays are too bad. I'm afraid Saturday afternoon's no good.   RUPERT

[1] V. H. Mottram.

To MRS BROOKE　　　　　　　　　[*Grantchester*]
　　　　　　　　　　　　　　　Thursday, 3 November [*1910*]

Dear Mother,

*　　　*　　　*

I don't know when my poems will be published. I haven't even found a publisher yet: though machinery to secure one is in motion. The real difficulty is that I want to finish off a dozen more before I print, and I can't do it. At least, I do it very slowly. But I daresay they may appear in March, if all goes well. It depends on the publisher. Perhaps it *is* best not to talk about it much in Rugby until everything is settled, and announced.

*　　　*　　　*

E. M. Forster the writer has just been staying here two nights. He's a very charming person—an old King's man of 27 or 28. Get his new novel 'Howard's End'. It would interest you. Can you send me some more of my money for the year? I have still a fair amount to receive, and the University won't pay me my second half of the Oldham [Prize]. And I want to pay some bills. I received 30s. from the *Nation* this morning. But I'm not writing much for papers.

Did I tell you, though, that I got two books on my period to review for the Spectator?

I've just received the bill for typing my Puritan Essay—£2.13s.0d.! So, with the expense of printing—when that comes, which won't be just yet—I don't get much change out of the Harness prize! But, of course, it's a very good Certificate.

*　　　*　　　*

I don't think there's anything more to say just now. It has been very cold lately: and, today, rain. Did I tell you about my 22 new little pigs?　　　　　　　　　　　　With love
　　　　　　　　　　　　　　　　　　　　RUPERT

To HUGH DALTON　　　　　　　　　　*The Orchard*
　　　　　　　　　　　　　　　Monday, 7 November 1910

Pejorism is the Art of thinking things Worse than they Are in order that you may thereby be the more powerfully impelled to Better them.

You may have a meal with me. *Not* Wednesday tea or dinner. *Anything* else. I am here all Thursday. Let me know which meal, immediately. You may have it in the room, and I will communicate with you by signs through the closed window.

Your lack of any sense of individuality in style has betrayed you. *I* wrote the Circular to freshmen. It is highly successful.

Give — all my love and half my sympathy. He will find — in his Bed one night: and then she will force him to marry her to save her Repper.

I have had a long letter from Reid about Henley. '*Have* the words "the rich quiet of the afterglow"[1] got a reference to human immortality?' I told him 'No'; but agreed that much of Henley was fine.

I have lost the Art of writing Poetry: but acquired the immense serenity of the Cow. Human Life is a fretful thing. But I have developed the Foreknowledge of Death, since my last birthday.

RUPERT

To JACQUES RAVERAT *Ye Olde George Hotel*
Chatteris
Tuesday, 8 November 1910

Mummy[2]

As those of old drank mummia,
     To fire the limbs of lead,
Making dead kings from Africa
     Stand panders to their bed;
Drunk on the dead, and medicined
     With spiced and royal dust,
In a short night they reeled to find
     Ten centuries of lust.

So I...

And there I've been for half an hour. And now I must talk to pretty Mrs Hoskins about Neapolitan Carpets!

And I suppose I shall never see any of you again.

Extremo tempore
RUPERT

[1] In 'Bric-à-brac', Henley's *Poems*, 1904, p. 112.
[2] Printed with additional stanzas as 'Mummia' in *The New Age*, 16 November 1911, and in *Poems*, 1911.

To GEOFFREY FRY   *24 Bilton Road, Rugby*
                                     Thursday [December 1910]

My dear Geoffrey,

It is amazingly good of you to give me the luckless Mr [A.H.] Bullen's lovely books.[1] A thousand thanks. I read them when I ought to be learning German, and I writhe with vain passion and with envy. How did they do it? *Was* it, as we're told, because they always wrote to tunes? The lightness! There are moments when I try to write 'songs', 'where Lumpkin with his Giles hobnobs', but they are bumping rustic guffaws. I feel that sense of envious incompetence and a vast angry clumsiness that hippopotamuses at the Zoo must feel when you stand before them with your clouded cane and take snuff. They're* occasionally so like the Anthology; and oh! I can see why Headlam loved them.

Your whispers of hymns and dances suggest strange revelries and devilries to me. What does it all mean? I may see you yet in England. For I don't go till January 8 or so. But when I go, aha! England will never see me more. I shall grow my red whiskers and take to Art. In a few years you may come and stay with me in my villa at Sybaris or my palace near Smyrna or my tent at Kandahar or my yacht off the Cyclades. But you will be a respectable lawyer. You will waggle your pince-nez and lecture me on my *harem*. Then a large one-eyed negro eunuch will come and tie you up and pitch you into the sea. And I shall continue to paint sea-scapes in scarlet and umber.

Farewell. Rejoice with me that we are going to get rid of the Lords at last—And mourn that my Muse is dead.

Ever

RUPERT

One poem in those lovely books you sent is incredibly bizarre—about a love-affair between a crab and a frog. Did you read it? In the end the crab bit off the frog's four feet morosely, and retired in silence.[2]

Why do you say your telegraphic address is 'Winsome'? Indecorous family.

* The song-books: not the Hippopotamuses.

[1] Anthologies of Elizabethan songs.
[2] *Lyrics from the Song Books of the Elizabethan Age*, ed. A.H. Bullen, 1891, p. 204.

To E. J. DENT *24 Bilton Road, Rugby*
15 December 1910

Dear Dent,

Either my boastfulness or my Keltic melancholy has misled you. I *have* met some of the minor Irish players, once. But they wouldn't remember me; and I feel vague about their names. Anyhow they wouldn't be the people who could help. I don't know any of the leaders of the 'movement'. I know that Lady Gregory has lately brought out a volume of translations, mostly Molière. They are in Irish guise, and speak with a brogue. Files of the Times Literary Supplement might help. I think it's within three months. If La Locandiera is in that volume, you'll find it in the shops, I think; or get information from Maunsel & Co. Dublin. You could get into touch with the Irish Theatre through Godwin Baynes, who knows Yeats and the lot. Or through Iolo Williams who's a friend of, at least, Padraic Colum. I expect, though, Lady Gregory *will* answer letters, and give information. I'm sorry I can't help.

By the way, did you see an article by Yeats on *Tragedy* in the Mask? It's worth reading. He's one of the few men who can write English prose. Splendid supple stuff!

Among the Johns did you see the one Jacques bought, an unfinished one of a woman on a cliff, oil on wood, I think?

I'm here for a bit, then going off with Jacques for a week or two to write. Then Germany. Have you seen the Grafton show yet? I'm going to, soon. Ever

RUPERT

To KATHARINE COX *24 Bilton Road*
Monday [December 1910]

Second-bests, even the loveliest, are so bloody. No; That's not good. I will certainly come. On the 26th. It will be splendid.

Only, look here, suppose on Christmas Day I *knew* I was, and was going to be for a week, just [*word erased*]—well then I should only do Jacques harm and please nobody and then I shouldn't come. So I daresay I shan't—eh? So go ahead and get Justin and Gwen. I may find I've got to work harder than I could if there was anyone to talk to.

I'm glad Jacques has got off. I'm glad he's coming to you for Christmas. Because that'll be calmer than either Lulworth or Frances, and calmness is what he wants, most.

Worried? I am sad for that, though I ought to be more so. But many are worried. But what hurts is thinking her wicked. I do, you see. Not very judicially, but I do. And what's to be done if you think a person you know so well is wicked? I don't see what I'm ever to do about Margery [Olivier]. I thought I was going to go to *The Champions*[1] this week-end, when I want to avoid School Festivities. But—I suppose I shall just go off to Kineton and walk. And in January.

And, awfully, *oughtn't* one to write to people who are wicked and explain they are; else—obviously one ought. And—oh, we are *quite* out of sight and this is simply a turning *off* a turning, such as I always got into when I rode out canvassing—*full* of mud, and I kept side-slipping. You're therefore right 'we'll not say any more about this'. Don't be black. Give me your blackness: it won't be noticed. And I deserve it (that is, at least, you don't). Just be a tinge grey about a minute a week....

So tired I got, working at our election all day and half the night. I did 'conveyances'. And we had twenty motor-cars promised; and *twelve* came! (The constituency is vast, containing 90 villages, and thousands of removals.) The Tories had over 100 motor cars. My God! Man after man we had to give up. Couldn't get them to the poll. A dozen waiting in Coventry, six at Northampton, and so on. The next day came pathetic letters, reproachful. 'We was waiting in the rain for three hours for that motor.' They can't afford railway fares.

The upper class women here take Tory leaflets round to their 'districts'; the people they vouchsafe 'charity' to at other times, very poor people. Also the clergy....I have cut off the only man in Rugby I know at all well, for he was a Tory and very wicked just now. Elections are as bad as...

It is not true that anger against injustice and wickedness and tyrannies is a good state of mind, 'noble'. Oh, perhaps it is with some, if they're fine. But I guess with most, as with me, it's a dirty mean choky emotion. I HATE the upper classes.

Ever

RUPERT

[1] The Oliviers' home at Limpsfield.

To A. Y. CAMPBELL   *24 Bilton Road,*
                                              Rugby
                                   21 December [*1910*]

My dear Archie,

Why do you write in crimson ink from Weston-super-Mare? It is *too* bizarre. And then to go to the Castle of Comfort! What century, or centuries, do you think you live in?

I agree about Dudley's incapacity for modern civilization. I may add to your list of charges that he sometimes does not see my jokes, and often bursts into shrill gawkish laughter when I make profound statements. His handwriting, as you say, is a disgrace. He plunges straight into a letter illegibly, uglily, *sans* ceremonious address, and without the slightest idea how it's going to end—just as, in fact, twenty-odd years ago, he (or anyone else) plunged into the world. God, however, (the clown!) was the penman then. What a world!

I'm sorry we gave you such little warning. The election rather tangled my affairs: and suddenly I found I could, and must, leave this hole for a week-end. I wired to Dudley to wire to you. Alas! it availed not. Nor, I fear, can I come for the beginning of next year; though I can think of nothing lovelier than hearing you sing Auld Lang Syne on December 31st 11.55 p.m. in the correct brogue. But I've promised to go on Monday for a week or ten days to Lulworth with Jacques, Justin and Katharine Cox. Many thanks, though. I wish I could come.

Your analysis of the situation in the [Cambridge] Review is profound and final. For such emotions the sudden-simple-last-line trick is incomparable.[1] My companion sonnet ending —'That was because you did not blow your nose' appears next term.

I hope you saw my review in that number of forty professors. It was dull. But I managed to call Prof. Saintsbury a hippopotamus.[2]

                                              anon

                                              RUPERT

If ever you write to me again in the next nine years, my address will be, The Den of Despair, Slobbington, Hell.

[1] '—And then you suddenly cried, and turned away', in the sonnet 'The Hill', the *Cambridge Review*, 8 December 1910.
[2] Review of vol. VI of the *Cambridge History of English Literature*, p. 188: 'Professor Saintsbury's chapters among the rest stand out like a hippopotamus in an expanse of mud, clumsy and absurd, but alive.'

Brooke was busy at Rugby at the beginning of the year, but was about to go to Germany for several months. His letters to Katharine Cox begin to show that their relations were becoming more than friendly, his feelings for Noel Olivier having been damped (as he thought) by the intervention of her sister Margery. In a letter to Reginald Pole he mentions that his first volume of poems is being considered by the firm of Dent, but this came to nothing and it was ultimately published on 3 December by Sidgwick and Jackson. One letter of 20 September to Frank Sidgwick is all that is now available from Brooke's side concerning the negotiations preceding its appearance.

By 14 January Brooke was in Munich, living in a *pension*, and for the next three months was writing long letters to his friends describing his life in Germany. In March he became deeply envious of Jacques Raverat and Gwen Darwin, who were to be married. The sense of his own loneliness—since he could never decide, to the end of his life, to take the plunge himself—was accentuated later in the year by the engagement of Dudley Ward to Annemarie von der Planitz, sister of Clothilde von Derp, the dancer, and by thoughts of the Cornfords in their new Cambridge house, Conduit Head, off the Madingley Road. In April he moved on to Vienna to stay with E. P. Goldschmidt, a Cambridge friend, who afterwards became a learned and eminent bookseller, and he had intended travelling further, perhaps to Dalmatia, when he was diverted to Florence to be companion to his old friend and schoolmaster, Robert Whitelaw.

Some time in May Brooke returned to England, and established himself in Grantchester at the Old Vicarage, the decaying house by the river, afterwards made famous by the poem 'Grantchester' composed in Germany in the following year. There he was looked after by the tenants, Mrs Neeve and her husband, and the house became his permanent home. After his death the property was bought by Mrs Brooke, who bequeathed it at her death in 1931 to Dudley Ward. In July he had begun to work at a dissertation on Webster and the Elizabethan dramatists to compete for a Fellowship at King's. During the summer and autumn he made several visits to Rugby and elsewhere, and in London frequently saw Diaghilev's Russian Ballet company at Covent Garden. Immediately after Christmas he joined a party of friends at Lulworth. Here an incident occurred (not recorded in the letters now printed) which first in-jected poison into Brooke's relations with Ka Cox. She had arranged with Lytton Strachey that the painter, Henry Lamb, should be invited to stay near by, at Corfe Castle, where she could visit them. Strachey's part in this earned the resentment against him expressed by Brooke in his later letters and caused a complete break in their relationship. The details of this episode are made clear in Christopher Hassall's *Life of Brooke*.

To KATHARINE COX   *24 Bilton Road, Rugby*
                                    Thursday, 5 January 1911
                     *   *   *

We drifted away, I all the time too (somehow) lost and shy and
perplexed ever quite to seize a chance of saying one or two things
that I was on fire to say. I wanted passionately to know that you
were painless and vacuously cheery. All yesterday and today
(though—do *you* find it?—half a day and eighty miles are all time
and space for the veils they hang between oneself and one's yester-
self) I'm red and sick with anger at myself for my devilry and
degradation and stupidity. I hate myself because I wickedly and
unnecessarily hurt you several times. (I don't mean that I'm sorry—
for my own sake—for all that happened; or that I'm an atom changed
from what I said and suggested. That stands.) But I hurt you, I hurt
you, Ka, for a bit, unforgiveably and filthily and infamously; and
I can't bear it; I was wild to do anything everything in the world to
undo the hurt, or blot it out (but what could I do? I waved my arm
in the bookshop at thirty books—but that'ld have meant nothing.
And I couldn't, as I wanted, take hold of you and put mouth hard
to mouth, for you had somehow put that aside, and it would have
confused other issues, and—I daredn't.)—Oh, tell me that you're
unhurt, for I hurt you in *such* a way, and I was mean and selfish, and
you're, I think, one of the most clear and most splendid people in
the world.   RUPERT

I go to the Champions on Monday or Tuesday, perhaps; not for
the week-end.

To KATHARINE COX   *Rugby*
                                    Sunday [*January 1911*]

I'm afraid this will not help you much, getting so late to you. But
I expect you may have found out about my movements before this.
Your letter arrived by the last post *in* last night, and I had gone out
to dinner with Mr Whitelaw, in dress clothes and shyness, and
didn't get back in time to catch the last post *out*.

I'm staying—I don't know how long, at the Champions. Till Wednesday afternoon or Thursday dawn. In any case I shan't go to
[Germany] till Thursday 9 p.m. from London. So you can have what
hours on Thursday you will: or perhaps Wednesday evening. So
you can stay for this damned play: which I shall see.

I come down by the 2.25 from London tomorrow, so I shall reach Limpsfield almost as soon as this. I shall see you at the dress rehearsal. Then on Tuesday we'll arrange an hour and day. It will be good. And there are things to say.

The first letter wasn't 'silly': though I *did* nearly wire about 'I' and 'day' rhyming. The poem—if I were Frances I might say I thought it 'brave and true'!: as I'm I, I'll confess it seemed 'witty'. Didn't you think it worked out rather admirably?

Oh, all right, I'm not sad. You can't stop me being ashamed. But so long as you're not hurt, the world's very fine. Nor can you stop me having my opinion of you. But I'll put the balance leveller one of these days by writing you a letter describing all the horrors that are in you—as seen from without and below.

Now I'm going to Limpsfield. It is very unpleasant. The atmosphere at *Priest Hill* and *The Champions* is too damned domestic. I love the people and cough the atmosphere. Orphanage (orphanhood? -dom? -ity?) should be state-regulated and compulsory. So ought monopaedy (= the state of being without brothers or sisters). Now I find I've been a devil to Margery, as well as in every other way. She says she never interfered (after a momentary impulse). Noel agrees. Ecco! Where am I? Perhaps the Archbishop was right; and 2+2 hardly *ever* makes 4, except occasionally in the evenings. But really!...I flickered a satirical protest: but it was a butterfly to a steam-roller. I *am* a beast, after all. Worse than ever. But apologizing to Margery is a little thing; finding oneself in a mere Chaos of disconnexions is the horror.

(But don't *you* speak a word of this. I'm going to close it all, with Margery. Most happily.)

And then I've a million things to clear with Noel:—oh *far* more than telling this last heroism. (But for saying I could, thanks, Ka! One *has* to be open. When everything is, life's so fine, my God! how fine!)

La! I shall be glad to be in Germany, at peace. Rest means being where no one knows you. For there one's actions have no effect either way. But when one finds oneself tangled up with so many other clumsy people...It's horrible being partly responsible for other people's souls. One feels so timid.

But hurrah for the World! It's fairly bubbling and glittering round me! I'd do anything anywhere a million years.

RUPERT

To REGINALD POLE   [*Rugby*]
                                      11 January [*1911*]

I'm just off to Germany, for ever. I was amazed and delighted to
see in all the papers that you had got through an exam, which
sounded of great importance. Are you now an M.A.? or only
a D.D.? I'm sorry I didn't see you when I was in Grantchester.
I live entirely for politics, now, and entirely by reviews, so that my
life is wholly and merely sordid.

Yes, you may certainly shout any of my poems with Homer & the
rest. I hope all London will hear them. Dent, I think, will bring them
out in the next six months. But I don't at all know when. It's all
very dim. I should like them to burst upon a furious world while
I'm safely on the Continent: but I daresay not. I'm glad (for the sake
of things in general) that you're not going to decay on a stool at
a desk. It's brave of you to face things out on a better level. I hope
it'll succeed immediately. Let me know if good theatrical things are
going to happen, ever, that you're mixed up in. The London theatres
just now are pretty deplorable. Perhaps the Munich ones'll be better!

                                      Ever

                                      RUPERT

To DAVID GARNETT   *24 Bilton Road, Rugby*
                                      [*January 1911*]

My dear David,

                  *   *   *

It is a thousand years since I saw you; and it will be more before
I see you again, for in three days I go to Germany, and from there
I shall wander South and East, and no one will ever hear of me more,
save that mariners who ply among the Cyclades will bring back from
time to time strange tales of a bald red-bearded man sitting on the
rocks in the sun, naked, chaunting little wicked Latin poems and
playing on a pipe most execrably. It will (you must never breathe it)
be me—'be I' as you literary people say. A faint reflexion of me,
however, will remain in England in the shape of a volume of lovely
and indecent poems that will almost surely appear this year. Many of
them you read with shrill cries of affected approval at Grantchester.
But you have forgotten.

The last time I heard from (not of) you, you were living in the wilds and exulting in *Joseph and his Brethren.*[1] I read it two years ago, and I liked it. I didn't put it very high, though, in spite of Swinburne. Except for a few gems, I thought the verse was rather flat and easy. And the man hadn't much width of imagination. It seemed a little second-hand. But of course it was rich and fine in its way, and oddly unaffected by his contemporaries.

The only time I have moved from dead dreary books and pedantry was to go and see poor Mr Masefield's play about Pompey. I thought it just failed, really. Though the acting didn't give it much chance. I wonder if you saw it. The sentimentalities just spoilt the finenesses. And sometimes nothing was happening. But there were good things. Pompey, however, occasionally exhibited a clergyman's mind. His banality was incredible, at moments. When he's going to his death, he asks his wife what was that fine sentence they read in a book together twenty years ago. Everyone tries to remember, and you think some superb jewel is coming, to stay him in the face of Death, and crown the play. He remembers at last, and it turns out to be 'Really Nice Men scarcely fear Anything' or words to that effect. He goes off repeating it, consoled. What tameness!

But you, are you still learning the scientific way of growing cabbages? Can you rub a little subtle chemical mixture on the earth and make it produce roses? Or do you only sit under hedges and produce ecstatic poetry? I expect that what you want in order to make your young soul flourish and leap like a lamb is ethics. Metaphysics might do. Read great books on them, and get to think clearly. Think! Think! Think! David my dear, and then you will be both good and happy   Like

(ever thine)

RUPERT

To DUDLEY WARD   [Postcard]
[*addressed to: Dudley & Jacques*]

[*Postmark:*
München, 14 January 1911]

I was sick at midnight; once. But oh, my dears, it turns out to be quite slight—*nothing* to the other thing.   RUPERT

I crossed with a very rich simple young business-man who told me the tale of the Bishop and the Little Girl. He also said that if we had

[1] By 'H. L. Howard' (Charles Wells), 1824; edited by Swinburne in 1876 (World's Classics, 1908).

not spoken to each other 'two souls might have gone to the grave and never reached out to each other'. 'Human companionship'...he said, and left me, on the gangway.

I have baffled this nation at every turn so far. Each time I slipped out of the waiting train to get a bun or a postcard, at Frankfurt, the train slid round to another platform. Each time I found it. Figure me across country and by forbidden ways pursuing it, the officials me. I was Caesarian.

To A.Y. CAMPBELL   *Pension Bellevue, Theresien Strasse, München*
[postmark: 17 January 1911]

England? England? I seem to remember that name...But 'alas! and oh, alas! my dear' I'm beyond week-ends here. In ten years perhaps, when I return...

>   I that dwell
> Ten leagues beyond man's life: I that from London
> Can have no note, unless the sun were post
> —The man i'th'moon's too slow—till new-born chins
> Be rough and razorable—[1]

My heart will be at Reading for the week-end; but my stomach, that most important thing, will be in Munich: immense, round, German, strange, swaying, calm.   RUPERT

To KATHARINE COX   *Pension Bellevue,*
30 Theresienstrasse
München, Bavaria
Sunday, 22 January 1911

I resist the temptation, Ka, to begin with a bit of German. Take instead my favourite verse in Keats. I expect you know it. He (too) wrote it to some ladies he believed to be occasionally thinking of him. (Its true though, you've never given me a shell, alas!)

> 'For indeed, 'tis a sweet and peculiar pleasure
>   (And blissful is he who such happiness finds,)
> To possess but a span of the hour of leisure
>   In elegant, pure, and aerial minds.'[2]

Oh, Ka, be it noted (for future reference) that the supper was

---

[1] *The Tempest*, act 2, sc. 1.
[2] The last stanza of 'To some ladies', *Poems*, 1817, p. 31.

a mistake: and be it known that I am a baby. Oh, *damn!* It is sickening to be a baby. I don't mind giving way to emotion if there's nothing else to do. When I'm seen off anywhere in a train, I always 'cry in a corner of the carriage as it steams away—even if it's only Aunt Fanny I've left standing on the platform. But when there is something else to be done—oh, it's too *gauche* and wasteful to be overcome by the situation. (It's really rather wicked, too, to mind, for two hours, going off into an amazing world, when life's so fine for me.) But I'd made myself rather hysterical. Saying good-bye, any-how—I'm as lopsided as Justin in the opposite way.[1] God, who probably doesn't understand the latest methods of indexing, got wrong over the Brookes' qualities. Oh, one's rather justified, under the circumstances, since (it is credibly reported) nothing is ever quite the same (until the Grand Cycle (29,900 years) has swung round) and when I return (*if*) you'll be in an emigrant-ship, and shall have a beard, and Jacques'll be in the French hills, and Lady Olivier'll be in England, and Margery'll be married, and Dudley dead by his own hand. And, to take only one part of it all, Noel and I meet so rarely and shortly, and in the great intervals *anything* may (and does) happen; so that unloosening hands and going away *is* (in this dangerous world and with 1910 not returning), just as you turn, rather a wrench. (As a sign, I was for two days miserable because (I had persuaded myself) the taxi-driver had abducted her. *That*'s not very level-headed!) In fine, being rather tangled, I wanted to walk rapidly, a relieving thing; and couldn't say good-bye as com-pletely as . . . as, you know, one has worked it out in one's Handbook to Life (v. Chapter x, §§ 14, 15. On saying Goodbye to Ka.)

I hope you didn't think me too unthinking—you didn't mind? Oh, *and* I hope (and hoped in the train) most feverishly that the working-men had a fine lecture? And are still progressing? I feel certain they are. If you have all the vices of the Victorians, you have (I have *always* maintained) some of their virtues. They *were* com-petent. (I'm always wanting to make you my Literary Executor, instead of James [Strachey]. Perhaps, however, he has his Finger most on the Public Pulse.)

'I wonder if you would like to hear about my life here.' All my letters begin like that. But it would be silly to think that, because it's laughable, it's not sensible. I *will* tell you about the World—if it's only to show you how fine Life is and what a Superb Fellow I am. I grow in culture daily.

[1] J.B. had once said he had never been sorry to say goodbye to anyone.

[*The end of the letter is missing*]

[*Written alongside*]

Go and see la Philippi do [Ibsen's] John Gabriel Borkman. It's a damn interesting play. I like it. (Of course, it *is* a bit '96. . . .) I've just seen it in Dutch.

To MRS BROOKE   *Pension Bellevue*
                                                [*Munich*]
                                        Tuesday, 31 January 1911

Dear Mother,

The last thing you forwarded to me (which got here on Tuesday morning) was a sample of five cigarettes! They might have been opened in the post, I think, and confiscated or taxed. I have got hold (through Professor Schick) of a German student called Ludwig Dellefant. We meet for two or three hours every day, sometimes more. Did I tell you all this? He is a pleasant youth, not highly interesting but very amiable, and, luckily for me, *very* meek. In fact, though we are supposed to exchange German for English, I continually have to pull myself up and talk English, to avoid cheating him. Otherwise he submits to German all the time, quite placidly. We go walks or sit over coffee or beer in *cafés*. Last night he took me to a '*Kneipe*'. The students who are working at some special subject band together to form a club. Dellefant belongs to the 'Neuphilologisch Verein' or Modern Languages Club, because he studies Modern Languages. Every Monday evening this Verein has a 'Kneipe', a meeting. Yesterday was, more or less, a visitors' evening. Professor Schick was there and Professor Siepers, the two Professors of English here, also a Professor Keys and his two sons from Toronto, who are working at various subjects in this university for a year. There was a paper on 'Victor Hugo' (I couldn't follow much of it!) then a discussion, and then songs, etc. All the while we drank beer, and smoked—at least, the rest smoked. The Germans put away an enormous amount of beer; but it's light stuff, and they didn't get drunk in the same way that English undergraduates do. Some of them got rather 'jolly' towards midnight. They were all extremely friendly. The students' songs were great fun. They have a book with about a thousand in, new and old; and every quarter of an hour we all sang one, Professors and all. I could [not] help the contrast of [Lowes] Dickinson's 'King's College Discussion Society' continually cropping up in my mind! It was extraordinarily different. That's partly King's, though. The German students are extremely simple compared with English undergraduates. They are more like very simple, fat, and hearty public-school boys; docile and sentimental.

Yesterday, also, I went to tea with Frau Ewald and her son, the people Dent gave me an introduction to—I think I've mentioned them. She's a widow and a portrait-painter, a very homely, but intelligent, person.[1] Her son—my age—was up at Caius for a year. She knows all the interesting people, and has promised to take me to a *salon* which is held every Thursday, to which all the German poets and painters go. Unfortunately they don't speak English, so I shall have to wait some weeks before I can understand them.

* * *

All Munich—all Germany—is highly excited about *Der Rosen-kavalier*, Strauss' new opera. It was first performed in Dresden on Thursday, and the first performance in Munich is tomorrow. I don't think I shall be able to get a ticket. But I'm going to the second performance on Saturday. On Sunday I went to Wagner's *Flying Dutchman*. I see the *Times* every day in a *café* here, so I am well up in English news. I was sorry Dilke died. I saw that Erskine Childers' child had arrived, and that Housman was Professor of Latin, and that Hugh Russell-Smith had got his prize. I was immensely pleased about that. Today (I think) I shall pay my dutiful call on the Semons. They nobly treated me to an opera on Thursday—*Tosca*. I could have found one more to my taste; but they were very kind. They are jolly, simple, people, and were delighted to find that I knew all the Cambridge people whose work they knew—Bateson, Frank Darwin, Punnett, etc. They were also a good deal puzzled that an under-graduate (practically) should know the big people whose work wasn't on the same lines as his. Professors and people in Munich—perhaps in Germany?—seem rather limited in that way. Frau Ewald, the painter, Professor Schick the English professor, and Professor Semon the psychologist, have none of them more than heard of each other, and don't know anything about things outside their own sub-jects. Very different from people like Frank Darwin and Dickinson!

With love

RUPERT

[1] There is a portrait of R.B. wearing an enormous hat by Frau Ewald at King's College, Cambridge, but it is a very poor likeness.

To GEOFFREY KEYNES   *Munich*
January 1911

First German Exercise

Ich sagte 'Herz, wie geht's?'
            'Ach! wunderbar!
Besser als Aepfel! Hoch!'
           Es war nicht wahr.

(Specimen from Herr Brooke's 'Idiomatic German and English Poetry for Beginners'. Dent. 2*s.* 6*d.* net. Pp. xi+176.)

Letter to A SHROPSHIRE LAD   *February 1911*

A Letter to a Shropshire Lad[1]

(Apropos, more or less, of a recent appointment)

     Emmanuel, and Magdalene,
       And St Catharine's, and St John's,
     Are the dreariest places,
       And full of dons.

     Latin? so slow, so dull an end, lad?
       Oh, that was noble, that was strong!
     For you'd a better wit to friend, lad,
       Than many a man who's sung his song.

     You'd many a singer's tale to show it,
       Who could not end as he began,
     That thirty years eats up a poet,
       And the muse dies before the man.

     Such gave the world their best—and quickly
       Poured out that watered best again,
     —And age has found them, tired and sickly,
       Mouthing youth's flabby dead refrain;—

     Or lived on lads whose song's long ended,
       Who will not blush for all they say;
     Or damned the younger songs and splendid;
       —Oh, lad, you chose the better way!

[1] Submitted in a competition set in the *Saturday Westminster* for 'the best new and original letters to live poets'. The prize was awarded to R.B.'s alternative composition 'Letter to a Live Poet' (*Collected Poems*, 1918), which appeared in the *Saturday Westminster* for 4 February 1911. The 'Letter to a Shropshire Lad' was printed in the issue of 13 May. A. E. Housman had been appointed Professor of Latin at Cambridge.

Let fools so end! Leave many a lesser
  To blot his easy-bettered page!
But play the man, become Professor
  When your ailment is your age!

You turned where no tune yet is clinging,
  Where never a living song was sung;
E'en Greek might tempt a man to singing,
  But Latin is the lifeless tongue.

You may stir that dust to laughter.
  The lonely wreath that once you made,
—Unsmirched by feebler song born after—
  We have it, where it will not fade.

Those who don't care for song now hear you
  In curious, some in languid, rows.
Undishonoured, clean and clear, you
  Teach and lecture, safe in prose.

For, lads of harsher voice or sweeter,
  They'll all together find one crown,
And hold their tongues from wagging metre
  In this—or in a dustier town.

No lad has made a song-book
  To please the young folks there,
No living tongue is spoken,
  And it's little one will care.

And there's time enough to dawdle in,
  And there, there's plenty o' dons,
And it's drearier than Magdalene,
  And a long way duller than John's.

To FRANCES CORNFORD   *Pension Bellevue, etc.* [*Munich*]
                            (only for a week more)
                           c. 10–15 February 1911

    The worst of solitude—or the best—is, that one begins poking at
one's own soul, examining it, cutting the soft and rotten parts away.
And where's one to stop? Have you ever had, at lunch or dinner, an
over-ripe pear or apple, and, determined to make the best of it, gone
on slicing off the squashy bits? You may imagine me, in München,

at a German lunch with Life, discussing hard, and cutting away at the bad parts of the dessert. 'Oh!' says Life, courteous as ever, 'I'm sure you've got a bad Soul there. Please don't go on with it! Leave it, and take another! I'm so sorry!' But, knowing I've taken the last, and polite anyhow, 'Oh no, please!' I say, scraping away, 'it's really all right. It's only a little gone, here and there—on the outside.... There's plenty that's quite good. I'm quite enjoying it. You always have such delightful Souls!...' And after a minute, when there's a circle of messy brown round my plate, and in the centre a rather woebegone brown-white thin shapeless scrap, the centre of the thing, Life breaks in again, seeing my plight, 'Oh, but you can't touch any of that! It's bad right through! I'm sure Something must have Got Into it! Let me ring for another! There is sure to be some in the Larder....' But it won't do, you know. So I rather ruefully reply 'Ye-s-s, I'm afraid it *is* impossible. But I won't have another, thanks. I don't really want one at all. I only took it out of mere greed...and to have something to do. Thank you, I've had quite enough. Such excellent meat and pudding! I've done splendidly....But to go on with our conversation. About Literature—you were saying, I think...?' and so the incident's at an end.

Dear! dear! it's very trying being ever so exalted one day & ever so desperate the next—this self-knowledge (*why* did that old fool class it with Self-reverence and Self-control? They're rarely seen together)! But so one lives in Munich.

And then your letter came! So many thanks. It made me shake with joy to know that Cambridge and England (as I know it) was all as fine as ever. That Jacques & Ka should be sitting in a *café* looking just like themselves—oh God! what an incredible lovely superb world! I fairly howled my triumph down the ways of this splendid city 'Oh! you fat muddy-faced grey jolly Germans who despise me because I don't know your rotten language. Oh! the people I know —and you don't! Oh! you poor things!' And they all growl at me because they don't know why I glory over them. But, of course, part of the splendour is that—if one only knew it—they, too—these Germans—are all sitting in *cafés* and looking just like themselves. That knowledge sets me often dreaming in a vague, clerical, world-mystic, spirit over my solitary coffee in one of the innumerable *cafés* here in which I spend my days. I find myself smiling a dim gentle poetic paternal Jehovah-like smile—over the ultimate excellence of humanity—at people of, obviously, the most frightful lives and reputations at other tables; who come presently sidling towards me. My mysticism vanishes and, in immense terror, I fly suddenly into the street.... Oh, but they're a kindly people. Every night I sit in a *café* near here, after the opera, and read the day-old *Times* (!) and drink—prepare to hear the depths of debauchery into which the young are led in these wicked foreign cities!—HOT MILK, a large glassful. Last night I spilt the whole of the hot milk over myself, while I was trying to negotiate the Literary Supplement. You've no idea how much of me a large glass of hot milk can cover. I was entirely white, except for my scarlet face. All the people in the café crowded round & dabbed me with dirty pocket-handkerchiefs. A kindly people. Nor did I give in. I ordered more hot milk and finished my supplement, damp but International.

Oh! no! Cambridge isn't very dim and distant, nor [E.J.] Dent a pink shade. I somehow manage, these days, to be aware of two places at once. I used to find it wasn't worth while; and to think that the great thing was to let go completely of a thing when you've done with it, and turn wholly and freshly to the next. 'Being able to take and to let go and to take, and knowing when to take and when to let go, and knowing that life's this—is the only way to happiness' is the burden of the Marschallin in *The Rosenkavalier* (the rage of Germany just now!). There's some truth in it. But sometimes, now, I find I can weave two existences together and enjoy both, and be aware of the unique things of each. It's true that as I write, there's an attitude of Jacques' or a slow laugh of Ka's or a morn at Grantchester or a speech of Dickinson's, that I'd love, and that I'm missing. But there'll be other such, no doubt, in May and June—and what if I'd not met the lovable Mr Leuba (and so differently lovable from an *English* unsuccessful journalist!) or the fascinating Miss Van Something or Other of Paris, or the interesting & wicked de Ravelli, or Dr Wolfskell who is shy and repeats Swinburne in large quantities with a villainous German accent, but otherwise knows no English, or that bearded man in the *café*, or the great Hegedin or Professor Sametsen? And what if I'd not seen Bozetti as Octavian, and Steinhals as Hans Sachs & Craft as Salome, and Steindruck as John Gabriel Borkman and the El Greco crucifixion & the Forain drawings & the good Diez's fantasies.

Eh, but I have grown clerical & solemn & moral. That is because I've been seeing so much Ibsen lately. I apologize. They do Ibsen here a lot—not so well as I'd been led to expect. The acting is, all round, nothing like as good as the English acting. Still, they do Ibsen: that's the great thing. I'm old-fashioned enough to admire that man vastly. I've seen five or six of his plays in four weeks. They always leave me prostrate. But if the Cambridge Stage Society want a stage-manager for Ibsen, they'll know where to come!

No. I've not yet been proposed to by young ladies in plaid blouses, not even one at a time. Still, your warning has made me tread cautiously. As a matter of fact I know only one or two such. Most of the people I see are working at some sensible thing like writing, music or painting, and are free and comradely. I made one or two incursions into German & Anglo-German Philistia, & came hurriedly forth. I'm damnably sorry for the plaid blouses (who *do* exist there and who are, at present, so much better than their mothers). I saw two stifling and crying. But I'm not going back to rescue them.

But in ordinary, & nicer ways I meet a lot of jolly people. It's true, a lot, I think—what you say about friends: but, oh dear people! it *is* fun going away and making thousands of acquaintances. I never talk or read a word of German. But I enjoy life hugely. There's Miss Grove, now: who has such a queer view of Cambridge & so hates it. (But what of the good part she *knows*, she likes.) She turns out, on cross-examination, *not* to be an illegitimate daughter of Mrs [J.G.] Fraser's, only a daughter by an earlier, & French, husband. Fancy being introduced to her in Munich! We swop Cambridge scandal. Then there's dear Professor Semon & his nice wife. 'There is one person in Cambridge I correspond with', said he at tea, 'do you know Pr-r-rofessor Doctor Fr-r-rancis Darrrwin?' I thought for a long time, & then it slowly dawned on me that I did. He produced a letter from your father to prove that he lied not.

I finish this tourist's effusion at 2 o'the morning, sitting up in bed, with my army blanket round me. My feet, infinitely disconnected, & southward, inform me that tonight it is freezing again. The bed is covered with Elizabethan & German books I may or may not read ere I sleep. In the distance glimmers the gaunt white menacing Ibsenite stove that casts a gloom over my life. The Algerian dancing-master next door is, for once, quiet. I rather think the Dragon overhead (the Dragon = that monstrous livid faced screeching pouchy creature of infinite age & horror who screams opposite at dinner and talks with great crags of food projecting from her mouth: a decayed Countess, they say) is snoring. I have this evening been to *The Wild Duck*. It is not as good, I rather thought, as most. *Do* read 'John Gabriel Borkman'!

I'm glad about Vaughan-Williams: & that the play's going on.[1]

[1] F.C.'s *Death and the Princess*.

I've not got far enough really to appreciate the difficulties, I think. I spend my time on lyrics—there's nothing new complete enough to send yet, though. Have you wholly left such things for your long flights? My labour is wasted: for though I've been inspired a lot lately, it's poor stuff; & moreover Dent[1] is now wanting me to leave out 'some too outspoken' poems! I am taking a Dignified line.

Oh, I sometimes make up a picture of Conduit Head, with Jacques in a corner & Gwen on other cushions and Justin on his back & Ka on a footstool & Francis smoking & Frances in the chair to the right (facing the fire)....It stands out against the marble of the *Luitpold Café* & then fades....But say it's true!

All love to both. Even with an enormous stomach & a beard in Munich.

Yours

RUPERT

To MRS BROOKE

Ohmstrasse 3, Gartenhaus I
[Munich]
Ash Wednesday
[1 March] 1911

Dear Mother,

I am comfortably settled in my new rooms. They are very quiet and light and nice, though somewhat expensive. Today Carnival is over. Yesterday being the last day was a great occasion: *Confetti*, everybody in costume, processions, crowds, and so forth. Luckily the weather was very fine. Benians,[2] of John's, is staying in Munich a week on his way round the world on one of these Kivet Kahn Travelling scholarships. I am showing him round. He was too shy to wear clothes of a riotous kind, but I put on a white and scarlet Pierrot costume, and we both spent our time between the streets and a masked ball in the *Deutsches Theater*. The latter ended about one, with the ceremony of 'The Burial of Prince Carnival'. It was all great fun, and Munich was rather a lovely sight. But I am glad to get to a period that uses up less time and money! I went to the 'Bacchus-Fest' in Greek dress. That was a very beautiful business, because all the dresses harmonized in kind, and all were good. People look so much better in Greek than in modern dress! There were a few English there and I talked broken German to German young ladies. I strolled home in my incongruous dress along

---

[1] The publisher.   [2] E. A. Benians, afterwards Master of St John's.

Leopoldstrasse—the chief big street here—a little before seven in the morning, when the night was beginning to get a little grey. The ball hadn't ended, however! It went on to about 8.30!

I have delivered my introduction to Professor Brentano, who has invited me to dinner tomorrow, I am glad to say. This afternoon I am going to the weekly 'at home' of one of Munich's chief poets; where one meets the most extraordinary people, I hear. It should be amusing.

I hear fragments of news from England. *The Times* and *The Morning Post* seem to approve of *The Knight of the Burning Pestle.*[1] Did you hear anything about it? I wonder if my preparatory article on the play got printed in *The C. Review?*[2] It may have come too late. I am sorry to hear about the new tax. It seems a bad one to dig up— £1% extra on property *not* left to widow and children would be sensible. But we're not in a position to complain.

* * *

With love

RUPERT

To DUDLEY WARD   [Postcard]
[*Postmark: München
6 March 1911*]

Elderly *marcheur*, where is my Oxford book of ballads?
Yours in the common way of lust.   R.

To DUDLEY WARD   [Postcard]
[*Postmark: München
14 March 1911*]

Heliogabalus, my little little Ballad book?—lest worse fall!
R.

To DUDLEY WARD   [Postcard]
*Atthidian Heliogabal,
Luxor incapillate.*
[*Postmark: München
22 March 1911*]

Where is my little Book of Ballads? Beware!   R.

[1] Performed by the Marlowe Dramatic Society at Cambridge.
[2] It was printed in the *Cambridge Review*, 23 February 1911.

To KATHARINE COX   [Postmark]
3 *Ohmstrasse, Gartenhaus I*
Wednesday
[*Postmark: 8 March 1911*]

Did he, goddamn him! did he? What a rotten man he is—Dudley! What a bloody rotten man! What rotten men and women you all are! I heartily believe Jacques is the only clean-minded person in London. I shall wire to him to come to Munich, and he and I will paint Germany red, and London will rot and rot, and God will burn it. Oh!

I've got so much to do and so many letters to write.... Almost I came to London. It would be fine.... The inside of a day there. But this afternoon I meet a German poet in a *café*: and on Friday I give a Swinburne reading...I feel so old and unwise; as one who ran (a little cursorily) through the whole of Life six years ago. It is metaphysically true that everything is worth while. But (on alternate days) I feel quite flat. It turns out—did I tell you?—that I am No Good. Otherwise everything is all right. To be no good, of course, is nothing—what journalists call a mere bagatelle. But to be no good through time is tiresome.

I meet the English trains every day, just in case....

RUPERT

What's going to happen to everybody all the summer?

To JACQUES RAVERAT   3 *Ohmstrasse, Gartenhaus I*
[*Munich*]
Wednesday [*March 1911*]

I really love you very much. I also love Gwen very much. And Ka...I even went so far as to write and tell her so—a little circumlocutionarily. I thought it'd balance letters out a bit—that you'd be getting more than she. Oh yes! I ought to have written to you before. Oh yes!...yes! yes! But I've been...oh!...If you only knew what my life was! If you only knew! *Si jeunesse savait!* as (perhaps) your nasal mother tongue says.

*   *   *

It is awfully queer to sit here and love people over eight hundred miles—cleverer and queerer than the telephone, though not so clever as Marconigraphing. So that I agreed, you see, with your remarks [on] Mankind—as typified in its finest specimens. As for you being God—I disagree. It's not much of a matter anyhow. But I rather offendedly claim, my dear, that I'm much more so. The essence of being in München is that one is, precisely, God—ignoble but at peace. You're too much *there*. You are central. In and outside you things happen. Nothing happens to God. He is afar and watches the world; the theory—the pretence—always being that He understands everything. He watches the little figures.... And about once in a blue moon HE has just the dimmest little divine shadow of a suspicion that He's really incredibly 'out of' it, and that He simply hasn't an atom of an idea of what anything important feels like. In Infinity there are no points. And Points are Everything. Let us be pointed. Let us *have* a point. Let us always be *on* a point. Punctuality (or whatever the substantive is) is the New Religion. And so God begins to have this queer glimpse of a fancy that the dirtiest impotentest beggar woman in a gutter who's too bloody tired to scratch her lice, is, in her soddenest moment, eternity ahead of Him....And then the Archangels (who are sexless, remember) begin to talk very loud all at once. And he forgets, again. 'In Heaven there is neither marriage nor giving in marriage.'

Oh, the analogy doesn't hold far. Still, I, in München, *am* more like God than you. Puh! Froggy!

I certainly look more like. Dirty Jacques! Rotten Artist! Sanctissimus Rev. Jack Raverat, Episcopus in Partibus Infidelium, etc. etc.

You once sent me a rotten postcard to say I must write, because I was having a million new experiences and you none. I hope you're ashamed of it now. Even at the time I of course knew you were being clumsily humorous and lazy; or else I should have feared the malign influence of Dudley was creeping over you. It is one of his favourite sentimentalities. Oh yes! my dear Jacques, I've had innumerable new experiences. What a thing travel is! The Munich architecture is awfly interesting. I'm awfly fond of drinking beer, here. It's most extraordinary what a lot of beer they drink in Germany; quite different from England. Awfly interesting to see them. Very fat, the Germans. By Jove, I met an awfly interesting German girl the other day. And I saw some German gypsies—ye Gods! they were fine people. Sometimes I go a walk at night from here to the theatre. The Germans are awfly Impure. Its awfly interesting to see them. By Jove, I met a simply splendid Woman, with eight splendid kiddies (does Dudley say 'kiddies' yet?)....

As if I didn't come here *exactly* to escape 'experiences'. I'd been having too damn many! Here I have none—except the ordinary ones in new dresses—and no responsibilities. 'Experiences'—one stays in England for *that*. One comes abroad to be...God.

But I'll catalogue my experiences, such as they are, as you demand that I'll write about me and not you.

Verhaeren's[1] god-daughter tells me he has written a play about Helen of Troy. It sounds rather good. The Point is that poor Helen can't escape love. There's of course Menelaus, and the Troy business, and then afterwards people fall in love with her more and more. Everyone does it. It's her only relation with people. Even all the women turn Sapphist for her....She decides to die—prays for death. The Gods answer with the greatest alacrity. They are, it appears, waiting—a *queue* at the Further Gate, so to speak. Zeus promises her a magnificent time in Heaven. Venus, Juno, and the rest will have to play second fiddle. There waits, divinely, for Earth's most beautiful woman, an Eternity of ever renewed coition, endless pleasure with the most glorious and lusty and untiring and devoted of lovers, the Olympians....

And she's so sick and bored and tired of passion, and sick, sick, sick of love.

I move among the München P[ost] I[mpressionist]s They got up an exhibition of their French masters here last year; and go pilgrimages to all the places where Van Gogh went dotty or cut his ears off or did any of the other climactic actions of his life. They are young and beetle browed and serious. Every now and then they paint something—often a house, a simple square bordered by four very thick black lines. The square is then coloured blue or green. That is all. Then they go on talking. They are all rather rich and all marry very pretty silly people from other worlds. The Women in the movement, obviously always become old maids. They can't, or won't, marry pretty men from other worlds. They become rather bitter. It is all very queer and important.

No child under fifteen in Germany is allowed to hear a Beethoven symphony (except the Sixth). When the previous item on the programme is finished they all get up and trot out and remain in the cloak room till it is over. Then they come back.

Have you heard about the good Jagon and the magazine called 'Pan'? It is a good tale. I also know about Briand and about the Queen Mother. Do you? (They are two affairs, not one.) The

---

[1] Emile Verhaeren, the Belgian poet.

Catholics here found it was the centenary of God, or something. So they got up a vast meeting to explain to themselves that they were all right; and advertised it all over München

TRIED
and
TRUE
to the
GOOD
Old
CHURCH

or words to that effect. The Agnoggers were

awfully sick; and got up an opposition meeting advertised in even larger letters

TRIED
and
TRUE
to the
GOOD
OLD
TRUTH

I, of course, went to both, and applauded discreetly from the back of the hall.

Then, there's me and the sculptress. I don't know what to make of that, quite. To begin with, you must know that we have Carnival here, in February. Joy. Youth. Flowers.... Do you know the play of John Gabriel Borkman? Therein is a youth who will fly from his mother in order to LIVE (it happens in Norway also). At intervals he says, the twenty-one year old, 'Ich muss leben, Mutter! Ich muss leben!' They played it here. In came the youth, hat and coat on, and cried that he must live. To emphasize it, he waved his hat. He was, in a circle on the back of his head, bald. He unbuttoned his coat. You saw his figure was so. He was thirty-five and his face lax and fat [drawing of a man with a paunch]. He whined on—Ich muss leben, Mutter!...

It was a Horror. That, my dear, stands for München in Carnival. The theory's all right. But these smooth, baggy, tired faces in the streets with the watery obstinacy 'It is *Fasching*. We are Enjoying ourselves' in the eye....I, anyhow, felt I'd like to be Gay, Young, a Part of it, lightly taking and leaving Joy, like a Greek. So I took off my clothes and went to a Bacchus-Fest, where all was roses and the apparel second century A.D. The young lay round in couples, huggin' and kissin'. I roamed round, wondering if I couldn't, once, be even as they, as the animals. I found a round damp young sculptress, a little like Lord Rosebery to look on. We curled passionate limbs round each other in a perfunctory manner and lay in a corner, sipping each other and beer in polite alternation. I felt that I wasn't really quite the Perfect Greek—that, you know, one wants, if one's Grown-Up, something more than the undraped half of the damp outer expanses of no-one-in-particular, kissing isn't enough, one wants to kiss X or Y. We've got to the point of heightening every such thing by Personality—one doesn't feel 'A NECK!', one feels it's precisely, wonderfully, exactly, and uniquely HER (or HIS) Neck that I am biting (whoever the momentary Her may be). All this, in fact—for she knew no English—I said to her. (In that way it was the Height, better than anything anyone could ever know—the only occasion when I have ever been or shall ever be able to say, absolutely frankly to the person *all* that is in my mind...) We roamed and sat and even danced and lay and talked, and the night wore on. We became more devoted. My head was in her lap, she was munching my fingers, when suddenly I became quite coldly aware of my position in the Universe. 'I, M. or N., who know—and—and—'...the whole thing came to me. I knew there was a Crisis at hand. I turned and said 'My dear Lady Rosebery, this is the Grand Climacteric. By the shaking of your enormous melancholy mouth I see that is also true for you. I haven't the dimmest idea what sort of a Grand Climacteric a Dutch Sculptress has: but I may as well say, frankly, now, that, though I'm really a long way beyond Greece, and I find the point of things rather distinctly elsewhere, and I demand more especially that keen mixture of intimacy and sensuality, body and brain, which Cupid has given us now that we moderns have unblindfolded him, yet, since, even if *one*'s a bit intellectual, it's all right so long as the *other* of the pair—you in fine—is happy, I am, my dear, quite ready...eager...to—to put it colloquially—"go on"!' But then, we put hands on each others' necks and shoulders for the millionth time and found them quite cool, and she raised her watery protruding eyes to mine, and I suddenly realized of her—and she of me—that she was in exactly the same state, that she, too, was trying Greece, was quite a conscious, sensible intellectual, real, modern person—might, in fact, in other circumstances, have been almost, not quite, one of Us—'we found', in short—to quote one

quite admirable sonnet I wrote on the whole thing next afternoon—
'that *we*,

> Were *you* (who-ever *you* may be!) and *I*!'

And, as one can't very well begin a new game at five in the morning,
we very solemnly and pathetically kissed each other on our quiet
intellectual lips and hugged a space and so parted: she to her Mother
(a quiet incredible figure, of whom otherwhen) I to seek the Nubian
who had thrown oranges at me. But she, too, had gone off with
a man: So I wandered down Ludwigstrasse home. It was just short
of dawn. There were nine dustmen, me as a Greek, naked and cold,
and a crapulous moon. I felt rather tired.

This is all true.

And so dull that I've not the heart to tell you anything else. Not
even about the German language. Except that *dudeln* is a verb that
means to play the bagpipes. It has a substantive. When you want to
say: 'What you say is merely a droning ugly lengthy noise without
rational content', you say '*Das ist Dudelei!*' I have yet to find if the
phrase is more than a year old.

And I've no time or space to write to you about your letter and
your damned soul. I had years ago, a scrawl from Gwen: which
I may answer. A nice scrawl. But I was shocked because I thought
the Woman's E.B.'s were wrong—quite wrong. Her M.B.'s[1] anyhow.
Yes: I must write about it. I live such a—somehow—flat life in
München, away from people I know, that it is rather fine to think of
you as living highly. That's rather what I meant by *elevation*—the
way it struck me. I find it gives me something to live on—fills the
trams and streets and the fat German faces with certainty and life. The
white and purple lamps down Theresienstrasse in the dusk—I saw
them, in such a queer coloured evening, the day Ka and Gwen and
Frances wrote. The street hit me violently, being so lovely, and
I flung out arms and gulped. Angels were walking in it. But it
seemed to stand alone and signal to all the other beauties or realities
in Europe, beacons winking at each other above the world. So are
good things in touch. I fantastically thought of the great people
I loved in England burning then so amazingly. 'Jacques...' I informed a prostitute. 'Gwen' I added, to a policeman. Neither
seemed to grasp my point at all. But I was dancing. For a part of

[1] E.B. and M.B. probably mean Ethical Basis and Moral Basis. A bishop who had
been to a lecture by Shaw wrote afterwards to someone at King's that he had been
much interested, but would like to know more about Mr Shaw's ethical basis. Shaw
replied on a postcard: 'Tell the old boy my E.B. is the same as his own.'

such things—a part that appeals to solitaries in Munich, though it's secondary on any real scale of values—I speak as one who adds a little apologetically, that the altogether so glorious landscape is, also, very notable for its cabbage-bearing proclivity—is that it provides one (viz. the solitaries, the, in the hypothesized case, *un*central) with a firmness in life. I sit on you. When—it is part of the game that it comes oftener here—I realize my vileness, I can reflect that, even without me, the world has its points. It is pompously evident that we are all, rather vaguely, carrying Banners of it's never quite clear what Causes against very dimly realized Enemies with great enthusiasm and very probably—in no quite intelligible way—Upward....And solitaries who had previously thought themselves lonely umbrella stands of Banners, scramble up from the mud they relapsed into, and hurry after the retreating dust cloud and the shimmer of what startling drums!...

In a word, Rupert, in München, scores more heavily off God than ever.

*   *   *

I hope you'll be clever and dexterous. Oh, do be clever about marrying, you two. Forbear to buy a house in Hampstead on a 99 years' lease: and oblige yours faithfully   RUPERT

I love you both.
I hope Dudley'll get my card of you two on a walking tour—
Love to that Bald Man and to Katharine and all.

To GEOFFREY KEYNES   *Ohm Strasse 3, München*
                          March [*1911*]

Jeph, my Bird,

Your defence of stamp-collecting was magnificent, but not war.[1] That is to say, it was unprovoked. A guilty conscience! Hast no drug therefore? Can neither balsamum nor mandragora cure the sinful Soul?—Physician, heal thyself!

Yes, I am quite ready to attack the antiquarian, the bibliophile. H. A. James & Sayle stand ready to my axe. Only—I did not. I merely attacked the people who like 'quaintness' in works of art. There are points of resemblance, I admit. Both quietudes are essentially Evasions. But I was not thinking (e.g.) in what *edition* you read Donne: but whether you read him for poetry or for 'prithee's' and 'quotha's'. A different question, eh? Ask Dent what he thinks

---

[1] I had defended collecting the early editions of Donne and Sir Thomas Browne.

about people who like 17th century music for its 'quaintness'. Have you ever seen Americans in a picture-gallery? They're out for quaintness. You've surely found people who like even Blake's prints that way? And Chaucer, and the Ballads, and 15th century prose.... Oh, my God! I could write for hours about it. But I won't. 'What in my youth we used to call not caring about literature.' My Gyff, it's the Last Leprosy. I'm glad *The Knight* went so well. Yes, Dent told me in his thin handwriting, incisively, about it. I always imagine Dent as the Serpent telling Eve about the Apples 'My dear Eve...' pointing out all the blemishes on them, with back-hits at God & Adam, & a rumour that the Holy Ghost was *enceinte*. But so kindly. He ended, however, with a sighed suspicion 'wasn't he too hard on pink people,[1] too intolerant? Mightn't he be doing more harm than good?' I fancied those great spectacles dim.... Wonderful! What's happening to Cambridge?

But I'm sorry to hear some want to go on doing comedies. It is said on all sides 'what a success' the M.D.S. is. Isn't it time we were unpopular again? It's not a good sign, being a success.

My life in München isn't wildly thrilling. I don't emulate Dudley with women. I sit alone in a café or my rooms & read or write. I write about one line a day—very bad. I move occasionally among P[ost] I[mpressionist] artists: & know no German. Rupert in München is quite remarkably like Rupert in other places.

Of course there's Elizabeth [van Rysselbergh]....

But then there's always somebody....

But there's never anybody *quite* like Elizabeth....

Oh! Oh!

But as she's spoilt my life, and given me a devilish cold in the head, let's pass to pleasanter topics.

I don't like your remarks about Eugenics: & I don't see how Jacques has exploded them. His case may have exploded the Eugenists—but we all knew they were fools. There are & always were only three possibilities. (1) we know Jacques *ought* to have children—in which case he *must*; or (2) we know he *oughtn't* to, in which case he *mustn't*; or (3) we don't know—in which case we'll risk it!...I admit the cases shade into each other. But I can't see that Jacques' rotten emotions have anything to do with the matter. Are the Eternal Laws of Good & Bad to be put aside because Jacques thinks he's got a passion for a square-headed woman who cuts wood?

---

[1] Will Rothenstein had remarked to F.C.: 'People are so different, one wonders they aren't quite different colours—some pink and some blue.'

No.

Eh, there'll be quite enough rot shrieked by soft-headed bladders against Eugenics in a few years. The Church'll declare that God gave every man the Right-not-to-use-Preventives. And the Rich will discover that to have an income of less than £100 a year is an hereditary disease: & will try castration to prevent its transmission. And both sides will have as little logic as they have over vivisection. So if the anti-eugenists are as bad as the anti-vivisectionists—let's prevent the Eugenists from sinking as low as the Vivisectionists!

Have you read poor old Shaw on this latter question? He's the only man I've ever heard say any sense on it. And he only goes part of the way.

I'm in Munich. Did you ever feel, when you were a child, about once every six months, a sudden waking, and a knowledge that you were, somehow, on a higher level, & that all the rest of the time you'd been thinking you were living, but really asleep. There were two grades of life, A & B, & the A periods signalled to each other across the valleys. But it was only in A you really knew the difference. So one feels here. I more than exist; I live. Good & bad things happen: & I'm not at all wanting to return to England. Only...there's the suspicion that it's all just not very interesting—that it's B. Or do you remember 'stopping out'?[1] One was there, alive and conscious.

One's whole personality was there—only, somehow, without the point. One was curiously *uncentral*. So, you see, I'm here; only— England's central. And I feel rather on the edge.

This may be true: or it may be a cold. Anyhow, it's undignified. Today is very hot & the children have appeared in spring clothes. I'm restless. I shall shortly vanish. I shall settle in Venice a bit: and return to Munich for the summer. I shall probably find, by then, that as Milton wittily put it, 'The mind [is] in its own place'.[2]

Now, in the name of God the Father....

When you see Godwin [Baynes], give him all my heart & add that the Ewald family send him passionate greetings. Do not forget this.

Love to the Corpses.[3] I write only short poems on the Resurrection morning.

Love to the Census, the Coronation, Cambridge, the Keynes family, Ka, & all else that commence with that noyse.

Thine in the Cause
RUPERT

---

[1] In the sick-room at Rugby.   [2] *Paradise Lost*, Book 1, l. 254.
[3] A reference to the realities at St Bartholomew's Hospital, where I was a student.

To E. P. GOLDSCHMIDT   [Postcard]
3 Ohmstrasse, Gartenhaus I
München
15 March [1911]

Splendid! Can you really support me? I am almost intolerable—
the complete tourist. I pass from Sight to Sight with clammy
British eyes. I have even developed a slight American accent, since
I've been in München. But it is almost impossible to talk about
plans. God! How should a man know where he'll be in a month?
At present I mean to scamper round by Constantinople. But it may
all fade.... Anyhow, I stay here till April 6, on which day they finish
doing The Ring. Then I'll come on to Vienna. But alas! I can only
stay 6 or 7 days. I've an appointment in Bucharest: and another in
Dalmatia! Will that suit—April 7th? It would be noble if you
could give me an attic to sleep in, and tell me the least worst pictures
to see. Most of the day I shall read fantastic books. I do that here.
The books are generally by the sad Keats. I told my family I came
here to learn German. But it is not true. I speak, read and hear only
English. Oh, and write it, so exquisitely!

Do not disturb your Venice plans—I may not come East—if all
my plans crumble.   R. B.

To MRS BROOKE   [*Munich*]
Tuesday, 16 March [14, 1911]

Dear Mother,

Thanks for the *Cambridge Review*. It didn't give a very long
account of *The Knight*. But the performance seems to have been
a success. Half-a-guinea more out of the Westminster[1] for me! I enclose a special postcard which Bavaria had printed for the 90th
birthday of the Prince Regent. That event occurred last Sunday and
was celebrated with great rejoicing. All the streets were decorated
and there were illuminations in the evening and brass bands. And
at midday a man flew over the town and dropped flowers over the
Residenz. Personally I sat in a *café* and read Keats. This postcard is
one of a limited number that were printed. Everyone was very excited
to get one, because it is said they'll go up in value. They're now up to
two or three shillings each! Of course, I didn't get one: but Mrs
Semon, when I was at lunch there on Sunday, gave me one, very

[1] For a translation from the French, 11 March 1911.

kindly. I am advised to send it in an envelope, or it will be stolen. The Semons are very nice. The more I see them, the more I like them. They are so extraordinarily alive, and interesting.

I am going to Vienna at the beginning of April, to stay with Goldschmidt, a very rich and clever Jew who used to be at Trinity. I meant to go right at the beginning of April, but now I find Wagner's *Ring* is being performed then, here, so I think I shall stay for it. Today I went with a Swiss Journalist called Leube, whom I see a good deal of, to Grünwald, a spot 10 miles from Munich and walked for a couple of hours. It was rather a nice change from Munich life: and the country was lovely with the beginning of Spring. It made me remember that every Easter time so far for years I have gone off on a walk or a reading party, and I began to feel my feet itching. I shall wander a bit after Vienna, perhaps. I am sorry you've got such a bad cold. It's a better time to have it, perhaps, than two months earlier. Still, it's annoying, especially missing Beatrice Webb.

* * *

A few hours after I got your letter, I developed a cold, in sympathy. Today I woke speechless: but it is not bad at all. If I'd been in England I might have walked it off. But it is impossible to walk *anything* off with a German (or Swiss)! Their idea of an enormous walking-expedition is four miles in a great-coat and a bowler.

* * *

My ordinary Munich life is progressing as usual. It is startlingly like life elsewhere. Except that one spends so much time in *cafés*— not that that's wasted time, for one's either talking or reading German papers.

There is no other news except that the German wash has shrunk my best flannel shirt literally a foot. It is the most amazing thing I've ever seen. I don't yet see how it's possible.

With love

RUPERT

To CLIVE CAREY [Postcard]
Ohmstrasse 3, G H I München
31 March 1911

Rather! I'm with the Ewalds every other day. They are bubbling with memories of you, and send all their love.

Yes: it *was* Munich in Carnival. I came late home from a *café* one night, and round the corner of a deserted street came a Pierrot and a Pierrette, a Harlequin, a Negress, and a Man in a Top Hat, all in Indian file, stepping in time, very softly, toes pointed, and finger on lip. Whence they came and whither went, I don't know. But it was wonderful.

How's London? I go off Eastward soon. But I return to England in May. Come and bathe at Grantchester. I'm glad *The Knight* was such a success. Did you see Shakespeare in Munich? Hamlet?!

With love

RUPERT

To E. P. GOLDSCHMIDT [Postcard]
Ohmstrasse 3, G.H. I
[*Postmark: 4 April 1911*]

Splendid. I don't find myself able to decide anything. But I feel I shall almost certainly appear on Friday or Saturday at 7 or 9 p.m. In a day or two I'll let you know which. Let it not interfere with your life, anyway. Oh, and I'm not going to—except under extreme pressure—bring dress-clothes with me. For I'm travelling light. So let me know if your way of life requires them.

I can understand German, when simple words are spoken slowly. But I can look as if I understand *everything*. R. B.

To E. P. GOLDSCHMIDT [Postcard]
Wednesday [*Postmark:
München, 5 April 1911*]

The promptings of the Almighty require me to reach Vienna on the evening of *Friday*—the day after tomorrow at 9.30 p.m. The same authority demands that I should go to Servia for ten days—or somewhere—alone to ponder—
I shall certainly miss my train.
München is Hollow. RUPERT BROOKE

To FRANCES CORNFORD *Near Vienna*
[*April 1911*]

There's a high hill which is the extremest edge of the Alps. On it I sit. Five hundred feet down flows the Danube. Westward the ridges I stand on stretch many hundred miles. East there's the endless Hungarian plain: and no large town till you get to Peking. Which is all very wonderful. But I am coming home one day. In May. I thought of you people on Dartmoor, continually. I was stuffing in cities, and hated you. I have a perpetual cold; which is so undignified in a young man seeing barbaric countries. Were the sunsets *awfully* yellow? And did you see Mrs Hern, of Becky Falls? I cough. Oh, damn. Have Jacques and Gwen and co. vanished from the world? I go to Italy. Oh! oh!   RUPERT

To KATHARINE COX   [Postcard]
IV Heugasse 12, Wien
12 April 1911

To begin with, I'm going to return in the middle of May or before or just after: so, the only 'foreign town' you could 'wander into' then to find me'll be 'just dear old Cambridge'—Otherwise it wouldn't quite have bored me. Oh Ka, you should have come sooner!...Lord, it would all have been otherwise! though how anything will be I don't know. I've got to go out and look after a very fine old man[1] in Florence etc. for a fortnight. His wife died in January; they'd been together 42 years, and he's rather broken. He stood a term....(He's my godfather.) He's almost never been abroad: but now Alfred's deposited him in Italy and the good Rupert's going to bring him home. But the good Rupert's plans are smashed. Oh! God! No *rück-sack* tramping through Dalmatia, no Constantinople; just dreary old Florence again; 'Dreary old Florence' is good, isn't it?

Anyhow, you don't come in.

One day between now and June you'll have to give me breakfast —a purely Continental one, I assure you, no eggs.

'Miss Cox, who has begun to make friends with my sister...', extract from a letter from E. J. Dent.

Is there anyone in Venice or Florence or Siena this year?

James [Strachey] told me that Virginia [Stephen] had become a...what is it? 'Neo-Pagan'?...

Lord! Lord! goodnight, children!   RUPERT

[1] Robert Whitelaw, of Rugby.

To E. J. DENT   *c/o E. Ph. G.*
IV Wien, Heugasse 12
13 April 1911

Dear Dent,

Many thanks for the introduction to Maddalene. I am only here for a few days, but I shall try to use it. The Munich introductions were invaluable—most especially to the never sufficiently to be valued Frau Ewald who is my mother and all my aunts. Through her I got to know enough people to make that side of life happy at Munich—the rest being most pleasant anyhow. I was infinitely lethargic but contented there, and I have culled a thousand facile and shallow generalizations about Munich and about Germany with which I won't bore you now. They're mostly not very favourable to the Germans as a race. I need scarcely say, though, that I can't speak a word of German.

I was going to write anyhow—I meant to write before—about your other letter. Yours was the only account (bar a few words from Geoffrey Keynes) I had of *The Knight*. It gave me a very clear idea of it, though. I'm awfully glad, and awfully frightened, that it was such a success! And furious that they want to do another comedy. We've drifted into a habit of electing only actors: and actors are apt to be *geschmacklos*. So that I'm terrified of the whole thing getting out of reach, unalterably controlled by a circle of people who are utterly delightful in themselves and wholly dead collectively. A company of perfect gentlemen delightfully acting the romantic comedies of three hundred years ago—is that anything different from a Twentieth-Century A.D.C.? Isn't it our duty to be unpopular, at length? 'An audience composed of Heads of Houses' gives me the sudden chill consumptives have when they strike a match and find blood on the pillow. Do you remember the description of Keats doing that? But I've a plan for next year I'd like to discuss when I get back, which is, A Triple Programme. It was suggested to me when I saw a Schnitzler one-act play called *Die Letzten Masken* in München. It will exactly suit us—only one female part and that easy, middle-aged and unimportant. It's a quite good (tragic) psycho-logical piece. Some of us could translate it. (It's in *Lebendige Stunde*, which I possess.) Another piece might be a medieval mystery: and the third, farce or comedy. It seems to me a scheme that'd get us out of the rut we're in, without being too risky, and would also give a lot of light for the future.

Your account of Hampton Weekes fills me with suspicion. I detest historical accuracy and the whole Cockerell business: also all artists when they get to moving objects. *The Magic Flute* ought to be great. I feel horribly useless when I think of it. *Ich bin*, my conversations in Munich always laboriously began, *ganz unmusikalisch*. But I daresay you may find you want manual or ambassadorial help in the later part of the year. If so, you can use me. It's sometimes useful to have a few assistants who *don't* want to be stage-managers: and it might set a good example in Cambridge!

*   *   *

I return to Cambridge in May: to the Old Vicarage.

Here I stay with the sad Goldschmidt. He has decayed dreadfully in mind, through living in Vienna. He knows mostly his race, which is absorbed in business. Other people don't talk to a Jew. I have met a hundred Jews; and two other people, who were compensatingly nice, Grete Wiesenthal the *danseuse* who is perfectly charming, and a young artist whom she has married—both Gentiles.

Goldschmidt is very sad because he thinks he offended you very much a year ago. Why is it you can almost *see* a Jew's tail go between his legs? No doubt it's our fault.

We came together, I saw, in the [Cambridge] Review. My article was very scrappy and bad; but it's a difficult play to write about. I didn't mention the music because I knew you were going to. I hope you appreciated my remarks about 'quaintness'—which some people have attacked. Beyond the article and two poems, I have written, as I have read, nothing. How one's character decays in the absence of the stimulus of people one can argue with! Love to Cambridge and London. You'll suddenly find me appearing to lunch one day soon.

Ever

RUPERT

To JACQUES RAVERAT   [Postcard]
München
en route for Hotel Berchielli
Lung' Arno, Florence
Thursday [*20 April 1911*]

Writing to Dudley, the day before yesterday, I forgot to say that I'm sending a box to you—or, more accurately, to me care of you. It may reach you any time between April 26th and the end of May. The cream of the joke is that you'll no doubt have to pay. The key is in my pocket. If the Customs people want it, I'll send it. But no doubt it'll be better to let it lie in their cellar till I reclaim it.

Today it thunders and rains and I'm ill and broken and I go to Florence. Oh, oh! Dudley said you were sitting and thinking of a number of things, at Tintagel, you and he: and thereamong Godwin. Why Godwin? Has Godwin brought himself especially into the public eye lately? Married?

I suppose the Russian Ballet's the only thing that'll happen in England this summer. I'm coming back to see it. I have discovered that I share the Old Vicarage with the Labour Exchange man. Will you come and share it and help squash him for a while? I have found a new profession for you, which I want to tell you about. It is to manage a theatre and design plays and dances. It is quite simple: but there are not very many intelligent people at it yet.

Whereas you'll never be more than a rotten literary painter, if you stick to *Malerei*.

Will Florence be lovely or beastly? Shall I be sick in the train? Will you be in Civilization during the summer? Is there a God? What is man? Cui bono? What porridge had John Keats?

RUPERT

To EDWARD MARSH   *Florence*
                                              25 April 1911

Dear Eddie,

I hope you learnt in Cambridge that I was not faithless, only travelling; & that you did not tramp out to *The Orchard* in search of me. The truth was that in January I determined to fly; & hurried to Munich to learn German & to find a soul. I did not learn German, & I did not find a soul. But I found a stomach; and in three months heard a deal of music.   *   *   *

I have led a most noisome life in Munich, crawling about in trams, eating, & sleeping. I never thought, & barely ever read. I worked hard in an intermittent, doleful way, but never accomplished anything. I spent two months over a poem[1] that describes the feelings of a fish, in the metre of *L'Allegro*. It was meant to be a lyric, but has turned into a work of 70 lines with a moral end. It is quite unintelligible. Beyond that I have written one or two severe & subtle sonnets in my most modern manner—descriptions of very poignant

[1] 'The Fish', *Poems*, 1911.

& complicated situations in the life of today, thrilling with a false simplicity. The one beginning

'I did not think you thought I knew you knew'

has created a sensation in English-speaking circles in Munich.

I have sampled & sought out German culture. It has changed all my political views. I am wildly in favour of nineteen new Dreadnoughts. German culture must never, never, prevail. The Germans are nice, & well-meaning, & they try; but they are SOFT. Oh! They ARE soft. The only good things (outside music perhaps) are the writings of Jews who live in Vienna. Have you heard of Mr Schnitzler's historical play?[1] They act an abbreviated version which lasts from 7 to 12. I saw it. A Hebrew journalist's version of *The Dynasts*; but rather good.

I hear dim rumours that England exists. Is it true? They tell me of a poet who lives in a Breton windmill & writes about London lodging-houses. It sounds charming. I read Shaw's latest. We seem to have left him behind as a dramatist. I want to see our brother [H. O.] Meredith's poems.

Here I live in a pension surrounded by English clergymen & ladies. The pens they use are abominable. They are all Forster characters. Perhaps it is his *pension*. But to live among Forster characters is too bewildering. The 'quaint' remarks fall all round one at meal-time, with little soft plups like pats of butter. 'So strong', they said, next to me, at the concert last night, of the Fifth Symphony, 'and yet so restful, my dear! Not at all what I should call *morbid*, you know!' Just now the young parson & his wife, married a fortnight, have been conversing. 'Are you ready to kick off?' he said. How extraordinary! What does it mean? I *gathered* it merely meant was she ready to go out to San Lorenzo. But does the Church talk like that nowadays?

So I am seeing life. But I am thirsting for Grantchester. I am no longer to be at *The Orchard*, but next door at *The Old Vicarage*, with a wonderful garden. I shall fly from Florence, which is full of painstaking, ugly pictures. But before I go, I've got to settle the question, 'Shall I lay a handful of roses on Mrs Browning's grave? and, if so, how many?' These literary problems are dreadful. And the English Cemetery is so near!

I shall see you in London or Cambridge.   Ever

RUPERT

[1] *Der junge Medardus, dramatische Historie in einem Vorspiel und fünf Aufzügen.* Berlin, 1910.

To GWEN DARWIN *Florence*

[*28*] *April* [*1911*]

'I used' said Iris Runge meditatively, 'to correspond with Gwindolin Darwin.' It was a delightful little party in Frau Ewald's studio, and Fräulein Runge had been playing on her lute and singing French and German folksongs, and in English one or two. In the intervals, just to fill up time, I fixed her with my eye and repeated my difficulter poems in a swift harsh voice. And, of course, the good Frau Ewald sat and made kindly remarks, and Paul was intelligent and enjoyed himself very much. So, as Dent had introduced me to Frau Ewald who introduced me to Iris Runge who had once corresponded with Gwindolin Darwin who, with Dent and me, makes the group of the three Graces (Music, Painting and Literature: it's an allegorical group I recommend to you) in Cambridge, we all felt that, somehow or other, the wheel had come full circle; and so we were very cheerful and happy. But all that, oh dear, was in Munich, and so long ago, and so very far away, as far as—anything else beyond the next street but one, where, they very credibly report, Space ends, and after which all things are equidistant; and it's the same with the day before yesterday. 'Youth! Youth!...Pass the Port!' (Quotation from Mr Conrad.)

* * *

Oh, my God! I do long for England! In Cambridge one meets them in every street. I hear nothing about England except that you contribute pictures to the absolutely latest papers whose pages are the size of postage stamps, and that you are going to marry a foreigner.[1] I'm all for marrying foreigners. The result is said to be good, by experts. Sir Sydney Olivier (himself a Frenchman) has written a book[2] which proves that when a nigger(-ess) marries a white, the offspring are frightfully bright. Is your man a nigger? I was told; but I forget. Myself, being forbidden by my conscience to be endogamous and marry a Scandinavian, have spent years looking for an Iberian—but they're all too Bloody, the Iberians. Now I come to think of it, you (among others) informed me. I thought your letter was red with crime and dark with forebodings. You said you'd all three felt, that week, as if you were in the hands of some external power, rushing you on. External Power? What? God? The Life-Force? Oh, my Gwen, be clean, be clean! It is a monstrosity. There is no power. Things happen: and we pick our

---

[1] Jacques Raverat.   [2] *White Capital and Coloured Labour*. London, 1906.

way among them. That is all. If only you'd been at Camp last year, you'd have learnt that one can sail eight points *into* the wind. To be certain of it is the beginning and end of good behaviour. Oh! Oh! I implore you to extend the flickering fingers of derision at the sky. Did that vapid blue concavity make Brunelleschi build the Pazzi chapel? No! no! Derision's for God. But if it's really that madder horror, the Life-Force, that you're so anthropomorphically female to, even derision won't do. Laws do not wince. When you jeer, they wear the set, tired smile of a man who politely listens without hearing what you say. It only remains to cut them—cut the L.F.

But there aren't laws. There aren't. Take my word for it. I saw— I lifted up the plush curtain and looked behind—nobody, only dust and a slight draught from the left. (*Dust and a little draught* rhymes with *laughed* in the metrical version.) There are no laws; only heaps of happenings, and on each heap stands one of us and crows—a cock on a dung-heap or a beacon on a hill (in Lord Macaulay's poem)[1] according to taste.

So!

It wildly enhances life when one realizes one's free-will (psychological *not* metaphysical). 'Realizes' not intellectually, but again psychologically, as one does with generalizations and moral rules. You learn them till they're so much part of your mind that you've forgotten them. You unconsciously regard or disregard, just as you aren't nowadays aware of disregarding the telegraph-wires in looking at a landscape. So you aren't saying all the time 'This is the only time in all Eternity I shall be in Verona in the Spring' but your nearly-unconscious awareness of the fact heightens all your staring at the Scaligers.[2] Pfu! And so you aren't always only thinking 'I *can* choose which street I go down'; but the background knowledge of the choice deifies the street you do go dancing down. It's queer that *all* the important things somehow partake of the same nature—metre, moral rules, meandering, and all—in involving a well-lit individual thing on a background of unconscious consciousness. The Puritans dimly try to build up the background: the hedonist flaps inconsistently for the thing. *We* go for both; we join up Puritan and Hedonist: we have (once more) only connected.

Well, as for Life. (It's the beginning of summer: and you're making a great splash: So I may as well tell you.)

The great thing about Life is to realize three qualities in things:

---

[1] Macaulay's 'The Armada', 1848.　　[2] Three seventeenth-century Italian painters.

(1) this controllability I've mentioned; (2) Uniqueness; (3) Transience. All things are so; pins, moments, paramours, letters, intimacies, lamps, spinach. I saw Giotto's tower with the sun on it this afternoon. *I saw Giotto's Tower* on April 28, 1911, with *6.0 p.m. sunlight* on it. I needn't have done it. I splendidly came out of all the ages, I hurtled out of the darkness to do it. It was half a second—it changed as I looked; and so did I. It and I and the light won't be quite the same again.

If you let the principles fairly sink in, and begin to realize Life, it leads to fainting in Restaurants, screaming before a wall-paper pattern, and madness in the end.

So I will not show you that great work of mine called 'The Infinitely Transient Pin', which depicts a Universe composed of the following: (a) Four billion immortal consciousnesses.

        (b) The I.T. Pin.

This Universe lasted for nine million years, during all of which, of course, all the consciousnesses were conscious: but the pin only appeared for an hour and a half, exactly in the middle of the nine million years, on an October afternoon from 2.30 to 4, when the light wasn't very good. And it's very apparent how frightfully the Universe was worth while. . . .

I agree with you: this is dull stuff. Why I should write it (and to a Female Artist) I don't very well know. Except that I've got a passion for telling the Truth, and that I love you a great deal. I love you, too, for being joyful, as I sit and imagine you are. Sometimes, at least, I applaud that. Generally I hate you for it. This too is true. You have no conception of the depths of horror of the mean and egoistic human heart. One day—when you are seventy and famous and referred to in the papers as the 'Rosa Bonheur of latterday England'—I will tell you the Whole Truth about the Average Human Heart. And you will die.

But perhaps you've already discovered the Great Secret—the Horror—that joy's as incommunicable as sorrow. Loneliness. Crying alone is bad enough: but that's an old story. It's when one suddenly discovers that one must always and for ever laugh alone. . . . That's one of the things that, two by two, people sooner or later learn, and never tell, for the sake of the young. The other deadly secret is even simpler—everyone finds it out, but the young must *never* be allowed to guess, lest they kill themselves—it is quite simple and very tragic, that people cannot kiss and see each other at the same time.

It's so late: the stars over Fiesole are wonderful: and there are quiet cypresses and a straight white wall opposite. I renounce England: though at present, I've the senile affection of a godfather for it. I think of it, over there (beyond Fiesole). Gwen and Jacques and Ka and Frances and Justin and Dudley and Dr Verrall and the Master and Lord Esher and Mr Balfour...good night, children.

RUPERT

To KATHARINE COX

The Old V[icarage
Grantchester]
Tuesday [*May? 1911*]

Could you read and direct this?

It's terrible that I can't happily write a short letter. I always want to achieve a literary whole, with ἀρχη, μεσον and τελος,[1] all complete, you know. Why can't I just scratch down a typical bit of nothing, quite often, as you do?

I'll try.

I'm still convinced you are abominable about your portrait. What is it? Is it again this unpleasant side of you one occasionally splashes into, this English Ladyhood? Are you for ever playing for safety? Ah, don't be mistaken about English Ladies. They don't say 'I really don't think that sort of thing is at *all* nice...'. That's the Maiden Aunt. The Lady says 'Of course, dear, *I* don't mind personally, but...'. They're quite advanced, you know.

Why shouldn't Geoffrey have a picture of you by Duncan [Grant]? Why wouldn't it 'do'? What *would* people say? (I omit, in writing, you see, your half of the dialogue.) That he's in love with you? Let them say it. Perhaps he is. And when they *have* said it—or said that you're engaged—what then? What follows? Nothing. Nothing. Frightfully nothing.

Oh, come. The group of people we're part of may be awfully honest and genteel and chaste and self-controlled and nice—but at least we're far enough ahead for that. We don't copulate without marriage, but we *do* meet in cafés, talk on buses, go unchaperoned walks, stay with each other, give each other books, without marriage. Can't we even have each other's pictures?

You seem to me to want to make the best of both worlds. You don't seem to realize that being right involves not being always wrong. You cannot serve both G$_{\text{eoffrey}}^{\text{od and}}$ M$_{\text{rs K.}}^{\text{ammon.}}$ Being right

[1] i.e. beginning, middle, and end.

involves shocking the wrong—oh, within limits. You don't seem to me to be in danger of pushing the limits too far, you know.

You see, you're better than Geoffrey. Don't, because you're more conscious, be worse. Portraits are poor things, and it's permissible to refuse on that ground—to urge him to get a refusal of Duncan's forthcoming *genre* pictures till he finds one he likes. But for God's sake don't refuse on the 'It wouldn't do' ground, *nor* on that other wildly irritating one which almost crept in—'can't think what you see in poor little *me!*'!

I bore. I meant to talk about the Apostles—I thought you might be hurt at the way I boomed and trampled—or anyhow at the whole thing. But that and my poem against you can wait. That we'll discuss—on Friday? But don't discuss it otherwhere first, please. I'll explain as far as I can. But be what you so disdain—secret.

Your loving uncle
R.

To KATHARINE COX   O[ld] V[icarage] [Grantchester]
Monday [12 June 1911]

Daphne on a bicycle, Margery, Ethel [Pye] and Hugh [Popham] in a punt, have vanished to Cambridge, to dress for the King's Ball. They were very nice; but so is solitude.

I went to say good-bye for a month, to Frances and Francis last night. They said they weren't coming back till July 9 or 10. You're going to them then for a week. I rather gasped. I thought you were coming about the first, for a fortnight. Does that mean you're going elsewhere for a week, in Cambridge? Here? or at least the Orchard? That'd be splendider than ever: especially if—But anyhow, say you're coming *somewhere* from July 1st....

It's nice of Aunt Annie to remember me. But I wonder what she'd say if she heard how we talk to each other—the things we relate or propose. What'ld even Frances say?... What a hidden, distressful world it is, where people don't know what others do, or might do, and say, and be! O my dear, we'll, in any case, be so intimate, so *damned* intimate.

That's what's called a *cri de cœur*. Oh, how I'll try to cut off all the outside, and tell you truths. Have I ever seemed to you honest? That was when I got one layer away. There are nineteen to come— and when they're off what? Patience! patience! I grow cleaner, perhaps.

What drivel! But it's better than thinking on the old round—
'How many people can one love? How many people should one
love? What is love? If I love at 6 p.m. do I therefore love at 7?
If...' Pah! if you were here, and I, that's all; and then all's clear.
Isn't it damn silly to destroy anything by thinking?

You *must* come this week-end. Then we'll talk: and laugh. You'll
have thought by then. Oh, come, come! Never mind Aunt A.

Come! and talk! and love me—a little. 'Never give all the heart
for love' says Mr Yeats,[1] or sings. Don't give more than I, or
I mayn't dare to look you in the face. And that's wrong again.

Come. We'll be wholly frank. If you don't understand quite—
nor, you know (don't tell anyone) do I. We'll explain and discover
and guess, everything. Pride's irrelevant. Come!

We're very wise and good, though I never see you again after
August. Doesn't God admire us!   I wish you were here

RUPERT

To DUDLEY WARD   *Grantchester*
                                    Wednesday night [*June 1911*]

It seemed to me that if Ka happens not to go to Manchester, or to
go too late, through her disease, I could write to poor Oscar Eckhard
and tell him to show Clothilde and A. M.[2] Manchester. I expect he'd
love it. And otherwise they might find it dull....

It is 10 p.m. and I have worked since 10 a.m. and Anthony is
playing hymns and my brain is—

The only lively thing in this house and garden ever, was the
kitten. I return to find it silent, its limbs queer and a Look in its
eyes....A doctor has been staying here, Mrs Neeve said, and was
consulted. He diagnosed 'Infantile Paralysis'. 'Sometimes think
I oughter put th' pore thing out of its mis'ry' reflected Mrs Neeve.
But she doesn't.

So that's what we've all got—Mrs N., and the hen, and the cat
and the bat, and the house and the louse, and Me and the tree—

Infantile Paralysis

I'm still slowly re-sorting my view of the Universe, after your
unexpected intelligence. I thought it charming of you to dash in on
Sunday morning (it would be, wouldn't it, *too* irrelevant to mention

---

[1] The first line of a poem of that title in *In the Seven Woods*, 1904.
[2] Clothilde 'von Derp' and her sister, Annemarie von der Planitz.

that I reached King's Cross at 11.50—to find, luckily, that since your
Bradshaw saw light the time of that train, like the rest of the world,
had shifted on?). I felt avuncular. My eyeglass was dim—and
I stroked (I remember) my moustache. I was most glad to see you
both. You had (the good part) the air of slight distinction. And you
so refreshingly hadn't, as people generally have under such circumstances, a vista in the background. Generally, I see the haloed
figures—and all their future stretching behind them. You, my good
Peace Investigator, I can see down successive years, balder and
madder ever, but with no fixed *Umgebung* as you recede. You live
in the present; like me (an Infantile Paralytic) and Mr George Meredith (now, alas! dead). I'm so glad you aren't married for a time
yet; and still secretly hopeful you'll cohabit in spells first. Half a year
in St Petersburg, and half alone exploring the Pacific tendencies of
Northern Tibet. Superb existence! 'I shall be with you, and that
merry crew: under the same old flag we used to fly!' As I said to
you once, on the Avon, one Sunday afternoon.

I imagine you're happy: in any case, you're (very likely) alive.
'Dance, my girl, oh, dance! oh, dance!' as the drunk Herr Dillinger
sang to me. 'Usumcasane and Theridamas, Is it not passing brave
to be alive.'[1] Dudley Triumphant! 'Hilda Lessways'[2] out tomorrow.
Me promised £35 for translating. Put your teeth into it, man. And
spit at   George Meredith
           Percy Shelley
           Richelieu
           Stolypin
           Abraham
           Habakkuk
      and Adam

Why? Because they are dead.   R.

To KATHARINE COX   *The Old Vicarage*
                                    Monday night [? *June 1911*]

I started so bad a letter to you on Saturday. There were only four
lines—then I thought for an hour and a half; then I went and bathed.

But today I'm a better person. Though why I should be, God
knows. For Jacques and Gwen were here for half-an-hour: and, at

---

[1] Altered from Marlowe's *Tamburlaine the Great*.   [2] Arnold Bennett's novel.

7, rode off for ever leaving me drooping in front of the Old Vicarage and very sentimental and jealous....But afterwards I've been so lofty and so full of thoughts about Immanence and Transience and the Larger Outlook and so—occasionally—selfless—in a word so very like Ka, for an hour—that now I'm ready to face it with the best of you. In fact about 8.45, down by the Mill House South Walk, I had such an Access of Energy that I saw quite where I was Wrong and determined on nine new things.

Mourning and moping—*Lord!!* How Damnable that one should ever do it. The time that's wasted! The time that's wasted in *anything* except tasting passionately! God, I'll never be flat again. As for last Wednesday and Tuesday, I was too despicable. Never mind, at least you've learnt something. The wise Ka has discovered what a Man of the World's like when he's tired. Or did you know even that before? Or—No: I was too despicable—to collapse on you. Oh! Why do you invite responsibilities? Are you a Cushion, or a Floor? Ignoble thought! But why does your face invite one to load weariness on you? Why does your body appeal for an extra load of responsibilities? Why do your legs demand that one should plunge business affairs on them? Won't you manage my committees? Will you take my soul over entire for me? Won't you write my poems?...

But it's—or something's—cured me. Worse thought than ever! —if spiritual valetudinarianism's to be the rule! Better to marry for health than to use Ka as a remedy for tiredness—or are we to face even *that*? Why not? Perhaps it's even the Ultimate Compliment: After all, if ever you get much fatter, some one of your friends'ld have to cut your toe-nails: which is the same sort of thing. So you might be that as well as everything else—and nothing anywhere be lost....After all, whatever we find each other, I'm better than Galahad, you than Beatrice. So, once a year, as a pat of butter (this weather) plops on a plate or (in Mr Swinburne's lovely words) as night sinks on the sea, I'll sink on you, flabbily, and you'll be a moment's Atlas: and all will be well—as long, Ka, as you don't believe in it at all.

There's something! And I'll give you so many things—oh what can't and won't I, I'm so strong and so clever?—amazing things, glittering, smelling, vast, triumphant...if...if, if...oh, you funny old thing, or anyhow...I write driftingly and madly. I wish you were here. Damn! where *are* you? careering over Wiltshire behind the O'Malley? I've lots of cheery things to say: and also lots of angry things. I shall write you an angry letter. Oh, but I want to see you. Just now I'm scribbling this merely to say that I think you're really a most lovely and splendid and superb and loved* person. Ka. What can I give you? The world? a slight matter....But do hurry to Cambridge, or I'll to London, *soon*. Damn your aunts! Life's so bloody short. Come! Meanwhile I greet you: du wunderschön und allerliebste. I append my list of the best things in the world—a sketchy list: and, of course, generalities have an unfair advantage—

(1)   Lust
(2)   Love
(3)   Keats
(4)   Weather
(4½) go
(5)   Truth
(5½) guts
(6)   Marrons glacés
(7)   Ka

...(29) RUPERT

* By me.

To KATHARINE COX   *24 Bilton Road, Rugby*
Tuesday [*? June 1911*]

Such a fine fellow I am and full of good sense and wisdom and an excellent adviser for puzzling people (until you find out what I've been doing and thinking and feeling, when it all rather falls to pieces) that I really ought to have had the determination to plunge up North. But a foreigner gets that *caught* in London, and each moment I might have rushed for a train there was always someone and something to be done next moment so...I didn't rush. And finally I selfishly chose to go to Limpsfield. And then Cambridge. And then Ma.

Oh, and a few searching conversations with various Londoners convinced me (a not much changed Rupert) that I, alone in the world, quite understood the whole situation, and especially your condition and thoughts from moment to moment. So I *must* meet you, and we'll settle each other's business. I've got the rest off my hands! I've told Jacques about Marriage and Dudley about Women and Gwen about Babies and James about Wisdom, and I've brought Cambridge up to the level in European culture. Now for you! Besides, we'd mitigate each other's loneliness. I stayed at the Grange with Gwen and Jacques: and I'd a bad touch of that disease you too'll have known. The ignoblest jealousy mixed with loneliness to make me flog my pillow with an umbrella till I was exhausted, when I was shut into my lonely room to read myself to sleep, and they went roaming off to tell each other truths. Oh, it's too damnably irrelevant! But we might convalesce together....

I guess it'd be better for you to see me before you get to London. I go to Cambridge Saturday morning. The good Dudley insists on bringing up his German goddesses[1] to stay with me. But if you'll tell me which half-day you'll come, I'll clear it, and we'll slink off together. You might also come to Conduit Head[2] on Sunday evening: and at 10 we'll go off to Madingley Hill to watch stars. And if you'd stay till Monday afternoon, there'd be as much of Monday as you'd time for.

And I will tell you about Literature: and you will show me your latest poems.

Oh, quite soon, I pray you: and if you can't stop in Cambridge the week-end, won't you break your journey there for five hours, one day?

Auf wiedersehen

I *am* mean.

RUPERT

To KATHARINE COX

[Postcard]
[*Grantchester*]
[*Postmark: Trumpington 18 June 1911*]

You're to come quite early on Monday. I'm getting, occasionally, some of the people you ought to see.... You'll have quite a gay time. Goldie [Lowes Dickinson] comes to tea on Tuesday. I think I'll get Lytton [Strachey] to lunch tomorrow. Myself, I shall be on my dignity. I step down, now, for a moment to inquire if my toothbrush is in Hester's[3] room. Then I ascend again for ever. As (once more) Mr Yeats says[4]

> 'Love's law being broken, I shall stand alone
> Upon the eternal summits, and call out,
> And you can never come there, being banished.'

Do you see my handkerchief, aloft, in the distance? Oh—I shall often wave! R.

---

[1] Annemarie von der Planitz and her sister.   [2] The home of the Cornfords.
[3] Hester Cox, Katharine's elder sister.   [4] *Deirdre* (1907), lines 622–4.

To EDWARD MARSH *The Old Vicarage*
Grantchester
Wednesday [5 *July 1911*]

That week-end, the 23rd, turns out to be perfectly all right. You'll find me quite wild with reading and the country. Come prepared for bathing and clad in primitive clothes. Bring books also: one talks eight hours, reads eight, and sleeps eight.

The food is extremely simple and extremely unwholesome.

R

To KATHARINE COX *Grantchester*
Wednesday [*July 1911*]

Rising earlyish, and bathing at noon, and a heavy lunch, make me so sleepy now (2.30) that I'm sure I'll miss the 2.55 post. Lying on this rug I'll alternately scribble a line and doze. After all, it's only just a sort of feeble attempt to cheer you. There is no wind and no sun, only a sort of warm haze, and through it the mingled country sounds of a bee, a mowing machine, a mill, and a sparrow. Peace! And the content of working all day at Webster. Reading and reading and reading. It's not noble, but it's so happy. Oh, *come* here!

* * *

What's the H[eart] to H[eart] to be about, this time? Oh Ka dear, my principles are always stiffening me up to be on the point of disapproving of you and snarling—I mean rebuking—but I always rather break down when it turns out to be about, after all, *you.* And I'll not have you sad. Oh, my dear, my dear, you mustn't be sad.

It's evening. Sheppard, Taylor and Shove dropped in and demanded tea. I'm going on to read Webster. Farewell. Shall we have supper here and a walk, on Friday? RUPERT

To DAVID GARNETT *24 Bilton Road, Rugby*
July [*1911*]

My dear,

(I called you *Bunny* because I thought it meant you had a mind like a rabbit; and I agreed. {Note: it's not the same as having a mind like a rabbit's.})

(But I apologize, God forbid I should have any connexion with the Oliviers. I am English: and a logician.)

I'm rather glad you haven't my razors. For you would only have cut your admirable amorphous indeterminate chin. And then you might have turned out to have *Haemophilia,* and have bled to death.

* * *

Why do you write, I wonder, on paper that is either an advertisement of a Roumanian paper-merchant or a Home-Rule Manifesto?

Why do you write, I wonder, sitting on the ground with your chin over the edge of the table? You will only bite your tongue.

As for this monstrous modern movement against my handwriting —I hate it. And despise it. For the occasion I have stooped to an even more round-hand copper-plate than ever. It only requires a *quick* reader. You people stumble and chew. And you—individually— after all can read like a Man and not like a savage (like the rest of them). You said so. A Novel an Hour. Nor is your own handwriting lady-like, except in as far as it is literate.

It was, after all, your grand*mother* I meant. Unless indeed she—or rather, in that case, the other person—lied. One of them, anyhow, thought well of my father's schoolmastering. Perhaps you *do* know the Curwens[1] . . .

Oh, David, Life (as my uncle once said) is very Strange. Americans are DEVILS.

Solipsistically

RUPERT

I'm afraid Hindhead's too far East. But if after the 16th inst, you're free and require peace, *come* to us, West of Winchester, I fancy. There'll be only Dudley & I. We'll give you our address to find us on any day.

To KATHARINE COX

Rugby
Saturday [?*July 1911*]

* * *

Schéhérazade[2] was thrilling again. Bryn and Daphne, of course, didn't like it. What sloughs they must be, within, the Glorious, really. And how good one is—we, I mean, are.

And now, I'm going once more. On Monday with Margery and, probably, Noel. We feed at 7.15, Eustace Miles. James'll be there,

---

[1] Boys who were at School Field, Rugby.   [2] The Diaghilev ballet.

I hope. Won't you? And anyone you're going with. (I trust you have tickets.) I'd like to see you. I've got to go to Cambridge at 9.0 next morning. Won't you? (Where are you till the 14th?)

Your sonnets—where are they?[1]

Yesterday I got up at 4.30—bathed above Oxford: worked in the Bodleian, went to the Grafton Galleries, saw Schéhérazade, called on Geoffrey, talked to James, and caught the midnight train down here. At 2.30 I walked up, strung with bags, this mile and a half. It was incredibly hot. I crept to bed at 5.30: after a cold bath, and claret and soda. Living is sheer ecstasy. How one packs things!

Your letter—it's half castrated by your punctuation; but I made out some of it.

Ka, they've been Talking, about You and Me. Talking! Awful. If you only knew what James said Virginia said So and So said...! These mediate ignorances! But your repper, my dear, is going. Oh, among the quite Advanced. I, it is thought, am rather beastly; you rather pitiable. How otherwise, you see, can a situation be explained where two people have, in no Morning Post, 'arranged a marriage'? Isn't it too monstrous? They gibber night and morning, teleologically. 'How will it end?' They impudently ache for us. There are, you must know, only two 'endings' for this or any other case. (1) Marriage. (2) Not. (1) is entirely good, (2) entirely bad. And the goodness and badness are *ever* so retrospective.

All the worst things drive them on. The furtive craving to interfere in other people's lusts, the fear of unusual events, and the rest. The mother and the clergyman are at one in these kind hearts. False ethics and funk have Raised one another. They live for the future like Puritans and judge by the end like Parsons. Is there no SIGN to give them, that each minute is final, and each heart alone? Sonnet? I'll sonnet ye!

> 'Marriage was on their lips and in their eyes.
> Churches they scorned! their hearts unshackled stars
> Scurrying, fearless down bewildered skies
> To Love's own sanctuary, the Registrar's.
> The kind souls trust that "all will end all right":
> "No painful sequel" hope the timid souls:
> Two good friends wed is the dear souls' delight.
> Not for the game they play, but for the goals.

---

[1] K.C.'s sonnets were a standing joke because she was so utterly incapable of writing any.

"Will Ka and Rupert marry? Let us pray!"
If Ka or Rupert loves, they hardly care;
Whose morrows lead to—our least yesterday!
Who pray for day all day, till night is there.
"The Means! How will it *end*?" And all the while
The Eternal End goes by: We love, and smile.'

Hurried dreariness. We will talk. Do not fret. That's hardly worth
the saying. We are covered from sight by a blazing veil of rightness.
We hold what immeasurably trump cards! But have no mercy, if
Virginia starts (supposing she really *did* (don't tell him) on James)
on you.

You're, it comes to me, 'comfortably furled a million miles away
from this damn world'. Are your lips six red roses on one stalk?
I wish I knew your address; or you.

I suppose you'll never get this.   R.

To ERICA COTTERILL   *The Old Vicarage*
                                    Grantchester, Cambridge
                                      18 September 1911

Damn! I've lost your letter, and this'll have to go round about.

Your invitation trickled round England after me. Finally—long
after the day you'd invited me for—it ran me to earth in a camp ten
miles north of Dartmoor. Now I've returned to comparative civilization and absolute sanity, I'm trying to answer it. And I've lost it!
Oh! Oh!

I should have liked to come. But it was anyway impossible. But
I'll see you in London. I shall be there every now and then through
the autumn—perhaps living there, I too, a week or so, working in
the British Museum. Tell me where you're living, & I'll let you know
when I appear. You will hate me. I have developed into a ferocious
man. I live a dark, passionate, sudden life, compounded of scholarship & tragedy. I often shout suddenly and leave the room. All the
Spring I lived in Germany & learnt strange things. All the summer
I alternated between seeing the Russian Ballet at Covent Garden and
writing sonnets on the lawn here. This is a deserted, lonely, dank,
ruined, overgrown, gloomy, lovely house: with a garden to match.
It is all five hundred years old, and fusty with the ghosts of generations of mouldering clergymen. It is a fit place to write my kind of
poetry in (exactly what, and how frightfully modern, it is, you will

learn in October or November if you have sufficient money to buy, and intelligence to understand, my book).

I'd like to see you again. Several times during the summer I vaguely thought of telegraphing. . . . But there's no office here, and I never could remember your address.

I rather liked your book:[1] which some unheard-of publisher produced. I never, you know, applauded your literary style throughout. But when it comes off, it carries more conviction than most. And the subject seemed interesting (which it doesn't in most books) in spite of circumlocutions—which sometimes made it difficulter to follow than if you'd been able to call a spade a spade. Oh but this is very disagreeable and conceited of me. I wish, though, also, you'd finished the play as a play. Perhaps you're doing another in your omnibuses? I hope your constitution's improved enough to allow it. Anyway, I liked this '*Account*' book.

Oh, I'll see you somewhen, and give you bags of advice: as an Old Vicar should. My dear, I've a superb grip of Life; a pellucid and lovely literary style; a vast stock of information; and an immense happiness.

They are at your disposal

RUPERT

To FRANK SIDGWICK   *The Old Vicarage*
Grantchester
Wednesday, 20 September 1911

Dear Sidgwick,

Is the objection to 'Lust' only that it's bad as poetry, or also that it's shocking as morals? I can't see that it's any worse as poetry than the rest of the book[2] (except one or two poems). Technically it's not much, I admit; but any fool can write a technically good sonnet. And I hoped that the newness of the idea might counterbalance that.

If it's thought to be improper, it must be sadly misunderstood. Its meaning is quite 'proper' and so moral as to be almost untrue. If the title's too startling *Libido*[3] or 'Ἐπιθυμία could be substituted; tho I'm afraid that would only make it more obscure.

My own feeling is that to remove it would be to overbalance the book still more in the direction of unimportant prettiness. There's

---

[1] *A Professional Socialist*, New Age Press, 1908, a play by E.C.
[2] *Poems*. Sidgwick & Jackson, 1911. In a letter dated 13 July 1911 Sidgwick had also objected to including a poem called 'The Seasick Lover'; this was, however, printed as 'A Channel Passage'.   [3] This suggestion was adopted.

plenty of that sort of wash in the other pages for the readers who like it. They needn't read the parts which are new and serious. About a lot of the book I occasionally feel like Ophelia, that I've turned 'Thought and affliction, passion, hell itself. . . to favour and to prettiness'. So I'm extra keen about the places where I think that thought and passion are, however clumsily, *not* so transmuted. This was one of them. It seemed to have qualities of reality & novelty that made up for the clumsiness. The expression is only good in places. But the idea seemed to me important and moving. I know a lot of people who like my earlier work better than my present. They will barely notice this sonnet. There are others who prefer my present stuff. I've shown the sonnet to some of them. They thought it good (by my standards, whatever they may be!). And they weren't, I assure you—though they were of all ages and kinds—shocked.

I should like it to stand, as a representative in the book of abortive poetry against literary verse; & because I can't see any aesthetic ground against it which would not damn ¾ of the rest of the book too, or any moral ground at all. If your reader has misunderstood the sonnet I will explain it to him. If you really think it finally ruins the chances of the book, I suppose it ought to go. If you think it will only decrease the sales, we could make some additional agreement about the number sold within the year, or something. If it's too near the beginning, it can be buried.

Yours

RUPERT BROOKE

I should like to know if the acknowledgement at the beginning is all right.

I can come to London (preferably Thursdays or Saturdays) if there's anything that needs discussion.

To E. J. DENT   *The Old Vicarage*
                                   Grantchester
                                   20 September 1911

Dear Dent,

I know you are out of Cambridge for some time—so at least the King's Porter said.

I'm going to be here till the beginning of term: then I'm going to be in London four or five weeks, spending week-ends here, and returning here for the last three weeks of term to finish up my

Dissertation. I thought it would be a nice occupation while I was working to take singing lessons. I don't want to sing much; and I don't imagine I should ever be able to. But I want to be able to get hold of airs; and chiefly I've an idea it might train my dreadfully uneducated ear a little. Which would be useful.

At present I've got the rudimentary beginnings of an ear; and no control at all over my voice. It might all turn out, after a few attempts, vain. But I should like to try.

I thought you might be able to tell me where to go for a teacher. I've very little money: and peculiar times. But I shouldn't want anyone very fine. If there were anyone in Cambridge I could start with them now and continue in term on Saturday afternoons and Monday mornings. If I could find someone in London I could go to them in October and November.

*   *   *

I've come back from camping in Devonshire to work in comparative civilization. In the intervals of Webster I correspond with my publisher, who's always discovering new indecencies in my poems and demanding omissions.

Yours

RUPERT BROOKE

To KATHARINE COX   *Grantchester*
                                Friday night [September 1911]

'You know', he finally said—abruptly, after a silence and a conversation on the General Aspects—with a funny proud shyness, rather red, 'she only weighs six stone thirteen—no, eleven!' He was almost unconscious. I said 'Good Lord!'

I *didn't* get much sleep that night, and I've been—in consequence of that, and work—very ill ever since. We walked it all out over—what's it called? Hampstead Heath! There were three of us: Dudley, myself, and a cat that attached itself to us, and kept getting between Dudley's legs. He was always going back to a new explicatory tangle in the infinite involutions of the summer; and always the cat tripped him. 'And then—oh! that was the simply beastliest time of the lot. I didn't know—(oh, *damn* the beast!) Oh Gaw-awd! it *was* bloody', etc. I was so tired that I didn't evince or even feel, proper surprise; or interest. I think I was rather beastly. But he was quite central and preoccupied, and also tired. I don't think he noticed much.

I *was* surprised, though. I'd (and even, I think *you*'d!) never glimmered a suspicion. I'd noticed Anna Marie (how *is* she spelt?) was cheerier than in July. But an Engagement!...

Luckily it's not very definite. Dudley won't give up his freedom for some years yet. But I'd so idolized him. I'd made such a speech about him to James, that afternoon. All these others, A. Y. Campbell, Bill Hubback, Jacques, Donald [Robertson]—how dull they were, in varying degrees! How their life was ended, their feelings domesticated! How superbly Dudley, with his real emotions, his thrilling life, shone out against them! The Romance! The Supremacy! The Glory!

James was one shrill cheer the whole time. And a few hours later 'You see...(It's funny it's so damned hard to begin)...Anna Marie and I are going to be married...'.

Into one of the privatest most frequent shrines in all my chapels, with a pink light ever burning therein, the deity himself threw such a bomb-shell!...My last hope gone! I felt so awfully lonely.

But I didn't, of course, say so: nor shan't, till he's recovered and rested. (I'm very sorry you're not going to see him in Manchester now.) Next morning they he and she (A. M. deliciously insisted on it, I gathered) dashed round *Adieu ʒu sagen*. The ladies were off to Manchester at 12: I at 11.45 to Cambridge. Male and female they stood suddenly before me, hand, I almost think, in hand. So, of course, I cried. (They were *so* small!)

Hush! Hush!

I really like her so *very* much. She's the nicest stranger I ever met, almost. I only occasionally drop a tear for the great wild days of Clothilde (who's not 1/20 so nice—so *nice*, you know).

And they won't ever marry, I rather believe. Of course, that means groans and tears in 1912–13. But it's now, now. Hurray!

But I didn't mean to write about that, at all. We'll nod over it, one day, soon. And you'll, I know, pull everything very slowly to pieces. (I've an irresistibly vivid picture—from natural history books of remotest childhood—of a Bruin scooping wild honey from a hollow tree-trunk with long slow sweeps of the paw—oh! and licking it.)

I beg pardon.

Nor do I want to answer your letter. It would require time and emotion. And I want to give them both Mr George Chapman. Oh, I did like your letter. Though there were bits—notably a passage on *unconscious idealists* and *undergrowth*—I could make *nothing* of.

But...oh, my dear, I can't answer that sort of letter, when I'm working. I only—oh, want to see you (over in that chair...). And I feel rather ashamed....

*   *   *

Tell me immediately what's to happen. And send me all your addresses. I may have to telegraph.

I say, *do* think of something romantically exciting and interesting. I'm getting excited. Lincolnshire? The Peak? The Fens? East London?...

Good-night
RUPERT

Lulworth, if you like. But *somewhere*.

To KATHARINE COX *[Grantchester]*
Saturday midday
[September 1911]

A note from James. Belgium was too much for him. Life always is—knocks him down again and again. As Mr Johnson will the Bombardier.[1] (And then we lose S. Africa.)

*   *   *

I keep reading Hilda Lessways instead of work.
Write: a ard.
I hope you are very well. I am very well. I must stop now.

RUPERT

I've just written and ordered two amphitheatre seats for the first Ring. To be on the Safe Side. Dates and prices in today's Times. I mistrust James' Box. Will you come to one? which?

P.P.P.S. Correspondence with Frank [Sidgwick] over the sonnet entitled *Lust*. Did I tell you? He wanted it left out. Said a woman's smell was an excrement. I wrote an *immense* letter, saying it was the only serious poem in the book, and a million other things. This morning he's come down like a shot possum. Compromise: It's to be printed, but called *Libido* (Latin)! Let us Pray.

[1] Two prize-fighters, Jack Johnson and Bombardier Billy Wells.

To KATHARINE COX [*London*]
Memorandum from Rupert [*September*] *1911*
In bed To Ka

It's really very little after 11; and I've had to throw *two* rugs off,
I'm so hot; and the bed's so comfortable (and so big. . . I beg pardon)
—so you may turn off the mother spout. Yourself, you're having to
listen to Hester's tales, and to laugh and soothe her and love her—oh,
not grudgingly. . .but you ought to be ten minutes off sleep as I am.

I'm so ashamed of myself. It's a thing of character you see: not
physical. If it were just being bodily tired. . .but *you're* bodily tired,
but you don't give like me.

It's so maddening not to be able to keep up to the liveliest level
always, when one knows there's no *reason* why one shouldn't. Why
isn't the brain always dashing about after new ideas? Why isn't one
always tasting very consciously? And what'll one say in the
gutter
grave   } when one remembers how things were wasted
vase (if cremated)
—opportunities—on that day, and that—

To have such Mondays and Tuesdays, and to be grumpy on
Wednesday; oughtn't I to be wiped up? And I spend my time in
thinking I'm putting others on their right paths. An Influence.
What a comic figure!

I'm determined to live like a motor-car, or a needle, or Mr [Arnold]
Bennett, or a planetary system, or whatever else is always at the
keenest and wildest pitch of activity. When you see me foolish pinch
me and go away to sensibler things! I shall always object to you
wasting your time in being too often charitable to other people: but
I'll kill you if you waste it being charitable to me.

Oh, I *will* startle you. I'm going to be so damn intense. I'm going
to crowd more into every remark I make to you or bite I give your
finger than even you have in a whole fat day. I'll make more out of
roll and butter in this A.B.C.[1] (it's morning now, and breakfast) than
you'll ever get from your eggs and fruit and home-made jam. I'll
liven you!

You're so fine.

But I'll wake you up a lot yet. And I'll tell you all the secrets of
Hell: and you shall tell me unmentionable things.

Nothing matters except the moment.   RUPERT

[1] An Aerated Bread Company's restaurant, known as an ABC.

To KATHARINE COX   *67 Belsize Park Gardens*
                                            Hampstead, N.W.
                                            [*September 1911*]

Date: Friday midnight.

I lingered on at Camp and then went across and stayed with Lytton and James and Becky: and this evening James and I reached London, in time for the Fifth Symphony.

After which we picked up old David [Garnett] outside—solitary and sad—and introduced him to the National Liberal Club. And, as we all sipped our hot milk there, in, of course, trotted Dudley. 'Had we had news of Ka?' he asked. 'Ten days ago.' He fairly triumphed over us—oh, he'd had recent news, *most* exciting. I was white, prepared to hear you'd contracted a Scotch marriage with a Duke or a—what are they?—gillie. Should I swoon? or cry? But it was only (or even) a dirty card saying you were—ill. *Ill*—you—oh my Ka! Are you? what with? how ill? Why are you so damned far off? Oh, come down to England! And this evening, during a Bach thing, it suddenly came on me you were drowned (trying to save Frances). I felt certain, for five minutes. And then Dudley's tidings brought it all up again. I knew it was a telepath. You've died of typhoid. Woman, you're lying dead now. I've thought it all out, all the damned details. Oh, Lord, Lord! You're not to be dead; it won't bear thinking on. I *will* sleep...I can't help thinking of the idea of that funny slow strong body having stopped. Oh God, it's madness to figure your eyes. But think (I'll be sane) how extraordinarily confident of immortality we slip round corners and away for whole months. And any silly tangle of chance may do for us. That you stopped loving me, or I you—that'd be a little thing. But that we'd never more for all ages know that queer lovely laughing absurd craning peering wrinkled wise kindly Christian clever old slow thing called Ka—it's a devilish unmentionable monstrous idiocy that only comes to tired fools like Rupert—after—the Fifth Symphony.

I'm foolish tonight. I'll write better tomorrow.

To CLIVE CAREY   *24 Bilton Road* [*Rugby*]
                                          Thursday, 12 October 1911

Clive dear,

I've come, lately, to that period of life at which every young man stops short and looks round. I have turned the corner. I am on the way downhill. In short, I am twenty...whatever it is: I forget for the moment. And it seemed to me I ought to learn to control my voice. With death so near there isn't a moment to lose. I must learn to sing. Or, if that's impossible, learn to hear. It seemed to me that if I was taught singing by some sensible person who understood all the time that I couldn't ever sing properly whatever happened, I might gain anyhow two things (1) be able to hear music (which I've begun to try to do) with as much appreciation as is possible for a non-musician, (2) have a better and more manageable reading and speaking voice.

Both would be worth while.

I asked Dent, and he advised me to write to you. I thought you'd probably be too full, and anyhow not wanting to waste time on an unmusical person. But Dent thought you'd at least, if that was so, know of somebody. What I want is somebody intelligent, who understands voices—as one can see these ordinary teachers probably don't. What I am is a very poor, quite sensible, but (at present) almost entirely earless and unmusical prospective pupil; who is working rather hard at other things. I shall be in London for some five weeks, beginning during next week. What shall I do? If you've any advice to offer me, and time to offer it, could you send me a line about it, and, perhaps, eat with me in some insalubrious cookshop?

I'm here till Saturday. The Old Vicarage, Grantchester, the week-end; and London on Monday, and again on Thursday, onwards. King's or Grantchester always gets to me. Ever

RUPERT

To KATHARINE COX   *The Athenaeum*[1] [*London*]
                                              [*1911*]
Dear Miss Cox,

It was more than kind of you to let me see some of your work. I need hardly say how much I was interested in it. Your thought seems to me elevating and restrained: your style subdued and digni-fied. It is obvious that you have studied with profit the masterpieces of our great stylists. You have shown me a work of indeed notable promise; and I have spent many happy hours with it. If I say that, with all its merits, it seems to my ears, unused, I know, to modern fashions, a little *unfinished*, I hope you will not put me down at once for an 'old fogey'!

---

[1] This address, like the letter, is not to be taken seriously.

I hope very much you will go on steadfastly in the path you have chosen for yourself. The profession of a woman of letters is an arduous, sometimes even a *dangerous*, one. But I feel sure you will, in old age, be able to look back with contentment, feeling that your life has not been altogether ill-spent. And you will always have the satisfaction of knowing that you have chosen for yourself the walk of life for which your aunt has always destined you. I need say no more: but remain   *Yours very sincerely*

RUPERT C. BROOKE

P.S. I must just add that the unassuming and silent way in which you left your little essay among my papers, to catch my eye when it might happen, has touched me as being so delicately and tactfully what only *you*, if I may say so, could have done.

R. C. B.

To KATHARINE COX   *Grantchester*
                                Sunday dawn [*October 1911*]

Damn you, I am not tired! I am as lively as God, and working like an engine. If ever you pretend I am tired or lay your large pity on me, I shall suddenly remove your pince-nez and burn them, and then you will never be able to distinguish me from Owen [O' Malley] again.   *   *   *

This letter was interrupted, in the middle. Do you smell soot? I've been the last half hour with my arms up a chimney. The beam in the kitchen chimney caught fire. 'These old houses!' we kept panting. It was so difficult to get at, being also in part the chimney piece. Only Mrs Neeve, I, and Mr Wallis at home. Mr W. dashed for the Brigade on his motor-bike. An ever so cheerful and able British working-man and I attacked the house with buckets and a pickaxe. The bowels of the chimbley are now on the kitchen table, charred but out. And, worst horror, the Brigade's somewhere crashingly on the way. I was masterful at the always slightly wrong minute—but gave very decisive directions for the rest of the day.

Chapman,[1] now.

You on Wednesday.   RUPERT

P.S. There are a lot of men in such *wonderful* clothes in the kitchen. Taking the rest out. I admire them *so* much. One is so

[1] The Elizabethan dramatist.

beautiful, shining.... Mrs Neeve says: 'There is no doubt we were all Lying in Danger last night.'

Mrs Stevenson says: 'Thank Goodness it's morning and not night, *now*!'

And I—I see—was so dreadfully irrelevant all the time. Oh!

To KATHARINE COX   *The Union Society*
                                          Cambridge
                              Tuesday [*November 1911*]

I worked till 1: and then ran nearly to Haslingfield and back before lunch, thinking over the next bit. There was such a clearness and frosty sun. Some men under a haystack, eating their lunch, shouted how fine a day it was. I shouted back it was very cold; and ran on. They roared with laughter and shouted after me that with that fine crop of hair I oughtn't to be cold.... It was wonderful and very clean out there. I thought of all you Londoners, dirty old drivellers. Now I'm come in to rehearse my nigger part and to work. I've realized that taking part in theatrical performances is the only thing worth doing. And it's so *very* nice being an intelligent subordinate. I'm a very good subordinate—it's such a test. I'm thought not to dance well: but my intelligence and devotion have brought me rapidly to the front. I am now the most important of 7 negroes.

*   *   *

RUPERT

To KATHARINE COX   *Rugby*
                                    [*November 1911*]

I wonder if it *is* very degraded—or very annoying—to send you this.[1] Not annoying, I think, because you after all needn't look at them. It rather pleases me, sending them. If you've time and pleasure, look at them. I really want (but not badly) advice about corrections. If you do look through, say what you think about *Capitals*, and *Italics*. And special points. Or say nothing. You may touch anything, from commas upwards. And you may write or draw on the proofs. These don't go beyond me.

'Town and Country' *may* be rewritten.

[1] Proofs of *Poems*, 1911.

In any case, I want these back on Wednesday. To get here on Wednesday.

The dissertation is moribund.

I am very much excited.

You are Ka—

dein

RUPERT

If James is with you, show them him, if you like. He has Judgement. But not to anyone else, probably, *because* no one else has already seen all. And it's nicer to see them clean and whole, first view. But of course (and it's that that's so extraordinarily nice) I don't explain or enjoin about them, to you. I merely enclose them.

It's rather a score, woman, to have the feeling of motherhood before you!

I think *Kindliness* and three more so *good*.

To MAYNARD KEYNES

76 Charlotte Street
Bloomsbury
[*13 December 1911*]

Dear Maynard,

Signor Bekashy[1] (as it's pronounced), I, Noel, Bryn, perhaps Margery, are going to start the reading-party on the 27th (or so). Ka appears some few days later. James for a week-end; may be. But some (e.g. Ka and Margery) will not overlap; so there'll not be too much of a crowd.

I hope you'll come. You can stay on and sample Gerald if you like: later. But it's only in that first week we'll go decent walks.

I'm going to write a play. If it fits your dates, could you bring Duncan [Grant] along? I find that Creative Artists are so particularly *sympathisch*.

*   *   *   RUPERT

P.S. I appear in your house tomorrow at dawn.

[1] Ferenc Békássy, a Hungarian undergraduate of King's and a poet, killed in the Bukovina in 1915.

To BILL AND EVA HUBBACK   *24 Bilton Road, Rugby*
20 December 1911

Bill!

Eva!

I'm sending you a book.[1] It is horrible of me. If you hate it, burn it. Anyhow, never refer to it.

I made all arrangements to go to the *Alcestis* on Friday. And that idiot James Strachey, to whom I left negotiations, forgot to post a letter. So I missed it. I'm very angry with James and sorry for myself.

(Eva! I once let you, didn't I, take off H. O. Meredith's poems, my copy? Eva, *WHERE IS THAT BOOK?*)

I shall never see you again. I am going to the University of *Weiss-nicht-wo* for a Term, to learn Callisthenics. I have to leave England, because of my book. It is too Pure. And my Godfather and seven other Rugby masters cut me in the street yesterday.

RUPERT

To SYBIL PYE   *24 Bilton Road, Rugby*
22 December 1911

Dear Sybil,

Your letter threw the only rays of joy for months into the grey life of a literary archaeologist. It gives me the mean and degraded joy of a parent (ugh!) when people like my poems—the ones I like, I mean, and the ones by *me*, not by a frail pleasant youth of the same name who died in 1908. I am ashamed of being so pleased by your comments; but I cannot suppress it. The compliments, even, of those who do not understand poetry fill me with a comic and irrational pleasure; the compliments of those who do, make me determined to continue to write poems and plays, however little I earn. I'm glad—now that you're liking some of my later poems in the way you do like them, makes me think you understand poetry—to remember that I knew so, anyhow, before I knew what you'd say or feel about them. The most cynical part of my reason confesses there may be something in it.... Huh! I shall write much better things in the next year or two, now I've time to practise the thing seriously and continually.

When you see copies of my book, will you surreptitiously change 'greasy' to 'queasy' (p. 35 last line), insert 'so' before 'fair' p. 32,

[1] *Poems*, 1911.

and write LUST for LIBIDO p. 34? The first two are misprints; the last is a sacrifice to my publisher's pudency. Other mistakes you may have spotted.

You'll notice I *didn't* alter the title of *The Goddess in the Wood*, or add a note. But it wasn't for want of thought. I thought, on the whole, it was best to leave it to leak out what it was about.

I wish I'd been at the Russians that day. I'm glad you saw them. I went some fifteen times during the year. They, if anything can, redeem our civilization. I'd give everything to be a ballet-designer.

I, at that time, was labouring in The Old Vicarage (a House of Ussher this weather). I'm now sleeping off the effects of months of horrid and increasing toil. I have slept 15 hours of the last twenty-four, mostly in arm-chairs. This may excuse the stupid state I—obviously—am in, just now. I am glad you liked the recent poems.

Love to Ethel,

RUPERT

To EDWARD MARSH
24 Bilton Road, Rugby
22 December 1911

Dear Eddie,

Your letter gave me great joy. It was very good of you to write. I horribly feel that degrading ecstasy that I have always despised in parents whose shapeless offspring are praised for beauty. People are queer about my poems. Some that I know very well & have great *sympathie* with, don't like them. Some people seem to like them. Some like only the early ones—them considerably, but the others not at all. These rather sadden me. I hobnob vaguely with them over the promising verses of a young poet, called Rupert Brooke, who died in 1908. But I'm so much more concerned with the living; who don't interest them. God! it's so cheering to find someone who likes the modern stuff, & appreciates what one's at. You can't think how your remarks & liking thrilled me. You seemed, both in your classing them & when you got to details, to agree so closely with what I felt about them (only, of course, I often feel doubtful about their relative value to other poetry) that I knew you understood what they meant. It sounds a poor compliment—or else a queer conceitedness—to remark on your understanding them; but it's really been rather a shock to me—& made me momentarily hopeless—that so many intelligent & well-tasted people didn't seem to have any idea what I was driving at—in any poem of the last few years. It opened my eyes to the fact that people who like poetry are barely more common than people who like pictures.

I'm (of course) unrepentant about the 'unpleasant' poems. I don't claim great merit for *The Channel Passage*; but the point of it was (or should have been!) 'serious'. There are common & sordid things—situations or details—that may suddenly bring all tragedy, or at least the brutality of actual emotions, to you. I rather grasp relievedly at them, after I've beaten vain hands in the rosy mists of poets' experiences. Lear's button, & Hilda Lessways turning the gas suddenly on, and—but you know more of them than I. Shake-speare's not unsympathetic—'My mistress' eyes are nothing like the sun'. And the emotions of a seasick lover seem to me at least as poignant as those of the hero who has 'brain-fever'. 'Whatever', I declare simply and rather nobly, 'a brother man has thrown up, is food for me.'

The 'smell' business I don't really understand. Four hundred poems are written every year which end 'The wondrous fragrance of your hair': & nobody objects. People do smell other people, as well as see & feel & hear them. I do, & I'm not disgusted to think so. It's part of amazing emotions... *Quid plura*...? (Your suggestion for the recasting of *Dining-Room Tea* shall receive consideration when I'm preparing the second edition!)

I rather agree about one of the anapaests you pick out, 'Smiles you wel(come)...'.[1] It's meant to be carried off by the queer prosody of the line before...'The stróng dówn'...And the whole two & a half lines is supposed to be 'onomatopoeic', in a way—to express a kind of change to reality.... But I think it doesn't come off. I was trying consciously to write on a much looser & more happy-go-lucky, Anglo-Saxon basis—like Lascelles Abercrombie—than usual. The other anapaest, in *Finding*, seems to me all right, & undistinguishable from all the rest in the poem; though I'll admit the metre of the whole poem is impressionistic. Many thanks for pointing out the omission of 'so' in *Menelaus*. No one else had noticed it. It was entirely my fault; & I'm very angry. Two other misprints (*HAVB* in the Index, & 'Gtae' in *Failure*) were success-fully inserted by the printer after I had seen the final proofs.

I'm so sorry I never saw you again. The last part of November & the first of December I spent in writing my dissertation at Grant-chester. As I had a Soul Crisis as well as Insomnia & other things,

[1] In 'Paralysis', *Poems*, 1911.

I couldn't do it at all well. I came to London in a dilapidated condition for a day or two after it was over. Now I'm here, over Christmas. About the 27th I go to Lulworth with a reading-party for a fortnight. Then to the South of France, then Germany... & the future's mere mist. I want to stay out of England some time. (1) I don't like it. (2) I want to work—a play, & so on. (3) I'm rather tired & dejected.

So I *probably* shan't be in London for a long time. If I am, I'll let you know.... I'm going to try to do scraps—reviewing, etc.—in my spare time for the immediate future. I suppose you don't edit a magazine? I might review Elizabethan books at some length for *The Admiralty Gazette*, or T.A.T. (Tattle Among Tars), or whatever journal you officially produce?... At least I hope you'll issue an order to include my poems in the library of all submarines.[1]

Ever
RUPERT

To KATHARINE COX

Rugby 50 (Telephone)
Christmas Day
[*25 December 1911*]

Letter and P.C. to hand.

*   *   *

I bring—War and Peace (with you).

> Crime and Punishment.
> Milton.
> Donne.
> Verhaeren, a volume—A German trans. of *Szanin*.

Possibly Browning, Ben Jonson, a little Keats.

[1] E.M. was then working in the Admiralty as private secretary to Winston Churchill.

The episode mentioned as having occurred at Lulworth at the end of 1911, or very early in 1912, had upset Brooke's emotional life so seriously, as is reflected in his letters, that he had fallen during January into a severe nervous crisis ('a foodless and sleepless hell', as he afterwards described it) and had been to see a 'nerve specialist', Dr Maurice Craig. A period of rest abroad had been prescribed, and the first letter of 1912 was written from Paris while he was on his way to join his mother at Cannes on the Riviera. During January all his letters, of which comparatively few have been chosen for inclusion here, were written to Katharine, and express, sometimes incoherently, his mounting excitement, while he planned to escape his mother's vigilant eye and meet Katharine in Verona, whence they were to go to Munich. He finally broke down his mother's opposition to his leaving Cannes, though it is uncertain whether she knew he was to meet Katharine. Most of February was passed in Munich, and there are no letters covering this period. On 17 February they left Munich to stay for a short time near the Starnbergersee, and this was the scene of a further crisis concerning Katharine's relations with Henry Lamb, whom she had been seeing while Brooke was at Cannes. Yet he was afterwards able to remember this visit with satisfaction. At the end of the month, back in Rugby, he again began to write to his other friends, but by then he was experiencing an emotional reaction. It gradually becomes apparent that he had not achieved the happiness he had expected, and for the rest of the year his emotions veered to and fro, his mind being at times possessed by so frenzied a jealousy of Lamb's influence in Katharine's life that he seemed to his friends to be almost out of his mind. He still sometimes contemplated marriage with Katharine, but at others confessed that his affection for her was dead, and that he was filled with weariness in her company.

In March he stayed twice for a few days with James Strachey in Rye and made an abortive attempt to call on Henry James at Lamb House. In April he had news of his failure to obtain a Fellowship at King's and for the rest of the year he moved restlessly from place to place, both in England and abroad. In May he was back in Germany, Katharine Cox joining him for ten days in Berlin. Part of the time he stayed with Dudley Ward, who was about to be married—the awareness of others' happiness adding to his own misery. Nevertheless in Berlin he was able to write his most famous poem, 'Grantchester', scribbled while sitting in the Café des Westens. In July he was for a time at the Old Vicarage, but afterwards returned to Berlin in August and again in November.

Towards the end of the year he was becoming calmer and more able to think about poetry and literary affairs. In September he wrote for Harold Monro's *Poetry Review* a defence of Lascelles Abercrombie's poetry against an attack by Ezra Pound, and, as his friendship with Eddie Marsh ripened, was taking great interest in the projected volume of Georgian poets. In December he first made the acquaintance of Cathleen Nesbitt, a young actress. He spent Christmas with his mother at Rugby. From an early date in this year Brooke began to refer to his mother as 'the Ranee'. The name, first used, I believe, by my brother, was on the analogy of Rajah Brooke of Sarawak and suited Mrs Brooke's strong personality.

To KATHARINE COX

11 Villa Aublet
Rue Laugier [*Paris*]
Thursday morning
[*January 1912*]

Dearest,

I slept eight hours; I have had a hot bath and several meals; and I am going on this evening.

Elizabeth[1] was very kind, and waited some eighty minutes for my late train, and packed me into a cab. She has gone out to telegraph, and reserve me seats, and change me money. I sit by the fire and read the original MSS of Mon. Verhaeren and Gide.

I'm glad I didn't go straight on. To get as far as this was sufficiently tiring. I'm only a little cross that I'm in a way imposing on Elizabeth. I find myself so unmoved and kindly with her. All the passion I had once and the horrible mixture of lust and dislike I had at another time are gone so far away. I'm only tiredly well-meaning and slightly responsible.

I want so to turn altogether to you and forget everything but you, and lose myself in you, and give and take everything—for a time. Afterwards—doesn't matter. But I'm so wanting that security of Heaven. I'll make myself so fine for you. And I'll find and multiply all the many splendours in you.

Goodbye woman. I'm only scratching French lines to say I'm all right; and that by Friday noon I'll be comfortably in bed at Nice, resting and well. If the carriage is hot and horrible tonight, I shall think of your eyes and hands and mouth and body and voice; and sleep instantly and happily.

Rest in the week-end, Ka dear. We'll both be so strong and wonderful at Munich, that we'll be able to burn or tear or hurt each other; and laugh.

Don't mind my being here a day. I'm not loving Elizabeth.

In three weeks I'll get my body and soul fit for you.

It's so funny the two things combining—that I'll give you things you never dreamt of and you'll make me the wonderfullest person in the world, *and* that you've those funny blue infantile eyes that almost shame one. That you should be at the same time both everything in the world *and* Ka. I love you so. I kiss your lips.

RUPERT

[1] Mlle. Elizabeth van Rysselbergh, whom he had met the year before in Munich; see p. 291.

To KATHARINE COX   *Hotel du Pavillon, Cannes*
                                      Saturday, Morning–evening
                                      [*January 1912*]

Dearest,

I should take all the morning and most of the afternoon telling you how cleverly I travelled here; how the Duchess of Padua was opposite me and her lady's maid on my right (the maids of the Ordinary Rich go second, with you and the normal me), and M. Bonnard the celebrated painter (a delightful fellow) beyond the lady's maid. At noon yesterday the Duchess (who spoke excellent American) offered me a banana—ah, I needn't tell you what *that* meant; but she was so old and I've taken such a turn (you know) lately; so I truthfully said I was lunching in the dining-car. At Nice the Ranee, Alfred, M. Cook and all their luggage were on the station. They'd decided to take me straight back here. I lie and eat and sleep. It's all so precisely what I expected. Summer and comfort. The Ranee pushing my book in the English portions of Cannes, and bawling English with incredible success to crumbling foreigners. She has also entirely subdued eight solitary and separate maiden ladies in this hotel.

       *   *   *

Outside there are large numbers of tropical palms, a fountain, laden orange trees, and roses. There's an opal sea and jagged hills with amazing sunsets behind—the Esterelles they said they were. Wide open windows, and a balcony to lie on in a day or two. And quiet. I read two hours a day, negligently. Patience and water-colours give me occupation. Why aren't you here to teach me knitting?

I find myself—what *is* this degradation?—wanting you at each moment, to tell you exactly what I think about what I'm reading or about some person. The pleasure of telling you about things is so extraordinarily great. What does it mean? Keeping telling you everything would, it seems, make such a wonderful and golden background for everything else between us. I've such a longing to get out of myself, my tight and dirty self—to put it all out in the sun, the fat sun. And it's so hard to tell the truth, to give oneself wholly away, even to you. So one wants to chatter and pour everything out. . .and then perhaps truth may slip out with it.

Oh, I lie and am placidly stupid; and I'm hardly ever touched by that uneasiness. I've put everything away, and I'm concentrating on getting well. Two dangers I see. There's the danger of writing too

long letters to you, every day. I *will* be continent. And there's the
danger of too great vitality and avidity. Sometimes as I lie and pant
like an overfed puppy, thoughts of you and Munich and—I don't
know what, storm so irresistibly in; and I can't help feeling such
amazing energy and life in all my limbs and mind, that I'm racked to
be up and off to meet you at the *Hauptbahnhof*. You go burning
through every vein and inch of me, till I'm all Ka; and my brain's
suddenly bursting with ideas and lines and flames, and my body's
all for you.

'Sh-sh.' I hold myself in, and wait, and grow fatter. But I'm
certainer than ever that I'm, possibly, opening new Heavens, like
a boy sliding open the door into a big room; trembling between
wonder and certainty. (I can express *nothing*.) Oh, I'm seeing, or
thinking I see, how mad I've been. I'm beginning to see why I so
mysteriously—with all the best things in the world for me—*wasn't*
happy last year—was irritable and perplexedly wretched at times.
I know now how beastly I was both to you and to Noel; and
that one must choose—choose, being human—one thing at a time.
'One'=I; for everyone's different. I've been unhappy. I couldn't
give to either of two such people what I ought, which is 'all'. Now
I've got a sort of peace, I think; because I shall be able. I shall know
these things more clearly as each day comes. And a million times
more clearly when your face comes—in a fortnight? . . .

I'm more sane, a little, about the world. Oh, far from sane: but
better. I'm convinced that sanity is the most important thing there
is. I'm so hampered and spoilt because there are things I dare not
face, and depths I daren't look into. The sane person can go anywhere and imagine and write anything. By God! *you're* sane, with
your splendid strength and beauty. But I've been half-mad, alone.
Oh, it's all mixed up with this chastity, and everything's a whirl, and
still I'm mad and tiny and frightened. But I'm clambering up to
sane light. You've given me such sanity already—sometimes when
you didn't know it. But you will give me more. I'll be able to do
everything and look at everything, if you'll give me that strength.
Oh, give it me Ka! It'll be for a time. Afterwards you may give
what you've made of me out to the world; and anything may
happen—, no harm can, then.

* * *

Love me! love me! love me! Goodnight, Ka. I love you so much.

RUPERT

To KATHARINE COX

[*Cannes, January 1912*]

Saturday evening.

I posted a beastly letter to you this morning. Since, I've been thinking and looking at you. I see better how feeble and silly and mean I am. And how fine in your slow way, you. I'm sorry if my letter worried and hurt you, Ka dear. I'm just writing for half an hour this evening to put myself in a better light.

You have been so wonderfully nice, your presence has been so cool and happy to me, these weeks when I've been a devil to you—I'm ingratitude, dirty, dirty, dirty—

One changes so, if one's ill and on a rainy Riviera. Two nights ago I had (after a German consultation with Evelyn) a Hot Bath. I was so radiant, getting out of it. I almost rushed to you. I looked at myself, drying, in the glass, and I thought my body was very beautiful and strong, and that I was keeping it and making it splendid for you. And I knew that if I rested a night on your breasts, and then caught fire from you, my mind and heart too would be able to give you a million things that only I in the world knew of and could give. I was so happy. I was happy thinking of Munich. I thought of the whole of Ka, inside and out. I was so happy.

And then at other times I lie and *ache* to twist my thoughts onto Shakespeare, a poem—anything; and they always go back to the blackness, till I can't bear it and from thinking of suicide then, think of it immediate, to cut the thing clear and set you free from a fool.

Eh, I *do* want your presence, you know, to keep me fine and sane, just now.

But tonight I *know* I shall get to Munich. I can see the Ranee thinks she's going to keep a hand on me for a month or six weeks. But I give her ten days at the outside. I shall have to be beastly to her, I suppose. . . .

A quarter of an hour to dinner. . . .

'. . . with a sort of fero-defiance (My dear, *I* don't know), he is often, as in — and — and —, ineffectively ugly and unpleasant. And once or twice he is merely nasty. . . . He dares to be a Daniel (?), however, and it is enormously to his credit that he has managed to stagger free from convention. But if he is content with the merely surface freedom of speech and manner; if he is content with his present Puritan ignorance of passion and his own body, and pursues the phantom of sensation, his power of concentration will gradually leave him, he will stagger back into the conventional fold, and eventually, sick of 'mad magenta minutes', be received into some great hospital (Rome?) for men's souls...' He may, on the other hand, it appears, turn out a Poet. There's a lot more; Yes. It's what a gentleman in the *Observer*[1] thinks about

Your lover

RUPERT

To KATHARINE COX

Hotel du Pavillon, Cannes

[*January 1912*]

Monday evening.

*   *   *

Your letter—of Thursday evening; if you remember it. (It'll seem so long ago to you—with many things, and the sea, between.) My dear, *you* come out so in your letters; so kind, and wonderful, and real. And your last sentence (bar postscripts)—I want to kiss your hands, so—You know, I get rather frightened. Anyone can fall in love with anybody; granted. But once in love with you (precisely like anyone being in love with anyone else, so far) one has, I find—since you are uniquely you—to go further and further. At least, if one's me. Loving you implies a geometrical progression. One gets worse and worse. You grow on one, so. It's a pervading, irresistible thing, 'Ka'. It's like having black-beetles in the house. 'I've got Ka in the body....My dear, I've tried *everything*....Put down carbolic? My dear, *Yes!*...' So, I tell you, I get frightened. Where's it to stop? Am I to plunge deeper and deeper, for ever? Damn you! And it's so nice to—sometimes nice even if you don't care and won't have anything to do with me (save pity). That's queer. I'm happy; but also I'm frightened, Ka.

You and your letter! One of the reasons, I always suppose, I get deeper and deeper in, is that I *know* you—what you're like, and the whole good truth (= facts) of you. And then comes along something quite unexpected, that I'd never conceived to be in you, some queer corner in that round. And I'm tumbled over. Who'd have thought that you had a prose-style that was a superior combination of The Old Testament and poor Mr Wilde. 'Virginia was more

[1] In a review of *Poems*, 1911.

fantastic than an army of apes and peacocks.' What an image! *What* a mind! God! I wish I could write like that!

I shall finish this tomorrow morning. I've a faint idea, oh! less than a hope, there may be a card or note from you tomorrow: crawling round through Nice or somewhere—though you *have* stupidly lost my address. Die unfähige Ka! Oh, I don't really expect one tomorrow—posted, it'd have to be, Saturday evening (and you tired). I thought it out, that you might send me news from your retirement at Woking, writing comfortably on Sunday...posting perhaps on Monday or via Nice...I shall get excited—oh, infinitesimally—at the approach of the Wednesday posts. I expect nothing till Thursday morning.

Oh, and you, Devil, were tired on Thursday night! I wish I knew how you were now. On Friday night I think you were being tired, somehow. I had the horrors, then; so I think maybe something was happening to you. Were you.... But I had the horrors. And again curiously, this afternoon (but that may be because I dreamt, horribly, all last night, about you—no, not altogether horribly; only some. But you were at Woking, asleep).

My dear, my dear, you've got away, away from all of us, now— when you receive this. Perhaps you'll find it, late on Wednesday night, and be too sleepy to read it; but I think it'll more probably come on Thursday morning. Oh, after all this last week and then the journey, I'm afraid you'll be so dreadfully tired, even you. Sleep, dearest Ka—I wish I could make you sleep. I wish I could kiss your eyes and make you rest. Think that I'm doing it, now, where this paper is. Oh, Ka, Ka, please rest, forget everything a bit, and rest, and sleep and be happy. There's so much to amuse one in Munich. Ka, do tell them you're very tired and have been—say 'worried', 'ill', or what you like—and then you'll be able to rest. You *never* sleep enough. Do drop your silly English habits. Eight full hours every night, and ten the first two or three. And you might make them give you breakfast in bed. Ka! don't laugh. I insist. I—Ich, der Mann—$\frac{\text{command}}{\text{beg of}}$ you to do this thing.

It's Monday night. I'm going to turn off the light and sleep. At this moment you're at Oedipus. I want to hear about it, from you. (It *is* funny that you should be in that great dark building listening to *Oedipus*; and I in a bedroom over the Mediterranean.) I hope you're enjoying it. Ka at Oedipus. I forget if you've ever read a paper on the Greeks to the Friday Club? I can imagine what you'd say—oh, not the words, but the furry atmosphere of your inconsecutive ideas. Ka on Sophocles. Oh, I should like to hear it all. How good you'd think them all. And would you find Creon 'nice'?

*　　*　　*

Goodbye. I love you.

RUPERT

To KATHARINE COX

[*Cannes, c. 20 January 1912*]

*　　*　　*

Friday morn.

Damn! A Bad Night. It followed on Depression yesterday. For five hours yesterday I was convinced that it was all something right inside the head, and that I was either going to have a stroke, or else going slowly mad. It may be true: and one's so damnably helpless. Any other illness, one can suddenly shut one's teeth and one's hands and throw off. One can say 'I'm *not* going to be ill any more' and one isn't. But madness—means that it isn't up to 'one' to say anything. And yesterday (and part of today) I felt a cloud in my head and about me that seemed to mean it too certainly....Come to think of it, it's very possible. Jacques, being Jacques, went mad for half a year. I, being tougher and slower, defied chastity a bit longer, and then, naturally, would take it worse—in a slow dull way. Ich bin Englisch, wissen Sie. It'll be a curious comment on civilization or women or something if I do go. And, if it is that, I expect even your 'medecinal' methods wouldn't cure me, Devil and God.

Friday even.

In Munich and in health these plaints sound silly, I guess. But here it's always raining, and I'm alone, in a way, and I'm fighting such a bloody slow hopeless sort of fight, and there's a long time in the day that it feels entirely one of the credible things—like fine weather tomorrow, or 30 seats on the second ballot, or anything ordinary—that I am going mad. Oh, my dear, I find I'm still so ill and weak. And oh! I'm so far from you.

I'll write other things. For there's many hours in the day when I'm cheerful—knowing I will get to Munich, whatever happens, so that something, oh, my God, and perhaps all—will be all right.

I went to a Classical Concert at the Casino: this afternoon. Music, you know, has more of a nervous appeal than most things—directly in a queer way—even for the *unmusikalisch*. So at first I nearly gave in. But I stuck it out—it's part of a long scheme to hoodwink the Ranee. And the after effects are that I'm brighter than the rest of the day. You know it's *doing* things—mildly—and not thinking that may pull me out in time. Damn the rain!

I've been ransacking Cannes for a Munich paper, to see what's happening for you. Can't find one. Damn! Oh, most exciting. You know about the Romance of my Life. I know I told you, because I remember how beastly you were about her—Miss Phyllis (is it Phyllis?) Gardner. Everyone was so beastly that I hadn't the heart to meet her. She went to tea day after day in St John's Wood, and I was always too sulky and too *schuchtern* to go. So it all ended, you think. Ah! but you don't know Phyllis(?)! Today I received, through Sidgwick and Jackson, a letter. It was from an elderly woman, who said she had been led by a reviewer's hatred of *A Channel Passage* to buy my book, that she thought it all *frightfully* good (particulars) and would I go and see her, or her husband, a Professor at University College, or both, anywhen, anywhere...addressed from Surrey and signed Mary Gardner. Es ist alles sehr einfach, nicht wahr?

Oh, I've put it in the hands of my solicitor (Miss Noel Olivier) who has been acting for me in this matter throughout.

Tra! la! la!

That's what modern Mothers are!

(A thought has struck me. Do not consider yourself bound to write me at equal length. I exercise an invalid's privilege, in these vast reams. I desire very short, but not too infrequent statements of your existence and happiness. Oh, and *letters*; as short as cards, but not cards. The Ranee, you know....)

Women are funny. Really, I suppose, they're not. But men are very unimaginative—at least, I am. One doesn't think of some of their (women's) points of view. It gave me a queer half-pleasant half-painful start when you said you'd often thought of a child—of ours. I'd never thought about that, do you know? (thought about = imagined, felt) I'd often thought (more and more—on the whole— as months went on) about us living together—a week—or ten years, in every sort of way. And never that. I'd thought—agonizingly once or twice—of you in childbirth: and not—except in the background— of a child.

Now you've put it into my head: and it's a part of the imaginations and stories, wanders in and out. In pretty well all of the alternatives we have put, or put, or shall put before us, there's the possibility of one such thing appearing, I think? He (is that wicked?) he figures as very strong, and rather beautiful, or more. Good God, I am old. You've a lustful lower lip, Ka. Why do I imagine his arms unusually long? Pince-nez; Damn! Do you know, I lie for *hours* trying to put the walk, the gait, together. I *can't* quite imagine it.

But it's all nothing to you. I suppose you think of it as a fifth that size.   *   *   *

You and your permanent thinking. I *don't* understand, of course. But I'm still mad and scary, incapable of any impersonality. Oh, Ka, I wanted to come so strong and clean and sane and well to Munich and to pay back a bit by helping you—in both ways, by common sense and the other subconscious business. I could. But I'm not getting better. I'm only just what I was 10 days ago: and 10 days more'll see the end of January. And I don't want to come ill and foolish and beastly as I was, to weaken and worry you and sponge on your strength. And yet I *can't* keep always away and let everything drift by and get worse and worse, for not seeing you. What shall I do? I think the sight and presence of you might put me right again in a day or two. It's so ghastly lying here, struggling and thinking, fruitlessly, while these gray days go by; and nothing but your tired, kind cold letters to stay me. Oh, my dear, I'm sorry. I know we're waiting and you're thinking and I oughtn't to bother or complain. I've no faith and no strength. If only you were with me an hour, I'd get both; if you were with me a day, I'd be well again; a year, and I'd be the most wonderful person in the world.

Gwen once thought me 'sane', did she? I've always enjoyed that healthy serene, Apollo-golden-haired, business.[1] But, my dear, our relationship's based a bit deeper! My face—do what you like with it. But you, and only you in the world, understand my horrible nature. It's so importantly my humiliation and my—safety, joy, what is it called? I may be, and shall be, perhaps, sane and every thing else one day. But, the dirty abyss I am now—I've let you see. Don't pretend you don't know me, fool.

I suppose I oughtn't to post this. I think I shall. I'll write better, tonight and tomorrow. I think, soberly, I am a trifle better today—if it matters.

I suppose you'll be despising me. Or are you still wise enough to distinguish between actualities and potentialities? Even then—But I'll behave decently, if ever I get to Munich.

[1] A reference to Frances Cornford's well-known poem: 'A young Apollo, golden haired...' in *Poems*, 1910.

Monday morning this'll get you—in bed? (I know your neck and shoulders, so.)

Goodbye and forgive and expect a cleaner letter.

After all, you *don't* know what it's like—being where *you're* not. It's horrible!

Does one still say 'with love'?

RUPERT

To KATHARINE COX [*Cannes, 21 January 1912*]

Rupert to Katharine,

How vain, most adorable creature, is the pursuit of pleasure in the absence of an object to which the mind is entirely devoted, unless it have some relation to that object! I was last night condemned to the society of men of wit and learning, which, however agreeable it might have formerly been to me, now only gave me a suspicion that they imputed my absence in conversation to the true cause. For which reason, when your engagements forbid me the ecstatic happiness of seeing you, I am always desirous to be alone; since my sentiments for Katharine are so delicate, that I cannot bear the apprehension of another's prying into those delightful endearments with which the warm imagination of a lover will sometimes indulge him, and which I suspect my eyes then betray. To fear this discovery of our thoughts may perhaps appear too ridiculous a nicety to minds not susceptible of all the tenderness of this delicate passion. And surely we shall suspect there are few such, when we consider that it requires every human virtue to exert itself in its full extent; since the beloved, whose happiness it ultimately respects, may give us charming opportunities of being brave in her defence, generous to her wants, compassionate to her afflictions, grateful to her kindness; and in the same manner, of exercising every other virtue, which he who would not do to any degree, and that with the utmost rapture, can never deserve the name of a lover. It is, therefore, with a view to the delicate modesty of your mind that I cultivate it so purely in my own; and it is that which will sufficiently suggest to you the uneasiness I bear from those liberties, which men to whom the world allow politeness will sometimes give themselves on these occasions.

Can I tell you with what eagerness I expect the arrival of that blest day, when I shall experience the falsehood of a common assertion, that the greatest human happiness consists in hope? A doctrine which no person had ever stronger reason to believe than myself at present, since none ever tasted such bliss as fires my bosom with the thoughts of spending my future days with such a companion, and that every action of my life will have the glorious satisfaction of conducing to your happiness.

To KATHARINE COX

[*Cannes, January 1912*]

Thursday night: latish.

Very little tonight. This'll reach you Sunday morning—with luck it may be my last letter that gets you!

I'm such a coward, when I'm like this, you see. I sit opposite the Ranee with things on my tongue, and just daren't utter them; because it'd mean five minutes' row. But I *will* put it to her tomorrow: 'Sunday' I shall say, 'Sunday night', and if there's too *awful* a row I'll yield hour by hour and day by day. But Monday or Tuesday or Wednesday morning I shall be seeing you.

*   *   *

Bring a rück-sack, stuffed with clothes and Dostoieffsky.

This is all drivel: but what can one write? Scraps, one remembers. I *don't* know Hugh's address. You're to begin making arrangements for having meals out a good deal. For I shall have to; and that's the romance of Munich, partly. Also, how will you know I eat as much as Dr Craig wants me to: unless you're there? The man's written to the Ranee, in answer. (Not about staying at Cannes.) '...Your son was obviously in a state of severe nervous breakdown when I saw him. He was hyper-sensitive and introspective. (Was für ein Mann!) He must not recommence literary work for some months yet.' etc.

So what the devil am I going to do after Munich? Of course, I *shall* commence literary work, only not the exhausting kind.

(And I've such a damn good poem rustling away under the bracken, in my head.)

Introspective. Ha!

It's Ka I'm going to see. You're going to make me so amazingly strong and fine. And I'm going to give you undreamt things.

When each hour and feeling, lying in front, is black and strange (only black with strangeness): it's so wonderful walking into them with another person, in this way, to talk to. That, damn it, doesn't express. I'm thinking about Companionship, when it's there as well as everything else.

One does get further and further in with you: as I've said. It's all very queer: looking quite remotely backwards. We toiled up the Andermatt toboggan-track together the second day. When we, alone, got to the top, you sat on the toboggan, looked out to your left (to the pass to Italy) and said, rather self-consciously, I thought, 'Damn!' I looked at you, and pondered what your (or any young woman's, but, then especially your) mind was like.

Then there was an evening in the late autumn of 1910 (I think then; anyhow before the first Lulworth). I know precisely where you were standing: by the curtain that screens the Door (in the Flat), your back to it and to the wall-edge, facing West. There were probably other people there: Jacques perhaps. You'd for some reason, got on a low dress. I looked at the firm and lovely place where your deep breasts divided and grew out of the chest and went down under the dress: your columnar neck rising above it, and Ka somehow behind or in it all...and I was suddenly very giddy, and physically hit with a glimpse of a new sort of beauty that I'd not quite known of, a sort that shook me in a vastly deeper and fiercer way than Miss Lena Dare. It rather faded, I suppose. I wondered if you knew what was happening in those few seconds.

* * *

I'll remember that the more I rest here, the more I'll enjoy with you: and stop and sleep. I could go on so! But there's Verona platform, and the *Café Bauer*, and a Carnival evening, and—such mixed things ahead. I'll be ready for them; and do just a very little more than you think right. I'm going to be such a burden to you, in that way. You're to be the Ranee and Dr Craig and everything else! Goodnight, dear. In a few days—

Friday morning.

* * *

Oh, but *two* letters this morning!

I'm bothered about your Wednesday ball. It's so likely that it'll clash with Verona, I see. Oh, Ka: I don't want to stay here two or three days longer than I need. And I don't want to make you not go to your ball through duty to the engagement for meeting me. And I don't want to hurry through Verona and get back to send you in bright yellow to a ball while I spend my first evening in solitude in an hotel: being jealous of you at a ball, with so many naked men there. Virgins like you, you know, give in immediately if they see a naked man.

I'm rather silly: but it does seem an extra tangle you see, the ball'll be great fun. (Though it'll be greater when we go alone to one later: (one of the Wicked Ones, maybe).)

Oh God, I see I shall have to break it all at lunch, and wire this afternoon.

So when you've got this, all'll be settled, perhaps. But remember, I'll be very happy anyhow; so if you'd rather not break some Munich engagement, ball or other, you're to wire when you get this, if you haven't done, and if there's time.

I'd even wait at Verona! I've set my heart on it—on Italy—you know.

I expect I shall write a little by the next post. I ought to get up and go out now. A Concert this afternoon: Mendelssohn and Mozart, Ravel and Saint-Saens. Very Cannes. I want to write you such great flaming letters. I know how mean and dull these are; and how little they're what I want to say. But I'm not really up to it yet; writing down things. It's so difficult and requires such power. Only don't think I'm as flat as I sound. And don't think I'm going to be as flat as I am. Health, you know, makes a great difference in those things....Even now, I know I love you more and more over-whelmingly than anyone ever can or has or will. There's a lot in me, I'll tell you, Ka. My strength all goes out to you. I blaze out more to you....Everything seems to be coming back. The other night, in the rain, a man was singing between my window and the sea. And suddenly I felt that shiver; and romance (the keenness and darkness and life) came back. I knew how dead and flat I'd been, how long. And walking home in the evening from the *Californie* on Monday (your telegram was waiting for me) I suddenly smelt. I hadn't smelt little things—trees and rain and the sea and wet gravel—for ages. It all goes for fuel.

My God, if you'd stay with me, somewhere down on the coast by Venice, while the spring woke: on and on! What we'd be, there! (Oh, there's cafés in Venice—Florian's in front of St Mark's.)

I can see myself going up and up, these days and weeks in front. There's no stopping—with you in the Universe, and nearby.

This'll get to you in two days. Two days nearer our meeting. It may be so very close, then.

Hey for Life and Italy!

I'm all reaching out to you, body and mind.

RUPERT

P.S. Bring a lot of money to Verona. I've a letter of credit I can't cash till Munich.

P.P.S. I do want to talk to you. I want to know what the *Hell* you see in [Gide's] *L'Immoraliste*. *The Dynasts*: Ka, I don't think it'll do, quite.

To KATHARINE COX

[*Cannes, January 1912*]

Sunday morning.

You are quite certainly the nicest person in the world, and absolutely right. And I am a beast and a toad.

Why do your Munich activities and Ka-isms give me such pleasure? I feel slightly ashamed—as of a sign of feeble-mindedness, you know.

I'll take you point by point. It's so important not to miss things. I did it all, so exactly, you know, a year ago. That Post-Office business—! well! well! Reflect, when the panics come, on the figure of me suffering likewise, only more gauntly—very red in the face; consider me conscious, in Cannes, of your paroxysms, and giggling.

           *   *   *

You may spend some time in the Alte Pinakothek: two mornings (with a rug) in the Glyptothek; an hour (if you're strong) through the Neue Pinakothek; then a morning each for the Secession and three private galleries. Then you'll be through for January.

I haven't Hugh's address, but I sent him yours. Only it'll take ages to get round to him. I'm so sorry. I'd have got it through earlier if I'd had the sense to think of you wanting it. I only thought of *him* wanting it, and dallied! But you'll meet him in the galleries.

Concerts, you know, you can quite well go to alone. Also most theatres, if you've got into the tricks of them. The *Residenz*, for instance.... Miss Grove did, occasionally! Of course, *she* was on the look out for adventures. But then she always funked them; more than you would.

Concerts you find out by scanning advertisement boards, or revolving pathetically round those towers. They're often not in the papers.

Sunday evening.

I wonder if they'll let you have two cups and four biscuits at 4.30, after a bit? Shall I come for the 'work' there? I'm not sure. I dread treading into the lair. Joanna would make a third, too often. My room (if only I can get my old one!) will be safer.

When you meet Alexander, and get him and Joanna together, pour out a few names, Van Gogh, Cézanne, Mattisse, Derain, Girieud, etc.; and they'll accept and admire you. Wonderful, the effect'll be: and the result cheap at the price. Try it.

Oh my dear Ka, Ka with that particular hair and head and neck, and a certain walk, and a special way the clothes have of going down over the hip, and strong hands, and a hundred other things, Ka peering about and saying 'Hoo!', Ka whom I know so very well, and whom I've been so beastly to, and whom I love so, I wish I could see you, red streamers out and head a little forward and solemn-eyed, Ka-ing down past the Siegers-Thor and the Library and eyeing the Residenz and noting the ladies in charge of the streets and round with joy at four Bavarian privates doing the goose-step salute past an officer (is that still to come?) and finally poking [in at] Theatinerstrasse and tentatively buying soap—a laborious 'Wie viel?' and then the tender of 10 marks to be changed, to cover your ignorance of their reply. I wish I could see you.

Joanna.... It's not what *I* call a decent way, if it's what it was. But I daresay I'm particular. So she and 'all Munich' are still in love with me? Can it be? A whole year. These things must last longer in Deutschland.

I'll endeavour not to feed their passions. I've developed an extraordinary monogamy of soul-tone lately—a pathetic and belated offering, my dear. Evelyn, who is Italian and talks beautiful German to me is utterly charming—even with Evelyn I have been stern to myself. And that though matters were precipitated—just as they were last January with Professor S——. God! God! God! Have you bumped into that horror yet—

*   *   *

but wait, wait!)? I'm referring to the du–Sie fandango. If one's talking to a mere acquaintance and slips a Du, you know, it's a proposal, and they're expected to retire at once with you to the bedroom. The Professor, luckily, was due to start for Bucharest in 40 minutes, was in fact saying 'Leben Sie wohl!', and I accursedly slipped a *Dein* for *Ihr*. His dark little hand was at my trousers like a flash; I—but

I've told you it all before. Evelyn was more feminine. For a married woman she's *so* fond of me. I was ordering the bath when it happened. She was all red, under the lovely brown, and began to murmur that the bath would be there, and herself all naked in it—when I cried *Ihnen* three times so loudly that Miss Barker put her head out of No. 84, to see what was up—and then I rushed to my room and locked the door. Dear, dear, how one goes on! I'm sure I hope I haven't tired you. It's getting so late. I shall read my chapter and turn the light out and pray for a better night than last night. Tomorrow I'll tell you about the Play.

Goodnight, my dear. I need you so. I write 'my dear', I daren't and can't write how very much I love you. Goodnight.

Monday morning.

Noch ein Brief! You *are* nice. And you won't be getting my long one till just now (I'm breakfasting in bed, too). I'm going to give up all reading and writing, and only write to you, in future. All day and every day.　　　*　　*　　*

With love
R.

I had to end there: it was such a good ending. Really, I've five minutes more.

My dear, I shall be entirely gay in Munich.

Damn Joanna and my cheeks. I never even let her kiss them. Why am I old and dead and ugly, and why do they think me a lovely Child. The Rev. W. Christie on Wednesday thought I was twenty-one. And old Mrs Woolaston (of whom more later) thought Alfred and I were twins aged eighteen, she confided to mother in the *Salle de Lecture*, after I'd tottered to bedder. 'He has a skin like a girl's— He looks very like a girl'...'in his *Face*' put in Miss Barclay.

God! God!

Gwen, oh, yes! I wanted to tell you (I want to tell you everything). Gwen impressed me as much Cleverer than I'd guessed. About Frances. She was so delightfully uncharitable. I *was* impressed.

Dinner.

Goodnight; my dear.

I wish you'd come to an Italian villa, from March 20 to September. I should write the greatest play in the world.

Goodnight.

To KATHARINE COX

[Cannes, January 1912]

Monday: nachmittag.

A seat: the Esplanade: aber ein bissel kalt.

*   *   *

My dear, with your resting and your work, you can stand solitude
a bit; so, Ka dear, *don't* get mixed up and dutifully socially entangled
with a lot of people. Say you've a *devilish* lot of work to do. They'll
all be freezing on to you, because you're so divinely the nicest person
in Europe, these Grahams and Poultons and things. And then, when
I come, you'll always be conscientiously disappearing, '. . . besides,
they're really quite nice, you know'—Ka dear, *don't*, for God's sake!
Let's have those few days—apart from work, etc., for laughing over
Munich. We'll descend on a German or two, out of our fastnesses;
but let's have each other. So don't, for once, be so wicked and
unfeeling and unimaginative, as to be soft. You've done enough
harm with your tolerance.

*   *   *

Indoors (resting).

I'm really getting on very well: my body ('nerves'). But I wish
you were here to look after my soul. It'd pay the Ranee (if only the
poor dear knew!) to pay you to telegraph, say four times a day;
once 'I am very well; and you?', and once 'Goodnight', and once
'Munich is so very nice', and once, if you cared, perhaps, 'Noch
lieb' ich dich'. She could balance the cost by knocking off my extra
milk and baths: and I'd be 15 stone in no time.

We get on very well, the Ranee and I. Half the day she spends in
reproducing to me verbally her conversations of the other half.
She's only still a little sore about my tie. She says it is 'so con-
spicuous'. I pretend it is my only one. And it is understood that
(a yellow like that!) I bought it at Liberty's on my way through.

*   *   *

Just back to find your telegram. And now from telegraphing;
I must send this tonight, in case you don't come: as I hope.

For I diagnose that my beastly letter upset you. I'm worthy of
treading to death in dung. I *was* ill, and am a bit: but I'm much
better. I *will* get to Munich in a week. I'm really all right: only very
rarely morbid. I'm so sorry. If it's other business, to tell me some
best or worst—But it can't be.

I'll write after dinner and post tomorrow. Your penultimate word came 'baisse'—I now guess *trains*.

Oh, I'm sorry. I'm a devil. I *have* suffered. But I'm a devil to have worried you. Please, Ka, all's well. I love you so. I love you so.

RUPERT

To KATHARINE COX

[*Cannes, January 1912*]

Tuesday afternoon (rain).

I lie waiting for a telegram. I think I may, anyhow, as well give you the news of the day.

No: I don't give readings, or even talk cricket. I'm not known as a poet. Mother let out one evening, after I'd gone to bed, that I was going to take up 'writing' as a profession. But it hasn't been referred to. And old Miss Fox, who is so fond of me, thinks I look like William Poël, whom she's also *so* fond of, knows his family. She took me aside, in fact, and said she knew all about William's married life 'which has been very strange, yes, and interesting'. I was highly excited; listened attentively for 40 minutes. All she could tell me was that he had had two children (one died) and his wife is a great invalid. I professed enthusiasm. But I don't really see what it means. 'Don't they ——?' I wanted to ask. But, even if they don't, you know, it's not very interesting. Dear! dear! Perhaps I don't understand.

And there aren't many Colonels. One Anglo-Indian (old Hullar) but a *very* progressive one. 'That fellow, *Keir-Hardie*, now, you know. Of course, what he says is poison. Poison, Sir! But there's a dear old friend of mine, old John Simple (Sir John Simple) (one of the best of chaps), who has a province out in Bengal; and, y'know, he had to entertain the fellow—Keir-Hardie. He didn't like the idea, one bit. But, you know, he told me afterwards, that he really wasn't at all a bad chap, just like anyone else, quite a decent chap to have stay with you. Really! 'Straordinary, isn't it? Oh, I'd like to get to know some of these Labour Leaders, as they call them. I sometimes think perhaps we don't hear both sides of the question, down at Cheltenham, you know.'

The Ranee gets madder daily. She now runs the whole Hotel. I am lost in wonder: and more determined than ever that she must marry Gerald. I have never met two people so made for one another. He will be Prime Minister in 1922.

It will give me extraordinary pleasure to tell you my whole day.

At about 8 I wake. Till nine I drowse. At 9 there is a knock and the Liftboy brings a letter from you. I kiss it dimly and put it unopened in the bed (the shutters are still shut, against mosquitoes) and murmur, in a rather maudlin way, about you, till 9.10. Then Evelyn appears with hot water: and hurls the shutters open. I remark in German that it's still bloody weather. She agrees with immense vivacity. At 9.15 Fritz appears with Chocolate

Four Rolls

One Egg.

As he vanishes I get out and wash and produce the Ranee's private jam from the wardrobe. I return to bed, search it for your letter, and open letter and egg together. Funny about ritual. I read, eat and drink very slowly; laughing slightly. Your letters are so *very* like you, you know. And I can visualize it all. Also, it's so extremely nice that you really were writing to me two days ago.

It's gloomy coming to an end of one of your letters. But then one reads it again; or yesterday's for a change. And there's such a quantity of acute pleasure to be got out of them—your letters. I get very pleased and well, and swallow great cups of chocolate, saying (in a mixture of frightenedness and triumph) 'She does, you know, love me. Ka! It *will* be all right!'...etc.

At 9.45 I'm towards the end of breakfast. The Ranee knocks. I conceal your letter and make out I'm reading *The Dynasts*. She enters in a magenta dressing-gown and brings yesterday's *Continental Daily Mail* (which appears with her breakfast). For an hour I alternately read the Mail and lie thinking.

*　*　*

Goodnight. I love you so.

RUPERT

To KATHARINE COX

[*Cannes, January 1912*]

*　*　*

Thursday morning.

It was (your letter) most extraordinarily nice, though. Oh, Ka! But you, all Monday evening, in such a fever. Ka, you *mustn't*. I'm a fretful child: you mustn't, *you*, be worried by me.

Oh, I am a beast.

We went up to a distant hotel that afternoon, Monday, to tea. We successfully saw Mr Balfour! Returning, we found no train, so we had to walk a long way. We got back here at six. The Ranee solicitous. I was to lie down till dinner. But your telegram was waiting. (I don't know when it arrived.) I stared at it—it required some taking in. 'Nothing'—I answered, '—er—from James, you know: about a thing....' We both talked to Mrs Digby a minute. Then I slid swiftly to the door, muttering vaguely 'Just answer it, you know...take a tram.' The Ranee was half in tears. But I'd gone. There weren't any trams. (It's only half a mile.) I thought and thought, as I walked.

I'd provisionally settled the Ranee, if you did come. It was to be that you were on your way from England to Italy and had so kindly come a rather longer way to see if I wasn't better. What simpler?

My dear, it's so nice of you to say you'll come here, if I don't come to Munich: before you go back to England. But, you know, I *must* come to Munich! (Of course you know it.) Here, we'd see each other two hours in the day. That'd have been possible, now, with Munich ahead. But, with only separation ahead—oh my God! you going back to England. It wouldn't be bearable—all the restraint.

No: I'm coming. It's the only thing: and entirely possible. And you're not to write that I'm 'not to try the journey for a fortnight'. That, fool, means four or five days more away from you. You know, I might be with you now, this very very second, but for this damned collapse.

And it's all right about my health. I'm not going to be ill or sad till I've seen you again. If by any mad chance I *do* get very ill, I swear I'll telegraph. But I can't possibly get like that. And I'll keep my letters from being sulky or sad. If they are, you fool, you mustn't fret. Reflect that I'm (especially now) a changeable thing—in spite of healthy cheeks: and that it was only an hour's indigestion when I was writing, soon done. Think I'm a sulky fool: and leave me, to get clear again.

You were right to believe my telegram. I *am* much better. I'd not insult you by being kind. I tell you the truth, always (or try to). I lie to people worse than me, or strangers. And you're better than me: and not a stranger.

Your letters—I do love you so, Ka. It's mad, mad, mad, that we shouldn't be together: *now*, and continually—

Verona: see here. I'm going to take a *train de luxe* to Verona or Milan.

* * *

(If it's Verona 11.55 a.m. we could just change and go on to Venice, where we'd get at 2.15!)

My dear romantic. The whole thing's very much in your style! I'm ready for *anything*. Oh, it will be fun. Just say what you want. I know Italy so *very* well, that it's for you, novice, to choose where you'd like an absurd day or two.

Let me know. I'm so excited. Ka. I must get up and go out. (It's stopped raining.) I shall write again, oh, sometime. I shall read your letter nine times before lunch. I hate myself for making you unhappy: and I'm so happy because I'm going to meet you so soon. You're very lovely and wonderful and dear to me.

RUPERT

One thing, wherever you come to meet me, *bring a German postcard*: I shall immediately write on it and enclose it to Munich to be posted. You must find someone for me to enclose it to. Hugh, perhaps.

To KATHARINE COX

[*Cannes, January 1912*]

Thursday evening.

This'll get you Saturday.

There's only two seconds to write in.

You see, your telegram's come. I don't know what to do. I'm afraid I shall laugh all dinner-time: or sing.

Verona—

* * *

Once I meet you, I'm in your hands. I give up responsibility. You may do what you like. So choose *precisely* which you like; and wire on Saturday, 'Verona' or 'Milan': or if you've some additional details. Then I'll sometime wire the day. We meet on either station.

Ka! It will be good. I shall be infinitely gay and well. I look Italian. You look merely German.

Oh! but to see you again and touch you!

We shall be splendid.

Love

RUPERT

To KATHARINE COX

Friday night: in a hurry.

Awful scenes with the Ranee. But, as wired, I'm coming. At first she was horrified. Then in wild despair she came down to only a week. But I've bought the ticket!

I get into the train Monday evening (as you do).

I shall write tomorrow. My last letter.

My dear, it's so splendid.

I'll know tomorrow where we meet. I think the arrangements are obvious and fixed. I don't want you to wire too often: for suspicion's sake. *Anyhow* don't wire after 1 on Monday. The dance— I explained. I don't want you to miss it: and I don't want us to have to start Wednesday dawn for Munich. Que faire? But you'll decide —have decided. I'll be happy anyhow.

I'm rather tired—it's so beastly hurting people, as I do the Ranee. But it's got to be done. You'll 'look after' me so, when I tiredly fall into your arms in Italy. I wish I could tell her that. Three days from now I start. Within 90 hours I see you. My god! Italy!

Oh my dear; I must stop: and go to go on fighting. But all's so very well: because I'm to be seeing you. Everything leads to that.

Please do just what you like: and anyway don't fuss or worry.

Oh, my dearest. I can't write I'm so happy.

RUPERT

To KATHARINE COX

[*Cannes, 26 January 1912*]
My last letter to you: I think. Hands and lips, next. Only invalids know what time is. A hundred years have gone over since I saw you at Victoria. I've forgotten you, so. But I know that I'll find something so extraordinarily kind and lovely and comfortable. I've that long-ago feeling of a 'lap', a place you hid your face in, and shelved responsibilities. All's confused and tiring, and unimportant for a bit, in front; and then you! It's like the last ten minutes in a muddy House-match; or the last two miles on a long walk.

These things go on round, the Casino, and walking back in the rain, and Miss Barker on Mendelssohn, and Mrs Digby on India, and Mrs Fox at Bridge, and Ovaltine. But in 85 hours I'll see Ka. Tomorrow morning I shall get your letter written after hearing about Verona. I'm so excited. Friday night. I wonder what you're ridiculously doing now: reading German grammar, or at a theatre.

Oh my dear I'm going to rest so wonderfully these three days. And be so finely strong as I prance down the platform. You know, it would be too absurd for us to keep apart a second longer. It's been monstrous we've kept apart so long. I've even thought I ought to have hushed it all up (my 'nerves') and rested ten days in England and come straight to Munich. Only there were depths I got into, I couldn't fight in. And I, even I, was a little ashamed of trading on your strength and goodness. Even now, I feel at moments a bit, a bit ashamed—but, I think—know, that's irrelevant, nonsense, wicked even, between you and me. Isn't it?

Tuesday! I wonder how you'll find me? As much better as you thought? Will you be pleased or disappointed? I'm really so much better, I think, than three weeks ago: and yet something short of what I'll be.

'S! But we'll talk and laugh.

Oh, Ka, I *won't* be a bother to you this time, a whining baby on your hands. Please look forward to it only with happiness—and not a sigh too, that you've the great load of me to carry.

Oh, my dearest, it's so splendid in all the hurry and the doubts and the incompletions, and mistrust and funking and sham to find one thing that stands out clear and certain and great. One thing clear in all the tangle. By God, it's good to have one thing you can take and shake in God's face, with 'Here's one thing that, without "ifs" and "mights", *is*!'!

I'm lying in bed now in this funny room (no, it's not very large). When I shut my eyes and whisper your name over, I can feel your hands and face and hair above and about me. Oh, you must be thinking of me now. You must know. I think of you in a million ways. I know just how you'd like one French family in this hotel better than anyone else in the place, for a certain quality—I do, too. And I think of your eyes when you say something. And I think of your gentle strong soft body—my thoughts are entirely indecent and entirely clean. I see you with your head thrown back. I put my bare arm round your bare back; and my arm's infinitely strong and the curves of your back are the loveliest things in the world.

Oh Ka you've taught me and given me such a lot. I wish to God I could give you something. I love you so.

But you love me and we're going to meet, and there's nothing to write but happiness. If I were stronger!—for I'm weak, so that

I can only cry for the sheer happiness of it. That we should exist, be going to meet.

Ka, Ka, Ka, you're so fine and glorious and beautiful. I've done you a million wrongs, and it hurts like Hell to remember some of them (during last year, oh my God!)—but I can't remember or care for that now. I'm only happy that we'll meet, and that you exist.

Ka, it's all so clear. Can't you chuck Hester and everything and come off till at least the Autumn? Italy and Greece and Spain we'll wander and work in. And afterwards in some English hut a bit. One only makes plans for a year or two. Then, perhaps, we'll go off. We'd be able to then, with a good thing behind us. You'd have given me the strength and sanity, and I'd have given you—oh God, *something*! But that, now, for it's clear and good. Oh, Ka, we'll know even better soon, in Munich: and talk. But I know it! I know it! I know it!

Dearest, it's so late. I must sleep. I shall do so, happily and well. I'm all cool-burning with love for you. I know you so. Oh, I wish I could write—I couldn't even say it. But touching does. If you were here!

I kiss every inch, every inch of you, and every thought of your heart. Goodnight.

Saturday morning.   [*27 January 1912*]

Ach! it's been so beastly. The Ranee was dispirited, and generous over money, and the rest. She's entirely given in. I suppose you're disliking me for it all. But what could I do? What would you have done?

Your letter of Wednesday night–Thursday morning, this morning. And one from poor Mr Masefield. His writing's so far more feminine than yours. Your envelopes may be seen by the Ranee; she thinks they're from Hugh. But if she sees his—oh! she'll think it's the old story. Bryn, you know. Did I ever tell you that Hester's not the only one who knows the truth of my tragedy? Each time I get a telegram (and what with you and the Apostles there's a lot) the poor Ranee thinks that Bryn's so brilliantly (one can see her) going to swoop down and carry me off.

Well: in half an hour I go to be weighed: and get the Ranee's money. (I'll enclose my weight in a postscript.) So I'll end off. The Ranee's leaving for England on Wednesday: so we may dodge the postcard. But you must bring one, an envelope for it, and prepare someone to dispatch it from Munich.

Your duty's so very simple. You get into the 10.40 p.m. (having discovered from Cook's if it goes) on Monday night (I'll be at Nice then) at Munich. Then we commence rushing towards each other. I suspect both trains'll go just a little faster than usual. If you settle on Verona: you get out at 10.0 Tuesday morning and go for 115 minutes stroll, then you return and I fall out of a carriage into your arms. If you've wired 'Milan' you (perhaps) change at Verona, and get to Milan at 12.25 p.m. There you'll see me waiting. We lunch hard by the Duomo. And if you decide not to come; you can be on the Munich platform at 10.14 Tuesday night.

But you are coming! I'm upset about the dance. But I'm leaving all to you. You *did* wire 'any day and hour'! It will be such fun. And Munich! You're to be incredibly sour to Frau Kanilot, hinting you never wish to see her. You don't mind my letters, do you?— I mean it's so hard sometimes, to know how other people are feeling. Oh, but I know it's all right.

*   *   *

Just 3 days; one from when you get this!

You and your tickets! If you go so rarely, just buy more expensive seats at the Booking office. If there's anything at the end of next week, get *two*. . . .

Goodbye, dearest. No more letters! You. I shan't even wire much. You are so splendid: and you're going to make me so well: and I love you so.

RUPERT

*   *   *

To JACQUES RAVERAT   *24 Bilton Road, Rugby*
                                        End of February [*1912*]
                    *   *   *

Children!

I heard from that Cox-woman. She seemed to say she'd seen you. . . .

Oh well, you see, it's this; only it sounds so beastly. *I* wrote to *her*, about her perhaps trickling down to Rugby, and how it was really too beastly for anyone to come to, and how if it wasn't too horrible for any but the strongest nerves, I might perhaps have asked a Foreigner or two like Jacques. . . only wasn't he ill? or wouldn't it anyhow be too horrid and too insolent of me. . . and so on. I was being frightfully dim and wandery and solilocutory. And then it was crossed, you see, by *Her* writing to *ME* (I hope this is all *quite* clear) to say she'd seen you and how he—that is *you*—I mean *Jacques*—had said he almost thought of looking me up. . . .

O, it's all too horrid, and I'm so acutely aware that my poor mind isn't *all* what it was and that it wanders so, and I often catch people nodding and winking at each other—finger tapping forehead—when I'm talking, and then the *things* the little boys shout after me in the streets! . . . So, you see, I naturally don't want to burden at all the healthy and living with my presence (oh, I *know* I saddled myself on Ka (metaphorically) and played on her hospital-nurse instincts, damn her! in Munich—but I *assure* you I was very helpful in showing her German Life and didn't, almost at all, lean on her Christianity) —especially with this Victorian *entourage* (French) and with the Ranee so devastatingly president at dinner. Only I *am* a lot better, and almost bright by London standards: and it's a very quiet little house, and there are a lot of fields two hundred yards down the road. What, in fact, I wanted to say—oh, not to *say*, to let fall, to whisper, to hum, to indicate—was that if London was too beastly, you could, if you liked (only I don't see you could conceivably *like*) drop—drip—down here a day: either or both or all three (V. could have the Bath room?) with your easels and things—and just go on living you know, painting in that field, and talking to me now and then—almost as if you hadn't really come anywhere on a visit. The Ranee's very often out: and anyhow there's my untrodden brown room at the top, where only I am allowed, and the lady who brings me tea. There's a spare bedroom with a *lot* of beds, and another (bedroom) which the Ranee said Monsieur was to use as a dressing-room—(I said couldn't he dress in Madame's presence? and then there was such a *dreadful* scene—silence and redness and so on. I *wish* I knew about married life.)

Oh, it all sounds too beastly: you'd have to wear a tie, Jacques (of course, you've been through it all before—this house isn't quite so lugubrious as School Field was, though: but it's uglier, even; and smaller).

No. You mustn't even let the idea of coming enter your heads: unless you suddenly thought Not-London would be good for you, either of you, And unless Jacques is in absolutely supreme health, this Hell would be the end of him.

This next week-end there's a man coming. The week-middle after that (a week today)—the Ranee's away in London all the Wednesday —and subsequent week-ends are void—or vaporous.

Oh, it's so horrible being supposed to be unwell: I'm so gaspingly afraid you might, one of you, conceivably come and visit me because you absurdly thought I (in any way) *wanted* you to—Oh God!

RUPERT

P.S. Please burn this unread.

To EDWARD MARSH   *24 Bilton Road, Rugby*
                                          Saturday–Sunday
                                         end of February
                              [*Postmark: 25 February 1912*]

Dear Eddie,

Your letter found me in Munich. I was at Cannes for two or three weeks, Munich two or three more, & now I've unexpectedly come home.

Alas! your tidings of me in rude health at Cannes were far from accurate. I find I was getting ill through the autumn & winter—& I don't know how long before—with work & things. The final rush for my incondite & incomplete dissertation finished me. I went to Lulworth after Christmas for a 'reading-party'. There I collapsed suddenly into a foodless & sleepless hell. God! how one can suffer from what my amiable specialist described as a 'nervous break-down'. (He reported that I had got into a 'seriously introspective condition'! and—more tangibly—that my weight had gone down a stone or two.) I tottered, being too tired for suicide, to Cannes, not because I like the bloody place, but because my mother happened to be there. I flapped slowly towards the surface there; & rose a little more at Munich. I've come here for a month or two to complete it. After that I shall be allowed (and, by Phoebus, able, I hope) to do some work. My cure consists in perpetual overeating & oversleeping, no exercise & no thought. Rather a nice existence, but oh God! weary. I detail all this to account for my recent silence & my present lumpishness & banality, & to illuminate any future reports you may hear of the dead & doltish remains of the shipwreck.

Your letter & review gave me immense & slightly pink-cheeked pleasure. It is absurdly kind of you to face the terrors and pangs of parturition (at, you report, so advanced an age for a first confinement!) for me. Either innate & long-hidden genius or else the continual & earnest study of the masters of English (me & Trollope & Crashaw & the rest) has given you, though, a finished & practised wit & clarity of style that'll fairly prick the honest stammerers who neighbour you in the Poetry Review. (For, oh yes! I know it: I've taken it in since January, as it happens; so that, alas! your review will sell only 3,999 fresh copies of my book.) I love your account of Beauty running behind the cab of modern poetical points of view. Mr Galsworthy or another crying 'Whip behind!' I suppose?

I liked the review very much from my own point of view, & of course felt passionately in agreement with it. But one feels so distorted & uncertain & oblivious about one's own work, that I'd rather, in any case, offer only thanks & not comment. I've an insistent queer feeling of having got rid of poems I've written & published—of having cut the umbilical cord—that they're now just slightly more anybody's concern than mine, & that everybody has an equal right & a faintly greater opportunity of understanding them. But with this reservation, & in the spirit of two *Philologs* discussing some musty classic, I'd like to make two suggestions. One is that there wasn't any intention of having 'the beloved' at the table in that Dining-Room. If she was (as I'll confess she happened to be on that imagined—or generalized—occasion), it was rather in her capacity as one of a few very close friends, than as anything more intimate—& more disturbing. If you think the situation demands a central figure, all right. But it seemed to me to be a group.

Then there's *Town & Country*. The point is, what time of day do they go off their heads? You suggest midnight. 2.30 p.m. was rather my idea; with all the horrible stillness of hot sunlight. But that's again rather a matter of choice. . . .

London sounds rather bright just now. But I don't think I shall be in it for more than half an hour for weeks & months. I'm going to grow fat & serene here. Anyway, I've got a turn against London just now:—against England as a whole, rather.

Funny your finding George Mallory. I've known him so many years, discontinuously. I'm rather fond of him: but I never have a warm enough affection—no, it's a sharp enough interest I lack— to see him a great deal—I've meant to go & find him at Charterhouse, but never done it. I always, or generally, have a vague feeling in his presence—as if *I*'m, momentarily, dull, not he, especially. But what's one to do? But I like him.

I'm very glad Gosse & Austin Dobson liked the book. Wasn't it perhaps your skilful advocacy? I've always had a sort of respect for Gosse, in spite of an almost irresistible tendency to despise anyone who was writing about English Literature before 1890. He seems to keep an unusual combination of sanity & vitality in his taste, or outlook. Does he think my Muse one of those 'Decaying Maenads in a throng' who 'shout a startling and indecent song', that I seem to remember he recently wrote about?

I suppose I shall see you some day. I can't say what I'm going to do after I leave Rugby. I expect I shall go abroad again.

I forgot to say I had a letter from the Editor of the Poetry Review saying he was going to put in a long review (yours) in April: & asking for poems to print in the same number. Of course I haven't any, & I don't suppose I shall be writing any by then.

I'm vaguely thinking of writing a few articles & reviews & things in intervals to keep myself going. I suppose you don't know of any editor who requires occasional absolutely true & infinitely brilliant accounts of books & things, written by a man of immense learning?

Oh, yes about *Dead Men's Love*. You're entirely right, as to the meaning of it; in all ordinary meanings of the word meaning. I suppose it was just an idea—that they only found out they were dead by discovering the absence of bodies in that way, & that Hell just consists in such absence of bodies. But if anyone, realizing that the point of Hell is that you have precisely similar desires in the absence of the means of satisfying them, can't help thinking of cis-Stygian embodiments of the horror—let him! I say. For a poem is essentially, I take it, tended by millions of strange shadows, just as poor Mr W. H. was; & I'll not deny this was one of the shadows. But it was only a shadow: not in any way the substance. So I hope your elderly friends'll be assured that I've not the smallest doubt they'll still for a long time be able to say with Ovid

> Decepta est opera nulla puella mea.
> Saepe ego, lascivae consumto tempore noctis,
> Utilis, et forti corpore mane fui.[1]—etc.

I think there's no news to tell you. Mrs Cornford tried to engage me in a controversy over the poems—she & her school. They are known as the Heart-criers, because they believe all poetry ought to be short, simple, naïve & a cry from the heart: the sort of thing an inspired only child might utter if it was in the habit of posing to its elders. They object to my poetry as unreal, affected, complex,

[1] *Amores*, II, 10, 26–8:
No maid has been beguiled through my doing.
Often, after a night spent in dalliance,
I rise in the morning with no diminution of my body's vigour.

'literary', & full of long words. I'm rewriting English Literature on their lines. Do you think this is a fair rendering of Shakespeare's first twenty sonnets if Mrs Cornford had had the doing of them?

Triolet

'If you would only have a son,
      William, the day would be a glad one.
It *would* be nice for everyone,
If you would only have a son.
—And, William, what would *you* have done
      If Lady Pembroke hadn't had one?
If you would only have a son,
      William, the day *would* be a glad one.'

It seems to me to have got the kernel of the situation, & stripped away all unnecessary verbiage or conscious adornment.

                                             Ever

                                        RUPERT

To KATHARINE COX   [*Rugby*]
                                        [*March 1912*]
Noon: Friday

Nothing today. Do I deduce that you were tired last night? Ka! It raineth. Jacques is not yet here: he comes at 2.15, I hear. Silence, as Mr Ivanov so wonderfully says, is more than Words. So, though you hear nothing, think of me loving you a good deal during the week-end.

It's so hard to write just now: for I'm all the while occupied in soothing a new inmate, who was pretty disconsolate till she met me. A Cat. She arrived last night. Tell James. She kisses the end of my chin as I write. She kisses less well than you. I read a story about a woman who knew 127 different ways of kissing. I suppose you don't know of a book about it or anything?

The Ranee was so excited about Disestablishment last night, that she forgot you. And this morning, so far, she's lain pretty low.

I sit in here like a weather-beaten mariner, thinking of the stormy sea. Do you know it's less than three weeks since we were at Starnberg? The things—the adventures, Ka, we've been through together! It's quite certain no other two people in the world could have done it. I'm so old and proud and strong.

I forgot to tell you, I went to tea with Froylein on Tuesday and we talked Germany, and she was very keen on the *Rosenkavalier* and I was suddenly ferocious and talked of Nietzsche.

An Interlude. The Ranee entered from the rain, screaming 'Here's Mrs Bullock'. So I winked and put my tongue out; and the Ranee, as Mrs Bullock entered behind her, jigged and grimaced and shouted, in a stage whisper, 'You'd better go upstairs'. So here I am, upstairs. We don't like Mrs Bullock. But the Ranee's sorry for her, and helps her.

The Ranee, I'm glad to say, has given up the lost-child craze. At one time she used to wander about the streets accosting all small, lonely, tearful children. With infinite patience she used to discover they came from the other end of the town. Determinedly the Ranee would grip the lost baby, and march it back two miles to its hovel. Sometimes she'd meet an upper-class acquaintance bound in the same direction. 'Mr (or Mrs) Bradby's going in your direction. How fortunate!' the Ranee then roars to the amazed baby. Then to the sky, 'It *says* it lives in Paradise Court, and its name is Wilkins.' She would press the dirty small hand into the clean large one; and rush in the direction of the next small lonely creature: leaving a hot-faced wrathful young master or master's wife, and a hot-faced frightened baby to tread their joint paths in silence. But generally she followed it out to the end, scolded and made friends with the Mother, and adopted the whole family.

Thanks for St John's Wood. You seem to expect *me* to expect the whole family to be in mourning, tears, and insomnia. No. It's not done, or thought of, in those circles. I'm sorry Noel's looking ill.

I cease. It will be very nice when you come. *Do* behave, though. Will you remember *not* to call me 'Dearest'? Think it. I think it continually. I'm very well; and loving you very much; and quite happy, and only thinking that these days are going by, wasted a little, when one's well and twenty-four, and you're in London.

Go on resting—and loving. You are very splendid.

RUPERT

To VIRGINIA STEPHEN   *24 Bilton Road, Rugby*
                                         9 March 1912

Virginia dear,

I'm told—in the third-hand muffled manner I get my news from
the Real World—that you've been, or are, unwell. It's not true?
Let me implore you not to have, as I've been having, a nervous
breakdown. It's *too* unpleasant—but you're one of the few people
who, of old, know what it's like. ('Hypersensitive and Introspective', the good doctor Craig said I was.) I feel drawn to you, in this
robust hard world. What tormented and crucified figures we literary
people are! God! how I hate the healthy unimaginative hard shelled
dilettanti, like James and Ka.

It was a pity you couldn't come to that House Party long, long,
ago, at Lulworth—not that you'd have enjoyed it: it was *too* horrible.
But you might have made all the difference. I fell into an abyss
there. Bruin Cox[1] (who, robbed of her offspring by the authorities,
was diverted into being general wet-nurse for the ricketty gathering)
pulled me out and dispatched me to the South of France. There,
among Mr and Mrs Roberts, Miss Barker, old Mrs Wollaston, Mrs
Paxton, Colonel Hullar, old Miss Fox, and the two Americans,
I rallied a little. (One day I shall tell you their life-histories.) But it
was Munich that brought me in sight of shore: and Ka that brought
me to Munich. I showed her life there—i.e. Carnival. She took
a slow but intense part, and hugged several men of her own size in
mid-street. She even went to several costume-balls, disguised as
a human being. She waltzed—I watched her—with slow relish: the
gay petticoats only rarely whisking aside and giving a glimpse of
furry pelt beneath.... She talks Deutsch now as if it were Urse.

It's nice being in a foreign town—the irresponsibility of it. It's
like standing in the wings after you've done your scene, and watching
the next performers. Other people's lives are in the centre, instead
of your own. It's as good as being old.

I'm not really in England. It's only an interim between two
½-periods abroad. One gets into the state of mind for being abroad.
I've carefully got into it for a period of some twelve months. I happen to have come to Rugby for a month in the middle, in order to
get my health back. It doesn't really interfere, or break the abroad-
ness. I *am* abroad, and I generally put 2½*d* stamps on my letters.
I stay out here, on the Continent, for a year perhaps. So, unless you
could escape England and come out I shan't see you again; which

[1] V.S. had always thought of Katharine Cox as being like a bear.

gives me a great deal of pain. A year = for ever. It would be horrible not to see you at all in 1912. If I'm in Germany in July, couldn't you represent the Daily Press at the Mozart and Wagner Festspiel?

Rugby is not very interesting. I drink stout all the morning, and slumber all the afternoon. My mother occasionally brings in tales of the devastating cyclone they call Life in these parts—tales in her usual vein. Would you like to hear of old Mrs Enticott (the ex-gardener's wife), and the operation on the Lower Part of her Stomach, in a Public Hospital, and how they pulled the stitches out too soon, and what the other patients said to Mrs Enticott, and how Mrs Enticott said to the Nurse, every two minutes, 'Please, Miss, do you think you could just let me die? I think I'd rather die'?

*   *   *

There is no really exciting news. I was present at a rehearsal of the first Act of an undiscovered Gilbert and Sullivan opera, last night, in my dreams. But I have forgotten the tunes.

Drink stout—it is the only way. I have a deal more to say to you, but I can't think what it is. Maybe I shall one day see you. I hope so.

Ever

RUPERT

To KATHARINE COX   *Mermaid Club, Rye, Sussex*
                                        (Oh yes!)
                                        Saturday night
                                        [*March 1912*]

My dear,

We're in a Smoking Room. They're all in evening dress: and they talk—there *are* these people in the world—about Bridge, Golf and Motoring. They're *playing* Bridge—

But then the *most* extraordinary thing is about 'Colonel' Aldington, May, Anabel, and Dick. Because—it turns out—*they* keep the Inn. ('Very *Old* Place—you see these beams?') She's written a book of poems and *several* novels. And Dick—but Dick's been a flame of James' for years.

One's almost further from you among the upper classes than elsewhere. Oh Lord! And in the Dining-room.... But James, or I, 'll tell you about it all.

I've been feeling a lot better to-day. I got a morsel afraid Jacques or Gwen 'ld attack you—worry you. But I guess, you'll allow for (it's not unknown in you) their love—

Jacques, my dear, was extraordinarily nice to me. It seemed a comfort—when one had (I feel, you know) spued it out—that he was there, one's friend, loving (you and me), meaning well, suffering —in the world. The Universe seemed to oscillate less than it has.

('I think you made a mistake in putting that ten on, partner.')

You've, dear, a lot of thinking—quiet—to do: about arrangements in Berlin. *What's* to happen, and how. (I swore Jacques to deadliest secrecy about all that. I think your repper's safe for a time.)

About rooms—the number and situation. I can always give my address as Dudley's you see.

Jacques was very eager we should all meet—take Dudley off for a week or two—in the Tyrol in June.

('Having no clubs, partner?' 'Having *no* clubs!')

Oh, yes: and I persuaded (*I* persuaded) Jacques to go to my doctor—

A hurried glance through the Club Visitors' book discloses 95 Colonels, Sir E. Ray Lankester, and Horace A. Vachell.

(It's a question of minutes till they ask James to make up a four. You've *not* taken quite all the joy out of the world, Ka.)

We shan't be here *later* than Monday evening. I'll wire the next address.

('My hand was *mud*!' 'MUD, sir?' '*MUD*!!')

If I'm going to you Wednesday or Thursday, though, I shall be *chez* Noel till then.   *   *   *

I've got rid of my headache fairly well: and, as I told you this morning, I feel mentally better for being beastly to you. I'm (for the tension—my foolishness—is soon passing over) better and decenter rather. I'm loving you extraordinarily—one pulls the barriers, and it comes full flow. I'm thinking—oh, my dear, your lips and mine—it's only twenty-four hours ago—of Germany. I'm going to write— when you're there—such poems and things!

*   *   *

(Enter, Anabel, with a parcel. Dear, dear!)

I suppose there's no chance of this going tonight—or getting to you before Tuesday.

('No Trumps, Partner—*distinctly!*'...'"Distinctly!" I *like* that "distinctly". *I* should have said "*stinkingly*".')

(I'm awfully sorry. It's merely verbatim. My dear, *I* can't help it).

James has just found the Spectator.

You know, when one sees a lot of one's fellow-*men*, one comes round to the women, a bit. As intelligent anyhow: I suppose these Colonels wouldn't steal one's purse.

(James is writing to Bryn.)

Thursday I shall see you—it'll be nice.

I want, I extraordinarily want—it's too degraded—to *work* for you. Do a lot of hard things—a Treatise on Prose Rhythm—a Play —An Epic—and watch you read them. Then if each made a thousand pounds and I gave you ⅔. Damn!

But Happiness is defined as you reading my proofs.

(That'll make her sick: nothing about *her* proofs:...but one's done that, in a way....)

It's the turning point when one starts trembling *not* from pain, but from lust.

One's distracted—I wanted to say, sometime, that they told me (J and G) that your paper had every now and then, queerly, stuck in the middle, a sentence entirely in my style. Very noticeable. I feigned indifference—contempt. Really I *sweltered* with pride within. Fairly ooozed.

('By-y *Jove*, Gran' Slam'...'Dirt is Trumps: Ha! ha!'...And a Phonograph from the Lady's room. James is in Hysterics. Oh! oh!)

Dearest: think of things. I love you *very* much, oh my dear.

RUPERT

To KATHARINE COX   *Mermaid Club, Rye, Sussex*
                        Sunday [*March 1912*]

Dearest,

I'm just out a walk to Winchelsea. I don't know *where* I'm going to settle this week-end. But will you write to me chez Noel and say if Wed. evening or so 'ld do for you (and say other things too). I leave here, you see, on Monday evening.

I thought I'd like to get rid of that woman before I came in to you. I'll crawl in for comfort—the old game!

I'm sick about Noel. I, even I, find my theories true—she gets hold of one—oh, I know what I'm doing, it's all right! I admire her rather extraordinarily. Sentimentality they tell me.

You, you'll be in Woking this time tomorrow. I may hear from you tomorrow. You'll (damn!) not have heard for ages.

It's come out, by the way, that the Ranee *didn't* like your clothes—

I've got to go out. Trains *are* difficult. I *think* I get to Noel tomorrow evening.   *   *   *

Do you know about the General and the Aide de Camp who shared a Bed?

Dearest: I'm getting ravenous with passion. *Oh*, I love you.

I'm feeling clearer, too. Love, love, love: it takes me like a tide. I'd sweep you away.

Good: bye. I love you so—

RUPERT

You'd better marry me before we leave England: you know. I'll accept the responsibility. And the fineness to come....

To KATHARINE COX   *Mermaid Club, Rye, Sussex*
                              Sunday evening [*March 1912*]

Oh God, we've been searching for Rooms in Winchelsea. No luck. It's the most tiring thing in the world. (I wish *you* were going to Berlin first, to do that sort of thing.)

We're going to telegraph to Mrs Primmer—

Oh, and Winchelsea's so lovely. On the road back we met a small lady who was lost, and I was (nervously) Kind to her, and restored her, practically, to her mother. Ha!

I read *The Way of All Flesh*, and talk to James and think of you. James nibbles at the past—oh, the Remote past—and I throw him scraps.

You swim about one in your strength and vitality and loveliness and kindness.   *   *   *

One tires, still away from you. (Oh, I'm *much* better!) People wrangle 'You want *Company*', 'You want *Peace*'—But the answer never given, is always that in solitude one frets to illness, in company one talks...and then gets tired and collapses. 'There's only *Ka* to be with: then all goes straight—will go straight....'

I wonder if to send this to Woking or London. I suppose you'll come down late evening. Tired. Or will you put it off till Tuesday? You're a bother of a Ka.

I'll be soon seeing you. You're to say if you want to get rid of me sooner than I suggested.

James and I have been out this evening to call on Mr Henry James. At 9. We found, at length, the House. It was immensely rich, and brilliantly lighted at every window on the ground floor. The upper floors were deserted: one black window open. The house is straight on the street. We nearly fainted with fear of a Company. At length I pressed the Bell of the Great Door—there was a smaller door further along, the Servants' door we were told. No answer. I pressed again. At length a slow dragging step was heard within. It stopped, inside the door. We shuffled. Then, very slowly, and very loudly, immense numbers of chains and bolts were drawn within. There was a pause again. Further rattling within. Then the steps seemed to be heard retreating. There was silence. We waited in wild agonizing stupefaction. The House was dead-silent. At length there was a shuffling noise from the Servant's door. We thought someone was about to emerge from there to greet us. We slid down towards it. Nothing happened. We drew back and observed the House. A low whistle came from it. Then nothing happened for two minutes. Suddenly a shadow passed, quickly, across the light in the window nearest the door. Again nothing happened. James and I, sick with surmise, stole down the street. We thought we heard another whistle, as we departed. We came back here shaking—we didn't know at what.

If the evening paper, as you get this, tells of the murder of Mr Henry James—you'll know.

One day James, or I, will tell you the story (overheard this evening) of the Dynamo and the Two Household Pussies. . . .

No Bridge this evening: Sunday.

* * *

You, oh you. You fill one's horizon—one's narrow horizon— and one's life. Ka, and her dresses, and her walk—it comes round and over one. I think of living very close to you for long, knowing and being known, seeing a child; knowing your mind, knowing your ways and thoughts round me. Taking things, strength and rest and love—and giving love and a thousand things—the great things I'll do.

RUPERT

To JACQUES RAVERAT   *Rye, Sussex*
                                                Sunday, [31] March
                                                      [1912]
My dear,

I leave here tomorrow evening. I go to Noel's, then to Ka Wednesday evening? till Friday? Then I don't know where:—Winchelsea or the New Forest. I'll tell you where I'm going when I *know*, you know.

You're such good people to have in the world—supposing the world's going to exist without me...

Tell Ka that if she's not married me by the 10th of May you'll burn England and come across and shoot us both.

                                                      RUPERT

To JACQUES RAVERAT   *Hook Hill Cottage,*
                                              near Woking, Surrey
                                          Good Friday [5 April 1912]

Your letters—you're both very good. You stand when most things rock and slide—I love you, also.

I'm going tomorrow to c/o Mrs Primmer, Beech Shade Bank, Lyndhurst. James'll be there a day or two, then Bryn. I'd promised James already.

I'm going to leave Ka alone till she's rested and ready for Germany. I found her (I came yesterday) pretty bad. To rest, as far as she will, is the best thing for her: (and for me). She sees—anyhow —what other people think. It can stay there for a bit. Time starts—

I went to Limpsfield a few days. I talked to Noel. She was astounding. Being there—and she—gave me extraordinary rest and strength: I found. I feel all ways vastly stronger—I'm at Bank till Thursday (?), then I'm going to Limpsfield again a day or two— I want to see Margery. Then I come through London *en route*. Will you be there?

I'll write soon. This is to say that all's...'well'.

                                                      RUPERT

To MAYNARD KEYNES   *Beech Shade Bank, Lyndhurst*
                        Wednesday after Easter
                        [*10 April 1912*]

Dear Maynard,

You were very good to give me tidings about the Fellowship, the Expert Manuscript book, and other matters of importance. I have forgotten the first and write the third in the second all day. How difficult that is to understand. I didn't come to Cambridge: I wasn't fit. I'm not fit for anything. I have suffered a Seelebruchenleide— or, as the sailor said to me last Thursday, I've done myself in.

I sit here in the country eating and sleeping and occasionally going on with my task of translating Mr Swinburne's First Poems and Ballads into German. I think I shall go on my travels very soon. England will never hear of me again.

*   *   *

My poor mind isn't at all what it used to be (all of you, of course, think that a trifle: but, Lord, it was all I had!) When it has recovered —if ever it does—I shall write a short play, before the End. My next year's dissertation will have no more facts but ninety pages more epigrams, so *that* won't take long.

I'm here, under the charge of Brynhild, at present. Most charming. And about my intellectual level. Oh, no, a little above it. A month with the Ranee nearly finished me. I heard you were at Bewley in France—but then that you were back. Very queer. What is Bewley, anyway? And did you see Mrs Woolaston there?—she's somewhere on that coast—

Oh, oh! Mrs Primmer's five-course dinner is on the table—funny she should be the best cook in England. Brynhild, a little nervously, sends you her love. ἀσπαζεσθε τους ᾽Αδελφους μιτ εἰνεμ εἰλιγεν κῦσσεν.[1]

Love to Duncan if you're at Brunswick [Square].

                                        Tenebriously
                                        RUPERT

[1] Mixed Greek and German: 'Greet the Brothers with a holy kiss'.

To HUGH DALTON

C/o Mrs Primmer,
Beech Shade Bank, Lyndhurst
Easter 1912
[*Postmark: April 11*]

Dear Hugh,

You were good to write to me. It doesn't matter about the scientist who got a fellowship for two reasons.

(1) Nothing matters.

(2) They will give me a fellowship next year. The electors seem agreed upon that.

The scientist, you see, had no more shots. I have one more. Both our dissertations were extremely good. He discovered a very important thing about the Blood of Coal Miners. It needs far less Oxygen than you think. And, it follows, they can live far longer and far oftener when the Worst happens, than you suppose.

Friend of my laughing careless youth, where are those golden hours now? Where now the shrill mirth of our burgeoning intellects? and by what doubtful and deleterious ways am I come down to this place of shadows and eyeless pain? In truth, I have been for some months in Hell. I have been very ill. I am very ill. In all probability I shall be very ill. It is thought by those who know me best (viz. myself) that I shall die. Nor do I greatly want to live: the savour of life having oddly left it, and my mind being worn and flabby, a tenth of anything it used to be.

I do nothing. I eat and sleep and rest. My thoughts buzz drearily in a vacuum. I went in January to a slightly American nerve-specialist who said I was deplorably unwell. He made me drink stout and swallow the compressed blood of bullocks. In consequence I am now enormously fat. Boys laugh at me in the street. But that is partly, also, on account of my manner. For I am more than a little gone in my head, since my collapse.

I go back to Germany soon. They are a slow race and will not know I am stupid. I shall never appear in England again. I shall never write poetry or limpid prose again. I may ultimately become sub-reader of English Philology in the Johns Hopkins University Wa. (or Ma., or Ra.).

I am a despicable toothless creature: and I mock at the Spring.

I salute you from these depths. Give my love to the Middle Temple.

Ever

RUPERT

To KATHARINE COX *Beech Shade* [*Lyndhurst*]
Wednesday morning
[*April 1912*]

No: You've got the address right.

James left yesterday. He was very freakish—what they call delightful—when he was here. But at the end 'a sense of impending doom' seemed to hang over him. That was partly because Bryn had played the woman's part, and *not* been kind—nor (oh, alas!) kissed me. She is in Wales. And James had to leave me to solitude.

But she may be coming tomorrow. I sit and read and write.

I'd like you to bring the dissertation out, if you will.

I shall either buy a Baedeker, or appropriate Dudley's. So don't you get one.

It is fine but not warm. The beeches are in bloom. Also the junipers and arbutuses and so forth. We went walks and enjoyed the scenery. James pointed to a clump of larches, and said: 'Birches!...ah! Birches! Birches are a wonderful tree....'

'You should see a birch in Autumn, my boy!' he said, rather simply. 'I *have*', I said, with some irritation.

Mrs Primmer is, of course, the *most* amazing cook in the world. Four-course dinners, absolutely perfect. One eats a lot. I think of staying here for ever. I shall at any rate not leave before Saturday or Monday (unless Bryn doesn't come at all). Then Limpsfield. So I've still a week in England, it seems.

*   *   *

RUPERT

To KATHARINE COX [*Germany, in the train*]
[*c. 25 April 1912*]

Sunday

4.40 p.m. The good man says. So I've slept two and a half hours more. Gott sei dank! I got a very doubtful hour last night. I've just woken by kicking the old lady very violently under the knee. My reflexes played that trick that seems to be chronic with them now. (You'll be pretty well bruised after a bit, my dear.) The old lady has gone an extraordinary light greenish yellow, and is staring into the *Ewigkeit*. Mother of God! What can I say, in German? *Liebe Frau, es tut mir furchtbar leid das Sie ganz grün-gelb sind.* I wonder if she will die.

But here's the edge of Berlin.

If Dudley doesn't meet me—I shall cry.

My delicious sleep (she's obviously had all her joy in life) has prevented my writing. But I will do so.

Monday

In Dudley's favourite pension. The room is immense. I find I shall be very comfortable.

Dudley is going to be married on May 11th in Munich; and is going to leave here on the 6th or 7th. So you *must* come quickly, Ka, to see him some days. He's going for about a fortnight to Venice, after the marriage and then back here.

I'm going to get my luggage, buy Ovaltine, ink, etc. I'll write more connectedly, once, to-day or tomorrow. I don't know *when* these letters 'll get to you.

Berlin's full of theatres: oh! *Der Rosenkavalier*, Ka! So come quickly; to see Dudley. And then we can arrange at leisure. I'll think things out.

I feel so ready to give and take happiness.

You'll be getting happy, now, on the Downs.... Will you have tea at the Duncton Inn and talk about cricket?

It was difficult, in London. I'm sorry. So fine, it'll be, here.

Dear

RUPERT

To KATHARINE COX [*Germany*]

Monday [April 1912]

I am travelling in a square box at 10 miles an hour between Brandenburg and Ketzür. I shall walk back from Ketzür. That will suffice for this part of the country. I think it is too flat. Though the lakes *are* rather remarkable. I say, we'll do some sailing? We could have a lot of fun that way. Fancy knowing how to sail.

The worst of this job is that I'm sure to be lynched as an English spy. I sit with maps, looking out of the window, and taking voluminous notes.

We shall bathe. *I* shall dive.

Why am I sitting by the road halfway between Ketzür and Brandenburg? It seems very odd. I have a very large yellow train book and

a Manchester Guardian for Saturday under my arm and a Baedeker
and a Donne in my pocket.

I am here because I love Ka and she is coming to Germany and
we are going to live in a house together, and I must find one, and
this looked a good place on the map. . . .

I am here because at Fettes, in the seventies, Willie Brooke and
May Cotterill got thrown together. And then they had a son and
a daughter, and the daughter died, and while the mother was
thinking of the daughter another child was born, and it was a son, but
in consequence of all this very female in parts—sehr dichterisch—me.

It none of it seems to hang together.

I've just seen a smaller crested wren.

Two soldiers are bearing down at the double. On! on!

The train again.

I can see that one will get fond of the country round here very
quickly. The woods and small hills and great sunsets and the lakes.
This particular region probably won't do. It's nice enough. But
I can see the others'll be nicer. The villages are rather lovely. I don't
know what German rooms are like in the country. I want slightly
bigger hills.

There's five such silly men with me in the carriage: and a placid
baby in the corridor.

I shall go these expeditions every alternate day till you come:
God with me, and a decent amount of sleep given.

You, you'll come, I know, and bring colour and things with you.
There'll be all that, I can see. You do want me a lot: and I you. And
we know a great deal.

I'm just passing through Potsdam. I've a fancy you may be, just
now, in Grantchester. I envy you, frightfully. That river and the
chestnuts—come back to me a lot. Tea on the lawn. Just wire to me,
and we'll spend the summer there; with Goldie to tea every Saturday
and a fancy dress ball on Midsummer night.

I went and saw The Rosenkavalier last night. They do it so *much*
worse than in München. It's scarcely worth seeing. Oh, oh. But
I think of going to *Frühlingserwachen* tonight. Perhaps you, silly,
don't know what that is. James'll enviously tell you.

Just here we pass through miles of pine forests: and under each
pine tree there is a paper-bag.

When you come, you must register to, and get out at, the Zoo-
logische Garten station. It's fifteen minutes before Friedrichstrasse.
I think you pass there from Hamburg.

What shall I say to you? I think, of course, that you've been drowned in a dewpond or savaged by a sheep on the South Downs. I shall know you haven't though, when I have a letter, in a day or two.

Come, woman, come. I want you.

RUPERT

Oh yes: bring as many biscuits as you like.

To KATHARINE COX

bei Dudley Ward
Kantstrasse 14/Gh
Charlottenburg, Berlin
Wednesday [1 May 1912]

*   *   *

I think I'd answered all your questions. Ben Jonson and Ford to add to the list of books I have with me. If you're in Berlin any time I'd like to make you go to Frühling's Erwachen by Mr Wedekind. I *think* James only has the American translation: but if he *has* the German, you might take it from him.

At 2 this morning I entered the house (I'm sorry: I'd been talking to Dudley:) and collided with the loveliest lady in Berlin. She took me up in the lift (I'd, of course, never been in it before, because I was frightened—it's worked by oneself, with Buttons on the Wall.) It stuck half-way; so, of course, there was only one thing for a gentleman to do. Between Heaven and Earth—with vague reminiscences of Maeterlinck's Bees—I did it—you don't object?...

The story's really much longer.

Dudley....I've been hearing his plans. 1913, a Professorship in China. 1914 War Correspondent in the Balkans—1915 A house in Cambridge and a Caravan in Turkestan...etc. I can only gape.

RUPERT

To JACQUES RAVERAT

bei Dudley
Kant-strasse 14/G.H.
Charlottenburg, Berlin
Freitag [April–May 1912]

I sit in a luxurious pension near Dudley's, and write plays about murders in Lithuania.

My letter to Ka did *not* get her in time at Woking; and my covering note to Harley Street was confiscated by Hester. So that Friday she only knew I was, silently—she thought—in London. At lunch she looked out of a window and saw me on a bus-top. It was the final stroke, for (it appeared) she'd been thinking of nothing but me for four days, ever since her letter. She telephoned in the afternoon to the N.L.C. that she *must* see me. We met for half an hour—in Trafalgar Square and the Park. When we met she collapsed and had to lean behind a lion, against Lord Nelson's pediment, till the crying was over. I think she thought I'd suddenly decided not to bother about her at all: and it brought her round with a jerk. Next day (oh, I missed Friday's train, of course) she'd had my letter and that had put her back up again, a bit. But she seemed really relieved we were going to proceed with the German visit, I thought. Her revulsions are queer. I've not heard from her since. So we tug and jerk. But (in a callous moment) I thought the weather seemed to be clearing....

On the Friday night James and I took Margery to Harry Lauder. Margery spent Friday in arguing with James and me alternately against my going abroad. There were telegrams from Bryn to the same effect. The whole of the South of England seemed to be in a turmoil about it. But I went: seeing the Finger of the Lord. I made a defence to Margery, as we walked London that night. It was, perforce, untrue. But she accepted it. Oh, but she was pleasant!

I've mapped out the surroundings of Berlin into five parts. I shall trot out into one every day, and explore. I ought to have gone to-day: but I was too tired. I don't sleep; often. And that debases. (It produces, you'll have marked, an epistolary style like Dent's.) Mostly I enjoy myself. Sometimes the Depths open.... Berlin, you know, is *frightfully* out of date. What do you think is the thrillingly latest sensation here? A picture-exhibition just opened. By some young Italians. Who call themselves the Futurists. Wirklich! Fancy being pursued by those old phantoms! And Signor Marinetti delivered his famous lecture on Monday. Elsewhere, a Cézanne exhibition: most of which was in London in December. He paints apples best: then men: then landscapes. I don't believe in his land-scapes—oh, I miss the point, I know. Figaro's Wedding: The Magic Flute: Offenbach–Reinhardt: Ibsen.... The Magic Flute about nine times as bad as in Cambridge. *Café's* most of the day. Occasional calls on Dudley, who is always churning out things on his typewriter.

*   *   *

Annemarie and Mrs Ward are about. Mrs Ward is a nuisance
and A. M. is tired. There's going to be a real family wedding in
Munich. Poor Dudley! But he's bearing up.

They go to Venice for a fortnight. (He's married May 10.)
Then back here. He's in an agony of unsuccess about writing to
you. He nearly cries when he mentions it. Then he lights a cigar
and goes to the café, tears in his eyes. You figure him.

*   *   *

My love to you both
RUPERT

To DUDLEY WARD

[*May 1912*]

*   *   *

Things have, in almost every way, been entirely for the best.
Ka's been slightly tired at times; but I've regulated her life so damn
well, and forbidden her to do so much, that that's pretty well gone.
She's enjoyed herself a lot; and found her feelings—physical and
mental—were sixty (her figure) times livelier than she thought
they'd be. And she has climbed down a lot about Lamb. Tonight she
said she didn't feel much interest in him now. She still says she
doesn't think him a beast and that she'll always have immense
affection for him.   *   *   *

So she says that even if she and I don't marry, she'll almost certainly
have nothing to do with him—beyond occasionally seeing him.
But—though she's wiser—I think of course, she'd get trapped fairly
soon, on those terms. But she'd promise never to see him again, she
says, if we married. And I'm pretty sure she'll marry me, if I want.

The crux is that that absolutely dead feeling I had when I was in
Berlin before she came, hasn't vanished. I was afraid, beforehand,
I might—when I saw her—be dragged down into that helpless
tortured sort of love for her I had all the first part of the year, and
had just crept out of. The opposite. I remain dead. I care practically
nothing for any person in the world. I've anxiety, and a sort of
affection, for Ka—But I don't really care. I've no feeling for anybody at all—except the uneasy ghosts of the immense reverence and
rather steadfast love for Noel, and a knowledge that Noel is the
finest thing I've ever seen in the world, and Ka—isn't. But that
doesn't come to much.

So—that's the fix I'm in at present. Time may clear things a lot,
and waken them. From Neu-Strelitz we're going a week's walking,

probably. After that we may or may not continue together, just now: things being as they are. I've sometimes a wish I could take the last step—exact a promise she'd not *see* the man again—and then go off and sleep in some unknown place for six weeks.

But next week, walking'll be great for both.

Love to A. M. and the gondolier—with love   RUPERT

To JACQUES RAVERAT   *A lake North of Berlin*
                                 Friday before Whitsuntide
                                 [*24 May 1912*]

My dear   *   *   *

'God', in His own inimitable way, has answered your prayers.

I was in a mere stupor those weeks in Berlin; dead, dead, dead. I hadn't a flicker of emotion left for any living person. I'd not have cared if the whole lot of you'd had your necks broken. A Peaceful state, but not pleasant. Ka came, and we spent 10 days in Berlin and looking for places in the neighbourhood. Good days, in a way. Ka was a bit tired at first: but she soon perked up, and was extraordinarily happy, and in body and mind, hundreds of times (she said) more lively than she'd thought she was going to be. We lived in the present; only twice, shortly, mentioned past things.

But you know, I was and am still dead (especially towards her). I go *about* with the woman, dutifully. I've a sort of dim, reflected, affection for something in her. But it's all sufficiently dreary. I can get up a sort of pity when I see how weak she is. But that won't do. Love her?—bless you, no: but I don't love anybody. The bother is I don't really *like* her, at all. There is a feeling of staleness, ugliness, trustlessness about her. I don't know. Dirt. —hu—

Oh, it's all nonsense, in a way; and of course we get on very well and I'm fond of her. Only—there's some mud wall between us. Or rather, my faculty for loving her got cauterized too far.

I thought things'd wake, if I went on. But I only seem to get deader. I've a sort of hunger for cleanness.

She is, in general, so much better. And I'm as certain as I am about anything that I could make her promise to marry me within a month. So things have come down pretty well on this side. Only I'm still dead.

On Monday we started off for—at any rate—a week's walking tour, to clear our minds: and to seek a house perhaps.

*   *   *

I got a nice sidelight on you two in a good letter from Noel. You seemed to be shining along.

I hope you'll take Margery to France. It struck me she ought to make a Weltreise. So I've been planning one. Couldn't you send her along to Dudley from you? It's be very good for both. Thence she might find me, if I'm still on the Continent: or, conceivably, Ka, at Dresden. One could keep her out of England for months!

I gather Noel went to Virginia's for a week-end. I suppose she's got too much sense—and she's got you and other wise people—to get spoilt in any way by the subtle degradation of the collective atmosphere of the people in those regions—people I find pleasant and remarkable as individuals. Do you keep on her the eye of responsibility which (you and I know) the old owe the young?

With love
RUPERT

Ka sends her love.

To JACQUES RAVERAT *c/o Dudley, Berlin*
Monday [May 1912]

Your letter was nice to get.

Ka went to England a week ago. I, or what they call me, am here. I thought she'd see you in England; or I'd have sent another 'bulletin'. Though there's little to report.

I think I wrote from Feldberg. We were there for 11 days: ten of them in lovely rooms. We had agreed to part, anyhow, by now, for a bit. She was to have gone to Dresden: but her sister's engagement was broken, so she had to go back to wipe up. I am staying out to give a decent interval, between her arrival in England and mine. For I'm going back to rest in Grantchester. Marriage or Murder, you say. Well, we've tried both, in a way. I don't at all want either. Though it's true, I don't want anything else. I forget what facts I told you. Ka found she was livelier and happier than she thought she'd be. She changed incredibly in the time. We spent a night with Dudley and A. M. on the way back. That finished the process, and she suddenly appeared the old Ka.

She was happy, sometimes, during Feldberg. She also, at the end, professed herself (to Dudley as well) cured of Lamb. Even that she could see him more or less as he is, it seems. (I needn't say, by the way, that we lived entirely in the present, at Feldberg.)

I felt utterly without 'love' for her: and extremely dead. So we agreed we'd wait and get as well as we could, and I as clear, before deciding. I suppose that's what we're doing. She wrote a sad note to Dudley a day or two ago, in which she seemed to be feeling the strain frightfully. I think there may be something in your ideas of us. Not much in some, though. I think really my love for Ka was pretty well at an end—poisoned, dead—before I discovered she was after all in love with me: before that is, I came to Germany. It just died, because—because one can't go on loving a person like Ka made herself indefinitely; love can be suffocated in a dung heap like anything else; and because I got back among sane people, out of my dirty lonely imaginings; and because, anyway, emotion of any kind died.

I thought then I was just suspended—that it'd all come back (I was so *frightened* it would!) when Ka and I were together. But it's dead all right.

What's one to do? It may be, you see, that I'll wake up if I rest and see good people for a month or so—that I'll wake up, and reality —emotions—will come back; and that among it. I feel so extra-ordinarily now as if I'd been asleep—or delirious—for six infinite months. Nothing's real. Dudley's just a silly little man. You're a dim and stupid invalid. Ka's a weak silly female. Writing or work —is a thing one used to do, or think of. There's no difference between you or Dudley and, say, Sayle; or between writing plays and writing notes on dates of Webster. Everything's just as it appears to me in a fever—there, only infinitely dim and far off. Only I'm not at all in a fever.

I *know* what things are—what you are or Dudley is: in an intellectual way. That is, I know what I should feel, if I were I. There it stops.

What's one to do? Dudley thinks—as we're doing—wait till I'm in a fitter state to judge. In a month or so I may—if ever I do—get near a normal state. Then I must decide if there's any hope. It seems rather silly to make a decision like that when I'm like I am— unless that's permanent.

I have such a wish to get away from the whole thing—I'd like to blot the last six months out if I could. But at least I keep feeling that Ka's done her bit: it's mostly to the bad: now the best thing is to be clear of it all, wind it up. She writes to Dudley that now she's, any-how, glad it all happened. That's something (if it's true). I envy her: and want to let it rest at that.

And also, it's hard to get up love for anyone whom one associates only with the evil things of one's life: and whom one always catches oneself thinking degraded, slightly noisome or at least contemptible; and for whom one has—all unwillingly—continual feelings of unforgiveness.

And then—I'm terrified of leaving her. She is weak and silly and has no one to look after her. I feel infinitely responsible. If she drifts off, I feel that Lamb could get hold of her easily again in two or three days: if he said he was ill, for instance. Or she'd float along: food for any feeder. A — — next, or any other little ladies' man... What's one to do? But we'll decide something by a given date in July or August: I promise.

I'll write to you about Dudley and A. M. sometime. They're in a fairly bad way.

I leave here in two days and wander. Rugby address... England in July.

I'll write again, less tired.

> With love
>
> RUPERT

To ST JOHN LUCAS

Germany
[*Permanent address: Rugby*]
May — [*1912*]

Who'd give his heart to a pedant? Who'd trust an anthologist? You've no innards, spleen nor marrow nor good blood.

It's now, I declare, five months since we parted in the romantic Hillmorton Road; and I've been four months on the bed of sickness and great pain; and wandering lonely in hideous lands, and even again in Rugby for a while. But I have heard nothing of you. Inscrutable, hideous enigma; old as the Sphinx and thrice as passionless; how are you? It was even rumoured that you appeared in Rugby to celebrate—as usual—the holy feast of Quinquagesima, that you saw your grotesque father, your lascivious step-mother, your twisted and malicious step-brothers, and even the debonair, the Satanic, the Hellenic, the infinitely beautiful Arthur—and were too stony-hearted to come and sit awhile by my heated bed. Pfui! Why is this? What have I done to you? has it got round to your ears that I called you a mingy and coprologous Oxford poetaster. It is true. But you should not have believed it. Or are you envious that my anapaests were livelier and lither than yours? Or did you loathe my too intricately modern poems, Nestor, so much that you swore to abjure me? Or do you only detest all my friends—but that should hardly be a cause for division, for I do, too. Write to me, St John, write! I demand a postcard, as my right, for I am ill, and have been sick to death, and I am in exile, and I have written no word of verse since August. I desire to know that you live: that you have started the Oxford Book of Norse Poetry: that your dramas are going to be staged with great splendour by Mme Sarah Bernhardt; that your eyes are well: that your brain is superb: that your taste is impeccable: that you have taken silk: and that I shall see you this summer. I'm in Berlin now. I don't know how long I shall stay. I may come back sometime to England. If I do I shall swoop on you and extract you from your gloomy attic. You've falsely, smilingly, promised a hundred times—I shall grip you firmly, this time, and make you tramp three days, or live on a sunny lawn in my clerical residence a week, and write pastoral plays full of sin and smut, and bathe at dawn. You shall see no one from Cambridge. I will disavow all the Professors I know for your sake. Even O.B. shall not be allowed to have tea with me.

Or if you're coming abroad, and I'm out here, let's meet a bit. We can scoff at the unwashed foreigner together. I may slide down to Italy soon. (Perhaps you're enigmatically there already.) Tell me what you're going to do.

I, I have been infinitely forlorn. I'm still a listless corpse. I can't work decently: and the springs of emotion are dried within me. Waken me!...*Ich habe unglaubliche Dinge erlebt*, as they say out here—ἄρρητα δὴ πέπονθα,[1] as your curved lips more exquisitely put it. I had a 'nervous collapse': which is scientific language for the lowest Hells Dante could feebly imagine. De Profundis clamavi, Sancte Johanne, Sancte Johanne, audi meam vocem.

I thirst to see your hawklike brow: or at least your uncultivated Victorian handwriting—

Thine

What was

RUPERT

Do you ever see that enamelled butterfly Fry?

*   *   *

Give him my devotion.

R.

[1] i.e. I have undergone sufferings unspeakable.

To KATHARINE COX   *bei Herrn Dudley Ward*
                                      Kantstrasse 14/Gh
                                      Charlottenburg, Berlin
                                      Sonntag
                                      [May 1912]

Nothing's come from England since I came—except a packet from
the Ranee. So I expect I gave my address wrong. No, I expect no
one's written. But I mistrust the German post office. If my letters
leave out 'bei Ward', they are confiscated. Even Dudley's don't
arrive.

Oh, I don't really want you to have written. You've been walking.
I hope you're all right.

Annemarie I've just said goodbye to. It's frightfully difficult to
express one's sympathy with people. I thought I'd like to. She
seemed to be going out into unknown wilds. Oh, she's all *right*, of
course, with old Dudley—damn her! And I daresay I'd no right to
do anything but dislike her. But it came on me (in the Conditorei)
suddenly that, if you take a calm view, everybody's a pretty lonely
figure, drifting in the gloom: and even the people who think they're,
wonderfully, in pairs—there's not much difference between them
and the rest. '...echoing straits...enisled we mortal myriads
live alone...between us—thrown...to be, the unplumbed salt
estranging sea.'[1] (I *wish* I could remember quotations.) You catch
the drift?...Of course, it's entirely untrue. But I felt it (consolably).
So, at the corner of Kantstrasse, I took her hand (which disap-
pointingly, had a glove) and pressed it and said 'Goodbye. Good
luck!' and my eyes dimmed. And she, she didn't catch a bit what
I was driving at. She was thinking of her journey to-night, or of
Mrs Ward. She didn't notice the sea, hear the murmur of the billows,
spy a white flutter on the horizon. She thought it was Berlin. They
trotted off. I trailed up my Wohnung steps, and watched them for
fifty yards. They didn't turn round. Damn.

She's tired, as I said. But better, now a flat's found. They marry
on the 11th, have 6 days in Venice, and return. So (she remarked)
she'll be seeing you. She seemed dull several times I saw her. But
one moment cheered me. We three went to lunch. Dudley led the
way in, trotting stiffly, ferociously, up between the tables; so straight.
You can see him. Annemarie followed 3 yards behind, I three
behind her. I watched them and felt rather fond of Dudley, and
wondered what she felt. In that instant she turned, smiling, and

[1] From Matthew Arnold's *Isolation, or To Marguerite, continued.*

caught my eye, and slightly motioned towards her man. 'Dudley', we signalled to each other. She turned her head back again, still trotting. Dudley was unconscious to the end. The second of sympathy seemed extraordinarily nice. I loved her through lunch.

To FRANCES CORNFORD   *bei Dudley Ward*
                                           Spichernstrasse 16 G.H.
                                           Charlottenburg, Berlin
                                           May–June [1912]
                                           (*about a week altogether*)

Dear Frances,

The book came.[1] Many thanks. I was officially summoned to the District Post Office, Section F, Subsection 4 (Parcels), Division 2 (English). I repaired thither with my passport, my bank account, and a visiting card. After filling up thousands of forms, I got it: and carried it rapturously home. I've not read it: more than the preface, the chapter summaries, and the twenty odd first pages: for I had to finish a review book first, and since, for three days or four, I've been trailing through these neighbouring pinewoods, seeking repose and inspiration. But I've already read enough to see that my worst suspicions about the Greeks are going to be confirmed. I'm going to enjoy it a lot. I like sensible books about people's minds. There aren't many. Who's going to write the companion volume showing how Huxley and Spencer wrote in terms of the English Church?

I shall write about the book when I've finished it: probably the sort of letter Dent writes Forster after each of his novels. '. . . Surely the Italian quotation on page 476, is not quite grammatical; and I thought I detected a misplaced comma on page 223. . . .' Meanwhile, I'm happy, among these Prussian streets, to be in touch with England and Sense.

I kept trying to write to you after your penultimate (April ?) letter, but it was so difficult. And my former letter was so grey and stiff (my flatness, by the way, wasn't, I think, a dim jest or affectation: I was very prostrate). You see, the matter was this. (I was in that sick state when the whole world's rotten with mistakes and dirtiness, and any additional unfittingness rubs along your nerves like a new noise when you're in a fever.) I thought you disliked and were foolishly unjust to Noel Olivier—and apropos, in a way, of me. I couldn't bear that then, somehow. I knew it was so entirely

[1] F. M. Cornford's *From Religion to Philosophy*, 1912.

wrong. Things weigh so, when one's ill. What do entirely healthy and entirely wise people do when people they love misjudge one another? Oh, I don't think I mind much anyone wronging someone I love. It's only when you love someone and have been infinitely beastly to them, given them evil and wrong in return for fineness— that you can't *stand* other people wronging or badly misjudging them. Isn't that so? That's what it all was then. It was so difficult to *say* that: and so horribly difficult to go on without saying it. So, anyhow, it's clear now. Among a hundred other horrors, I had been so wicked towards Noel; and that filled me with self-hatred and excess of feeling seeking some outlet. I was very angry with you. I suppose it was weak and fretful of me.

But don't misjudge her. She's very fine. Ask even Jacques, who knows her a bit. He's the only person in the world who knows her well. I can see her faults and virtues (and everyone else's) with an absolutely clear and cold eye, as dead people do see. I'm very grateful to her; for she's given me a great deal of good and very little bad, and, in the end, that's fairly high praise for a human relationship. That's all. Don't be angry at my having written this, Frances. For it was right to do so. Though writing's so cold and unfriendly compared with talking.

I'm sorry the play's not going to come off this summer. Poor old Justin! I have a vague feeling all we nerve-collapsers will meet in some high-walled padded quiet place one day soon—Virginia, Justin, Jacques, and I; and gibber and mow at each other while the nurses push pap down our mouths.

But can't the play be done in September? Anyhow, I'd like very much to see it. I'll even, protestingly, put marks at the side where the lines have a foot or two short—though you've written 40 times as much blank verse as I; and I'm increasingly of the opinion that (in the words of the Book) 'no man may save another's Blank Verse alive: for that he must let alone for ever'. I sit here in Berlin—in the Kensington of Berlin—and niggle with plays, too. But mine are severely in prose, and they are full of characters ..., who murder strangers with hammers.[1] But they don't go ahead much. I mostly try—for journalistic practice, and to start a Career—to write Articles. One endeavours to be Delightful. It's all very unpleasant.

But I don't really do much work. I read a bit. But I still feel pretty dead: and very unenergetic. And most of my time is spent in

---

[1] A reference to his play, *Lithuania*.

trying to go to sleep. Once or twice I've taken a rück-sack and gone out into the country for a day or two; which is rather refreshing. And soon I think of getting a boat and going through the rivers and canals and lakes that are all round Berlin, for a week.

It was when I'd wandered to a lake just South of Potsdam that I composed the poem I enclose. It is called, indifferently, *Artistic* or *Die Natur.*[1] It may amuse or enrage you. Otherwise, I've written nothing. I scrawled in a Café a very long poem about Grantchester, that seemed to me to have pleasant silly passages. I sent it to the King's May week Magazine Basileon: so, if it got there in time, you may have seen it.

I am here superintending the alliance of the English and German races, in the persons of Dudley (whom you don't know very well), and a very small woman called Annemarie. I think I've got them fairly well settled in by now. So I shall soon depart. I've a fancy for trying one of those queer Northern lands—Denmark, or Sweden, or England. But I don't know.

Here I consort with journalists: the Berlin correspondents of various English journals. It has finally cleaned me of all respect for, or belief in, a newspaper. They are, personally, these correspondents, rather amusing people, who are always knocking about the world doing journalistic jobs, sometimes getting £1000 a year, sometimes a pound a week. They have good tales.

Ka appeared in Berlin to help tie up Dudley and Annemarie. Then she fled to the North—some rural spot discovered by Dudley—where I hope she is resting. She seemed rather gloomy, and still ill.

I'd like to know, if you answer, how long and when you're going to be at Conduit Head. Aren't you, perhaps, going to lecture to the Extension meeting about the British Empire, on 'Heart-Cries under the Red White and Blue', or some such title? If I come to England ever, I'd like to know if anyone's in Cambridge, for deciding whether to live in Grantchester or not.

By the way, you were wrong about me and Bertie Russell. When I said his praise of my dissertation was the 'final insult' or some such phrase, it was only my dim and tired attempt at a joke. Really, and secretly, I was, of course, frightfully pleased. I rather like him in a way; and I greatly enjoy being with him. I used, till recently, to dislike him a little; for the sole reason that he disliked and despised me. Now he approves of me more, I do of him! It's the way one works!

[1] Published with the title 'By the Lake. A Music for three voices' in *The Eye Witness*, November 1912.

What more—oh! yes! behind *Artistic* I copy out the only fruit of a Spring project of mine—to turn all famous English literature into heart-cries. You leave out all the literary language and long words and queer ideas and so on—you know. So it rather shortens it. This is the first 20 sonnets or so of Shakespeare, distilled into one *cri du cœur*.[1] I hope you won't mind.

That's all. There's no real news, much. The world's a dirty enough place. And I'm too grey and old to be worth your—if you're inclined to it—being angry with. But. I'm settled and sedate, in a flat way, now.

Love to everyone.

Yours

RUPERT

It'll be very nice to see you again, if ever I do. I shall, soon, I guess.

To GEOFFREY KEYNES   *Kolner Hof (Köln a. Rh.)*
                          Sonntag, 24 June 1912

*   *   *

Jeffiello mio,

Your letter has just come, forwarded in the strong womanly handwriting of the Ranee. It relieves me to know that my description of Grantchester is true. The mind of man decays & grows uncertain with disease & the quiet lapse of time, & I had become more than a little doubtful if it had ever happened that I was in such a place, or if I had but dreamt it.

You will observe I have been reading Mr Belloc. Indeed, I laid *The Four Men* down, to open your letter. I am in bed, dimly wondering whether to get up, or to lie & watch Dudley washing. Dudley & I despatched Frau Ward to Munich, & came off here to see the largest exhibition of the moderns ever held—they begin with Van Gogh (110 pictures) & come to the later painters & newer schools. Frightfully boring.

Later: in a train.

I am now *en route* for Haag (the Hague, you call it). I've determined to come to England again. There's not much point being anywhere...but writing about Grantchester gave me a bit of

---

[1] The 'Triolet' already printed on p. 362.

Heimweh; & your statement confirmed my dim remembrances that England held some nicish spots—& even some niceish people. And that is less true about Germany. I am going to be taken to see the Rembrandts at the Hague by James—oh yes, James is on the Continent. Then I shall slide across, & through London, & perhaps soon to Grantchester—I may be there next week-end—shall we bathe? I haven't bathed since November. There's a lot to wash off.

Dudley grunted recognition of your existence. He very much desires to see you as you pass to the Tyrol, or as you come back, if you can do it through Berlin. Do see him. He's sad, & wants cheering. His wife's a nice girl.

My health is now perfect. My soul is on its last legs. Have you any cure for syphilis of the soul? I have tried several injections of spiritual 606. But still I stink; & still I peal [*sic*]. It may be there is a herb growing at the bottom of the river just above the pool at Grantchester, & that if I dive & find it & bring it up—it will heal me. I have heard so. I do not know. It seems worth trying.

I have no emotions. But my indifference to the universe seems to diminish infinitesimally when you swing into the view. So come & bathe: & perhaps I will tell you the tale of *Weisheim an der Eider*. Poor old Jeff!   Thine

*ex-*RUPERT

To EDWARD MARSH   *Old Vicarage, Grantchester*
                                   [*11 July 1912*]

Good God, I must have been carrying this key about for ages. I'm most awfully sorry.

Here's this hurried stuff.[1] Will you send it back to me sometime? It's my only copy.

I'm here till the 24th or so.

RUPERT

To MAYNARD KEYNES   *The Old Vicarage*
                                   [*19 July 1912*]
Dear Maynard,

There are two things—no, three. One is that they *will* fall into my bed and get in my hair. The hot weather brings them out. They climb the walls and march along the ceiling. When they're above me

---

[1] 'Grantchester.'

they look down, see with a start—and a slight scream—that there's another person in the room, and fall. And I never could bear wood-lice. Mrs Neeve sprinkles yellow dust on my books and clothes, with a pathetic foreboding of failure, and says 'They're 'armless, pore things!' But my nerve gives.

And then, I ought to be getting off about the 4th—because I've got to get a week then, and my early date is determined by my latter date, which is determined—etc.

And then, I gather that Noel's going earlier than was arranged—on, in fact, Monday week.

So may I come earlier than you noted down (I'm not at all certain when that was)—on Wednesday, in fact? I may arrive on foot.

Denham [Russell-Smith] is dead: the Ranee has cut me off with £26: Hilton [Young] is with Alfred in the Black Forest: and the youth of Grantchester quote my local patriotic poetry to me as I ride by on a bicycle. There is no other news—save of my continued *Gehirnschwachheit*.[1]

> Ever
>
> RUPERT

To FRANCES CORNFORD   *Whitney*
                                          Friday night
                                        [*3 August 1912*]

I began to answer your letters—or rather write to you—It never got far. There were things to be said, perhaps. It seemed as if it didn't matter, though—

You'll anyhow have gathered from what of the story you heard (& you didn't hear it all, if only that Ka doesn't know it all), that we were waiting to get clear a bit—It seemed useless to prolong the strain—I know it's all no use—So today I went, *en route* for Rugby (I missed a train, & am stranded here), with Justin, in his motor, & saw Ka for four hours; and told her. I can't love her, you see. So now it's all at an end. And she's passed out of my power to help or comfort. I'm so sad for her, & a little terrified, & so damnably powerless.

Oh Frances, it was Hell. Ka, whom I loved, whom I love so still, is in such hopelessness & agony. My God, it was awful. When one's seen people in pain like that, one can't ever forget it. Oh, to hurt people one loves, so. I feel as if I can't go on loving, for the despair

---

[1] i.e. weakness of the brain.

of it all. I feel like a criminal (though I know I'm not). She spoke wildly—one does at first, I know—it was terrible. I'm aching so for her.

She was so fine. It's so easy to be bitter & mean, especially after a strain; I've been bitter & tiny often these months; she has, sometimes; but she wasn't bitter—only nakedly bare & true, simple, she was fine.

She's in such agony. No one can comfort or help her. It tears at me so, to think of her.

I daresay this is all very confused. I'm going to the Murrays in Norfolk (if I don't collapse) on Wednesday. I've got to pick up dress-clothes in Grantchester. Can I stay Tuesday night with you? I can explain things, & talk about Ka. You're the only person. She doesn't like Gwen & Jacques (she's foolish: & they). You'll be able to guard her in the future. No one else. You can't do anything now. You might write (saying I've told you that we're ended) & praise her. Don't discuss it all. Just say what you think of *her*, as herself— tell all the truth of how great you think her, & then lies. Pile it on, it doesn't matter if it's true—love & praise. It's the only sort of thing that helps human nature in these bloody moments. It sounds silly: but it's true. Not that anything'll do much. And it's impudent of me to write in this way. I'm all exhausted & worn with the pain of it.

Saturday—Oxford station

I'm going to be at 24 Bilton Road, Rugby. You might let me know, there, if I can come on Tuesday.

I doubt if Ka will go to Savoy. I wish she would. But we'll talk. It is incredible that two people should be able to hurt each other so much.

I expect I shall see you.

RUPERT

I'm twenty-five today.

To HUGH DALTON   *bei D. Ward*
                                              Charlottenburg
                                    Berlinerstrasse 100, Berlin
                                    Thursday, 7 August 1912

A German word

I gather from postmarks that Frau Neeve kept your card for four days, and my mother for two. It has got here at length. You will have sought some other older man by now. To whom you will talk of law. Alas. But perhaps it is as well. For, yes, I am, as you say, dead. Further processes even have set in

> 'Though one be mild as Moses
> His meekness clouds and closes:
> In the end he decomposes;
> And he is sure to smell.'

As Swinburne or you or some one of the romantics puts it.

I am under pretext of doing my dissertation here. Actually I have not done a word. I spend my time in making love to female dancers. They pirouette scornfully away....

After the 10th of December I shall come to London. Then I shall sit one night and repeat poetry to you: you will repeat dirty stories to me: till 3.30 a.m. then I shall go to bed. In January I go to America for three years.

Cambridge must be full of people one knows. Perhaps it is nicer not to be there. I am sorry not to see them capering in the Greek play.

I have discerned the real division of mankind; into the Petrine and the Jesuine; those who are crucified head downwards and those who are crucified right way up. It is immensely important. Perhaps the greatest discovery of the Twentieth Century. Beyond that I have done nothing: written but one line, but that a good one.

> 'Ah Love, there is no something in the Sun!'

It ends a sonnet. (But what sonnet?) It is the truest line in English except Meredith's 'And Life, some say, is worthy of the Mews.' Be in London in December.

                                              RUPERT

To SYBIL PYE   24 *Bilton Road, Rugby*
                                       [*Postmark: 21 August 1912*]

End of August

Dear Sybil,

They've always told me that to understand everything is to pardon everything. I know now it is untrue. For I understand completely why I haven't answered your letter this month—the infinite listlessness, the state of feebly desiring to do things, and yet only having the mental force to sit and watch the minutes and days drift by—I've written nothing and read nothing. . . .

But I find I can't pardon it.

Oh dear! I collected information (which you desired) about poor old Strindberg, so long ago. And I've just been too dead to write it to you. Have you been pining and thirsting all these weeks for the cool waters of Norwegian anti-feminism? I am so sorry.

I find I concluded that one could start on Strindberg with the following (besides the three in that translation): *The Father, Comrades, Fräulein Julie, Inferno,* and *There are Crimes and Crimes. The Father* is to be got in English; whether the translation's good I don't know. My private information about the trade of literature in England includes the fact that Stephen Swift is going to bring out a volume of Strindberg's plays, including some of those I mention, in a month or two—translated by a Jew. They can all be got in German; and some in the 2d terracotta *Reklam* edition—you know it?

It was very good of you to tell me about Sturge Moore's views. His selection puzzles me—but so does everybody's, almost. I see the point of plunging into *Dust*[1] at verse 3, and letting you gather that they're dead—as you do in an Ibsen play. But I've thought of the thing so much as it stands, that I *can't* quite get round to seeing it otherhow. It seems like lopping the head off someone I know, to make them more interesting. . . . But I'll note it for the memorial edition.

I saw Ethel [Pye] for a smoky moment the other day. She said you were all going to be in Limpsfield all September—so I may see you sometime. Or do you ever come to London? I often pass rather hurriedly through it: filthy place.

I crawled here a day or two ago with ghastly headaches, in collapse. I think I shall summon up enough vigour to drag myself on to Scotland tomorrow. But I'm not sure. But it seems a pity to

---

[1] His verses with that title in *Poems,* 1911.

collapse altogether again, sooner than I need, so I expect I shall continue my journey. Oh dear! this is fretful. But it's horrible to be in this condition. Did I ask you if you'd seen—and did you see—a long lanky lax-limbed set of verses I wrote about Grantchester and published in a King's magazine? If you've not seen them, I'll try and find my dirty copy of them to send you to look at, if it'd amuse you.

I see no hope of doing anything more in the way of work for a long time.

Ugh!   Ever

                                            RUPERT

To DUDLEY WARD   *N[ational] L[iberal] C[lub]*
                                   27 August [1912]

Yes, I've not written. I've often thought of doing so. But my will seems to have gone even more to pieces lately.

You may have heard from Ka. We waited till the beginning of August. I felt infinitely flat and emotionless about everything: and gradually felt surer I couldn't marry her. Finally I found I was in love again, after all, with Noel: so if emotions of a sort did begin to stir in this cesspool that is my heart, and still no feeling for Ka came —it seemed time to end the strain. I saw her and told her. She thought I was wrong not to marry her. One can't. She was pretty bad for a bit: but she is better now, I gather. I think she's fairly *well*, which is the main thing.

Frances Cornford, who is the only decent person in this country who knows about it all, and understands, and is good, is a great blessing. She turns out to be a fine person. The only emotion I have nowadays is thankfulness for what good people there are.

                    *   *   *

Frances wants me to go to America or somewhere for a year for Ka's sake, for mine, and for everybody's. America means, if possible, some physical work and little or no mental. California....

It's not made imperative—I really think—by the prospect of either Ka's dislike of occasionally seeing me in England, or mine of occasionally seeing her. (She's in London with Margaret [Cox] till December. Then she probably goes abroad.) That wouldn't be much evil. But it's thought that if I stay in England I shall only get iller and iller—and also that a year's absence (and returned health) 'll make all my affairs straight.... There sounds something in it. I slide into doing it. I feel unable to make up my mind.

The other elements in the situation are these. I am, it appears, in love—unwillingly and unhappily enough—with Noel. She, very justifiably, has got tired of me the last year or eighteen months.

* * *

I daresay I could work it. There's a good deal of love for me to go on.... Supposing, they say, I came back in a year *well*; all would be clear, and all might turn out successfully—and anyhow I'm too weak and exhausted to bear reverses now....

* * *

Then comes my crux: that my nerve has gone.

It's that. Do you see how I'm racked? There's poison round. And my nerve's gone. If I go away, Ka'll fall back, perhaps. She *says* she's clear of it all, and sees all the filth.... But she's only a woman. That'd be bad enough. But for that, perhaps, I've already given up my power or right to hinder. But Noel. That would kill me.

So there I am—staying will be one long drag of misery. Going seems impossible. I daresay I shall know some time.

I have written nothing since I came back and read not a single book, except two novels. I get worse.

You once seemed to write for a book by Perris on *Foreign Policy*. I deliberated some weeks and sent off Perris on *War and Peace*.

I dined last night with Squire. He is part of Stephen Swift, the publishers. I told him to secure the copyright of Wedekind's translations. He thinks they may want me to do some: 3 or 4 to start with. I didn't accept: but I got the refusal of it. I thought, if I did it, I'd come out, if possible, and go over it with Anne (paying a suitably small share of the profits!). But I may be too far under. I should have to do it before proceeding to California—Squire'll be writing to you about getting the translating rights—I hope A. M. is getting on. My love to her.   Thine

RUPERT

To JACQUES RAVERAT   *Scotland*
                                          Sunday [*August 1912*]

I have been touring round this dismal country with Norton and
Norton's Aunt. I go to England soon, tomorrow or so. Rugby, or
a cottage Justin's in—I don't know.

I kept trying to write off to you. I heard Ka had, so I knew you'd
know. I've been too flabby to write. I've just tried and tried, dimly,
and been too dim to put the thing down on paper.

It's all so old and desolate now, I can scarcely remember. I waited
till the beginning of August, still dead to Ka and everything else in
the world. Then I found that not only was I still dead to her, but
also I was after all, in love, sicklily, with Noel. So I thought I'd
better wind up with Ka. There was no use dragging on.

She thought me (and perhaps still thinks) wrong. She felt bad at
the time; but I believe she's better now.

I expect she'd better just lie quiet a bit. If her friends prevent her
sliding into the miasmic circles she feels drawn to, things'll be as
good as they can. Don't worry her with all your bright intellectualist explanations, generalizations, and theorizings about what
Should and Shouldn't have been, about her Nature, about mine,
about Woman.... She's had her little fling, and, for the moment,
she'll lie quiet.

Love me, if you will, for suffering (and you—with very few
more—*can* do so, because you understand feelings of all these kinds);
but I think it's foolishly romantic to honour one for it.* Suffering's
a dirty business. It only weakens and destroys, at best—and worst,
poisons. Nor do I at all love life.

Frances, you'll have heard, was a stand-by. I thought she was
fine. She was the only person left in England who was good and
grown-up, and so could comprehend anything.... How it sifts
people!
                          *   *   *

Frances, of course, doesn't understand male feelings; queerly not.
But it doesn't matter. She's very helpful, and fine.

Frances, and others, want me to go abroad for a year and, for
a bit anyhow, do some sort of manual work. Cleaning oranges in
California is a type. I can't do any 'work'—writing or reading—
for some time I think. I've done none at all all these horrible
months. I daresay I shall go. It seems very vague and dim in my
mind; and I have no will.

I'm supposed to be going to translate some German plays: so

I may have to go to Berlin for a week. At present I feel more like going to bed or into an asylum for three months. I feel half mad, most of the time. I don't fancy myself in Holland. I might come to Prunoy in October; but I expect I shan't be able to make the effort, or, if I do have strength enough, I shall use it in getting right away.

I'll let you know sometime how things go. I'm infinitely miserable, and ill. And very tired.

With love

RUPERT

* It's all part, I suppose, of that babyish Dostoieffsky-craze that afflicts Lytton Strachey, Ka, and you, and the rest of the moderns.

To FRANCES CORNFORD   *Scotland*
                                         Tuesday
                              [*August–September 1912*]

'Generous' 'angry' 'beastly letter'...bless the woman! What does it *mean*? what does it MEAN?

Do you really think one flames up, at this time of life—oh, what *do* you really think? 'Generous'—you use words that have no meaning.

You are so stupid. Isn't the situation clear? I have, and Ka has, been through a bad time, and we're both, more or less, for the moment, in a bad way. One's friends may help—who else can? You can't expect the Sultan of Turkey or Mr Balfour to take much interest in us! One's friends are limited in number. Knock out, for the purposes of the present, those who haven't grown up. Knock out those who aren't good. There's a handful left.... What can one do but take their love?... Oh, don't you see? Let's have no more of it. You're good; and you understand things—more or less, as human beings can. That's all. You can't, now, make me 'angry'.... You can only make certain comments, give certain advice. I can only say 'Yes, thank you' or 'No, thank you'. Either of us may be right, or wrong. And beyond that there's love and strength and one or two things, one can get.   *   *   *

I had a very nice letter from Jacques. I think he's the only person in the universe who understands precisely parts of the story and some of my feelings. Partly because only a man can understand the grisly and poisonous ways men can suffer. This sounds as if it's meant to be an insult to you. It's not!

I'll try to write again some time.

With love

RUPERT

To FRANCES CORNFORD

National Liberal Club
Whitehall Place, S.W.
Midday: Tuesday
[*September 1912*]

Dear Frances,

*   *   *

I shan't write much now. I'm in an infinitely tired, muddy, flabby state. I got into London at 8 this morning, and I'm reduced by the miseries of the journey to pulp. Several times this morning I've almost taken the train to the North Pole—but now it's lunch, and for the rest of the day I'm going to attach myself firmly to several friends, and refuse to be left alone.

Your letter was so nice to get. I'm so glad everything's right in that—division of the Universe, especially as everything's wrong in such a large number of others.

Oh Lord, this England place you all talk so much about, turns out to be grey with rain and drizzle.

I've been so thirsting for England (not that I've really got much feeling for place—but England = places + atmosphere + people I know). I've an idea I may work in Grantchester. Do you know the feeling when one's looked forward to a thing very much a long time, and pictured it vividly, and then, when it comes (a party it used to be perhaps) you're a little tired possibly, and you've thought about it too much—and it doesn't come off. Everything's *there*, just as it ought to be, only—the emotions don't come. There's the ices, and the games, and the lights, and the decoration, and the laughter, and the supper-table, only—where's that happiness business? It's really a state of tiredness. It generally passes in a minute. I've now got it. I expected England and my friends to be—so wonderfully fresh and beautiful and invigorating...and now I'm here, and there's only the Strand, and the National Liberal, and X. and Y. and Z.—trotting their round....

Oh but people one knows are very nice. Even this horrible stucco ghetto of a smoking room seems to me homely and kind.... But the Jews oppress one a little.

It will be very nice to see you.

I hope you're both well; and happy.

Yours nationally

& liberally

but wrong

METHUSELAH

To KATHARINE COX

Under the Chestnuts
[Grantchester]
Saturday [September 1912]

When I got your letter—midday, yesterday—I was fairly on my last legs. I'd been working for ten days alone at this beastly poetry. Working at poetry isn't like reading hard. It doesn't just tire and exhaust you. The only effect is that your nerves and your brain go. I was almost a mouthing idiot. I couldn't think or sit still or stop eating. I had reached the lowest depths possible to man. You just saved me. I worked out that you'd not be accessible till Saturday, and then only with babies and probably Ethel. So I wired for James. He is reading about Prisons on my right, now. Dudley, from London, is expected any moment. He wired last night!

I've not dared to write again yet. I've been talking and playing. But I'm going to risk half an hour at a sonnet after tea. I am made of wet paper, and I longing to walk or camp. Oh! oh! I wish you were here. I'm not so damp as I've been. But I'd like to sink back.

Hush! I must write business. I am a Man. Your letter was almost impossible to understand. Virginia comes here (I'm rather nervous) on Monday till, say, Friday. By the following Tuesday I start for Camp.   *   *   *

I do, you know, wish you could come to Camp. We must talk. Anyhow two or three days.... If you did, we might send everyone away but Noel, Bryn and Justin and Geoffrey, and have James and Virginia and Duncan for a week-end. That might come at the end, perhaps.   *   *   *

R.

To KATHARINE COX

[*Grantchester, September 1912*]

Tuesday night

Geoffrey [Keynes] popped in on Sunday & lunched. I thought him extraordinarily nice. Today Gwen told me (don't be angry with her) of your fuss with *him*. It was that, I suppose, you nearly wrote about. It doesn't distress me to know about it. I'm concerned lest in any way it should end in him not seeing you. He's a good person— & so unique in London—the London you & I know.

When I've thought of you, what you could be doing, I've some-times suddenly thought 'She may be with Geoffrey', and glowed content. I don't see the point in him not 'knowing'—unless you fell in love with him. I wish you would. His devotion to you makes me rather happy. When I feel desperately helpless to aid or sustain you it's the one thing I can fly to, the thought of the immense love and reverence people have for you—Gwen, Frances and the rest.

It also rather sends him up in my estimation.

There's a thousand tiny things. I'll write again, for it's late now. Frances is superber than ever. And oh! Dudley...!

When I meet Jacques and Gwen I love them very much. And then suddenly they throw an arm around each other's neck, or touch hands: & I go sick with envy, & blind—and generally say something to hurt them.

Or yes, Eddie. *Georgian Poets* 3*s*. 6*d*. net ready in December. Brooke, Abercrombie, Masefield, Gibson, Chesterton, S. Moore, & the rest. He's really got too many rotters in. But we all think our fortunes'll be made—I send a fragment that may adorn December's *Rhythm* with this. And November's *Poetry Review*, I've told them to send you.

My only friend is A. C. Benson. We had an infinitely affecting *tête-à-tête* dinner last night. He implored me to write to him. I nearly kissed him. Both were drunk.

*   *   *

To ROSALIND MURRAY   [*September 1912*]
                         London
                            for a moment
                            and
                         Rugby

Dear Rosalind,

This is the note you promised to send on to 'Hetty'. Hetty was a genius at packing: but, like a genius, she overdid it. For she packed, with all my books, the box of writing-stuff in my room, autochthonous. Oh, I'm far from complaining! And it's not enough —some envelopes and some scribbling-paper—to be worth while solemnly packing up and returning.

I have wandered through many places since I left Overstrand:[1] but none so nice. It was a very good week there. I am sorry I was a little ill and rather flabby. It takes the edge off one.

I write no poetry, not even dreadful modern stuff with jokes in it. And I read no books. Horrible! And at the moment I'm extremely irritable: because the Times this morning says I'm very *very* healthy —and as a matter of fact I've got a dreadful headache and oh, it's not true!

The only consolation in life is—did you see about him?—that a man who found bathing in the morning and evening rather dull, purchased a musical-box to cheer the proceedings. But the scheme was a failure, because the thing could only play *God save the King*, so he had to stand up all the while. Otherwise life is grey.

I was sad that I forgot to say good-bye to the fair Agnes.[2] Did you convey my farewells?

I passed through London two days ago. It was grimmer than a nightmare. I feel so sorry for you.

Autumn—death—despair. Even the fact you're all (I gather) drowned can scarcely make this black world blacker.

                                        Yours
                                    RUPERT BROOKE

[1] A village on the coast of Norfolk.   [2] R. M.'s sister.

To FRANCES CORNFORD   *24 Bilton Road*
                                         Rugby
                                         25 September [*1912*]

                    *   *   *

I've been meeting a lot of poets in London. They *were* so nice: very simple, and very goodhearted. I felt I'd like, almost, to live with them always (and protect them...). But London won't do.

Also I saw Rosalind [Murray] several times. She's just started on her own: so infinitely eager about Life and its Adventures, that I almost couldn't bear it. I've retired to Rugby, where I'm, comparatively, not more than middle-aged. But Rosalind's absurd humour (an entirely paternal inheritance) and eager joy in things, are such a blessing to witness. I thought her delightful and mad.

The Winter's Tale.... Oh, there's a lot of tattle, for when we meet.

Oh, but Ka said Justin had collapsed again. Damn! I saw Noel. I'm quieter about her, every way—though not very cheerful. I do believe, just now, that God's giving me a kind of respite. He seems to have ceased to fiddle with me for the last week or ten days. I have time to look at things, and do a bit of work, even; and write some letters. A queer feeling. And once a week I even have a touch of energy.

So you'll gather I'm well.

For the moment. One can't—I can't—be properly and permanently all right till I'm married. Marriage is the only thing. But, oh dear! one's very reluctant to go into it without love—the full business. Love, love—I feel so awfully hungry for it, sometimes. To have had it once—the complete thing—does seem so much more important in life than anything else. And life's very short. Marrying without love seems like shutting such an irrevocable door on all that matters. So that even peace and freedom to work scarcely count. I think, you know, love's more important for men than for women. You, if you miss that in its fullness, have probably, children: and half your life's fulfilled. But we've only the one thing to pray for: and, if we miss it—work and so on.

It comes on me that it's rather a truism that Love's an Important Thing. I'm sorry. It's a remark I found I *couldn't* make to Mother at dinner: and one must work off one's loneliness somehow! But, as Bryn disgustedly observed to a sister, after a long general conversation with me some weeks ago, 'Rupert holds such dreadfully conventional views nowadays!' So again, I'm sorry.

I'll be seeing you soon. I hope you're both radiating health and energy. Make an extra bow of reverence to Thos. Hardy from me.

With love

RUPERT

To HAROLD MONRO *24 Bilton Road, Rugby*
28 September 1912

Dear Monro,

Yes, I'll do an article on Abercrombie if you like. But by when? I haven't his things at hand (except *Emblems of love*) & I shan't get to them for nine days. Will that do? I could plan out the thing, & supplement it by a glance at his works, & send it off very soon after. I'm not so fervent an admirer of Abercrombie's as many people: but perhaps that's all the better, as I *do* think him good.

Do you want it in the form of a letter or how?[1] I see a little difficulty in introducing myself. Do you want just an honest & discriminating defence of Abercrombie's muse, prefaced by a few remarks about Ezra's sneer? I'm glad you're not cutting it out. I'm sure it's the best course. The editor in you typewrites the curt & businesslike letters; it is the poet who omits to sign them. Shame! But I recognized the inimitable prose-style, & was corroborated by *Poetry Review* writing paper!

Yours

RUPERT BROOKE

To EDWARD MARSH *Rugby*
Saturday, 28 September [*1912*]

Dear Eddie,

Thanks for your last note. I've written to Sidgwick & Jackson.

I think your sandwiching will do admirably. How are you going to arrange us?[2] & in what immortal throne shall I find myself at this Parnassian ἔρανος?[3] Not next Gibson,[4] I hope; for he's an octo-syllabler, too, for the most part. I'd like to be shouldered by some five-foot giants—or perhaps we're alphabetical.

Do you want it called *The Sentimental Exile* or *Grantchester*?

---

[1] A letter from R.B. in reply to Ezra Pound's article on contemporary American and English poets was printed in *The Poetry Review*, November 1912.

[2] In *Georgian Poetry*.   [3] Symposium.

[4] Wilfrid Wilson Gibson, poet.

I'll sit & think: but I fear it's too old for revising. If a couplet or two could be taken out of the last part & shoved in elsewhere, it'd improve the balance. . . . I fear it'll have to remain its misbegotten self. I get so excited, wanting to scrap those poems, & write you much better ones, that'd fairly boom the book & obliterate poor Jan [Masefield]—but I shan't.

I fear I shan't be in London for some time—I do want to be.

You know, I don't rate Bridges so highly. I think Yeats worth a hundred of him. But he's a fine figure: so perhaps it'd be all right.

I wonder if you've seen *The Winter's Tale* yet?

RUPERT

To A. F. SCHOLFIELD   *24 Bilton Road, Rugby*
                                    Monday, 30 September [1912]
Dear Scho,

India? What *is* this craze for the East? Lowes Dickinson, and Forster, and now you. . . . Why should King's be stripped in this way?

*   *   *

I'm considerably perturbed that the Empire has claimed you.[1] Shan't we see you for years? Cambridge becomes increasingly a barren and friendless place. And how the play will suffer! I'd really hoped there'd be a good one at last.

I've got to go to Grantchester in about a week, to pick up some books; and also to London in these days, somewhen. Is there any chance of catching a glimpse of you in either place before you entirely *verschwind?* I'd like to: for when you return from the East, yellow, old, leathery and livery, you'll find (if you remember to look) that the work of disintegration, which has already begun in me, will have completed its course. I shall be Laureate, or married, or dead. . .Send me, if you can spare time, a hurried card, saying when you'll be in Cambridge or London, before you start: and I'll plan if we can't have a swift meal together, if you've time.

Yours
RUPERT

[1] He was about to take up an appointment in India.

To EDWARD MARSH   *Rugby*
                                    Friday [*4 October 1912*]

Dear Eddie,

You townsfolk leap too easily to a facile contempt for us of the country. I scorn you. *Of course* I've seen *The Winter's Tale!*—the first night! And, as a matter of fact, I'm going to it again on Tuesday —more or less by way of excuse for seeing Scholfield, who's off to India—but you don't know him—That brings me to my request. I'm going to Runcton Cottage tomorrow for the week-end. Can I stay with you on Tuesday &, probably, Monday night? Tuesday, as I say, I'm going out. But I suppose the Tigers[1] won't want me longer than till Monday: so, if I can, I'll appear then, &, if you're doing nothing, we might dine together—I don't know if there's anything to see? But anyhow I'll see you in the evening & at breakfast: & talk about the Georgian poets then. I find myself believing I can make a rival better selection from the same poets! Of course, I can't set up to advise you; but I can taunt.

*   *   *

                                              RUPERT

To EDWARD MARSH   *The Old Vicarage*
                                  Monday [*28 October 1912*]

Dear Eddie,

Thanks for your comments.[2] Even if I hadn't had them first, I should have guessed whence Monro had got what he had to say. *Sexless* I've changed to *radiant*. It was that, originally. I put in *sexless* when I was working with my nose too near the poem. *Wire* I leave. I don't mind it: and my *Crivelli* picture doesn't suggest flowing hair. *White, Lightning...light* seems to me rather nice in sound.

All I've thought of for *ecstasy* is *fury*. I don't think it's good.

I'm coming through town for a day or so this week. Can you possibly give me a bed on Thursday night, & perhaps Wednesday? Let me have a card.   RUPERT

---

[1] Middleton Murry and Katherine Mansfield, living at Runcton Cottage, Chichester.
[2] On the poem 'Mary and Gabriel'.

To EDWARD MARSH   *bei Dudley Ward*
                                          Charlottenburg
                              Berlinerstrasse 100, Berlin
                                               Friday
                              [*Postmark: 9 November 1912*]

Dear Eddie,

What a confusion! However, I've got the thing now: so all's well. Many thanks.

When I lie awake o' nights—as I sometimes do—I plan advertisement for 'Georgian Poets'. I hope you're going to get it reviewed on the Continent. Certainly the *Nouvelle Revue Française* ought to be urged to write about it. Gosse could write a note to one of the people connected with the N.R.F.—he must know them all—to draw their attention to it. Or you could get at Coppeau, who's in London just now, through Roger Fry. Or I *could* get round at them through people I know. I expect there are one or two more French papers. I'll try to see if there are any German papers any good. I'll mention it in the paper I write for, if they'll still admit me. I'm sure with a little pushing, a good hundred copies could be sold in Germany & France.

I hope you're getting Gosse to do *The Times*, & Hewlett, & the others you spoke of—& getting hold of Northcliffe, & so forth. My series of inspirations included these: that 'Q' should introduce himself to Cambridge by reviewing it at some length for *The Review*. I could write to the Editor of the Review, if you liked, & persuade him. Failing 'Q', Benson. I'll make the *Granta* & *Cambridge Magazine* flourish headlines, too. Couldn't you make Raleigh write about it from *The Oxford Magazine* (or elsewhere)? He's keen on— or keen to be keen on—modern poetry. I expect he'd do it.

I forget all my other ideas: but they each sold some twenty-five copies. I have a hazy vision of incredible *Reklam*, secured by your potent wire-pulling & ingenious brain. I have always averred that any of the Society could beat Patent Medicine vendors on their own ground, if he chose. I feel sure you ought to have an immense map of England (vide Tono Bungay) & plan campaigns with its aid. And literary charts, each district mapped out & a fortress secured— John Buchan to fill a page of the Spectator: Filson Young in the P.M.G. (we shall be sixteen things that matter in italics): etc. etc. You'll be able to found a Hostel for poor Georgians on the proceeds.

Here it snows: and I sleep.   RUPERT

Love to Wilfrid, & the Tigers: when you see them.

To FRANCES CORNFORD

bei Dudley Ward
Charlottenburg
Berlinerstrasse 100, Berlin
Wednesday [*November 1912*]

Dear Frances,

*   *   *

I heard from Ka. She *did* seem better—especially for the decision.
And she always *is* much quieter and happier after being with you,
I think. I'm relieved, immensely, I shall sit and work quietly now:
and not badger her more—just give her news now and then.

Her desperateness to Gwen wasn't Gwen's fault. She was very
like it to Dudley, too....I think I understand it. It was part of
a phase. One does go up and down a lot.

But she's all right—considering—I think.

*   *   *

It's nice with these two little people—save for those moments
that occasionally come to us celibates when we stay with married
people—when they talk together—or something—and one suddenly finds oneself four million miles away from any human companionship, on the top of a frozen mountain, among stars and icicles.
Oh, well. I shall work.   Ever

RUPERT

To CLIVE CAREY

bei Dudley Ward
Berlinerstrasse 100
Charlottenburg, Berlin
23 November 1912

Clive dear,

It's been weighing horribly on my mind. After I left London
a year ago I got filthily ill for a long time: and I've been abroad and
semi-convalescent for most of the year. So I never paid you all the
gold I owe you for gallantly enduring me last autumn. I've not the
faintest idea how much. I don't even know how often I went. Do
tell me; and I'll send you a cheque. (It's awful how an illness puts
an impassable abyss between this year and last—I can scarcely
remember anything in detail before six months ago.)

*   *   *

Oh, oh, I that was musical as was Apollo's lute am now as harsh
as any raven. If ever I'm within reach again, I shall try to make

a longer spell possible, and be at you again. But I don't know when that'll be. My naturally pure baritone will have risen to the super-treble of second childhood ere then. . . .

I hope you're licking them into shape decently in the Greek play.

I loved your dances in Winter's Tale. I saw it more than once. I'll get a sight of Twelfth Night when I return. Did you help them in that, too?

I shall be in Cambridge right at the end of term again, a few days, dispatching my resurged Dissertation. Then perhaps a week of London. So I may see you again.

The Russians[1] are here. But nothing else endurable.

Thine
RUPERT

To EDWARD MARSH

bei Dudley Ward
Charlottenburg
Berlinerstrasse 100, Berlin
Monday [*25 November 1912*]

Dear Eddie,

I rejoice to hear that things are going well.

*   *   *

Hulme[2] has arrived in Berlin. I show him round & talk to him. He's an amiable creature, & a good talker; though I don't think much of him as a philosophic thinker. But he has an extraordinary power of observation, & a good memory. German literary circles are so entirely cut off from English that it's difficult to get any connexion. I've mentioned Georgian Poets in a sort of letter-article I wrote for one paper. I couldn't go into it *too* much, as I have to initial the letter. I know what papers it might be worth sending the book to for review. I shall still *try* to get hold of some literary cove.

*   *   *

Yes, I've seen a poem or two by Luce.[3] 'Wilful' an elderly person like me calls 'em. But brilliant.

A belated review of me, commendably short, has just appeared in the Oxford Magazine. I give myself the pleasure of copying it exactly for you.

---

[1] The Diaghilev Ballet company.   [2] T. E. Hulme, philosopher-poet.
[3] Gordon Luce of King's, who afterwards lived in Burma as a teacher at the University of Rangoon.

'Mr Rupert Brooke's *Poems* show a good ear for metre, but otherwise have little merit. The language, though forcible, is not only vulgar, but often positively savours of the gutter. The book is full of bad taste, and is at times positively revolting. Especially disgusting is "Dead Men's Love", a matter which, if treated at all, should be treated with reverence, not with ribaldry.'

The last sentence is mysterious.

I should think the thing for abroad, is to get a copy or two in bookshops in the big places. The Tigers' list of bookshops would be a good beginning.

*   *   *

If Austria & Russia fight, I shall try to go as a war-correspondent. I thought of wiring to the M[anchester] Guardian. I suppose you don't know of anyone who wants a war correspondent out there?

My love to the bards.   Thine

RUPERT

To ROSALIND MURRAY   *24 Bilton Road, Rugby*
                                    Friday, December 1912

My dear Rosalind,

It wasn't wrath that kept me from writing, but a mixture of busyness and flatness. I assure you I considered all your arguments against my going abroad, with the utmost gravity and seriousness. Aren't they minimized by a telegram from Denis[1] saying that you and he are going to Panama tomorrow? What, my dear Rosalind, of your Literary Future? Think of your Career as Novelist. Oughtn't you to keep steadfastly in Touch with our Manysided English Life? I shall discuss your project with Mr Galsworthy.

But perhaps it was all a *blague*.

No, I'm *piqued* with curiosity. *Are* you all going to the New World? Because I certainly am, during the next two months. Perhaps you'd better come. Panama's as good as anywhere. In any case, I shall come down and call on you.

*   *   *

[1] R.M.'s brother.

I had started a slow (and dull) letter to you when the telegram (I found it here) shook me out of my stupor for a puzzled moment. I vaguely awaited an explanatory letter.

I want to stay in England a few weeks past the new year, to try to write something to leave them to think about, while I'm in the wilds.

Solve my perplexity. Say what you are doing and where going to be—Panama or Parnassus. I tend to deduce that Denis has shaken off Barrow?

I've a plan for making a fortune in the South Seas. Absolutely certain. You and Denis, if you assisted, could have a quarter share each—about £200,000.

I'm rather ill.   RUPERT

Anyway, a Happy New Year to everybody at Beckhythe Manor.

To EDWARD MARSH   *24 Bilton Road, Rugby*
                                            Christmas Eve, 1912

Dear Eddie,

I entered & cleared out of the flat yesterday, leaving the key on the hall-table, small pieces of paper on the floor, & my heart all over the place.

I liked Seabrooke[1] very much. I thought he had as good a nature as anyone I'd met for ages. Also I kept thinking he'd make a very fine [rugby] forward (the handling code).

I lunched with Monro & [Arundel] Del Re & went into the Poetry Shop again yesterday. I couldn't get my copies of *Georgian Poetry* of course. Even *Deborah* they'd ordered for me & lost before I could get it. I fear they are rather too unbusiness-like. If they *do* buck up, I'm more convinced than before that they'll make a success of it. The most extraordinary people keep dropping in & spending immense sums.

A thing dawned slowly on me during Saturday. I attended breakfast that day in a state of great slumbrousness & exhaustion. You & Seabrooke & the eggs were phantoms on the horizon of my muddled consciousness. At one point you seemed to take something out of a box & say 'Buz buz buz this buz buz buz Christmas present buz buz...'. I remember thinking you had said that Russian toys were your this year's Christmas presents...and vaguely saying '...oh!...'

[1] Elliot Seabrooke, actor and painter.

What else could a young man say with his eyes full of sleep & his heart full of Cathleen [Nesbitt]? As the morning wore on, it came to me that *possibly*—and later *probably*—you had said it was your Christmas present to *me*. For it sat on the sideboard in an expectant way, & was very attractive.

If that's not so, the situation's awkward, for I have the thing, very firmly. If it is so (& you couldn't have the heart to deny it now!) I'm sorry I seemed so very ungracious. It was my stupor—I am sorry.

Here I rest somnolently.

You are rioting, I suppose.   Ever

                                           RUPERT

I carried the toy about in buses, shooting it round the neck of acquaintances. A foreigner who shaved me was intensely interested in it, & said 'It is vary Beautifool', rather solemnly.

BIOGRAPHICAL PREFACE 1913

Early in January 1913 Brooke was staying in Cornwall, still suffering from complex emotions, unable to love, but tortured by remorse for the pain he had caused. Soon afterwards, however, while staying with the Raverats at Croyden, their home in Cambridgeshire, he asked Eddie Marsh to arrange a meeting with Cathleen Nesbitt, then a promising young actress on the London stage, whom he had first met in Marsh's company on 20 December 1912. In her company his more normal feelings revived, and she was from thenceforwards to play the main part in his emotional life. Nevertheless, he was still determined to break away from his friends and surroundings in England and to spend a year travelling in North America and the South Seas. During the first four months of the year he was preparing for this change of scene.

Meanwhile he was greatly interested in the welfare of various literary periodicals, particularly *Rhythm*, which became the *Blue Review* and *Poetry and Drama*, a successor to Monro's *Poetry Review*. To all these he was a contributor. He was also taking part with Lascelles Abercrombie, Wilfrid Gibson and John Drinkwater in a plan to publish their work in a new periodical to be called *New Numbers*, which began publication in the following year.

In February and March he stayed with Marsh in Gray's Inn and made many new friends. His revulsion from 'Bloomsbury' was compensated by his introduction through Marsh to the set of young people centring on 10 Downing Street, Asquith being then Prime Minister. Violet Asquith, afterwards Lady Violet Bonham Carter (now Baroness Asquith of Yarnham), in particular won his friendship with her charm and vitality, and to her he later wrote some of his most witty letters. On 8 March he was at length elected to a Fellowship at King's College, but this did not alter his resolve to go abroad. He therefore spent some time at Rugby with his mother, making excursions to London; during one of these a series of portraits was taken by an American photographer, Sherril Schell, some of which have since become well known through their inclusion in various editions of his poems. At the end of April he was staying in Albert Rothenstein's flat in London, and a farewell party, to which all of his available friends were invited, was arranged for 21 May. He sailed for the United States on the following day.

He had been commissioned to write a series of articles on his impressions of the United States and Canada for the *Westminster Gazette*, and on his arrival in New York on 31 May his first thoughts were directed towards this task. A dozen articles duly appeared while he was still absent in the South Seas, and were reprinted after his death as *Letters from America* (1916) with a preface by Henry James. In his private letters he wrote more freely than when composing for publication in a newspaper, though, as usual, his natural ribaldry often led him into saying more than he really meant. He had been given a number of introductions to potential friends, among whom were Russell Loines, Professor Chauncey Wells of the University of California at Berkeley, Duncan Campbell Scott, a Canadian poet and man of affairs, Leonard Bacon, another poet, Sir Wilfred Laurier, the Canadian Premier, and the Marchesa Capponi. Loines was a New York lawyer who took him soon after his arrival for a camping expedition on the Delaware River and was of assistance throughout his travels in sending him the necessary funds. All these names appear in his letters, which, together with those written to England, tell the story of his travels in the United States and Canada, and from California to Hawaii, Samoa, Fiji and New Zealand. On Christmas Day of this year he was in New Zealand nursing a septic foot following an injury sustained in Fiji.

To HAROLD MONRO   *9 January 1913*
                                 Cornwall (returning to Rugby)
Dear Monro,

* * *

I enclose a cheque for 16*s.*, which is my bill with you: to show I'm
an honest man & no poèt. (I don't know if you're the proper person
to send it to: but I suppose it'll do.) I ordered 4 Georgian Poetry &
only received (& pay for) 3. I'd like, sometime, that other. No
hurry. I hope you're amassing orders. Hewlett's letter was good, to
Marsh. I hope he'll review it somewhere. The W[estminster]
G[azette] was good, though dull. But why did she say we all
believed in God, like 'Young Oxford'? Damn her!

Did you see Dixon Scott's (of the M. Guardian) review of Q.[1] in
the Liverpool Courier? It was sent me. If you haven't seen it, I'll
show it you. It's all about you & me, of whom the creature
humorously professes not to have heard. Screamingly funny!
'These Brookes & Monros...' one fine paragraph begins. Very
favourable, in a way. But hadn't we better send him G.P.?

Fare thee well. Love to Arundel. I hope that you're well, & that
he's good, & that you're both more businesslike, & that the P.B. is
making an immense sum by selling my book.

RUPERT BROOKE

P.S. Frances Cornford is enraptured by Lake Leman. She gives
me permission to tell you.

P.P.S. Bowes & Bowes have started sending me the pink new
Poetry Review. I have reprimanded them & bid them cease. But
will others not be taken in?

To GEOFFREY KEYNES   *Cornwall (address Rugby)*
                                 9 January 1913
Geoffrey!

Your letter got to me as I was on the point of dashing off here to
the Francises, from Rugby & the Ranee. I nearly called at Cowley
St:[2] but just hadn't time. I'll be in London in a week or two though,
and we'll roar over a sardine or two at Gustave's.

* * *

[1] An anthology by Quiller-Couch.
[2] My lodgings at 14 Cowley St., Westminster.

Your literary criticism is very good when you praise me, & ridiculous when you blame.

I have written nothing for months, till I came here, except a fragment which I composed soon after I left you in September (August?): it's called '*Motoring*'.

> 'The part of motoring *I* like,
> Is luncheon near the Devil's Dyke.
> —The country's really very fair,
> From beyond Ditchling Beacon there:
> The view is very *sweet*, and very
> *Pretty*, from there to Chanctonbury:
> But still, the part of it *I* like
> Is luncheon near the Devil's Dyke.
>
> ...   .
>
> Chicken & sausage-roll laid out,
> Pudding, and stout, oh Jesus, *stout*!
>
> ...   .
>
> Above my head the clouds they pass:
> My table-cloth is the green grass.
>
> ...   .
>
> My mouth is covered with stout-froth—
> The green grass is my table-cloth.'

It went on a long time: but I omitted to write it down: & have forgotten it.

I've been meaning to write to you about Prof. Grierson's *Donne* which I'm reviewing:[1] to know if you've anything of interest to point out about it—beyond his intermittent dimness about your name. But we'll talk of it.

I have written a very good play, here.

The purpose of this letter is this. I'm trying to buy a Gill. He's done an extraordinarily good cast for a bronze—a Madonna. If he can only sell *one* cast he has to charge me an immense sum, which I can't pay. If more, it gets cheaper. He can sell six at £8 or £10 each. If you're wanting to buy a Gill, now's your chance! I sent my photograph of it to Maynard, with instructions to send it on to you. I knew you a potential Maecenas. Send me the photograph back, will you? You don't know of other possible Gill-buyers?

There's an idea of a party of (*secretly*) prospective purchasers, you,

---

[1] In *Poetry and Drama*, no. 2, June 1913.

me, Justin & Eddie, all in a motor, one Saturday or Sunday—the old road to Ditchling. (Eddie to stand lunch—don't tell him.)

We meet soon. Thine (in health)   RUPERT

To KATHARINE COX   *Cornwall*
                                                    [*January 1913*]

Dear child, you'll have to put up with my views on 'women' and love. I can't unlearn what I've learnt. It's no good basis for an understanding to pretend that last year never happened. I see—not only through you—a lot of things about women. I can't pretend I don't. Nor is it an argument put forward, or anything. I just see them. My 'faith''s all right. I've got 'faith' where faith's due. But it'd be silly to try to work up 'faith' that women can't be raped, or that human beings don't bleed when pricked, or any other comfortable untruth.

Also, I know about love. It's all right if one can be taken in, enough; and all happens to go happily. But one can't keep it at that. Love *is* being at a person's mercy. And it's a black look-out when the person's an irresponsible modern female virgin. There's no more to say.

You don't quite understand about promises. If love helps 'to keep you straight'—my dear, very good! Where it didn't help, I meant, was in enabling you to *see* good and bad, as you now blessedly can. But promises—don't keep saying that, if yourself can't keep you right, 'promises' are no good, or whatever it is you say. Promises are a great thing, a great comfort, things all good people can make & keep. Infinitely important. They're things one keeps because they're promises, not because they concern the sort of action one's character leads one to do or avoid. They're things one keeps blindly without seeing the point, essentially. Supposing you didn't want me to fall in love with anybody, & were especially afraid of Frances. Well, you couldn't make me promise not to fall in love with any-body. But you *could* make me promise never to see Frances. I should say 'It's all nonsense!'; but I should go away, & never see her—if I was a decent enough person to be honourable about promises. It wouldn't keep me 'straight'. But it would help, just as avoiding a measly house helps one to escape measles, & it would comfort you.

Isn't it all perfectly plain? And isn't honour about promises *essential* to any relationship between decent people in the world?

Oh, dear, I tend to drop into a pedagogic and parsonical tone with you, so. But you *are* a child.

*   *   *

To JACQUES RAVERAT   *Cornwall*
                                Thursday [*9 January 1913*]

O dear, yes, I'm certainly coming. But when? I really don't
know. On Saturday I leave here and stay in London a night.
Sunday I probably go off for three days—Then home to catch
Aunt Fanny. Then it'll be the 17th or so, and between then and the
end of the month I'll spend a bit with you, I guess, and a bit in
London. I suppose I shall get clearer some time. I had a spasm of
warmth for you both a fortnight ago yesterday.* I am very well,
and working, even. Writing very good plays. Cornwall's so nice,
three hundred miles away from anywhere. It's as peaceful as being
abroad. Why are you so damned central—*Royston*!

I was in a room in London—very distinguished—there were there

> The Editor of Rhythm
> His Paramour
> Me
> Mr Gilbert Cannan
> Eddie
> Two painters
> A poet

The room was plastered with woodcuts by Gwen. We all looked at
them and said 'What Power!' Then I said, offhandedly,

'Known her for *years*.'

They all respected me.

Subsequently I had tea with William H. Davies, a one-legged man.

*   *   *

RUPERT

P.S. Did I tell you that I'm, oh, so much in love with Cathleen,
and she simply won't look at me?

* Not that I generally hate you—but that I practically never feel
warm towards anybody.

To GWEN RAVERAT   *Oxford to Rugby*
                                Sunday [*January ? 1913*]

Gwen, ol' dear,

Albert tells me he's written to you and not heard from you.

I rather see you hesitating for two reasons. (1) your natural

churlishness, (2) your anti-Semitism. I approve of the second, but
not the first. But I hope you'll contribute to *Rhythm*.

It's being reorganized, you see. It has had some good things in it.
It will have more. Albert is in charge of the organization of the
pictures—three or four of us of the literature—all under the editor.
The staff poets are me, Gibson, Davies, De la Mare and Abercrombie,
all good poets, all good men, and all Europeans.

*   *   *

Nearly all the people connected with it are your people, we poets,
Eddie, G. Cannan, Noel Rooke, Lees, Ferguson, etc. My great fear
is that Albert will make it too much New English and dreary. Gill's
doing some lettering, and Albert's going to try Cookham,[1] and
I hope very much he'll have got you. Then it'll be savingly broadened.
The little man's only in that position because he's such an industrious
organizer (vide *Comus*). He's nice enough—in this capacity—and
commendably keen on your work: and he's not speaking for himself,
but we all demand through him. Answer us with assent.

With love, and to Jacques,   RUPERT

To EDWARD MARSH   *c/o J. Raverat*
                                          Croyden, Royston
                                  Saturday [*25 January 1913*]

Yes, I'd like to have lunch with Gosse on Wednesday.

I enclose, ere I lose it again, and in case anything happens, the
ticket. Do you think it'll be possible & worth while to exchange it
for the next seat to Ervine's two—in the 2*s*. 6*d*. seats?

*   *   *

It *had* just occurred to me, that, as Mrs Ervine has to go on from
us to the theatre, & we shall probably pick her up there afterwards,
and as they know her, & as it's so ridiculously convenient, we might
include in the party, on one or other occasion, quite incidentally—
oh dear me!—Cathleen. But no doubt it's quite impossible—I
suppose she dines with Millionaires every night—I can see a thousand
insuperable difficulties—it was scarcely worth while mentioning
it. . .   Ever
                                                     R.

[1] Stanley Spencer.

To GWEN RAVERAT   *Rugby*
                                                     Sunday
                                    [*January or February 1913*]

Comic characters, rustics. And it's awfly funny, for an agnogger, about Gill. It'll all come right, though. *I* know about the religious temperament. People who've taken religion are hard to get on with for a bit. They're so precious keen on their new-found salvation. (Witness the English-Catholic recommendation of 'The Lord's Prayer' to a poor sufferer like Ka!) Converts. Converts. Converts are always inhuman. (All this is probably the best reason for becoming a Roman Catholic, because, damme, you can't get converted any *further*: there's no madness beyond it, unless Satanism: so you rest.) But they come back: they come back: to humanity. I from Stracheyism: Gill from Roman Catholicism. I bet you'll be able to work with him in two years, when he's got over it a bit. Old Belloc works with English Christians, Agnostics, and Atheists, to establish Truth in certain directions. So can Goddites and No-Goddites and Pope Goddites work together to produce beauty—which all leads round, you perceive, to what *I* mind about *Rhythm*. I've told them to send you March, April and May, so that you can see in what way it's changing. The Cover *is*, as a matter of fact, to be altered: to only lettering (by, I believe, a Roman Catholic, called Gill). But I hope the things you hate in it, the 'modernness and desire to shock' will continue. Of course it's modern. It's all by people who do good work and are under thirty-five. It shows there are such, and that they're different from and better than the *Yellow Book* or the *Pre-Raphaelites* or any other body. Do you think it ought to look as if it was written by Gosse and Tennyson and illustrated by Whistler and Madox Brown? I'll tell you why it is better than *Country Life* or *Home Chat* or the other things you prefer: because in *Rhythm* we're doing work because we think it's good, and in *Country Life* poor devils are put down at a salary to write what it's thought the subscribers want, whether they like to write or not, and aren't allowed to say anything they think true or good, if it's thought subscribers won't like it. And the result is mush and poison. It's mere wickedness to exhibit with a little coward like Brimley Johnson (the Little Gallery) who isn't 'modern' or 'shocking' because he daren't be, and not to contribute to *Rhythm*, on such grounds.

As for 'shocking', it's impossible to put forward much good or true work in this modern world without shocking all the bloody people more or less. Nor is it true that you are too good for a magazine, to which Gilbert Cannan, and Wibson,*[1] and I contribute.

So, when you've seen a number or two, neglect Albert, and send in an occasional thing; though you don't bind yourself to contribute three a year. It won't interfere with your sale.

I'm going to London on Wednesday. (I've been here for some time, at the beginning with a sort of influenza.) I have such a passion for various women in London, that I shall live mainly there, for a bit. I want passionately to go to the South Seas: and it's *awfully* difficult tearing myself away. I shall take every third day in the country. If your relatives are still too young for your husband, you can pack him off to me for any two days or three, and I can either entertain him in London or walk him on the hills: and I will not let him drink alcohol, and I will put him to bed early.

Also I may pop down for a day to Croyden, some time. But I centre in London.

I have done no work for ages.   Love to both

                                        RUPERT

* I know all about nervous diseases, and can cure him, you remember.

To KATHARINE COX   *Jacques'*
                                        Thursday morning
                                        [*February 1913*]

No, my dear, I'm not ill. I'm sorry I've not written. I suppose I ought to have. I haven't been too busy. I suppose I've been too unconscious. The days slide past, and there's never any more point in doing one thing than another; and so one does nothing at all. No work: and no letters. I occasionally hope I'm 'resting'—but I doubt if it is that.

All the same, it is rather peaceful to have you out of the country, and to be able to spend days together without supposing that you're paying the penalty of being unprotected. I suppose you *are* a bit better off in Germany.

I'm sorry to hear you're ill. Berlin isn't really a good place for health, and Dudley lives unrestfully. But what's to be done? You can't be trusted to take care of yourself in England. It's the penalty of being incompetent. I hope in a few months you may be hardened

    [1] Wilfrid Gibson.

over a bit. That's the hope. Otherwise, you'll continue being that burden to your friends you deplored being recently.

I leave here this afternoon; Cambridge; London; Cambridge again. After Monday I don't know. You'd better address to King's till further notice.

I've been fairly comfortable with these people. I've even given them a few hints on sensible living—for they're apt to be too fidgetty, and when Jacques' nerves are too bad for painting, he thinks it sensible to dig in the garden all day! Their opinions seem to be modified in the direction of sense, and they're a little, gracefully, ashamed of God. After all, they've got moral taste, and nothing else matters much. One discussion on God, in which I with difficulty controlled myself, and one on Socialism wherein I explained a few elementary things to Jacques and left him disturbed and humbled. I have hopes that most of his errors are due to his health. The only real difficulty of living here is, of course, the loneliness—they do walk hand-in-hand so, and occasionally kiss. I reflect that they, being fairly good and clever, got what they deserve, and I have got what I deserve; and so I look the other way and think about literature.

I went to King's for the week-end. I hoped to meet Lytton and insult him. But there was only James, who is so defenceless that it is no sport kicking him, after a bit. Otherwise, the usual gang.

I went to London to hear the Shaw–Belloc debate. They were both a little wary, and they talked in different directions. I went with my latest acquaintance, Mr Ervine, the dramatist.

* * *

Geoffrey came here a bit. He seemed fairly well. Jacques and I spent one evening explaining to him about the female question, suffrage etc. He was very much upset, and nearly cried. It was rather unfair on him, of course, for whenever he appealed to what females think or feel, Gwen gave verdict against him. He's now gone off to stay with David Pye, and writes that David's views are much more feminist and fair and a great relief after ours. But I expect it'll sink in—

Frances I met in the market place on Monday, looking about 22. I suppose *she* isn't with child?

Justin got on Gwen's nerves. Hugh Russell-Smith is engaged to be married. No other news.

I'm a little frightened about Anne, as the time comes. I'm very glad you're there. Could you send me a telegram afterwards? Or is that silly?

I have had the play by me for three weeks and not the energy to copy it out. So I suppose nothing'll come of it.

I rather shrink at the idea of your tramping Russia with a female. I like the lingual companionship idea much better. But you needn't quit Berlin too soon?

Don't fuss about me. I'm not ill, and never shall be again. I'm permanently as I am.

I don't see what I can do, to help you to sleep. I wish there was anything. But you'll just have to learn to sleep, on your own account. If ever we meet again, it's got to be from strength—not weakness. Goodbye child.

With love

RUPERT

To FRANCES CORNFORD   *c/o E. Marsh*
5 Raymond Buildings
Gray's Inn
Wednesday [February 1913]

Dear Frances,

It was awfully nice of you to write and tell me.[1] It has prevented me—the joyful contemplation of it—working for some two hours this afternoon.

But—if it's not too ungracious to say so—it wasn't news! Something—the aspect of Francis, and also a sudden feeling about it— had convinced me, oh, some nine days ago (or is it sixteen?). So I wrote and told Ka; knowing how much hopes of it filled her. She heard from you, later, and wrote to say I'd felt truly—two days ago I got her letter. She was wrought up with gladness—and tears. It made her very happy.

You'll not accuse her of betraying secrets to me! It's very good. I AM glad.

O Frances, you seem to have lived very successfully. Did you square the gods, or anything? It must be wonderful to have perfected life.

I'm coming to Cambridge this week-end. To read a paper (a week early) to the Heretics. I'll stay till Monday afternoon, if you'll

---

[1] F.C. had told him she was expecting a baby.

give me Monday lunch? I don't like to suggest Sunday meals: for wisdom has taught me that I shall be writing all Sunday to get the paper done.

Let me know.

I've no plans to tell you. One doesn't rise to plans in this slough of existence. I still flirt with the idea of an European War. And I intrigue with theatrical people.

But I've a heap of foolish tittle-tattle to retail.

For myself, I shall have twenty-five children: all sons.

I've got to go out.

With love
RUPERT

To GEOFFREY KEYNES

c/o Eddie
5 Raymond Buildings
Gray's Inn, W.C.
Tuesday [*February 1913*]

Dear Geoffrey,

*   *   *

The M[ary] & G[abriel] poem came out (with one or two more things) in the *November* number of *The Poetry Review*. Price 6d.

I don't know when, or even *if*, *The Nation* will print J.D.[1]

The play's type-writing. I shall see Clive anyhow. The more places perform it, the better, say I. Do you think I shall be making as much as £50 a week? I'll send you a stall. But you'll have to dress.

I am not cynical about d[as] E[wig] W[eibliche]. Cynicism implies thinking a thing rather unimportant. Some Socialists are cynical about Tariff Reform; they think it silly, & that it won't make the slightest difference either way. But a King's don isn't cynical about T[ariff] R[eform]. He thinks it a deadly menace. It's about as cynical to hold my views about females, as it is to put fire-guards in front of a nursery fire.

Nothing like getting words right.

I had lunch with Hugh-Smith,[2] & his *fiancée* yesterday. Also present, Elsie Smith & (!!) her *fiancée* (*sic*), Geoffrey Marchand, an old Johnian & Fabian acquaintance of mine; also his sister, Hilda Marchand (*Pappagena* of Magic Flute) who is engaged to Hugh's other great Johnian friend, Burton—whose brothers & sisters, no doubt....

---

[1] His article on Donne, printed 15 February 1913.   [2] H. Russell-Smith.

They're all right, you know. Their hearts are sound & their views not at all feminist. Central, they. From that rightness are divergencies, you & I on one side, Denham [Russell-Smith] on the other, the hearts of both not being sound & *our* views tainted. Oh, we have our work, & Denham his worms. So things go *on*.

How nasty it is addressing an envelope to you as I address this.[1] Pray hang up carbolic sheets in your house.

RUPERT

To JACQUES RAVERAT   [Postcard]
Gray's Inn
Tuesday [*25 February 1913*]

Coming back from dining with—well never mind whom—I saw, suddenly, a poster outside a newspaper shop. I reproduce it—

SCIENCE
SIFTINGS

No. 24.   Feb. 22

SEX
DIFFERENCES

SHOULD THEY BE
DONE AWAY WITH?

1*d.*   Monthly

I do not comment.   RUPERT

To HAROLD MONRO   [Postcard]
c/o E. M.
26 February 1913

Donne be blowed. I've spent two weeks trying to review Wilfrid [Gibson]. Blast it! I've never had so hard a travail—a fortnight's

---

[1] Addressed to Brunswick Square, where I had a room in a house inhabited by Adrian Stephen and others of the 'Bloomsbury' set.

continual use of the forceps. But I've ground out some fairly good stuff (I think).[1] I'll rush it round tomorrow morning. It can go in in July, if not now; Donne[2] certainly can. I didn't know you were going to print that 'note' in full. *I* thought it needed compression & a new foreword. But as you like.

Yours,

Alive but feeble—

R. B.

To E. J. DENT

c/o E. Marsh

5 Raymond Buildings

Gray's Inn, W.C.

[February 1913]

Dear Dent,

*   *   *

Rhythm, which is being reorganized on a fuller basis, but equally advanced, is having occasional articles on music—not so much reviews of concerts as enlightenment on modern or ancient good things— They'd heard of you as the only good writer on music nowadays— one of the only people who both was musical in a sincere sense and also could convey his meaning to—us intelligent ἀμουσικοι [unmusicals], let's say. They were delighted to find I knew you and 'ld ask you. I've an idea of the *sort* of thing they'd like, which I could explain in conversation. But I expect you understand. They don't pay! But they're doing good work—If you're again in London, we might talk. I've several ideas I could suggest to you of what the advanced public want telling about music!

*   *   *

To KATHARINE COX

Eddie's still

Thursday [March 1913]

It's a little late for writing. Still—I got a letter from Dresden today. You'll have heard from me by now. Oh, I was a beast not to write.

I am rather a beast. You mustn't mind my not writing. It doesn't *mean* anything at all. I think of you continually; almost every hour. But I aim at filling my life so chock-full that I don't have time for worry. I'm really rather successful (except when I tire

[1] Review of Gibson's *Fires* in *Poetry and Drama*.
[2] His review of Grierson's *Donne*, printed in *Poetry and Drama*, June 1913.

myself, and everything begins to go). But such a mode of life keeps me from writing letters.

Nay, I'm a beast.

The thought of you grows lovelier day by day.

My plans don't get ahead. Mr [Granville] Barker has declared his admiration for my play[1] in conversation with friends; but keeps it and is dumb. So do Manchester.

O, a message to you from Mr Yeats. He drew me aside, as I, with others was leaving, Monday night, and asked where I got my shirt from—'A present' said I. He so wanted to know where he could get such stuff—he needs a dark flannel semi-pyjama garb to wear in the mornings about his house—I promised to find out where he could get the *stuff*—'You'll never get anyone who can make it as this is made' I flung at him, as I vanished. But tell me something, weises Weib.

On Wednesday to hear Newbolt lecturing about me: there who should tread on me but your Frances Graham.[2] You'd said she was nice, so I was less stern than my wont. Also present, Mrs Barlow, Eddie, and 115 Duchesses.

Eddie brought my letters in one morning, and complained that they were—as usual—from myself—from Germany. You, of course! It was far more like my handwriting than my own is, he complained. For he often gets letters from me that—from the envelope—he can't make out who the devil it is. But your handwriting he always knows for mine instantly.

Friday morn

Two letters from you!

Oh my dear, you *didn't* hurt, really. It's only that one's so callously unimaginative and material. One doesn't take much notice, if anyone gives their life or happiness—but if they give *money*, it seems so overwhelming.

I'm ashamed of myself in front of some people, especially you. That's all.

I don't know that there's much to be said. My plans—the War seems fairly far off. I got Nevinson to promise to take me, if it happens. But I think I won't wait for it.

But I *do* rather want to wait for my play to be settled.

I'll be all right in California. I'd better go, you know. I'm not doing anyone any good here, myself nor nobody.

---

[1] *Lithuania*, written in 1912.   [2] Soon to be Mrs Cosmo Gordon.

It'd be nice for you to go walking in the Hay or wherever it is. Perhaps it *is* the sound of the *Black* Forest. Do try to get hold of someone to go with. It *is* beginning to be weather for walking. Even I feel.

If ever you're in London and meet W. W. Gibson be nice to him. He's the only nice person in London, and he is so very nice. Like an untruculent Dudley. One keeps looking after him.

You'll be advising Dudley about Eddie's picture scheme.

I write dully. I am dull, I must leave London.

You're a lovely old thing. It *is* good if you're getting stronger.

I've hurt you so: oh my dear—wasting years of your loveliness. I hate myself.

Be well, child—
dein RUPERT

To GEOFFREY FRY

c/o Marsh
Monday [March 1913]

My dear Geoffrey,

*   *   *

It's very good of you to congratulate me[1]—you can't think how I despise you mere civilians, now. Jetzt bin ich Professor. A grey look of learning has already settled on my face. And I wear spectacles.

*   *   *

I salute you

RUPERT   F.K.C.
D.D.
G.P.
BBB etc. etc.

I'm in London till Saturday: unless I'm summoned to King's to be churched.[2] They wanted to do it today. But I didn't learn of the ceremony till too late to go. I fear they may refuse me altogether now.

---

[1] On having been elected a Fellow of King's College.
[2] i.e. to be admitted as a Fellow.

To KATHARINE COX 5 *Thurloe Square*
Sunday [*March 1913*]
Dear child,

Going off walking interrupts one's life so; from Thursday morning to yesterday evening, I trod the South Cambridgeshire hills with Jacques. And now I can't remember when I wrote to you last, or what has happened since, or in what order things have happened.

(Not that anything *has* happened.)

Oh, dear, we walked a great way, and cooked sausages in woods and on Roman roads, and now I'm very rustic and stolid and unemotional. I've scarcely worried about anything since I got up, three hours ago. So forgive this letter being dull.

I'm sending the *Quarterly*[1] with Calderon's article to you. It's even bloodier than I remembered. Still, you may as well have it. If you're not a better authority than he, on Russians, I shall expose you in the public Press.

Jacques and I spent our time in telegraphing and writing to Dudley, making appointments, and demanding plans. We never heard anything and I suppose I shall have to go on sitting here till he appears. He must be even less capable of managing life than before he became a father—Jacques and I plan to have him removed to the country for a little. It is thought he is interviewing people all day, under the impression he is important—or they.

* * *

Jacques (to his and Gwen's great joy) has become very fat in the last three weeks. I believe my words on the right way of treating nerves are the cause. His *face*, too—quite fat. Gwen I thought tiredish: but all right. Doing rather a good *Pieta*. They seemed shy of the subject of Roman Catholicism.

My dear child, don't worry about me and Ottoline Morrell.

* * *

No, you needn't feel alarmed, child. There are many things possible in a bloody world. But that's a thing that's impossible. If you like, I'll even promise not to 'discuss' you, or would, if you didn't so despise promises.

But I won't promise not to discuss you, with Gwen and Frances and such. It's part of the penalty of your weakness. As a matter of fact I don't practically. As a matter of fact everybody I know goes miles out of their way rather than mention your name to me. But

[1] *Quarterly Rev.* (1912), CCXVII, 21–42, 'The Russian Stage', by George Calderon.

with Frances or Gwen—you see, there are moments when I'm overwhelmed by the horror of your incapacity, and the pain's so great that I want to tell the people that *do* care for you, that if anything goes wrong with you while I'm away, I'll kill them (and you) when I come back. Oh, I won't go on. But there's so many things: my extraordinary and tearing thankfulness, sometimes that there *are* people who care so for you—that has to find expression. And practical points: whether you'll be made ill by being alone in Russia for more than a week (as some think)—I say, you can, and ought to, stand a month.

But past things aren't ever opened, child. Self-protection forbids my doing that.

This is very long and ill-tempered. I daresay it's the last letter you'll get from me. For on Friday I go to take my M.A. And it's not probable an M.A. would condescend to write to a quite degreeless lady. Meanwhile the London news is—a new American Revue (it's funny to think that rag-time means, perhaps, nothing to you), Mr Henry James' seventieth birthday, rumours of more Marconi revelations, my supper with Mr Gosse tonight, and my lunch with Jan [Masefield] tomorrow. Oh, Mr Bennett's new play[1] is very lovelily acted, by Ainley and an adorable Cockney genius discovered on the Halls. *Rhythm* is coming out as *The Blue Review*. And my second edition is now on the market.

* * *

With love, child,
RUPERT

To EDWARD MARSH

24 B.R., Rugby
Tuesday noon
[*10 March 1913*]

My dear Eddie,

I've waited till today to write because I've been waiting to see how a bad cold I've been having would turn out. It must have started on Friday or so, & I was rather bad at the Murrays. I think it must have been a kind of flu. I still feel very groggy, hoarse, and katarhoeic. I don't think I dare try a walk of three days while I'm like this. I should knock up after a day of it with fever & a bad throat. I feel

---

[1] *The Great Adventure*, a dramatization of his novel, *Buried Alive*.

very sick about it. I've to go tomorrow afternoon to King's to be enrolled, & spend the night there; I'd meant to join you in London, & travel down to Gloucester—I think I must come back here: & stay till I'm whole. I'm sorry to let you down.

*   *   *

Oh, dear, even through the stupidity of a cold I begin to hanker for London. Mustn't I write you a Collins, saying it was so nice of you to put me up during my fleeting visit of two months?

Breakfast with you, lunch with Wilfrid, tea with Cathleen— a round which the Ranee finds it rather hard to compete with, & which even now takes on the colour of old time & romance— Cathleen has become a lovely dream, and Wilfrid and Violet Asquith rather plain dreams—but how fascinating!

I grow maudlin. I gave up my keys to Jack Tiger[1] with a curse of jealousy.

This must catch the post. A card tonight, or a telephone tomorrow will find me. I go to King's in the afternoon.

Your

RUPERT

To AELFRIDA TILLYARD [MRS CONSTANTINE GRAHAM]

24 Bilton Road, Rugby
18 March 1913

Dear Madam,

Many thanks for your letter and your congratulations.

I *did* get your letter a fortnight ago, & put it aside to answer. But I forgot. I'm very sorry.

I am afraid I cannot give you any of my unpublished poems. There are only five: and I have promised them all to various journals.

I've a rule always to charge a guinea a poem for anthologies. I'd like to be in your book, for I'd find myself with friends there, I suppose. So you may have what you like of my published work (within reason) for half a guinea per poem, for poems of under fifty lines each, and a guinea a poem for poems of above fifty lines each. If you like I will send you references to the six poems by me that have been published in various places since my book appeared, so that the field of choice may be wider.

[1] John Middleton Murry.

If you want to include anything by me on these terms, I should like to see & agree to the list of what you select, before it is decided (there are a few misprints in my book, which should be corrected). And also, if you choose any poem that has not previously appeared in book form, I suppose you will confirm me that I retain the copyright of them (I am uncertain about the law on this point).

I hope the delay has not been a nuisance.

Yours truly,

RUPERT BROOKE

To FRANCES CORNFORD   *Buckinghamshire*

Monday [*20 March 1913*]

Dear Frances,

Thanks for your letter. You *have* been good. What can one say?
I heard from Ka, too. She is very wonderful and beautiful.
This pen is beastly. A pencil is better.

I write in *The Pink and Lily*.[1] The hill drops a few hundred feet in front, and beyond is half Buckinghamshire, Berkshire, and Oxfordshire. In this little room is the publican, asleep and rather tipsy. Outside there's a lot of wind, and sun and rain alternating.

*   *   *

I left the Murrays on Friday. I was rather ill when I was there: and very unpleasant. Gilbert was lovely, Rosalind very funny and childlike and nice, and the rest of the family pleasant.

*   *   *

I slide along in the same way. I do no work. I seem to take it for granted that I'm going away. I sort of drop enquiries out. But I can't say I've faced the thing—in my own mind—yet. When I try to, it seems unbearable. What I 'owe' to Ka—or to myself—or to the world. Oh, it seems very far away, all that sort of idea. But I think perhaps I'm rather mad. Things do happen, obscurely, in the brain.

I often think that going away 'll only be an intolerable agony for me, and 'll do no good. But I know staying won't, either.

But this isn't a discussion. It's just a bulletin to say I'm all right.

RUPERT

[1] An inn near Great Hampden in the Chilterns where he wrote the poem 'Never came there to the Pink' (*Collected Poems*, 1918).

Rupert Brooke in the garden at the
Old Vicarage, Grantchester, 1911

Rupert Brooke declaiming poetry to Dudley Ward
and Jacques Raverat, Grantchester, 1911

Katharine Cox, 1912
from a drawing by Henry Lamb

Edward Marsh, 1910
from a drawing by Violet, Duchess of Rutland

Cathleen Nesbitt, in *Quality Street*, 1913

Rupert Brooke, 1913
photograph by Sherril Schell

Duncan Campbell Scott and Rupert Brooke,
Canada, 1913

Rupert Brooke (second row, second from left) in the
Hood Battalion, 1914

Rupert Brooke's grave on Skyros, 23 April 1915

To CATHLEEN NESBITT
24 *Bilton Road, Rugby*
Thursday [*20 March 1913*]

φαίνεταί μοι κῆνος ἴσος θέοισιν
ἔμμεν ἄνηρ ὅστις ἐνάντιός τοι
ἰζάνει καὶ πλάζιον ἆδυ φωνεύσας ὑπακούει.[1]

So, verstehst du denn kein Griechisch? Armes Mädchen! Kein
Deutsch, auch? Darum kann ich alles was ich will sagen; und du
kannst nicht verstehen. Gut. Du bist wunderbar. Du bist das
schönste Weib im ganzen Welt. Ich kann dich nicht anschauen. Du
machst mir weh. . . .

So: that's for you. Just to teach you a befitting humility in the
presence of the learned.

It was a very nice letter you wrote me. Yourself comes out through
the fall of the sentences. One hears the tone—and the silly Irish
accent you sometimes put on, you know.

Lord, Lord!

I was in Cambridge last night—I really got admitted at length,
not having a dinner with you to put it off for! I dined solemnly
with very old white-haired men at one end of a vast dimly-lit hall,
and afterwards drank port somnolently in the common-room, with
the College silver and seventeenth-century portraits and a sixteenth-
century fireplace and fifteenth-century ideas. The perfect don, I.
You'll hardly recognize me, when we blessedly next meet.

I'm going to stay here till I'm entirely sound again. My fever's
left me with a cough. Oh the weather at Cambridge was Spring—
wonderful. And I wanted to be out, walking, taking you with me.
Your account of your walk fired me with a mad hunger for the
country, and with a devasting fire of jealousy against the man who
was with you. Damn him! What good deed did he ever do to be
rewarded by hours and hours of your company on the Surrey hills?
What deed *could* any one do good enough?

But that other people should see your face turning and changing
hour by hour, wonderfully, and I not be there. Nash's Magazine
(my only reading) is but a makeshift. Woman, I will *not* have you
blaspheming. You have done it in two letters. If you don't know
that you're the most beautiful thing in the world, either you're
imbecile, or else, something's wrong with your mirror. But I refuse
to let you deny it, impiously. If you try, I shall kill you. Your
beauty—it's only the insensate poverty of the English language and

[1] In my eyes he is the equal of the gods, the man who sits opposite you and hears
your sweet voice from near at hand. (Sappho, 10, 'Anactoria'.)

the feebleness of my imagination that prevent me describing it to you. Helen and Deirdre—evoking names can only document it. How can one catch and preserve and pin down a living thing? Is it an insane chance that your features and attributes all happened to meet?

> 'So may your mighty amazing beauty move
> Envy in all women, and in all men, love.'

(That's old Donne.)[1]

But there aren't any words, most radiant. I can only measure it by its result—as one records the light of the sun on photographic paper, or the rain of all the heavens in a little water-gauge. There have been evenings when two or three hours of you left me as if I'd run ten miles, panting, knees trembling, and entirely exhausted. That's your damned face. Do you understand that?

*   *   *

I'm sending you, as far as these Festal posts allow—Belloc's *Four Men*. I wonder if it'll convert you to him?
Good-night.

I have no doubt I shall dream of you as usual—'How can a woman *live* with such a face?'

Do not blaspheme. It offends me—a worshipper.

RUPERT

To GEOFFREY FRY   *24 Bilton Road, Rugby*
The Saturday
[21 March 1913]

My dear Geoffrey,

Are you enjoying Christ's sojourn in Hell down in the country? I sit here and blow my nose and cry. And it rains.

I went to King's and was admitted and dined with Nixon and Corbett and Heycock at High Table. My God! my God!

It's come upon me that you were asking in what papers had my poems appeared and would they, and—if it's not too repetitive— what papers held the cream of modern literature: and that I promised to let you have details. Here are forms concerning each. If you subscribe to *Rhythm*, do so from the beginning of the year, for I wrote in January on a Puff-Puff.[2] *Rhythm* is being reorganized,

---

[1] Sapho to Philaenis, ll. 62–3.   [2] 'The Night Journey' (*1914 and other Poems*, p. 47).

and permanently draws, hereafter, on Gilbert Cannan, L. Abercrombie, W. W. Gibson, me, W. H. Davies, Walter de la Mare, Hugh Walpole, Dent, A. Rothenstein, Duncan Grant, D. Lees, and a hundred more artists. It's going to be very good. The other thing is the old Poetry Review, extended.[1] A poem by me to come in the second number.

Subscribe to these, and you will be on the tip-top of modern Art and Literature.   Ever

RUPERT

To CATHLEEN NESBITT   *24 Bilton Road, Rugby*
                                      [24 March 1913
                                      Easter Monday]

Bankollidy

My dear Cathleen (what a thing to begin a letter with!)

Ere I forget them, two pieces of news.

One is that Ethel Levey is out of *Hello Ragtime* all this week— I expect you know. I thought it worth while preventing your disappointment, in case you didn't know. And I can rest easy in Arcady, knowing you're not stealing a march on me.

Another is that I'm going to see *Hamlet* on Wednesday, April 2nd. So that rather hints that I shall be in London next week, anyhow. And I've a suspicion that I shan't be able to tear myself away by the first train on Thursday morning. I need hardly say I'm very much at your disposal. Infinitely so.

(I can even imagine that there'll be a very fine Spring day in the country on the following Sunday, and no Stage Society production.)

Here I sit and read Wedekind, and try to screw out poems: and they won't come.

I'm sending you back, tomorrow, the two books you lent me, the American and the French. I told you how the American shocked me. I like Benda.[2] The dinner-party's fun. The end's queer. Do you suppose that *Eleuthère* dies in the duel? I'm not good enough at French to know if it's implied in the atmosphere. The *Présidente*— oh, it's very maliciously nice. But that queer second chapter sticks in my mind the longest: so unexpectedly outspoken, and subtle. How did you know of Benda? I'd like to know more about him. . . .

---

[1] Presumably *Poetry and Drama*. Four poems by R.B. appeared in no. 4, December 1913.   [2] Julien Benda, *Dialogue d'Eleuthère*, Paris, 1911.

There's the question of the condition I return the book in. I took it about in my pocket so much. . . . Oh, but it was *very* dirty before, the cover, I swear. Awfully dirty. I couldn't be entirely *positive* that when you gave it me, some of the leaves had come unstitched. It's really quite possible. Or it *may* have happened in my possession.

Oh, I say, I'm awfully sorry if it is my fault. I'm terrified you'll be angry. I thought of getting it bound, but I daredn't decide the colour. What colour would you like to see it in?

We can talk about the book when we meet—about the contents, I mean. One more to the million things to talk about!

My God, it's ten blooming bloody days since I saw you! Can the mind *imagine* greater self-restraint? And another eight or nine till I see you again. Oh! oh! Every day that last week I saw you: every golden day. Except Saturday; and then I heard you.

Tell me, assure me, that you look just like you did; but better (and less white). Beer and early sleeping and country-walks, and the Cheshire Cheese—you've probably become entirely a country maiden. Shall I meet a bouncing red-faced plump hearty rustic wench in a print frock and a sunbonnet, who'll dip a curtsey and grip my hand and shout 'Whoi, 'ow's 'ee, laad?'—and it'll be you? I drivel.

I do not wholly acquit you of being provocative of drivelling. But my letters are absurd. I wish I could write letters. They spin out so long: and there's nothing in them. There's more in one sentence of your letters, than in a page of mine. Damn you.

That reminds me. I write you frequent letters, because—I like to; and I'm alone in the country and have plenty of time. But don't feel bound to answer them. You're in the thick of London, and haven't the same opportunities—I'd hate that you felt I desired (—but I *do* desire)—aimed at, I mean, or claimed, replies. Oh damn it, I get tied up. You *do* see what I'm driving at, *don't* you?—you're an intelligent old thing, for all you make out you don't know what goes on inside my only too transparent head. I'm very happy if you don't have time to write: and very very happy if you do. So don't fash yourself.

Oh, but they've been nice, your letters.

There is, though, that one drawback to them, that they almost *intolerably* make me want to talk to you. You keep raising points that I want to reply to *at once*! And I can't. It's then *I* bite my pillow—just to work some of it off: not from sheer joy—not even at old Gilbert Cannan—like you.

Oh, your pillow!

Your reflections and resolves—I admire your resolves. They make my blood leap. (They do say, anyway, that it's Spring. And out in the country on Sunday, I noticed things.) To *live*—' *Die junge Leute*' . . . they say in the *Rosenkavalier*, which means 'Those young people'—When one's getting on for fifty, one sighs twice or three times before starting out on any part of life—you'll know one day. I rather doubt if your programme of falling in love once a day, and out once a month, will work. An Acquaintance with mathematics much slighter than Miss Cathleen Nesbitt's (*vide* the press, *passim*) assures me that you will be in love with 353 people in a year's time. And that takes doing. I was once in love with *3* people: and that wasn't all jam. But 353!

But oh my dear there are things to be done! I want to walk a thousand miles, and write a thousand plays, and sing a thousand poems, and drink a thousand pots of beer, and kiss a thousand girls, and—oh, a million things: I daren't enumerate them all, for fear this white paper 'ld blush. I wish I could get you from the theatre for a week, and we'd ramp over England together, and wake the old place up. By God, it makes one's heart sing that such a person as you should exist in the world. Could a thousand poems repay God for your mouth?

Eh, it's late: and I must run out and post this. I always go on and on in my letters, and hardly ever get to any of the things I want to say—even of that small proportion of them that I *dare* say. I wanted to comment on your account of the attitude of women to love. It'll keep.

What else is there? Have you been to the Alpine Galleries (I *think* it's there)—the latest English Post-Impressionists? If not, let's go and laugh together. May we?

What else?

Oh, nothing.

Cathleen, goodnight.

In a week you'll see me, bounding with energy and joy. It'll be Spring.

Oh, goodnight, goodnight.   Your

RUPERT

P.S. There's a place downwards from the corner of your eye, and inland from your nose, and about half an inch North East from your mouth—that's entirely adorable.

To CATHLEEN NESBITT *Rugby*
[*March 1913*]
Tuesday evening

Sweetheart,

I'm really dreadfully sorry to write to you so *often*. Do you hate it? It's awfully nice for *me*, feeling in communication with you. This time it's with a purpose—or, at least, an excuse. You'll *not* deny it's an excuse. It's this. The Brownes[1]—I promised them that I'd be seeing them again, seeing them off on Thursday, perhaps. Oh, but I shan't. It becomes more and more apparent that I'll not be able to get to London till Thursday afternoon. So if they go off up to time —I'll never see them again.

But you're nearer the centre, and you may chance to see them ere the end. If you *do*—stroke most maternally, their young heads, and give them my valedictory love. Tell them to be good, to love men and women, hate God, observe the Rules of Thought, revere major premises, space out the Undistributed Middle, wear light colours, read Milton, drink in the *Café des Westens* Berlin (a place renowned in English Song),[2] wear life-belts over the Atlantic, be kind to Germans, sing loudly in railway-carriages, and to repeat to themselves night and morning, before sleeping and on waking, the immortal words of Bishop Berkeley

'Everything is what it is, and not some other thing.'

Bid them also remember me, tolerantly.

And for yourself, child, sleep well, eat better, and learn Deirdre very well indeed. And, now and then, love me.

You are very lovely to me. I would like to put you into your quiet bed tonight, and smooth your hair, and kiss your two eyes shut, and leave you to good dreams. Perhaps my soul will do it. You'll feel a breath in the room, and hear a whisper. Goodnight, child.
RUPERT

[1] Maurice Browne and his wife. Browne was afterwards Director of Chicago Little Theatre. [2] R.B. had written 'Grantchester' there.

To KATHARINE COX   *Rugby*
                                          Tuesday after Easter
                                          [*25 March 1913*]

Two letters this evening, from you: full of energy and walking tourishness. So of course I, who had to give up my walk, for a cold, am very grumpy about it.

One letter contained two dead violets and an ivy leaf. Hypatica's an unlikely name for a flower, my dear.

Old Mrs (I forget her name) from next door wrote today offering the Ranee some Spanish (or French?) poppies for the front border. Ranee awfully bucked. Mrs Forrester (next door the other side) sent in some tulips. But Lady Molesworth said 'My dear, I can't think how you can make friends with such people!'

A lot of gossip about Mrs Whitelaw and this that and the other. I go to London a week tomorrow to see Mr Forbes Robertson play Hamlet. Everybody's very respectful about it.

Germany sounds very nice; and you healthier. I'm glad. Though I don't think it right for you to be walking alone with a young man. Today you'll have got back and found letters from me. Love to Dudley and Anne. There's precious little news in this blamed place. I think of going across to Birmingham to see the new Repertory Theatre. They're doing a *Hankin* now. Alfred Douglas' libel trial comes on next week; and the whole business'll be fetched up again. But that's out of your line. More in it are some good dirty stories Eddie amused the week-end with. But I'll not copy them out here. Frances has sent me five poems, to choose from for *Rhythm*. They're not good. (Don't tell her.) Good bits. Women aren't meant to write, I suppose. The funny thing is she seems, at times, to have come under your influence. (Not the 'a glint, a tint'—business, I mean; but more your prose style and tricks of thought.)

There's even in England (I had a walk on Sunday) a sort of perfunctory ritual of green shoots, blue skies, showers, etc. I however, have become very very bald, in the last three months. (You may tell Dudley.)

The queer thing is, that now I've hardened myself a good deal, and cut off other emotions fairly short, ambition grows and grows in me. It's inordinate, gigantic. It's no use; it doesn't even make me work. I just sit and think ambitious thoughts. As I used to sit and think lustful thoughts.

I'm egotistic tonight. Sorry.

I've had a dreadful note from James.

Retain that health the country's given you: and sleep well, child.

RUPERT

To GEOFFREY KEYNES   *Bilton Road (with a cold)*
Saturday (J.C. in Hell)
[Received 25 March 1913]

Thank you, my dear.

I was sorry you couldn't come to my little party—I'm in the middle of a correspondence with Aelfrida [Tillyard]. I *did* answer her in the end: & demanded money for my poems. Damme, I have to live by it! Now she writes by every post, cajoling, threatening, & bargaining. And I reply twice a week, raising my rates by 6*d.* a line.

*   *   *

Love to Godwin [Baynes].

I'll be in London again; & we'll arrange ahead that your ladies shall abstain from fecundity one evening.[1]

wie immer, dein
RUPERT

Spit at Bloomsbury from me.

To MRS CONSTANTINE GRAHAM

24 Bilton Road, Rugby
Easter Sunday [1913]

Dear Mrs Graham,

I expect the other people you are including in your anthology aren't trying to live by their writings. I am. It makes a difference.

'Q' probably doesn't know much about anthologies; except his own. I know at least one poet who demanded a guinea a poem for inclusion in the *Oxford Book of Victorian Verse* & got it. Most of us didn't, because we felt it was in a sense a national affair. But it was an exception. Masefield told me it was the only anthology he hadn't got a guinea a poem, or more, out of. It's the same with most poets; except amateurs. So much for the general rule: a very good one, in my opinion.

---

[1] I had been prevented from coming to the party by having to go and deliver a woman. I was then a student on 'the district' at St Bartholomew's.

Poems by me have appeared, one in *Rhythm* for January: five or six in *The Poetry Review* for November. I have these papers somewhere, in Grantchester or in London, I suppose: not here, as far as I can see. If I had them here I would send them you.

Other poems will be appearing in the *New Statesman* & *Poetry* & *Drama* & *Rhythm* during the next few months. If you don't go to press till June, I will send you a list before then, if you want one.

I really don't think I shall be able to write a special poem for your anthology. I'm very sterile just now & have great difficulty in filling my engagements even.

I don't think I can go lower than half a guinea for the shorter poems. Your first letter said something about dividing the profits, if any, among the poets. If I were paid for mine, I should, of course, lose all claim to that: so perhaps that might be counted in as diminishing the final expense of paying me.

I suppose you know of an anonymous Cambridge Book of Poems —Χαριτεσσιν—published last year, which contained at least one good poem?[1]

Yours truly,

RUPERT BROOKE

To HAROLD MONRO   *24 Bilton Road, Rugby*
                                               27 March [*1913*]

Hail!

I was staying with Gilbert Murray a week ago & discovered he was another person who'd approved of the old P[oetry] R[eview], & hated the new one, & didn't know about *Poetry & Drama*. I explained, shortly, & tried to sow a subscription. But I don't know him well enough to pursue it far. But if you sent him a form for *P & D*: & a short typewritten cold note 'Dear Sir...' saying you believe he subscribed to the old P.R., & that the tradition of that is being carried on in P. & D. he may like to take it in: & that the present P. & R. has nothing in common with the old, bar the name—I guess he'll subscribe. Only don't make it personal or warm, or mention my name: or he'll think I've been touting. These Oxford People are so damn Difficile.

*   *   *

RUPERT BROOKE

[1] This small volume did not contain anything by Brooke.

To EDWARD MARSH   *24 Bilton Road, Rugby*
                                     Sunday, 30 March 1913
Dear Eddie,

Denis [Browne] only lent you his copy,¹ didn't he? Would you care for this, then, as an oddity? I'm absolved from suspicion of touting for a place in the next G[eorgian] P[oetry] by the date of this. Of course, you can sell it when you've done with it.

V[iolet] A[squith] is very witty. I tried inventing Masefield stanzas with *disgraceful*; but couldn't. I've had a note from her. I shall certainly appear on the 15th. Will it be immense, the party? I'm so excited. My health is now perfect: which is more than my industry & inspiration are.

What is this reception of Lady Plymouth? Will all these bloody people of the Contemporary Art Society be there—Bells & such & artists? But I suppose there'll be others. Oh, today's so lovely! I wish you were here to make an even wonderfuller Sunday walk. I'd not stop short of twenty miles today.

Give me hours & times for Wednesday, when you send the key. I shall probably appear in the morning, for I've to lunch with a man. Dinner at Simpson's? I'm going to tea that day with Cathleen in her dressing room. Isn't that TOO romantic! I've never been into an actress's dressing room in my life before!

Murchison's sent two bloody & immense photographs. I'll show them you. An American photographer, Sherill Schell (!) is at me now. Perhaps I'll have better luck with him—

                              With love
                              RUPERT

To CATHLEEN NESBITT   *24 Bilton Road, Rugby*
                                   Sunday [30 March 1913]

You can't *think* what Sunday's like in Rugby: the tidy clothes we wear (except me): the solemn walks, collared and hatted and gloved: the immense meals: the church-bells. . . . Sunday, Monday, Tuesday, WEDNESDAY. Yes, I'll come to tea on Wednesday. Rather. At 27½ minutes past four I shall walk in and demand of 'that two-handed engine at the door'* to be conducted to your room. Will he do it?

* I've made it a note, because it'd break the sequence of thought *too* violently in the text. But Milton's most frightfully good. Did you know? It's the only thing I can read. If you'd learn *Paradise*

¹ Of *The Bastille*.

Lost by heart and repeat *that* to your Duchesses, there'd be some point in you.

———

I'm terrified. But you don't know how romantic it is for me, having tea with a real actress, in a real dressing-room. My dream of the height of romance. And to you it's the most utterly ordinary thing in the world. Romance to you is walking down a Reinhardt path, with coloured electric lights, singing 'Then, come to the stage-door to ni-ight!' And to them that is commonplace, and Romance is— what would it be? Being a Fellow of King's, possibly! It's as bad as the foot of a rainbow, or the top of a hill. In Heaven, perhaps, I shall for ever have tea with actresses, and you will walk an eternal Reinhardt path, singing, and they will wear M.A. hoods and gowns —and yet none of us will lose the illusion.

I suppose you aren't going to Lady Plymouth's Contemporary Art Society reception after your Wednesday night show? Eddie and I may be going on after Hamlet: but I don't know if it won't be too boring.

If your photograph looks *too* ridiculous, I may go mad and break it. So beware! How many photographs do you have taken a month, I wonder. What a life! Even we literary men, though, have our little moments. My celebrated amateur photographer who took me for his collection of Eminent Poets has just sent me two gigantic works of Art, on eternal paper—a new process—depicting a tortured elderly man reflecting in prison on the earlier plays of M. Strindberg —me, he says. I shall present them to the nation. Now I'm bombarded by an American photographer called Sherill Schell(!). You know all about America—does he exist? He says he's in London for a month—I suspect him of being a fraud.

Astonishing and alarming woman, to prefer Strindberg to Ibsen. I do. I do. But how the Hell do *you* know that he's preferable? That you should be right, as well as—but we'll have a truce about your other characteristic. Only, you mustn't blaspheme, saying that your neck is rough and yellow, again: or I may do sudden violence upon you. I can't really agree that *Married*[1] is cheerful though: all those little stories. But I think what most depressed me was that they're so much written on a thesis, that there's little else. And though the thesis is sound, it's coloured by the awful loveless character that his experiences had left the man with. One keeps coming down on this inelastic background—it's depressing in the

———

[1] Strindberg's *Married. Twenty Stories of Married Life.* Trans. E. Schleussner. London, 1913.

way preaching is depressing—I can't quite explain. I think that I think they're artistically inferior to most of his work.

I've got all the English (American) translations of Strindberg here. The Dance of Death: The Dream Play: Creditors: Miss Julia: Crimes and Crimes: and the Father. Would you like any of them? The first two are the best. But I suppose you've read them. I've just finished for a second time the translations of Tchekoff's plays. The late ones move me so. You know them? There are many things in them that—well, you *just* wouldn't bite your pillow, perhaps, for he's very restrained: but you'd certainly wriggle. Oh, and at the end of *Uncle Vanya*, you'd throw the book behind the wardrobe. There's a lovely old nurse who comforts the love-sick girl, when all's at worst, and everyone's at odds with everyone, and they've all messed their affairs, and everybody's talking and worrying—

> 'It's all right, my baby. When the geese have cackled they will be still again. First they cackle, and then they stop.'

Isn't that divinely lovely? I weep at it.

I've so much to say, like you. What shall we do, when we meet? Shall we both talk at once, for an hour. Or shall we have to lay down rules, like the Shaw–Belloc debate?—first you half an hour, and then me half an hour, and then you twenty minutes and me twenty minutes and you ten minutes and me ten minutes and then I'll propose a vote of thanks to you, and you to me, and we will carry them by acclamation. Or shall we each talk into phonographs beforehand, and then exchange them, and turn them on in tubes and places when we're alone? Have you ever heard your own voice from a phonograph? It's dreadful: dreadful. Oh, it'd sound so funny if you babbled into a phonograph, and one turned it on: for you've the silliest mind.   *   *   *

I see we shall scarcely know *Hello Ragtime* when we see it again: for Ethel Levey has introduced *Waiting for the Robert E. Lee*, in her own version; and some new performers have appeared. 'Eheu fugaces, Caitilin. . . .'

(I thought your Russian boy's verdict on Ethel Levey and her understudy perfect and beyond price. Why is it one can express things so much better in broken English?)

(Also I thought your ballet very lovely: but you know, *allerschönste*, it's not fair to put lovely words into their mouths. You can't do it on the stage. It's like Barker's stage directions. But you *did* make it sound desirable.)

What else?—the Prize. It was but for the best poem that appeared in *The Poetry Review* last year. Seven judges judged: and thought my poem on *Grantchester* the best. (You saw it in *Georgian Poetry*.) A double satisfaction: in defeating Sturge Moore and James Stephens and Gibson and Abercrombie and several others who are *really* better than I, and in receiving £30! (When I get it out of the Editor, I'll give you a champagne supper) (which reminds me, I sedulously hint to Marsh how nice another supper party in his rooms'd be. I hope it'll bear fruit in time).

Oh, oh, I shall stop this letter swiftly: ere I remember any of the thousand things I've got to say. We'll plan glorious things on Wednesday. I *may* scribble you a line before then, conceivably. Tomorrow I go to the Birmingham Repertory Theatre, to see *Press Cuttings*[1] and *Countess Cathleen*![2]

Life is superb. The spring makes me almost ill with excitement. I go round corners on the road shivering and almost crying with suspense—as one did as a child fearing some playmate is waiting to jump out and frighten one—I fear Green—

Stop! stop! Goodnight, Cathleen. All the blessings of all the Gods be on your head—(whether it's done with short hair or the other way). RUPERT

To KATHARINE COX *Rugby*
Sunday–Monday [*April 1913*]

You'd better get out of your Pension. It sounds bloody.

My dear: how can I break it to you? 'Bald' doesn't rhyme with 'lord'. It doesn't, really. It's a pity for the first two lines were nice; very nice.

There are ninety little points. I wonder if I can remember them all. One is—don't jump at my conclusions about Rosalind. It's really entirely dim: and my sexual egoism makes me believe that all young women I know are oozing for me. With her, it was just her general appreciation of me, and the fact that when I put her in a bus in December and said I might or might not be on this side of the world when she returned from her trip, her eyes were very large and shiny and wet, and she said very little.

And there's the feeling it in the air.

Oh, I expect it's all fancy.

[1] By G. B. Shaw. [2] By W. B. Yeats.

Anyhow, it's quite faint and undeveloped. For God's sake don't let it choke you off her, if you want to see her in Russia, or anything. It's infinitely subcutaneous.

I thought (nine days ago) why you were so much more attractive than other women. It's because you're much more female. They're all feminists, these creatures. You're just very female, mind and body: not a bloody hermaphrodite. That's why you blot them all out.

I don't yet trust your Russian country house, from your account. If there's only an imbecile and a bachelor, it's too intolerable. Do find out, clearly, that it's all right. Have you got an introduction to Ursula Cox, who lives in Moscow or Petersburg? She'd be awfully useful. I thought her fairly nice, and much better than her cousins. Margery Olivier'd give you an introduction, you know. See about it.

I didn't carp at your walking with the Oxford youth, silly, because I thought you bad for him. Of course you're not. But because I thought it *improper*.

What is there in the way of news. I go to Birmingham a night to see their theatre, tonight. On Wednesday to London, to Eddie's, to see Mr Robertson as Hamlet. A cultured Life. Eddie'll be my address till further notice.

Yes: I heard from Gwen: nominally about something else; really about Gill. I laughed like anything and wrote them a letter that'll make them *awfly* sick (ragging them). I shall get hold of Jacques for a day or two sometimes: for I hear he's not too well again: and I'm the only person who can put him right.

*　　*　　*

You sound less bad than you've been. If you look back, *aren't* you quieter and better for exile? I am, for your exile. So I hope you are! I do think you must be. You've got to get quieter, so much, before you come back.

This is a snippy letter. But information's good in letters. I might have given you my views on Tchekoff, or said Spring was here. It is, now and then. It suddenly was on Thurday; and I got so excited, walking up and down Bilton Road. So I didn't sleep properly; and was prostrated all next day. I wish I was a woman and didn't feel things. (Oh, they suffer, yes. At least, you do, child.)

Good be with you. You're fine. And a silly child.

With love

RUPERT

A dull letter. I'm sweating over an account of Verrall, for Francis. Be good and happy: my dear. Love to those two.

To CATHLEEN NESBITT　　　*Clouds, East Knoyle, Salisbury*
　　　　　　　　　　　　　　　Saturday midnight (in bed)
Dear child,　　　　　　　　　　　　　*[April 1913]*

Champagne and port and whisky make one too sleepy to write. Nor is there anything frightfully important to write about—except the fact that you are incomparably the most lovable and lovely and glorious person in the world: and I've a dim, sleepy, idea I may have mentioned that before. I've been discussing literature and politics with my host all night: and to send myself to sleep I'm going to continue making up a poem that's in my head. In this interval I write.

Outside the wind's howling like anything (this place is 700 feet above the sea). It's been raining. And it keeps coming on me that your retreat into the country is being spoilt by bad weather. Still you *are* in the country.

Nothing's happened: except that my American photographer has sent me a photograph of me—very shadowy and ethereal and poetic, of me in profile, and naked-shouldered.[1] Eddie says it's very good. I think it's rather silly. But anyhow, I don't look like an amateur popular preacher—as in those others.

And no one will ever be able to put it into an interview, with the words 'We want great serious drama' underneath.

My literary labours haven't been progressing very well. The only complete poem I've produced lately is

> 'There once was a lovely Cathleen—
> I don't think she can ever have been.
> It's not *likely*, you know.
> P'raps I dreamt it was so.
> There aren't *really* such things as Cathleen.'

It rather expresses my occasional state of mind.

The Champagne was good. The Port was *very* good. But I'm thirsty for you.　　　　　　　　　　　Dearest child, goodnight
　　　　　　　　　　　　　　　　　　　　　　RUPERT

---

[1] Afterwards used as the frontispiece in *1914 and Other Poems*, 1915.

To KATHARINE COX *Eddie's*
[*April 1913*]

It's not *assonance*, you know, as far as I can remember, that I noted in your poem. There's a nice chap called Flint[1] who does assonance here. He rhymes *boom* with *moon*. Silly, I call it. He's done it for years: in the Post Office. What you did, didn't you? (your letter's in Rugby, locked up)—was to rhyme on the unaccented syllable: e.g.

'we blindly cannot see the things that they see:'

rhyming with

'But either I have you, or you will have me'

like rhyming *murder* with *father*. But perhaps I get confused.

* * *

With love
RUPERT

To CATHLEEN NESBITT *Rugby*
[*April 1913*]

Dearest love,

Isn't writing coherently difficult? I must try. At any rate, it's good writing to you. I know you'll understand. It's wonderful saying *everything* to a person one absolutely trusts.

I've two reasons against your going to America. The first is (I *think*) impersonal. I mean, it would apply even if I didn't exist. *Two years with damn bad plays in America* is a very alarming idea. I think you underrate your capabilities and chances in England. And also, I think you're probably not very clever at working a 'career'— I mean, at judging what sort of a figure you are, and how the world runs. Actors and actresses live in a queerly improvident and blind little world. You seem to me to have got a curiously (!) wide and sound reputation for the very short time you've been in London. You've contrived to charm the normal person in *General John Regan*, and, I suppose, in *Quality Street*. You've got a queer reputation with the critics (who really *are* stupid) for being an 'intelligent young actress'—through having been in the advanced drama crowd. (You *may* be an intelligent actress: I don't know, 'cause I've only seen Perdita, which *might* be an accident: and I don't suppose the critics know.) And—through being in yourself *supposed to be* (I don't

[1] F. S. Flint, one of the 'Georgian' poets.

venture on debatable ground!) both very beautiful and quite intelligent—you've got into touch with places and people unknown to the ordinary good actress: places and people which—coldly and cynically—must in the long run be extremely 'useful'.

(I'd better state, before going further, that as a matter of fact I loathe women acting in public.)

There's so very much to build on, there: both from the point of view of good work, a 'career' (as long as you choose to take it up), fame, and money. And you'll lose a great part of these advantages if you go off for a long spell to America.

What I want to impress on you, is the necessity of taking a 'long' view, and not snatching at things as they come. Taking the most lucrative affair at the moment is the most hopeless way of proceeding. It's as if I should spend my whole time writing the most careless and swift journalism, and so making £1000 a year for the next two or three years. Even from a financial point of view, I mean, it's imbecile. If the choice lay between starving idle in London and making a lot of bad money in America, the latter might be the better of two evils. But it doesn't—not even as much as I pathetically think. I mean (of course, I'm ignorant of some conditions) you're *bound* to get good work in London. It's a world where things turn up unexpectedly, and one has to count on that. You'll make some money by touring: and other things will appear. For instance, Barker's theatre will almost certainly begin after the New Year (this is secret: but Violet [Asquith] assures me it's so—the benefactor is buying a knighthood—don't breathe a word). It'll be on a large scale, and you're sure to get work there. Of course he doesn't want you *now*, because he hasn't anything for you. And he daren't engage people, because it's not *quite* certain till the New Year's Honours are out.

For you *qua* Actress to stay in England is much better, I'm sure. For you *qua* person, even more so. (The two react on each other!) And the latter seems to me (*still* impersonal!) far the more important. For, child, while I suspect you might be a very good actress (which *you* really *don't* believe, even so, to be the main object of your life) I KNOW you may be—*are* in your transient stage—a very wonderful person. It's a thing you're the last person to be able to see, but *I* can see with immense clearness: the development of *you*. Heavens! I don't mean that I know the mystery and depth of beauty of you, any more than I know a flower: only, I can see whether the flower is beautiful, and whether it's flourishing or sickly. Women are blind: and you're very much of a woman. But even you must be able to see how much good food and how much unsatisfactory there is for the soul to eat: and how much of both is in sight for you. You—oh *child*—are *very* credulous. Even for a woman. You not only trust and believe in *people*—which is mad enough—but you trust and believe in the world, which is madder. You take, so much, what's offered you. Oh child, child, child—and in the very taking you're more wonderful than anybody else in the world. But you're getting a kind of sense of things, and realizing where the wonder of life is, and where the dullness. My dear, if you put cut flowers in red ink for water, the blossom goes red: and men are even more coloured and made by their surroundings, than flowers: and women even more than men, and *you* more, far more, than most modern 'women'. (Frances Cornford wrote, in her excitement, that you were 'really, really, a woman, and that is the most lovely and rare thing in the world'.) You don't know how I *ache* that you should be fed with the most beautiful and radiant things in the world—like the children in Plato's Republic. We all *ought* to be, of course. But *you* above all. For so many of us couldn't grow into anything much worth having. But *you*. . .

And how empty of all that's worthy of you, of all except what's poison to your loveliness, is *A Pair of Silk Stockings* for two years in America! Those filthy bloody plays—for you. And that empty land. I can't bear the thought of you coming back after two years hard and dwarfed and starved and all the splendour faded and thwarted. By God, it mustn't be. England is full of rottenness: but there are things worthy of you. And you're beginning to distinguish. There are some lovely places, there are a few books, there are some fine people and groups; there's after all *me*!

But when I think of 'me', I definitely drop the impersonality. I *do* think of you, and believe that I have given, give, you things. And, still more, I think of us, and what we build. But most, I'm afraid, I think of what *you* mean to *me*.

I tried to explain a little. But if you could see sometimes in my mind, you'd understand how desperately frightened and miserable I become at the thought of you going away. Dear love, I've been through evil places, and I cling all the more graspingly to the peace and comfort I find more and more in loving you and being with you. It grows as I see love in you for me grow. Love in me grows slowly, and differently from the old ways—I thought the root was gone. But it's there. It's the one thing I've got, to love you, and feel love growing, and the strength and peace growing, and to learn to worship you, and to want to protect you, to desire both to possess every atom of your body and soul, and yet to lose myself in your kindliness, like a child. It might be that, in the end, it wouldn't do, and we'd find that I didn't love you enough, or you me. But there's the hope and the great chance. We're so far towards it. The more I know you, the more I love. And the more I know and love, the more I find you have to give me, and I to give you. How can I let this growing glory and hope be broken, and let myself go adrift again? Dear love, I *daren't* go wandering. You don't know what a helpless poor fool I am. It's only in love and marriage I can find peace. The rest is Hell. I want to love and to work. I don't want to be washed about on these doubtful currents and black waves or drift into some dingy corner of the tide.

You know—

> 'Lest once more wandering from that heaven
> I fall on some base heart unblest
> Faithless to thee, false, unforgiven,
> And lose my everlasting rest.'[1]

But that's only a little part of it. It may not be 'faithless to thee', but it's a faithlessness to—something. I don't know what. And the wandering is so grey and helpless: and things get washed out of one. And the best visible, is that in 1916 or 17 we might meet again and perhaps build it up from the bottom again, if we still can, laboriously —with the two best years of our life gone.

Child, you can't do that.

I mustn't prolong a personal plea. It's unfair. The situation is this. There's only one *possible* argument for going to America: the financial one. Well, that isn't very great, if you remember that it costs twice and a half as much to live there; and that you probably will make a good deal, with luck a great deal, in England. Also, I've tried to show that you'ld sacrifice in various ways, things a hundred times more important to you than that much money. What you ought to do, young lady, is to stay in England, act many parts as well as you can, make a little money, and in a year or so marry some good man (*me*, for I'll be there) who'll make money for you, while you go on the stage once every few years, if the whim seizes you, and have lots of lovely children and a thousand deep experiences meanwhile.

Finally, my dear—and this is serious—if you really want money

[1] The last stanza of Rochester's 'Song' (Absent from thee I languish still— *Oxford Book of English Verse*, no. 413).

after you've been in England half a year or a year, I can give you as much as you want. I can make as much as I like (indeed working for *you* would give me what I've been wanting all my life, something to work for) and I've a lot of capital I can give away without missing it. And by God! it would be cheap at any price—keeping you in England.

Read all this carefully, dear one. I give you leave to tell your Impresario, that you *may* go at a large salary, for three months, *but no more*. And I forbid you to sign anything, even that: till we've had lunch and talked on Thursday.

Forgive me if I've written selfishly, dear love, or if I've been stupid. I want your welfare *very* much. And I love you. Goodnight.

It's very late. Even you must be asleep by now. I kiss your lovely face and breasts and hands. I wish I could take you right away from theatres and everything and have you all to myself and make your beauty grow even more perfect. Goodnight, child.

RUPERT

To CATHLEEN NESBITT *24 Bilton Road, Rugby*
Wednesday night (in bed)
[April 1913]

What really beats me is that you can write letters like that in a theatre—between calls, or whenever it is.

Thursday night (in bed).

I *could* go on for a page, and pretend I wrote it all last night. But I'll be honest. I wrote that one sentence, and then I looked at the paper, and at your photograph, and at the paper again, my mind full of things to say, for twenty minutes. Then I turned the light out, and slept.

Still, it *does* beat me. Your Monday evening's letter was amazing.

But oh, but oh, *such* a day, Cathleen! 'Spring come complete, with a leap, in a day', said the wisest and nicest man in Warwickshire, my godfather, an aged scholar[1]—seventy—infinitely learned in Greek, Latin, English and Life. He said it was a quotation from Browning. It certainly fitted. I took him a walk. The air had changed all in a night and had that soft caressingness, and yet made you want to jump and gambol. *Alacer* and not *acer*[2] was, we agreed, the epithet

---

[1] Robert Whitelaw.   [2] i.e. *brisk* and not *stinging*.

for the air. (Latin *is* one of your accomplishments?) And all the evening from tea to dinner I wandered up and down the road glorying, and grieving that you were shut up in a town, far from this. Oh, it's *mad* to be in London, with the world like this! I can't tell you of it. The excitement and music of the birds, the delicious madness of the air, the blue haze in the distance, the straining of the hedges, the green mist of shoots about trees—oh, it *wasn't* in these details. It was beyond and round them, something that included them. It shall be like that on Sunday week, and I'll take food in a *rücksack* and we'll eat it under a hawthorn-bush. It's the sort of day that brought back to me what I've had so rarely for the last two years, that tearing hunger to do and do and do things. I want to write ten pages to you: to finish a play of Tchekoff's: to write several poems: to start a play I've thought of: right through the night: tasting it all: anything so long as I'm *working* at it. And at dawn to run three miles and bathe. You wrote the other day that you were going to LIVE. I understand now. By God, there are such things to do! Witch-child, you know too much. Yet you're not wholly right. It's true about women's hearts: but not wholly true. There are sometimes lovelinesses there, of which the owner knows not. And with men: it may be that they'd made the song before they met you. And yet—and yet—it wasn't meaningless that they should offer it you. Nor wholly by chance. Oh my Cathleen, I'll even grant your elderly wisdom that it's not to you but to your beauty that we kneel. Not to poor unimportant little Cathleen Nesbitt: but to Beauty that has taken mortal shape upon itself, is manifest in place and time, most rare and most to be worshipped. Oh, but you know—or you've *heard*, woman—what beauty is. One gets muddleheaded before it. How's a poor mortal man always to distinguish between it and you? One's brain spins; one's heart thumps: one's breath goes sobbing— isn't it pardonable that I sometimes cannot distinguish between the beauty of your lips and your lips, Cathleen? Even I am sometimes too young to be a philosopher.

But perhaps this is that alcoholic writing I was to avoid. But why should I care if it does make you a trifle drunk? Drunkenness is a fine thing—and April coming in! We'll be drunk together. You'd be fine, drunk. By God, I'll make you Bacchante, one day.

My pen is unruly, and would write a deal I shall not let it. Good-night, you nice Cathleen.   RUPERT

To EDWARD MARSH 5 *Thurloe Square, S.W.*
Sunday [*4 May 1913*]

Dear Eddie,

Cathleen was delighted & charmed at the idea. I have made her swear to get up late on Wednesday & to rest between the matinée & evening show (she's still an invalid) so she'll be pretty fresh, *hoffentlich*. She, being a lover of the past, could think of nobody she particularly wanted to meet *chez toi*, save Gilbert & Harry Ainley. She has a passion for Gilbert I entirely deprecate. I suppose one couldn't lure de la Mare away for the night? He could sleep with you, & go straight to his office on Tuesday. He might be enticed if it were represented to him that it was the last time he'd see me in this world.... Denis occurs to me (or did you say he'd be away?).... Are you getting Society, in your weekend party? If so, let's have enough of the Arts to balance them. (You couldn't wire for Steuart?)[1]

I didn't mean to spring a great supper on you—costly champagne & nightingales' tongues. 'Twas only to evoke or consummate a not wholly hellish period...period, as Sir John Daw says of poems, should 'chime well and cry tink in the close'.[2] (But perhaps the moderns, like M. Vildrac, would deny it.) But we can consummate on Beer—I met Raleigh in the street on Saturday, & lunched with him. I *nearly* invited him to sup with you—but he'll not be in London. Who should come to lunch but—Violet! Delightful surprise! It was the tenth meal she'd had with me in three days: so she must be sick of the sight of my face (not, I flatter myself, of the sound of my voice). *My* passion grows with feeding.

Raleigh was wonderful.

I'll be in all tomorrow morning as far as I can see. I think Wilfrid's poem on Solway Firth awfully good.

What'll you be doing late tomorrow evening?

RUPERT

The supper-party you were so dreadfully excluded from, was, at last, complete...& not a success!

---

[1] Steuart Wilson, now a professional tenor.

[2] Ben Jonson's *Epicoene, or The Silent Woman*, Act II, Sc. 3: Clerimont says of some lines by Sir John Daw, 'How it chimes, and cries tinke i' the close, divinely.'

To CATHLEEN NESBITT   5 *Thurloe Square*
                                Tuesday afternoon

Dear child,   [*April 1913*]

*   *   *

I shall very probably go off into the country on Wednesday evening, till Saturday evening—as I get a holiday from you! I shall come back incredibly healthy and vigorous. Come here on Sunday morning about ten. Edgware Road to S. Kensington—it only takes ten minutes. Then we can sit and think what to do. If we're energetic, and it's fine, we can go out to Richmond Park—or where you like. If otherwise, we'll sit here and read Swinburne, or do the balcony scene from *Romeo and Juliet*, or anything we damn well like. You can wear your laziest clothes: this sofa is extraordinarily comfortable: and if you go to sleep, I shall sit and write poems about you, and kiss you once every half hour, very softly (as I did yesterday).

No: I'm no good for Wednesday night (though you're adorable to have asked me). Not even if I'm in London, and you're fit to go (which you *won't* be). I gave up dancing when I reached the Byronic, sick-'o-the-world, old, old, stage, at nineteen. And I've never taken to it since, again: being too lazy (except for student-balls in Munich at Carnival-time, when we all go naked: but that's a different thing).

But I'll turn up for 5.30 tea: if you're fit to receive.

Don't look ill and white, Cathleen.

Oh, I've just had a letter. And I'm going to walk the South Downs from tomorrow evening to Saturday midnight with a French Artist, and a doctor, two superb people. We shall shout! I hardly bear to tell you. It's what you ought to be doing, instead of having diphtheria in London, child.

I'll give you an address, when I see you tomorrow. Send me a line to the wild—I had only two letters at all this morning, one from you and one from the King: and your's was much the nicer. (His Majesty's was curt, I thought; and on the subject of telephones.)

*   *   *

It gets worse, I find. I do love you so: and yet I'm going to leave England in May. I've got to go, for a bit. Because I promised. I got mixed up with a woman. Do you know how human beings tear each other? I've been so torn, and torn so. But everything's very complicated, and one day I'll explain, maybe. Anyhow, there's my promise: I've got to wander a bit.

You chain one to England horribly.

Dearest child, good night. Be quiet and happy and well. I love you in so many ways.

But I will not love you if you look white.

RUPERT

You can't think how lonely one's hair feels without your hand in it.

To JACQUES *and* GWEN RAVERAT

5 Thurloe Square, S.W.
[April 1913]

Dear children liebe Kinder,

I'm not coming to see you before I go away.

I'm so packed with things, and the world has me by the ankle. And I've to hurry down to Rugby to pacify a bitter and enraged Ranee (it'd be good if Jacques, in his secret confabulations with her over my welfare, could hint that my evanishment is for the good of my soul and body, and not an idle whim). I shall be in London on and off till the 22nd: if you're passing through (mostly between the 18th and the 22nd). Otherwise, we may meet again in this world— I brown and bearded, you mere red round farmers. When that'll be, I know not. Perhaps in six months. Perhaps in six years. Or we may only find each other in a whiter world, nighty-clad, harped, winged, celibate—oh, dear, oh dear!

> 'Shall we go walks along the hills of Heaven
> —Rücksack on back and aureole in pocket—
> And stay in Paradisal pubs, and drink
> Immortal toasts in old Ambrosia,
> Fry wings in nectar on the glassy sea,
> And build the fire with twigs of amaranth.'

I suppose it'll be easier to fry on one another's 'glories'—the tongues of fire, you know. Fried pigeon. But I shock you.

And anyhow women certainly have no souls, unbelievers probably not, and Frogs very likely not. So we'll sleep sound enough: and never meet.

No: let us not die.

As for Ka. I suppose it'll be better for her to come back pretty soon. I think she's fairly bad: though, perhaps not quite so bad as Dudley makes out. I don't suppose it's quite true—his account of things, that they helped Ka all the time for three months, and she not them at all.

I think the sooner she gets quite clear of me, the better. But I think the idea of 'leaving her to work out her own fate' is silly. It doesn't apply to young women. If it's really possible to leave her without her going to the devil, very good. If not, what's one to do? I hope to God she'll get something decent to do in England, and be kept where there are clean people and good to look after her. I shouldn't be surprised if she married Geoffrey one day.

Be gentle with her; remembering she's a feeble fool; for if you aren't, she'll mix with the people who flatter her—the other kind of her friends.

I shall write to her once before I go; and then distance and time will work the break, gradually. I shall write once perhaps, or twice; and so cease. It's a bloody world.

*   *   *

I hope if Gwen thinks the Blue Review gets cleaner, she'll send them a woodcut.

My address will always be *via* Rugby.

My literary agent is Eddie.

My heart is yours.   With love and goodbye for a time
                                                    RUPERT

To FRANCES CORNFORD   *5 Thurloe Square, S.W.*
                                                            [*May 1913*]

My dear Frances,

You nearly frustrated the main purpose of my going to Canada; which is to grow a beard. Thanks for relieving me, though late.

I shall send you a letter, or a card, from time to time: may be. A card anyhow: if I'm near civilization. Once, in the middle of my exile, you might send me tidings of the world. After your child comes, perhaps.

I hope you'll have a lovely quiet summer, and be able to write something.

Now for one thing. Ka is in a bad way still; I gather from Dudley Ward, and, indirectly from her. I don't think she's appreciably better than she was at, say, Christmas. (If she'd stayed in England all the time, she'd no doubt, be worse.) I rather hope she'll come back soon: and settle into some job in England, and see her clean friends.

Most young women have husbands to look after them, or fathers and families. Ka has no one—her family know nothing of her real life, and she won't see much of them. So her friends have to look after her. I can do it. I can keep her from doing stupid or wicked things: because she loves me. But it is unfair to her, keeping her on loving me, in order to keep her straight. I can't ever marry her: because of the great evil she did me. So I must get apart from her, I find, even to the extent of not writing; to be fair to her. So I (not willingly) shovel the entire responsibility of Ka on to the shoulders of all you, her friends. I don't mean that they all ought to go and live with her! But she's the sort of person who is blind and helpless and lovely as a vegetable. If you feed her with a constant stream of obvious love—continual letters etc.—she'll flourish on it. Otherwise she'll decay and go bad on whatever uncleanness may surround her.

Don't be misled by the fact that she gives you more than you give her. She's helpless for all that. Really, Frances, you can't think how utterly she's a child, hiding things, breaking promises, and lying, all half innocently. She needs direction, and patient love, so. Oh God, she's in such a bad way, just now!

I only mean in that she's lonely and miserable. Do often write to her and help her and look after her. And make other people do it.

And I hope she'll come to you two for advice, if ever she needs it. I shall try to make her.

Don't tell her I told you all this.

I don't really feel going off to be nearly as 'Hellish' as you imagine. I've really got quite callous in my feelings by now. I'm not excited by travelling. But I've the feeling of shaking the dust of a pretty dirty period of my life off my feet. And that makes up for any tear there may be.

Good-bye: and good luck to your journey.

I hope you have a son. I shan't be away long, I think.

Best love to you both.   RUPERT

To CATHLEEN NESBITT   [Postcard]
                                         6 May 1913

> 'The way that lovers use is this,
>   They bow, catch hands, with never a word;
> And their lips meet, and they do kiss.
>   —So I have heard.

> Sure, they must find some healing so,
>   And strange attainment in the touch.
> There is a secret lovers know.
>   —I have read as much.
>
> Tears are no more, nor joy, nor smart,
>   Changing nor ending, night nor day:
> But mouth to mouth, and heart on heart...
>   —So lovers say.'
>
>   R.
>
>   (A title, please!)¹

To EDWARD THOMAS   *5 Thurloe Square*
                                      South Kensington
                                  Thursday [*15 May 1913*]

Dear Thomas,

I couldn't come down to your parts. London gripped me too firmly by the ankle. I have been inextricably tangled in the web of this existence—Maya, the Orientals call it, don't they?—often, not even escaping for week-ends. I'm sorry. I wish I'd been able to come.

Now, I'm off to America. I sail next Thursday. I shall stay— I don't know how long. Perhaps next March's primroses'll fetch me back.

I'm rushing round buying things: & making farewells. Will you be in London any late evening at the beginning of next week? If so you might charge me with some message for the continent of America & for Ella Wheeler. And I could leave the muses of England in your keeping—I do that anyhow. Feed the brutes. If I don't see you, farewell.   RUPERT BROOKE

To EDWARD MARSH   *N*[*ational*] *L*[*iberal*] *C*[*lub*]
                                  Monday [*19 May 1913*]

Dear Eddie,

I write from an evil place. I have been rushing round all day, buying outfit and making bloody farewells. And I shall do the same tomorrow. Oh! Oh! I went to take my leave of the Ranee last week.

---

¹ Printed as 'The Way that Lovers Use' in *Poetry and Drama*, December 1913, with variations, and in *1914 and Other Poems*.

Your postcards are lovely. I'd always heard Dalmatia was divine. But oh, I've booked my passage in the Cedric (cabin 50) and Fate is under weigh. *Vires acquirit eundo.*[1]

I have written nothing and done nothing. I hope you will find your various books at Gray's Inn when you return.

Frederick Whelen wrote suddenly to me and said he'd been informed I had a play[2] he and the Stage Society should read. I sent it him. He replied, 'Could he submit it to managers.' I said 'Yes: by Gum!' There it rests. With Barker it has apparently set up its everlasting rest (which reminds me that I'm broken-hearted that his inauspicious 'star' hasn't followed up his invitation to supper at the Garrick).

I gave Whelen your address. I'm sending off copies of the Revised Version to Drinkwater and the Glasgow man—Abercrombie has chucked Liverpool. So I leave that.

If there's an extra copy of the R.V. I'll send it to your rooms. One I take to America—I think there's no more business. I shall write from the boat. I told the Ranee to write to you if she wanted to know about my literary affairs.

I find it very hard to cut one's life abruptly at a certain point—|. I shall be back by January, I think. Perhaps America's nearer than I think, though.

*   *   *

I commend into your keeping all England, especially

> Wilfrid
> Cathleen
> The Nine Muses
> and the Spirit of Wisdom and Goodness

—some others, but I forget for the moment.

I've already roughly planned out my *Tristia*. I would send V[iolet] A[squith] my love, if I didn't think it might be lacking in respect. Is she witty in foreign parts? I can imagine her amazing about the blacks—(the natives of Cattaro, and Athens, and elsewhere). She sent me such a nice note before she started.

Thine

—though senilely—
with love

RUPERT

[1] i.e. it acquires strength as it goes.   [2] *Lithuania.*

To W. DENIS BROWNE   *8 Thurloe Square, S.W.*
Wednesday [*21 May 1913*]

Under Gambrinus between 10 & 12 tonight. And Euston, 11.40–12 tomorrow, noon: are the last two chances of my beholding your round & musical face again. For when we write for an even Bluer Review in Heaven, we shall have, they say, no faces at all. So let me see you once.   RUPERT

To GEOFFREY KEYNES   [Postcard]
5 Thurloe Square, S.W.
6531 Western
Wednesday
[*Postmark: 21 May 1913*]

My dear,

From 10 to 12 tonight I sit in the Restaurant underneath Gambrinus, surrounded by Gibsons etc. (but not entirely surrounded). At noon tomorrow I leave Euston by the Boat Express.

If you want to take a last farewell of my elderly face, look in, if it be but a minute, on one or the other occasion. If you come for half an hour in the evening, I will pay for your Beer.

      RUPERT

To W. DENIS BROWNE   *On board S.S. 'Cedric'!!*
22 May 1913

My dear Denis,

It was noble of you to see me off & aid me in so many ways, even to purchasing me the most tasteful notepaper Euston could produce. Did you find those letters? They were, I think, all on the top of the Cabinet of drawings: & all in two heaps. I trust they're registered & on their expressest way to the Broadway Central Hotel, New York, U.S.A. They'll probably arrive before me. For I find that all boats that end in -a go twice as quick as any boat ending in -ic. If you have seen to them, may God reward you by making you (at length) Controller of the Music of the Spheres—which reminds me, I hope you're composing hard, & variously. For one day soon we must do some show together—some theatre show—where poetry & music & ancient & modern & wit & tragedy & satire and suffering & dirty jokes & triumphal processions shall be so mixed together that the public won't know whether it's on its head or its heels for joy. We might do a Georgian Pantomime.

Oh we're all going to wake England up when I return from the West.

The orchestra is playing rag-time—an excellent preventive of seasickness, I find: for it makes it impossible to feel Rhythmic. I cease. RUPERT

To CATHLEEN NESBITT *S.S. 'Cedric'*
Sunday [24 May 1913]

Dear love,

You'll not take it in a bad sense if I tell you that there was never anybody so nice to go away from as you! *Really*, my dear! I arrived solitary on the boat. After it had started I asked at the office—more to show that I existed than in the dimmest hope of getting anything —were there any letters for Rupert Brooke. And out, astonishingly, came a letter and a telegram; and both from divine *you*. And the letter you'd been writing all those last good days, secretly! Was there ever so nice a person? The *fact* you'd written it upset me more than I can say. And then the letter itself! I sat on my bed and laughed and cried over it. And two hours later I went past again and there was, stuck up, a list called 'Unclaimed Mail'. (I thought it sounded as if a lot of knights who had promised to equip themselves for the quest of the Holy Grail, had missed the train, or married a wife, or overslept, or something)—and at the top of the list 'Mr Rupert Brooke'. 'Good God!' I thought, 'there *is* somebody else who has remembered my existence!' But there wasn't! There was only that absurd Cathleen again, sending a silver boot, of all mad things in the world! You can't think how it cheered me up, this string of communication with you. It felt as if your love was so strong it reached with me all the way. It's queer. I do feel as if [there] was a lovely and present guardianship all the time. My darling, you give me so much more than I deserve. But it does make me feel so quiet and secure.

Blank-day.

Time is no more. I have been a million years on this boat. I don't know if it's this month or last or next. Sometime, in a past existence, I was on land, and loved Cathleen. But this is another existence.

(I remember, though.) Yet I have my joys; Cathleen, today I ate Clam Chowder. That's romance, isn't it? I ordered it, quite reck-lessly: I didn't know what it was. I only knew that anything called *Clam Chowder* must be strange beyond words.

'If you were like Clam Chowder,
And I were like the spoon,
And the band were playing louder
And a little more in tune,

I'd stir you till I spilled you,
Or I'd kiss you till I killed you,
If you were like Clam Chowder
And I were like the spoon.'

But you don't know Swinburne.

'Clam Chowder', my God! What *am* I coming into?

My dearest loveliest child, your mothering of America (in your letter) is almost as nice, and even funnier, than your mothering of me. You really are the Cathleenishist Cathleen ever thought of.

Another day.

Yes, I'll be gentle with America for your sake, my dear. 'Any friend of Cathleen's. . . .' I'm even gentle with myself for your sake, dear child. And when I get despondent, or angry, I retire into a corner, and slap myself on the back (it's not easy) and say 'Cath-leen loves you; so cheer Oh!'

And oh Cathleen, I've been sick and sad today. I feel sore and angry. I want your comforting. Will you put your lovely hands round me and your lips on mine and comfort me? I want to put my head in your lap and shut my eyes and feel you hush me and bend over me. For I've been writing a letter.

O child, it's hard work cutting off from people one's been intimate with. (I told you I'd been with a girl I loved—and you'll not ever tell anyone about it, child: for it's not wholly my secret.) I've got, I feel, to stop even writing to her, for her sake, to give her a chance to get free. Oh, it's bitter destroying and breaking things two have built together—intimacies and trusts and friendliness. It's like cutting something out of oneself. And I feel so responsible for her.

Child, beyond a certain point men and women shouldn't go, unless they marry. Not if they're people of human feelings. Or they pay overmuch in irretrievable ways. That's the one thing in the world I know surely.   *   *   *

Later.

I haven't told you much about my voyage, have I? There's not much to tell. I felt (*before* I got your letter) a trifle lonely at Liverpool. Everybody else seemed to have people to see them off. So I went back on shore, and found a dirty little boy, who was unoccupied and said his name was William. 'Will you wave to me if I give you sixpence, William?' I said. 'Why, yes!' said William. So I gave him sixpence, and went back on board, and when the time came, he leant over his railing on the landing stage and waved, and I leant over the railing on the second deck and waved, and now and then he shouted indistinct messages in a shrill voice. And as we slid away, the last object I looked at was a small dot waving a white handkerchief (or nearly white) faithfully. So I got my sixpenn'orth, and my farewell. Dear William!

On board, there's Richard le Gallienne, and some Jews, and some women, and a peer, and a lot more people.

* * *

There's the American youth who came up to me the first day and said 'Say, are you a Peer?'

I said I wasn't.

He said 'I guess you'll find A*mur*rica vurry different from England. In A*mur*rica we reckon one man's every bit as good as another.'

I was very kind, and didn't remind him of the cars which are half for white and half for coloured persons. I just said 'Oh!....'.

Then he said 'Would you like to hear me re-cite the American Constitution?' 'Yes!' I said. Cathleen, he recited it!—or a lot of it. It begins. 'All men are born free equal and happy.'

Another day.

My dear, the weather was *bloody* yesterday. So about six I went and lay down...oh no, I wasn't *sick*: just quietish, and I had a bleedin' headache. Sat up in bed and had a little fish for dinner.... Oh dear, I did so want a nice lovely practical Cathleen to come and soothe me and tell me I wasn't very ill, and life wasn't a failure, and I had my good points.

But today it's all right, and they say we're passing the Nantucket lightship; and there *is* a little unexplained boat in the middle of a great Ocean; and we get somewhere tonight, and somewhere else at dawn, and on to land at 10 a.m. tomorrow, and boxes must be packed by nine, so I've got to go and pack, and it's all very exciting. And in two days or three, I'll send you the fullest account of America and Me.   *   *   *   RUPERT

To EDWARD MARSH   *S.S. 'Cedric'*
                                              26 May [1913]
My dear,

Behold me fairly launched on the Great World. Your letter was very nice. I like the *arid aunts*. You're having a more romantic and pleasanter voyage than I. It does sound too lovely. I have my little romances though—a school of porpoises, and a whale spouting. And one of my fellow-passengers is Richard Le Gallienne. Oh Eddie, he *is* a nasty man. He mouches about with grizzled hair and a bleary eye: and Mrs Le G., an ex-Golden Girl, follows him with a rug. And Miss Le G. plays deck-tennis with the American 'girls'. He eyes me suspiciously—he scents a rival, I think. We've not spoken yet. His shoulders are bent. His mouth is ugly and small and mean. His eyes are glazed. His manner is furtive. Is it to that we come? I feel like the knights in Orcagna's picture (isn't it?) who ride out, and come on a hideous corpse, and hold their noses as they gallop past. I think I will drown myself at thirty: or turn schoolmaster speedily. I do not care for the fate of the poet. An American and I watched him crawl along the deck. The American spat, and said 'He's the man, who said his face was like the Moon in a grove of Pine trees.' Imagine that, in an American accent: a fitting Epitaph. I have started a *ballade*, in imitation of Villon: but it may not be printed.

I found sitting next me at table a little man of fifty with a cold light-blue eye, with a pleasant turn of American humour. He appeared to be interested in theatres, so I took him into the smoking-room and delivered a lecture on Modern Drama in England, America and Germany, on Theatre-managing, on Commercialism in the Drama, and many other such topics. I got on to *The Great Adventure*: which he thought the best entertainment in London. I patted him on the head. 'Yep', he said, 'I've just sent a marconi-*gram* to buy that play for America.' I said, 'Oh, have you a theatre in America?' He said, 'In New York I own the Grand Opera House, the Metropolitan Theatre, the Knickerbocker Theatre, the Gaiety, and seven more. I have some in every big town in the States. I'm coming back with a new Lehar, a Bernstein, two German comedies...' I forget the rest. He turns out to be Klaw, of Klaw and Erlanger. I felt a little like Dominic [Spring-Rice], when he saw a lonely girl at a fancy-dress dance the other day, and took her out to dance, and it was Karsavina.

Otherwise there's not much to chronicle; except the Canadian girl who takes me into a corner to sing the Canadian national anthem:

> 'Splash me! oh splash me!
> Splash me with the ocean BLUE!
> Mash me! oh mash me!
> And I promise you that I'll mash YOU!'

I feel nervous about my visit to Canada.

I ordered to be sent to your rooms: six books of yours (Cathleen is responsible for returning two more), a photograph of me, and a typescript of *Lithuania*. All large envelopes coming to me c/o you, had better be opened: for they'll contain *Lithuania*. I met Barker, and talked about it. He advised getting it done, if possible.

Also will come to you my gilded Madonnula from Gill. Will you keep it, till further instructions?

I promised Monro to talk, if I could get at them, to Macmillan's about publishing *Georgian Poetry*. Have you any backstairs influence on them?

Also I'm going to see Kennerley about my book. Nothing like a campaign to civilize the Yanks.   With love

RUPERT

To MRS CONSTANTINE GRAHAM

On board S.S. 'Cedric'
May 1913

Dear Mrs Graham,

I forgot to mention one or two points. If you are giving a list of people to whom you acknowledge permission to reprint, could you include *The Poetry Bookshop*, publishers of *Georgian Poetry*, for 'Grantchester', and *Sidgwick & Jackson* for the other poems?

The correct text of *Grantchester* is in *Georgian Poetry*. The version printed in a King's journal[1] last June, was incorrect. I forget if you

[1] *Basileon* H.

are printing *Dust*. If so, the *Georgian Poetry* version of that is more correct than the one in my book. The other poems are all right in my book, I think.

If you want me to correct the proofs I'll do so with pleasure. But it means three weeks till you get them again. If you want any correction or authorization in a hurry, Mr E. Marsh, of Raymond Buildings, Gray's Inn will give it you. He is looking after my literary affairs while I'm away.

I copy out the one of my recent poems[1] I'm told is the best, in case you want to add or substitute it. It is the property of *The Blue Review* and is coming out there on July 1st. But they'ld let you have it, I'm sure, if you don't (as I suppose you won't) publish *before* then. In any case, I expect most of your readers won't have seen *The Blue Review*. And if you don't want it—why there's no harm in having copied it out. Best wishes for the anthology's success.

Yours sincerely,
RUPERT BROOKE

To GEOFFREY KEYNES   *S.S. 'Cedric' Off Long Island*

May 1913

*   *   *

Geoffrey, what do you think I had for dinner yesterday? I had *Clam Chowder*, Geoffrey!

It was nice of you to come to my little Bierundgerösteteschwein-fleischlebwohlnehmengesellschaft. Weren't they a rum lot? *Temperament*. What ho!

I've already begun an interminable series of poems about England, entitled *Nostalgia*.

> 'In England oh the cauliflowers
> They blow through all the English hours,
> And all New York's clam chowder is
> Less dear than Rugby strawberries.'

I can keep it up for days.

All transatlantically thine
RUPERT

[1] 'The Busy Heart'.

To CATHLEEN NESBITT *Broadway Central Hotel,*
New York
Saturday, 31 May [1913]
6–7 p.m.

We got into dock at 8.30 this morning, and then there was a lot of loitering about the luggage: and finally I got here. And it's a beastly hotel: and I'm in a beastly room over a cobbled street where there's the Hell of a noise; and I've been tramping this damned city all day, and riding in its cars (when they weren't too full); and it's hot; and I'm very tired and cross; and my pyjamas haven't come; and my letters of introduction, which I left behind *en masse*, haven't come; and nothing's come; and I don't know a soul in New York; and I'm *very* tired; and I don't like the food; and I don't like the people's faces; and I don't like the newspapers; and I haven't a friend in the world; and nobody loves me; and I'm going to be extraordinarily miserable these six months; and I want to die.

There!

Oh, it's Saturday evening, and if I were in England I might be lying on the sofa in Kensington, or on the floor in Gray's Inn, and my head in your lap, and your face bent down over mine, and your hands about my head, and my eyes shut, and I only feeling your hands going to and fro in my hair and your kind lips wandering over my face. And I'm here in a dirty room and lonely and tired and ill, and this won't get to you for ten days.

I'm crying. I want you. I don't want to be alone.

RUPERT

To CATHLEEN NESBITT *Noo York*
Sunday [1 June 1913]

This place is certainly forgotten of God. But I'm better. Nevertheless I enclose my letter of yesterday. After all I wrote it—one of the 'I's. And you'd better see them all.

Today I have wandered in cars and on foot, noting details and throwing off hurried, vast, entirely satisfactory generalizations. If I meet a man with a twisted lip, down it goes 'Americans have twisted lips'. In the end I shall shake them up in a bag, paste them on sheets of paper, and send them to the Westminster [Gazette] at 2 guineas a column. Such is my trade.

I'm still a lonely wanderer. My bleeding letters of introduction have not turned up. I subsist on American drinks, sightseeing, and your good wishes. The last are the most substantial—I sit in my room (I've got into a new, stuffier, but quieter room) and contemplate the vision of you, your face your ways your voice and your character, with great satisfaction and quietude of soul.

Yesterday I couldn't walk straight. The pavement rolled steadily beneath me, and I vacillated like a drunken man. Also, I nearly fainted three times. Today, I have got my land legs.

My dear, this is *not* a land for a civilized man. There are three things worth some praise; the architecture; the children's clothes; and the jokes. All else is flatulence and despair and a living Death. I discovered a nice public library, and went in and read their literature—*The International* and the rest. It is written by women and by apes; neither of which classes are any good at writing, *allerschönste*, though the apes are perhaps the less distressing.

I met an American literary man on the boat—did I tell you? A nice fellow—He said 'Being a poet in America is merely having a succession of haemorrhages'—which sounded true.

*   *   *

RUPERT

To W. DENIS BROWNE   *Broadway Central Hotel*
                                  Broadway [New York]
                                  3 June 1913

My dear Denis,

The New York Post Office invited me to go and inspect a parcel addressed to me. I went this morning, & proved to them it was not saccharine nor pig-iron nor 'underwear' (did you know the Americans spelt 'pyjamas' '*pajamas*'?) & brought it back. It is my thousand letters. Many thanks.

Denis, America is no place for a gentleman. To begin with, the lower classes (many of whom are BLACKS) insult one. And the combined effort of New York in Music or Art or Drama is far below that of Rugby. Even in Ragtime, they've sent all their best people to London.

And Literature—
Oh my God!

But on the Boat I met a man who is a Personal Friend of

> (1) Ethel Levey
> (2) Frank Tinney
> (3) Lew Hearn

So I have not lived in vain.

Love to everybody
RUPERT

To EDWARD MARSH

Forgive The Envelope [with a picture of the Broadway Central Hotel, New York]

Tomi, Ia, U.S.A.
6–10 June 1913

My dear,

I'm expecting to hear soon that you're home again and that you had a wonderful cruise. I am so immersed in the gritty refuse-heap of reality that Greece is incredible to me, and even London a lovely half-forgotten dream. America—or at least New York—is round and over and on me. New York is ridiculously inchoate. Do you know it's the biggest Greek city in the world except Athens, and the biggest Italian city except Rome, and the biggest Jewish city except Vienna, Salonica and Tring? I scarcely ever hear a word of 'English'. But in nine days I go to Boston.

I've met a few nice people, and a few mediocre ones, and made many notes. Today I went into the chief store here—like Selfridge's, only bigger. There I met the head of the advertising staff, who made a speech about American poetry. He thought it was shortly going to effloresce. Young American poetry, Eddie, is divided into four schools. The Humanist, headed by George Sylvester Viereck, and Blanche Schoemaker Wagstaffe (friends, by the way, of Jack's);[1] the Mystical, which worships Crashaw, Francis Thompson, and— Stephen Phillips; the Lurical (*sic*), headed by Shamus O'Sheol; and the Romantic, a body of youths who worship Ezra Pound!

But on looking through it I haven't found much.

England seems to be disappearing rapidly. The chief topic which excites America, is, Who (if anybody) is to be Poet Laureate. All the papers have immense articles, with pictures of Masefield and Noyes.

---

[1] J. C. Squire.

They mention everybody as possible, except me and Wilfrid. Even Will Davies. I'm going down to the Stock Exchange tomorrow, where I hear they're betting on it.

But I was shocked last night, to hear about Wyndham.[1] It seemed abrupt. Well, I don't expect many of you'll be left alive by the time I come back. It seems an age till next Christmas.

I never had any introductions from Violet—I don't know that I need any more for this part of the country, anyway—but I got a postcard with a picture of the island where Calypso dwelt, and you, I gathered, all bathed. I shall retaliate with a postcard of Tammany Hall, or Teddy [Roosevelt] looking at the statue of Liberty, or whatever stands for Romance in this land. We don't go back very far here. But we enjoy what we *have*.

Did you say you were going to introduce me to a rich widow in Canada? I remember something—dimly. I go North in a fortnight.

With love

RUPERT

To CATHLEEN NESBITT   *Near the Delaware river*
                               Dawn, one Sunday
                               [*June 1913*]

O little I slept tonight; and it wasn't the thought of you kept me awake, bad luck to you (though I'm equal to saying it was); but a bloody little Mosquito. Now the little white wisps of mist are creeping and curling along the face of the great wide river to my right, and the hills and woods over to the left are solemn and new and mysterious in the inhuman morning light. They look as if they'd just come back—where from?—and were lining up to perform their dull daily task of background, a little perfunctorily. They're like supers who despise both play and principals, yet have to stand there performance after performance. Where *do* they go to at night?

Yesterday morning I escaped with an American lawyer[2] to this river. Seventy miles from New York City. We found a canoe of his and paddled down, and bathed (oh, my dear!) and paddled on—nearly four hours. We fetched up by a pub and ate there. Such eggs. The kindly woman said 'Come *right* in, boys!' and, later, 'If you two boys would like...'. And the lawyer is middle-aged, and I, as you know very well, am not *at all* young. So we were very pleased.

---

[1] George Wyndham, Conservative politician, died 9 June 1913.
[2] Russell Loines.

Then we paddled on and landed and decided to sleep out in this field. Which was bold, for we hadn't come prepared for sleeping out. But we just put our overcoats on and lay down, and I looked at the stars and the fireflies and made a poem, and the noise of the frogs was *deafening*, and I thought of you a bit, and said your name once or twice, not very loud; and so I fell asleep.

And at midnight four great black dogs came pounding along, and the other man saw them and shouted and I woke and they ran away and I *was* frightened.

Oh Cathleen, if they'd come on and the other man hadn't woken, I might have been eaten and you wouldn't have had your Rupert.

And twice a frog jumped on to me, and I screamed.

And once a little short snake wriggled from under me. Oh, God! And now it's 5.15 and we're going to cook breakfast.

Monday.

My God! My God!

I'm still half dead. We paddled from exactly six a.m. till 11.15— five sanguinary hours. Then we bathed and eat half an orange each: and paddled another ninety minutes, and then got to our objective, an artist in a lonely farmhouse, and had lunch.

Twenty miles we paddled without stopping, under an impitiable sun. And today there is no skin on my forearms, but only a swollen redness. I wish you were here to kiss them.

But it was great. And a million things happened. Once, we came round a wild turn of the river, and there was a voice singing wonderfully, and when we got round, we saw a little house, high on the bank, with an orchard, and a verandah, and wooden steps down to the great river, and at the top of them was a tall girl, very beautiful, standing like a goddess, with wonderful red hair, her head thrown back, singing, singing. I love her wildly. I have found the passion of my life. Oh! Oh!

Also we shot rapids.

*   *   *

To JACQUES RAVERAT [Postcard]
Boston
21 June [1913]

Unanständig, aber sehr Amerikanisch, nicht wahr?

> 'Across the sea, across the sea,
> My heart goes out to J. and G:
> All the way, from Americay,
> My heart goes out to G. and J.'

Good people, good people: I am homesick once a week, for an hour: and this is the hour this week. Pray for me.

Love
RUPERT

To HAROLD MONRO *New York*
25 June 1913

My dear Harold,

This morning came this from Macmillan's. They hold most of the copyrights themselves. But perhaps G.K.C. & one or two may be bothering them. Or perhaps they just don't want it.

Anyway: I'm sorry I failed.

I rather think America's no good now. These copyright laws are the most bloody silly things in the world. Kennerley's shop *is* selling G[eorgian] P[oetry]: but illegally! Macmillan's can stop them as soon as they discover.

For *G.P. II* I recommend Kennerley, & a simultaneous publication over here. I think that would be possible to carry through: if negotiations were put in hand early.

I leave New York in four days. Anything you want doing in America, I'll try. Though I don't suppose it's any good bothering about G.P. now Macmillan's has refused.

I largen the sale of G.P. though, a little!

* * *

One poet in America I've found: E. A. Robinson. Do you know his work? I shall boom him when I return. Don't forestall me! Good luck.

Yours
RUPERT BROOKE

To CATHLEEN NESBITT   *New York*
                                      Wednesday, 25 June [1913]

> 'Now the hot labour of the day is done
> How nice it is to lie with nothing on
> Except a thin, a yellow dressing gown,
> And listen to the noises of the town,
> And think of what I've done and where I've been
> And write a letter to my dear Cathleen.
> Cathleen! loveliest creature! nymph divine!
> Unhoped for, unapproachable, yet mine!
> Fount of all beauty, vision of delight,
> Whom I love all the day and half the night;
> Child, and yet goddess, woman, saint, and witch,
> (Rhyme too obvious—)
> Perplexing compound, teasing wonderment,
> Wiser than God, and baby-innocent,
> Sweeter than love, and bitterer than death,
> Lucrezia Helen Mary in a breath.'

Oh, dear, I'm so sorry. I've a sort of feeling that I'm a poet and ought to write to my beloved in verse; for then it'll come out in my 'Life and Letters', and be printed in an Appendix to my collected works, and they'll all say 'How wonderful to write letters in verse! and how beautiful she must have been!'...

But it's no good. For I cannot say half the things I want to. I have to drop into mere prose; where there's a larger stock of words to praise you in.

                    *   *   *   RUPERT

To KATHARINE COX   *America [New York]*
                                      June
                                      [Postmark: 25 June 1913]

Oh, child!

I've kept thinking how to write in such a way as would be best for you. But I won't try to. There are disadvantages in telling the truth. But between us it is still the best.

My dear, I've been worrying so about writing. And almost every night as I crossed I dreamt about you. And you always seemed in pain. I hope to God nothing extra is wrong.

Being alone, I incline to get mad ideas. But also I'm getting to see all the past more steadily. So I'll try to stick to that, and minimize the former. And I'll try to put my feelings and ideas as clearly and honestly as I can before you. Forgive them if they hurt (I don't think they especially will): and forgive them where they're bad.

Well Ka, there are, as far as I can see, three purposes that drive me in what I do to or about you: (1) to be myself as little as possible worried or spoilt by uselessly keeping wounds open; (2) to see to it that you're able to keep clean and guarded against evil; (3) to see that you get clear and as happy as maybe, as soon as possible, and have the best and swiftest chance of realizing the loveliness and greatness of you.

I needn't go into the feelings on which these purposes are based. You know them.

The first I know is selfish, and whenever I'm conscious of it, I minimize it. I know what I owe to you and me (this is all very academically written). And I know that however we buy peace or anything else, you pay most.

I've tried for the second and third, as far as I could do anything. I thought I could secure both by not seeing you, and yet being in touch, writing.

I liked it too, my dear. It remains that we know each other better than anybody else. It was nice, writing and understanding.

But it has come upon me that it won't do. To realize the third purpose, I've got to leave the second out of my control. I've got to leave it to you.

You *must* get right clear of me, cease to love me, love and marry somebody—and somebody worthy of you.

Oh my dear, let's try together to put things right. It's so hard to know what to do—one's so stupid and blind and blundering.

What I feel about you is this—I'm not arguing if it's true, I just state it as it comes to my heart—'Ka is more precious than anything. She has marvellous goodness and greatness in her. She has things so lovely it hurts to name them. She is greater and better, potentially, than any woman I know: and more woman. She is very blind, and infinitely easy to lead astray. Her goodness makes her a prey. She needs looking after more than anybody else in the world. She's a lovely child.'

And with that in my heart I have to leave you. It's very difficult. Oh Ka, you don't know how difficult it is! So have pity on me. And forgive my breaking out like this.

I have your promises and your experience, and the love of your friends for you to comfort me. No one could ever draw friends to them as you can. If it comes to this responsibility question, my dear—you've a great deal of responsibility.

And now—though I'm a bit hysterical—I've a clearer view. And what you wrote gave me strength. You give strength. You said, I mean, that we're free to go—but only to clean people. Oh, it's true, child. I feel it now. It comes of my seeing something of what I owe you.

Oh God, I'm such a coward. I funk writing to you. Because it makes me concentrate on thinking about you. And that gives me pain—thinking about you. I haven't touched this letter for days and days.

There's nothing to say, but what I've said. It's only that. You're not getting better. I don't know how I can make you get better. I'm helpless. I can only leave you altogether. I do not do you any good or help you by being in touch with you. And I harm you by keeping myself too alive in your heart. The only good I do is by keeping you sensible and straight with advice—oh, take that from other people, and that's all I want.

Dear child, dearest Ka, whom I've loved and known, you must get well and happy, and live the great life you can. It's the only thing I care for. Oh, child, I know I've done you great wrong. What could I do? It was so difficult. You had driven me mad.

I'm sorry for the wrong. It's the one thing in the world I'm sorry for: though I've done a lot of evil things.

I can't bear it that it is I have hurt you.

But you'll grow, and be the fine Ka.—In the end I know you, that you can't be broken or spoilt, I do know you.

What is there? Unless in the two weeks' mail that's waiting for me somewhere, or in reply to this, there's something from you that needs reply, I shan't write again. In a few years we'll meet. Till then —we can dodge each other. If we meet—we're big enough to manage that. The creatures who watch won't get much change out of us. If I irritate you or you want me out of the way—tell some body, or me. But it won't happen. And if you see writings of mine —don't ever feel they're about you, and be hurt. I only write about suggested things and imagined you know.

There's one thing. Do you mind? I want to break the rule and give you a thing. A statuette of a mother and a child. It's now kept for me by Eddie. A tiny thing. He knows you're going to send him an address to send it you at. So when you're in England, will you send him the address?

I give it you; because you'll be the greatest mother in the world. And I'll not be anything but sad, till I've heard you're happy, and with a child of your own.

Let it stand: not for what we did: but for what we learnt.

I thought at one time I'd only learnt bad from you: now I know that before and after and over it all I learnt good—all that I have.

I've got to leave you. But if ever it happens you're in ultimate need of help—it may—you know I'll come, at any time and from any place, if you want it.

I'm very happy and well, travelling. And in the end I'll get back and work. Don't think of me.

Please, Ka, be good and happy: and stick to and be helped by your friends. That's the last thing I ask.

This is so bad a letter: and I wanted to make everything clear. Do believe. See what I've tried to write.

Preaching and everything aside, let's just be Ka and Rupert for a minute: and say good-bye so. I'll be loyal to the things we've learnt together: and you be loyal. And life'll be good.

Dear love, good bye
RUPERT

To EDWARD MARSH   *The Montreal Express*
                                     29 June 1913

My dear Eddie,

Two letters from you, came yesterday. So I feel entirely *au fait* with London life now. It was *very* nice to get them.

*   *   *

Now I'm shut up in my upper half of the sleeping-berth, I'm empty but a little easier. Beneath me sleeps—oh, a mattress and a plank between us—a fat old lady. Every other berth in the car is shared between married people, so it is—naturally—the prevalent opinion that the fat woman is my wife. It causes her even more embarrassment than me. I'm clad in my new *batiste* pyjamas which are a dream. So I have some consolation in life.

Ruminating on my 'impressions' of New York and Boston for letters to the W[estminster] G[azette] has made them so stale that I can't bear to put them down for you. They aren't very amusing. When I'm alone I sink into a kind of mental stupor, which may last for months. I shan't be really right again till I get back to you all.

Business. I heard from Waring who is enthusiastic about my play, and will do it as soon as he has a chance. Will you send the *Madonnachen*—the gold one—to Katharine Cox, *when* she sends you her address. I don't know when she returns to England. And, as a matter of fact, there's no particular need for you to mention the fact to anybody: if you don't mind.

My activities *in re* G. Poetry I wrote to Monro. Copyright is the difficulty. And they wouldn't quite realize the value of the book. I hear you've got hold of Macmillan—I fear too late.

I spent today in the country outside New York, flirting with Louise. It's the first time I ever flirted with anybody called Louise, so I'm rather tired. I've been diving into many sides of New York lately. The low foreign part is rather fascinating. Bohemia in New York rather cheap—even worse than in London. Theatres not very good: *revues* the best thing they do. I've found one poet and some poetesses. But I shall explore that more thoroughly later. It's very queer how utterly they depend on us for literature. Masefield, Galsworthy, etc. are *precisely* what they are in England. The magazines are filled with English writers, and all the critical articles are about English stuff. They simply don't exist. The Laureateship is discussed ardently and continually. They think Le Gallienne is in the running otherwise they're fairly sane. Except that everybody here thinks Noyes a *big* poet: bigger than Yeats or Bridges for instance. I can only gape. They also all love him personally. I haven't come across him.

I say, do just see that the Laureateship is kept. It would be a *frightful* scandal if it were abolished. Why not Bridges? I hope Violet'll see that it's all right—Kipling'ld be fine, too.

By the way, I had a card from Violet before I started, depicting the place where Ulysses met Nausicaa. What a thing to send to a person going to America! The only retaliation in kind I could think of has been a picture postcard of the stone by the wayside near Boston where Bishop Berkeley sat while composing the celebrated line 'Westward the course of Empire takes its way'.[1] But, though the place was pointed out to me, I couldn't find a card of it.

[1] George Berkeley, *Verses On the Prospect of Planting Arts and Learning in America*, 1726.

Your news of Rosalind Murray[1] was a surprise. It detached just a morsel from an already sadly diminished heart. *A propos* of hearts, give Cathleen my love if you see her, and a fatherly hand on the shoulder from yourself. She needs looking after, poor lady, being tired and rather troubled with certain things that have been about her way...but that's all private.

But I want sometime, from *somebody*, (1) an account of her in the new play, (2) an account of the reception of Wilfrid's play,[2] (3) the Dinner.

I'm glad Stephens is getting the Academy prize. The *Crock of Gold* deserves it—Stephens, Masefield, de la Mare, all G.P.'s! Aren't you proud of us?

Everybody—even Mrs Brooke—is asleep. So I shall stop this scrawl. I *will* try to write some stuff and send it soon—I go Westward fairly rapidly now.

I thought the June *Blue Review* quite distinctly good, especially Katherine [Mansfield]. She *can* write, damn her.

With all love
RUPERT

Give Wilfrid and Denis my love.

To CATHLEEN NESBITT   *Château Frontenac, Quebec*
                          3 July [*1913*]

I don't mind telling you that I had a bad fit of home-sickness this morning: for about two hours, from 9 to 11—I got into this boat at Quebec at 8. Bad. I threw up quite a lot of slobby old memories. Partly, today too the nearest I've yet been to you—well, to England.

[*Pen and ink plan*]

I'm going by the dotted line down the St Lawrence, and up the Saguenay to Chicotimi—just for the trip. And oh! we're on the Saguenay now, and it's *too* terrifying. My dear, it's not a river: it's a part of Hell, got loose. It's very narrow by Canadian standards, varying from ¾ mile to 300 yards across (the St Lawrence is eighteen miles wide where we leave it). And it's just the same depth—varying between 200 yards and a mile. Each side there are terrific cliffs, sometimes two thousand feet straight out of the water, of black granite. Pines occasionally but mostly bare. The water in

---

[1] Her engagement to Arnold Toynbee.   [2] *Womenkind*, 1913.

the river is jet black and absolutely smooth. This goes on for fifty miles. It's like some ghastly dream of Dante's. 'Fair gives me cold feet.' As evening came on and everything got blacker and stranger, and the mountains grew wilder and the river more sinister, I got restless and started prowling round the ship. Then I noticed the face of the river was queer, and as I watched it, I began to think I could see things coming out of it—large black things you know—I don't know what—turning and looking at you and bellying—so I came and shut myself in here, in my cabin, and read Jane Austen, and started this letter to you. Now I'm going to sleep. God guard you— and me in this place. I don't like these foreign lands—Not whole-some. Pray for me. RUPERT

To HUGH DALTON
[Postcard]
Canada
5 July 1913

You'll be pleased to know I'm looking round the Empire, won't you? Rather in your line.. . . But they're a rough lot, Hugh. Their manners.

But you should hear me sob when they speak of The Old Country. As they continually do.. . . And I am expert at singing 'O, Canada!' in English *and* French. RUPERT

To EDWARD MARSH
Ottawa
9 July [*1913*]

Mein lieber Eddie,

I picked up a letter of June 23rd or so from you here this morning: which brightened my grey life a moment or two. I got on well in New York and got to know a lot of folks: but here I'm rather astray. With my usual improvidence I omitted to get any introductions for Canada. One to Sir Wilfrid Laurier is all. And he isn't here for a day or two. So I've been—in Montreal and Quebec for the last ten days —rather dull. The Canadians are a churlish race. I find that when I'm alone and don't see my friends, I don't get very miserable or go to pieces (save for occasional bouts of home-sickness just before meals): but my whole level of life descends to an incredible muddy flatness. I do no reading, no thinking, and no writing. And very often I don't see many things. The real hell of it is that I get so numb that my brain and senses don't record fine or clear impressions. So the time is nearly all waste. I'm very much ashamed of it all. For I've always beforehand a picture of myself dancing through foreign cities, drinking in novelty, hurling off letters to the W[estminster] G[azette], breaking into song and sonnet, dashing off plays and novels.... Lord, Lord—I've not really given the Canadians much chance yet. But my impression *is* that they have all the faults of the Americans, and not their one lovely and redeeming virtue, 'hospitality'. That 'hospitality' is often sneered at in the Americans: but it merely means that with the nice ones, you can be at once on happy and intimate terms. Oh dear, the tears quite literally well up into my eyes when I think of a group of young Harvard people I tumbled into—at Harvard—they were connected with the theatrical movement there, and they had the charm and freshness and capacity for instantly creating a relation of happy and warm friendliness that, for instance, Denis has. It's a nice thing. But these people here.... However, I fancy the West may be better. And I'm gradually becoming convinced I must get across there very swiftly. I'm going to stay to see what can be got out of Laurier. After that, I guess I shall shoot through my other places. Especially as I hear there's unemployment in the Middle West; so I couldn't get a job on a farm.

*　　*　　*

July 11th. I find a mail goes.

I enclose the first-fruits of my exile. Poor stuff: and more of the kind is on the way.

E. V. Knox, subediting the Pall Mall *Magazine*, writes that they're pulling up their poetry, and will I, etc. Also 'upon what terms'? So you might send them two or three of my slighter things sometime, marked two guineas each—except *There's Wisdom*,[1] which might go at a guinea. That's after they've passed through the Blue [Review] sieve, and others—I've told them you're my London agent.

You, at home, have no conception how you're all getting a sanctity and halo about you in my mind. I dwell so much and so sentimentally on all the dear dead days, that I'm beginning to see no faults and all virtues in all of you. *You*, my dear, appear perfection in every part. Your passion for anagrams is a lovable and intellectual taste. Your acquaintance with Ottoline Morrell a beautiful thing.

[1] 'There's Wisdom in Women', *New Statesman*, 18 October 1913; reprinted in *1914 And Other Poems*.

Your lack of sympathy with the Labour Party turns to a noble and picturesque Toryism. Even your preference for gilded over-comfortable chairs loses something of its ugliness in my heart. Of you and Wilfrid and Norton and the Society and Duncan [Grant] and Cathleen and even Alfred I think incessantly devotedly and tearfully. Even of figures which, to be frank, have hovered but dimly on the outskirts of my consciousness, I am continually and fragrantly memorial. I miss Elizabeth Asquith immensely. The face (though not the name) of Wyndham's secretary dwells in my mind, tenderly guarded. Tears often come to my eyes when I think of either Miss Gosse. I make up little minor pitiful songs, the burden of which is that I have a folk-longing to get back from all this Imperial luxury to the simplicity of the little places and quiet folks I knew & loved. One very beautiful one has the chorus—

> 'Would God I were eating plover's eggs,
>   And drinking dry champagne,
> With the Bernard Shaws, Mr and Mrs Masefield,
> Lady Horner, Neil Primrose, Raleigh, the Right
> Honourable Augustine Birrell, Eddie, six or
> seven Asquiths, & Felicity Tree,
>   In Downing Street again.'

Waw, waw, the Post.

With love

RUPERT

To HAROLD MONRO

Ottawa
July 1913

My dear Harold,

Will you tell one of your minions to send Hardy's Poems, the little 2 f. edition comprising the first two volumes he issued, to the following address, & put it down in my account—

Russell H. Loines
Dongan Hills
Staten Island
New York, U.S.A.

Indeed, you might note the name & address, as one keen on things. I left him ordering *G.P.*

I hope all goes well with you: & that my poem caused the July number to sell several thousand. I have not seen it, nor anything even remotely connected with ease, refinement & the life of a gentleman for weeks. This is a —— Philistia. I'm just off to dine with the only poet in Canada. Duncan Campbell Scott—a very nice fellow. He may be visiting England later in the summer, if so, I'll send him in to see you. He's quite a big man in the civil service here. Be nice to him. My English news trickles out slowly: & my mail has missed me for more than a fortnight now. I suppose it's somewhere on this Continent. I live on in the confidence that you're all alive & intermittently kicking.

Love & a kiss to the Muses.

R. B.

To MRS BROOKE   *King Edward Hotel, Toronto*
                                   Monday, 21 July 1913

Dear Mother,

I hope you got my postcard, saying my next mail was to go to me at Vancouver. At least I forget if I did say that. But that's the next thing. My movements are

> Niagara Wednesday–Saturday—
> Winnipeg   Wed. 30th for three
> c/o Howard Falk   days or so
> 301 Edwin Street

Then I go to   Edmonton,
                  Calgary,
(The Rockies)   Banff or Laggan,
(The Selkirks)   Glacier
                  Vancouver

I may get to Vancouver by August 15, or any time up to the end of August. (My birthday I'll probably spend on the train between Winnipeg and Edmonton!) The uncertain parts are my tours off the line. From Calgary I shall go off for a day to an Indian settlement, for certain. From Edmonton I *may* go North into the wild part for ten days. And I shall stop at either Laggan (or Banff) or Glacier, or both, for a few days, to rest, enjoy mountain scenery, and write. In Vancouver I shall stay a few days, and go across to the Island. Then to San Francisco. They're doing a Greek play in the Greek theatre near San Francisco about September 7th; and I want to see it, if possible.

*   *   *

Laurier was a nice old man—a bit of a 'politician', playing the party game, but not so much as the others. I don't trust his policy, because I don't believe he *really* wants to pay anything in any form towards the Navy. He's very French in sympathies. I saw Perley, the acting-Premier on the other side. Borden was away. I had been told by Masefield that he knew (by correspondence) the Canadian poet Duncan Campbell Scott.

*   *   *

One letter you forwarded was from George Calderon, introducing himself, praising my work, saying he'd heard I'd written a play, and inviting me to meet an American actress in London looking out for plays. So there's another chance of making my fortune gone! But it was nice of him to write.

Gibson has been staying with Abercrombie, and has got a great idea that he, Abercrombie, Drinkwater, and I should combine our publics, and publish from the Abercrombies (Mrs A. does the work) a Volume four times a year.[1] A. has done it with some of his own stuff, and finds he makes most money that way. The other three seem to be keen on the idea. Rather a score for me, as my 'public' is smaller than any of theirs! But it's a secret at present.

I haven't been writing much out here—Rather bad letters to the Westminster. Perhaps they'll refuse to print them.

*   *   *

With love
RUPERT

To CATHLEEN NESBITT   *King Edward Hotel, Toronto*
[*July 1913*]

To Cathleen

'When she sleeps, her soul, I know,
    Goes a wanderer on the air,
Slips where I may never go
    Leaves her lying, still and fair,

[1] *New Numbers*, published in February 1914.

Waiting, empty, laid aside
Like a dress upon a chair. . .
This I know. And yet I know
Doubts that will not be denied.
For if the soul be not in place,
What has laid trouble in her face,
And, sits there nothing ware and wise
Behind the curtain of her eyes,
What is it, in the self's eclipse,
Shadows soft and passingly,
Round the corners of her lips,
The smile that is essential she?
And if the spirit be not there,
Why is fragrance in the hair?'

R.

To EDWARD MARSH   [*Toronto*]
                                 22 July 1913

Oh Eddie,

The truth is, you're on a higher level of civilization than I. I've got into the habit of roaming off & living away & never giving my friends any sign or news for months & months & then turning up & expecting to take up the old relationship just where it stopped. . . . But your letter-method is the nobler & wiser: & I, at least, derive pleasure from it (& money too, I hope: if my plan of having your letters printed in a New York paper as revelations of high life, comes off). So I'm ashamed that I write so spasmodically. My way, I assure you. I write regularly to no one—not even my four young women.   *   *   *

I've found here an Arts & Letters Club of poets painters journalists etc., where they'd heard of me, & read G.P., &, oh Eddie, one fellow actually possessed my 'Poems'. Awful Triumph. Every now & then one comes up & presses my hand & says 'Wal, Sir, you cannot know how memorable a Day in my life this is.' Then I do my pet boyish-modesty stunt & go pink all over: & everyone thinks it *too* delightful. One man said to me 'Mr Brooks (my Canadian name), Sir, I may tell you that in my opinion you have Mr Noyes skinned.' That means I'm better than him: I gathered a great compliment, here. But they're really quite an up-to-date lot: & very cheery &

pleasant. I go on, tomorrow, to the desert & the wilds. My next letters will take a week longer on the way so they won't reach England for a long while after you get this.

Niagara. July 24th.

Were you ever here? It's very queer. The things are very very low & broad & gloomy. I write with the sound of them monstrous in my ears; one is across the river opposite, one to the right. A dizzying affair. Funny to think that this noise has been continually sounding, & that I'm hearing the *same* noise as Washington & Poe & Goldie Dickinson, only a little later on.

*   *   *

With love
RUPERT

P.S. The most unpopular person in Canada is Winston. Ever since his lecture-tour. They *do* hate him.

To WILFRID GIBSON   *King Edward Hotel, Toronto*
                              23 July [1913]
My dear Wilfrid,

Two letters from you awaiting me here: one about roast-duck, and one about Gallows Garlands.[1] I think the G.G. is a great idea. I'm all for amalgamating our four publics, the more that mine is far the smallest! I'm afraid I shall be outwritten by you fluent giants—

> 'Modern poets outscrawl and outbawl me,
>   And old Wilfrid makes mouths at my speech.'

(A.C.S[winburne])

I foresee that the average number will read as follows—

Index

1. Lascelles Abercrombie: 'Haman and Mordecai'   pp. 1–178
2. John Drinkwater: 'The Sonority of God: An   pp. 79–143
   Ode'
3. W. W. Gibson: 'Poor Bloody Bill: A Tale'   pp. 144–187
4. Rupert Brooke: 'Oh, Dear! oh, Dear! A Sonnet'   p. 188
5. Lascelles Abercrombie: 'Asshur-Bani-Pal and Og   pp. 189–254
   King of Bashan'

---

[1] Afterwards called *New Numbers*.

6. John Drinkwater: 'William Morris: an Apprecia-   pp. 255–377
tion in verse'
7. W. W. Gibson: 'Gas-Stoves: No I. A Brave Poor   pp. 377–594
Thing'

Finis

Then there would be three hundred pounds profit, divided proportionally to the amount contributed:

W. W. G.	£130.	10.	6
L. A.	£94.	7.	4
J. D.	£74.	11.	11½
R. B.	£0.	10.	2½

And *that's* how the money would go.
'But not the fame.'
Phoebus replied, 'It is not *all* a plant'—
(How does it go?)

Anyhow, I'm very much pleased and excited about the scheme,
and I'll 'come in', right in, without knocking: if ever I write anything again. But there's plenty of time by December. (Shall I prepare a list of addresses?)

The only poet in Canada was very nice to me in Ottawa—Duncan
Campbell Scott, aetat. 50, married, an authority on Indians. Poor
devil, he's so lonely and dried there: no one to talk to. They had
a child—daughter—who died in 1908 or so. And it knocked them
out. She, a violinist, never played since: he hasn't written, till the
last few months. Their house was queerly desolate. It rather went
to my heart. Canada's a *bloody* place for a sensitive—in a way 2nd
rate—real, slight poet like that to live all his life. Nobody cares if he
writes or doesn't. He took me out to a Club in the country near, and
we drank whisky and soda, and he said 'Well, here's to your youth!'
and drank its health, and I nearly burst into tears. He's a very nice
chap (especially away from his wife, who's nice enough): and he's
thirsty to talk literature; and he's very keen on all our work. He saw a
little of the 1890–1905 men—he's caricatured in Archer's book[1]—and
he finds us *far* better! So he's obviously to be encouraged. He's
probably visiting England Sept–Oct for a week or two. I gave him
letters to Eddie and Monro, and told him you'd insist on talking to
him and giving him tea in your attic. So get hold of him and cheer
him. He'd love it. And, if there's not much on, make Monro (or

[1] William Archer, *Poets of the Younger Generation*, 1902, pp. 385–93.

Eddie) get up a little dinner or lunch of the quietest nature with de la Mare and you and whoever of the immortals is about. It'd be a nice thing to do. Reserve a chair and a plate of soup or blood for me: and you'll see a faint shade lapping at the plate and hear the dimmest of American accents wishing you all well.

I must go out to lunch at the Toronto Arts & Letters. It's a club, Wilfrid, where they have HEARD of US! And one or two little men possess our Works—not G.P. but our own—Canada's looking up!

I'm glad your Gloucestershire holiday was good. It sounded splendid. (One year we'll go camping a week in the New Forest, or Dartmoor, shall we?) It sounded far nicer than wandering from Hotel to soulless Hotel, wondering why the Devil one has put the thick of the world between oneself and those one loves—

which is the experience of

Yours

RUPERT

To DUNCAN CAMPBELL SCOTT

The York Club, Toronto
23 July [1913]

Dear Scott,

(Dropping the Mr is to be interpreted not as a mark of irreverence, but rather as a recognition of the Brotherhood of Poets—it is nicer, isn't it?) Your introduction made Toronto very pleasant for me. Morris was indefatigably kind to me, and he and McTavish took me to the Arts and Letters where I found a lot of jolly people. Willison I only just caught before he went away: but I had a good talk with him.

I'm hoping to find some photographs at Niagara. My Winnipeg address will be

c/o Howard Falk,
301 Edwin Street,
Winnipeg.

I shall get there Tuesday 30th and stay a few days—after that—the void. I'll decide then if I can make the trip North of Edmonton, and wire if I want a letter beyond there.

Morris was very urgent I should take a trip from Calgary to see the 'Stonies' (is that right?) and said you would give me a note to the Indian agent at Morley. Would that be a good idea? I'd like to see them in their proper state. I feel a sort of sympathy with them, and friendliness. Morris would give me a message to the Indians themselves.

I want a card sometime to say if you definitely *are* going to England. My envy goes with you, if you do. You'll find a copy of my book put aside for you at the Poetry Bookshop, if you care to take it. And I'll write my name in it, on the good occasion when we next meet. If you happen to go to or from through Rugby (which is improbable) or Cambridge, you must let me know. There are a lot of people in Cambridge who would like to see you—there's a nice mad poet in King's called [Iolo] Williams who'd welcome you, and take you up the river to Grantchester! I write this, as a matter of fact, as I'm being borne towards the roar of Niagara. I'm rather excited about it.

I shall be eternally grateful to Masefield, for having sent me to you. I'm beginning to feel sad I shan't be with the men in London to welcome you. I told Gibson, if you all ate together, an empty chair and a plate of soup were to be put aside for me. You'll see my faint ghost lapping at it, like the ghosts in the Odyssey, and hear my shadowy plaudits.

I hope Europe'll inspire you—perhaps to write about Canada. I always find I write warmly and longingly about England as soon as I get out of it. I hope you'll both enjoy the holiday anyhow.

    With best greetings to yourself

and your wife

Yours ever

RUPERT BROOKE

To A. F. SCHOLFIELD   *Toronto*
July–August 1913

Oh, Scho!

(It sounds like the beginning of a musical comedy song.

    'Oh, Scho!
    Why do you go,
    Cat'loguing books for the Nig-u-ars?')

Behold, I also am in exile. A third of the way round the world in the other direction. It is true that the people I am among have skins of a dingy white: they're not niggers, such as you, with that tendency to perverse tastes we have always deplored in you, have taken up with. But their ways and tongue are almost as alien from those you and I share, and they have no souls. I have been on this continent for two months and shall be six more, perhaps. Oh! oh! *Quisque suos patimur Tomos*: which does not, my scholarly friend, mean 'we each bear our own Thomas', but 'Everyman his own Náso'— I assure you that I drip horribly with *Heimweh*, nearly the whole time. Don't you? I have the advantage (?) that I can write—and do—vast quantities of nostic verse,

My heart is sick for several things
Only to be found in King's...

I do recall those haunts with tears,
The Backs, the Chapel, and the Rears...

O Places of perpetual mire,
Localities of my desire,
O lovely, O remembered gloom
And froust of Chetwynd lecture-room,
Dear haunts with old romance aglow
Where first I viewed the passing *show*.* (paranomasia)
O spots my memory yet is gilding,
O Jumbo Arch! O Wilkins Building!

. . .

descriptive of the Natural Beauties

Ah, how my memory floods and fills,
The Hills[1] and Brookes[2] and little Sills! (1) A. V. and W. D. P.
The Olive and other greenery[3] (2) R. C., A. C. & A. E.
And Canes complete the scenery: (3) e.g. The Birch
And, in my dream, stretch far away

The poet, to hide his emotion, drops into latin

Montes et Knox perpetua...

There we pursued the Truth amain,
With Dialectic and Champagne,
And, through the young and purple night,
Still holla'd after 'What is Right',
And played the young philosopher
From Hesperus till Lucifer,
And stalked and startled from her nest
The subtle bird, *quod verum est,*
And linked, with the new risen sun,
τὸ καλόν with τὸ ἀγαθόν...

(but this is getting bawdy: and the rhymes aren't all your pedantic
ear would wish; besides, you're laughing at my accents. I know you!
German! Yah! So all End, all End!)

> Dear Home of my Rememberings!
> O Kings! O Kings! Oh Kings! O Kings!   (my style when
>   they pay me by
>   space)
>
> Spot where I cheered the College Bumps,   (not I! 'tis but
>   for the rhyme)
>
> Place where I read First Less'n in pumps!
> Founded the New Jerusalem!   (with Schloss.
> And breakfasted at 3 p.m!   Reitlinger, etc.,
> Haunts where I drank the whole damn night! etc.)
> Place where I catted till the light!
> Dear spot where I was taken short,
> O Bodley's Court! O Bodley's Court!

Enough! and too much! I can only excuse myself by the fact that
I'm writing near Niagara, the spray of which is wafted gently over
my paper. There is romance for you! A letter dewy with Niagara
read by a corpulent turbaned rajah of a librarian under the deodars
of Taj Mahal. (Local Colour.) But it shows you what the British
Empire is! (I am become (1) a strong Imperialist, (2) a rabid anti-
Canadian, (3) a *violent* Englander). But, o Scho. I'm so impressed
by Niagara. I hoped not to be. But I horribly am. The colour of the
water, the strength of it, and the clouds of spray—I'm afraid I'm
a Victorian at heart, after all. Please don't breathe a word of it: I want
to keep such shreds of reputation as I have left. Yet it's true. For
I sit and stare at the thing and have the purest Nineteenth Century
grandiose thoughts, about the Destiny of Man, the Irresistibility of
Fate, the Doom of Nations, the fact that Death awaits us All, and so
forth. Wordsworth Redivivus. Oh dear! oh dear!

I complete this scrawl in the wilderness, eighty miles N E of
Winnipeg, by a lonely lake where I'm living wild and fishing with
an old Rugbeian I found in Winnipeg. And it is August 3 and I am
twenty-six years old today. 'So little done, so much to do!' as
I wittily and originally observed to a chipmunk this morning.
I swear, I will have written two plays, a novel, and a long poem by
this time next year. 'Swelp me Bob. That last is a quotation from the
writer who gives me my only idea of India—Kipling. Seeing it
through his eyes, I fear for your virtue. Scho, you must not marry
an Anglo-Indianess! I forbid it. We should all die. As it is, we take

your absence badly. Geoffrey Fry was wilting day by day, ever balder and ever shriller. King's went mad with grief, and, still distraught, elected me a Fellow (for your letter of felicitations, many thanks). I succeed Waigers—another Amurath business—and try, however humbly, to fill his inky and downtrodden shoes. But oh, the one thing which, with all my charity, I *cannot* forgive you, is that you did not finish that dissertation, and make them elect you— Come back soon. *I* return next year, probably. You must get a job in England. We need you. Meanwhile herzliche Grüsse.

R. B.

To SYBIL PYE [Postcard]
Niagara Falls,
25 July [*1913*]

O dear, I'm old-fashioned after all. Perhaps it's the first fruits of Q. dubbing me Victorian....But I really am deeply impressed and moved. Just at old Niagara that I've heard of since I was two! I'm secretly ashamed. But, you know, it's really the colours that fairly knock one: dark rich green at the top, frilling down to dazzling white, and occasionally great streaks of purple. Oh! Oh! Oh!

Love to Ethel and David. RUPERT

To HAROLD MONRO *in the train* (*America*)
24 July [*1913*]

My dear Harold,

* * *

I gave Duncan Campbell Scott, the poet of Canada, a letter to you. He'll probably be in London about the end of September. A very nice, quiet, sad, fellow. He's very keen on G.P. & wants to meet the younger literary people in London. So introduce him to some. You might give a small lunch, perhaps...but you know what to do. Be kind to him. He's rather shy: & he's gone quiet & melancholy through lack of people to talk to. But he has done good stuff. He has a wife. I always tell everyone I meet to call at the Bookshop. So if anyone says I told him: it's probably true. It doesn't mean I want them entertained for my sake! unless they've got letters. But they're always nice.

There's an *Arts & Letters* Club here, full of jolly people. I gave them a spare G.P. They know of it, & they knew our work. The leading newspaper interviewed me. Fame! Fame! A Canadian interview is a Solemn Thing.

My latest intelligence is that Bryn Mawr, the leading American Girls' College, is *wild* about Georgian Poetry.

Oh, you might find it worth while to make Scott give a reading. But I warn you, he doesn't read well. He spoils the metre rather, & has a hard voice.

Will you put aside a copy of my book, & give it him, & charge it to me? Also send one (my account) to Edmund Morris, 43 Victoria Street, Toronto. I promised them both.

By the way, if you send photographs of a Georgian or two, of the Bookshop, to Canadian & American papers, when the book goes for review, it might be a good idea. They print them a lot.

I'm sorry I was only represented by my Donne article in P. & D.:[1] it wasn't very good. I *may* have enough by December: though I've written only 16 lines since I left England. Some ways it'd be safer to put it in September: but do as you like. I think that's all. I'm glad things are going well. You got my note about the book to Loines?

Ever

RUPERT

To EDMUND GOSSE

Lake Superior
27 July 1913

Dear Edmund Gosse,

I'd just planned a call on you, before I left England—in May, but it seems to me a thousand years ago—and when I consulted Eddie Marsh as to the best time to find you at home and at leisure, I discovered, to my dismay, that you had gone to Paris. I was, and am, very sorry I didn't see you again before I crossed these gulfs of water, and of spirit. I had a very good time in America. I didn't see Noyes, but I heard of him on every side. He made a great impression, and people were praising him with enthusiasm, in equal proportions for the goodness of his poetry, for its Englishness, and for his personal charm. I left them all quite certain he would get the Laureateship, and quite angry with anyone who suggested that there were more worthy candidates. I didn't see Howells, who had

[1] Review of Donne's *Poems*, ed. Grierson, *Poetry and Drama*, no. 2, June 1913.

gone off to his summer country house, so I couldn't give him your message.

The Americans just now seem almost entirely subsistent on England for serious literature, just as this soulless 'Dominion' is on the United States for *all* literature. I could discover, in the briefest of searches, almost nobody alive, younger than Howells, of any mark. Except one man, a poet, Edward Arlington Robinson—a protégé of Roosevelt's! But with your wide view over the world's literature, you probably know him. Roosevelt, with his fine large return to good old ways, having read a volume of Robinson's, put him into the Government Customs Department. When the superior officials, after a trial, objected that he was entirely incompetent and very idle, they were told that he was to stay there while he wrote good poetry. However, Robinson cleared out on his own account very soon. But what an example to modern Governments! Robinson has a queer kind of intimacy with the small objects and affairs of life, very like de la Mare's; and a similar, but less subtle, musical power over common words and phrases. There's one divine thing 'On a Dead Lady'—I haven't the book with me—

> 'The forehead and the little ears
> Have gone where Saturn keeps the years;
> The breasts that had no need of love
> Have done with rising and with falling'—

It rings the feminine rhymes beautifully.

I recall, as typical, a poem that narrates his meeting a large jolly man in the street—each greets the other warmly, then each finds that he has mistaken the other's identity—they *don't* know each other; so they part. It's a not unknown situation in real life, and very poignant, with a peculiar tinge of emotion of its own—but how rarely treated in poetry!

I'm writing on Lake Superior. We're steaming along in a little low fog, which just doesn't come up to the top deck, but completely hides the surface of the sea. Occasionally little cones and peaks of the mist float by, and the sun catches them. It is slightly uncanny; like everything in these great lakes. I have a perpetual feeling that a lake ought not to be this size. A river and a little lake and an ocean are natural; but not these creatures. They are too big, and too smooth, and too sunny; like an American business man.

But this is garrulity. I hope you're well; and that England (of which we hear little over here) is still healthy. I become more passionately English, the more I'm absent from England.

I go to Winnipeg, the Rockies, Vancouver, and, I hope, the South Seas. And I'm not writing anything.

Yours sincerely

RUPERT BROOKE

To CATHLEEN NESBITT   *Lake George*
                                1 August [1913]

My dear,

You'll excuse me if this letter is smeared with dirt or mud or blood. I've all of them on my hands. The blood may be mine or may be a caribou's. A caribou is a sort of stag—at least, the male is. I'm writing in bed, by a lake forty or fifty miles from the nearest town, N.E. of Winnipeg, at midnight. The way it happened is this. I found a man, an old Rugbeian, in Winnipeg. He had been working very hard for a long time. And Winnipeg was *very* hot. So we decided to take a holiday. So, first by rail, and then by a truck on some lines to a Power Station by a lake, and then on foot and then in a canoe and then on foot, we got here. It is the 'Club House' of a Winnipeg Hunting and fishing Club. There's no one here now, except the man and his wife who keep it, for it's not the good fishing season. It's just a wooden low house, built on a granite cliff, over a little lake, 2 miles by 5, amidst great woods. There's a family in a shack across the lake, and an Indian and his son on the river two miles away; no other neighbours. Beyond the lake there are low hills all wooded, and other lakes, and hills, and woods, for hundreds and hundreds of miles; all wild; filled with caribou, and moose, and red deer, and BEARS, and timber wolves, and minks, and all sorts of things. All the woods around us are full of bears, which is frightfully exciting. My friend and I bathe all day—diving off rock into the clearest and sweetest of blue water—and row and fish, and try to sail a canoe and get tipped up, and light great fires at evening, and listen to stories and sleep and eat. The man here is a trapper; a fine fellow with a handsome face and a shock of curly black hair, who has hunted and trapped over the whole of North America, and can find his way anywhere, shoot anything, and do anything. He found a little Liverpool scullery-maid who'd emigrated and was working in a town out West, and married her. She is just blossoming into a primitive in-touch-with-Nature squaw woman—very funny. Tonight the trapper and an Indian who lives near here set out in a canoe after 'supper'—about 5.45 p.m., to hunt. About 10.30 p.m., after our bonfire had died down, came a hail from the landing stage in the darkness below. The woman went out on to the rock we stand on to answer it, and came back with the news that 'the boys were to come down'. (It's very nice to be addressed 'Say, boys,—.') We went down the steep path, I ahead. By the boat-house in the darkness was Bryan (the trapper) wading ashore, tugging the canoe with two dark forms in it—the Indian, and, as I peered through the dark, something crouching with a vast head of horns. The woman said ''Ave ye shot anything?' Bryan replied 'Yaw. A rat.' (His form of humour.) The canoe came right up, and we distinguished an immense deer, the size of a small pony, dead, strapped into the bottom of the canoe. It weighed 500 lbs.: and they had paddled the canoe six miles, all round by the shore, the water up within half an inch of the gunwales, from the place where they'd shot him. They emptied him out into the muddy edge of the water; we lit a great fire of birch, spruce, and tamarack wood to see what was going on; and we all set to work to string him up for the night (he had been disembowelled.) For two hours we pulled and hauled at this creature, tugging at a rope over the branch of a birch. Then the trapper got an axe and hacked the beast's head off: with the great antlers it weighs some hundred pounds. At length we got the carcass hanging up and supported it with sticks. I got cut and scratched and smeared with the creature's inside. It was a queer sight, lit up by the leaping flames of the fire, which the woman fed—the black water of the lake, muddy with trampling at the edge, and streaked with blood, the trapper in the tree, this great carcass hanging at one end of the rope, my friend and an Indian and I pulling our arms out at the other, the head gazing reproachfully at us from the ground, everybody using the most frightful language, and the rather ironical and very dispassionate stars above. Rather savage. Bryan said, once 'Brought it all the way home so as *you* could see it, kid', to his wife; so she was in an ecstasy of delight all evening.

August 3.

Today, o my heart, I am twenty-six years old. And I've done so little. I'm very much ashamed. By God, I'm going to make things hum, though.

But that's all so far away. I'm lying quite naked on a beach of golden sand, six miles away from the hunting-lodge, the other man near by, a gun between us in case bears appear, the boat pulled up on the shore, the lake very blue and ripply, and the sun rather strong. We 'trolled' for fish coming, which means, you may know, putting out a piece of bright twisting metal with hooks and letting it drag after the boat. It rotates, and flashes, and large fish think it a little one, and swallow it. So! we caught two pike on the way out, which lie picturesquely in the bows of the boat. Along the red-gold beach are the tracks of various wild animals, mostly jumping deer and caribou. One red deer we saw as we came round the corner, lolloping along the beach, stopping and snuffing the wind, and going on again. Very lovely. And the meat wasn't needed, so we didn't shoot at it (I'm glad—I'm no 'sportsman'). We bathed off the beach, and then lit a fire of birch and spruce, and fried eggs and ate cold caribou-heart, and made tea, and had (oh!) blueberry pie. Cooking and eating a meal naked is the most solemnly primitive thing one can do.

And—and this is the one thing which will make you realize, that I'm living far the most wonderfully, and incredibly romantic life you ever heard of, and *infinitely* superior to your miserable crawling London existence—the place we landed at is an Indian Camp. Indians when they go away from a camping-ground take the strips of birch-bark which answer to canvas in our tents, but leave the poles standing for the next visit—just like Pictures [*sketch*] and this birch-grove has six or seven of these, with litter inside, temporarily uninhabited—oh, but only temporarily! Any moment a flotilla of birch-bark canoes may sweep round the corner crowded with Indians—braves and squaws and papooses—and not these lonely half-breeds and stray Indians, who speak English, mind you, but the Real Thing. Shades of Fenimore Cooper! But if you don't like Beer or Kenneth Grahame, perhaps you also dislike or don't know Fenimore Cooper. What a woman! My dear one, I'll write you a shaky letter from the train while I'm hurrying across the boundless prairie. But God knows when it'll get to you.

My mail will reach me sometime. Then more news from you! Hurray! I want so sometimes, to get in touch with you.

I hope you're very happy and very well and very good and still in the country. Sleep much.

Dear lovely child, good evening.

With love
Your RUPERT

To CATHLEEN NESBITT

A note not a letter.

Edmonton

4. p.m., 13 August 1913

The Foyer of the King Edward Hotel

Child,

I got in here this morning, from Saskatoon. Edmonton, which is one of these new towns—200 in 1901, 25,000 in 1911, 50,000 in 1913—frightfully pleased with itself. There's a 'Fair' on now, I find: so everywhere's frightfully full, and I've not yet got a room. *Therefore* I am in a bad temper.

One thing, however, I have been saved. I decided, after lunch, that I *must* finish a Westminster article (on Montreal!—oh Gods of Incapacity, Laziness, and Procrastination!).[1] So I sat here, trying to get that done before I went on to the Fair. And as I finished it, down came the rain. So the other guys have gotten wet, but not me.

So, as I've done some work, and there's nothing in the world to do, I'm reduced to writing to London actresses...

It's very hard to give *news* of my travels, I find. I'm really much amused by all the things I see. But I've got a damn bad eye and mind for detail, and I just *can't* describe people's dress and faces. Edmonton is full of the most extraordinary toughs, for the fair. I just leant against a building this morning, and surveyed them. I find I'm becoming very thick-skinned and bold and the complete journalist. I've just been interviewed by a reporter. I fairly crushed him. I just put my cigar in the corner of my mouth, and undid my coat and put my thumbs under my arm pits, and spat, and said 'Say, kid, this is some town!' He asked me a lot of questions, of which I did not know the answer. So I lied. I gave the poor old West-minster, for instance, a circulation of a million, and a reputation that would make Spender's few prim white hairs stand horrid to the heavens, if he knew. Also, I am become very good at bearding people. I just enter Railway offices, and demand free passes as a journalist. And I stamp into immense newspaper buildings and say 'I want to talk for an hour to the Chief Editor'. And I can lean across the counter with a cigarette and discuss the Heart with the young lady who sells cigars, newspapers and stamps. I believe I could do a deal in Real Estate in the bar over a John Collins with a cleanshaven Yankee with a tremulous eyelid and a moist lower-lip.

In fact, I am a Man.

[1] Perhaps an allusion to Samuel Butler's line, 'Oh God! Oh Montreal!'

As for *you*, I have received my first report from my confidential Enquiry Agent in London (Mr E. Marsh). It says 'Cathleen was looking very happy and healthy.' So I pat your little head, and approve.

It's clearing. I must go out. I'll write from a train.

> With love
>
> RUPERT

To DUNCAN CAMPBELL SCOTT

> *King George Hotel, Calgary*
> *15? August [1913]*

Dear Scott,

It comes upon me slowly and awfully that I may not have acknowledged those photographs. Or was it the letter of introduction to Waddy I didn't acknowledge? or both? I get so fuddled travelling about, and seeing a new place and thirty new people every day. It seems ages ago since I was in the quiet of Ottawa.

Anyway, it's very nice to have those photographs. I don't know why the one of me alone should have caught me at a moment when I was trying to look like Arnold Bennett. In one of the groups Mrs Scott has turned her back on me very markedly: which wounds me deeply. But they're very pleasant to have and keep. Thanks very much. I hope Masefield appreciates the compliment of the gift!

I do hope very much that you've started off for Europe. I'm sure that if you can get away you'll both enjoy it very much. I envy you England. My latest news from there informs me that *The Blue Review* has gone bust, through lack of support, and Gibson has gone to live in the country near Abercrombie; but I hope he'll be in London for a day or two when you're there. He's the most lovable and simple person in the world.

Out West I have sloughed the poet, and become the Political Thinker. Why, I don't know. The papers all interview me on The European situation and the Navy Question; and print columns and columns of what I never did and never could say. So if, out East, you hear me reported as saying 'Old Laurier's some guy' or any such thing, you'll know it's a libel.

> Yours ever
>
> RUPERT BROOKE

To EDWARD MARSH   *Calgary*
                                            16 August [*1913*]
My dear,

My progress is degenerating into a mere farce. The West insists on taking me seriously as a politician & thinker. Toronto, which is in the East, started in on me as a Poet, with an Interview which I'll send you if I get a spare copy. It's only fairly funny, though it gets better when it's copied into *The Saskatoon Sentinel* & the rest, in fragments, as it does. Every little paper in Western Canada has started its Society Column with 'Dust' sometime in the last three weeks. Solemn thought. But in most of these towns they know me chiefly as a Political Expert. I average two reporters a day, who ask me my opinion on every subject under the sun. My opinions on the financial situation in Europe are good reading. And there are literally columns of them in the papers. I sit for an hour a day & laugh in my room. When I come back, though, I shall demand a knighthood from Winston. I've been delivering immense speeches in favour of his naval policy. What's really wrong with these damned Canadians is that at bottom they believe it's all play, & that war is impossible, & that there ain't no such place as the continent of Europe. They all live a thousand miles from the sea, and make an iniquitous living by gambling in real estate.

But the papers here are applying a nice story to Lloyd George. I'm only afraid they got it from London. *I'*d never even heard the story before. Is it current 'over there'?—A mouse (L.G.) pursued by two cats takes refuge in the darkest corner of the cellar, gets drunk on whisky-drippings, & is seen staggering up the cellar steps saying 'Where are those dam' catsh that chased me?'

I have been lying in bed for half an hour practising to become American; the spittoon on the floor beside me. It is a lonely sort of game, & I'm not very good at it. I'm becoming the most expert of travellers, though. I've even started washing my own clothes. On Tuesday I get out of this plain up into the Rockies. There I shall rest awhile & try to write. It's so long since I've written anything, except a little painstaking dreariness for the Westminster. I left Pegasus in a horse-van at Port Arthur. Which reminds me that I don't *think* I should value Flecker's volume so highly as you seem to (I got two very nice letters from you at Winnipeg). I expect I'd find him too fluid. The first quote was good, though. Give him my love.

England—I dreamt, last night, that at Vancouver I got sick of the trip & came back to England, & landed at Grantchester (you should have seen how we drew up at the Boat-house), & wired to you that I was going to stay a night with you in London, & caught the 4.55—&, oh, woke. Would you have been there? I've a sort of idea you'll go to Venice or some lovely place in September. I envy you. You can't think how sick one's heart gets for something *old*. For weeks I have not seen or touched a town so old as myself. Horrible! Horrible! They gather round me & say, 'In 1901 Calgary had 139 inhabitants, now it has 75,000': & so forth. I reply, 'My village is also growing. At the time of Julius Caesar it was a bare 300. Domesday Book gives it 347 and it is now close on 390.' Which is ill-mannered of me.

Oh, but I have adventures—had I only anybody to tell them to! For a day I travelled with a Scotch Whisky manufacturer, a Radical. At Euston he had got into the carriage with a woman who had turned out to have nursed the late Duke of Sutherland up to the last. 'And she gave me most interesting particulars about the Duke's passing away.' Isn't it extraordinary what things complete strangers will say to each other? * * *

I suppose you won't be sailing the Admiralty Yacht, near 'Frisco this September? Can't you persuade Winston to inspect the Panama Canal? & I'd come down & join you. It's frightfully important.

With love

RUPERT

To ROSALIND MURRAY
Chateau Lake Louise
Laggan. Alta. Canada
1 September 1913

Dear Rosalind,

They say you're engaged to be married. I'm glad. For I suppose you're very happy. It is very nice (I remember) being engaged to be married. And being married is far wonderfuller and lovelier, I suppose. It must be. So, as you're happy and are going to be happy, I'm happy. For most of happiness is because one's friends are happy: so that spiritually—whatever the damned Economists may say—we *do* live by taking in each other's washing.

So I'm very happy: thank you very much: and God be with you.

Yours

RUPERT

P.S. Do *not* come for your honeymoon to Canada. Some time soon I will write you a letter describing this country...Oh! oh!

To CATHLEEN NESBITT

Chateau Lake Louise
Laggan, Alta. Canada
2 September 1913

Liebes Kind (that's German for dear child),

I'm much pleased with myself, because I've just upset a whole hotel by missing a train. I came into the lounge about ten minutes after the train started and found all the porters and bell-boys and room-maids standing there with my rugs and coats and screaming, and they all said 'My God, you've missed the train!' and *I* said 'Then I'll take the next one', and they fainted with wrath and dismay. The next one is twelve hours on, so I just sit here, and write some of the letters I ought to have been writing these last ten days.

Lord, Lord, how one's life (if one's a wanderer) goes in ups and downs. I've been 'down' for a week and a half—submerged—but oh! very happy. Just lounging and staring at the lake and the mountains and the snow. It is the most beautiful place in the world. Just sheer beauty. So I eat and chatter and roam and look. Occasionally *one within me* says 'Rupert, you ought to be writing an article for the Westminster!' or 'Rupert! Kathleen (for I've an American conscience) hasn't had a letter from you for God-knows-how-long.'

And I say a line from Anacreon which signifies that nothing matters, and that I shall continue to sleep.

So I've written to nobody (not to you, and therefore, *a fortiori*, to nobody else) and not a line or a word of prose or verse has flowed from my pen. I am just one of the idle rich. Tra! la!

Oh, and while I've been doing this, you're probably sweating away in a hot and stupid London rehearsing a not very clever play (for Calthrop's[1] a bit of a fool, you know, at bottom) and generally plunging yourself in the hurly-burly of life. Ma pauvre enfant—(is that right?) I demand that you write and tell me all about it, or rather that you have written, and that I find it in Vancouver, where my letters for ever so long are waiting. And especially about Mr Shaw's new effort. I've *nothing* to tell you, except that the mountains are...and the lake is...and the snow and the trees are...but it would take me weeks to get out what they are, and I haven't time, for I want this letter to go today or tomorrow. Suffice it that they

---

[1] Dion Clayton Calthrop, artist, novelist and playwright.

are wonderful. Did I tell you that I spent a day in an Indian reservation when I was coming through here! I had a letter to the agent—they always have an agent, a white man, to look after the Indians. The reservation is about 15 miles by 8, and contains 600 Indians. The agent was a queer restless fellow called Waddy, who had been all over the world, served in South Africa, etc. When he was talking to the Indians—he had to do it through one of them who knew English, for most didn't—he said 'Ask him, did he buy that yesterday...' So I shouted, 'You're Irish': and he was. 'Ask him did he'...funny nation the Irish. This one was typical of you all, restless, lively and without humour, and nice.

Oh, but the Indians. They were so fine looking, and so jolly. They kept coming into the store-office to ask for things—the agents are father mother aunt priest doctor lawyer M.P. housemaid and God to the Indians in their charge. An Indian in a blanket and fur and gaudy trimmings would sidle into the room. Then for ten minutes he would stand silent. You must never hurry an Indian. Then he takes the pipe out of his mouth, says 'Um' and puts it back again. Five minutes pass. Then he looks at the ceiling, and says: '...Um...Salt. Um.'

The Agent. 'Is it more Epsom's Fruit Salts y'r wanting?'
Indian (*nods*).
Agent. 'But ye had som th'ither day—'
Indian (*blank*).
Agent. 'Is y'r stomach onaisy?'
Indian (*nods*).
Agent (*getting up, taking jar, pouring out some salts into paper, and wrapping them up*). 'There you are.'
Indian (*secretes them in some pouch, without a word*).
Agent sits down again.
Indian stands for ten minutes silent and immobile.
Indian (*suddenly*) '...Um...'
Exit slowly.
Enter 2nd Indian, cautiously.

(*da capo*)

But they're far nicer than the other inhabitants of this continent.

This is a stupid letter. What I want to do is to write you letters as follows

(1) on Good
(2)   „

(3)   ,,
(4) on Truth
(5) on Love
(6)   ,,
(7) on Dramatic Art
(8) why all modern actors and actresses are so bloody bad.
(9) why you may be some good, if you're carefully educated
(10) what you're like—
(11) what I'm like.
(12) what Life's like.

There's 12 letters. I wonder if I shall ever write them.

Anyway, from Vancouver (which I'm nearing) I'll write again, better.

For the present, my lovely child, Good be with you.

Your

RUPERT

To MARCHESA CAPPONI   *Vancouver Hotel*
Vancouver, B.C.
Thursday afternoon
[4 September 1913]

Κορίδιον μου[1]

I write on the paper you gave me, and by me is the envelope we directed, in the woods.

Field was a Failure. It rained—God! how it rained. I couldn't get to the Emerald Lake without getting drenched. And I knew if I did get there I should see a view of about one hundred yards of pine, and then clouds for ever. So I boldly took the midday train (which was of course some two hours and a half late)—and here I uneventfully am. It rained the whole way.

*   *   *

I was lonely after you'd gone. I turned straight and climbed to Lake Agnes, and there sat and looked at the valley down which your train had vanished. After a bit seven females rushed up and said 'We have seen a bear. Will you protect us back to the Hotel S?' I replied 'I want to be alone. There are already too many females in the world. Go. And I hope you meet the bear.' They went. And

---

[1] i.e. my little girl.

I could not see them in the hotel that evening. I suppose they did meet the Bear. Elsa and I were lonely, and tried to comfort each other.

In the train a lady from Chicago gave me some peanuts and said she supposed I should have to get back to England in time for the restarting of school. So I blessed her for thinking me under twenty, and wept.

I was afflicted by inspiration all yesterday in the train. Sehr peinlich. For I had ideas for seven poems and was too tired to write any. Now, I am waiting for my big luggage to appear. When it does, I shall have a bath, and change. I pass the odd few minutes in writing thus dully to you. There are only two chairs in my room. I am sitting on one. I wish you were sitting on the other.

I was greeted here by a letter of last Thursday from Ewald, asking me to lunch. *Der Arme.* He has vanished now.

At Field an Eastward train came in, labelled—Minneapolis and St Paul... When no one was looking I stole behind and affixed a tiny kiss to the rear buffer. Did it get to you? I feared it might fall off.

Love to Stanley.

Be happy: Rest

RUPERT

To EDWARD MARSH   *Hotel Vancouver*
Vancouver, B.C.
6 September 1913

Dear Eddie,

I 'blew in' here yesterday, & found about nine letters from you. One of them demanded an answer by Sept. 6th as you were bound for Spain then. Well, you can't have your answer. I hadn't enough money to telegraph. Glückliche Reise, all the same. It's a better journey than mine.

You have done me great wrong. Why the Devil weren't you taught American as well as French & Greek? 'You bet your' is a sentence.[1] Your nothing. Neither boots, nor buttons, nor bottom, nor balls, nor hopes of beatitude. Just 'You bet your'. I don't know why. But it's so.

And now my reputation's for ever gone. Hell!

[1] E.M. had added 'boots' in an article for the *Westminster Gazette*.

But I'm glad you like the articles. I think they're pretty bad. But they have some jokes.

As I write, I suppose you're in Paris. Oh Eddie, did you do all I said about the statuette? I hope so. But there's one thing—I *think* I never paid Gill. I'm horror-stricken. He may be dead of starvation. Will you find out as soon as you return? And pay him, if I didn't? Then I'll repay you, if you let me know. It's either £10 or £10. 10s. 0d.

As for my poems. I know I've only sent three (for you've got, somewhere, 'The way that lovers use is this...' that might go in somewhere). But damn it, what's the good of a friend if he can't sit down & write off a few poems for one at a pinch? That's what I count on your doing, if the editors press.

By the way, I'd like a few to go to the Nation, if there's a superfluity. Squire mustn't have *too* many. I've a lot half way through, to be finished when I have leisure. I *ought* to have done them in the Rockies. But I had an Episode with a Widow, instead. My unfinished ones aren't much good, except one or two. I contemplate two short Sonnet Sequences (one including *Aeterna Corpora*). One or both might grace the Cooperative Concord or whatever its last name is. (I think it's silly changing it from Gallows Garland.)

By the way, you seem to be a great comfort to my mamma, as my literary executor. So if she worries you, be sustained by the thought of the good you're doing.

By the time this gets you, I shall probably be half-way across the Pacific, never to return. If I *do* get back to America, I've to stay. For Cathleen's coming out in January at latest. So Europe will not have the pleasure of my company for a long long time.

Give my greetings to Jim Barnes, if you don't think he'll be offended at such effusiveness from a comparative stranger.

There is no news. Vancouver is a wicked city. And I am very lazy. The weather is intermittently good. God be with you.

Thy loving grandpapa
RUPERT

The only bright thing I've done for two months, is to write a letter to my last but one, beginning 'Dear Penultima...'. Make her sit up, damn her eyes. Pretty smart—what?

To EDWARD MARSH   *Hotel Vancouver*
                                                Vancouver, B.C.
                                                8 September [*1913*]

Isn't it extraordinary—after the months that have been separating
us—I got your letter of August 26th just now; from the bed of pain.[1]
Isn't ligature—or is it ligament?—a lovely word?

> 'Is it prudent? is it Pure?
>   To go & break a ligature?'
> 'With lissom ligament
>   My lovely one she went
>   And trod the street
>   On quiet feet'—
> 'Torn, like a ligament, his random mind'...

Oh, it sets one singing.

But this is to say that I've heard nothing from Cathleen about my
play. It would be heaven if she did it—Drinkwater has a copy.
James B. Strachey has a copy. Granville Barker has a copy. And
I *thought* I sent you a copy with those photographs.

I hate you lavishing all your mad aunt's money on those artists.
Don't forget those woodcuts of Gwen's you were going to buy.
One day instead of buying pictures with these dubious legacies you
must give a Show (something such as I'm going to give for my
Wedding, on the Grantchester lawn), with words by me & music by
Denis & dancing by Clothilde & acting by Cathleen & costumes by
Cookham.[2]

I'm really writing because I'm so charmed by the picture of you
in bed & Geoffrey binding you up & Wilfrid smoothing your brow
& giving you chloroform, that I sat in this lounge & laughed till
Sir Gilbert Parker looked askance at me. What a nice lot you are in
England!

What fun though, if both Wilfrid & Cathleen join me in these
parts in the autumn. How denuded England will be! And how rich
I! I think Cathleen'd better learn up *Womenkind*. And then in
every town I'd be interviewed, Wilfrid'd read, her portrait'd come
in the papers, & then, in the evening, she'd act *Lithuania* & *Womenkind*. And next day we'd share out the profits. Will you be advertising agent & courier?—

'My paper warns me to conclude.'   RUPERT

[1] E.M. had sprained his ankle, on account of which he became my first private
patient (see *A Number of People*, 1939, p. 294).   [2] Stanley Spencer.

To MRS BROOKE   *Vancouver Hotel, Vancouver*
—and the boat to Victoria
8 September 1913

Dear Mother,

A whole heap of stuff awaited me in Vancouver, and another letter has come since. Somehow, I only seem to be eleven or twelve days from you. I'm very glad you like the W.G. articles. They're not always very well written, but I think they're the sort of stuff that ought to interest an intelligent W.G. reader more than the ordinary travel stuff one sees. I hope they won't annoy people over this side. Canadians and Americans are so touchy. But it's absurd to ladle out indiscriminate praise, as most people do.

*   *   *

I had several introductions in Vancouver, and only four days. It's a great place, rather different from the rest of Canada. More oriental. The country and harbour are rather beautiful with great violet mountains all round, snow-peaks in the distance. They interviewed me and put (as usual) a quite inaccurate report of it in the paper, saying I'd come here to investigate the Japanese question. In consequence about five people rang me up every morning at 8 o'clock (British Columbians get up an hour earlier than I) to say they wanted to wait on me and give me their views. Out here they always have telephones in the bedrooms. One old sea captain came miles to tell me that the Japanese—and every other—trouble was due to the fact that British Columbia had neglected the teaching of the Gospels on the land question. He wasn't so far out in some respects.

*   *   *

B. Columbia returns 39 Conservatives and 2 Socialists to a local house of 41 members. The Conservative majority was got by turning the population of every doubtful constituency out to build roads for high wages at the public expense for six months before the elections. McBride, who's now in England, the premier of B.C., had practically no money when he entered politics a few years ago; and now he is a millionaire. People have done the same all over Canada.

I'm going on to Victoria, on Vancouver Island, for two days, then to Seattle by water, then to San Francisco by train down along by the American Rockies.

*   *   *

I'll be about there for some time. I gather there's a lot to be learnt in California. Vancouver is full of Chinese and Japanese and Hindus. The Hindus wear their turbans. There is a lot of feeling against all the Orientals. They come in and underbid the white labour, and get rich and buy land. Some trades they've taken over altogether. When British Columbia, California, and Australia get working together against Japan, there'll be trouble out here. They have anti-yellow riots occasionally.

I shall be rather glad to get down into the States again. Canada is a most horribly individualistic place, with no one thinking of anything except the amount of money they can make, by any means, in the shortest time. The States are pretty bad: but they do have a few people trying to do some good, or to do good work or follow ideas for their own sake. The University'll be meeting again when I get down to 'Frisco: and I believe they are rather an interesting lot.

                    *   *   *
                              With love
                                   RUPERT

To SYBIL PYE   [Postcard]
                              [*Postmark: Victoria, B.C.*
                                 12 September 1913]

You think B.C. means before Christ. But it doesn't.

I'm sitting, wildly surmising,[1] on the edge of the Pacific, gazing at mountains which are changing colour every two minutes in the most surprising way. Nature here is half Japanese.

I had a letter from you the other day. It *did* get to me, by a sort of accident.

Southward now.   RUPERT

To RUSSELL LOINES   *14 September 1913*
'Shasta Limited'   (Southern Pacific
                    Ogden & Shasta Routes)

Dear Loines,

Your letter to Winnipeg finally reached me in Vancouver. Thence I've started South, & am now rushing in the utmost luxury through Washington (a dry State, on Sundays anyhow, damn it)—*en route* for 'Frisco.   *   *   *

----
[1] A reference to Keats, Sonnet xi.

I'm glad, in a way, to be out of Canada. Theoretically, I hold that Life is more important than Art, that intellectual snobbery is the worst kind, etc. etc. But in practice I do like occasionally seeing people who have heard of, say, Shakespere before, even though we don't discuss it. And the U.S., even where they're ghastly vulgar (as often), are apt to show some—not very healthy—vitality & liveliness. The Canadian is *sehr steif*, as my German friends say of me. Well, I guess the Westminster has started printing my insults now: & you'll never speak to me again. They held it up for some time, but my mother writes that she has had proofs, now. Don't take anything personally. I may have quoted your remarks. I forget. But I probably put them in other people's mouths. It's all a composition.

I'm sorry you think my Muse less at home with women than with fish. For I write more about the former. And now that I've got on to plays, I'm advised that women characters present less difficulty in the staging than fish. But perhaps the reason is that I've met nicer fish than women, on the whole. I'm very glad you like W. W. Gibson. I hear there's some idea of him crossing the Atlantic to give a few readings of his poetry—if he can get guarantees. (He's quite penniless.) If so, I'll tell him to get you to take him up that great building & show him the Kingdoms of the World, shall I? He's very nice. And, by the way, now the *Blue Review* has stopped, he, I, Lascelles Abercrombie, & Drinkwater, are going to bring out our poetry together in a quarterly publication, beginning January. THE event of the 20th Century.

Say, do you know anything of Goldie [Lowes Dickinson]? I keep watching out for him on this coast. I suppose he'll have to get back to England across here? If you know anything of his movements, *do* let me know. I'd like to intercept him.

Love to all.

In the immediate future I'll be in San Francisco. After that I don't know.   Yours

                          RUPERT BROOKE

To MARCHESA CAPPONI   *San Francisco*
                                          17 September [*1913*]

I don't know what I do wrong. Perhaps it's because I always open my mouth to scream, and that makes me choke, and *that* makes my eyes sore. . .or perhaps the water here is bad—but my eyes always look very red afterwards, and I feel all of a tremble. You'll have gathered that I've just been washing my eyes in a basin of cold water, and so am driven to think of you...

I found your letter here; and loved it, though it was so bad. (It's funny that women can't write letters.) There is so much of you that doesn't get into a letter (and a lot that does). I was lonely (and *very* hot—why did you all say California was cool?) the first day or two. I nearly wired for you. (Dash it all. I need you as much as S—— does, now he's got other people. If his mind isn't well yet; my soul isn't.)

But now I've found some kind University people so I crawl along.

I love you for two reasons. Or rather—since one does not love for reasons—I have two excuses for loving you. And they are good ones, however much you deny the first or avow the second. One is that, do what you will, you're a woman. O Rarity! I hate these men-women. And can admire only a few men, the fine ones. And women do not make fine men.

The other is that you're good. There are only two things in the world I think beautiful. One is a woman's head and body, and the other is goodness. I don't really care a damn for mountains or poetry or anything else. Only those two. And I cry when I think of them. And in you—I adore you and them in you. And I want to bathe my eyes in your beauty (instead of the basin here): and I want to bury my face in your goodness and sleep and sleep. Is this nonsense?

I like California, the people are kindly, the women are lovely, and the scenery (*outside* the city) is romantic. This will still be my address for a letter.

But I guess I shall be off to the South Seas.

For that note-book which contained 2 months' notes on my travels, and unfinished sonnets, and all sorts of wealth I lost it in British Columbia—yessir, isn't it *too* bloody. I've been prostrated with grief ever since. And God knows how I shall get through my articles on Canada.

So I doubt if I shall be able to start back to Europe in the beginning of January. What's to be done?

I must see you. One day I will send you a poem—for I feel that one day (if God spares me) I may finish one. A short one anyhow. But not for some months. It is very dreadful to be red...I hope you are resting and lovely and happy—

RUPERT

To CATHLEEN NESBITT   *Mount Tamalpais, near 'Frisco*
(rhymes with nice, ice, or fice)
27? September [1913]
night

Dear loveliness,

When I got to San Francisco (the lights of which I see shining eight miles away, far down) I found a letter from you, written just before the *première*, saying how bad you were going to be. They don't go in for English papers much here, and the only ones I saw thought Shaw important enough to exclude mention of Calthrop (not indefinitely); except the *Sketch*, I think, which had an abominable caricature of you. But several private letters inform me that you were, of course, perfectly bewitching, and gave a stupid part more beauty than it merited. I can imagine you, oh most diffident and most lovely of ladies. It's really a very good idea. I have had plots for several plays which required that the audience should know an immense deal beforehand. I had abandoned them as hopeless. But now I see that all that is necessary is to get Cathleen to come forward beforehand and say 'Dear audience, in order to understand this play you must know that (a) four hundred years before the curtain rises the economic condition of Jutland was remarkable in, roughly, the following seventeen ways (i) the marginal value of cornland...' and so on for an hour. And they'll listen enraptured. And no wonder. I know that voice. And that ridiculously unmeaning (un-aesthetic-ally-meaning, I mean) smile. Absurd. What's a smile? It is absurd, and offensive to one's human dignity, to suppose that a Stores Catalogue read by Cathleen is better than Keats read by anyone else—

'But I'm in San Francisco
And oh, 'tis true, 'tis true!' (misquotation).[1]

Oct. 7?

So far I had got, and let things slide, miserably. You know how one does? One puts off and off writing. And meanwhile I've had a letter from you, written shortly after the first night: and yesterday evening, just in time, a telegram. For I start today—in an hour—on the good ship Sierra, for Honolulu. I'm going to write you a big long letter from the boat. It ought to get you in about a fortnight. Meanwhile, my child, I desire that you be good and happy. Your telegram is really quite extraordinarily nice. You can't think how it cheers me.

[1] From A. E. Housman's 'When I was one-and-twenty' (*A Shropshire Lad*).

I was like you, blank a bit, and then, like you, woken to the realities of life. You by the peasant and wife and children in the train after your first night: I by the news that my two greatest friends had had their first baby—the Cornfords, I think you've not met them. It is good to be brought back to reality, things that matter. (It's funny you're so like me.)

* * *

Your

RUPERT

To EDWARD MARSH

San Francisco
1 October [*1913*]

My dear,

A postcard from you, via England & Vancouver, arrived yesterday. It displayed a divine place called Tarragona—far lovelier than these gaudy sky-scrapers. How perfectly imbecile I am to wander over here, when Europe is infinitely more romantic! I began to realize it last week. I've gone soft through loneliness. I tossed up—back to England? or out to the South Seas? The latter prevailed: so I leave for Honolulu on Tuesday. Then Samoa, Fiji, Tahiti, and a resting-place at the bottom of the Pacific, all among the gay fish & lovely submarine flowers. Will you all come, like the Titanic widows, & drop some wax flowers, a Bible, & a tear or two, on the spot where I'm reputed to have gone down? I hope so.

You may continue writing to me. Letters will reach me occasionally, I suppose. And you may figure me in the centre of a Gauguin picture, nakedly riding a squat horse into white surf.

I forgot to comment, didn't I?, on your meeting old Schick. I was frightfully excited. He has been one of my most intimate friends for years. Dear, dear, how it brings back the old Munich days. I was frequently in his drawing room (my first German jest was one about Schick-saal), flirting with Wilhelmina, or whoever she was—his daughter—(isn't the bitterest part of it that one forgets their names?). He is rather a silly old loon, but pleasant, in some dreadful way.

I've had a letter from Naomi. (I always supposed she was called Nellie. Naomi—good God!) She writes—she is Miss Royde-Smith, by the way—that Spender is away, that they won't begin printing me till October at least,[1] & that they never have more than six in

---

[1] 'Letters from America' in the *Westminster Gazette*. Thirteen were published, October 1913 to July 1914.

a series. Isn't it beastly? I supposed I was going on once a week for months & years. I could read me once a week for ever, couldn't you? She holds out a faint hope of a second series after January.

I shall go on writing them: & I shall send them you. So if & when she wants them she can ask you (or rather *they* can, for I suppose Spender will see to it). If they finally don't want them, Jack Squire or somebody might. Lots of them will make good single articles. And I want money.

I sent Wilfrid a sonnet.

Eddie, they have atttacked us in *Punch*. Who was it? Not poor Arthur [Eckersley]? I thought it intensely feeble—except for the joke about Ezra. Perhaps it's a good advertisement. And one gets immortality, as England knows it, on a level with politicians, music-hall artistes, & publicists. But oh—

* * *

California is nice, & the Californians a friendly bunch. There's a sort of goldenness about 'Frisco & the neighbourhood. It hangs in the air, & about the people. Everyone is very cheery & cordial & simple. They are rather a nation apart, different from the rest of the States. Much more like the English. As everywhere in this extraordinary country, I am welcomed with open arms when I say I know Masefield & Goldie! It's very queer. I can't for the life of me help moving about like a metropolitan among rustics, or an Athenian in Thrace. Their wide-mouthed awe at England is so touching—they really are merely a colony of ours still. That they should be speaking to a man who knows Lowes Dickinson, who has met Galsworthy, who once saw Belloc plain!... What should we feel if we could speak with an *habitué* of the theatre at Athens, Fifth Century, or with Mine Host of the Mermaid? All that they have with me, the dears! Yet I don't know why I write this from California: the one place that *has* a literature & tradition of its own, to some extent.

Which reminds me. Who do you think I'm going to meet at dinner (probably) on Monday? Mr & Mrs Winston Churchill. Yessir. Will you be there? I have a faint hope... Won't it be fun?

And on Tuesday—the Pacific.

I'll write thence—but God knows when it'll get to you.

Farewell—ever

RUPERT

To CATHLEEN NESBITT   *S.S. 'Sierra'*
                                    Sunday, 12 October [*1913*]
                          The Pacific
My very dear,

   I scribbled a few lines to you just before I started. But I gave the
letter to a frightful rough-neck who was hanging about the wharf—
we were just off—so he may have pouched the stamp and destroyed
the letter.

   The Pacific has been very pacific. God be thanked! So I've had
a pleasant voyage. Three passionate Pacific women cast lustrous eyes
towards me: but with a dim remembrance of the fates of Conrad
characters who succumbed to such advances, I evade them. I pass
my hand wearily through my long hair: and say 'Is not the soul of
Maurya a glimmering wing in the moth-hour?' or words to that
effect. The Celtic method is not understood in this part of the world.
We are an extraordinary mixture of races. Imagine me, I pray you,
walking up and down the deck arm in arm with (1) a Russian Jew
who emigrated to New York thirty years ago and is now (I fancy)
dying of consumption, (2) a Bavarian priest, one of three such who
have drifted, Heaven knows how, into these seas, (3) a youth whose
ancestry is in these proportions 1/4 American (Danish), 3/8 Hawaian,
3/8 Southern Chinese. (Rather a good mixture, for looks. But the
poor devil has too many bloods fighting in him to be happy.)
There's a crowd of Hawaian and Hawaian × Chinese boys on board,
and in the evening they sit in a row and one strums the piano, and
the others thumb their little semi-mandolins, and all sing their
strange sad Hawaian songs, which are all vowels. And the moon
shines out on queer Pacific waters, and there are banks and banks of
strangely coloured clouds, and flying-fish flicker along the waves,
and the stars are very near.

   And you, my dear—I suppose you're nightly making lovely
a rather dull part in a stupid performance.

   I wish you were here. Wouldn't you like to join me in surf-riding
on the best surf-beach in the world tomorrow?

   But I've your telegram and your letter. 'God Bless you Dear
Heart Cathleen'—just six words, and in the handwriting of that
shameless hussy at the 'Frisco Western Union. Funny it should be
so very moving. But it is. It's queer, too, that it should have, in
many ways, so much more power than a letter, although a letter is in
your own ridiculous handwriting, and reaches me just as it left you.

I suppose it's this silly business of time. The letter comes three weeks old. One thinks 'September 8. What was I doing then? I was at the last place but six—or seven—I can't just remember. And *she*—it's three weeks ago. She may be dead now.' But a cablegram or a night letter is in the same plane as one's present existence. And one can think 'Just six hours ago, just as I was breakfasting, Cathleen was thinking "Dear Heart".'

And your letter. My dear, my dear, I wonder if you know how very pleasant your letters are, even when they're sad. They're so very you. Who else would have picked out all those bits from Francis Thompson, and all the best bits? (Several I didn't know, or had forgotten.) Why is it you always ridiculously know what is good in poetry? I know why it is. But I will not tell you.

* * *

It's very easy writing to you. Because you're wise and good and one trusts you, and you understand. Only it's so damned hard ever communicating with another human being.

* * *

And yet, oh loveliest fool in the world, you're wise. And you wrote wise things to me. For it is true, what you said about the evil of a woman gratifying her instinct of kindness by ways that may wake other things in the man—the danger of it, anyway. But how's she to know, poor lady, till she gets wise in the ways of the world? It's a bad business. I told you I was in love with a girl for three or four years, and then she got tired of it—of the little she'd ever found in it? Once, towards the grey end of that—I'd sort of put my love away, numbed it, for I saw things were going ill. But I was desolate and rather hungry. And one day—we were staying in the same house —we'd arranged to get up *very* early, and go out and pick mushrooms together in the summer dew, for breakfast (oh youth! youth!)— I crept along, having woken and being unable to sleep another hour, to her room, some little while before dawn. She was sleeping. I knelt down by her and kissed her forehead to wake her, and put my head on her hand; and she woke, and felt fond of me I suppose, and pulled my head against her heart and held me a minute. And I thought I had found heaven. And all my love woke worse than ever. But she didn't mean anything, you know. Only she felt fond of me. But it made the breaking about nine hundred times harder; we both paid a lot for it, I most. Luckily, that was all we had to break. For she was too wise, and something in her heart too strong, for her to give herself to me, because she loved and pitied me in that way; nor did I love her little enough to want it given—in that way. Else it would have been a thousand times worse: as I know from later things.

But I put it—the episode—into a sonnet, in a series about imaginary people...At least, the sonnet's not done yet. But it ends with this—only it'll be changed and better (I hope)

> 'Child, you should not have done't! for the poor gain
> Of that short moment's soon forgot delight
> And sleepy mother-comfort. Could you know
> How easily Love comes laughing from the night
> With eyes of hope! And love that's wakened so,
> Takes all too long to lay asleep again.'[1]

(Clumsy, clumsy!) But it *does* take all too long, my dear. It's not worth it. Yet, there was another time when I was in trouble, and she gave me strength and calm. One *can* help. I suppose a woman has to judge by the particular case. But I think she ought always to go a little less far than she thinks she can, unless she knows men *very* well. For men catch fire quicker than women, though they may not burn so long. Lady, is it not true?

I will tell you a secret, two secrets. They are very important ones. One is this, a man is a child. The other is, a woman is a child. The second you know: but the first takes learning. I knew the first long ago, but have learnt the second, hardly. And each (but especially the man) is a child in this way, that he doesn't know what is good for himself. It's so hard to learn that—that one must treat men and women as children, who do not know what is good for them, but cry and whimper for things—and that one must give or withhold without regard to their cries. I suppose it's harder for woman to learn, than for man. For a woman tends naturally to think a man a responsible being, and also has a craving to hush crying. But she's also told by nature how to manage children, if she'll but listen. That's what she's for. Those women that fail, betray their final trust. That is the final rule of life, the best one ever made. 'Whoso shall offend one of these little ones'...remembering that all of the eight hundred millions on earth, except oneself, are the little ones.

My dear, we loved well, didn't we? The loveliness without and within you—I loved it so, those months. Oh child, what great

[1] 'A Memory', *1914 and Other Poems*, p. 32.

things you have given me! My heart and my belief were so deadened, before I found you. I thought there couldn't be people like you in the world. And then you showed me. I wish I could pay you back, sometimes. You give great riches.

Now we're apart, with the memory of those months, and each finds the image of the other rather faint with the interval of time and distance. But it won't be long before we see each other's dim faces again—two months, perhaps, from the time you get this letter. Then we'll be able to talk together, and find out what's to be done and what we want, and what the world's like. It's not very long to wait. Meanwhile—there's that to sustain us, the memory that certain things were, though we can't just remember how it was so. It's like the mountains 'back of' the coast here. (I write in the Hawaian islands). Above two thousand feet or so, they're shrouded by cloud, and one thinks that they are not much higher. But about once a day the clouds lift a little and one sees the great peaks. And the rest of the day—one takes it on trust that they are there, remembering.

I would like to make a litany of all the things that bind me to the memory of holiness—of peaks. It would run—'The Chilterns—Hampton Court—Hello Ragtime—Raymond Buildings' and a few more names. And it would begin and end with 'Cathleen'. It's a funny sort of mixed chain to hang on to heaven by: but very human. Repeat it, when you want to know values clearly.

Those are the things that hold one. For those reasons I can't ever accept smaller things. Isn't it so? Aren't we bound to be faithful to each other, whatever happens? I mean, 'though I marry elsewhere, and marry often', as they say in *The Importance of Being Earnest*, I shall be true to you, because I can't, now, do less than the fine things. Do you think this all nonsense, dear child? Be forgiving to my awkward attempts to express myself. I demand forgiveness, as one human from another. We're all in the same difficulty, this inability to express onself decently without sham or awkwardness or sentimentality.

I write just a few feet from a wonderful blue and green sea. I'm sitting under a busy 'Hau-Tree' (pronounced 'How'). In the sea are two or three Hawaian women wading and swimming for sea-weed, in sadly diaphanous garments. Occasionally a few Japanese wander past in neat kimonos. It is very hot.

You are very far away. I hope that all is well with you. May all the blessings of whatever gods there be rest on you, and may my prayers be always about you to shield you. I pray you, love good and keep away from the evil things of the world, for my sake and for your sake and for our sake. Bless you.

Your lover

RUPERT

To RUSSELL LOINES

Moana Hotel, Honolulu
15 or 20 October or so [*1913*]

Dear Loines,

I didn't write to you on board ship, as I meant. Oh dear, the essays & poems & plays & letters that were to be written on that boat! But the sea always makes me very stupid. I've got over the stage of qualms & headaches, especially on this nice Pacific. But I sleep fourteen hours & gaze vacuously at the sea for ten, quite well & as intelligent as—well, as if I were a Fellow of some other College, not King's. It's due partly to the monotony of the scenery & the motion, but mostly—since this is a realistic age—I think, to *constipation*. However, I hardly used my pen once; so I make amends now I've got my land-legs again.

I hope you got my cheque, & that you're able to feed your starving family again. It was very good of you to send the money so promptly & so effectually. I spend it riotously on picture post-cards of highly-coloured fish, with which the water is full, & on pine-apples, which can be got here for ten cents each, perfect ones.

I was disappointed by your news of Goldie. I'd got an *idée fixe* that I was bound to meet him somewhere & when on my peregrinations, & I'd quite figured it out that I was going, in the surf here, one day, to see a small slightly bald head pop out of the foam near me, & hear a persuasive Kingsy, Modernly Symposiac[1] voice say to a mildly surprised brown Kanaka—you imagine the *pince-nez* being adjusted meanwhile—'I think yours is a *very* interesting point of view'...alas, it may not be. But I fancy you'll see him before I do —in which case, give him my love. For I work out that I won't be in California again till January, so I shan't blow in to New York till at least February. That means that I shall lose the chance of crossing with you, if you stick to your present plans: which is a nuisance—for me. It would be *too* ridiculous if we missed both in America & in England. If you get to London, before I see you, go to the Poetry Bookshop, in Devonshire Street, & enquire for Gibson, when he'll

[1] A reference to Lowes Dickinson's *A Modern Symposium*, 1906.

be in London, & get hold of him. I'll tell him to look out for you. He's the most simple & delightful of people: & perhaps you'll be able to advise him where to go in America, & see if he's fallen into good hands. You'll find him entirely charming.

*   *   *

Both the Wells & Seward have been extraordinarily kind to me. The former at least I shall see again.

Love to all

RUPERT BROOKE

To HAROLD MONRO   *Honolulu*
                                     October the latter half, 1913
My dear Harold,

I *cannot* write when I'm travelling. This is all my harvest for months: except one sonnet I sent to Wilfrid, I guess you'd better defer me till March. If not, do what you like with these. I will send a few more to Eddie from Samoa—whither I'm just starting. But they'll barely reach him before December. If you don't use these, or if there are some of them you don't use, you can hand them over to him. *The Way that Lovers Use* is old & he *may* have planted it somewhere. Find out from him. God be with you.

Hastily

R. B.

To CATHLEEN NESBITT   *28 October* [*1913*]
                              The Pacific
                          about 17° North
                      and 162° West of Greenwich
My Darling,

Having lain in my bunk writing sonnets an hour or two, I just wandered up, and in the saloon I found a man and woman playing duets, hard—members of your profession I fancy, a touring company, she with a back as broad as it's long. And *that's* what you'll come to, my dear, second lady in a company wandering the Pacific, as broad as you're long, and crowned with bright yellow hair. And what were they playing? Why 'Hello Ragtime', in a piano score, right through! I retired to my bunk here again, in confusion and tears.

How those foolish melodies—for we had them all, from *Military Mary Ann*, up—or down—to *Dixie*—bite at one's heart! What does it all mean? There's such a glow over it—over such an immediate past.   *   *   *

The beginning of November.

The sea made me stupider and stupider: and I found I couldn't get a letter to you till God knows when. So I put off writing till I should get on land. And here I am in Samoa: I left the *Ventura*, my boat, at Pango-Pango, which is the port in the American island of this group. The loveliest little harbour in the world: great hills covered with thick forests all round, and a little lake of blue in the middle, and a queer air of tropics over all, and the loveliest people in coloured loin cloths trotting round. I went a walk under the coco-nut palms, with a naked baby of five or six holding each hand (one said his name was *Fred*), and several more twining round my ankles. I had a coco-nut—for it was hot—in the house of a white trader who had married a native. Have you ever sent a chocolate-coloured youth up an immense almost perpendicular coco-nut palm to pick a baby coco-nut, and then drunk the milk? It is the most refreshing thing in the world, on such an occasion.

In the evening, the wharf was covered with torches, lamps, and a mass of Samoans, all with some 'curios' or other on little stalls. The sailors and passengers from the ship wandered among them buying or bartering. The Samoans were rather indifferent about money, but would give anything they had for old clothes. Great bronze men, with gilded hair, and godlike limbs lay about on the grass, while their women held up pieces of 'kapa'—which is bark beaten into a stiff cloth, and covered with a brown pattern—and grinned and beckoned and gesticulated. And the whole was lit up by these flaring lights against the tropical nights and the palms and stars, so that it looked like a Rembrandt picture—you know those things where there's a light on the immediate figures and faces, and the rest are in inky darkness? After dinner six girls and six men came on board and performed a *siva-siva* on deck, before the astonished eyes of the American and Australian passengers. A *siva-siva*, my dear, is a Dance. But not what you (poor stepper of hideous American stuff) or I or M. Nijinsky mean by dancing. Nearer M. Nijinsky's, but far even from him. Much of it I could not understand; some

I felt it my duty, as an English gentleman, not to. Both girls and men were naked to the waist, and glistening with coco-nut palm oil. The dancing was on a background of high nasal wailing—which seemed to be telling a story—hand-clapping, and convulsive rhythmic movements of the body. This was carried on sitting, to begin with; but at the exciting moments they leapt to their feet and careered jerkily around. Their eyeballs stared and they indulged in strange pantomime. The men frequently pretended to be animals, leaping about on all fours. One of them took it into his head to be a dog, at one moment. Approaching the chief woman performer with howls and barking, he threw up his hind leg and went through the motions of a dog who throws up his leg against a wall, she being the wall. That was a humorous episode. Most of it consisted of the women facing each other, in a crouching position, wailing rhythmically, and making very slight rhythmic motions with their hands, feet and thighs. As the crisis approached, the movement grew slighter, and in proportion, more exciting. Which is queer. It was all very thrilling and tropical and savage. I felt strange ancient raucous jungle cries awaking within me... The dancers vanished, after half an hour, precipitately into the darkness. The *Ventura* went on to Sydney. I poked round and found a tiny schooner that was coming across to Apia—whence I write—the largest town in these islands, 80 miles from Pango, and on another island. The schooner started at midnight. She was about seventy feet long and took, that night, 80 passengers—mostly natives. The journey lasted twelve hours. I slept 'on deck', in the open, on four sugar casks. Sugar-casks are a hard bed.

Good God! an English mail! The only one for a month from here. I continue from Fiji, whither I go next. My love to you. This is Samoa, by a full moon. You're in London, in a fog. Both are very wonderful. I love you. 'Be good to yourself' as we say in saying good-bye in America. Oh, my dear, I love you all the time.

RUPERT

P.S. I won a lottery on the boat for a Marconi letter via God-knows-where: and sent it you. I had to write it hurriedly. As you may have seen!   R.

To MRS BROOKE   *28 October 1913*

The Pacific

Dear Mother,

I'm off for the South, though just what I'm going to do, and where, I don't yet know. I shall probably get off at Samoa, and trust to luck. I find I probably can't get to Tahiti without going by New Zealand. I wonder if the Pember Reeves are there now. Tahiti's the place I'm keenest on seeing; I have introductions there, I want to see Stevenson's place, and I want to hunt up traces of Gauguin, the painter. But I'd like to take a look at Samoa, and Fiji, even, too.

I got a whole lot of mail on from San Francisco, at Honolulu, just before I started, yesterday, and one Westminster (with nothing of mine, yet). Honolulu itself is a dreadfully American place, just like any city in the States or Canada. But the people in the streets are interesting, and as soon as you get outside the city, the country is very fascinating for a stranger. It really *is* tropical in character: like some of the gardens and places at Cannes, on an immense scale. Great palms of all varieties, especially coco-nut ones; banana trees, immense fern-trees, great vines, a great deal of hibiscus, and other flowery trees. The climate is the same all the year round, and very even in heat, about as hot as a fairly hot July day in England. The evenings are generally cooler, but not chilly, very nice to sit out in. I lived out at Waikiki Beach, four–five miles from Honolulu (a tram-line): except for four days when I went over to the island of Kanai. That is one of the islands about seventy miles away, and I had an introduction to a man who owns a plantation and a great deal of land there: from a Professor of English in the University of Cali-fornia, who knows him. I stayed in his house and got taken round the place in motor-cars. One day I went with three white youths and two Hawaians a great expedition inland up a valley to some falls. We went as far as we could by car, and on for some hours on horse-back. No road for the horses; but a 'trail', which sometimes lay over great boulders, and kept crossing and recrossing a river, which was up to the horses' bellies. English horses couldn't stand it— they'd have broken their legs. But these were used to it. When we got to the water-fall, which was not very voluminous but very pretty and some two hundred feet high, we bathed in a pool, under the waterfall, and had lunch. The scenery was very wild and lovely, and I enjoyed the excursion very much, though I was extremely sore next day!

October 31st.

Over the equator today! The people on board, mostly Australians, got up a ceremony in honour of the event—King Neptune coming on board, and so on—with comic dressing up, and horse-play. It's not *very* hot, though the weather doesn't dispose one to *violent* activity. I get to Samoa on Sunday, have to find a boat across to the chief island of the group, and there I shall stay a little. I've an introduction there. It is where Stevenson lived, and is buried, so I shall go and pay my respects on his grave.

The sea is still very smooth. This afternoon a school of whales were spouting a little way ahead and to the left—nothing very exciting, just occasional little columns of foam. But anything that happens on a voyage is exciting.

November 2nd.

We get in at two this afternoon, and then I shall be able to post my letters. I find I can get a little boat across to the bigger island tonight. Yesterday evening I saw the Southern Cross for the first time! I enclose a few scraps of photographs. Some of them I got in Honolulu; they aren't much, but they give a good idea of the way things look there. The others are my own first-fruits. They were before I learnt how to use the camera properly. I know better now, so my others will be improvements on these out-of-focus things.

With love

RUPERT

To EDWARD MARSH   *Samoa*
                                              2? November 1913
Dear Eddie,

These to go to Wilfrid immediately. A few more are half out & shall follow somewhen. I am becoming indistinguishable from R. L. S., both in thinness, in literary style, & in dissociation from England. God have mercy on my soul!

I have crossed the Equator, & so am a Man at last. The rest of my life is to be spent in bartering cheap coloured handkerchiefs for priceless native tapestries, & gin for pearls.

To all those you may meet whom I know, my love, be they never so insignificant or so remote. For I have a great love for them all.

...   .

I hope the world is well. This is—but it's another world. I'll write, some day.   Yours barbarically

RUPERT

To EDWARD MARSH   *S.S. 'Torfua'*
                                                15? November 1913
Somewhere near Fiji

Dear Eddie,

I'm conscious I haven't written to you for a long time—though, indeed, my last letter was *posted* only a short time ago. When it, or when this, will get to you, God knows. About Christmas, I suppose, though it seems incredible. My *reason* tells me that you'll be slurring through London mud in a taxi, with a heavy drizzle falling, & a chilly dampness in the air, & the theatres glaring in the Strand, & crowds of white faces. But I can't help *thinking* of you trotting through crisp snow to a country church, holly-decorated, with little robins pecking crumbs all around, & the church-bells playing our brother Tennyson's *In Memoriam* brightly through the clear air. It may not be: it never has been—that picture-postcard Christmas. But I shall think of you so. You think of me in a loin-cloth, brown & wild, in the fair chocolate arms of a Tahitian beauty, reclining beneath a bread-fruit tree, on white sand, with the breakers roaring against the reefs a mile out, & strange brilliant fish darting through the pellucid hyaline of the sun-saturated sea. Oh, Eddie, it's all true about the South Seas! I get a little tired of it at moments, because I am just too old for Romance, & my soul is seared. But there it is: there it wonderfully is: heaven on earth, the ideal life, little work, dancing singing & eating, naked people of incredible loveliness, perfect manners, & immense kindliness, a divine tropic climate, & intoxicating beauty of scenery. I came aboard & left Samoa two days ago. Before that, I had been wandering, with an 'interpreter'— entirely genial & quite incapable of English—through Samoan villages. The last few days I stopped in one, where a big marriage feast was going on. I lived in a Samoan house (the coolest in the world) with a man & his wife, nine children, ranging from a proud beauty of 18 to a round object of 1 year, a dog, a cat, a proud hysterical hen, and a gaudy scarlet & green parrot, who roved the roof & beams with a wicked eye, choosing a place whence to shit, twice a day, with humorous precision, on my hat & clothes. The

Samoan girls have extraordinarily beautiful bodies, & walk like goddesses. They're a lovely brown colour, without any black, Polynesian admixture: their necks & shoulders would be the wild envy of any European beauty: & in carriage & face they remind me continually & vividly of my incomparable heartless & ever-loved Clotilde. Fancy moving amongst a tribe of Clotildes! Can't you imagine how shattered & fragmentary a heart I'm bearing away to Fiji & Tahiti. And, oh dear, I'm afraid they'll be just as bad.

And Eddie, it's all true about, for instance, coco-nuts. You tramp through a strange vast dripping tropical forest for hours, listening to weird liquid hootings from birds & demons in the branches above. Then you feel thirsty. So you send your boy—or call a native—up a great perpendicular palm. He runs up with utter ease & grace, cuts off a couple of vast nuts & comes down & makes holes in them. And they're chock-full of the best drink in the world. Romance! Romance! I walked 15 miles through mud & up & down mountains, & swam three rivers, to get this boat. But if ever you miss me, suddenly, one day, from lecture-room B in King's, or from the Moulin d'Or at lunch, you'll know that I've got sick for the full moon on these little thatched roofs, & the palms against the morning, & the Samoan boys & girls diving thirty feet into a green sea or a deep mountain pool under a waterfall—& that I've gone back.

Romance. That's half my time. The rest is Life—Life, Eddie, is what you get in the bars of the hotels in 'Frisco, or Honolulu, or Suva, or Apia, & in the smoking-rooms on these steamers. It is incredibly like a Kipling story, & all the people are very self-consciously Kiplingesque. Yesterday, for instance, I sat in the Chief Engineer's cabin, with the First Officer & a successful beach-comber lawyer from the white man's town in Samoa, drinking Australian champagne from breakfast to lunch. 'Today I am not well.' The beach-comber matriculated at Wadham, & was sent down. Also he rode with the Pytchley, quotes you Virgil, & discusses the ins & outs of the Peninsula campaign. And his repertoire of smut is enormous. Mere Kipling, you see: but one gets some good stories. Verses of a schoolboy kind, too—

*　*　*

I may pick up some mail, & hear from you, when I get to New Zealand. I'm afraid your post as my honorary literary agent, or grass-executor, is something of a sinecure. I *can't* write on the trail. I hope I get in enough, to select something for *New Numbers* from. I'll slip a poem or two more into this or my next letter.

There's one thing I wanted to consult you about, & I can't remember if I mentioned it. I'm giving up the National Liberal Club: because I hate the Liberal party, & the Marconi affair, & the whole mess, & Rufus Isaacs as Lord Chief Justice. I want some Club, to take an occasional stranger into, for a drink, & to read the papers in, &, sometimes, to have a quiet meal in. I thought of asking Raleigh to put me up for the Authors' Club: I don't know what it's like. Or Albert might for the Savile ———. I want somewhere I needn't always be spick & span in, & somewhere I don't have to pay a vast sum.

There's nothing else in the way of my European existence, I think. That part of it which is left, out here, reads Ben Jonson. Kindly turn up his 'New Inn' (which is sheer Meredith) & read Lovel's song in Act IV. The second verse will dispel the impression of the first, that it is by Robert Browning. The whole thing is pure beauty.

No more. My love to everyone, from Jackson down to—if you've made her acquaintance yet—Helena Darwin Cornford. And to such as Wilfrid & Denis & yourself & a few more poor pale-skinned stay-at-homes, a double measure. I have a growing vision of next summer term spent between King's & Raymond Buildings: a lovely vision. May it be.

Manina! Tofa!   Thy

                                                       RUPERT

To DUDLEY WARD   *S.S.* '*Torfua*'
                                                November 1913
                         Off Leruka

Dear Dudley,

I've been in Samoa. I meant to write to you from there. But my time was taken up with a thousand things. I got in there some weeks ago. My heart leapt back instantly a few thousand miles to those villages on the Spree and the Isar. Echt Münchener to drink, a Bier-Abend on Saturday, and 'Mahlzeit!' as you sat down to table! Oh, I was fairly in my element! Dudley, I have beaten you. I have been in *the* German colony. It is a good 12 miles across, and almost 30 long; and there's another island as big. We are an Imperial nation. Hoch!

Lord, lord, it's funny. They seem to me to govern it much better than I thought they would. The first governor was a wily man, studied Fiji, and started German Samoa entirely on British lines—in '90, or whenever the great divide was (about which the Germans are awfully sick, because they think they were out-diplomatized). And the tradition has been kept up.

There are certain people with certain grounds of complaint against the Regierung. The private traders say it doesn't foster the trade and prosperity of Samoa enough, 'Under British or American rule we'd have four times the trade...' etc. etc. The German private traders say this as much as the English. It probably has some truth: though it partly means they aren't allowed to exploit the natives. But the German officials aren't very adaptable to other people's points of view...And the natives prefer the English, personally. But that is merely on personal—and to you and me, comprehensible—grounds. They *say* they are taxed more than the Fijians, sometimes; but it's only in direct taxation; in indirect the Fijians are worst off. Anyhow, the Samoan head of the family has only to pay £1 a year, and 5s. each for his offspring, in taxes: which means three days' work picking and drying coco-nuts for copra: so they needn't kick. The Samoans are richer, and far far happier than the average European. Life here is just one long, long, picnic. The plantations have to be worked by indentured Chinese coolies, because the Samoan can, and will, live without working. He puts an hibiscus in his hair, twines a gaudy loin cloth round him, takes a few bananas and a coco-nut, and goes off bathing with the girls, saying as he goes: That is the end of life! Tra! la!

They're certainly the happiest people in the world, and among the nicest: and very well-treated by the Germans. Which makes their conduct in gloriously fêting the crews of British cruisers, and being merely polite to the German crews, the more ungrateful and reprehensible. But it's damn funny. So, also, is the painstaking way in which the Germans forbid English and teach German in the schools in Apia; and the natives cheerily forget the German and remember the English as soon as they leave. English is the language here still: and will be, for a long time: though the larger half of the white men are Germans. The real ruler of the place is 'The German Firm' D. H. & P. G.—Deutsches Handel und Pflanzen Gesellschaft—which pays 60% to a few people in Hamburg, and owns most of the islands. Most people round the Pacific, and in Apia, agree that the German Customs Officers in Apia are incomparably more courteous than the English in Fiji; and that the German officials round the Samoan Governor are easier to get on with than their English brothers in Suva. Explain it how you can. I suggest that the manners of the Middle Classes are better than those of a sham aristocracy, such as the cubs who surround a Governor of Fiji are apt to be. Anyway, the German government in Samoa is so remarkably attentive and nice to the English, that it's generally thought they have special instructions from Berlin to that effect.

On the whole, my dear, I'm agreeably surprised at the excellence of German control here. I daresay you knew of it. I'd drunk in that 'Only We can Colonize' dope (excuse my Americanisms). I suppose they can afford to take trouble and give time to what they *have* got. The only thing is, they may not be able to keep it, as we could. The Germans don't seem adventurous. They come out here, do their bit, and get home again. But, even here, the English stay, some of them. If the German *does* stay, he gets denationalized—I met several such. (They say there's a brother of von Bülow on the beach, but I didn't strike him.) But the Englishman strikes roots, imagines he's in a story by Kipling, and elects himself perpetual vice-consul. There are lots about here, mostly married to natives. One was sent down from Wadham in '83, ordered out of England, cut off by his father (of the Landed Gentry). He still dresses for dinner, among his chocolate brood. My country! my country!

One thing more. I've discussed your wife's family's ancestry. You know how there's a mixture of Vendish blood—or whatever that very alien tribe not far from Berlin is; you said there was. Well, the Samoans turn out to be mere Venns (or whatever). The same faces and figures, and—being tropical—a trifle richer brown! I've *never* seen anybody so like Clotilde, in face form and manner, as half the girls here. It's too perplexing. You may imagine how I'm crucified hourly. Especially as they're so *very* friendly.

I cease. God be with you and your wife and family. I send them my love. I hope Europe's well. I suppose you know nothing of Ka. I heard vaguely that she was healthy.

God damn the Lord Chief Justice. I heard of it, a week ago, and got quite drunk with another Englishman, trying to drown the shame. I've written to resign the N.L.C. and I insulted a Jew merchant on board. Otherwise I am impotent. When I return, is unknown. I have no money and no energy. The South Seas are heaven, but I no angel. With love

Yours antipodesily

RUPERT

To EDMUND GOSSE

[Picture of a sailing boat full
of Fijians—palm trees, etc.]

McDonald's Hotel, Suva, Fiji
19 November 1913

Dear Edmund Gosse,

Forgive this gaudy tropical notepaper. It's all I can find. I've just got into this place, from Samoa. I said to myself 'Fiji is obviously the wildest place I can get to round here. The name, and pictures of the inhabitants, prove it.' And lo! a large English town, with two banks, several churches, dental surgeons, a large gaol, auctioneers, bookmakers, two newspapers, and all the other appurtenances of civilization! But I fancy I'll be able to get some little boat and go off to some smaller wilder islands. This place and the country round have been stocked with Hindus, to work the plantations. Fifty thousand of them. For the Fijian has that curious quality, inexplicable and abhorrent to the white man, that he will not work for other men, as long as he has enough to live on without. And in this magic part of the world, so long as he is left with a few patches of land of his own, he can do this. He has only to shin up a coco-nut tree, and pull out a root, and there's food for the next week. Perplexing country! At home everything is so simple, and choice is swift, for the sensible man. There is only the choice between writing a good sonnet and making a million pounds. Who could hesitate? But *here* the choice is between writing a sonnet and climbing a straight hundred-foot coco-nut palm, or diving forty feet from a rock into pellucid blue-green water. Which is the better, there? One's European literary soul begins to be haunted by strange doubts and shaken with fundamental fantastic misgivings. I think I shall return home.

But if I *do* return, I know I shall be wanting, every now and then, to slip away to the South Seas once more. The attraction's queer. It's not really Romance. At least, I associate with Romance, something of veiled ladies, and moonlit serenades, and narrow Venetian or Oriental streets. Something just perceptibly feverish. But this is quite another world. It's getting back to one's childhood, somehow: but not to the real childhood, rather to the childhood that never was, but is portrayed by a kindly sentimental memory; a time of infinite freedom, no responsibility, perpetual play in the open air, unceasing sunshine, never-tiring limbs, and a place where time is not, and supper takes place at breakfast-time and breakfast in the afternoon, & life consists of expeditions by moonlight and diving naked into waterfalls and racing over white sands beneath feathery brooding palm-trees.

Oh, it's horribly true, what you wrote, that one only finds in the South Seas what one brings there. Perhaps I could have found Romance if I'd brought it. Yet I do not think one could help but find *less* trouble than one brings. The idea of the South Seas as a place of passion and a Mohammedan's paradise is but a sailor's yarn. It is nothing near so disturbing. It is rather the opposite to alcohol, according to the Porter's definition;[1] for it promotes performance but takes away desire. Yet I can even understand Stevenson finding—as you put it—the Shorter Catechism there. One keeps realizing, however unwillingly, responsibility. I noticed in myself and in the other white people in Samoa, a trait I have remarked in schoolmasters and in the 'agents' who are appointed in Canada to live with, and look after, the Indians. You know that sort of slightly irritated tolerance, a lack of *ir*responsibility, that mark the pedagogue? One feels that one's a White Man*—ludicrously. I kept thinking I was in the Sixth at Rugby, again. These dear good people, with their laughter and friendliness and crowns of flowers—one feels that one *must* protect them. If one was having an evening out with Falstaff and Bardolph themselves, and a small delightful child came up with 'Please I'm lost and want to get home', wouldn't one have to leave good fellowship and spend the evening in mean streets tracking its abode? That's, I fancy, how the white man feels in these forgotten—and dissolving—pieces of heaven, the South Seas. And that perhaps is what Stevenson felt. I don't know enough about him. His memory is sweet there, in Samoa; especially among the natives. The white men—mostly traders—who remain from his time—have—for such people—very warm recollections of his personality, but—with a touch of pathos—avow themselves unable to see any merit in his work. Such stuff as the *Wrong Box* they frankly can't understand a grown man writing. I went up the steep hill above Vailima, where the grave is. It's a high and lovely spot. I took a Samoan of about 20 to guide me. He was much impressed by Stevenson's fame. 'That fellow' he said 'I think every fellow in world know him.' Then he looked puzzled. 'But my father say', he

* Vide R. Kipling *passim*.

[1] 'It provokes the desire, but it takes away the performance.' See *Macbeth*, act II, scene 3.

went on, 'Stevenson no big man—small man.' That a slight man of medium height should be so famous, puzzled him altogether. If he had been seven feet high, now! Fame is a curious thing.

I go round to Tahiti soon, and so back, to the bustle of the States. Then gradually nearer home. Many thanks for your last letter. It's nice to know that England, in spite of everything one reads in the papers, still stands! A Merry Christmas! My best greetings to the whole household—   Yours ever

RUPERT BROOKE

Oh, *do* forgive the envelope![1] My own—in this awful climate—are all fast stuck, tho' never filled, like an English churchman's mind. And I'm reduced to these fantastic affairs.

To W. DENIS BROWNE   *Suva, Fiji*
20 November 1913
Fiji Club
Denis!

Do you still live? are you still writing the Times? I hate your opinions on Home Rule, but I thought one of your leaders on the Land Question very tasty. I got a nice letter from you that was written in September & found me in Honolulu or somewhere, in October. I've been cruising about these islands, Samoan, Fijian, & the rest, for some time. It is mere heaven. One passes from Paradise to Paradise. The natives are incredibly beautiful, & very kindly. Life is one long long picnic. I have been living in native villages & roaming from place to place. I know now, entirely, that it is better to leap by moonlight into a green & silver cool strange sea, with hibiscus in one's hair & the coco-nut palms nodding magically above, than to write rotten little poems or to compose bloody little tunes. And I prefer watching a *Siva Siva* to observing Nijinsky. Oh dear, I so wish you'd been with me for some of these native dances. I've got no ear, & can't get the tunes down. They're very simple—just a few bars with a scale of about 5 notes, repeated over & over again. But it's the *Rhythm* that gets you. They get extraordinarily rhythmic effects, everybody beating their hands, or tapping with a stick: the dancers swaying their bodies & tapping with their feet. None of that damn bounding & pirouetting. Just *stylisierte* pantomime, some-times slightly indecent. But *most* exciting. Next time I get sick of

[1] It has the same picture on it as the paper.

... to J.C.

Think of me :   I am
exactly the opposite
side of the earth , + upside
down

England

But still, though
arsie-versie, as the
Elizabethans say,

your

Rupert

England, I'm going to bring you along out here, & we'll settle in a village somewhere for a few months & work the whole thing out. These people are nearer Earth & the joy of things than we snivelling city-dwellers. There's a thing or two to be learnt from them. I'm off now to the outlying parts of Fiji, to see how they do their dancing. I have to spend the night on a very small cutter in a very rough sea: so I shall be extremely ill. You will not know me, when—if ever—I return. Many things I have lost: my knowledge of art or literature, my fragmentary manners, my acquaintance with the English tongue, & any slight intelligence I ever had; but I have gained other things, a rich red-brown for my skin, a knowledge of mixed drinks, an ability to talk or drink with any kind of man, & a large repertoire of dirty stories. Am I richer or poorer? I don't know. I only regret that I shall never be able to mix in your or any intelligent circles again. I am indistinguishable (except by my poverty) from a [Trinity] Hall man.

Is London all right? Is Wilfrid as nice as ever? and Eddie as young? & Clive as lively? & Dent as *rococo*? & Cathleen as lovely? are you, you?

I trust so.

Many happy returns of the day to J. C.

Think of me: I am exactly the opposite side of the earth, +upside down.

But still, though arsie-versie, as the Elizabethans say,

Your

RUPERT

To EDWARD MARSH *McDonald's Hotel, Suva, Fiji*
22 November 1913

My dear,

This'll get you, I gather, just in time for Christmas. A merry one! I have heard, & shall hear, nothing from England for ages. I go off this afternoon on a cutter to Kandava, an island seventy miles away, to see feasts & dances, & I shan't be back till after the mail leaves. I enclose one of my further articles on Canada. I told you about them I think. You're to keep them till the Westminster wants them. If it never does, as is probable, let them lie, & I'll make something out of them another day. Others shall follow.

Suva's a queer place: much civilized: full of English people who observe the Rules of Etiquette & call on third Thursdays & do not speak to the 'natives'. Fiji's not so attractive a place as Samoa, but more macabre. Across the bay are ranges of inky, sinister mountains, over which there are always clouds & darkness. No matter how fine or windy or hot or cheerful it may be in Suva, that trans-sinutic region is nothing but forbidding & terrible. The Greeks would make it the entrance to the other world—it is just what I've always imagined Avernus to be like. I'm irresistibly attracted by them, & when I come back from my cruise, I intend to walk among them. Shall I return? If not, spill some blood in a trench—you'll find the recipe in Homer—& my wandering shade will come for an hour or two to lap it.

Making enquiries about Tahiti, I discover a predecessor, a painter, on my tour. He passed through Fiji lately, & is now heard of in Tahiti. Who but Stephen Haweis! Mrs, I gather, is not with him. He writes that he has found things of Gauguin in Tahiti. So I'm forestalled by three months. Isn't that sickening?

However, I shall go along: & if Stephen Haweis is still there, knock him on the head & take the boodle. I hear he's quite a small man.

The sunsets here! the colours of the water over the reef! the gloom & terror of those twisted mountains! & the extraordinary contrasts in the streets & the near country—for there are fifty thousand Hindus, indentured labour, here, emaciated & proud, in Liberty-coloured garments, mournful, standing out among these gay, pathetic, sturdy children, the Fijians. The Hindus, who were civilized when we were Fijians: & the Fijians, who will never be civilized. And amongst them, weedy Australian clerks, uncertain whether they most despise a 'haw-haw Englishman', or a 'dam nigger', & without the conscience of one or the charm of the other: secret devil-worshippers, admirers of America, English without tradition & Yankees without go. Give *me* a landed gentry, ten shillings on wheat, & hanging for sheep-stealing: also the Established Church, whence I spring.

Talking of affairs at home (of which I think continually, to the exclusion of Romance), there's nice things in the Cornhill article on Wyndham. I wish he hadn't died.

*   *   *

I'm sending you a box of things. It may turn up any time before May. It is not for you: only stuff I don't want to carry about with me. I'd *rather* nobody saw them till I came home, but I guess it'll be better if you open them (show them no one) & see nothing's smashed, & dry the tapa's & stuffs, lest mould & moths be in them. They're not very good.   All love

RUPERT

To CATHLEEN NESBITT   *McDonald's Hotel, Suva, Fiji*
                          Monday, 24? November 1913

My sweet one,

My last letter to you ceased suddenly. This is a Christmas one, so they tell me. And, child, it's *so* hot here!

And perhaps it won't get you in England at all, but in your loved land of disgustingness, America: and in January: oh! oh!

So you're Olivia. How badly you'll play it. And how bloody that you should have to. Oh, you'll play it better than most people. But it's a thankless part, I imagine. (Which reminds me, I'm writing such a nice little one-act comedy; and it hasn't a part for you. What's to be done?)

I say, if your Mr Barker says such damn silly things about Shakespere, I shall cut the last link with intellectualism, and become a Tariff Reformer, an Anti-Socialist, and an admirer of Mr Lewis Waller. 'O withered is the garland of the war!' etc.—not meaning anything indeed! The cad! The green-eyed cad! How the devil *dare* he talk like that. Not 'mean' anything. I could take you— even you, a mere woman, and Irish at that—through the whole speech, word by word, and explain *exactly* what it means, each phrase, line, and sentence. And by God that a man who wrote *The Marrying of Ann Leete* and some of the darker portions of *Waste* should complain that A & C[1] doesn't mean anything. The swine! the goat! the actor-manager! the stay-at-home, puking, God-forgotten, grease-paint-stinking, clod-pole! Were I by him, I should say 'Brother-in-law!'—or the Hindu word for it—which is a very severe and compendious Indian insult; it implies (1) that the person you're speaking to possesses a sister, (2) that the sister is of light virtue, (3) that you, the speaker, have had personal proof of it. Ingenious, isn't it? Reminds me of another compendious insult I heard the other day.

A. (to B. a drunken-looking, grey-eyed lout). 'I suppose you're Irish, aren't you?'

[1] *Antony and Cleopatra.*

B. 'Irish, is ut? No, bedad!'

A. 'Then there must have been an Irishman on tour with your mother.'

Again the triple insult, you see, (1) You're Irish, (2) Your mother was an actress, (3) Her virtue, as we say in Canada, wanted sandpapering.

Well, it's since I've written to you (I think) that I've been living in Samoan villages, and losing my heart to brown maidens. I had a great time in Samoa, sharing the sports and festivities of the naked brown savage. 'That's the life for a lad like me.' Now I'm here, and bound, in a few hours, for the island of Kandava. It is a very long way away, and I shall go in a very small boat, and shall probably be very very unwell. No matter. *Man muss leben*, as the bald-headed young man says in one of the late Ibsen's plays. But you don't know what it means. Tut! Tut!

Child, I see that I'm going to have the Hell of an uncomfortable life. I want too many different things. I keep, now, pining after London and all the things you've been seeing and doing. I want to talk, talk, talk. Is there anything better in the world than sitting at a table and eating good food and drinking great drink and discussing everything under the sun with wise and brilliant people? I want to sit at the table at Eddie's, with you there and Violet Asquith's brilliance, and Gilbert's wise silences, and Eddie's monocular stories —and TALK. Oh, but I'm going to have such a time when I get back! I'm going to have the loveliest rooms in King's. And I'm going to spend 5 days a week there, and three in London (that's 8, stoopid) and in King's I'm going to entertain all the mad and lovely people in the world. And I'm never going to sit down to dinner without a philosopher, a poet, a musician, an actress, a dancer, and a bishop, at table with me. I'm going to get up such performances, that'll turn old Cambridge upside-down. I'm going to have Yeats and Cannan and Craig and Barker to give a lecture each on modern drama. I'm going to have my great play in the Grantchester Garden, with Clotilde dancing in it. I'm going—oh, Hell, I don't know what I'm going to do. But every morning I shall drift up and down the Backs in a punt, discussing everything in the world, with anybody who desires.

Meanwhile, I'm in Suva. It's the 'capital' of Fiji: full of imported Indians, staid English officials, heavy with the White Man's Burden, and jolly grinning fuzzy-haired Fijians, who care nothing, and know nothing, of burdens, Empire, or responsibility, nor that they are a dying and defeated race. They merely like sunshine, and people, and fishing, and food and especially swimming in the sea. It's so queer, seeing the thin, much clothed, ancient, over-civilized, silver-bangled, subtle Indians, and these jolly, half-naked, savage children of the earth, working side by side in obedience to the Clifton and Trinity, or Winchester and New College, man, with his 'Doesn't do to be too friendly with these niggahs, you know. You must make 'em respect you!' That is Empire. We have two picture shows a night, a Carnegie Library! and a daily paper; mail twice a month, regulations about calling on first and third Thursdays, and *very* strict *caste*. And across the bay are range and range of strange black mountains, always misty and sinister, inky abodes of ghosts and demons, through which few white men have ever passed, covered with impenetrable bush, and crowned by fantastic crags. I'm going there, when I get back from Kandava.

*   *   *

RUPERT

To JACQUES RAVERAT   *Suva, Fiji*
                                        1 December 1913
My dear,

This'll get you next year, won't it? Fancy us all having waded through as far as 1914!—perhaps we shan't though, even yet.

I wander, seeking peace, and ensuing it. Several times I've nearly found it: once, lately, in a Samoan village. But I had to come away from there in a hurry, to catch a boat: and forgot to pack it. But I'll have it yet. Fragments I have found, on various hills or by certain seas. It would be wonderful to find it.

*   *   *

Oh, I shall return. The South Seas are Paradise. But I prefer England. I shall return when I'm certain. I'm nearly certain now. I'd once thought it necessary to marry. I *approve* of marriage for the world. I think you're all quite right. So don't be alarmed. But not for me. I'm too old. The Point of marriage is Peace—to work in. But can't one get it otherwise? Why, certainly, when one's old. And so I will. I know what things are good: friendship and work and conversation. These I shall have. How one can fill life, if one's energetic, and knows how to dig! I have thought of a thousand things to do, in books and poems and plays and theatres and societies and housebuilding and dinner-parties when I get Home. Ho, but we shall have fun. Now we have so painfully achieved middle-age, shall we not reap the fruits of that achievement, my dyspeptic friend? By God! yes. Will you come and walk with me in Spain next summer? And will you join me on the Poet's Round, a walk I've planned?— One starts from Charing X, in a south-easterly direction, and calls on De la Mare at Anerley, on S.W. and find Davies at Sevenoaks, a day's march to Belloc at Kingsland, then up to Wibson on the borders of Gloucestershire, back by (Stratford), RUGBY, and the Chilterns, where Masefield and Chesterton dwell. Wouldn't it give one a queer idea of England!

Three months in a year I'm going to live with you and Gwen, three with Dudley and Anne, three with the Ranee, and three alone. A perfect life. I almost catch the next boat to 'Frisco at the thought of it.

And there is no man who has had such friends as I, so many, so fine, so various, so multiform, so prone to laughter, so strong in affection and so permanent, so trustworthy, so courteous, so stern with vices, and so blind to faults or folly, of such swiftness of mind and strength of body, so polypist* and yet benevolent, and so apt both to make jokes and to understand them. Also, their faces are beautiful, and I love them. I repeat a very long list of their names, every night before I sleep. Friendship is always exciting and yet always safe. There is no lust in it, and therefore no poison. It is cleaner than love, and older; for children and very old people have friends, but they do not love. It gives more and takes less, it is fine in the enjoying, and without pain when absent, and it leaves only good memories. In love all laughter ends with an ache, but laughter is the very garland on the head of friendship. I will not love, and I will not be loved. But I will have friends round me continually, all the days of my life, and in whatever lands I may be. So we shall laugh and eat and sing and go great journeys in boats and on foot and write plays and perform them and pass innumerable laws taking their money from the rich.

I err. I praise too extravagantly, conveying an impression that friendship always gives peace. And even at the moment I [have] a hunger too rending for complete peace, to see all your faces again, and to eat food with you.

* = of many faiths, *not* bespattered by a parrot, O Greekless!

No homesick exile I, though. God, no! I've my time and emotions filled to overflowing with wandering through the strange and savage mountains of this land, or sitting and watching the varied population of the streets, Indians imported for labour cringing by in yellow and pink silks and muslins, and Fijians swinging along half naked with bun-faces and heads of hair just like Francis's and the women with a gait like—oh, like no one you've ever seen in your misty tight-laced feminist lands.

But I'll not tell you of Abroad. Come and see it yourself. I do but write to tell you that I love you both very much, and that I live, and that any moment I may turn up and demand to stay with you for a year, so lay a place for me, and have a bottle or two of stout in.

Oh, I forgot—I've got to have rooms and live in King's for a term or two or three. I'll make 'em sit up. I'm going to get up lectures by Impossible People on all Subjects outside the Curriculum. Wibson and I are going to lecture on 'Poetry', W. H. Davies on 'Fleas', Harry Lauder on—Whatever he likes, and you and Gwen on 'Art'. I'm going to turn that damned hole into a Place of Education. Oh, and Eddie on 'Manners'. When you go through London, see that man—although Gwen's so bloody supercilious about him. It's eccentric, I admit, to conceal a good heart beneath good manners, but forgivable, surely. And he'd love to see you. He's really so nice, and deserves well. I fear lest you children get cut off too far from the world, without me to look after you.

Farewell, farewell, my dears. Won't 1914 be fun!

Talofa—with love
RUPERT

Tell me, sometime, that you've seen Ka once or twice, and that she's well.

To VIOLET ASQUITH   *Nearly half-way*
                                      through December [1913]
           Somewhere in the mountains of Fiji.

Dear Miss Asquith,

Forgive this paper. Its limpness is because it has been in terrific thunderstorms, and through most of the rivers in Fiji, in the last few days. Its marks of dirt are because small naked brown babies *will* crawl up and handle it. And any blood-stains will be mine. The point is, will they....It's absurd, I know. It's twenty years since they've eaten anybody, in this part of Fiji, and far more since they've done what I particularly and unreasonably detest—fastened the victim down, cut pieces off him one by one, and cooked and eaten them before his eyes. To witness one's own transubstantiation into a naked black man, that seems the last indignity. Consideration of the thoughts that pour through the mind of the ever-diminishing remnant of a man, as it sees its last limbs cooking, moves me deeply. I have been meditating a sonnet, as I sit here, surrounded by dusky faces and gleaming eyes:

Dear, they have poached the eyes you loved so well. It'd do well for No. 101 and last, in a modern sonnet-sequence, wouldn't it? I don't know how it would go on. The fourth line would have to be 'And all my turbulent lips are *maître-d'hotel*'—I don't know how to scan French, I fancy that limps. But *all* is very strong in the modern style.

The idea comes out in a slighter thing

> 'The limbs that erstwhile charmed your sight,
> Are now a savage's delight;
> The ear that heard your whispered vow
> Is one of many *entrées* now;
> Broiled are the arms in which you clung
> And devilled is the angelic tongue;...
> And oh! my anguish as I see
> A Black Man gnaw your favourite knee!
> Of the two eyes that were your ruin,
> One now observes the other stewing.
> My lips (the inconstancy of man!)
> Are yours no more. The legs that ran
> Each dewy morn their love to wake,
> Are now a steak, are now a steak!...'

Oh, dear! I suppose it ought to end on the Higher Note, the Wider Outlook. Poetry has to, they tell me. You may caress details all the main part of the poem, but at last you have to open the window —turn to God, or Earth, or Eternity, or any of the Grand Old Endings. It gives Uplift, as we Americans say. And that's so essential. (Did you ever notice how the Browning family's poems *all* refer suddenly to God in the last line. It's laughable if you read through them in that way. 'What if that friend happened to be— God?', 'What comes next—Is it God?', 'And with God be the rest',

'And if God choose, I shall but love thee better after Death'—etc. etc. I forget them all, now. It shows what the Victorians were.) So must I soar—

> 'O love, o loveliest and best,
> Natives this *body* may digest,
> Whole, and still yours, my *soul* shall dwell,
> Uneaten, safe, incoctible.'

It's too dull. I shall go out and wander through the forest paths by the grey moonlight. Fiji in moonlight is like nothing else in this life or the next. It is all dim colours and all scents. And here, where it's high up, the most fantastically shaped mountains in the world tower up all around, and little silver clouds and wisps of mist run bleating up and down the valleys and hill-sides like lambs looking for their mother. There's only one thing on earth as beautiful: & that's Samoa by night. That's utterly different, merely Heaven, sheer loveliness. You lie on a mat in a cool Samoan hut and look out on the white sand under the high palms, and a gentle sea, & the black line of the reef a mile out & moonlight over everything, floods and floods of it, not sticky, like Honolulu moonlight, not to be eaten with a spoon, but flat and abundant, such that you could slice thin golden-white shavings off it, as off cheese. . .and among it all are the loveliest people in the world, moving and running and dancing like gods and goddesses, very quietly and mysteriously, and utterly content. It is sheer beauty, so pure that it's difficult to breathe in it —like living in a Keats world, only it's less syrupy. Endymion without sugar. Completely unconnected with this world.

There is a poem:

> 'I know an Island,
> Where the long scented holy nights pass slow,
> And there, twixt lowland and highland,
> The white stream falls into a pool I know,
> Deep, hidden with ferns and flowers, soft as dreaming,
> Where the brown laughing dancing bathers go.'

It ends, after many pages,

> 'I know an Island,
> Where the slow fragrant-breathing nights creep past,
> And then, twixt lowland and highland,
> A deep, fern-shrouded murmurous water glimmers;

There I'll come back at last,
And find my friends, the flower-crowned laughing swimmers,
And...'

I forget. And I've not written the middle part. And it's very bad,
like all true poems. I love England; and all the people in it; but oh,
how can one know of heaven on earth and not come back to it? I'm
afraid I shall slip away from that slithery murky place you're (I suppose) in now, and return. Ridiculous.

I continue in a hot noon, under an orange tree. We rose at dawn
and walked many miles and swam seven large rivers and picked and
eat many oranges and pine-apples and drank coco-nuts. Now the
two 'boys' who carry my luggage are asleep in the shade. They're
Fijians of twenty-three or so who know a few words of English.
One of them is the finest made man I've ever seen: like a Greek
statue come to life: strong as ten horses. To see him strip and swim
a half-flooded river is an immortal sight. Last night we stayed in the
house of a mountain chief who has spasmodic fierce yearnings after
civilization. When these grow strong he sends a runner down to the
coast to buy any illustrated papers he can find. He knows no
English, but he pastes his favourite pictures up round the wall and
muses over them. I lectured on them—fragments of the *Sketch* and
Sphere for several years—to a half-naked reverent audience last
night (through my interpreters of course). The Prince of Wales,
looking like an Oxford Undergraduate, elbows two ladies who
display 1911 spring fashions. A golf champion in a most contorted
position, occupies a central place. He is regarded, I fancy, as a rather
potent and violent deity. To his left is 'Miss Viola Tree, as Eurydice',
to his right Mrs Granville Barker as Jocasta (or whatever the lady
was called), looking infinitely Mycenaean. I explained about incest,
shortly, and Mrs B. rose tremendously in Fijian estimation. Why do
people like their gods to be so eccentric, always? I fancy I left an
impression that she was Mr H. H. Hilton's (is that right? you're
a golfer) mother and wife. It is so hard to explain our civilization to
simple people. Anyhow, I disturbed their theogony, and elevated
Lillah [McCarthy] to the top place. How Eurydice came in puzzled
them and me. I fancy they regard her as a holy ghostess, in some sort.

It's very perplexing. These people—Samoans and Fijians—are so
much nicer, and so *much* better-mannered than oneself. They are
stronger, beautifuller, kindlier, more hospitable and courteous,
greater lovers of beauty, and even wittier, than average Europeans.

And they are—under our influence—a dying race. We gradually fill their lands with plantations and Indian coolies. The Hawaians, up in the 'Sandwich Islands', have almost altogether gone, and their arts and music with them, and their islands are a replica of America. A cheerful thought, that all these places are to become indistinguishable from Denver and Birmingham and Stuttgart, and the people of dress and behaviour precisely like Herr Schmidt, and Mr Robinson and Hiram O. Guggenheim. And now they're so. . .it's impossible to describe how far nearer the Kingdom of Heaven—or the Garden of Eden—these good naked laughing people are than oneself or one's friends. But I forgot. You are an anti-socialist, and I mustn't say a word against our modern industrial system. I beg your pardon.

I go down to the coast to catch a boat to New Zealand, where I shall post this. Thence to Tahiti, to hunt for lost Gauguins. Then back to barbarism in America. God knows when I shall get home. In the spring, I hope. Is England still there? Forgive this endless scrawl. Don't read it. You'll be far too busy. It gives me pleasure to write it.

I suppose you're rushing from lunch party to lunch party, and dance to dance, and opera to political platform. Won't you come and learn how to make a hibiscus wreath for your hair, and sail a canoe, and swim two minutes under water catching turtles, and dive forty feet into a waterfall, and climb a coco-nut palm? It's more worth while.

Yours from Polynesia

RUPERT BROOKE

To MRS BROOKE　　　　　　　　　　*About 15 December 1913*

R.M.S. 'Niagara' a day from Fiji

Dear Mother,

I've had a great time in Fiji, wandering, living in native villages, etc. Everyone has been very nice to me. I made one trip to Kadava (pronounced—and sometimes written—Ka*n*dava) with Armstrong, who is in the Native office here, and was going to hold an annual meeting. In consequence we were very ceremoniously received and treated, and there were chiefs from all over the island there. (I *think* my last letter was before that trip.) Kadava is a large island 80 miles from the central island of Fiji: and has only two white men on it— 7000 natives, I suppose. We stayed in the chief's house, eat native food—taro, and yam (sorts of potato), turtle, chicken, and Fijian puddings—and saw native dances. I was there 5 or 6 days. We went in a cutter, a boat about 14 yards long and 3 or 4 wide. I slept on deck (there *was* a tiny stinking cabin, *filled* with cockroaches) and only woke when we dipped more than usual and a wave broke over me. Roughing it! In Kadava I played cricket! The Fijians play a good deal, very wildly and without great regard for the rules, but they have good eyes. Then I went for a day and a half with some of the chief people here to Taviuni, another island (we had a small steamer to go on that time) to see a very rare and rather impressive ceremony. A Fijian princess of high rank died, and they had a big funeral. She was only 20 or so, very charming and accomplished, people said. She'd been educated in New Zealand. Pneumonia, as so often with these natives. The Governor was there, at the funeral.

The last week before leaving Fiji, I went a walk. That I enjoyed best of all. The mountains and scenery are wonderful. It's rough walking, and I'm lame with blisters. I went alone, with two native 'boys' to carry my bag and rug and guide me. The photographs of that trip are better than what I enclose, which are a poor lot. But I've not had time to have prints made. I stayed in native villages, climbed a mountain (not 'climbing' in the Alpine, dangerous sense), and walked anything from 14 to 24 miles a day in the great heat. So I'm thinner now, but very well and healthy, save for a sore foot. I don't think the photographs want explaining more than I've done. *Yagona* (pron. Yangona) is the drink: same as Samoan Kava. It is made by pounding up a root, and is non-intoxicant, though *slightly* narcotic.

I tumbled into Fiji without knowing a soul and without any introductions, for I didn't know I was going there. The last few days, after my walk, I didn't have a meal in my hotel, bar breakfast, because I was always dining or lunching out. And I left behind scores of people I was quite sorry to part from: both white and native. The two 'boys' who came on the walk (both about 24: any native is a 'boy' till he is 60) I got quite fond of. The Fijians are a very lovable childlike race, less so than the Samoans, but still, nice. The women are generally rather ugly, but some of the men are superb, the finest I ever saw.

I finish this up in New Zealand. I thought I could catch a boat on straight away. But we missed it, owing to the strike, and other things. So I have to wait here for two weeks. I'm going off into the country, to put in a bit of work, and see some geysers. I have run short of money, owing to this wait. I may be able to cash a cheque with some people I know slightly. If not, I *may* have to cable to you. Some money awaits me in Tahiti, where I get to about Jan. 7. So if you've received the cable, you'll know all is well, it's merely a temporary hitch. My mail is all in Tahiti; so I'll hear news then.

With love
RUPERT

To REGINALD BERKELEY   *R.M.S. 'Niagara'*
                                     Tuesday [*December 1913*]
Dear Berkeley,

*   *.   *

During most of January my address'll be the Union Steamship Cpny's Agents, Papeete, Tahiti. But I don't know when this'll get you. The jade poi-pounder I'd love to have—as a possession, as a memorial, and to confound the experts. Pack it to me at Berkeley, or c/o E. Marsh (editor of Georgian Poetry, by the way!) as you think best: with, I beg, a precise account of its genealogy as far as known. So shall I confute the pedants.

I forgot to put in that list of books, James Stephens' *The Crock of Gold*. It is pure joy: make the Dixon's read it.

The S——s are very kind to me, have put me at their table, and mildly adopted me in general. She is a kindly and charming person, and—as nice stupid women are—delightful and warm-hearted towards individuals and, through absence of imagination, perfectly detestable in her attitude towards classes. I suppose she drinks in entirely her husband's opinions. He has been very nice to me. I can see no reason for his existence, and several against. I do not like people who have money, but neither heart nor brains. I suspect him of being a Public School and 'Varsity man—a 'gentleman'. If so, God help him—a gentleman who has nothing to do but make money. For a trader who makes money, or a member of the proletariat who makes money, there is excuse. They have not been shewn better. But for an English gentleman—give me, rather, the Sydney Bulletin and the Australian accent. They stink less.

An aside, that. I write only to give you a few golden words about life and literature. One can do it better, writing, and after deliberation. And who better than I? For one can only advise people two or three years younger. Beyond that—one has forgotten. They say the body changes completely every seven years. I believe it.

I've found Barker's plays on board, and read them again. Even in him I find myself detecting melodramatic sentimentality: so I'm inclined to think I'm a little morbid about it. So discount my finding it too often in *Education*: and forgive my lack of sympathy with the play. I think, on reflexion, it's the *obvious* that must be avoided—for it's generally sentimental, and it's rarely precise—the remedy for sentimentality. There's an admirable German playwright, Wedekind, who has violent and melodramatic modern scenes; but escapes sentimentality altogether. At the end of one Act, there's a murder in the next room (à la Ibsen) tragic and bloody. The murderer comes out, wiping his hand on a shirt: saying 'They don't even provide towels in this rotten place.' Prettier still: at the end of one play Jack the Ripper appears, cuts up the heroine, an amazing prostitute called Lulu, and almost smashes a woman, Countess Schwizzi, who loved Lulu sapphistically. Schwizzi comes to, at the point of death, knowing Lulu dead. She grunts:

'It's dark.

Dying, Oh, rapture! to float forever through eternity with the Beloved, to— [*blood comes in her throat*]

God damn.

[*Dies*]   *Curtain*'

An admirable use of sentimentality and melodrama—*but Wedekind doesn't identify himself with it.* He laughs at her fine talk, as much as an enemy could. Consider the end of *Othello*, too. It seems to me that we can either use reticence, or unobvious melodrama, but not obvious. Take it with obvious sentiment, such as Wilde *might* have done it (obvious intellectualist sentiment, I mean—not G. R. Sims).

Lord Otho Hell (*desperate*). Then, Dolly was innocent. My God!

Duc de Casse (*nearly breaking down*). Old Chap!—

Lord Otho Hell (*biting his lip*). She gave me Heaven, and I gave her hell.

Duc de Richelieu (*cynically*). Why does an emotional crisis always lead to Blank Verse?

Sir Jago. Ha! Ha! (*at Otho*)   (Jago might
                                                  be Gogo)
All. Brute!

Duc de Casse (*nearly breaking down*). Old Pal! (*his eyes are bright with unshed tears, his hands clutch the table, his face is white as of a man who has seen life*).

King Edward VII (*nearly breaking down*). Remember the child!

Lord O. H. (*white with a strange set look: very mysteriously*). There is only one thing to be done.

The Child (*in the background, and in a sweet childish treble*). Dadda, where's Mam-ma?

Lord O. H. (*with a strong man's pain*). Kill that child!
(*They kill the child*)

Duc de Richelieu (*cynically*). The English take *all* their pleasures seriously—even suicide.

Lord O. H. (*white to the lips*). This is a man's way (*shoots himself nine times with a revolver through the left temple: falls*).

King Edward VII
Lord Smith
Lord Jones
Emperor William } (*nearly breaking down*). Oatley, old pal.

The Queen Mother (*kneeling by his side*). He loved me too!

Edward VII (*abruptly*). Damn! (*leaves the room*).

Duc de Richelieu (*cynically*). Death is only one more expression of the Will to Live.

Duc de Casse (*nearly breaking down*). I'm only a bluff, strong, silent man, but he was my boyhood's pal, etc. etc.

Lord O. H. (*coming to*). Ah, if only I had learnt the rudiments of sexual physiology at my preparatory school! (*Dies*).

Curtain

No good, you know. Mr Barker would have done it very differently. Nearer William, I figure him—but how far!

O. Moore (*subtly*). Then *your* washing-mark is 31?

Manda Cassell (*asserting himself, but at sea*). The laundry decreed it.

O. M. (*calmly*). I took one of your vests away last time. I found it in my wardrobe last week.

M. C. Friends' property is common. What's the time?

O. M. (*flows on*). I might have suspected Desdemona!

M. C. (*tolerant*). Your...present?

O. M. (*grimly*). ...Yes.

M. C. (*pokes the fire twice.*)

O. M. (*cheerfully, as one changing the subject*). You remember that poisoned Dyak arrow I killed a nigger with when we were camping a few years ago. (*Takes arrow down.*)

M. C. (*untruthfully, banishing a momentary fear*). Yes....

O. M. I scratched him, curiously, behind the knee (*pulling up his pyjama leg*).

M. C. I hate niggers.

O. M. (*mildly*). Last Thursday I killed another person, by scratching them, oddly enough, in the same place—there! (*scratches himself*).

M. C. (*dreadfully*). Who?—I mean whom?

O. M. (*delightfully*). Desdemona. (*Dies*).

M. C. Oh! (*rings for the waiter*).

Curtain

W. S. himself did the melodramatic method, but how unexpectedly and how truly. Figure to yourself what a speech before death another would have given Othello—the lines of pathos, the regret, the despair, the prayers for forgiveness, the self-malediction...the too too easy phrases. Then read, how Othello bids them repeat that he was this and that, and that once for Venice' honour, he beat a Turk, 'took by the neck th' uncircumcised dog

And smote him—thus',

and so stuck himself. Thus gentlemen die...

I have been thinking.

I would advise you to practise scales and study counterpoint. We writers don't do it enough, as musicians and painters do. Write—for drama—many plays: aiming at different ends. Especially write one-act ones. They're quicker, harder, technically, and far better practice. And take, for the exercise, plots from somewhere—of modern plays; think for a week how you'd handle them; write, even, a page of dialogue; then read the original, and compare. For instance, here's Barker's *Waste*. A big politician, unmarried, leaves the Liberals over Disestablishment. He comes over to the Conservatives with a scheme for Disestablishing and Endowing Education on the proceeds, and is to be in the forthcoming Cabinet. Meanwhile, he has had a night with an attractive lady (in Society). She is with child: funks it: procures abortion, and dies. There is the possibility of scandal, and the feelings of those who know—he has to be left out of the Cabinet, and his scheme dropped. He shoots himself.

Write that out. Then read *Waste*, and (on the whole) admire. I beseech you, attempt reticence in situation, compression in the writing (*vide*, in some sort, my little play. I say this without conceit, for I went over the writing pretty carefully with Masefield and with Gilbert Cannan: so it's fairly well polished down), and some strangeness of imagination in the atmosphere of at least *some* plays.

For writing, do the Stevenson trick, i.e.—only for exercise—do occasional pages of deliberate imitation of various authors. Especially people with a thick personal atmosphere, like Conrad, or Henry James, or Wells, or Belloc, or back to Gibbon and Shakespeare and Sir T. Browne. It seemed to me that one of the things you needed to do soon, is to develop more individuality and depth of style. You've ideas enough, but they lose atmosphere in transition from your mind to your paper. It always happens, a little.

Finally, I charge you, be kind to life: and do not bruise her with the bludgeon of the *a priori*. Poor dirty woman, she responds to sympathy. Sympathetic imagination with everybody and everything is the artist's one duty. He should be one with every little clergyman, and the stockbroker's most secret hopes should be his hope. In the end, the words of Strindberg's heroine are the only motto 'The race of man is greatly to be pitied.' Isn't that true? Hatred should be given out sparingly. It is too valuable to use carelessly. And, misused, it prevents understanding. And it is our duty to understand. For if we don't, no one else will.

Forgive these impertinences: and the length of the letter. I rarely write. So you'll not be troubled again for a long time. I'm glad I met you in Suva. It made my visit much nicer.

Love to the Dixon's   Sa/mocc. [*sic*]

RUPERT BROOKE

To CATHLEEN NESBITT   *Grand Hotel, Auckland, N.Z.*
17 December 1913

Why, precisely, I'm here, I don't know. I seem to have missed a boat somewhere: and I can't get on to Tahiti till the beginning of January. Damn. And I hear that a man got to Tahiti two months ahead of me, and found—and carried off—some Gauguin paintings on glass. Damn! Damn! DAMN!

Also, my mail is at Tahiti—if anywhere—and I know nothing about anything for months past. You may be dead, wed, in bed or in America, child. In New York, now, being fêted, absurd lady—and I don't know.

When I did get to a few English papers of the latter part of October, they were singularly secretive and mysterious. *Androcles* and the Harlequinade[1] were going off: the *Witch* coming on. Very good. But Cathleen is not in the cast of the *Witch*: not for all her witchery. I nosed feverishly through portly and protesting *Times*. At length —a sinister paragraph down among the burglaries and absconding

---

[1] By D. C. Calthrop and Granville Barker.

deans. 'Miss Snooks is to take Miss Cathleen Nesbitt's place in
G. K. C.'s *Magic* at the Little Theatre.' But what of Miss C. N.?—
that's what the public wants to know. Not a word.

It sort of agitated me, my dear. Your letters are at Tahiti. Damn
Tahiti. And I've got to wander in this desolate place two bleeding
weeks. Are you dead or ill? It's so possible. Or were you thought
too bad? That's also possible. People are very stupid—and there
isn't me to tell you what old Chesterton means, and how to act. Or
were you snatched away to America? or to take the leading *rôle* in
Covent Garden? Oh! oh! oh! I *wish* I wasn't infinitely far from
everything. I HATE not knowing about you. I'm going to live in
London all the rest of my life, with a private telephone-connexion
to every theatre.... It's the farthest South, though, this: the farthest
from news of you I'll ever be. From Wellington, which I get to on
New Year's Day, I turn towards you. Thereafter the days bring me
nearer.

I hate not knowing. I hate being uneasy. Why did you give up
that part? You can't be ill. You're not.... I refuse to go on worrying.
I won't think of you.

My dear: my life's been getting madder and madder. I tumbled
into Fiji without a friend or an introduction: and left it a month
later amidst the loud grief of the united population, white and black.

Later.

Thank God for *The Daily Telegraph*. I have never praised and
lauded the *D. T.* before in my life. But I do now. I went down to
the Public Library, turned vaguely to a copy of November 7, and
found that *Quality Street* was to be revived, and you as the chief
person. Oh! oh! oh! I'm so excited (and it's so funny tracing your
career in this detective manner). So you deserted the very large man
for the very small. Was it a tug? Was it wise? I've a suspicion that
G. K. C. is better than Barrie. But you know. But oh that I could
draw! 'Miss C. N., proposed to by Barrie on one side and Chesterton
on the other, hesitating.' The picture is so vivid to my mind, and so
funny: and you so fascinating in it. ...

My dear, I suppose that now you're *far* the most famous person in
England. I'm so very happy about it. I just sit and gurgle—a very
unusual thing in New Zealand, by the way. Are you *very* nice in
Quality Street? I never saw it: it was before even my early playgoing
days. I suppose you're adorable; a man in the *Saturday Review* said
that your charm (in the Harlequinade, anyway) is the 'extremely

calculated attractiveness of an entirely conscious young woman' or something like it. I saw it yesterday, and cabled a challenge, instantly. Oh, I'm so pleased.

But, child, you're going back to the icy Barker, aren't you? You mustn't be wasted as a mere leading lady in the modern English theatre, too long. It's so bad . . . think what a waste Mary Ellen was. You're an elderly woman of 24(?): and you've such a lot to learn (on the stage). The man Barker—although he's such a cad as to say there's no meaning in a speech of Cleopatra's which staggers with meaning—but I've written about that—still he's the only person (unless you went off to Craig for a bit). So just make a fortune and an European reputation for a month or two, and go back to cheaper, better things.

I don't understand about America, I expect it'll be in my mail at Tahiti. I dimly see that you'll be crossing when I am, whenever that is. It's a way God has of arranging things: I know the fellow's tricks of old. If it does happen so, I shall leap from my boat and swim to yours. It's quite easy, especially now I'm such a good swimmer, practising with these brown people.

Yes, I wandered round Fiji and slept in native huts and climbed impossible mountains in my pyjamas and tennis shoes, umbrella in hand, under a torrid sun. What fragment of heart the Samoans had left me (which wasn't much) I left with the Fijians. What shall I do when I meet you? They are such a fine and delightful lot of people. The two 'boys' (aged 23 or 4), I took with me when I went walking through the centre of the island, to carry my bags, are my sworn and eternal friends. One of them ('Ambéle', under which I, but not you, can recognize 'Abel') was six foot high, very broad, and more perfectly made than any man or statue I have ever seen. His grin stretched from ear to ear. And he could carry me across rivers (when I was tired of swimming them, for we crossed vast rivers every mile or two) for a hundred yards or so, as I should carry a box of matches. I think of bringing him back with me as a servant and bodyguard to England. He loved me because though I was far weaker than he, I was far braver. The Fijians are rather cowards. And on precipices I am peculiarly reckless. The boys saved me from rolling off to perdition about thirty times, and respected me for it—though thinking me insane. Would you marry me if I turned up with two vast cannibal servants, black-skinned and perpetually laughing—all of us attired only in loincloths and red flowers in our hair? I think I should be irresistible.

They dance so well, the Fijians. All chorus and ballet dancing and singing at the same time. They make them up and practise them for weeks: except when they do old ones. Very subtle rhythms and clean gestures—like the Russians only sincerer, and no gymnastics. I *schwärm* for it; and no white in or near Fiji cares twopence for anything except money-making. So the dances'll slowly die out, as the Fijians drink in civilization more and more. I want to go out and study them and cinematograph them before they're lost. When you're making £1000 a week, will you fit out an expedition with me?

* * *

I go on to Tahiti on Jan. 2nd, on (probably) to 'Frisco in the middle of February. And thence as quickly or slowly as I like across the States. Quickly, if my present mood holds, for I shall be rather sad at leaving savagery behind me, and not inclined to dally long with that inferior thing, barbarism. But it'll depend on several things, chiefly on your whereabouts. I want to get hold of you, and take you out into the country from wherever you are, and watch something growing, and hear you talk Irish (which reminds me, I suppose you'll have learnt to talk Scotch too, from Barrie, now, and'll be quite intolerably conceited), and say poetry to you. I have a great desire to do these things. I figure that I shall spend Christmas alone at Wairakei. Fancy spending Christmas at Wairakei! Life is unutterably fantastic...New Zealand turns out to be in the midst of summer, and almost exactly like England. I eat strawberries, large garden strawberries, every day: and it's the middle of December! It feels curiously unnatural, perverse, like some frightful vice out of Havelock Ellis. I blush and eat secretively.

I'll describe New Zealand another day. It's a sort of Fabian England, very upper middle class and gentle and happy (after Canada), no poor and the Government owning hotels and running charabancs. All the women smoke, and dress very badly, and nobody drinks. Everybody seems rather ugly—but perhaps that's compared with the South Seas.

The South Seas—my dear, when I *do* get back you'll have to keep a firm hand on me, or I'll be slipping off again. Can anywhere, can even England, hold one from them for ever? I know there'll be times when I remember palm trees and the reefs and the moon, and I shall start looking up boats....

No: I want to get back and see you. That's all I want.

I hope you were *frightfully* good in *Quality Street*, and I'm awfully glad you're so eminent. As I do not trust you in the slightest, I believe you to be overworking. Don't.

*   *   *

RUPÊRT

To CHAUNCEY WELLS   *Warapei, New Zealand*
                                        Christmas Day 1913

Dear Mr Wells,

I'm sorry to have bothered you. I thought I should be able to get straight on to Tahiti, but my boat from Fiji was late. So I'm condemned to stay in New Zealand for a fortnight. That is why I ran short of money, and wired. But I'm all right now.

New Zealand is a queer place. If you go a walk along the road, and happen to look down at the puddles, you will notice they keep bubbling. Stoop down and put your finger in them and you know why. They're boiling. You turn to examine what looks like a rabbit hole in the wayside. Suddenly a strange rumbling proceeds from it. You stand back frightened. An enormous geyser of steam and boiling water bursts from it, plays a minute or two, and lapses again: to recur at a regular interval of 10 seconds, two minutes, an hour and a half, or whatever it may be. The whole country is built on a thin crust of rock and deposit, over thousands of feet of boiling mud and water. Occasionally one can thrust one's walking stick through. A terrifying place. I expect it will give soon. The people are pleasant, quiet, and affectionate. Very English, in accent clothes mind and everything. The women dress badly in precisely the same way the London suburban woman does. It's rather amusing to see. They're more civilized than the Canadians, and have some good laws.

I had a great time in Samoa and Fiji, wandering about alone among the natives. In both places they seemed to me extraordinarily nice and lovable, and in many ways—in manners, for instance—so much superior to oneself. It makes one inclined to believe in the Christian idea that we've come down since the beginning of the world, not up. They seem (especially the Samoans) curiously nearer the Garden of Eden than we. I want to start, or join, a Polynesian Defence Society. Its work will be principally destructive. It will mostly be occupied with leaving them to themselves, and with poisoning or ruining the swine who want to exploit them. The German and British governments seem to me to be working very decently and disinterestedly, on the whole, and protecting the natives. It's the independent trader or planter, whose only idea is to get in, make as much money as he can, and get out again, who is the evil.   *   *   *

I hurt my foot in walking in Fiji, and must have got some wretched and tropical microbe in it. For it *won't* heal. I'm going to see a doctor in Wellington about it. So I may turn up in February with a cork leg. Otherwise I'm very well and happy.

Best greetings to both, and a Happy New Year!

Yours ever
RUPERT BROOKE

BIOGRAPHICAL PREFACE 1914

Brooke had planned to leave New Zealand on the second day of January, but to his annoyance his ship was a week late. When at length he reached Tahiti he realized that he had found 'the most ideal place in the world'. He prolonged his stay there for over three months and his letters proclaim his intense satisfaction. He turned again to writing poetry, and sent home to Eddie Marsh some of the best of his later work. He had lost his heart to a girl named Taatamata, or Tuatamata, and it was not until well on in April that he sailed for San Francisco. He there resumed the role of traveller, visiting Arizona and the Grand Canyon; Chicago, where he renewed acquaintance with the Maurice Brownes and their Little Theatre; Pittsburgh, Washington, Boston, and finally New York.

At the beginning of June he was back at Rugby, feeling a renewed warmth for his mother after their long separation and an access of affection for his friends. *New Numbers* had started publication in February, the first issue containing several of his poems, and in July he travelled to Gloucestershire to stay with Wilfrid Gibson, from whose house their periodical was issued. Here they discussed the August number, which was to contain some of his South Sea poems. Later in July he was again at Rugby, but in London with Marsh on 4 August when war was declared. He was still worrying about the necessity for marriage, and now he was suddenly thrown into an agony of indecision about what part he should take in the war with Germany. His first idea was to obtain employment as a war correspondent and then he made efforts to join a Territorial Unit, but it was difficult amid the prevailing disorganization to find the best way of using individual talents. My last encounter with him was in a London street in the early days of August, when he was full of envy at my easy transformation into an officer in the Royal Army Medical Corps, so that I should land in France on 24 August to work there 'for the duration'. His difficulties were finally resolved through the good offices of Eddie Marsh and Winston Churchill. By the middle of September he had obtained a commission in the Naval Division (R.N.V.R.) together with Denis Browne. On 1 October they were with the Anson Battalion near Walmer in Kent, and a few days later experienced, though almost untrained, a brief and abortive expedition to Antwerp. For the rest of the month he was under intensive military training and attending to the equipment of his troops. Early in

December, after various changes, he was drafted to the Hood Battalion, then in camp at Blandford in Dorset, where he enjoyed the company of a number of congenial young men besides that of Denis Browne. These were Oc (Arthur) Asquith, the Prime Minister's younger son, Patrick Shaw-Stewart, Cleg (F. S.) Kelly, Charles Lister, son of Lord Ribblesdale, and Bernard Freyberg, a New Zealander. Of these Shaw-Stewart and Kelly had taken part in the Antwerp expedition; Lister and Freyberg had joined them later. On Christmas Day, writing to Cathleen Nesbitt from Blandford, Brooke confessed 'on Wednesday I (don't tell a soul) started a sonnet', but this was not one of the five famous War Sonnets. These had been written while he was on leave a few weeks earlier and had already appeared in the fourth and last issue of *New Numbers* (December). On the last day of the year he was on leave at Rugby writing to Eddie Marsh in an effort to decide whether to join him at lunch to meet the Winston Churchills or to fulfil a promise made to Cathleen Nesbitt.

To MRS BROOKE   *Wellington Club*
                                               Wellington, N.Z.
                                               7 January 1914

Dear Mother,

I'm just off to Tahiti. My blasted boat was nearly a week late: so I've had to spend three weeks in New Zealand. I went through the geyser district (I think I sent you a postcard) and then stopped at a place called Ruanni, a sheep-farm right away from everywhere on high ground near the foot of the big mountains in the centre of the North Island. It belongs to some very rich and upper-class people called the Studholmes, whom I met on the boat from Fiji (we had common friends in Fiji). Studholme cashed a cheque for me, among other things. It's useful having an honest face! Their house is quite large and old—twenty or thirty years old!—like a small English country house, with a lovely garden. (The Studholmes were one of the early N. Zealand families.) I went there meaning to stay two days, but my boat kept being put off and off, so I stayed a week: mostly lying out on the lawn and dozing. I got rid of a bit of chill I'd got—from coming too abruptly from the tropics, I suppose: and had a jolly rest. Not that I didn't do work, but I didn't take much exercise (I'd had plenty in Fiji) and I didn't 'see' anything—except the flowers and the sky and—one afternoon—sheep-shearing. Studholme was rather a typical rich English 'gentleman' and his views on the strike and labour were simply *filthy*. But they were very kind to me, so I didn't argue, and I mustn't say anything now.

By the way, I got to Wellington two days ago and have been reading up The *Times* etc. for a month. I'm catching up! I feel wild about Dublin. I always feel in strikes that 'the men are always right' as a man says in *Clayhanger*[1]. Of course the poor are always right against the rich. But often enough the men, in any particular strike, are in the wrong over some point of the moment (it's not to be wondered at). But Dublin seems to be one of the clearest cases (continued on board the *Tahiti*) on record, where the employers are in the wrong even by ordinary Conservative standards— in refusing the Askwith[2] suggestion. When the *Times* begins saying that the employers are in the wrong, they must be very unpardonably and rottenly so indeed. I do hope people are contributing for the wives and children in Dublin. I saw an appeal from a lot of people including George Trevelyan and Masefield. Erskine Childers is

[1] The novel by Arnold Bennett.
[2] G. R. Askwith, later author of *Industrial Problems and Disputes*, 1920.

a treasurer for it. Could you send two guineas in my name? I'll settle when I get back. But I'd like it done immediately. I expect you'll have sent some yourself. (What mad and maddening fools those priests are!)

I found a lot of Saturday Westminsters at the Club, here, and my eight articles in them. They were occasionally misprinted, but fairly good on the whole: though they ought to have printed them out in paragraphs more—it makes stuff look more interesting. I don't think the articles are *good* (except one or two). But they serve their purpose: and there's more in them than in most stuff of that kind.

Talking about journalism, by the way, I was shocked to see, somewhere, a report that they're going to run a strict party weekly because the *Nation*'s so independent. I do hope not, for it might kill the *Nation*, and I'm growing more and more to admire it. *The New Statesman* and Belloc's paper represent my views more, I suppose: but I can't help thinking the *Nation*'s a long way better written, both on its literary and its political side than *The New Statesman*. I disagree with Massingham on a lot of things, but I think he's very admirably and bravely independent—without being erratic—and consistent with his own views. And that's just the sort of person one wants writing.

The *Times* keeps having these articles on Prominent Canadians: and it had two in November that were useful on the Western Cooperative Grain Growers movement. I shall want those when I get home: so I hope the old Times aren't destroyed—or if they are that you'll keep Canadian articles. *Months* of correspondence etc. await me (I believe and trust) in Tahiti. If there's anything requiring immediate attention I'll send you a line—when I've read all the stuff —on by the same post as this (i.e. by this boat). After that you'll not hear for three weeks and a bit.

I wonder how Christmas is with you. It seems so odd having it hot and fine here. I wonder if you're going abroad at all, or if you're facing it in England. I gathered from the Australian papers that it was colder than usual. I hope you're keeping very well.

New Zealand isn't a frightfully interesting country, I fancy. It's run on more sensible lines than Canada: of course, it's much younger, and smaller. The queer thing is that they've got all the things in the Liberal or mild Fabian programme—eight hours' day (and less), bigger old age pensions, access to the land, minimum wage, insurance, etc. etc.—and yet it's not Paradise. The same troubles exist in much the same form (except that there's not much bad poverty). Cost of living is rising quicker than wages. There are the same troubles between unions and employers, and between rich and poor. I suppose there'll be no peace anywhere till the rich are curbed altogether.

*   *   *

With love

RUPERT

To MRS BROOKE   *Mataia, Tahiti*
                                              4? February [*1914*]

Dear Mother,

I have found a fine place here, about thirty miles from Papeete the chief town in Tahiti. It is a native village, with one fairly large European house in it, possessed by the chief, and inhabited by a 3/4 white man who worked in Australia and married an Australian girl. It is the coolest place I've struck in the South Seas (Papeete was very hot), with a large verandah, the sea just in front, and the hills behind. We have *very* good food—native mostly—and cheap French wine thrown in. 6s. 3d. a day. It is not a recognized hotel, but occasionally takes a few guests. Two other Englishmen are here, both from a few years' ranching in Canada. We go out fishing, and expeditions with the natives. And there's a little wooden pier out into the sea (which is thirty yards away in front of the house), with a dive into deep water. We bathe four times a day. The water is cool in day time and warm at night, and never very rough, because it's inside a reef (and sharks don't come !). The average day is this (they combine Tahitian and French customs here). Up at 6 and bathe. *Petit déjeuner* of coffee and fruit 6.45. Work till 10.30. Bathe. *Déjeuner* (=lunch) 11. Sleep 12–1 or 1.30. 1.30 to 6.30 work or some expedition. 6.30 dinner. Bed about 10 or 10.30, unless we go night fishing. So you see I do plenty of work. And as it's not very hot I find I can do it fairly well. I have got through quite a bit of reading and writing. We find every kind of fish about here, fresh water and salt, from sharks to eels and prawns, and we catch them in every conceivable kind of way, netting, spearing, and line. It's an ideal life. The half-caste and his Australian wife are very decent simple people. And the natives, though more civilized and more spoilt than in Fiji or Samoa, are many of them extraordinarily good companions and jolly people when you get outside the town.

*   *   *

I got your letter saying how you'd always wanted to go to Honolulu. (I don't know when I shall get any more letters.) I think you'd like it. The other South Sea islands would be too rough for you; but outside Honolulu, or the Waikiki Beach, there are one or two hotels which are quite as good as the ordinary Cannes or Nice Hotel—better—(but rather more expensive being American). And the weather and climate in Honolulu 'beats the Riviera all to pieces'. Ten days to Vancouver, and six on to Honolulu! And eleven or twelve of the sixteen days would be by water. You ought to do it some time. It's really no more strain than travelling to Italy or the Riviera. Next time there's a windfall from that mine, you and Alfred ought to do it.

I think I shall stay on here another month. I've several bits of work I want to do. I'll get to San Francisco half way through March. I hope England's rubbing along all right. I haven't had much news, except that W. W. Gibson's going to be married. I hope to goodness his young woman has some money.

Did I tell you I travelled as far as here on the boat with Clara Butt and Kennerley Romford and their family. I don't admire her singing, but I thought they were rather pleasant people. We had a goodbye dinner together at the restaurant in Papeete. She's over six foot high and must weigh sixteen stone and has a bass voice like a man's.

With love
RUPERT

Next mail four weeks.

P.S. They call me *Pupure* here—it means 'fair' in Tahitian—because I have fair hair!

To CATHLEEN NESBITT   *Mataia, Tahiti and Papeete*
7 February [1914]

My sweet one,

I've decided to stay another month in Tahiti: for two very good reasons. One, that I've found the most ideal place in the world, to live and work in. Two, that I haven't enough money to get out. I hope and believe that money is coming sometime. So you'll see my wrinkled face at your dressing-room door some day again before you're found out by the public, or I by Death.

A wide verandah over a blue lagoon. A wooden pier with deep clear water for diving—and coloured fish that swim between your toes. There also swim between your toes—more or less—scores of brown babies—from 2 years to 14. Canoes and boats. Rivers. Fishing with spear, net, and line. The most wonderful food in the world, strange fishes and vegetables, perfectly cooked.

*   *   *

Europe slides from me, terrifyingly. There are but one or two things that prevent me letting time flow over me here till I turn to white sand and scented dust and little bright fish: a friend or two, a certain worthless Irish lady, the thought of some enemies I want to smash, the ever-rarer memory of primroses and English hedges, a thought of running a theatre. . . .

Will it come to you having to come and fetch me?

The boat's ready to start. The brown lovely people in their bright clothes are gathered on the old wharf to wave her away. Everyone has a white flower behind their ear—Tuatamata had given me one. Do you know the significance of a white flower worn over the ear? A white flower over the *right* ear means

I am looking for a sweetheart

A white flower over the *left* ear means

I have found a sweetheart

and a white flower over each ear means

I have one sweetheart and am looking for another.

A white flower over each ear, my dear, is dreadfully the most fashionable way of adorning yourself in Tahiti.

Bon voyage, to the travellers! Good luck to everybody else! Tonight we will put scarlet flowers in our hair and sing strange slumberous South Sea songs to the concertina and drink red French wine and dance obscure native dances and bathe in a soft lagoon by moonlight and eat great squelchy tropical fruits—custard apples, papaia, pomegranate, mango, guava, and the rest—*urana*!

*   *   *

RUPERT

To EDWARD MARSH *Mataia, Tahiti*
7 February 1914

Eddie,

I've got stuck here. Not enough money to get on. And I don't know when it's coming. So I have to catch this post a fortnight earlier than you think, & forego the two weeks of solitude & work on the boat up to 'Frisco. I've two of the Canadian articles finished, but I'm keeping them till the rest are through. There's three fair-sized poems nearly done, too. I've found a great place for working & living here. I spend my time between swimming, working, & having astonishing medieval adventures with Tahitian beauties.

It's great about Wilfrid. I wish I had a letter from you about it. I want to know about the female. Has she money? Is she good?

But these & most other things must wait till I get to 'Frisco & find my mail.

The post goes.

I live in a loincloth & an old vest of yours, swimming or climbing or fishing. . . . Thy

RUPERT

To EDWARD MARSH *Hotel Lorina, Papeete, Tahiti*
7 March 1914

Dear Eddie,

I'm sending a registered package of stuff. There seems to be too much of it for the world to run a risk of losing. There's still The West: Vancouver: & conclusion: to come for Canada. I've been ill. I got some beastly coral-poisoning into my legs, & a local microbe on the top of that, & made the places bad by neglecting them & sea-bathing all day (which turns out to be the worst possible thing). I was in the country when it came on bad, & tried native remedies, which took all the skin off & produced such a ghastly appearance that I hurried into town. I've been lying on my back for eight or nine days suffering intensely while I swab my skinless flesh with boiling disinfectant. However, I've got over it now, & have started hobbling about. At first I had a bit of fever: but I feel very spry now.   *   *   *

I lie in a hovel at the back of the hotel & contemplate the yard. The extraordinary life of the place flows round & through my room—for here no one, man or woman, scruples to come through one's room at any moment, if it happens to be a short cut. By day nothing much happens in the yard—except when a horse tried to eat a hen the other afternoon. But by night, after ten, it is filled with flitting figures of girls, with wreaths of white flowers, keeping assignations. Occasionally two rivals meet, & fill the darker corners with cursings & scratchings. Or occasionally a youth intercepts a faithless lady & has a pretty operatic scene under my window. It is all—all Papeete —like a Renaissance Italy, with the venom taken out. They're three-quarters savage, but without savagery. No, simpler, light-come & light-go, passionate & forgetful, like children, but all the time Southern Pacific—that is to say, unmalicious & good-tempered. I have been nursed & waited on by a girl with wonderful eyes, the walk of a goddess, & the heart of an angel, who is, luckily, devoted to me. She gives her time to ministering to me, I mine to probing her queer mind. I think I shall write a book about her—Only I fear I'm too fond of her.   *   *   *

O my dear, I really do feel a little anchorless. I shall be glad to be back among you all, & tied to somewhere in England. I'll never never never go to sea again. All I want in life is a cottage & the leisure to write supreme poems & plays. I can't do it in this vagabondage. I wonder where you're going to be at Whitsuntide? In America, won't you? I'm sure it's a lovely place for a May holiday.

Fire the verse on to Wilfrid.

I've various strange happenings & a few good stories to tell you, but they'll keep for telling.

Ever

RUPERT

To PHYLLIS GARDNER   *Tahiti*
March 1914

My dear Phyllis,

You may be dead, or paralytic, or married to a peer, or anything. So may every one I know. I haven't had any mail since October. It's all waiting for me—news of death + sickness + joy + good + evil— in America. I've been rather out of reach of posts, for five or six months, roaming through the Hawaian Islands, Fiji, Samoa, New Zealand, + Tahiti, never knowing exactly where I was going to be a week or a month or a year later. I just escaped falling over a precipice in Fiji, & somehow I evaded the various tropical diseases here & in Samoa, & shipwreck everywhere, so I'm beginning to think that I'm fated to be hanged, & to drift back to England. Surprising thought! And disturbing. For unless the hanging takes place immediately, I shall have to *Work* to pay my debts, contracted in this unproductive occupation of travelling. And that, I feel, I could never do.... Do not ever wander, Phyllis. Or not for too long. It becomes a habit—landing in a fresh port with a light heart, a full bag, & an empty stomach. You stay there a few days or weeks or months, make some friends, see some queer things; & then, one gay morning, a boat blows in, & the rumour goes round that she's bound for the Islands of the Blest. And in you jump with your bag, heavier by a few memories, & the anchor's up & the folk on shore sing 'Goodbye, my flenni!' or 'Aloha oe!'—& out & on you go again. But now I'm frightened I may never be able to settle down to other desirable —more desirable—things—living in an English cottage & writing immortal plays. And oh! Lord if I *do* settle, it'ld be so much easier to settle here, than anywhere else. The South Seas have got into my blood: the lovely & gentle brown people, the flowers & the lagoons, & the moonlight. If only I *could* I'd like to hire a small boat & spend five years cruising about these parts. But five years would be too long. One could never go back to bowler hats & the Strand & the Daily Mail & tea-parties after that—& through America too! Even now the thought of landing in that harsh hysterical hell twelve days after I leave this Elysium appals me. And I'll get back to talk about Shaw & Matisse & Schonberg & the Russians & all the things I'm interested in, & away from all the things that make up life here, the things I only like—Damn!

Et tu, Phyllis? (We speak bad French here—though it might be Latin for the matter of that.) It may be I shall find a letter from you when I reach America. It may be not. In any case I hope you're flourishing, working hard & happy. For myself, I may drift into England again soon, or I may not. I seem to have given up writing with any enthusiasm. I do just a little, as I knock about. But it seems, somehow, more amusing just to live. What a fate for a poet!

I have still some shadowy remembrance of a place called England. I suppose I shall see it again soon. May it, & all the good things in it, flourish. And may you be happy & prosperous.

> Your friend,
> some 20 degrees S,
> RUPERT

To EDWARD MARSH   *Tahiti still*
                                                        March [*1914*]

My dear,

I've had—after all these months—a letter—& from you. All my other mail waits in 'Frisco. But this was sent from the address you blessedly—oh, expectation!—sent those books to. They sent me money (so at length I can escape hence) & with the money a letter from you & a note from Rugby. It's *so* funny: getting a letter of January 25, & not having heard any thing from anybody since October. Your letter of November announcing your marriage with Cathleen: your kindly Christmas information about the disastrous fire in Bilton Road & the disposal of the Ranee's & Alfred's cinders: your New Year's epistle announcing your, Wilfrid's, & Albert's Knighthoods; the later letter that recounted your series of conversations with Shaw, the Earthquake, the war with Germany, the Chinese Ballet, Stravinsky's comic opera, the new El Greco, Mrs Elgy's illegitimate twins, Gilbert's trial, Masefield's latest knockabout farce, Arthur Benson's duel...all these I have not yet had. They await me in 'Frisco. So I take up the thread at the 25th of January—now itself some way down in the heap of yesterday's seven thousand years. I study them rather confusedly. Flecker—Wilfrid—poetry—plays—Moulin d'Or—the Savile—*Hullo, Tango!*—they all stir, these names, some dusty memories away in the back of my subconsciousness. Some-when, they must have meant something to me, in another life. A vision of taxis slides across the orange & green of the sunset. For a moment the palms dwindle to lamp-posts.

> 'So a poor ghost, beside his misty streams,
> Is haunted by strange doubts & fugitive dreams,
> Hints of a pre-Lethean life, of men,
> Rocks, stars, & skin, things unintelligible,
> And the sun on waving grass, he knows not when,
> And feet that ran, but where he cannot tell.'

(You recognize the master-hand?)

I must come back, & see if I can take to it again. Plan out a life for me for next year, Eddie—beginning from the Dinner, or thereabouts. (May I stay with you for the Dinner? Thank you.) I must get a room in Fellows' Building & live in it half the week, & lecture. I've great schemes for getting up a series of lectures on the Theatre—public lectures—in Cambridge: Barker, Yeats, Craig, & Gilbert & one or two more: & Copeau & a German or two. Find out what the —— are at. It'd be rather fun to make Cambridge the Theatrical Centre of the World for a year. I'll buy little houses, & put Justin in one, & Denis in another, & we'll do nothing but get up performances the whole time. I'm *convinced* that I've a genius for organization. Oh, oh, & there'll be several Dreams of my life I shall realize. One is, a dialogue—in the King's Common Room, on Poverty & Wealth, between Pigou & W. H. Davies. The other half of the week I shall reside with you—I warn you.

But, my dear, I doubt if you'll have me. The Game is Up, Eddie. If I've gained facts by knocking about with Conrad characters in a Gauguin *entourage*—I've lost a dream or two. I tried to be a poet. And because I'm a clever writer, & because I was forty times as sensitive as anybody else—I succeeded a little. *Es ist vorüber: es ist unwiederruflich zu Ende.* I am what I came out here to be—Hard. Quite, quite hard. I have become merely a minor character in a Kipling story. I'll never be able to write anything more, I think. Or perhaps I can do plays of a sort—I think I'll have to manage a theatre. I feel very energetic: and very capable. Is that a great come-down? I think that what I really feel like, is living. I want to talk & talk & talk . . . & in the intervals, have extraordinary adventures. Perhaps this too, is a come-down. But haven't I, at 26, reached the age when one should begin to learn? An energy that has rushed upon me with the cessation of my leprous skin-disease & the approaching end of six months' peace of soul, is driving me furiously on. This afternoon I go fishing in a canoe with a native girl on a green & purple reef. Tonight from ten to two, spearing fish in the same lagoon by torch light. Tomorrow up into the mountains at dawn on foot with a mad Englishman, four natives, & a half-caste, to a volcanic lake in the interior. There we build a house & stay for two days. The natives return, & the M.E. & myself swim the lake & push on for a pass down to the other coast. Perhaps we get it. Perhaps not. In any case we hope to see some ghosts—they abound in the interior. They come to you by night, & as you watch them their bellies burst & their entrails fall to the ground, & their eyes— unpupiled balls of white—fall out too, & they stink & shine. This morning I have been reading *The Triumph of Time*[1] & *Bartholomew Fair*.[2] Yesterday I was in Papeete, spending the morning learning about Sapphism in Sydney from a stray Jewish chorus-girl (Tahiti collects the flotsam of all the oceans), the afternoon learning about

---

[1] Perhaps a misreading for *The Triumphs of Truth* by Thomas Middleton.
[2] By Ben Jonson.

Gauguin from a drunken beach-comber (the certain facts about Gauguin's death are that he was suffering from syphilis & elephantiasis: the probable points, that he had leprosy, & killed himself); the night. . . ..

Learning, learning, learning. . . is there anything else to do except *taste*? Will you come with me to Morocco, Persia, Russia, Egypt, Abyssinia, & the Aran Islands? I'm afraid I shan't be able to settle down at home. It'll be an advantage that I come to England through America. For then, I'll find it so lovely that I won't be hankering after sunlight & brown people & rainbow-coloured fish. At least, I won't for some months, or a year.

I'll learn at home, a bit. There's so much to learn there—if one's sensible enough to know it. And I feel hard enough to make the attempt. I want to love my friends & hate my enemies, again.

*   *   *

Alas, why are there no decent clubs? What do the jolly people all do? I want to belong to the same club as de la Mare. Where does de la Mare go? To Anerley, S.E., I suppose.

> 'There was once an a-metrist of Anerley,
>   Whose neighbours were mundane but mannerly,
>   They don't cavil the least
>   At a stray anapaest,
>   But they *do* bar his spondees in Anerley.'

I'll write about the books in a month or so when I get to them. They ought to charm away that desolating journey across the States. Or is that a desecration of Georgian literature? By the way, I hope you examined Monro's accounts sternly. £4 each for four editions comes to £16 profit on each edition: which seems to me ludicrously small. However, I hope my debt to you'll be still further wiped out by the time I blow into London again.

I'll post this, & send off my bundle of MSS., from 'Frisco. It'll get to you as soon as this. I hope my last lot of verse struck you as more 'objective'. It's funny, I'd intended to confine myself more strictly to 'love' than I have. I meant to do a series—sequence—on a more or less imagined & eventless love-story. But I've not had the peace of mind & the repose to think it out.

Adieu, & my love to you

RUPERT

To CATHLEEN NESBITT *The Pacific*
April [1914]

Sweetheart,

(Don't start. It's the usual mode of salutation in Tahiti.) The last boat went away two hours before it should have; so I suddenly found myself with this poor fragment of a letter, too slight to send you. I scribbled a line on the back of a previously written note to Wilfrid Gibson, explaining my faithlessness. So, my dear, forgive me—if ever you did get my explanation. Wilfrid's in love, so he mayn't have sent it on. In any case, forgive me. For though you mayn't want to hear the aimless wanderings of a vagabond poet in the South Seas, he considers it his bounden duty, and his great pleasure, to keep you informed about them.

They're ending—for the time. Alas!—and hurray!—they're ending. At length I got a credulous friend in California to send me some money, and I've got out of Tahiti—not without tears—and I'm pounding up the Pacific with a mixed crowd of Australians, New Zealanders, Americans and English. Last night I looked for the Southern Cross, as usual—and looked for it in vain (like the moon for Omar Khayyam). It had gone down below the horizon. It is still wheeling and shining for those good brown people in the Islands. And they're laughing and kissing and swimming and dancing beneath it. But for me it is set. And I do not know that I shall ever see it again. It's queer—I was sad at heart to leave Tahiti, but I resigned myself to the vessel, and watched the green shores and rocky peaks fade with hardly a pang. I'd told so many of those that loved me, so often, 'Oh yes, I'll come back...next year perhaps: or the year after...' that I suppose I'd begun to believe it myself. It was only yesterday, when I knew that the Southern Cross had left me, that I suddenly realized that I'd left behind those lovely places and lovely people, perhaps for ever. I reflected that there was surely nothing else like them in this world, and very probably nothing in the next: and that I was going far away from gentleness and beauty and kindliness and the smell of the lagoon and the thrill of that dancing and the scarlet of the *flamboyants* and the white and gold of other flowers, and that I was going to America, which is full of harshness and hideous nights and ugly people and civilization and corruption and bloodiness and all evil. So I wept a little: and very sensibly went to bed.

There's always, isn't there, the consolation that I'm going through that place—oh, sweetened by all the nice people I know and shall know—and shall get home to England and the people and places I really love, and among them one hideous and foolish woman, an actress, a popular favourite, a public character,˙ and withal, goodhearted....

Mia cara, or rather *tau here*, I greatly desire to see you. Your image in my heart breaks like a flower (*Masefield: adapted*). Do flowers break? Anyhow, what your image does is to dwell in some innermost corner of my heart and bloom there all the time and fill it with perfume. And that drowns—out-sings, out-perfumes, out-sweets—(*damn* the English language) certain other reprehensible corners of my heart, that whisper to me 'There's a village in Samoa, with the moonlight on the beach' or 'I've heard of a hill in Japan' or 'One said, there's an inn in Tibet, over a sheer precipice' or 'The Victoria Nyanza is an attractive Lake' or 'That trail in the North West, up the Mackenzie—Morris *said* he'd go, whenever I wanted' or 'I wonder if it's true, about that flower in the Andes, that smells like no other flower upon earth, and when once a man has smelt it, he can't but return there to live in those hills in the end, though he come back from the ends of the earth': and....

There are too many vagabond winds blowing through this evil and idle heart of mine, child. Do not let me wander. You are better than wandering. Or rather, wander a little with me. For that won't be wandering: I'll be Wordsworth's lark

> 'that soars, but does not roam,
> True to the kindred points of heaven and home.'

For I'll lie between your face and your heart, then; and your face is heaven and your heart is home.

La! La! these scraps of English poetry start whispering within me. That means I'm north of the Equator, doesn't it? It's a good sign, perhaps. English thoughts are waking in me. They'll fetch me back.

Call me home, I pray you, Cathleen. I have been away long enough. I am older than I was. I have left bits of me about—some of my hair in Canada, and one skin in Honolulu, and another in Fiji, and a bit of a third in Tahiti, and half a tooth in Samoa, and bits of my heart all over the place. I'm deader than I was, sweetheart. *Partir, c'est toujours mourir, un peu.* You, who know French, know that admirable, and true, proverb, don't you? A little old French-man, a friend of mine, lately Governor of Tahiti, told it me as we leant over the rail, and watched the waving crowds, and the red roofs, and the hills and the clouds, dwindle and vanish. He was going home to France for a year for his health. 'Home'—he'd be angry at that. 'Mon 'ome, c'est ici!' he told me repeatedly. He's married to a native woman, these fifteen years. No children of his own, but plenty adopted. She was so much finer than a white woman, he sighed. So lovely, so faithful, so competent, so charming and happy, and so extraordinarily intelligent. I told him what Tagore told me about white women compared to Indian, and he gave me his observations, and we entirely agreed, and forgot our sorrows in inventing bilingual insults to the swarms of ugly American and Colonial girls on board.

But I explained to him the exceptions, my dear; the rare ladies who aren't spoilt by feminism and riches. There's still you, and a few others. But when you and they die, I shall bury you in a little row, blow up Europe with one of Mr Wells' machines, and clear out for the East, or the South.

*   *   *

I babble on. I'll write from America. While I have written this page, the boat has ploughed five miles nearer you. And while I sleep tonight, it will go a hundred more. I wonder if you feel it.

*   *   *

RUPERT

To HELENA CORNFORD[1]   *5 April or so 1914*

About 10° S. and 146° N.
A boat on the Pacific.

My dear Helena,

Ἕλεναυς Ἑλενανδρος[2] but you know the old saw; and can quote it, no doubt, more accurately than I. My Greek is something rusty. Had it been Tahitian now, or Fijian. ...

Someday this will get to 'Frisco, and then hurry across to New York, & catch the Lusitania, fetch up in Southampton, win through to London, achieve Cambridge, and finally flutter into your eager hands, half the world away. In May? But you won't have gone dabbling in the dew, in Justin's car, at Overcote. No, indeed. You

---

[1] Daughter of Frances Cornford, aged six months.
[2] Ἕλεναυς = ship-destroying; Ἑλανδρος = man-destroying, an epithet applied to Helen of Troy.

young folks don't do these things. There *were* days.... But I weary you.

I hear you ask 'What are you doing?' It's nice of you. Though I really never quite know what I *am* doing, these days. This afternoon—well, I've been reading *Antony & Cleopatra*: & thinking. It was that place near the beginning—take down your well-thumbed copy and turn to Act 2 Scene II, Helen. It's where Antony suddenly becomes unfitted for fun—

> 'He was disposed to mirth: but on the sudden
> A Roman thought hath struck him.'

A *Roman* thought, my dear. Isn't that fine? Not only a thought about Rome—though that's included. But a *Roman* thought: a thought of that stern proud dark-brown colour & rigid shape. You could have a Roman thought about anything—it would be different from having an ordinary thought about it, & immediately recognizable. So you could have—a little less definitely—a Greek thought.

*   *   *

Lately, I have been having English thoughts—thoughts certainly of England—and even, faintly, yes, English thoughts—grey, quiet, misty, rather mad, slightly moral, shy & lovely thoughts. But very faintly so. England is too vague & hidden & fragmentary & forgotten a thing. One'll not be able to have really, such things as English thoughts while England's under that irresponsible & ignorant plutocracy which your aged parents so keenly support and obey.

It'll be good to get back to theatres and supper parties & arguments & hedges & roast beef & beer & misty half-colours. But oh! sometimes—I warn you—I'll be having Samoan or Tahitian 'thoughts'. When everything's *too* grey, & there's an amber fog that bites your throat, & everyone's irritable and in a high state of nerves, & the pavement's greasy, and London is full of

> 'Miles of shopping women, served by men,'

and another Jew has bought a peerage, and I've a cold in my nose, and the ways are full of lean & vicious people, dirty, hermaphrodites and eunuchs, Stracheys, moral vagabonds, pitiable scum—why, then I shall have a *Sudseegedenke*, a thought of 20° South, a Samoan thought. And in my heart there'll be a dawn of incredible scarlet, and a sunset of such gold and green & purple as you do not know in

England, and a lagoon shot with every colour under the southern sun, and a perpetual wind, a Trade Wind, blowing coolness against the shore. And the kind & lovely brown people with flowers in their hair will come & say 'we're going out fishing on the reef, come along!' & I'll wind my parea tighter round my middle & go & pull out the canoes & we'll all jump in, with our torches & spears, and go swinging & singing out over the parks & palaces of coral & the gaudy fish, and Marai and Pépé will wail a most untranslatable song. . .and I shall jump up and curse, & go to the *Cheshire Cheese*, & read Dr Johnson & Jane Austen & Milton & whatever is most English, & eat Porterhouse Steak & drink a great deal of Ale, & so get drunk, &, I hope, forget. Damn!

Helena, do not go beyond civilization. It is unsettling. Inside civilization one can realize the beastliness of it, and labour—if one's honest, as I hope you'll be—to smash it. But when you get *outside*, you realize the advantages of not being in it *too* acutely. My dear, to return to England, where the presence of people I love obscures the bloodiness of the state of affairs, I have to cross—how can I say it?—America. Land of Individualism, of Plutocracy, of ugliness. Shall I ever bear to do it? Helena, I have been in America, & I have been in New Zealand (a much better place), and I know what England's coming to. They are countries ruled by women. And I shall live to see the total prohibition of alcohol in England, which is the female idea of politics, and the establishment of Christian Science as a State Church, which is the female idea of religion. Helen, do not, as you grow even older, become a feminist: become, I pray you, a woman.

There is no news to give you. How can one give news of moon-rises and sunsets and winds and mountains and white clouds over the Pacific at night? One day is like another: and all are good. I am growing old, & so are you. Gather rosebuds while you may, Helena; I'm trying to. There are as many here, ten thousand miles away from you, as anywhere.

I wrote a little *ballade*. I send it you. Do you like that sort of stuff? It is a very tragical brief poem. I shall follow it to England, one day—I suppose. You'll see me rolling up the drive, yet. Live patiently till I come. Be good. And give my best love to your aged parents.

Ever

RUPERT

To HILTON YOUNG[1]   *Santa Fé*
                                                          April [*1914*]
                    The California Limited. En Route.

My dear Hilton,

It's not old age that makes my handwriting like this; nor is it, as it well might be, the beginnings of G.P.;[2] it is the motion of an American train. I am in Arizona. Extraordinary thought? We may, by the way, be waylaid and massacred by Mexicans up from El Paso, any moment. An even more extraordinary thought. I got back from a blessed letterless roaming in the too too romantic South Seas, and found a few days ago, amongst many less agreeable things, a letter from you, in December. True, it dwelt upon, and complained of, my Westminster horrors. But I forgive even that for the pleasure of getting it. Hilton, Canada *was* dull. It is *not* a nice place. I was infinitely bored (except, perhaps, by the Rockies) and I couldn't think *what* to write for that green green paper.[3] Do not ever go to Canada. Rather, when you're in the Cabinet, cut the painter, or whatever it is you little Englanders want to do. I'll give a helping slash. But do go to Samoa, and to Fiji, and to Tahiti. They are the only places left on Earth. 'Civilization' hasn't penetrated there. Savagery has vanished thence. They are just lovely barbarians. I have left my heart (and much of my skin, for the sun's Hot there) in those paradisal places. I've merely come away in order to persuade you—you're the only very rich man of my acquaintance—to buy a steam-yacht and come a cruise with me round the South Seas. I'll be there to persuade you in person sometime this year. Come! It is your only chance of salvation. 'Come, and wed some dusky woman, she shall teach your piebald brood: How to wrestle, swim. . .' damn, I can never quote properly: and the Santa Fé R.R. don't supply a copy of Tennyson's Works.

Can you dive for turtles? I will teach you. Can you climb a coconut tree with bare feet? I will show you how. Can you spear fish? eat octopus? dance obscene primitive dances, and chant in 7/11 rhythm? All these things shall be yours, if you will but buy a 2000 ton yacht and fit her out and take me as sailing-master. For myself, I shall return there for ever. I'm only coming back to put a bullet in Sir Edward Carson, and another in Mr Murphy, who

---
[1] Afterwards Lord Kennet of the Dene.
[2] General paralysis of the insane, known as g.p.i.
[3] The *Westminster Gazette* was printed on green paper.

smashed the Dublin strike. Then I shall bid farewell to plutocratic dirty England: and back to the lagoons.

Your last chance of escape. Mark it. Your

R. B.

To EDWARD MARSH *April* [*1914*]
(The California Limited)
(Santa Fé. En Route)

My dear,

The train disturbs my usually perfect handwriting. It was lovely of you to send me all those books. The reading is a thing of long ago to you: but the receiving is very recent to me. I read them all day & night, in this sad train. Flecker I reserve for stability. I've finished Gilbert [Cannan]. His peevish intellectuality sometimes irks me. *Old Mole*, not as spacious or good as *Round the Corner*, is it? I think the latter part's really the best: though I *loathe* the up-to-date moral that you aren't to wipe the floor with an Armenian Jew if he plays about with your wife. I'm going to write a novel called *A Dirty —— Thief*, or some such title, as a protest against all this 'Passionate Friends' business. I'd like to hear of a modern book which portrayed a fairly laudable passion that wasn't adulterous.

* * *

I like Gilbert's passionately pedantic, Kingsy, style of writing. He's good on actors, isn't he? (I'd had the passage sent me, before, in a letter from Cathleen, quoted oh! just a *little* protestingly.) He seems, though, to fumble with so many things, & not carry them through. It was to have been a modern picaresque: & suddenly shifted to social satire.

Sons & Lovers I've only just started. But it seems to appeal to me much more in my present mood. It's so extraordinarily vivid in conception of scenes. He's always *hectic*, isn't he, a little? But I must proceed. He's a big man—

I wonder how you eventually got on with Garnett. Not very well: I think. He's really gone a bit woolly on reviews & the *Cearne*.[1] Was it much of a shock when you discovered I was his only son's most intimate friend? or haven't you discovered yet?—It's a part of one of my many subterranean lives (all caved in, now).

Speculative Dialogues.[2] I've read three. *The beggar & the dog* the

---

[1] Edward Garnett's house in Surrey.
[2] By Lascelles Abercrombie.

best so far. Though I do *not* think I'm the Universe putting Its Tongue out. Do you? Why does he worry so about the Universe? His style loses, when he gets out on it. So like dear Shelley. In his somewhat. . . *Egyptian* sense of humour, too. You know, vast, almost to ponderousness. The poet's humour.

For the rest, I read books on *Indirect Primaries*, just to get the South Seas out of my blood. One must remember one has trousers on again. I had a faint thought of going to Mexico. But I guess it won't be much of a war. You'll be vanishing for Whitsuntide soon. A yachting trip to Ulster? I *do* hope you're going to let the Orangemen slit all the priests' throats first: & then shoot *them*. I'll enlist on either side, any day.   Best love

Your nostic

RUPERT

To EDWARD MARSH   *San Francisco*
April 1914

Oh, God! oh, God!

How I hate civilization & houses & trams & collars. If I got on the *Tahiti* & went back again, shouldn't I find a quay covered with moving lights & lovely forms in white & pink & scarlet & green? And wouldn't Taate Mata be waiting there to welcome me with wide arms? And wouldn't there be coco-nuts to drink, & *pota* & *puhe* & 'curry' & oranges (oh, those oranges!) & mangoes & *avoca* to eat? And wouldn't there be the huts & the palms & the trade-winds, & the lagoon to leap into? And. . .and. . . .

But I've found good friends in the quieter part of this region, who live in a garden filled with roses & hyacinths & morning-glory. So I'll rest a day or two & try to get over the effects of my first re-entry into civilization. And then I'll sneak away East & come home. I want to live in a hut by a river & work & pretend I'm Polynesian. Will you come & see me o' week-ends?

Oh! Oh! It's all very difficult. And I feel tearful.

Here's another. I see that Naomi [Royde Smith] started printing me irregularly in a diminished Westminster. The Ranee informs me I got 16 guineas for October. About four guineas an article. Pretty bloody, isn't it?

Oh! oh! I am old as death. Eurana!   RUPERT

To CATHLEEN NESBITT   [? *April 1914*]

En route

Dearest Sweet,

Earth more coloured than the sky. Sun a red hole, angry through dust clouds. Hills one side serene wrinkled, purple (later blue). Ground at one time bright violet. Occasionally little rich *black* hill-mountains rise in the plain. Slope between other hills and plains exactly like a gigantic ploughed field. Bushes, I suppose, resembling sods. Eastern sky dark blue. Earth *mauve*. Light dies. Sand mauve and green. Distant mountains misty blue. Others black outlines. Blue indistinctness sweeps over everything.

As light fades: ground (white sand with scrub) gets to look blue, as if in strong moonlight. But there is no moonlight. Electric blue or green.

West, low, sky a rich dull purple. Changing to a bruised colour. Dull dark pink and orange above it. The colour in the West lingers incredibly long.

Then, clouds and desert *very* black. Sky very clear blue with a belt tinted orange pink.   /

so black that they're green

To JACQUES RAVERAT   *Arizona*
April [*1914*]

My sweet Jacques,

I'm in the middle of a brick-red desert. I have been there for days, and I shall be there for days, and I have a headache, and the train jiggles, and I am bored. I am too bored to read, and to write to anybody else except you. For I cannot get up enough interest in a letter to anybody else, to enable myself to forget America.

I went without letters for many months (it *was* so nice). But when I got back to civilization (screams of laughter) I found a million. One was a very nice one from you. It made me feel that the world is not lost, though there *are* one hundred million persons in the United States.

'While three men hold together,
The plutocracies are less, by three.'

As Swinburne might have written: (Damn this train!)
You and me and Dudley, you know.

Your letter was full of false reasoning and bad rhythm. I accept, in part, what you say about friendship, though. I was using it to cover also that third stage, above acquaintanceship, that is friendship —the sort of relation one has to . . . Gill, or Hugh Wilson, or, perhaps, Bill Hubback—a stage I'm peculiarly apt to.

(Thank God, the train has run into a buffalo, and, for the moment, stopped.)

Thus:

(a) One loves   —one. [He! he! he!]
(b) One friends   —eleven.
(c) One friendlies—seventy-two [if one's me].
              —twelve [if one's you].
(d) One knows   —a thousand.

N'est-ce pas? (I say, I'm *so* good at French; I've been talking it in Tahiti.)

Yet I'll maintain two things, yet. One is that (c) is a very lovely, and safe, and good state—oh! one can't live by bread alone I *know*. The other is that, though hazardous enough, (b) is safety and serene peace compared to (a). There's risks enough, and bitterness. But one has a dozen friends, and paints a dozen pictures, in life. So one failure doesn't matter, *much*. But if you miss the other thing— damme (as the Judge said in defining an explosion), where are you?

And I'll agree with Grizzlebeard that estrangement is the greatest evil in life. And yet it isn't. But the worse ones are of such a nature that no gentleman would refer to them in the presence of another. Damn it, we're not muck-rakers or German novelists. So let us go on saying that estrangement is the worst thing in the world—if only on the poor little obvious ground that it's worse than death. But we know very well that it is not the worst thing in the world.

Well, my dear, I'll waive Spain: and walk with you in Italy and France. But we will *not* take Gwen with us. Or if we do, I shall bring my mistress. There are places and times when one should leave women. A walk with a friend is one. I will give her a pledge that I'll not let you drink too much wine (ha! there's virtue in that 'too'!): if *you'll* give *me* a pledge that you won't take me up any damn dangerous mountains. I want to live. I can't for the life of me remember why. But I remember I want to.

Your account of England is depressing, and confirms my worst fears. (I hope you saw what your bloody friends the priests did, to help break the Dublin strike.) Here is worse Hell. Yet, in a way, there's more hope. There have been several thousand miners under arms for some weeks, in the mining district belonging to Mr John D. Rockefeller Jr, (who is a great man for Sunday schools): and Mr John D's hired roughs and the State Militia have been fighting them all the time, and can't beat 'em. They've shot a few and succeeded in firing the strikers' tents and burning a score of their wives and children: but—queerly enough—that hasn't mollified the strikers. They are composed of sixteen different nationalities, and are officered by Greeks who were through the Balkan War, and know a bit about fighting. And John D. is losing money. There's fun. But, oh, it'll never happen in England. Or will it?

I sometimes wish I was a Christian, or of some known religion, to be able to *curse* these people. I wouldn't want to refer to all the bloody rot which Christians *believe*. But I'd like the weight of two thousand years *moral* force behind me. Then one could let fly. Christian morality—as emended by Mr Belloc—isn't so bad. I've had to make a few additions to the Beatitudes to make it worthy of a gentleman's acceptance.

> Blessed are the peacebreakers: for they shall have the fun of knocking a lot of bloody men on the head.
> Blessed are the unmerciful. *They* never get mercy.
> Blessed are the rich in heart: for they shall see some jolly men.
> Blessed are you, when men do curse you and despitefully use you...for you shall go back with a few friends and a big stick and knock hell out of them.

That makes it better, doesn't it?

Eh, well, I've been reading Boswell, lately: and I've discovered that Dr Johnson's the only man I love. An Englishman, by God. Do you know what he said, to the extreme annoyance of some anti-Papist Anglicans, on the subject of the Roman Catholic Church? 'Their theory and doctrine, sir, are indisputable and perfect. But their practice is abominable.' What a man!

As for me, if I believed all the rot you do—if, that is, I wasn't cursed with a mind that followed the good Christian tradition of believing only what it is reasonable to believe—I'd join the Roman Catholic Church like a shot: if it was only to annoy the Pope.

But as for 'keeping one's eyes on the Ideal Church', why, I'd as soon stay a member of the National Liberal Club (as I profoundly desire to do, it being so cheap), on the pretext of keeping my eyes on the Ideal National Liberal Club. Woof!

Jacques: I do not any longer like at all Industrial Civilization. But especially not the women.

These American young women.

* * *

They are dead and damned. Necrophily would be Elysian to it. Their conversation is *infinitely* boring. Their manners are tiresome. They dress richly and abominably. And they have no conceivable particle of beauty. They are hideously selfish: worse really than the American business man. They flirt unceasingly, drearily, disgustingly. Their religion is Christian Science—damme, I'm not reverent, I like lying in bed making up dirty jokes about God, but 'Christian Science' *does* shock me—and their politics is 'Prohibition', i.e. entire prohibition of the sale of alcohol...

I shall go back to the South Seas, where women are women, beautiful, intelligent, competent, and real—in the round—three-dimensional (at least): not silhouettes with pince-nez.

Or I shall come home.

Allerliebste, farewell. Prepare your walking boots and your dialectic. The thunder of my coming shall resound afar. On guard! On guard!

I'm so well and cheerful. I know nothing of anybody in England, and I think of them all with devotion and pleasure. No, I don't think of Ka with pleasure. It hurts to think of her—I often do it—because I feel so anxious about her. I don't want to think of her. I should pray: were there anything to pray to! With love

RUPERT

To RUSSELL LOINES *25 April 1914*
(El Tovar, Grand Canyon, Arizona)

Dear Loines,

It was pleasant to find, in returning to San Francisco from a long sojourn in the South Seas, two letters from you. I'm glad you enjoyed England. I've forgotten what it is like, and I know nothing of all the people. I shall depend on you for news. I'm very glad you met & liked Gibson. He really is, isn't he, the most simple & charming & good-hearted of people in the world. I'm so very glad that he is so tremendously happy. A mutual friend[1] wrote to me of

[1] Leonard Bacon.

him, during the engagement, 'The Muse, for a time, with a deplorable tactfulness, yielded her place to Miss T.' But I hope both ladies
enjoy his favours now, and without jealousy.

I'm coming, as you see, slowly across this country. I expect to
reach New York about May 16–18. I've booked a passage on the
Minnewaska on June 6th—Wells says she's entirely your property,
so I shall rely upon you to tell the skipper to be careful of icebergs
& things. Between May 18 & June 6, I want to go to Yale, & to
Boston for a few days: & I've rather arranged a week in Rhode
Island with some antique aristocrats* who are friends of the Wells,
& also teach 'Frisco youths & maidens the President's English. The
odd week or so, I'll be in or round New York. Please be there, &
you can't go careering back to England again—not until June 6th. I
want to see you again; & exchange experiences. It's nearly a year
since I saw you: & I've seen the Southern Cross since then.

I told my mother, who was frantic about my mail, which has long
been accumulating at home, to send it to me c/o you, at 49 Wall
Street. I couldn't think of an address where it would lie safely. Do
you mind? It won't fill more than one or two rooms. And there will
be no explosives in it, I expect. Let it lie there. I'll let you know my
Washington address, in case you want to warn me not to go to New
York, or anything. I'm going to the Auditorium Hotel, Chicago
(I can say Shickawgo now, quite perfectly): but I guess I'll leave
there about the 5th or 6th of May.

It'll be good to see you again. I can never sufficiently thank you
for introducing me to the Wells.

Best wishes to your wife.   Ever

RUPERT BROOKE

* only in family: they are actually middle-aged, about 28.

To MARCHESA CAPPONI   *El Tovar, Grand Canyon*
Arizona
Saturday, 25 April 1914

I sent you a telegram yesterday from some desert station. I hope
it got to you. There was *an* address in your letter. Either God (whom
you believe in), or the spirits (whom I believe in) is (are) keeping an
eye on us.

For your letter was thrust into my berth at Richmond, or somewhere, at 12.30 in the morning, after I had wiped away my tears at

leaving 'Frisco. How it got there, God (or the S.) knows. I read it by a match. Had I started a day earlier, as I intended. Had you written a moment later. Had... For my next address for mail is New York. So I might have been in Washington a week, and never known, tho you were within a few yards!

Well, I'm going on to Chicago tomorrow. I reach there Tuesday (?). I stay there perhaps, six days. Then one day at Pittsburgh—then Washington. That makes Tuesday or Wednesday May 5 or 6. I'll be more definite from Chicago. You'll write to me there? I'm told there is an hotel called the Auditorium. I shall go there. I suppose Chicago will be HELL. I shall reach Washington dishevelled, dirty, tired and bad tempered and in rags.

I am tired of doing things for myself. I've done it for eleven months. I shall require you to tell me what to buy and where to buy it, and how much to eat, and when to go to bed, and where to stay, and what to see, and what to say, and when to brush my hair and wash my hands. Will you?

I *can* get along without such things: but not very well.

It will be heavenly seeing you. I'm not going to write anything of news or information now. I'm going to put on my overcoat and sit in the snow and look at the Grand Canyon. It is very large and very untidy, like my soul. But unlike my soul, it has peace in it.

It was divine of you to visit the Ranee.

Was she cheerful? She seemed pleased that you'd been... I love her the more—the more I think of her.

I am going to see Stanley, if he is secure and well.

I'm tired by two nights in the train so I can't write livelily. Don't be *too* busy when I'm in Washington—Have you a house there?

I want to lie on a sofa and talk. There's lots of things I want.

Aufwiedersehn
RUPERT

To MRS BROOKE   *El Tovar, Grand Canyon*
Arizona
27? April [26 April 1914]

Dear Mother,

I found last week's letter amongst my papers. I'm sorry. But it won't have delayed it much. Anyhow I telegraphed. For some reason one can telegraph from 'Frisco to England for 7s.—a dollar and three-quarters. Isn't that extraordinary?

I'll be in Chicago in three days: Hotel Auditorium. In Washington in ten. I don't know the hotel. By the way, I'll probably see the Marchesa there. She's working with Madame Montessori at that new education game. Funny, her swooping on you. She's rather a pleasant person: a Western American who became civilized through marrying an Italian and living about Europe. She must have had rather a rough time, for she lost her husband and her only child. She seems to rush about doing good, now. It was rather refreshing meeting a woman who could speak five languages and knew Galsworthy, among all the American tourists in the Rockies.

This place is very remarkable. I'd like to come to this country some day, and roam for a month. The Canyon itself is gigantic: a mile from the edge where you stand to the river at the bottom. For we're 7000 feet, and the river is 2000 above sea-level. The opposite rim of the Canyon is 13 miles away, and one can see up and down it for some thirty miles in each direction. The hole itself shelves down in great terraces and thousand feet cliffs. It is filled with what would be respectable mountains—at least Snowdon's size—on the level: but here don't come up to the edge of the chasm. They are all of red sandstone—and the effect when the afternoon light strikes them is gorgeous. I arranged to get up and see the dawn this morning. But when they called me at five, there was a snow-storm raging. So I turned over and went to sleep again. It was the first snow I'd seen for fifteen months. I'd forgotten what it was like!

I'm going out now, to walk to a point three miles away. This morning I went down into the Canyon, some fifteen hundred feet. But it was a bit of a pull up. My cold has vanished: my legs are completely healed: and the skin has returned over my sunburns. Eddie sent me a lot of the latest books for a New Year's present; so I have plenty to read on these immense, ghastly, railway journeys. No especial news, I think. Wilson gets forced more and more into war. The newspapers are wicked. But there's nothing like the popular excitement a war generally causes. It'll be a 'sort of a war' —dragging on and on.

With all love

RUPERT

To MARCHESA CAPPONI   *Auditorium Hotel, Chicago*
Monday [*30 April 1914*]

Allerliebstes Kind   (Is that better?),

The reason I'm staying more than an hour in this mucky place: is that there are some perfectly charming young people here who are doing very good things in the theatre: and I talk to them.

I leave on Wednesday night for Pittsburgh. I shall leave there Friday sometime, and get into Washington Friday or Saturday. I'll wire a definite time later.

I'm at the Fort Pitt in Pittsburgh.

*   *   *

Yes, Stanley was very charming to me, and took me out twice in his car to see Chicago—(only it *was* so cold).

The young men and women in the Little Theatre are perfect dears: and make me feel so *old*—old enough to be your grandfather, child, instead of only your   Fond father

RUPERT

(Auf Samstag)

P.S. Why do you live in 'R' Street? Have you still a name? Or are people in Washington lettered and numbered? Shall I have to address you as X 4949 g?

To E. J. DENT   *Fort Pitt Hotel, Pittsburgh*
May 1914

De profundis clamavi: never say you've not had a letter from Hell. And I've recently returned, really, from heaven.

This note's for a purpose. An able and pleasant man, Maurice Browne (did you know him, in his dimmer youth?), and his charming most un-American wife, are running a *kleines Theater* in Chicago, and doing quite good work at it. They're making a theatrical tour of Europe, landing in England June 5, and scouring London, Paris, Munich, Berlin, Helleran [*sic*], Budapesth, Moscow, Vienna, Florence, and any other place that may be thought to offer attractions. I've given them a few tips: but, of course, I'm out of touch with European theatre activities, for this year. You're the man who'd be most likely to know—from your cell!—of any occasion for pilgrimage in Europe in June, July, or August. If you *do* know of anything, I'd be infinitely obliged if you'd write me a note about it. (I suppose *you* won't be in Berlin or Munich, in June. If you *were*, they might meet Stern through you?)

Well, if you do know anything informative and interesting could you scribble it to me, by return.

* * *

We *Theater-leute* must stick together.

I hope you're well: and that Cambridge is booming.

Ever

RUPERT

To CATHLEEN NESBITT

The New Willard
Washington, D.C.
14 May 1914
Night

My sweet child,

I am excited. I have been out to dine with the Ambassador, and O'Shaughnessy was there—you, poor insular fool, don't know who O'Shaughnessy is: learn, then, that he has just returned from Mexico, where he has been U.S. Consul—and we talked of Mexico, and I drank champagne, and got so excited that on returning here I had to have a bath and dance many obscene native dances, in lonely nakedness, up and down my room, to get sober. I feel restored enough to get into bed, and still too excited to sleep, and so—you. I should have to write, anyhow, tomorrow. For I have news. Oh, dear me! I *have* such news. It begins with Maurice Browne and his wife (whom I love passionately), going to Europe a week sooner than *I'd* planned to. We squabbled—I saying they should defer their departure a week, for the pleasure of going with me: they (ridiculously) that I should hasten my leaving this land some seven days, for the honour of their companionship. Neither side would yield, so we parted in wrath—they pettily, I with some dignity. Coming here, I found two engagements fallen through: and, last night, I dreamt very vividly that I arrived in England, and telephoned to everybody I knew—and they were *awfully* nice—and then went round and saw them—and they were *lovely*. Friends I had known long ago, between whom and myself evil and pain has come, greeted me in the old first way; and other friends, who have stayed friends, were wonderfully the same; and then there were new friends, whom yet

I had known and loved longer and better than any—and they were
—that is to say, she was—oh, my dear! I woke laughing and crying.
I felt I *must* get back—I telegraphed to Browne, flew to some agents,
and in consequence—I sail from New York on May 29: and reach
Plymouth (o blessed name o loveliness! Plymouth—was there ever
so sweet and droll a sound? Drake's Plymouth! English, western
Plymouth! city where men speak softly and things are sold for
shillings, not for dollars, and there is love and beauty and old houses,
and beyond which are little fields, very green, bounded by small piled
walls of stone—and behind them—I know it—the brown and black,
splintered, haunted moor. By that the train shall go up—by Dart-
mouth, where my brother was—I will make a Litany—by Torquay,
where Verrall stayed, and by Paignton, where I have walked in the
rain: past Ilsham, where John Ford was born, and Appledore, in the
inn of which I wrote a poem against a Commercial Traveller; by
Dawlish, of which John Keats sang; within sight of Widdicombe,
where old Uncle Tom Cobbley rode a mare; not a dozen miles from
Galsworthy at Manaton; within sight, almost, of that hill by Drew-
steignton on which I lay out all one September night, crying. And
to Exeter. And to Ottery St Mary, where Coleridge sojourned; and
across Wiltshire, where men built and sang many centuries before
the *aquila*. . . . Oh, noble train, oh glorious and forthright and English
train, I will look round me at the English faces and out at the English
fields, and I will pray. . .)—reach Plymouth, as I was saying when I
was interrupted, on Friday June 5.

Cathleen, keep that day in your heart. Do not tell it: but do not
forget it. Keep, if you are in London, that evening empty. No, do not.
Haven't we all Time before us? Shall we snatch at one short hour?

And yet do.

For perhaps my heart will burst, that night, for joy of returning.
And I would see you once again.

Carissima, I have dreamt of you. I want to see your face. Where
you are, or what doing, I do not know: for I shall get my recent mail
(D.V.) in New York tomorrow. I hope that you are well and happy.
I know that you are beautiful. I am so tired of seeing people and
going over buildings and observing 'significant' phenomena. I desire
to rest, and to observe only what is significant to Eternity—you, that
is. I am very hungry to see you. It is just a year—Dear child, in
three weeks!　　　　　　　　　　　Your loving

　　　　　　　　　　　　　　　　　　　　　RUPERT

To RUSSELL LOINES   *Hotel Bellevue, Boston*
                                       Wednesday [*18 May 1914*]

Dear Loines,

I'm leaving here tomorrow morning, staying one or two days in Yale, & getting into New York Friday night or Saturday morning.

Thanks very much for asking me to stay in Staten Island. I think what I'ld like to do best would be to headquarter in town—*not* because it's pleasanter! but because I've got my eye on two or three theatres I must go to: & continually trying to get back to Dongan Hills at one a.m. would become tiresome. And then on the *other* evenings, I'll pack a bag & join you on the 5 p.m. ferry, if it's possible, & help you dig your cabbages, or fell your trees, or discuss Post-Impressionism. Will you be in your office on Saturday morning? I'll ring you up, & discuss at closer range. Is Arthur Cotton in New York? I'd like to see him again, before I sail.

I find Bertrand Russell in Cambridge, bravely battling against Pragmatism & a belief in God.

*   *   *

I'm going—for the experience—to centre in the Hotel McAlpin (Broadway & 33rd) when I can't get out to you.

R. B.

To EDWARD MARSH   *Hotel McAlpin*
                                     Greeley Square
                                     New York City
                                     24 May [*1914*]

Dear Eddie,

I got hundreds & hundreds of lovely letters yesterday, & most of them from you. Yours were all very nice to read (some of the others weren't). They covered three months, very nearly. I grew green with envy at your account of L. Abercrombie's Saturday to Wednesday. Even the best of the best people in Ryton—nay, Dymock itself— must have seemed to him a little tame after that. Raymond Buildings must be littered with dropped smocks. May I add a well-worn *paréo* to the heap on Friday week—a day or two after you get this? I've just cabled to you to find out if you *will* be in London then. For the agony of doubt conquered my deep & secret desire to wander in on you, all unexpected, one lovely June morning. I am romantic at heart: but the practical lies deeper (*vide* F. Birrell *passim*). So I've determined to secure the future, if I may. Only, don't defer a cruise to the Hesperides for me. For I can probably only stay one night, at that time. And, of course, if the *Philadelphia* meets Atlantic roughness, we won't bite the Plymouth sand till Friday night, or Saturday, or Sunday.... Still, I'll go straight to London. If you haven't cabled me here, wireless the *Philadelphia* about your plans a day or two before we sight Scilly. Oh! these names! I'm travelling—did I tell you?—with Maurice Browne & his wife. They run the *Little Theatre* in Chicago, act nothing but Gibson & Abercrombie & Euripides, & are touring Europe (under my direction, not guidance) for theatrical enlightenment. They do good work. And they're friends of Wilfrid, of Cathleen, & of me—what greater recommendation is possible? (I don't *think* you've met them before.) Nice people. I'm a bit responsible for them. I suppose it's impossible to put them up for a night at R. Buildings. Perhaps they're 'fixed', anyhow. I may take 'em down to Rugby as a headquarters for Birmingham. If there are any theatrical lights about, can you corral them? Browne knows Barker, Gilbert Murray, etc., already. But perhaps not Basil Dean. And you must press *King Lear's Wife*[1] (*was für eine Frau!*) on him. (Not that I'm tied to them, wherever they are. I can easily get away, or put them to bed, & tell you all my adventures.)

I *may* want to go to Cambridge for the week-end: for the S–c—ty,[2] & to catch 'Q'. *   *   *. No English news: except that James Strachey's in Moscow, growing a beard.

*   *   *

I'm *awfully* glad Frank Birch was such a success. I'm sure he's a great man. Can't we bring him into the Renascence of the English Theatre? A Burbage to all our Shakesperes—have you got to know him?

My only private news concerns my *rapprochement* with Mr Clement Shorter. But not a word. It's a comedy that will keep.

Do not raise your ill-named Rooker's hopes too much. The only Foreign Thinkers I know or care anything about are Lucretius & Tahiti (not the place: a wise man who lived on the neighbouring island of Moorea). And I don't think Rooker'd care for them. I might ponder Strindberg, though. But, you see, I don't know any foreign language, & I hate all foreigners. So I'm rather out of court.

Or would G. L. D[ickinson] come under the heading—they say his grandmother...

---

[1] By Gordon Bottomley.   [2] The Apostles.

I *have* to be at Rugby a good deal when I return. I've such a warmth for the Ranee. Will you have a spare moment to come *there?* But anyhow she'll let me up to town for a day or two. God! how I hate most of the people in London, & love the rest!

I'm infinitely vigorous, & excited. I can't sleep for thinking of England. We'll make life sweet for the Brownes for a day & a night & a morrow. They'll have to depart for European shrines very soon.

Thy forward leaning
RUPERT

To MARCHESA CAPPONI *Rugby, chez the Ranee*
9 June 1914

I started a letter on board but my sea-lethargy forbade its being finished.

So I cabled, the day I got in just to let you know I hadn't gone down.

* * *

It was so lovely of you to send that telegram to me on board. I found it as the boat was going through the harbour. I was roaming about, both happy and sad in my heart, restless and excited. Did you send it that morning? But you ought to have been *asleep.*

* * *

I think of you as very happy and shining, going about your ways. Is that right?

I was so happy, all the voyage. We had splendid weather, and there were nice people on board. I thought of you and rejoiced. You give me great quietness and peace.

You are very good to me.

Shall I tell you of England? I don't know what there is to tell. I'm still a little dazed. The first two nights I scarcely slept at all for excitement.

Michael is married. The Ranee is younger than ever. There is no news.

I shall settle down and work soon. In July and August I want to go away into the country and write.

Send me your blessing. Here's mine—for what such a thing is worth! I'll 'write you' again when I've rediscovered England.

Goodnight
RUPERT

To JACQUES RAVERAT   *Bilton Road, Rugby*
                                     9 June [*1914*]

No Sirrr—(American). I'm rejuvenated and beachcomberish and
all that, and hard as nails, but I have *not* got back to the point where
I can enjoy gaiety. I will *not* come to the Races. You are married,
and can view the young with an affectionate pity. But I am still, in
a manner of speaking, a Bachelor. And I hate the toads. I will wait
till you get back to Croyden.[1] And come and talk like a man to men.
I've got to creep down to Cambridge, when the moil's over, to see
about my next term's rooms (don that I am). I'll leave them my
curse—and over the hills to Croyden. At present, I'm comforting
the Ranee for my long absence (she doesn't need it a bit: she's
younger and madder than ever); and taking short draughts of London once a fortnight.

Did you ever hear what the sheepish-looking man in the audience
said to the Anti-Personal-Immortality Lecturer?

Put on paper, I pray, your rough plans for this summer. We'll go
a canter (on our own hooves) over downs sometime? The South
Seas have left me with the hell of a good thirst, and four lbs. weight
to make up. You should see me making up. Golly!

The English really *are* rather nice.

*   *   *

                           Love to both
                           RUPERT

To FRANCES CORNFORD   *24 Bilton Road, Rugby*
                                     10 June 1914

Dear Frances,

A week or two ago I received a letter from you, which seemed to
hint that I wasn't in Rugby. But I *am* in Rugby. Of course I'm in
Rugby. Where else should I be? I've been in Rugby for ages. What
funny ideas women get hold of...

In fact, I'm really thinking I must have a change. I hate travelling:
but I'm not certain a trip to Boulogne wouldn't do me good. One
vegetates so. What a *cold* summer we've been having. Though there
were some nice days in early May. And wasn't April lovely? And
weren't Easter Sunday and Monday too rippin'?

[1] The village near Cambridge where the Raverats were living.

Well! Well! I'm sorry I 'depressed' you about 'government by women'. Never be depressed by things. I never am, now. I'm only infuriated. The worse the world is, the redder in the face I grow, & my eyes bulge. There was a nosy American young lady on the ship, who said to me 'You know, Mr Brooks, I've got vurry vurry modern ideas about Sex': & everyone thought I was going to have apoplexy, & threw water & things on me. Oh! oh! oh!

Do not be muddled, Frances. I am not insulting women. There *was* a period when I despised them a little, perceiving what fourthrate men they made. But lately I've cheered up, noticing what supreme women they make. Have you ever noticed? Think of Gwen. Think of Ka (all her glory woman-ish, & what weakness she had feminist). Think of—oh, dear! millions. No, Sir. I'm not insulting women. I adore them. I'm insulting feminists. I loathe them—that is to say I loathe that feminist part in many otherwise nice people which spoils them much & other people & things almost more. And I *do* assert that women are not very good at certain kinds of governing. Just as I assert that men are not very good at suckling babies. And if any ——, being a hominist (for if feminists are 'women' trying to be men, I suppose 'men' trying to be women are hominists) comes up & says 'Men *can* suckle babies', I shall say what we used to say in such cases in the good old days at school: *viz.* (all in one breath) 'Y'r-a-liar-and-y'r-feet-stink.' A very true & fine saying.

And what I particularly maintain (apropos of America) is that a drama whose audience is always 95 per cent. women is not likely to be a good drama. I'm sorry, but it's so. It's an unnatural affair. Now an audience entirely of men (as in Greece?), or half & half—or as 3 to 2, as in the Globe—these are healthy. I don't know why. Any more than I know why you can order lunch better than I, for all that I think about eating day in & day out. These things are hidden. I bear you no malice. God be with you.

Oh, yes. I'm very well, & full of vitality, & that sort of thing. They say you're going to see a doctor. Do not do that too much. Go for the summer to Ruan, & bathe often & fear neither God nor man. And I will come down and stay a week with you there, & tell you great lies about the South Seas. You are the only person, Frances, who ever believed *all* my lies. Nothing (short, perhaps, of incredulity) can shake my devotion to you.

Get very fat & well, & in August you & Francis & Justin & I will walk over the downs for five days: 12 miles & a sonnet a day each.

There is certainly a great deal to be done in life. I am highly excited about it.

All love to Francis & yourself   Palofa!

RUPERT

To FRANCES CORNFORD   [Postcard]
Sunday [*15 June 1914*]

I'm awfully glad you're better. It sounds a lovely way of being cured.[1] I wish I'd tried it in the old days. It's made me start a poem for you—

> 'The world may go from worse to worst
> *I* shall recline at Chislehurst
> And in a neuropathic attitude
> Feed my subconsciousness with platitude.'

Church villa sounds just the place. I'll be in Cambridge sometime— probably in July—to survey the position & clean my rooms. I may stay in King's but I'll eat food with you & talk. I want very much to come to Cley. It sounds lovely. I'd write another play, & be infinitely domestic & placid. And one day we'd walk over to tea with Lady Mary [Murray]. The future's a glorious pink—'protective coloration' says Jacques—mist at present. But I'll get clearer about my plans soon.   *   *   *

R.

To MRS CHAUNCEY WELLS   *24 Bilton Road, Rugby*
18 June 1914

Dear Mrs Wells,

I missed the Bacons in the East. I was sorry. I started back sooner than I expected to. And I very stupidly lost the introduction to the man on the Century;[2] so I was without means of discovering their whereabouts. I don't think you've seen New Numbers, so I'm sending these two copies—all that's out up to date. There's some awfully good Abercrombie in it: and we're rather proud of the whole thing. Some of the things I read you in April just missed this number and will appear in the next: and I shall have twenty or thirty pages in the fourth number. We have already more than enough subscriptions to cover expenses, and there's also the sale of odd copies —so all seems flourishing! I find England very lovely and quite

[1] Treatment by 'suggestion', to which F.C.C. submitted for a short time.
[2] i.e. the American journal of that name.

unchanged—except that the upper classes are a little more anarchic. The last few days here have been glorious, and the air is so heavy (but not sleepy) with the scent of hay and mown grass and roses and dews and a thousand wild flowers, that I'm beginning to think of my South Sea wind [as] pale and scentless by comparison! I am leading a fragmentary life—as soon as I get to London I want to be out in the country, rolling in the meadow, and when I'm there, I'm looking up the next train to London to lunch with some friend I haven't seen for eighteen months. I hope California is still beautiful. I suppose the hills are browning by now. I shall long remember what a mass of flowers Berkeley was when I last saw it.

Please let me know if your plans for coming to Europe next year solidify.

*   *   *

With best wishes
Yours ever
RUPERT BROOKE

To EDWARD MARSH   *24 Bilton Road, Rugby*
                                          22 June

later

What I forgot to say is: I *think* I left a small bottle in my room. It holds a congealed strangeness. Do not let Mrs Elgy destroy it. It is coco-nut oil, for my anointing, &—at 55° North—more precious than spikenard. My only comfort in a strange land. I have some here: but that's my London stock. Let it be stored.

R.

To JACQUES RAVERAT   *Tuesday*
                              (just back from the Pinque)
                                   [*July 1914*]
Cheero!
The snail (=Lytton Strachey)'s on the Thorn:
(& may he Stay There):
The afternoon is dew-pearled:
The Dud is in London
All's right with the World!¹
Cheeroh!

Yes *Sirr*. There was a knock—Friday evening—Naked, I opened Eddie's door. And there he stood. First he apologized for not having

---

¹ A parody of a passage in Browning's *Pippa Passes*, pt. 1.

answered a *very* urgent letter of mine, of May 10th, demanding some immediate theatrical information. Then—relations readjusted—he said 'Hullo!' He is Balder than ever. And far nicer. Oh, awfly nice. I laughed for hours at his account of everything. I *do* think Dudley has a *funnier* sense of Yumour than anybody I know. And he was even more shiningly good than before. I think Germany is not so bad as London, really. It's stupid and ugly: but goodness can flourish there—though it'ld never *grow* there. He blooms, a rose among Cabbages. But in London—the miasma poisons flowers. But he *is* nice. And infinitely busy about politics and Anglo-German relations and God knows what. Interviewing Sir This and Lord That. Writin' the most *important* articles.

I'm rushing across in my Car to Gloucestershire tomorrow, to stay with Wibson two days, to discuss our financial ventures with him and Abercrombie. Thursday I dart back to London. Thursday night I take Herr Ward to see the Bally—a new affair by his compatriot Strauss—who, by the way, isn't a Jew, so may be patronized. The Bally is going in more and more for decorations by Bennois (Benois?) and other decent people, and less and less for Bakst, the Jew; so it's improving, in *that* way. Sunday I take a young woman out into the country. Tuesday I have to be in London again. So it doesn't look as if I'll be seeing you in your house yet awhile. It's so *BLOODY* being celibate. One hangs hopelessly round young women one doesn't care for a scrap, and—at this date—sees through entirely. And if one *doesn't* do that: one's too bally restless to work. All very dull. Wish to God I was married.

* * *

But why don't you rush up to London to see Dudley and me? Dudley's always under the impression that he is too busy to leave London. But get him *in* London—as I did on Saturday—and you can keep him all day without him ever seeing a politician. The dear. Wire to him to get you a seat too for Thursday night: and we will dine, attend the Opera and uproariously sup together. And I will explain to you how to be Hard. I'm as hard as Hell. The intensest things rebound from me. It's quite easy: and great fun—except when it's lonely. I've a lot of the *silliest* stories—mostly from Eddie—if I can remember them. The sort that aren't at all illuminating: and only make you laugh till you're sick. There's not an extra bed free at Eddie's, I fear, because a true aristocrat is usurping it that night.

* * *

As for Land, my frog, we must have a Great Deal, held in common. It is good for men to work of themselves, but not too much *for* themselves. In my part of the world, if we want to build a canoe, we all put wreaths in our hair, and take the town hatchet, and Bill's axe, and each his own hunting knife, and have a bit of pig each, for luck, and a drink, and go out. And as we go, we sing. And when we have got to a large tree, we sit round it. And the two biggest men take the axes and hit the tree in turn. And the rest of us beat our hands rhythmically, and sing a song saying 'That is a tree—Cut down the tree—We will make a boat—and so on'. And when those two are tired, they drink and sit, and other two take their places.... And later is the hollowing of the canoe, and the fashioning of an outrigger and the making of benches and the shaping of paddles. All this is under the direction of the best carpenter. And when all's done, we go home and sing all night and dance a great deal. For we have another canoe.

And when you have got a lot of other Goddites together and started to build a Cathedral, why, you'll see what fun it is working together, instead of in a dirty little corner alone, suspicious, greedy, competitive, hating all the world, like a modern artist or a French peasant or a money-lender or a golfer.

* * *

Tra! la! do come, one or both, to see Dudley. He's the refreshingest thing. He tells me all about Art. For the time, he makes even London clean and lovely.

Thine, in the Cause,

RUPERT

To JACQUES RAVERAT

Telegrams: Hell
c/o Eddie
Friday night
[*July* ? *1914*]

My dear Child,

Your general remarks are absurd. I have no respect for young women. I have as little as a sick man has for that gruel which he has to take to keep him alive. I know *all* about them. And I hate them.

* * *

I desire to consult you about Marriage. I *must* marry soon. And

I can't find anyone to marry—oh, I suppose one *could* marry anyone: but, I mean, I can't decide whom to marry. It seems such an important step. Perhaps there's a better choice in Samoa.

With love
RUPERT

You'll be relieved to know that I pray continually. Twelve hours a day, that I may, sometime, fall in love with somebody. Twelve hours a day that I may *never* fall in love with anybody. Either alternative seems too Hellish to bear.

To HUGH DALTON

Off to
24 Bilton Road, Rugby
5 July 1914

My dear Hugh,

I find I can't get back in time for Tuesday night. I'm sorry. I am free as the wind on *Thursday* night. Are you? You can shelve your wife. Nothing shall occupy me on Thursday night till I hear from you. Write immediately to Rugby. All other times I am dining with E. Gosse, or H. James, or S. Olivier, and others of my contemporaries.

How horrible it is to be a bachelor.   RUPERT

To RUSSELL LOINES

24 Bilton Road, Rugby
6 July 1914

Dear Loines,

You will have received from Wilfrid Gibson a parcel of *New Numbers*, as you demanded. The thing is going pretty well: about seven or eight hundred of each number, which pays expenses very easily, and leaves a good bit for division. It goes on selling steadily, & I suppose it always will—I mean the back numbers will continue to go off. I hope so, for the more it's sold, the more poetry, & less reviews, Abercrombie & Gibson can write: & the better for the world.

*   *   *

I'm also sending a package which explains itself: 'Georgian Drawings'. I think, myself, it's going a bit far to call a lot of beastly artists *Georgian*, when the name has been appropriated for a nobler clan. And it's generally agreed that Marsh has got Georgianism on the brain, & will shortly issue a series of Georgian poker-work: & establish a band of Georgian cooks. Still, there it is (or will be): & it'll contain work by most of the good young people in England. So if you find anyone who is interested in modern English stuff— fire them one of the prospectuses.

*   *   *

England is very nice, & very like the South Seas: full of lovely scenery & nice people & nasty people. Some of the scenery & many of the nice people I have seen. Dickinson was amiable & enthusiastic as ever. His book's expected for the autumn. [Roger] Fry I found less tired than I have seen him, & as plausible & delightful as ever. Almost he persuaded me to be a—whatever the latest thing is— Paroxist, I believe. I went over the Omega Workshops: but I could see little except the animals, lampshades & rugs that pleased me. I thought the chairs & the cushions *too* shoddy.

I've stayed two days with Gibson. He is still in a Heaven of delight. I'm going down there again in August. He has been too happy to do *much* work (a state *I* don't quite understand: I can comprehend being too *miserable* to work). But he is starting to do a little. Abercrombie is full of reviews: too full. His wife is expecting a third child. You didn't see *his* cottage, did you?—only the Gibsons'? Abercrombie's is the most beautiful you can imagine: black-beamed & rose-covered. And a porch where one drinks great mugs of cider, & looks at fields of poppies in the corn. A life that makes London a very foolish affair. Yet I keep finding myself in London. There's nothing 'on' there: except the Russian Ballet. Shaw's Pygmalion I haven't yet seen. I'm going—without any very great hopes—next week.

There's some good stuff of Wilfrid Gibson's in next *New Numbers*. I doubt if there's any other news of *first-rate* importance. The appearance of the Nationalist Volunteers has transformed the situation in Ireland in a very ludicrous way. The Prime Minister & the Cabinet must be, secretly, enormously pleased. Everything else is rather stationary. No strikes, no wars, no nothing.

By the way, I'm going, when I get settled, to take in an American paper to keep me in touch. I *think* I shall take *The Nation* (U.S.). Have you any better suggestion?

The Gibsons send their love to both. So do I.

Ever

RUPERT BROOKE

To LADY EILEEN WELLESLEY   *Rugby*
                                        Sunday night
                                          In Bed
                                        [*July 1914*]

Oh dear, I've been so busy all day: & I can't quite remember why. This morning—this morning I read the paper: & then thought about it: & then thought about other things: & then it was lunch. This afternoon my brother drove me out in the car. And now it's tonight.

We looked at all the places thirty miles away. We'd decided we wanted to go thirty miles away. Finally I chose Hampden-in-Arden. I remembered once passing through a station of that name. And I've always wanted to see the forest of Arden...Hampden-in-Arden. What a name to dream about! Perhaps one shouldn't have *gone* there. Arden—it's ten miles north of Stratford—is a little tamed nowadays. No holly & horns & shepherds & dukes. We caught one glimpse of a hart weeping large-eyed on the brink of the Stratford–Birmingham canal. Neither Rosalind nor Audrey. And Orlando's in an O.T.C. on Salisbury Plain. Everyone else was Jaques: I a shadowy Touchstone.

But it *is* lovely. It's the sort of country I adore. I'm a Warwickshire man. Don't talk to me of Dartmoor or Snowdon or the Thames or the Lakes. I know the *heart* of England. It has a hedgy, warm bountiful dimpled air. Baby fields run up & down the little hills, & all the roads wriggle with pleasure. There's a spirit of rare homeliness about the houses & the countryside, earthy, uneccentric yet elusive, fresh, meadowy, gaily gentle. It is perpetually June in Warwickshire, and always six o'clock of a warm afternoon. Of California the other States in America have this proverb: 'Flowers without scent, birds without song, men without honour, & women without virtue'—and at least three of the four sections of this proverb I know very well to be true. But Warwickshire is the exact opposite of that. Here the flowers smell of heaven; there are no such larks as ours, & no such nightingales; the men pay more than they owe; & the women have very great & wonderful virtue, & that, mind you, by no means through the mere absence of trial. In Warwickshire there are butterflies all the year round & a full moon every night, & every man can sing 'John Peel'. Shakespeare & I are Warwickshire yokels. What a county!

This is nonsense; and I will grant to you that Richmond Park is lovelier than all the Midlands, & certainly better inhabited. For Hampden was just too full of the plutocracy of Birmingham, short, crafty, proudly vulgar men, for all the world like heroes of Arnold Bennett's novels. They were extraordinarily dressed, for the most part in very expensive clothes, but without collars. I think they'd *started* in collars, but removed them by the way. They rolled out of their cars, and along the street, none so much as five foot high, all hot, & canny to the point of unintelligibility, emitting the words 'Eh...' or 'Ah, lad...' at intervals. They were profound, terrifying, and of the essence of Life: but unlovely. But in Richmond Park there's you. It's too late. I must go to sleep. God be with you. You frightened me by coughing up a red stain in the cab. You're all right, aren't you? Please take care of yourself. Eileen, there's something solid & real & wonderful about you, in a world of shadows. Do you know how real you are? The time with you is the only waking hours in a life of dreams. All that's another way of saying I adore you.

Goodnight

RUPERT

To GWEN RAVERAT   *Rugby*
                                          Monday [July 1914]
My dear Gwen,

Life is extraordinarily easy for married people, isn't it?

Cathleen is coming to London on Thursday to see an American Impresario and to go with me to the P.M.'s garden party. But she has to go off to her performance at Eastbourne before dinner. So I *am* inextricably free.

I don't like your taste. 'Gustave's'—those very dirty little places, established by the Latin races, and frequented by would-be Bohemians. You romantic provincials! I can't *eat* there, but I'll come and watch you eating. Soho makes me sick. So does Mongolian music. I *do* think you're degraded. I'd go to that, even, for the pleasure of sitting next you and Jacques. But there's only one chance in 372 that I should be next you: and a greater chance of my being next a Str-ch-y—they also dote on Asiatic performances. I *might* get Margery to go with me. The only virgin I respect.

Anyhow, I'll see you at 'dinner'.

Cookham was asking if and when he could catch you two. I think he may have fallen among thieves by the way.

RUPERT

Could we go on Friday to the Frog-Art show at Grosvenor House? From the First Frog to Cézanne—no later.

> There once were two Artists said 'Ho!
> Let us Go, and eat Dirt, in Soho!
> Et après ça, allez,
> Ze Mongolian Ballet!
> O, *aren't* we Bohemian, O!'

To STANLEY SPENCER *24 Bilton Road, Rugby*
31 July 1914

Dear Cookham,

I got to the Marble Arch that day at 3.40: as arranged. I stayed until 4.5. Then I went away, as I got tired of waiting, and I had another appointment.

I spent my time in leaning against that large dust-bin, which is the other chief adornment of that open place: and composing a long poem against artists and all faithless people who defile God's fair world by parodying it with dirty smears of paint on little bits of wood.

I spent last week-end with Jacques and Gwen. They are wonderful. It is so refreshing, being with real and fine people. London is full of very nice, kind, indifferent people, like Eddie, tempered by a handful of disgusting and contemptible people, like —— or ——. When one gets away to the Raverats—it's like getting into the open air, after being in a rather pleasant airless room, which would be *all right*...if it wasn't rather stuffy and the cat hadn't made a mess in the corner.

Gwen is doing a fine *Pietà*—Christ's body with two women. You've probably seen studies for it. I like Jacques' landscapes better than Gwen's, and Gwen's figures better than Jacques'. I wonder if that's right? I wish I knew about painting.

I've left Raymond Buildings for months. I don't know when I shall go back. In October, I suppose. I'm glad I was there when you came. I'm going sailing or walking with Jacques, in ten days or so. At least, I want to. But this damned war business....If fighting starts, I shall have to enlist, or go as a correspondent. I don't know. It will be Hell to be in it; and Hell to be out of it.

At present I'm so depressed about the war, that I can't talk, think, or write coherently.

God be with you!
Yours ever
RUPERT BROOKE

P.S. Don't address me as 'Mr' Rupert Brooke. It makes me feel so damned old.

To FRANCES CORNFORD   *24 Bilton Road, Rugby*
                                              Friday
                                         [*31 July 1914*]

Dear Frances,

I'm sure I shall love Umgeni.[1] It sounds far more romantic than Fiji.

*   *   *

I shall be very happy with Miss Macdonald. I'd be very happy with anyone—except three or four persons, I feel you somehow aren't likely to have staying with you....

It will be nice. I'm afraid I'm very depressing & unpleasant just now. I'm so much depressed about the war.

Jacques & Gwen were splendid. I find Jacques the only entirely reasonable person in the world. I'm growing old & intolerant, & I find I can only *bear* staying with married people now. The world is divided into married people & intolerable ghosts.

quorum pars minima
RUPERT

To JACQUES RAVERAT   *Rugby*
                                 Saturday [*1 August 1914*]

My dear Jacques,

I think one *can't* go to Cornwall—unless a miracle happens, and the sky clears. Margery says the sailing there is the best in England; and she and Bryn *are* nice; so I rather hanker after it.[2]

But what can one *do*, if there's war? I go to Norfolk on Tuesday. Write to me. You know the Cornfords' address. I *must* get down towards Bristol by the 17th.

We might just paddle about in Norfolk, or walk the Cotswolds, or up the Thames.

Everyone in the governing classes seems to think we shall all be at war.

[1] The name of the house in Cley-next-the-Sea where the Cornfords were staying.
[2] A party of Brooke's friends were in camp at Manaccan in Cornwall, across the bay from Falmouth, and we were there on August 4, when war was declared.

Everything's just the wrong way round. *I* want Germany to smash Russia to fragments, and then France to break Germany. Instead of which I'm afraid Germany will badly smash France, and then be wiped out by Russia. France and England are the only countries that ought to have any power. Prussia is a devil. And Russia means the end of Europe and any decency.

I suppose the future is a Slav Empire, world-wide, despotic, and insane. Have you ever read *Sanine?* It's just going to be translated into English. That's what Russia is like.

God be with you
RUPERT

I didn't write to Gide. I don't suppose he's come. Anyhow I shouldn't have had time to get hold of him in London.

The Ranee says that the *Caillaux* trial proves that we can't trust France. And Jaurès!

To LADY EILEEN WELLESLEY   *24 Bilton Road, Rugby*
1 August 1914

Dear Lady Eileen,

Your letter has only just found me. Alas! If only I'd stayed in London a few hours longer, I should have received it there, and come racing round to get tea and the cigarette-case. But I left London for ever after lunch yesterday.

(It's *not* my cigarette-case, by the way. Mine lies before me at this moment. I've just taken from it one of those cigarettes that taste so much better out of your box.)

It is raining. Every now and then one goes out and buys an evening paper to find the news. And the news is always a little worse. Half the day I have been trying to read Maurice Baring on Russia; and the rest of the time I have sat staring at an unfinished long poem on the fact that mountains, & mules, & other people's ideas, really exist only inside one's own mind. A comfortable thought—perhaps. But the poem, like the reading of M. B., doesn't progress. I grow irritated with Russia, & more than irritated with myself & my poem. What a state of mind for the 1st of August! If war comes, should one enlist? or turn war correspondent? or what? I can't sit still. I wish I could fly. One feels as depressedly restless as in those dreadful pauses of a day or two after one's sent off a proposal of marriage, & before the reply comes. What *will* happen tomorrow? and whatever it is, won't it be dreadful?

In fact, I'm in too gloomy a mood to write a readable letter. I wish I were Irish. A Celt becomes melancholy beautifully. He thinks of the sorrows of Deirdre or Maurya, & the moth-hour, & the pale opal veils of dawn. But an Englishman melancholy is an uninspiring thing; a conglomeration of swear-words and uncharitable thoughts & awkward limbs. That am I. I hate the Universe.

Goodbye. It was very nice last Wednesday.

> Yours sincerely,
> RUPERT BROOKE

To EDWARD MARSH   *Rugby*
                                    Sunday [2 August 1914]
Dear Eddie,

I'm going (D.V.) on Tuesday to

> c/o F. M. Cornford
> Umtata,[1] Cley
> Norfolk

for at least a week. I give you my address, because I feel you're the one link I have with the heart of things at this bloody time. Send me a card, once, to say how things are.

Mrs Elgy, in a flood of affection for me at my departure, put any little gifts she could find into my bag. Frances Cornford's *Poems*, & *Les Caves du Vatican*, are the only ones I've yet found. Maurice Baring on Russia I took myself. All shall return to you, in time.

Also, I have your green trunk. I demanded the bag Shaw Stewart took away once. Mrs Elgy said, 'Ar. Mr Marsh 'e *thinks* Mr Shaw Stewart sent that bag back. But 'e 'asn't. But Mr Marsh *thinks* 'e 'as.' She spoke with gloom, as if it was a well-known monomania of yours. So she gave me your green trunk. I wonder if that is all right...You hold, as hostage, the Virgin Mary, Christ, & Oa-haka-mana-ia. Protect them against the brutal soldiery, if London is sacked. Now the thing has really come, I feel as if I *can't* sit still. I feel I must go as a correspondent, if I can't as a fighter. Tell me if you hear of any jobs.

Tomorrow, I'm twenty-seven.

I feel as if I'd left London for ages. I *did* enjoy July. It's now a far & lovely vision. I thought Violet quite adorable on Thursday night.

---

[1] The next house to Umgeni.

All these things are past. Do you have a Brussels-before-Waterloo feeling? that we'll all—or some—meet with other eyes in 1915?

I had a nice lunch with John [Drinkwater] & his wife. Except that I had to undergo the ordinary ordeal—'What had I read of his lately? & how did I like it?'

Keep Basil Dean up to the mark about Cathleen. It would be a glorious chance: if there *are* theatres still in December. She'll be eternally grateful. Will you have to start a series of Georgian Actresses? I suppose Violet would forbid it.

Ever

RUPERT

To LEONARD BACON   *3 August 1914*

Dear Bacon,

In going over and sorting my papers today, I found an immense envelope containing all the letters I wrote on the boat coming to England. This, I'm sorry to say, was one of them. I'm much ashamed of myself. May it explain unexplained silences and almost forgotten non-appearances.

I hope your muse is flourishing. From Europe the Nine, with the Arts and Graces, have fled shrieking before Bellona. God! What a time!

One's heart is too heavy to write. I hope you're having a good time. I wish I had seen you again. I shall, perhaps, next year? If ever you and your wife have a snapshot taken of you standing among the flowers in that secluded garden—send me one.

Love to the Wells'.   Yours ever

RUPERT BROOKE

To JACQUES RAVERAT   *Cley*
Thursday [*6 August 1914*]

My dear Jacques,

You mustn't get excited.

I asked Eddie about interpreters' jobs. He didn't seem to think anyone was wanted just now. He promised to keep you in mind. There may be such posts vacant when a few people are killed off,

I suppose. There'll be plenty of work to do, later on, when the strain begins: seeing that the poor get enough food, and that the rich don't get too much, and so on. Unless any country gets suddenly smashed, it'll probably be the people who hold out longest who win. So the best one can do is to try to keep things going levelly and sensibly.

One can't 'go and fight' in England. Volunteers are admitted neither to the Navy nor the Army. If one joins the Territorials now, they give you six months' training, and then let you garrison the chief ports and sea towns, *if* the Expeditionary Force leaves England. It *might* be worth doing, if the Expeditionary Force *does* leave England.

At present, I can't get a job as War Correspondent. I've tried, in various directions. I suppose, there too, vacancies crop up if the others get killed.

I'm afraid you've been seeing the *Times*. I wish you saw some other paper to counteract it. I hope you'll believe only a quarter of what you see in any paper, and an eighth of what you see in the *Times*.

As for Dudley, I hope he'll keep his head, and not quarrel with anyone. He certainly won't send A[nne] M[arie] to England, I should think. It'd be impossible to get here. I hope she gets away with her mother, somewhere quiet, and leaves him to his work, if he's still doing any. Perhaps *he'll* come across, somehow.

With love

RUPERT

To CATHLEEN NESBITT   *Norfolk*
Saturday [*August 1914*]

Oh my dear, I'm so sorry our meeting isn't going to come off. I was looking forward to it. It's so difficult in these doubtful days to know when we shall meet.

I shan't come West at all, I think. I'm leaving here on Monday. Then I go to Eddie's for a night, if he'll have me. I want him to get me a job of some kind. I'd like to go off with the Army or Navy, in some capacity. I know one man who is going with the Army as Assistant Post-Censor. I suppose if there's nothing else, one ought to train as a territorial. But it's rather a damnable waste of time (for a selfish person), to drill for half a year, and never see or do anything.

*   *   *

The papers report that Dudley Ward had rather a bad time in Berlin: he nearly got mobbed. You remember him, the spectacled youth who travelled with us to Princes Risborough, and loved you? I gather he's coming to England, and may be bringing his wife and little child with him. It'll be a bad time for *her*, poor lady. If you come back to London, you must be nice to her.

Oh, my dear, I wish I were with you. I feel dazed and troubled these days. The general uneasiness and tension of minds seems to take all the strength out of me. I feel 'dopey'. I have need of your companionship and loveliness.

The Cornfords have a child, a daughter, nearly a year old. It's queer to me, living near a baby; and it's impressive watching them with it. It must be strange to have a child out of one's own body.

*   *   *

When shall we meet? Give me the benison of your hands.

Be happy and well

RUPERT

To CATHLEEN NESBITT   *c/o E. M. indefinitely*
                                      Wednesday night
                                      [*12 August 1914*]

Dear child,

I've just been to a music-hall. I feed with Eddie every night from 9 to 10. Then he goes back to the Admiralty. Tonight I turned into the Coliseum. It was pretty full. Miss Cecilia Loftus was imitating somebody I saw infinite years ago—Elsie Janis—in her imitation of a prehistoric figure called Frank Tinney. God! how far away it all seemed. Then Alfred Lester. Then a dreadful cinematograph reproduction of a hand drawing patriotic things—Harry Furniss it was—funny pictures of a soldier and a sailor (at the time, I suppose, dying in Belgium); a caricature of the Kaiser, greeted with a few perfunctory faint hisses. Nearly everyone sat silent. Then a scribbled message was thrown; 'War declared with Austria. 11.9.' There was a volley of quick low handclapping—more a signal of recognition than anything else. Then we dispersed into Trafalgar Square, and bought midnight war editions, special. All these days I have not been so near tears. There was such tragedy, and such dignity, in the people.   *   *   *

RUPERT

To LADY EILEEN WELLESLEY   *c/o E. Marsh (again)*
                                   5 Raymond Buildings
                                         Gray's Inn
                                 15–17 August [1914]

It's not so easy as you think—for a person who has no military training or knowledge, save the faint, almost prenatal, remembrance of some khaki drilling at Rugby—to get to the 'front'. I'm one of a band who've been offering themselves, with a vague persistence, to their country, in various quarters of London for some days, and being continually refused. In time, one of the various doors we tap at will be opened. Meanwhile, I wander.

One grows introspective. I find in myself two natures—not necessarily conflicting, but—different. There's half my heart which is normal & English—what's the word, not quite 'good' or 'honour-able'—'*straight*', I think. But the other half is a wanderer and a solitary, selfish, unbound, and doubtful. Half my heart is of England, the rest is looking for some home I haven't yet found. So, when this war broke, there was part of my nature and desires that said 'Let me alone. What's all this bother? I want to work. I've got ends I desire to reach. If I'd wanted to be a soldier I should have been one. But I've found myself other dreams.' It was that part, I suppose, which, when the tumult & unrest in me became too strong, sent me seeking for a correspondentship. At least, it was some individualist part in me which said 'It's the biggest thing in your seventy years. You'd better see as much of it as you can. Go, for some paper, immediately.' Base thoughts, those: when decent people are offering their lives for their country, not for their curiosity. You're quite right. It's a rotten trade, war-correspondent.

I came to see that. I came to London a few days ago to see what I could do that would be most use. I had a resentment—or the individualist part in me had—against becoming a mere part of a machine. I wanted to use my intelligence. I can't help feeling I've got a brain. I thought there *must* be some organizing work that demanded intelligence. But, on investigation, there isn't. At least, not for ages.

I feel so damnably incapable. I can't fly or drive a car or ride a horse sufficiently well...

I've found, finally, several people in much the same condition as myself. The musical youth who would have been number four in that lunch party is one. Together we assail Territorial Bodies, O.T.C. corps, etc. Our names stand on various 'waiting lists'. (It's so much preferable to go in with two or three friends.) And some day, I suppose, somebody will find use for us. Oh, quite soon, I expect. But there's such a plethora of trainable people.

When one *is* accepted, one'll be taken away & trained for months: & then—perhaps—put to guard a footbridge in Glamorgan...Still, I may get to the 'Front' (wherever that'll be subsequently)—some-when. By then you'll be expert at sending gifts!

I seem to have put the preliminary machinery in motion: & I shall just have to sit tight till something turns up. Partly my busy-ness at seeking a job, partly a desire to have some definite information to communicate, delayed my writing to you. (Your letter followed me round most of England.) This is to give you the latest news of my situation. It's also to ask if you're in London, and, if so, if you've found any cigarette cases just lately, & can I learn for myself if you have—at tea tomorrow perhaps? (that's Tuesday)—or, at least, rescue that ghost of the other me. And it's also to say things—more difficult to express. It would be good to go to the front, and get cigarettes & things from you. I was very happy to get your letter. 'Officious'...Oh, dear me, no! that wasn't the first word which came to my lips. I'm so sorry for you. For the strain you'll have to be bearing, I mean. I don't know it, because I've no near friend fighting. I only know part of what it may be like.

Oh God! I'm sorry for everybody. I'm sorrier for the people who give under the strain. You're brave. So I'm less sorry for you. That sounds rude.

Please don't be ill.

If you answer yes, I'll come to tea tomorrow. If not, I shall con-clude you're not in London. I should like to come & talk. We might talk of Plato or Keats or El Greco, some soothing irrelevant things. There's enough about the War.

This is a badly-written, dumb, letter.

Yours ever

RUPERT BROOKE

To ANDREW GOW   *5 Raymond Buildings*
                                   Gray's Inn, W.C.
                                   Wednesday [*August 1914*]

My dear Andrew,

Many thanks. I'll hurry up Frank & Alfred. But it doesn't much matter about going in together. I don't know the difference between one 'unit' & another. I suppose one can send in without particularizing.

Andrew! pedagogue & official! They seem to be going ahead with the 500,000. My mathematical sense tells me that they'll shortly need 10,000 junior officers. As soon as there's any signs of new lists, or amplification of the old, I pray you send me a card here. And I'll rush up, & hold my personal interview with the Board, & have lunch with you. The sooner I can get something to do, the better.

I saw Bob[1] at Rugby. He was very funny about Hardy & Hawkesworth.[2] 'The War-Lords of Rugby, Oh! very terrible!' They keep offering themselves to Kitchener for the most *important* posts, & being refused.

RUPERT

To LADY EILEEN WELLESLEY *10 Downing Street*
Whitehall, S.W.
Saturday [19? August 1914]

My dear,

I'm very confused. I'm left almost alone here. A few grey secretaries: & an equally invalid Cys[3]—who, however, goes out a good deal.

I'd be free almost any time up to dinner tomorrow: sitting reading in these vast Governmental rooms. No, that's wrong, too: I'm going out to lunch with Henry James. Shall I be able to find you afterwards, 3, 4, . . .? I suppose *you're* not alone, that I could come in to tea with you? I couldn't very well get to R. Buildings, where there's no fire, & a Jew artist. We might go a *drive*; but I'm not wanting to wander about too much. I don't mind dashing from house to house, muffled.

* * *

RUPERT

To CATHLEEN NESBITT *Rugby*
Monday, 24 August [1914]

Dearest child,

I've been wicked, in not writing to you for a week. Damn. I've spent a fortnight in chasing elusive employment about. For a time

---

[1] Robert Whitelaw. [2] Two Rugby masters. [3] Cyril Asquith.

I got drilled on the chance of getting into a London corps as a private. But now I really think I shall get a commission (Territorial, probably) through Cambridge. The whole thing, and the insupportable stress of this time, tired me to a useless rag. I hadn't the heart to write. I've been having a sort of neuralgic earache. And in the intervals I've been dodging the young ladies who are in love with me. I wish I were a decent man. I suppose no unmarried man is decent, and 50% of the married ones. My subconsciousness is angry with every dreary young woman I meet, if she doesn't fall in love with me: and my consciousness is furious with her if she does. (Not in absolutely every case, this last!) I wonder if young women behave like that. I suppose it takes them in a different way. But no doubt they're nearly as bad.

* * *

[End missing]

To ANDREW GOW *24 Bilton Road, Rugby*
Monday, 24 August 1914

My dear Andrew,

I've filled up some of the less impudent questions you asked me. I've only two or three extra points.

(1) I'm volunteering for active service: if you've any way of noting that.

(2) My brother & Frank Birch are each signing a similar document and want to die with me; so when theirs come in, may it be noted that we want to serve together, if possible. (But I don't want to be retarded by the swine.)

(3) To Hell with the Prooshians.

(4) Can't I put on it that I talk German like a bird, & French like an Englishman?

If you hear of any other good jobs of a special nature, slip me in. Or let me know if there are commissions in other armies going.

* * *

I hope to goodness I get a job soon.

Yours
R. B.

P.S. To warn you—my brother Alfred'll be popping in some day soon.

To EDWARD MARSH   *24 Bilton Road, Rugby*
                                     24 August 1914

Unpacking or *Contemplation* or *The Store.*[1]

                       or whatever

In the rough:

     'When colour goes home into the eyes,
        And lights that shine are shut again
     With dancing girls and sweet birds' cries
        Behind the gateways of the brain,
     And that no-place which gave them birth shall close
     The rainbow and the rose;

     Still may Time hold some golden space
        Where I'll unpack that scented store
     Of song & sky & flower & face;
        And count, & touch, & turn them o'er

     Musing upon them; as a mother, who
     Has watched her children all the rich day through,
     Sits quiet-handed in the fading light,
     When children sleep, ere night.'

But I mayn't be back till Tuesday morning. *Perhaps* late Monday night.

                                    RUPERT

To CATHLEEN NESBITT   *c/o E. M.*
                        Thursday [*3 September 1914*]

Dearest child,

The note you sent found me in the hotel. It gave me such a...thrill. You've such a way of expressing yourself in *actions*. I felt suddenly so much in touch with you.

I deceived you—in a way. I found after I left you that the 9.0 p.m. reached Liverpool St at 3 a.m. A little *too* much! So I stayed in Lowestoft that night, went to bed early, and caught the early express next morning—long before your lovely head was raised from the dingy pillow.

My darling, do get yourself good lodgings in Yarmouth.

I've still to hear from Cambridge.

Do you want London peace news? I went to the first night of *Outcasts* with Eddie. A rather undistinguished audience. Gaby

---

[1] Printed as 'The Treasure' in *1914 and Other Poems.*

Deslys was in the front row of the stalls. I fell in love with her. Rather *too* vulgar of me, isn't it? But her wig was so wonderful.

The play was too foolish for words. Poor Ethel Levey had the part of a clinging soft would-be-good street-walker. Not a high-kick or a wriggle or a ragtime song in the whole thing! Gerald du Maurier took to drugs and was nervous and irritable and bit his fingers, all in the approved stage way. And of course he did it very well. There was a faint cry for 'author' at the end, and a pasty flaxen sweating Teuton, very young, hurried on to the stage, and bowed profusely. Mr H. H. Davies, I presume. I could have written a better play with my foot. There was a very irritating and incompetent actresss called Grace Lane who did her worst with an impossible part. I forget the rest.

Oh, I forgot *the* hit of the piece. Act III is in the flat of a *demi-mondaine*, infinitely typical. While she is playing the piano, Gerald du Maurier picks up one of her favourite magazines which is lying about—a French obscene journal. Tiring of that he picks up another, and holds it out in front of him, the title staring at the audience. It was *New Numbers*! I swear. Murmurs of subdued applause from me. Eddie had a *fou rire*. He was reading L. A.'s section, I'm glad to say. But there's no knowing which *she* read.

No other tidings. One of the less creditable periods of my life enmeshed me with the intellectuals. I hover on their fringes yet: dehumanized, disgusting people. They are mostly pacifists and pro-Germans. I quarrel with them twice a day.

I go to Rugby for the week-end.

Child, it was very lovely with you for that day. Don't forget it.

I kiss you. Be well and quiet and happy. It's a good world, even yet.

Good night, dear love

RUPERT

To W. DENIS BROWNE

5 Raymond Buildings
Gray's Inn
Wednesday [*3 September 1914*]

I should think you'd better come up on Friday evening, if you can, & we'll get away in good time on Saturday. You can remain in warmth & shelter on Friday night. Prodigious parcels, infinitely heavy, keep arriving. It will be the devil getting them down there.

I'll get the passes tomorrow. I don't think there's any worry, about going earlier.

Eddie has an immense kit bag, we might share *pro tem.* for extra things.

I have a sleeping-sack from the Cornfords.

Also I have a cold. I think the only thing is to get out into the open, & these things will vanish.

None of our contemporary sub-lieutenants have even been appointed yet.

RUPERT

To KATHARINE COX

c/o *E. M.*
Thursday, 3 September [1914]

Dearest Ka,

I hope you didn't mind, or misjudge, my not wanting to come to stay with you that week-end, nor my not seeing you now Anne's out of the way. We met rightly enough on C.O.S. work. And it's certain enough to me that it makes me feel a better, and in some ways a happier, person, when I've been in your company. Because you pour out from yourself an atmosphere of goodness; and I don't know more than one or two other people who do.

But there are other things to think of. One is, that when other people are there, besides us, I nearly always feel (and behave) extraordinarily uncomfortable and gruff and stupid. I don't know why.

And then, I often feel a sense of strain in you. Perhaps it's not there. But I can't help *feeling* it is.

And then, the thought of you—at least, if it's made vivid by your presence—makes me deeply and bitterly ashamed of myself. I don't know *why*—I mean, it's not that my mind condemns me, especially, in any way. I only know that—inevitably or not—through me you have been greatly hurt, and two or three years of your life—which can be so wonderful—have been changed and damaged. And I'm terribly ashamed before you.

And there's just the general case of old wounds: that everybody has a better chance, if they're given the best opportunities, to close and stay closed.

It's for these reasons, and only these, that I want not to see you too frequently or too much. I was afraid that my bad manners might have made it seem as if I thought you boring perhaps

*   *   *

That's very far from the case.

Anyhow, I shall be going off to train—sometime—when the W[ar] O[ffice] desires.

I don't seem to myself to do very much with my existence. And I don't know of anything I very much want to do with it. I think I find the world fairly good, on the whole, because that handful of existences I know about and care for—Dudley's and the rest— are, on the whole, happy and good. But of them all yours has to be the one which seems to me most important. Till I think you're complete, I shan't be happy. When you're married and happy, I shall believe that the world *is* good. Till then, I shall be conscious of— general—failure. It's the one thing I hope for, in a confused world. You see, you do seem *worth* so much. I shall probably see you, incidentally, in the next few days or weeks, in connexion with Dudley and Anne. Anyhow, I've tried to make myself clear.

*　*　*

RUPERT

To LADY EILEEN WELLESLEY　　　　*Rugby*
Sunday
[*Postmark: 14 September 1914*]

My dear,

This is all very confusing, & exciting, getting things for Camp Life. It appears my 'kit' won't be ready till Wednesday or Thursday, so I shall be in London till then. And will have Tuesday—till 10 p.m. I wrote that.

So you puzzled your foolish but lovely head to know what I meant by saying I was 'horrible'. Well, I *am* horrible. And occasionally it comes over me that I am. And then I feel—for a few moments—wretched. As to *why*—or *how*—I'm horrible: it's harder to say. There are so many things. I'm not especially *fickle*-hearted. I'm not—*doch*, I *am* rather—hard-hearted. I usen't to be. I think one of the things that appals me is my extraordinary selfishness: which isn't quite the same as hardness of heart, though it helps. I mean, I just enjoy things as they come, & don't think or care how they affect other people. That, my gentle and adorable child, is why I felt uneasy & frightened about you, at first. I knew how often I did harm to people, through carelessness & selfishness.

And another thing is (this sounds like a catalogue of German atrocities) I'm really a wolf and a tiger and a goat. I am—how shall

I put it—carried along on the tides of my body, rather helplessly. At intervals I realize this, and feel rather aghast.

Oh, it's all right if you don't *trust* me, my dear. *I* don't. Never trust me an inch.

Oh, I'm rather a horror. A vagabond, drifting from one imbecility to another. You don't know how pointless and undependable and rotten a thing you've got hold of.

Don't laugh. I know it's funny. But it's all true.

Well, child, if you're happy with me: that's something, isn't it? I'm certainly happy with you. We can have fun together, can't we? And supposing I go off & get blown to pieces—what fools we should feel if we hadn't had fun—if we'd forgone our opportunities—shouldn't we?

This is a stupid letter. I'm rather gray (I'm back in London, now, sooner than I thought, Sunday night): I've been bidding a modified farewell to my mother. Also, I'm tired.

It is so good being with you. You give me—much more than you know.

Be happy, child. Write about Tuesday. I love your variegated envelopes.

I kiss you good night. You'll get this in the morning. Never mind. All Heaven be about you.   RUPERT

To CATHLEEN NESBITT   *c/o Eddie's—still!*
                                    Friday [September 1914]
                But my uniform really *will* be done tomorrow
Dear love,

I've been spending the week in busy purchasings and a cold in the head. I feel so tired and stupid.

Winston was very cheerful at lunch, and said one thing which is exciting, but a *dead* secret. You mustn't *breathe* it. That is, that it's his game to hold the Northern ports—Dunkirk to Havre—at all costs. So if there's a raid on any of them, at *any* moment, we shall be flung across to help the French reservists. So we may go to Camp on Saturday, and be under fire in France on Monday! I'm afraid the odds are against it, though.

Your letter was a great comfort to me. I read it twice a day.

Queer things are happening to me, and I'm frightened. Oh, I've loved you a long time, child: but not in the complete way of love.

I mean, there was something rooted out of my heart by things that went before. I thought I couldn't love wholly, again. I couldn't worship—I could see intellectually that some women were worshipful, perhaps. But I couldn't find the flame of worship in me. I was unhappy. Oh, God, I *knew* how glorious and noble your heart was. But, I couldn't burn to it. I mean, I loved you with all there was of me. But I was a cripple, incomplete.

Child, there's something growing in me. You have given it me. I adore you. I love you in every other way: and I worship the goodness in you. This has been growing in me. I feel like a sick man who is whole again. It comes on me more and more dazzlingly how infinitely you're the best thing in my life: and that I might live a million years, and never find anything so glorious as you, for me to adore and pray to, nor anything so good in me as my love for you.

Child, oh my dear, it's very wonderful when we're together; and it's wonderful how strongly I lean on you and am thrilled by you, and live for you and hold you, when we're apart. For my sake stay well and happy. All my riches are in you.

Cathleen, if you *knew* how I adore you, and fight towards you. I want to cut away the evil in me, and be wholly a thing worthy of you. Be good to me, child. I sometimes think you can make anything in the world of me.

Dear love, I feel so happy in this new safety and brightness.

I kiss you, my dear and holy one.   RUPERT

To LADY EILEEN WELLESLEY

> *5 Raymond Buildings*
> *Gray's Inn*
> *23 September* [*1914*]

I *am* so glad you're feeling better. I don't know, of course, just how fit an orchestra of bassoons is. But it must be fitter than you seemed at the end last night.

I was so anxious for you: you seemed so tired.

It's a horrid story of yours about the telegram. Did I ever tell you of the telegram I sent to someone saying 'I'm in London. Would you like to come and see me.' And 'they' replied 'Extremely. I'll come at once Sophonisba' (*or whatever the name might be*) and it got to *me*, of course, 'Extremely ill. Come at once. Sophonisba.' So I came in a taxi. And so did Sophonisba. And we sat at each other's front doors sobbing for hours.

That is quite true. Only it was another poet, a man. But Sophonisba sounds better. Aren't I horrid? So I was yesterday. It's all a mannerism. I *want* to be very pleasant.

No news of my uniform yet. But I guess I have to get away in a day or two.

I've been sitting here reading dull books & writing letters for two hours of the evening, & not a sound. And yet last night—just 'cause we wanted to be quiet—a constant succession of alarms.

Have you been doing Belgians. I'd rather like to see you. Are you very majestic & cool & competent? Do you conceal your Rabelaisian mind?   *   *   *

I'll write again. Don't do too much, child.

Oh, I've got sleeveless socks on. They feel wonderful. Like what you told me. The sock like this [*drawing*] and my foot like this [*drawing*] & yet they fit!   RUPERT

To JACQUES RAVERAT   *London*
                                    24 September [*1914*]
My dear,

The Ranee gave me your letter a few days ago. I haven't precisely joined the Army: but I've joined the Navy—a more English thing to do, I think. I got going rather slowly. It's not a war that appeals to English people so immediately as to you, of course. I mean, you're fighting for France, we're only indirectly fighting for England. Oh, there's plenty to fight for: and Belgium's a thousand times enough. But also, against the pleasure of fighting on the side of France, has to be set, for us, the displeasure of fighting by the side of Russia. However, here we *are*. I'm afraid we'll never get a real chance at their navy. But we'll starve them; and keep on increasing our army. So there'll be quite a lot of us to avenge Belgium, or the Rhineland and Brunswick, and the rest.

It seemed it was going to be a serious and long business: and I felt that if we were going to turn into a military nation, and all the young men go in, I should be among them. Also, I had curiosity. So I put my name down for a commission through Cambridge and as a second avenue, joined an O.T.C. here called the Inns of Court: composed of lawyers. I drilled a time with them. Then Winston offered me a commission with the Naval Division. So here I am, a Sub-lieutenant R.N.V.R., if you please—for land service. I'm buying my kit. Tomorrow I return to our camp near Deal. In October we move to Blandford. We're promised to serve by January: but as a matter of fact—though this is a secret—we *may* go abroad any minute. The nucleus of the R.N.D. is marines, Naval Reserve, etc.—more or less trained men. Denis Browne is also in it: and a man who married Lady Dorothy Howard—who isn't Hilton. He wears a rather scared expression. I rather despise the Army. Britannia rules the waves. By the way, I'm generally referred to as the Handy Man.

Frank Birch (you know him?) is an interpreter on H.M.S. Vengeance. Alfred is a lieutenant in the Post Office Rifles (Active Service Battalion). His men, being the pick of English postmen, can march 45 miles a day for a month without noticing it. Hilton is decoding wireless on H.M.S. Cyclops in the Skapa Flow * * *. Hugh Wilson is a private in the Gloucester and Worcester Territorials and swears they'll be in France in six weeks: which I don't believe. Eddie is working 16 hours a day and has been with Winston to the Fleet and to France and God knows where.

*   *   *

As for Dudley, he's really all right. The only thing is, he was very much overworked, and very tired, before the outbreak of war. So when he reached London he was in a state of collapse. The way in which collapse takes him, is that he thinks he has a great deal of work he *must* do—collecting documents, writing articles, etc. So he stays in London, and gets worse and worse. I don't know how long it'll go on. But, of course, his ordinary incapacity for answering letters is magnified. He returned with a good deal of the German anti-Russian point of view: and he still knows the German case better than most people in England. In consequence, he's invited to pacifist meetings at Lady Ottoline Morrell's house. However, he dislikes all the pacificists very much. He is very eager to enlist, but daren't leave Anne and Peter. But he may go out as an interpreter when we get near Germany. The W.O. has his name.

There was a lovely scene when I was lunching with him in a restaurant: and James Strachey and Shove entered and sat down at our table and began arguing—that one had a 'duty to civilization', which was, not to fight: and that it didn't matter who won: etc. Dudley got so angry that he had to leave the restaurant in the middle of his pudding, scarlet and swearing. I followed him to try to assuage him, saying 'Never mind them. They've been influenced by

older people—Trevelyans, etc.—who call themselves pro-Germans.'
'Pro-Germans!' said Dudley, 'it's an insult to a noble name to call
those people Pro-Germans!' Isn't that a jolly insult.   .

He has now been to Holland—with Margery—and brought Peter
back. So he has his wife and baby: and all's well.

I hope you will get a gun-job. Tell me where you are, if you do.
For (this is a *deadly* secret) *if* there's any attempt to raid Dunkirk,
Calais, Havre, etc., we—the R.N.D.—will be thrown across to help
hold it, at *any* moment. So Winston says. It would be fun if I got
posted in a town where you were. You'll see me rolling up, with my
Tars, yet. I hope you get something you like.

Ever

RUPERT

To CATHLEEN NESBITT   *Anson Battalion*
                                Second Brigade, R.N.D.
                                Betteshanger Camp
                                Walmer
                                1 October [*1914*]

Dearest child,

Where are you? I've not heard for so long. At least, it seems
a hundred years since that Sunday. I don't even know your
addresses: and you promised to send them. Faithless woman!

I'm far too busy and tired to write to you. I'm kept at it all day.
This morning I was drilling like Hell. This afternoon I had to
inspect two hundred rifles. Now I'm lying on my camp bed
snatching a rest, before dressing for a 'night-attack'. We start out at
4.30, and have to 'fight' and march through the night, returning at
dawn. There'll be a full moon, and it'll be damned cold. In front, in
the sunlight, a sentry with fixed bayonet is marching up and down.
All these men are in naval uniform still. They'll get khaki in the end.
But at present they look rather jolly. I—*I*—am in control of some
fifty of them: awful ruffians, nearly all from remote parts of Scotland or—oh!—Ireland. When I try to get their names, they say
'Mghchnghchchch'. What a tongue, the Celtic! But they're very
nice, and I get fond of them. They have the reputation...

Good God! two days have passed: and we've been woken up at
5 this morning with orders to pack at once. If you don't hear anything from me for some days: it'll be because I mayn't write. I don't

know what's going to happen. We shan't be fighting, of course. So there's no need to worry. We leave here at 9 for Dover. Leave Dover at 2. Tonight I sleep in France.

Dear heart, I think of you all the time.   RUPERT

To LADY EILEEN WELLESLEY   *Anson Battalion*
2nd R.N. Brigade
Betteshanger Camp
Eastry, Kent
Saturday, 3 October [1914]

(Would you like to send me some cigarettes?)

Eileen,

I've had not a minute for writing. Did you think silence was horrid of me? You've not written either. Oh my dear, I've had such a busy week! I've been learning everything all at once, fighting all night, marching all day, drilling & God knows what. I've not had a minute to myself. This afternoon is my first free space. I'm going to creep out of camp with one of the Asquiths, who has also turned up as a sub-lieutenant, for dinner.

*   *   *

Child, I feel a strong silent sub-lieutenant. My mouth is like this, ⌒. My eyes are clear with perpetually gazing through spume & fog for rocks ahead. My skin is brown & hard. I think of nothing at all, hour after hour. Occasionally I'm faintly shaken by a suspicion that I might find incredible beauty in the washing place, with rows of naked, superb, men, bathing in a September sun or in the Camp at night under a full moon, faint lights burning through the ghostly tents, & a distant bugler blowing *Lights Out*—if only I were sensitive. But I'm not. I'm a warrior. So I think of nothing, & go to bed.

When I *do* think of anything, I think how lovely it was with you, & wonder how you are. This place is of the same sort of loveliness, partly, that Richmond has: especially at evening. Good God!

Write to me. And don't expect an answer by return.

Tired & dirty, but with love.   RUPERT

To FRANCES CORNFORD　　　　　　*Rugby*
Thursday [*13 October 1914*]

I have to report that your sleeping-bag was heavily shelled & demolished by fire in Antwerp last week. Awfly sorry. We all pay our little bit, these days.　　　Best love

RUPERT

To CATHLEEN NESBITT　　　*5 Raymond Buildings*
Gray's Inn
Sunday [*17 October 1914*]

Dearest child,

I've been very evil and idle in not writing to you. Indeed, I've been extremely slack and sleepy these last few days. I think it was the reaction after the excitement. Also, I caught *conjunctivitis*, alias pink-eye, in some of the foul places we slept in: and my eyes have been swollen, red, unlovely, exuding thick plum-tree gum, and very painful. I *hope* they're getting better. I did adumbrate, in myself, a project for dashing up to Ilkley? today. But my cold and my eyes constrained me to stay lazily and fuggily here, with a conversation with Masefield as poor recompense, and hourly lotions instead of the chrism of your kisses. I've my eye on Folkestone. I think—by hook or crook—I'll see you for an hour then; and tell you a few of all my marvellous tales, and refresh myself for my next glimpse (far enough off!) of death. It's only a fortnight ago!... We were pulled out of bed at 5 a.m. on the Sunday, and told that we started at 9. We marched down to Dover, highly excited, only knowing that we were bound for Dunkirk, and supposing that we'd stay there quietly, training, for a month. Old ladies waved handkerchiefs, young ladies gave us apples, and old men and children cheered, and we cheered back, and I felt very elderly and sombre and full of thoughts of how human life was like a flash between darknesses, and that *x* per cent of those who cheered would be blown into another world within a few months; and they all seemed to me so innocent and patriotic and noble, and my eyes grew round and tear-stained.

But by the quay we halted for hours, while the goods were being shipped, in a street composed of public-houses: so there was a nice busy time for all of us, keeping the men out of them.

We sailed that night, and lay off Dunkirk next morning, waiting for the tide: spent the afternoon unloading; and then sat in a great empty shed, a quarter of a mile long, waiting for orders. After dark the senior officers rushed round and informed us that we were going to Antwerp, that our train was sure to be attacked, and that if we got through we'd have to sit in trenches till we were wiped out. So we all sat under lights writing last letters: a very tragic and amusing affair. My dear, it *did* bring home to me how very futile and unfinished life was. I felt so angry. I had to imagine, supposing I *was* killed. There was nothing but a vague gesture of goodbye to you and my mother and a friend or two. I seemed so remote and barren and stupid. I seemed to have missed everything. Knowing you shone out as the only thing worth having...Men kept coming up and asking things. One said 'Please, Sir, I've a bit o' money on me. It's not much to me: but it'd be a lot to my wife: we've got fourteen children: and supposing anything happened to me, I wouldn't like them bloody Germans to get hold of it.' What should he do? We arranged he should give it for the time to the parson...We *weren't* attacked that night in the train. So we got out at Antwerp, and marched through the streets, and everyone cheered and flung themselves on us and gave us apples and chocolate and flags and kisses, and cried *Vivent les Anglais* and 'Heep! Heep! Heep!'

We got out to a place called *Vieux Dieu* (or something like it), passing refugees and Belgian soldiers by millions. Every mile the noises got louder, immense explosions and detonations. We stopped in the town square in Vieux Dieu; five or six thousand British troops, a lot of Belgians, guns going through, transport waggons, motor-cyclists, orderlies on horses, staff-officers, and the rest. An extraordinary and thrilling confusion. As it grew dark the thunders increased, and the sky was lit by extraordinary glares. We were all given entrenching tools. Everyone looked worried. Suddenly our battalion was marched round the corner out of the din through an old gate in the immense, wild, garden of a recently-deserted villa-château. There we had to sleep. The rather dirty and wild-looking sailors trudged over lawns, through orchards and across pleasaunces. Little pools glimmered through the trees, and deserted fountains: and round corners one saw, faintly, occasional Cupids and Venuses—a scattered company of rather bad statues—gleaming quietly. The sailors dug their latrines in the various rose-gardens and lay down to sleep—but it was bitter cold—under the shrubs. It seemed infinitely peaceful and remote. I was officer on guard till the middle of the night. Then I lay down on the floor of a bedroom for a decent night's sleep. But by 2 the shells had got unpleasantly near. A big one (I'm told) burst above the garden: but too high to do damage. And some message came. So up we got—frozen and sleepy—and toiled off through the night. By dawn we got into trenches, very good ones, and relieved Belgians.

Sweetheart, this is *very* dull. And it doesn't really reflect any state of mind. For when I think back on it, my mind is filled with various disconnected images and feelings. And if I could tell you those fully, you *might* find it wonderful—or at least queer. There's the excitement in the trenches—we weren't attacked seriously in our part—with people losing their heads and fussing and snapping. It's queer to see the people who *do* break under the strain of danger and responsibility. It's always the rotten ones. Highly sensitive people don't, queerly enough. 'Nuts', do. I was relieved to find I was incredibly brave! I don't know how I should behave if shrapnel was bursting on me and knocking the men round me to pieces. But for risks and nerves and fatigue I was all right. That's cheering.

And there's the empty blue sky and the peaceful village and country scenery, and nothing of war to see except occasional bursts of white smoke, very lazy and quiet, in the distance. But to hear, incessant thunder, shaking buildings and ground and you and everything; and, above, recurrent wailings, very shrill and queer, like lost souls, crossing and recrossing in the emptiness—nothing to be seen. Once or twice a lovely glittering aeroplane, very high up, would go over us; and then the shrapnel would be turned on it, and a dozen quiet little curls of white smoke would appear round the creature— the whole thing like a German wood-cut, very quaint and graceful and unreal. Eh, but the retreat drowned all those impressions. At 6.30 on the second evening the forts away on our left had been smashed and the Belgians had run away (probably) and the Council of War in Antwerp had decided that we'd have to get out. So we stole away from the trenches, across half Antwerp, over the Scheldt, and finally entrained in the last train left, at 7.30 next morning, thirty miles away. We had one hour's sleep, from 2 to 3, in a wet field: and we very nearly walked into a German ambush. It was rather a miracle we got away. But the march through those deserted suburbs, mile on mile, with never a living being, except one rather ferocious looking sailor, stealing sulkily along. The sky was lit by burning villages and houses; and after a bit we got to the land by the river, where the Belgians had let all the petrol out of the tanks and fired it. Rivers and seas of flame leaping up hundreds of feet, crowned by black smoke that covered the entire heavens. It lit up houses wrecked by shells, dead horses, demolished railway stations, engines that had been taken up with their lines and signals, and all twisted round and pulled out, as a bad child spoils a toy. And there we joined the refugees, with all their goods on barrows and carts, in a double line, moving forwards about a hundred yards an hour, white and drawn and beyond emotion. The glare was like hell. We passed on, out of that, across a pontoon bridge, built on boats. Two German spies tried to blow it up while we were on it. They were caught and shot. We went on through the dark. The refugees and motor-buses and transport and Belgian troops grew thicker. After about a thousand years it was dawn. The motor-buses indicated that we were bound for Hammersmith and Fleet Street and such places, and might be allowed to see *Potash and Perlmutter*. Women gave us apples.

My dear, I've a million things to tell you. We'll meet at Folkestone or in London. Are you glorious as ever? I so want to be with you.

I finish this at Camp. We're all training ourselves again.

Good-bye, dear love
RUPERT

To FRANCES CORNFORD

IMPORTANT

Anson Battalion
Second Naval Brigade
Betteshanger
Eastry

Trafalgar Day   [*21 October 1914*]

Dear Frances,

Awful rumours prevail here that The Old Vicarage is to be destroyed. I wonder if you could find out if that's so; by whose orders; & what steps could be taken in the way of saving it. I mean, could one buy it, or the land. It seems to me very important. Failing that, I want some decent painter to make a picture of it (I hear Dent has got some hack to paint it.) And if there are any good photographers about, you might turn them on. I wish Mottram was still there.

Rain, rain, rain. But it's all great fun.

Yours under Mars
RUPERT

Love to Anne.

To KATHARINE COX

Anson Battalion
2nd Naval Brigade
Betteshanger
Eastry
[*20 or 21 October 1914*]

Dear Ka,

I rather shamefacedly concluded it'ld be better to communicate with you directly. My train started a few hours earlier than it should, yesterday, and so there's a lot of little things I've forgotten.

(1) A little mirror, to stand or hang.
(2) A tin mug with a handle.
(3) A collapsible aluminium cup.
(4) Toilet paper.
(5) A bit of sweet-scented soap.

I don't think there's anything else. Perhaps I'll put it on a post-card, if there is. They're all very small, aren't they?

I'm to have my accounts for the other things, through Dudley? My eyes are suddenly all right.

I intrigued for a job for you. With Dudley. When he gets the War Office Clothing business he's after. You're to see we all get warm clothes and that nobody's sweated to make them.

Camp is very nice after the murk of London.

RUPERT

To FRANK SIDGWICK

Anson Battalion
2 Naval Brigade
Betteshanger
23 October 1914

Dear Sidgwick,

I've had an idea—in the intervals of picnics at Antwerp, etc. It occurred to me and to a friend of mine. So other people *may* be thinking of acting on it.

It's this. I've lived long enough in Germany to know how extra-ordinarily good and pungent criticism of things Prussian *Simplicis-simus* contains. I suggest a selection from *Simplicissimus* caricatures, since, say, 1900, under four or five heads—the Army, the Royal Family, Bureaucracy, the Prussian—some sixty of them: the whole to be called '*What Germany thinks of Germany*' or some such title. There are several places one can get old *Simplicissimi*. And it really does give the evil and ridiculous side of what we're fighting against, better than anyone else.

I wish I were at leisure sufficiently to ask if you'd let me preface such a book. But I'm afraid I'm not, at present. But there must be a lot of people competent. I think it's a book that *should* be published; and I think it would be a vast success.

Yours

RUPERT BROOKE

To G. LOWES DICKINSON

Anson Battalion
Second Naval Brigade
Royal Naval Barracks
Chatham
28 October [1914]

Dear Goldie,

I never thought to find myself in Barracks. Camp is all right: there's Romance in it: it's rather like 'camping-out'. But Barracks! (which is yet extraordinarily like College).

I looked in at Edwardes Square one morning two or three days after I got back from the Antwerp affair. But you'd just gone to Cambridge—I was sorry to miss you. I hope you don't think me very reactionary and callous for taking up this function of England. There shouldn't be war—but what's to be done, but fight Prussia? I've seen the half million refugees in the night outside Antwerp: and I want, more than before, to go on, till Prussia's destroyed. I wish everyone I know were fighting.

*   *   *

We go to camp near Blandford (also near Yeovil and Dorchester) in a week or two: probably for November and December. Will you be in that part of the world at all? It would be nice to see you.

Cambridge is very fine about Louvain.[1]

Ever

RUPERT

[1] The University had provided places for refugees from Louvain.

To E. J. DENT [Postcard]
Anson Battalion
R.N.D.
Royal Naval Barracks
Chatham
2 November [1914]

Your scare (reported by Denis) that the O[ld] V[icarage] was to be demolished, proves unfounded. It shall yet be left for that slower Prussian, Time, to reduce it. Perhaps I may buy it with my prize-money, after the war.

Love to everyone. Make everybody enlist, in some form. They'll be wanted. RUPERT

To MRS BROOKE *Royal Naval Barracks*
Chatham
Tuesday, 1.30
[3 November 1914]

An alarm about a German invasion in Norfolk, this morning. A lot of troops and sailors are going off now. We're waiting orders. If it's in Norfolk, we shall only be about seventh line of defence. If it's in Kent, we may get to the front. I hope so.

I'll write again if I get the chance. Very likely we shall stay here tonight. It seems pretty certain the German fleet has come out, anyhow. The Naval people are wild with joy. You'll probably find out from the papers what, if anything, is happening.

With love
RUPERT

To E. J. DENT *Anson Battalion*
R.N.D.
Royal Naval Barracks
Chatham
5 November [1914]

My dear Dent,

I have been much perturbed in soul by your letter about ——. In ordinary times, I'd be very glad to help him to Los Angeles. I gather it did his lungs good last year: and I feel certain it did his character good. He seemed much firmer and stronger. But these *aren't* ordinary times. I wouldn't for a minute have it inferred that I don't admire your great goodness of heart, in trying to help ——, as you've already very finely helped other people in the past. But I feel bound to put my point of view.

I feel it's not a time to be wintering in Los Angeles. I feel that if there's a ghost of a chance of —— doing some good by giving his life, he should try to give it. Also, that if anyone *has* any spare money, he should be trying to assist with it some of the outcast Belgian widows and children. I've seen those widows and children. I can't help feeling, I mean, that there's bigger things than bronchitis abroad. I know a girl who is consumptive. Her doctor said she'd probably die if she didn't spend this winter in a sanatorium. She's doing Belgian refugee organization and clothing in London: and is going to stay at it. One of her three brothers was shot through the head near Ypres a week ago, leading a charge. The other—who has spent a third of the last two or three years in consumptive sanatoria —is at the front in the Flying Corps: and will stick at it, till a bullet or consumption remove him—or till he returns, hale and hearty at Peace. There's nothing like disregarding weakness.

In the room where I write are some twenty men. All but one or two have risked their lives a dozen times in the last month. More than half have gone down in torpedoed ships and been saved *sans* their best friends. They're waiting for another ship. I feel very small among them. But that, and the sight of Belgium, and one or two other things makes me realize more keenly than most people in England do—to judge from the papers—what we're in for, and what great sacrifices—active or passive—everyone must make. I couldn't bear it if England daren't face or bear what Germany is facing and bearing.

If we weren't such a civilian country, people like —— might realize what I gather they (very naturally) don't, and what I've only just discovered. Namely, that 'military' life, in training, is quite 'soft', for officers; not nearly as 'hard living' as the larger part of my life has been: an existence endurable by anybody who can endure— say—college life.   *   *   *

Forgive my tirade. It inclines me to this. If you're satisfied that —— has tried every means to get military service, I (though not believing he ought to leave his country, even then) will contribute to your fund three pounds. If he waits, and goes when peace is secure, I'll willingly give ten. *Then*—it would be a good cause.

Denis is at Sheerness (and very poor). I'll send your letter to him. Geoffroi[1] has had a leg blown off. Péguy, the poet, is killed. Also various other poets. I am envious of our good name!

Affectionately ever
RUPERT

To CATHLEEN NESBITT

Royal Naval Barracks
Chatham
[*November 1914*]

[*First part missing*]

to make a list the other day, of all their 'kit'—to compare with what they should have. I soon found that questions about some of the articles on the lists were purely academic. 'How many handkerchiefs have you?' The first two men were prompted to say none. The third man was called Cassidy, 'How many phwat, sorr?'

'Handkerchiefs?'

'?'

'Handkerchiefs, man, handkerchiefs!'

(*In a hoarse whisper to the Petty Officer*) 'Phwat does he *mane?*'

(*P.O. in a stage whisper*) 'To blow yer nose with, yer bloody fool!'

Cassidy (*rather indignant*) 'None, sorr.'

They were dears, and very strong, many of them: the Scotch, too.

I feel so much what you say about hating acting at this time, child. It *would* be good if you could find anything to do instead. If you were a man, there'd be no excuse for you to go on acting. You'd be despicable. As it is, it's so hard to find what's to be done. You help by existing, my dear. Beyond that, it's difficult. Continue, energetically, to exist, I pray you. Avoid runaway steam-rollers, arsenic, Zeppelin bombs, and the novels of H. G. Wells.

You'd make a good nurse, and a good lady with the Belgians, I know well. Perhaps you'll hear of something, after a bit.

I'm rather disturbed, my dear one, about the way people in general don't realize we're at war. It's—even yet—such a picnic for us—for the nation—and so different for France and Belgium. The millions France is sacrificing to our thousands. I think—I know—that *everyone* ought to go in. I pray that there'll be a raid, or, at least, a score civilians killed.

[*End missing*]

[1] Charles Geoffroy Dechaume, the painter.

To CATHLEEN NESBITT
Anson Battalion
R.N.D.
Royal Naval Barracks
Chatham
Tuesday, 10 November [1914]

Sweet child,

I was deaf and sleepy and naval and block-like on Sunday. But oh God! I was happy. I got your letter this morning. I'm glad we seemed nearer, for a while. I know that feeling of suddenly per-ceived distance. It is disheartening. And we, wandering on different paths, have so little chance of weaving the threads of common knowledge and affections together. But I *do* feel near, often. With you, from a queer feeling of carelessness—'safety' perhaps—and certainty that all is well. Away from you, because you've a trick of coming suddenly round a corner in my mind—bursting without knocking into the grey assemblage of my thoughts—and reminding me that you're queen of the castle. Often enough, though, in these times, I have a passing despair. I mean what you meant—the gulf between non-combatants and combatants. Yet it's not that. It's the withdrawal of combatants into a special seclusion and reserve. We're under a curse or a blessing or a vow, to be different. The currents of our lives are interrupted—what is it—*I* know. Yes. The central purpose of my life, the aim and end of it, now, the thing God wants of me, is to get good at beating Germans. That's sure. But that isn't what it was. What it was, I never knew, and God knows I never found. But it reached out deeply for other things than my present need. There was some beauty and holiness it should have taken hold of. Perhaps you were near, or were, that beauty and holiness.

[*End of this letter missing*]

To LEONARD BACON
Anson Battalion
R.N.D.
11 November 1914

Dear Bacon,

It was a pleasure to get your letter: and more than a pleasure to know that you're all with us. The muses have fled to America, and are to be interned in that (technically) neutral country, I'm told, for the period of the war. Don't keep them forever. I've forgotten them—for this.

I've been in the Naval Division for some two months: went through Antwerp: and am training for further service. Where will that be—Cyprus? the Kiel Canal? the Rhine? Ypres?—and when, next week? next month? next year? No one knows. Anyway, it'll be good work, I hope: and (with the horror) fun.

It seems a most damnably long time since I saw that quiet garden off Piedmont Avenue. All my friends, but a few, are training or serving. One or two have been killed. Others wounded, and are going back. The best Greek scholar of the younger generation at Cambridge, Cornford, is a musketry instructor at Aldershot. Among my fellow officers are one of the best young English pianists, and a brilliant young composer. Gilbert Murray gets up every morning to line a hedgerow, gun in hand, before dawn. What a world! Yet I'm still half ashamed of England, when I hear of the holocaust of the young poets, painters and scholars of France and Belgium—and Germany.

It hurts me, this war. Because I was fond of Germany. There are such good things in her, and I'd always hoped she'd get away from Prussia and the oligarchy in time. If it had been a mere war between us and them I'd have hated fighting. But I'm glad to be doing it for Belgium. That's what breaks the heart to see and hear of. I marched through Antwerp, deserted, shelled, and burning, one night, and saw ruined houses, dead men and horses: and railway-trains with their lines taken up and twisted and flung down as if a child had been playing with a toy. And the whole heaven and earth was lit up by the glare from the great lakes and rivers of burning petrol, hills and spires of flame. That was like Hell, a Dantesque Hell, terrible. But there—and later—I saw what was a truer Hell. Hundreds of thousands of refugees, their goods on barrows and hand-carts and perambulators and waggons, moving with infinite slowness out into the night, two unending lines of them, the old men mostly weeping, the women with hard white drawn faces, the children playing or crying or sleeping. That's what Belgium is now: the country where three civilians have been killed to every one soldier. That damnable policy of 'frightfulness' succeeded for a time. When it was decided to evacuate Antwerp, all of that population of half a million, save a few thousands, fled. I don't think they really had any need to. The Germans have behaved fairly well in the big cities. But the policy of bullying had been carried out well. And half a million people preferred homelessness and the chance of starvation, to the certainty of German rule. It's queer to think one has been a witness of one of the greatest crimes of history. Has ever nation been treated like that? And how can such a stain be wiped out?

Well, we're doing our best. Give us what prayers or cheers you can. It's a great life, fighting, while it lasts. The eye grows clearer and the heart. But it's a bloody thing, half the youth of Europe blown through pain to nothingness, in the incessant mechanical slaughter of these modern battles. I can only marvel at human endurance. Come and see us all when it's all over. Love to the Wells' and to you both.

Ever

RUPERT BROOKE

To MRS ARNOLD TOYNBEE (ROSALIND MURRAY)

Royal Naval Division
just now at the Royal Naval Barracks,
Portsmouth

20 November 1914

Dear Rosalind,

I'm merely a sub-lieutenant. Still I blush with pleasure and pride when people call me lieutenant. So the mistake doesn't matter. Yes: I'm a sailor: like all your uncles. I met Geoffrey Howard a moment buying kit: Francis Henley several times. He's very nice.

He missed Antwerp. I was in it. A queer business. When shall I see you and tell you about it? I *tried* to notice the points of literary and psychological interest at the time. But actually I was thinking 'When will the men—and when shall I—get our next meal?'

*   *   *

I hope I get through. I'll have such a lot to say and do afterwards. Just now I'm rather miserable: because most of my school-friends are wounded, or 'wounded and missing' or dead. Perhaps our sons will live the better for it all

I knew of yours. I was very glad. I pondered it, and meant to write. But I was prevented by a sudden engagement at Antwerp. It must be good to have a son. When they told us at Dunkirk that we were all going to be killed in Antwerp, if not on the way there, I didn't think much (as I'd expected) what a damned fool I was not to have written more and done various things better and been less selfish. I merely thought 'What *Hell* it is that I shan't have any children—any sons.' I thought it over and over, quite furious, for some hours.

And we were barely even under fire, in the end!

Well, you've done it. Good luck to you: and my envious congratulations.

Will you give a message I wish you'd tell your father that I found his pamphlet 'How Can War ever be Right' (or some such name) the other day. I'd like to thank him for it. In all the bad stuff written or said *à propos* of the war, it was so good. And it said, so finely, many things I'd been feeling—or feeling towards—perplexedly in this welter. Oh, I *knew* them, I boast; but I couldn't express them. Now they're clear.

Cheeryo! (as we say in the Navy).

RUPERT BROOKE

To LADY EILEEN WELLESLEY   *Nelson Battalion*
Royal Naval Barracks
Portsmouth
Saturday [21 November 1914]

Dear Child,

I had a letter from you this morning. I read it with some attention: but couldn't help thinking 'How like one another the weeks are!' I looked closer: & lo! it was a week old. It went to Chatham & slept there.

I'm here for a day or two: or a week. I don't know. A sudden telegram on Thursday fetched me here (I'd just come back from Guy's, where I'd been visiting—who do you think?—de la Mare). I'm alone. Oc & Denis Browne are imprisoned elsewhere. But the whisper has just come to me that we meet in the end. So all's fairly well. I'm sorry I couldn't see you again, sweetheart.

My face is *burning*. I've been on the Range with Maxims, for four hours, in a wind far more unkind than human ingratitude. *That* never made me blush so—not even my own.

I wish you could come & cool my cheeks.

Carissima, the cigarettes have never come. We're 'standing by'. Do you know what that means? Nobody has leave, I can't go, tomorrow, to lunch with people a few miles away. For at any time we may be called to...Norfolk, to repel the Germans. They're expected hourly.

My best school friend was 'wounded and missing' yesterday.

You're in mourning. A hundred years hence they'll say 'What an age that must have been!' What'll we care? Fools!

Be well.   RUPERT

To DUDLEY WARD   *Hood Battalion*
                                          R.N. Camp
                                          Blandford, Dorset
                                          [*Before 15 December 1914*]

Dudley!

Last night I rolled about in this so-called bed. I've been bad lately with inoculation, a cough and things. And I dreamt I landed at Papeete, and went up between the houses, and the air was heavy with sunshine. I went into the house of a half-caste woman I know and she gave me tea, and talked. And she told me about everyone. And at last I said 'And how and where's Taata-mata?' And she said 'Oh —didn't you know?' And I said 'No'. She said 'She's dead.' I asked (knowing the answer) 'When did she die?' 'Months ago, just after you left.' She kept evading my eye. After a long silence I asked (feeling very sick) 'Did she kill herself?' The half-caste nodded. I went out of the house and out to the lagoon, feeling that a great friendliness—all the place—had gone against me. Then I woke with a dry throat, and found a frosty full moon blazing in at the window, and the bugle hammering away at the 6.30 *Reveille*. Perhaps it was the full moon made me dream, because of the last full moon at Mataiea (about which there is an unfinished poem: now in German possession). Perhaps it was my evil heart. I think the dream was true. 'There is no health in me' as we used to say in some Confession in Chapel. And now I'm not only sicker with myself than ever: but also I've got another bad attack of *Heimweh* for the South Seas. It's a bloody life. I'm really writing to tell you that the worst suddenly turned best. What *happened*, I gather (this is England), is that Papa Asquith who had been dimly amused by the whole thing, suddenly took the idea that his son had been insulted and ill used (as he had), sent for Winston, cussed him, and told him to put it right. So Winston damned an Admiral, who made blue Hell for the G.O.C. Marines, who wiped the floor with X, who—and finally two Sub-lieutenants Browne and Brooke were wired to, to join the Hood, where Asquith was. So here I am: for good, I trust. Asquith and

Denis are still learning musketry with fragments of the battalion. But we're one. It's worth while, being the P.M.'s son.

I'm told you're going to speak at the Union. Rub it in to poor Goldie. Hugh Smith (who told me) is going out in March. Pretty good.

We go out in January: probably towards the end. I gather we *probably* get leave for three days about Christmas.

I spend my odd moments in a grave perplexity, about marriage. I rather feel that if the war *hadn't* happened, I'd have gone on eyeing the brink, hesitating, and deferring, never quite blinded enough not to say 'Well, tomorrow'll do—' until I relapsed into a friendly celibate middle-age, the amiable bachelor, a Dent or livelier Sayle, or less distinguished Eddie, with my rooms and bedder and hosts of young friends. But oh! *this* threatens a hastiness of decision. 'Tomorrow Why tomorrow I may be, myself, with yesterday's seven thousand years.'[1] If it's true the war'll last two years more, there's very little chance of anyone who goes out in January 1915 returning. Now, if I *knew* I'd be shot, I'd marry in a flash—oh any of two or three ladies—and do my best to leave a son. How comforting it would be to *know*: and what delicious snatches of domesticity I could steal before January 20! But, oh, if I came back in a year, and found myself caught. It's easy to select a wife for a month: but for a lifetime—one must be a little more certain.

I agonize every night. At times I want to wire to almost anybody 'Will you be my widow?' And later, I sigh that I'll be free and the world before me, after the war.

It's partly dependent on my premonition. If I think I'll survive, I plump for freedom. When I feel I'll be killed (which is my general feeling and deepest), I have a revulsion towards marriage.

A perplexing world.

Are you the Censor now? It's very imprudent of you to try to become one of the most unpopular men in London.

Lebewohl

RUPERT

Dec. 15

P.S. All this some days ago. I find we don't have Christmas leave, as it now stands.

Love to Anne. RUPERT

---

[1] *Rubáiyát of Omar Khayyám*, 1859, stanza 20.

To JACQUES RAVERAT   *Hood Battalion*
                                          R.N. Brigade
                                          Blandford, Dorset
                                          3 December [*1914*]

My dear,

I've very often tried to write to you: and always been too tired. Very exhausting, this military life.

Oh, dear, it *would* be refreshing to see and talk to you. I rather gather, from Ka, that you may probably be accepted—for something—shortly. If not, do come to England for a little, and stay a Sunday at Blandford and take me a walk. I'll probably be here till January.

There's a lot to talk about, though I'm rather beyond talking. Yes, we *are* insular. Did you hear of the British private, who had been through the fighting from Mons to Ypres, and was asked what he thought of all his experiences. He said 'What I don't like about this 'ere Bloody Europe, is all these Bloody pictures of Jesus Christ an' 'Is Relatives, be'ind Bloody bits of glawss.' It seems to me to express perfectly that insularity and cheerful atheism which are the chief characteristics of my race.

All the same, though myself cheerful, insular, and an atheist, I'm largely dissatisfied with the English, just now. The good ones are all right. And it's curiously far away from us (if we haven't the Belgians in memory, as I have). But there's a ghastly sort of apathy over half the country. And I really think large numbers of male people don't want to die; which is odd.

I've been praying for a German raid.

To CATHLEEN NESBITT   *Hood Battalion*
                                          R.N. Brigade
                                          Blandford, Dorset
                                          Saturday, 5 December [*1914*]

My dearest,

I'm in a state of extreme depression. I was inoculated against typhoid (second time) yesterday; and it is a process which induces fever and despair. I tossed upon a dream-distraught bed all night: and woke feeling (as Harry Lauder says) like tuppence. I'm now so muddled in my head that I can't clearly remember when you're coming to Bournemouth—twenty-five miles away. Is it on Monday

—the seventh? Or not till the next week? Tell me. I'll get away for all Sunday, and we'll meet in Wimborne and walk wonderfully. It's a glorious chance: and the last. You'll be able to stay on the Sunday in Bournemouth, child?

There's no news, no nothing. I'm rather happy, really, in this new battalion. Oc is about: and I'm in a company with rather a good lot of officers. At the head, a New Zealand youth[1] who was fighting in Mexico, heard the news in August, walked 300 miles to the coast, got a boat, and turned up here. He is also an Olympic Swimmer: and *knows* the *South Seas*. Then there's a very nice Cambridge man of thirty who was biologist with Scott's South Pole expedition. Then there's a *very* charming and beautiful American youth, infinitely industrious and simple beyond belief. And finally there's a very hard bitter man, a poet, very strong and silent, called Rupert Brooke.

Carissima, they say there's a good inn at Wimborne. Let's get there *very* early on Sunday and sit in front of fires and walk and talk. You shall bring me a book to read me.   RUPERT

To W. DENIS BROWNE   '*Hood*'
                                    Monday [*7 December 1914*]
My dear Denis,

How many legs have you? Mrs Elgy says she has none. And *I* haven't any. I think you have too many. Centipede. Bring me some when you come.

I think it would be iniquitous if you were bribed to stay in that quomodo. The Howe is not a battalion, it is a query. I'm like Nigel (?) Beauchamp. 'He didn't care about fame. He knew all about that. He had seen a little cocked hat in the Louvre.'[2] I was not only second in command of a Nelson Company: but also Acting-Adjutant! I had the keys of Death & Hell, & laid them down for no. 3 Platoon A Cpny Hood. We're a merry band, & shall be merrier.

This place is fairly filthy. Nice country. I've had my second typhoid inoculation: & I'm taken rather bad.

Winston & Eddie expected. Be here for them.

                                    RUPERT

[1] Bernard Freyberg (Lord Freyberg, V.C.).
[2] Meredith's *Beauchamp's Career*, chapter 2: Nevil Beauchamp said, 'I don't care to win glory; I know all about that; I've seen an old hat in the Louvre'.

To REGINALD POLE   *Hood Battalion, R.N.D.*
Royal Naval Camp
Blandford, Dorset
7 December [1914]

*   *   *

I know all about the German case. I saw Dudley Ward when he returned from Berlin after the beginning of the war, a hot pro-German (till he read the White paper); & even helped him translate the German Blue Book (or whatever colour it was). There is no German case. And they have made folly & wickedness more foolish & more wicked by their treatment of Belgium. I've seen Belgium; & I know.

I'm all in favour of shooting the rich & tyrannical here, beginning with Sir Edgar Speyer. First I shall wipe out the Prussians & their supporters. So should every decent Englishman.

R. B.

To EDWARD MARSH   *'Hood'*
Monday [7 December 1914]

My dear,

I hear Winston's expected. *Insist* on coming with him. Don't be caught in your dress-clothes this time. You'd better both have lunch or tea with the Hood, to see soldiers (sailors?) at their noblest.

We must get Denis in. It's absurd to think of staying in the Howe for the sake of an extra stripe. I was *acting adjutant* of Nelson, & left it! I've been inoculated a second time, so has Freyberg. We're both rather bad, & spend most of our time in bed, groaning. I hope I'll be all right by the time you come & I hope it'll be one of our good muddy days, to let Winston see what life's like.

I see Lascelles [Abercrombie] is lecturing on War & the Drama. How is he? Won't you bring him down with you, as Assistant Clerk, or Admiralty Bard, or something? I'd like to see him.

Howe heard of the mud, & hasn't come.

Typhoidically
RUPERT

To MARCHESA CAPPONI

The Hood Battalion
Royal Naval Division
Blandford, Dorset
15 December [*1914*]

If you have any gifts for the troops send them me. I've a nice lot of scoundrels under me.

I expect to go out in the end of January again—make America help the Belgians—I saw their suffering. It is terrible. French and English suffering don't matter. But they're so helpless.

We're going to win. I hear the new armies all over England are wonderful.

In some ways it's a good thing.

I hope you are well, Agnes.

I'm very busy and tired.

With love
RUPERT

To MRS BROOKE

The Hood Battalion
Royal Naval Division
Blandford
Sunday [*20 December 1914*]

Dear Mother,

Many thanks. I'm very glad Aunt Fanny's put off. I *may* get away on the Tuesday evening: but I don't expect I could get further than London that night. I'm going to try to get somebody to give me a lift in a car to Salisbury, to catch the train. Shall I try to bring anyone down for a night to give colour to Aunt F. being put off?

About mince-pies and cakes—we're feeding half the company: about 120 men. Turkey, plum-pudding etc. at midday: *that's* arranged for. Mince-pies etc. for tea. Just as many as you can make. Dispatch them to get here on Thursday, if you can—to *Blandford* will do. I may be able to get Justin to call in and bring them down in a car. I believe he's going to stay with Ka Cox in her hut on Salisbury plain for 'Xmas. Will you wire how many men's teas you can get mince-pies and cakes for, to send me: 10, 20, 50, or whatever it is. I'll get some more elsewhere.

Also, please send me 3 bottles of my '87 port now. We might as well drink it in mess. Alfred says it'll go bad: so we might have it here.

With love
RUPERT

To JACQUES RAVERAT
Hood Battalion
2nd Naval Brigade
Blandford, Dorset
21 December [1914]

My dear,

I am a beast. I got as far as that, and hadn't a moment after, when I could summon the energy to think out sensible sentences. What a life! I sludge through mud all the day: and am continually too tired and too ill to think. Ka says you're coming to England, perhaps. I'm getting leave Wednesday Dec. 30 for six days. The first four I go home: then London. Where'll you be? Couldn't you come to Rugby for a day and a night? It would be good. Let's finish the Universe off. The Ranee'd like it, I know. I want to see somebody. I love no woman and very few men: only Mr Belloc and Dudley (sadly, that he won't join) and one or two more, and you. The large part of my fellow officers I rather hate, and wholly despise. They are very doggish, and tell dirty stories at breakfast: and their noses curve greasily and they lend money. (The others are good men.) But I want to hear of things. My mind's gone stupid with drill and arranging about the men's food. It's all good fun.

I'm rather happy. I've a restful feeling that all's going well, and I'm not harming anyone, and probably even doing good. A queer new feeling. The only horror is, that I want to marry in a hurry and get a child, before I vanish. Oh, oh! But *whom? There's* the question: to ponder in my sleeping-bag, between the thoughts on the attack and calculations about the boots of the platoon. Insoluble: and the weeks slip on. It'll end in my muddling that, as I've muddled everything else. Wow!

There is much to be said about soldiering, and nothing at all about Shakespeare. Let us say them. And I will tell you about the French National Character. I hear we're getting on pretty well together now, in spite of two hopelessly incompatible ways of fighting.

I want to ask a thousand things. What is Joffre like? And why isn't Gide at the front? And is Péguy a good poet? And how much reserve has Joffre got? And *where's it going in?*

See me next week.   Vale!

RUPERT

Telegram to KATHARINE COX [*December 1914*]

Send mince-pies for sixty men and a few cakes to me Blandford station immediately get someone to help you.

RUPERT

To CATHLEEN NESBITT
Hood Battalion
2nd Naval Brigade
Blandford, Dorset
25 December 1914

My darling,

You give me a great many Christmas presents, don't you? I'm the unworthiest of recipients. And what can I send *you* from this camp? A wet stick, or a little boxful of mud. Those are the only alternatives—You know, the flask was the usefuller present: but the photograph was the nicer. It sits on a box by my bed, and brightens that rather gloomy hut. It's not *much like* you, loveliest: but it *is* beautiful. One day you might get hold of a decent photographer, such as Schell or [H.] Oppé, and get them to take a proper photograph of you. It could be done—

* * *

Gilbert on *Love* seems rather crabbed. I'll look into it more: seeking the truth e'en at the Cannan's mouth, like the good soldier I am.

I spend Christmas in looking after drunken stokers. One of them has been drunk since seven. He neither eats nor drinks, but dances a complicated step up and down his hut, half-dressed, singing 'How happy I am! How happy I am!' A short fat inelegant man, in stockinged feet. What wonders we are!

I get to Waterloo 11.3 on Wednesday, with luck: and leave Euston 12.15. I owe a long visit to my mother. I'll be *through* London again on the Saturday, I think. And in it for thirty hours from Monday morning. Then—mud for a time—and the front. The Staff reckon for 75 per cent casualties in the Naval Division in the first three months! There's no news. Occasional scares. On Wednesday I (don't tell a soul) started a sonnet. If it gets finished, you shall see it. What a fall!

I had a letter from Masefield, saying he was proud to know me, because I'd done a fine thing. It gave me a queer thrill. But it seems an odd way of looking at it—Of course, the imputation that a Cambridge poet might be expected to funk, is rather beastly, and fairly true.   *   *   *

With love

Your

RUPERT

To VIOLET ASQUITH   *Hood Battalion*
2nd Naval Brigade
Blandford, Dorset
Saturday
[*Postmark: 26 December 1914*]

My dear Violet,

I'm sitting in the anteroom before dinner: and you can't, and I shouldn't like you to, imagine, precisely what that's like. But it's worlds away—universes away—from last Saturday evening, or the almost as great happiness of Sunday evening (my poor military brain!). It was fun. Or, *was* it, at all? Not '*was* it FUN?' but, 'W AS it?' The continuity of this mud is too convincing. I can't imagine that all my evenings since Antwerp weren't in here, and all my mornings on parade, and my afternoons lecturing sleepy, clotheless, embedded stokers. There was a dream of leave, and London, and lovely things. But it was no more: I woke to my servant's voice, 'Six-thirty, and you're Orderly Officer today, Sir,' and the corpse-like light that precedes these queer green chalky dawns.

Oc is my one comfort: a great one. His cheerfulness is unfailing. There emerges from the mud, Oc, backed by Denis Browne (playing *Petrouschka* of an evening) and the gnome-like, soulless affable Patrick. All else is flatness.

The conviction grows that we stay here for months, till the Division's completed. Hell. And many say we then go out in an Army with the Canadians and the Ulstermen. What a fate! And how bored one'll become here. Still, the months may bring another leave.

I must retire to my cabin to write the remainder of my promised sonnets. One more is turning out *fairly* good. It's rather like developing photographs. Forgive the dreariness of this letter. Shall I ever see you again?   Good night

RUPERT

To RUSSELL LOINES

Dear Loines,

It's more hopeful for us to wish you a Happy New Year than you us, with our daily casualty lists and khaki population. Still, your wishes may do more good. I started a long letter to you in August and September, in my scraps of time; a valuable letter, full of information about the war and the state of mind of pacifists and others. The Germans have it now. It went in my luggage to Antwerp, and there was left. Whether it was burnt or captured, I can't be sure. But it was in a tin box, with—damn it!—a lot of my manuscript. And it was fairly heavily shelled. I don't know if you'd heard of my trip to Antwerp. I entered this show (Sub-lieutenant R. Brooke R.N.D. at your service) in September and by the end of the month was in a trench hearing the shrapnel go screaming fatuously over me through a cloudless sky. A queer picnic. They say we saved the Belgian Army and most of the valuable things in Antwerp—stores and ammunition I mean. With luck we might have kept the line fifty miles forward of where it is. However, we at least got away, most of us. It really was a very mild experience.

* * *

England is remarkable. I wish I had the time to describe it to you. But this job keeps one so darned tired, and so stupid that I haven't the words. There are a few people who've been so anti-war before, or so suspicious of diplomacy, that they feel rather out of the national feeling. But it's astonishing to see how the 'intellectuals' have taken on new jobs.* Masefield drills hard in Hampstead and told me with some pride, a month ago, that he was a Corporal and *thought* he was going to be promoted to Sergeant soon. Cornford is no longer the best Greek Scholar in Cambridge. He recalled that he was a very good shot in his youth and is a Sergeant-Instructor of Musketry. I'm here. My brother is a 2nd lieutenant in the Post Office Rifles. He was one of three great friends at King's. The second is Intelligence Officer on H.M.S. Vengeance, Channel Patrol. The third is buried near Cambrai. Gilbert Murray and Walter Raleigh rise at six every day to line hedgerows in the dark and 'advance in rushes' across the Oxford meadows. Among the other officers in this Division are two

* No, not astonishing: but impressive.

young Asquiths, an Australian professional pianist who twice won the Diamond Sculls, a New Zealander who was fighting in Mexico and walked three hundred miles to the coast to get a boat when he heard of the war, a friend of mine Denis Browne—Cambridge—who is one of the best young English musicians and an extremely brilliant critic, a youth lately through Eton and Balliol who is the most brilliant man they've had in Oxford for ten years, a young and very charming American John Bigelow Dodge who turned up to fight 'for the right'—I could extend the list. It's all a terrible thing. And yet, in its details, it's great fun. And—apart from the tragedy—I've never felt happier or better in my life than in those days in Belgium. And now I've the feeling of anger at a seen wrong—Belgium—to make me happier and more resolved in my work. I know that whatever happens I'll be doing some good, fighting to prevent *that*. And I've a lot of friends in Germany: good people. That's bitter. It's rather indefinite when we go out again. Perhaps at the end of January. Or we may be kept back for less complete parts of the Division. The new Armies are shaping marvellously, I gather. We'll have great things doing in the Spring. But it may be a long job. Love to you both and Barbara. Will you be in England soon? Come down here for a day. I'd like to see you.

Good luck
R. B.

To VIOLET ASQUITH
Hood Battalion
2nd Naval Brigade
Blandford, Dorset
Xmas Day [Postmark: 11 January 1915]

My dear Violet,

I couldn't read in your letter *where* you were going to for Christmas (though I rather suspect you'll be in bed at Downing Street).

I get six days leave from Wednesday the twenty-ninth. I'm yet uncertain how much time I'm going to give to my lonely mother, to whom I'm going first. But are you going to be at Walmer for that week-end? On the Monday night I'm making my last revelry in London.

Never say we're not a hilarious nation. Christmas Day in the Naval Division is a revelation. The Battalion C.P.O., a very fat man, who has been drunk since dawn, is conducting the band in an Irish jig in the middle of the parade-ground. He can't beat time, but he dances very convincingly. He's slightly like Pelissier. Half my stokers are dancing half-naked in their huts. They spent the night on cheap gin. The surrounding woods are full of lost and sleeping stokers. I expect most of them froze over-night. Pathetic creatures.

Your Walmer week-end sounds too thrilling for belief. I wish I'd been there. But one can't get away from this mud-heap very easily.

My throat collapsed again and left me voiceless. I can only communicate with the outer world by Morse or Semaphore. Which do you prefer?

I've discovered that this is the site of a *Roman* Camp. Does that move you? It overwhelms Jan and me. I gave my platoon the slip yesterday morning (they were out gathering holly): and went a delicious country walk, decanting drops of a poem (don't report me)—

     ...   .

'And drowsy drunken seamen
Straying belated home,
Meet with a Latin challenge,
From sentinels of Rome—'

     ...   .

'In dreams they doff their khaki,
Put greaves and breastplate on:
In dreams each leading stoker,
Turns a centurion—', etc...

Good luck for next year.   RUPERT

To EDWARD MARSH   *Rugby*
                           Thursday [31 December 1914]
My dear,

I'd love to come to lunch with Clemmie[1] & Winston. I'd *rather* come another day, though: because I promised Cathleen Tuesday.

     *   *   *

For Monday evening: I'm so rich (thanks to the Admiralty starting to pay me for my lost MSS) that I think I'll give a dinner at (say) the Carlton—or Café Royal—Grill-room. I think the *Moulin*

[1] Mrs Winston Churchill.

D'Or isn't good enough for a last dinner before the wilderness. I go on Tuesday afternoon.

Desideration in regard to companions at the *Ambassadors* is divided into three parts.

(1) People one *likes* to be with. I have secured to me the only two there are—at least, the only two available.

(2) Amusing people (very important after Camp). If you knew how rarely desirable a good joke becomes to one after the mud—like a good liqueur or a divine sweet. If for instance Maurice Baring were back from the front. . . .

You & Denis aren't excluded from your natural place under (2) by the fact that you come under (1) (in this so delightful world) as you *are* excluded from—

(3) WOMEN.

There one hesitates. *Pro.* is the fact that one *aches*, after camp, for femininity: the sound of skirts, the twitter of the creatures, the *smell*. Oh, dear! *Against* it is the reflexion that there *aren't* many amiable ones: & that, at the best, they're not very nice companions—not fully possessed of a sense of humour.

What about—if you don't go back to the ships—Supper afterwards? Is there still any place one can drink alcohol out of tea-cups?

Do what you will. RUPERT

Is Violet in London? I've written to her at Walmer—wanting, really, to find out if she or anyone was going down on Saturday: so I could join them.

BIOGRAPHICAL PREFACE 1915

During the first week of the year Brooke was enjoying a New Year's leave at Rugby and with Eddie Marsh in London. He was back with his battalion by 8 January. A few days later he received a letter from the Tahitian girl, Taatamata, which had lain for several months in the wreck of the *Empress of Ireland* at the bottom of the Gulf of St Lawrence, and he was painfully reminded of the romance he had left behind him in the South Sea Islands. The Hood Battalion remained at Blandford through February, but Brooke was able to tell his mother that he expected soon to be on his way to the Dardanelles. On 1 March his battalion embarked on a Union Castle liner, the *Grantully Castle*, and by the 8th they were lying off Carthage. Brooke was fully aware of the risks he was likely to run of being killed on this expedition and he gave many instructions as to what was to be done in that event. He turned again to Katharine Cox as 'about the best he could do in the way of a widow', and gave instructions about his papers, since 'they *may* want to write a biography'. His hopes that she might marry and have a child were fulfilled when she became Mrs Arnold-Forster in 1919 and in due course the mother of a son. She died in 1934.

The few remaining letters describe the preparations for a Gallipoli landing which did not take place and mention the attacks of heatstroke and dysentery which very much weakened him early in April. His last letter, written to his mother on 20 April, tells her of the offer made by General Sir Ian Hamilton to appoint him an A.D.C. on his staff and of his refusal. The story is concluded with three letters from Denis Browne to Eddie Marsh. The first gives a full account of Brooke's last illness, his death on 23 April, and his burial the same evening on the island of Skyros. The other two contain Denis Browne's farewell to Marsh in anticipation of his own death. All the members of the group of friends surrounding Brooke in his last days were afterwards killed in the fighting on Gallipoli with the exception of Bernard Freyberg, who lived to gain great distinctions, including the Victoria Cross, and to become Governor-General of New Zealand.

To LADY EILEEN WELLESLEY   24 *Bilton Road, Rugby*
                                        1 January [*1915*]

Are you well, sweetheart? I've not heard from you for some days. Perhaps you've written to Camp. Did you get these debased & dingy photographs?

It is queer, having leave. Sheets. Hot baths. All sorts of *extraordinary* things. I've simply relapsed with a sigh into civilianity.

Tomorrow I go to stay the week-end at Walmer with Oc. Monday to Raymond Buildings, for one night. I'll get the place clear, I think. If you *don't* hear again, will you turn up there at four? Don't be late. For I'm going out to my last lush dinner on earth.

*   *   *

You asked about Life after Death; so, like a good sailor, I referred the question to Divisional Headquarters. They said there was no *definite* information: but that the Admiralty Regulations (para. 412*a*. (2)) lay down that it is only for the Church of England. So *I'm* all right. Are you? Apparently one can choose between huts & billeting. I think I shall try to be billeted. Of course, it's a risk. My brother (in this life) is billeted on teetotallers. Isn't that dreadful?

I'll find a note at Eddie's?   Your

                                          RUPERT

To THE REV. ALAN BROOKE[1]   *Rugby*
                                        1 January [*1915*]
Dear Uncle Alan,

It was very good of you to send a pound for my men. I consulted them—they're reserve stokers, tamed painfully to military use— what they would like, the fifty of them, for a Christmas present. Believing in liberty I left them a free hand. But they *didn't* choose beer. They bought themselves, halma, draughts (two lots), bezique, & various games of throwing rings on to hooks and balls through holes. And they amuse themselves very happily with these, when the weather's *too* dreadful to go out—as it very often is.

I'm having six days' New Year leave, sheets and hot baths & good food, a blessing. All's uncertain about the Naval Division, as usual. I may go out at the end of January again. Or we may be kept back for Divisional Cavalry & guns.

[1] Dean of King's College, Cambridge.

Will you tell the authorities who prepare the King's War list, to put me down *Royal Naval Division* (*R.N.D.*): for *R.N.V.R.* is merely the *channel* through which I get into the R.N.D. It means very little by itself.

A Happy New Year to you all. I'm feeling very confident about the war. Not so confident as the Staff at the Front, who predict a sudden cracking on the part of the Germans, & peace in April. But I think we should do it by August.

RUPERT BROOKE

To JACQUES RAVERAT   *New Year's leave*
                                                         Rugby
My dear,   *1915*

I'm only in London Monday morning to Tuesday afternoon. I'm going to Eat. The week-end I'm staying in Kent.

It wouldn't, anyway, be much good trying to see Belloc, I guess. When he's not in the London Library surrounded by Atlases, he's lecturing all over England. He'll be the richest man in the world by the end of the war: and swamp the Jews.

You'd better come down to Camp. You can stay in the Blandford pub a night, and I've most Sundays free. We'll hire a Car.

Nor shall I be sad. I'm very sorry for you, and it's bloody hard luck. But the world's going well: better than it did when we were younger. And a Frenchman is the one person in the world with something to be proud of, these days.

God be with you

RUPERT

To EDWARD MARSH   *The Hood Battalion*
                                                 Royal Naval Division
                                                 Friday, 8 January 1915
Dear Eddie,

*   *   *

London's a lovely dream. It was fun that night, wasn't it?

I spent, forwent, a lovely hour of the afternoon with Cathleen penning some absurd phrases about Flecker. I was grotesque & ornate: not having time to be simple. What a miserable task, writing a friend's obituary in the *Times*.[1] At the same table he wrote *Jasmin* in your book, the last time I saw him.

I jotted notes, & the *Times* interwove their gems. 'Educated at Balliol, (then me) his muse was stertorous with the lush slumbers of the east. His father is the Rev. W. Flecker. Apollo yielded to Marsyas, & fled crying strangely. . .' What a bloody jest: & a bloody world.

Will you tell Mrs Elgy to send my bag, EMPTY, *to my mother?*
A fine day for once!!   Lebwohl
                                                              R.

To DUDLEY WARD   *Hood Battalion*
                                          2nd Naval Brigade
                                          Blandford, Dorset
                                          10 January 1914 [*1915*]

Dear Dudley,

I'll tell the Ranee to let you know if I'm wounded or anything. And if you receive such news, will you keep communicating it to the damsel whose address is in this envelope? I promised her to arrange it in this way: so that not even a figure unknown to her should know her name *unless* it was necessary. So let the envelope lie among your papers, untouched, till it's splendidly necessary. When, and if, you *do* write to her, merely add your name and address.

It won't be for AGES, according to the latest intelligence; that we go, as a Bloody Division in April or May with—God help us!—the Canadians and the Ulstermen. So *we*, the Hood, have to wait. But when we do get out, will be used to break the enemy lines by numbers *à l'Allemagne:* so *that's* why they expect 75% casualties.

By the way, I suppose I *was* a bit unthinking to Ka. One forgets that women can't see jokes from the military point of view.

Later

The G.O.C. Division has just given us a talk: and we're to be here till the middle of March, AT LEAST: and that means the middle of April. Well, it'll be warmer. But it's TOO bloody, to have THREE more months of life, when one hoped for three weeks. There'll be lashings of time for you to come and see me, anyhow.

---

[1] Flecker had died at Davos on 3 January. R.B.'s obituary notice was printed in *The Times* of 6 January.

But it brings up the question of marriage again, which I thought I'd let slide altogether. Oh, God!

I hope I'll see Jacques, too, sometime. I left, of course, my French atlas in the train. Will you get and send me another? Instanter. Send me anything you come across really useful in the military way.

I wonder what's happening abroad. Why are you keeping back all news of Poland? It frightens me.   Ever

RUPERT

To DUDLEY WARD

The Hood Battalion
Royal Naval Division
Blandford
[13 or 14 January 1915]

My dear Dudley,

We started out at 8.30 this morning; and got home at three, after hard 'fighting' and marching. And waiting for me in the ante-room was a letter forwarded by the Dead Letter Office from Ottawa, 'recovered' by divers from the wreck of the Empress of Ireland. Rather frayed at the edges, and the ink much washed out. But it was a letter from Taatamata, which she gave to a man to post, who was going up to 'Frisco in a boat. And he posted it in Vancouver. And it went by the E. of I. down the St Lawrence, beyond the Sagonsac, where I bathed: and sank with Laurence Irving: and lay at the bottom from June to December. And this evening I puzzled out the French and English misspellings, and, being very tired and slightly drunk, gulped a good deal.[1]

---

[1] The letter, deciphered with great difficulty, is as follows:

Le 2 Mai 1914

My dear Love darling

I just wrote you some lines to let you know about Tahiti to day whe have plainty people Argentin Espagniole. and whe all very busy for four days. Whe have good times all girls in Papeete have good times whit Argentin boys. I think they might go away to day to Honolulu Lovina are give a ball last night for them. beg ball. they 2 o'clock this morning

I hope to see you here to last night, Lovina make plainty Gold Money. now. About Mrs Rosentale she is went to [?]anmoto whit Crower by Comodore before they go away to whe been drive the car to Lage place. Enton and I. Mrs Rosental Crower Williams Banbrige to whe got 12 Beers Bread Sardines only whe tout come right away to Lage the car Break and whe work down the beach. have drinking beer. Music and whe come away 5 o'clock morning [no sle sclep *del.*] pas dormir

I wish you here that night I get fat all time Sweetheart you know I alway thinking about you that time when you left me I been sorry for long time. whe have good

I think Life's F A R more romantic than any books.

Anyway she was alive in May (though the Germans shelled her since). And I can't decipher any reference to prospects of a baby. So that dream goes with the rest. And the world must rub along with Peter[1] and the rest.

Bring Jacques down: or Ka: or come alone.

RUPERT

To JOHN DRINKWATER

Hood Bn. R.N.D.
Blandford
18–25 January 1915

My dear John,

It was ignoble of me not to answer. But one becomes ignoble at this game. Or, at least, brutish. The mind becomes, not unpleasantly, submerged. The days go by. I plough through mud: march: drill: eat and sleep: and do not question more. There was some affair at Antwerp, I remember. I have a recollection of a burning city, the din of cannonades, a shattered railway-station, my sailors bivouacking in the grounds of a deserted château, refugees coming out of the darkness... But most of the time I was thinking of food, or marching straight, or what to say to the men, or, mostly, not thinking at all. It was rather exhilarating, and rather terrible. But I don't think one is very swift to sensations in these parts of life. Still, it's the only life for me, just now. The training is a bloody bore. But on service one has a great feeling of fellowship, and a fine thrill, like nothing else in the world. And I'd not be able to exist, for torment, if I weren't doing it. Not a bad place and time to die, Belgium, 1915? I want to kill my Prussian first. Better than coughing out a civilian soul amid bed-clothes and disinfectant and gulping medicines in 1950. The world'll be tame enough after the war, for those that see it. I had hopes that England'ld get on her legs again, achieve youth and

time when you was here I always remember about you forget me all readly oh! mon cher bien aimè je l'aimerai toujours

Le voila Cela partir pour San Francisco je lui ais donnè quel cadeau pour lui

he told me to send you his regards je me rappeler toujour votre petite etroite figure et la petite bouche qui me baise bien tu m'a percea mon coeur et je aime toujours ne m'oubli pas mon cher maintenant je vais finir mon lettre. parceque je me suis très occupèe le bateau par a l'instant. 5 heurs exuse me to wrrite you shot letter. hope you good health and good time

I send my kiss to you darling
xxxxxxxxxxxxxx mille kiss
Tatamata

[1] Peter Ward, D.W.'s son.

merriment, and slough the things I loathe—capitalism and feminism and hermaphroditism and the rest. But on maturer consideration, pursued over muddy miles of Dorset, I think there'll not be much change. What there is for the better, though. Certain sleepers have awoken in the heart.

Come and die. It'll be great fun. And there's great health in the preparation. The theatre's no place, now. If you stay there you'll not be able to start afresh with us all when we come back. Péguy and Duhamel; and I don't know what others. I want to mix a few sacred and Apollonian English ashes with theirs, lest England be shamed. But first, or anyhow, borrow a car, pick up Wilfrid and Lascelles one Saturday, and come to Dorset; and on Saturday afternoon, or Sunday, or both, walk over the Roman downs with me, and drink greatly, and talk once more, and bury New Numbers with a *Resurgam*. I *may* have only four weeks more in England.

Love to you both
RUPERT

To JACQUES RAVERAT   *Hood*
R.N. Camp
Blandford
19 January [*1915*]

Frog!

I am a kindly sailor. I went and looked at Stourpaine House. I do not think it would make a good froggery. I don't think it would be squelchy to your hops, nor re-echoing to your croaks, nor illuminating for the jewel in your head. I don't think it is batrachian enough. I don't think there are enough flies for you to catch. I don't think.

I took Denis Browne and an Asquith, brother officers. They were far competenter than I.

In answer to your questions:

(1) It is in hilly country, but rather low: nearly at the bottom of the Stour valley. You can see half a mile to a mile in most directions. It is not shut in: but not open.

(2) It is slightly deliquescent: and rather more disrepaired. But not badly: not Old Vicarage level. Uninhabited since two years.

(3) Water supply, rainwater and springs. Said to be good. Certainly beautiful.

(4), (5), (6) Other facts. Drains all right. *I* asked that (dreamer) —But Asquith, being a practical man, said 'Are there any ghosts?' To which the man returned an evasive answer.

The house is rather larger than you'd want: with too many queer little rooms. But one (two) large splendid rooms with immense windows opening on to a rather sweet lawn. Two good bedrooms.

But it *is* downhill: and there's now, a foot of water in the cellar. I think it would always be damp.

It's ugly enough to please you. *I* thought it had some points, though I wasn't all over it. But my companions said it was because to us hut-dwellers *any* brick house seemed glorious: and that it was really the worst house they'd ever seen.

It's got a nice lawn and field: but it's rather in the village.

I shouldn't think it'ld do. But I wish you'd come down and see it. Or at least come down. I have a great thirst to talk to you. I shall be here for ever. Appear. You can stay in an inn. Tell me when: for the Ranee comes one week-end. She adores you. But I don't want to dichotomize my time.

Dudley is gentler and lovelier than ever: isn't he? I wish he'd enlist. I'd like to enter the Hereafter with him. He would be sensible about God: if we met him. He's English.

You mistake about marriage. I'm entirely in agreement with you. My present difficulty is: should one marry without being particularly in love, before going to the front? How divine to have even a few hours of what the rest of life is a grey pre-existence to—marriage: with, oh! *anybody*. But how dreadful to return from Berlin to a partner for Eternity whom one didn't particularly *want*.

There is great difficulty in life. But I'm almost at peace. Come and talk. RUPERT

To EDWARD MARSH (*Blandford*)
26 *January 1915*

My dear,

Patrick told me the tale of the latch-key. It brought the horrors of civilian life very vividly home to me.

Thanks for your various illuminations. I'll touch on points. (I've a long evening. We went a night march. 3 a.m.—10 a.m. (I thought of a lovely poem on an empty room.) Now we have leisure: though great torpor.)

I don't 'see' Viola [Tree] as the Lithuanian. Nor would the public, perhaps. And isn't Lithuania one of our allies? But—it would be *rather* fun to see a play by me before I die. (I'm sure Quilter'd[1] give me leave!) However, Cathleen & John [Drinkwater] are the only people I know of who—probably—have copies. Mine has crossed the Atlantic. Next time I go sick I must write a play about Antwerp.

It *wasn't* a nice day, when you should have come. But it wasn't an untypical one. It was rather beastly to put it off for those shades called the first Brigade. I rather agree it'ld be nicer to go out with a clash in April or May, than to slink out to the mud now. Though I *do* share the impatience. The only thing is, the longer we stay, the more our officers seem to fade away. Especially the R.N.V.R.— though as a *rule* it's a good thing getting rid of them. I hope the authorities'll (1) block any *good* officers going off to other things, Naval or Army, (2) get decent people for the new officers. I'm sure if they got hold of the Artists or the Inns of Court or a University, they could get a good lot of young officers, & decent people. We get a very chance lot as it is: some good & some rotten, scratched up anyhow.

I think Paul would be quite good, it would be nice to have him. Popham isn't so lackadaisical as he appears. He's tough physically (you should see him diving thirty feet! He got the Cambridge championship). I don't think he'd be much good with these old stokers. But he'd be above the level of officers in the division.

I wish I could think of someone else, too. We have vacancies for four or five still.

Is it true Winston's coming next Tuesday? We—A Company— are going to a village 17 miles away to billet for the week-end: returning Monday. I don't yet know if I shall go. I've a bloody cold in my head. If it lasts, or if my temperature goes up, I shall be sent out of camp. We've found that bad colds take ages to get better in camp. Shall I go to Rugby or London? I don't know if Raymond Buildings'ld be a good place to lie up in (I shouldn't be infectious). I'd get more amusing visitors there than at Rugby: for the three or four days. RUPERT

Why not give Viola *King Lear's Wife* & prevent her acting, herself?

[1] R.B.'s commanding officer, Col. Arnold Quilter.

To VIOLET ASQUITH   *Hood Battalion*
                                       2nd Naval Brigade
                                       Blandford, Dorset
                                       Sunday, 25 January
                                       [*Postmark: 29 January 1915*]

My dear Violet,

Your letter was a great pleasure. The days have flowed by since: and though I've occasionally had the time, I've never had the mental life to write to you. If you knew how indistinguishable from Quilter (even in robustness!*) I'm getting. The only chance of possessing the last muddy drilled-upon corner of one's soul, and entertaining the remotest thin ghost of an idea, is to withdraw to one's cabin, roll up in the brown sleeping-bag, forget that one's Officer of the Day tomorrow, and—write to you—

Some days later

At that point I slept. And now—after days—and *nights*—of toil, I've deplorably got a cold* again. I'm in bed with it, stupid beyond military crassness, irritable, depressed and uncomfortable. And, this time, no chance of you swooping down in a car on Saturday to ravish me away to champagne and sheets and Lady Wimborne and all things light and lovely. My only glimmer of a malingering and unpatriotic hope, is that if I develop (as I so feebly *couldn't*, before, you remember?) a TEMPERATURE, I shall be packed off out of Camp promptly. They've discovered that no one *ever* gets better in these miasmic huts. In that case, instead of going through to Rugby, I think I should be wiser to turn Eddie's into a R.N.D.M.C. depot and wheeze there, swathed, in the great chair before the fire. Would you come one afternoon and read Shakespeare to me? I'm sure London's the cure for a bad cold—that they spring from the absence of anything one likes—except exercise—and that to be happy and amused is the remedy. Of course—as we're to be here till May— one'll get leave again. And there's a good chance of my going to Hythe for a fortnight to learn machine-gunning. Isn't that near Walmer?

My only solace here is in reading a book about the district. It appears that in Eastbury House—two miles away—lived—who but George Bubb Dodington!¹ Isn't that romantic? The Tower that

* Observe the penalty of ὕβρις.

¹ Baron Melcombe (1691–1762), M.P., wit and political pamphleteer.

had Two on it[1] is not far away. And at Tarrant Crawford a Queen is buried.[2] And Badbury Rings—which we attack weekly—is the scene of one of Arthur's greatest victories.

Trailing back from a night attack two days ago I made two verses of a rather good non-military poem on an empty room. That's fun. There are some other sonnets in New Numbers. None as good— one nearly as good—as the one I gave you. (I think you're right about 'gone proudly friended': but—there it is.)

I don't want a hot water bottle, thanks. My feet are always feverish. But I *do* want a book, one which is as amusing as Sterne and Jacobs and France and strong as Dr Johnson and lovely as Marvell and the Anthology, and Shakesperian as Shakespere. Can you find it? It's the only thing that could tempt me to interest enough to read it, this evening.

Forgive my immense stupidity—I'll write when this present cloud lifts. Write to me of you and London.

RUPERT

To VIOLET ASQUITH   *5 Raymond Buildings*
                                            Gray's Inn
                                            Tuesday [? *February 1915*]

My dear Violet,

Your letter woke me this morning. I think I rather *ought* to have gone to Rugby. But I didn't. Because, in part, I'm going to dine at Admiralty House tonight: and I thought I *might* be able to collar W[inston]'s ear for five minutes, and drip sense into it: for which it would be patriotic to sacrifice my health.

My life is semi-recumbency and pyjamas and wraps and visitors till night, when the bareness of the establishment forces me out to prowl for food. It begins to dawn on me that that's unwise. Certainly, my cold—influenza—or what not stays stationary. There's some harmony of the uvula and the Eustachian tube I yet miss. Yesterday I took my temperature a good deal: with the most varied and perplexing results. The thing is, *am* I, or am I *not*, ill? I'd like to consult you. Probably you'd know. If *not*, I should go back to camp tomorrow. If I *am*, I should go to bed.

---

[1] *Two on a Tower*, by Thomas Hardy.
[2] Joan, daughter of King John, wife of King Alexander of Scotland. The church was given to the abbess and nuns of Tarrant by Ralph de Kahaines about 1170.

I don't think I ought to come out (till dinner) this evening. I shall be sitting here. I'll ring you up. Or you me.

Poor Oc. He *was* getting bored. Can't he rake up one miasmic microbe?

RUPERT

To MRS BROOKE

The Hood Battalion
Royal Naval Division
Thursday, 18 February [*1915*]

Dear Mother,

Here I am again. Today and yesterday it has been raining like the worst days of December. But I'm feeling quite well, and refreshed by exercise. The last two or three days at Walmer did me good. It was very quiet and pleasant there. I had to get back here by Monday noon. So I had to come up—with Oc—to Downing Street for Sunday night. I dined with Winston and Eddie in Admiralty House. Eddie had to go off after dinner to work, so I spent an amusing evening with Winston, who was too tired for work, after preparing his speech (a good speech). He was rather sad about Russia, who he thinks is going to get her 'paws burned', and disposed to think the war *might* last two years, if Russia got at all badly smashed. But he was very confident about the Navy and our side of Europe.

He came down to review us yesterday. It rained all the time, but he was very much pleased. I saw 'Clemmie' in a motor-car for a second: and Eddie came to lunch with the Hood.

*   *   *

With love

RUPERT

To DUDLEY WARD

The Hood Battalion
Royal Naval Division
Blandford
Sunday, 20? February [*1915*]
[Feb. 20th was Sat., so probably 21st]

It's too wonderful. We're going in four days. And the best expedition of the war. Figure me celebrating the first Holy Mass in St Sophia since 1453. (But this is to your censorial ear.) Reviewed by the King on Wednesday. Off on Thursday. I may want some things. I'll wire if I do.

Anyhow I'll send you some letters and instructions etc. It should be a mildish affair. But one *might* get shot.

I want   (1) A waterproof sheet so slight that it folds up and goes into your pocket and weighs a pound—*but is not tearable.*

[This is crossed out and written beside in pencil:
'All right. Someone else is getting this.']

(2) Gillette-blades.
A tiny medicine 'chest' for the pocket. *Including morphia, or some such thing, if possible.*

Will you get these or make—say—Geoffrey Fry get them and send them off *immediately*. I *must* get them by *Tuesday*.

I enclose a cheque for 3 pounds. I don't know *what* I owe you. Get the money for these latter purchases from my executors. What bloody fun!   RUPERT

If I can't get someone to post this in town, I shall wire.

To MRS BROOKE   *The Hood Battalion*
                                         Royal Naval Division
                                               Monday
                                    [*22*(?) *February 1915*]

Dear Mother,
    My address will be, from *Friday*,

                Sub. lieut. R. B.—
                Hood Battalion
                2nd Naval Brigade
                Royal Naval Expeditionary force
                c/o The Admiralty
                Whitehall, S.W.
rather long, isn't it?
                        *   *   *

What follows is a dead secret (as is our day of starting). We are going to be part of a landing force to help the fleet break through the Hellespont and the Bosphorus and take Constantinople, and open up the Black Sea. It's going to be one of the important things of the war, if it comes off. We take 14–16 days to get there. We shall be fighting for anything from 2 to 6 weeks. And back (they reckon) in May. We may just lie with the Fleet off there and do nothing. Or we may get a lot of fighting. At any rate, it will be much more glorious and less dangerous than France. It is said—but this I don't *know*—that some Australians and New Zealanders and Regulars are coming with us. We are only taking 15 days' provisions (beyond what we have on the boats); so we obviously aren't expected to have a long campaign! I'm afraid we may be Reserves to Marines. We fight from the boats—i.e. we can always get taken off if we have to retreat, so we're pretty safe!

Please don't breathe a word of this to anyone. Don't tell Alfred *where* we're going—beyond the Mediterranean and the fact we're returning in May. The fact we're going out now makes it impossible to get him in now. He'd better stick to what he's at.[1]

We're taking our Camp Equipment, so it's obviously very possible we're expected to sit in Camp all the time.

I'm rather tired after a long day.　　　With love

　　　　　　　　　　　　　　　　　　RUPERT

To VIOLET ASQUITH　　　　　　　　*Hood Battalion*
　　　　　　　　　　　　　　　　2nd Naval Brigade
　　　　　　　　　　　　　　　　Blandford, Dorset
　　　　　　　　　　　　　　　　[February 1915]

Monday

Oh Violet it's too wonderful for belief. I had not imagined Fate could be so benign. I almost suspect her. Perhaps we shall be held in reserve, out of sight, on a choppy sea for two months...yet even that—But I'm filled with confident and glorious hopes. I've been looking at the maps. Do you think *perhaps* the fort on the Asiatic corner will want quelling, and we'll land and come at it from behind and they'll make a sortie and meet us on the plains of Troy? It seems to me strategically so possible. Shall we have a Hospital Base (and won't you manage it?) at Lesbos? Will Hero's Tower crumble under the 15 in. guns? Will the sea be polyphloisbic and wine dark and unvintageable (you, of course, know if it is)? Shall I loot Mosaics from St Sophie's (yes, I understood your telegram)? and Turkish Delight? and Carpets? Shall we be a Turning Point in History? Oh, God!

I've never been quite so happy in my life, I think. Not quite so *pervasively* happy; like a stream flowing entirely to one end. I suddenly realize that the ambition of my life has been—since I was two

[1] Alfred Brooke had joined the Post Office Rifles. He was killed in France on 14 June 1915.

—to go on a military expedition against Constantinople. And when I *thought* I was hungry, or sleepy, or falling in love, or aching to write a poem—*that* was what I really, blindly, wanted. This is nonsense. Good night. I loved your letter. But even more the news (in an arrangementary telegram of Eddie's) that I may see you on Thursday. I think I shall wire to you tomorrow for a book.

I'm very tired with equipping my platoon.

RUPERT

To VIOLET ASQUITH

The Hood Battalion
Royal Naval Division
Blandford
18 February [1915]

My dear Violet,

We're 'standing off' this morning, to 'mark and mend'. So, you see, I've time to write.

I'm incredibly healthy. You were an angel to me. I've never so much enjoyed being ill. Those last three days at Walmer were heavenly. Did you like them? It was such a moment of peace, against the pleasant excitement of London, and the remoter background of this dream-like war. It seemed a divine and Paradisal interlude, somehow, where hour flowed into hour unmarked by bugler, and never bringing one nearer anything, or farther away from anything.

Now I'm three days gone in reality—or this different dream. I come with quite a zest for it, I find with astonishment. Even yesterday—Winston's visit—barely damped me. What a day! Perhaps you'll have heard of it. A real Blandford day of the milder kind, mud rain and a hurricane. First old Paris[1] put the review off, because of the weather (but that was after we'd stood out a battalion of Lears, in the pitiless storm for half an hour). Then Winston turned up and demanded something. We were hurried out to an extemporized performance, plunging through rivers and morasses. It was like a dream. At one point I emerged from the mud, with my platoon, under the wheels of a car, in the midst of a waste. And in the car were what I thought were two children, jumping about clapping their hands whistling and pointing. It was Eddie and Clemmie. * * *. Eddie came to luncheon * * *, and was divinely civilian. He told us all the jokes from the *Times*, and all the atrocity stories: things we never hear. The wardroom was fascinated

---

[1] General Paris.

by him, and said in chorus, when he left 'what odd eyebrows'. It is rumoured Winston was 'pleased', and impressed by our (2nd Brigade) superiority to the other Brigades: and that we shall go out as a Brigade.   *   *   *

This is the letter of a sub-lieutenant—as dull as ditchwater. I wish I had even my civilian bright little interest in *anything*. I'm a machine, a clod, a platoon officer, a Jim Barnes, a title, an omicron, a jelly, a dry anatomy, a less-than-protoplasm. The only good news is that Patrick yesterday lost seven pounds at poker: today he has laryngitis. Oc is well. I am well. Quilter is roaring-well. There's a fine sun and a clean wind. When are you coming near, or to, Camp? Come and view my buffalo-like health, your handiwork.

RUPERT

Oh, thanks for the mess-tin covers.

To KATHARINE COX   *A Union Castle boat*
Avonmouth
5.50 a.m. Sunday
[*Postmark: 1 March 1915*]

At last I'm in bed. I've been working all night; and up since six yesterday morning, and I marched 10 miles from Camp (with what a 'pack'!) in the afternoon.

So I'll get three hours sleep. I'll try to find a cheque and envelope tomorrow. I telegraphed. I expect you'll have heard from Dudley. Wanting to write to you properly, I couldn't find time. Learn from him. Briefly, we're the best job of the war. We're to take Constantinople. Isn't it luck? I've never been so happy. 80, or 100, thousand of us altogether. And I shall attend the first Mass in St Sophia since 1453.

We're to be back by May; and it's a very unrisky job.

All this is a *dead* secret—except from Dudley and Jacques. And Jacques must keep it.

I'll find time *en route* to write. We leave in 12 hours.

Good-bye. Please keep well.   RUPERT

To EDWARD MARSH   *North of Tunis*
Sunday, 6? March [*1915*]

My dear,

Your last letter was very nice. It seems ages ago now since we said good-bye to you on our mottled parade ground. I saw Violet at

Avonmouth. We've had rather a nice voyage: a bit unsteady the first day (when I was sick), & today: otherwise very smooth & delicious. There has been a little, not much, to do. I've read most of *Turkey in Europe*. But what with parades, & the reading of military books, I've not written anything. Anyway, my mind's always a blank at sea.

For two days we've been crawling along the African coast, observing vast tawny mountains, with white villages this side of them, & white peaks beyond. The sea has been a jewel, & sunset & dawn divine blazes of colour. It is all too ridiculously peaceful for one to believe anything but that we're a—rather *odd*—lot of tourists, seeing the Mediterranean & bent on enjoyment. War seems infinitely remote: & even the reason, foreseeing Gallipoli, yet admits that there are many blue days to come, & the Cyclades.

I wish I were younger: then the five-pointed jewel would have been the height of my wish. Even now it thrills a little. I wear it.* Please thank Anonyma & say I'm quite sure it'll bring me luck. But what 'Luck' *is*, we'll all wait & see. At least, we'll all wait, & you'll see, perhaps. I can well see that life might be great fun: & I can well see death might be an admirable solution. At that, quote to her something appropriate from the *Apology*, & leave her to her prayers. But first give her a kiss† of pure gratitude from me.

If I write anything, I will send it you. I'm afraid I *shan't* write though.

Everyone you know is well. Patrick is the life & soul of the party —the life, anyhow. Denis is competent, Kelly silly, Johnny inquisitive & simple-hearted, & Oc Oc-like. While Freyberg (whose comment on you is that you're 'a white man'—a great compliment), often rushes across the room to say 'I say, do you think this is going to be a bloody good show? *I* do.'

Nothing amusing has happened. We bullied & cajoled & argued & implored the stokers into being vaccinated & inoculated.

*   *   *

In a fortnight, the quarter-million Turks.

RUPERT

If I'm wounded, or anything, & you have news, will you send it to (a) the Ranee, (b) to Dudley Ward, 33 Upper Richmond Road, East Putney. He's taken in hand the reporting my abrupter turns of fortune to one or two disconnected but deserving enquirers.

* Round my neck with my identification-disk.
† Hand or mouth at your discretion.

To VIOLET ASQUITH   *Hood Battalion*
                                                      2nd Naval Brigade
                                                      [*8 March 1915*]

Four days out.

All day we've been just out of sight of land, thirty or forty miles
away—out of sight, but in smell. There was something earthly in
the air, and warm—like the consciousness of a presence in the dark—
the wind had something Andalusian in it. It wasn't that wall of
scent and invisible blossom and essential spring that knocks you flat,
quite suddenly, as you've come round some unseen corner in the
atmosphere, fifty miles out from a South Sea Island. But it *was* the
good smell of land—and of Spain, too! And Spain I've never seen,
and never shall see, maybe. All day I sat and strained my eyes to see,
over the horizon, orange groves and Moorish buildings and dark-
eyed beauties and guitars and fountains and a golden darkness. But
the curve of the world lay between us. Do you know Jan's favourite
story—told very melodiously with deep voiced reverence—about
Columbus? Columbus wrote a diary (which Jan reads) and described
the coast of America (before Johnny Dodge's day) as he found it—
the divinest place in the world. 'It was only like the Paradise of the
Saints of God'—and then he remembered there was *one* place equal
to it, the place where he was born, and goes on—'or like the gardens
of Andalusia in the spring.'

Another day; off Africa.

My dear, I don't know when, after Malta, I shall be able to get
a letter through. We're in the dreamiest, most utter, most trustful,
ignorance of what's to come. Some even say it'll all be over before
we get there. I hope not: and certainly think not. Impossible.
I rather figure us scrapping forlornly in some corner of the Troad
for years and years. Everyone will forget all about us. We shan't
even be told when peace is declared. . . .

Africa looks too glorious for words. I shall go there the minute
the war's over—no, the minute our two-millions' plunge into luxury
and revelry is over—and spend months there. The mountains look fascinatingly old and wrinkled and ponderous and elephan-
tine: and lovely white mosques and walls and houses, all shining
sunward, are laid along their feet. The sea and sky are all the colours
of a peacock or a rainbow or a puddle of tar. I sit in a busy vacancy
and review my life and the condition of my platoon. And occasionally I dip into a book on the early heresies.

One's so entirely 'surrounded by the horizon of the day', even—perhaps more—in this odd little respite from war. I've not the strength of mind to withdraw myself from the current, and think. Perhaps I never have, even in peace. I'm a hand-to-mouth liver. God help me.   *   *   *

Do not care much what happens to me or what I do. When I give thought to it at all, I hate people—people I like—to care for me. I'm selfish. And nothing but harm ever seems to have come of it, in the past.

I don't know. In some moods that thought seems wrong. Generally right. I don't know the truth about that—or about anything. But somewhere, I think, there's bad luck about me.

There's a very bright sun, and a lot of comedy in the world; so perhaps there's some point in my not getting shot. But Also there's point in my getting shot. Anyway, you're very good to me.

The Staff-Captain is going to seal up the mail bag. Good-bye.

RUPERT

To DUDLEY WARD   *Off Carthage*
S.S. 'Grantully Castle'
8 March [1915]
[Postmark: Base Army P.O.
8 May 1915]

My dear,

Please thank Anne very much for her handkerchiefs. I shall tie them round my scimitar-lopped stumps.

There's nothing much to report about this idyllic respite. The Mediterranean is very blue, the weather very warm, and the mountains of Africa very mysterious. I think this part of the world is immense fun. I, or my ghost, shall often come here after peace.

It is my watch. I have just picked my way over forms recumbent on the deck, and under hammocks, visited twenty sentries, smelt the stale smell of sleeping stokers, and noticed the beginnings of the dawn over Africa. The sky is a grim silver: and beyond Carthage there's a muffled half-moon whirling faintly round in clouds.

I think of joining the Orthodox Church (I've been reading up Constantinople). It hates Jews, Mohammedans and Roman Catholics: all of which is to the good. But it is made up of bloody Orientals and Asiatics, which is bad.

There are a quarter of a million Turks awaiting us. We are ten thousand. This is some expedition. Next year, will Bulair[1] be the most famous name in History?

Take care of Ka.   Ever

RUPERT

I enclose another address for tidings of my casualties. The rest must find out for themselves, damn them.

I'll make Eddie give you tidings if anything happens.

To JACQUES RAVERAT   *S.S. 'Grantully Castle'*
                                        8 March [1915]

Near Africa. On Active Service.

This is probably the first letter you ever got from a Crusader. You expect to hear that we saw the sea-serpent off Algiers, that the Patriarch of Alexandria has blessed us, and that an outbreak of scurvy was healed by a prompt application of the thigh-bones and pelvis of SS. John the Divine, Mary Magdalene, and Chrysostom. Not a bit. But the early Crusaders were very jolly people. I've been reading about them. They set out to slay the Turks—and very finely they did it, when they met them. But when they got East, to the Levant and Constantinople, were they kind to their brother Christians they found there? No. They very properly thwacked and trounced them, and took their money, and cut their throats, and ravished their daughters and so left them: for that they were Greeks, Jews, Slavs, Vlachs, Magyars, Czechs, and Levantines, and not gentlemen.

So shall we do, I hope. But, for the present, we've been gliding through a sapphire sea, swept by ghosts of triremes and quinqueremes, Hannibal on poop, or Hanno. Oh, and we came down by Spain, and saw Algiers, and thought of the tribes of dancing girls, and wept for Andalusia. And now we've left Trinacria behind (you would call it Sicily) and soon—after Malta—we'll be among the Cyclades. There I shall recite Sappho and Homer. And the winds of history will follow us all the way. And you will be in Chelsea (pah!) painting gawky pictures (ugh!) of green-fleshed Northerners (wuff!). Poor devil! I'm a dark-eyed son of the South, hot-blooded and sweet-voiced. Come and see me among the vines, one day. Do not forget me.   Love to you both

RUPERT

Dr Johnson never came. But I have Latin and Greek and Shakespeare.

[1] Bulair (Bulayir) on the neck of the Gallipoli Peninsula.

To EDWARD MARSH   *S.S. 'Grantully Castle'*
                                              off Greece
                                           9 March 1915

My dear,

This is very odd. But I suppose I must imagine my non-existence, & make a few arrangements.

You are to be my literary executor. But I'd like mother to have my MSS till she dies—the actual paper & ink I mean—then you— save one or two you might let Alfred & Katharine Cox have, if they care.

If you want to go through my papers, Dudley Ward'll give you a hand. But you won't find much there. There may be some old stuff at Grantchester.

You must decide everything about publication. Don't print much bad stuff.

Give my love to the New Numbers folk, & Violet & Masefield & a few who'd like it. I've tried to arrange that some money[1] should go to Wilfrid & Lascelles & de la Mare (John is childless) to help them write good stuff, instead of me.

There's nothing much to say. You'll be able to help the Ranee with one or two arrangements.

You've been very good to me. I wish I'd written more. I've been such a failure.   Best love & goodbye
                                              RUPERT

Get Cathleen anything she wants.

To KATHARINE COX   *S.S. 'Grantully Castle'*
                                          10 March 1915

Dear child,

I suppose you're about the best I can do in the way of a widow. I'm telling the Ranee that after she's dead, you're to have my papers. They *may* want to write a biography! How am I to know if I shan't be eminent? And take any MSS you want. Say what you like to the Ranee. But you'd probably better not tell her much. Let her be. Let her think we might have married. Perhaps it's true.

My dear, my dear, you did me wrong: but I have done you very great wrong. Every day I see it greater.

You were the best thing I found in life. If I have memory, I shall

---

[1] The royalties from his book of poems.

remember. You know what I want for you. I hope you will be happy, and marry and have children.

It's a good thing I die.

Good-bye, child
RUPERT

To CATHLEEN NESBITT   *The Aegean*
12 March 1915

Sweet child,

It's a long while since I saw you. And you're a long way away. I've so far been having the most peaceful picturesque romantic unworldly time of my life. What a thing it is to be a soldier, and go lovely yachting cruises in the Mediterranean and the Aegean! We saw—they *said* we saw—very far away, Olympus. But with strong field-glasses I could not certainly see the gods. However, its head was shrouded in mist. Also, there was—I think—Parnassus: even farther away than usual, with Wilfrid and Shakespeare and the rest on it. And my eyes fell on the holy Land of Attica. So I can die.

And now we're—but I daren't say where: though I think they'll keep this letter till all information is quite un-risky. Suffice it that we're out of sight and hearing of war, in a lovely harbour on a blue sea, with lovely hills around and white peaks in the distance; and about us are various lovely warships—not triremes, though—resting between the spells of blowing Turks out of this world into Eternity. At any moment we may be fetched along to kill the Paynim. *Or* we may stay here, the world forgetting, by the world forgot,[1] till July. The latest opinion is that we'll be here, picnicking over the hills and sleeping on board, for a month. We have no news from the world: not even from the Dardanelles. What a peaceful affair the Naval Brigade is!

The queerest and nicest part of the voyage was Malta. We got in about 3 o'clock, and got leave ashore from 5 to midnight. My dear, it's the *loveliest* place in an evening sun. Softly white—grey-silver white—buildings, some very old and some new, round a great harbour, all very Southern: like an Italian town in silver-point: livable and serene, with a sea and sky of opal and pearl and faint gold around. It was nearer than any place I have seen to what a Greek must have witnessed when he sailed into a Greek coast-city. And in the streets—remarkably—was everyone one knew: all the people in

---

[1] Pope's *Eloisa to Abelard*, line 207.

other battalions, and a lot of creatures, last seen in London, who'd
been taken on at the last minute. And after a Maltese dinner we all
went to a very jolly Italian opera house, where *La Tosca* was being
played, and saw still more people we knew and waved and shrieked
and threw things to attract their attention, till the stalls and boxes
were one mass of Khaki-clothed laughers saying to each other 'How
in Hell did you get here'. (For each boat had come alone all the way.)
And then we went back happy to our different transports: and at
dawn next day started for—no one knew what. So. Such is life.
Tomorrow we may be off...But I fear a long pause.

With love
RUPERT

To DUDLEY WARD
[Envelope marked: 'If I die to be sent to Dudley Ward', etc.
There is also a copy of this letter]

S.S. 'Grantully Castle'
Lemnos
17 March 1915

My dear Dudley,

You'll already have done a few jobs for me. Here are some more.

My private papers and letters I'm leaving to my mother, and when
she dies, to Ka.

But I want you, now—I've told my mother—to go through my
letters (they're mostly together, but some scattered) and *destroy* all
those from (a) Elizabeth van Rysselberghe. These are signed E. v. R.:
and in a handwriting you'll pick out easily, once you've seen it.
They'll begin in the beginning of 1909 or 1910, my first visit to
Munich, and be rather rare except in one or two bunches.

(b) Lady Eileen Wellesley: also in a handwriting you'll recognize
quickly, and generally signed Eileen. They date from last July on.

If other people, Ka, for instance, agitate to have letters destroyed,
why, you're the person to do it. I don't much care what goes.

*   *   *

Indeed, why keep anything? Well, I *might* turn out to be eminent
and biographiable. If so, let them know the poor truths. Rather
pathetic this.

It's odd, being dead. I'm afraid it'll finish off the Ranee. What else is there? Eddie will be my literary executor. So you'll have to confer with him.

Be good to Ka.

Give Jacques and Gwen my love.

Try to inform Taata of my death. Mlle Taata, Hotel Tiare, Papeete, Tahiti. It might find her. Give her my love.

My style is rather like St Paul's. You'll have to give the Ranee a hand about me: because she knows so little about great parts of my life. There are figures might want books or something of mine. Noel and her sisters, Justin, Geoffrey, Hugh Russell-Smith. How could she distinguish among them?...Their names make me pleasantly melancholy.

But the realization of failure makes me *unpleasantly* melancholy. Enough.

Good luck and all love to you and Anne.

Call a boy after me. RUPERT

[Note enclosed in above letter:]

'Circulate these—
if I'm killed.
The last, little pecks
Make the beggars jump. R.'

['These' are letters addressed to several friends.]

To JACQUES RAVERAT
Off Gallipoli *18 March 1915*
My dear,

I turn to you. Keep innumerable flags flying. I've only two decent reasons for being sorry for dying—(several against)—I want to destroy some evils, and to cherish some goods. Do it for me. You understand. I doubt if anyone else does—almost.

Best love to you both
RUPERT

To MRS BROOKE   *20 March 1914* [*1915*]

Dear Mother,

All's going very well and quietly. I went to dinner on the large boat—a Cunarder—where the Divisional staff, among others, are—one night, and saw George Peel who enquired after you. Yesterday came a post, with a card from Aunt Fanny, and a *Land and Water*, all sent on from Blandford. Other letters are *said* to be waiting on the chief transport: and we shall get them tomorrow. The letters we send out are all censored now: not (I fancy) the letters we receive. A day or two ago we and certain others steamed off overnight to near an important spot on an enemy coast, and 'stood by' at dawn for landing. I felt very nervous, and rather irritated at getting up so early, and most excited. But nothing happened where we were for some reason: and off we went home. So really nothing's happening. I've had several good bathes.

*   *   *
                                  With love
                                  RUPERT

To KATHARINE COX   *19–24 March*
                          [*Postmark: 6 April 1915*]
                    Somewhere
Dear Ka,   (some way from the front)

Your letter of the 3rd of March has just reached me. Fairly quick. There are said to be 80 bags of mail still (parcels, if anything, I suspect) at headquarters (here). But your letter is the only letter I've had since we sailed. It *is* fun getting letters. Tell people—Dudley and such—to write occasionally. I can't write much. There's very little I *could*, of interest. And that, as a rule, I *mayn't*. This letter is to be censored by the Brigade Chaplain. It's not quite so nice getting letters here, as when I was in the South Seas, perhaps. Yet, I don't know. There one was lonelier, in a way. At least, much more solitary: here one has jolly and fairly *sympathetic* people. But there one's interest and appreciation were continually aroused: one was amused. Here three-quarters of the day is dullish—routine—and the society is unnatural—over a long period—all men. Anyway, it's nice to hear.

The same post brought Denis Browne a Working Men's College Journal, with a lecture by Morgan Forster, in it. It's odd seeing what the chrysalises think. You see *I'm* in it, and the Ranee (say)'s in it. But Forster's pathetically—where—on a hundred verges: or behind them. But he seems far nicer than most of them: though pathetically—outside. (The point of war is that it *brings out* their *exteriority*—which they *have* everywhen and everywhere, in the peacefullest of 1913 luncheons or nightmares.) They're like nice and nasty children outside a circus, who alternately try to peep under the flaps and explain to each other how they despise circuses. They've lost or given away their sixpences. It's rot to say Shakespere isn't English, or Wagner German. But he's nice about the soul of man. But oh! doesn't he *suspect* that the nobilities he whinnies for, come out more in war than in peace? I sometimes pray that some of these people may be allowed to see war: more often that they may see peace: but either is very unlikely.

Yes: this is romantic. (But I won't admit that Flanders isn't.) But I'm afraid I can't tell you most of the romantic things, at present.

My own lot have seen no fighting yet, and very likely won't for months. The only thing that seems almost certain is that one doesn't know from day to day what's to happen. The other day we—some of us—were told that we sailed next day to make a landing. A few thousand of us. Off we stole that night through the phosphorescent Aegean, scribbling farewell letters, and snatching periods of dream-broken, excited sleep. At four we rose, buckled on our panoply, hung ourselves with glasses compasses periscopes revolvers food and the rest, and had a stealthy large breakfast. *That* was a mistake. It is ruinous to load up one's belly four or five hours before it expects it: it throws the machinery out of gear for a week. I felt extremely ill the rest of that day.

We paraded in silence, under paling stars, along the sides of the ship. The darkness on the sea was full of scattered flashing lights, hinting at our fellow-transports and the rest. Slowly the day became wan and green and the sea opal. Everyone's face looked drawn and ghastly. *If* we landed, my company was to be the first to land... We made out that we were only a mile or two from a dim shore. I was seized with an agony of remorse that I hadn't taught my platoon a thousand things more energetically and competently. The light grew. The shore looked to be crammed with Fate, and most ominously silent. One man thought he saw a camel through his glasses...

There were some hours of silence.

About seven someone said 'We're going home.' We dismissed the stokers, who said, quietly, 'When's the next battle?'; and disempanoplied, and had another breakfast. If we were a 'feint', or if it was too rough to land, or, in general, what little part we blindly played, we never knew, and shall not. Still, we did our bit; not ignobly, I trust. We did not see the enemy. We did not fire at them; nor they at us. It seemed improbable they saw us. One of B Company—she was rolling very slightly—was sick on parade. Otherwise, no casualties. A notable battle.

All is well. Good-bye.   RUPERT

Later.

We're off to *Egypt*: for repose. For—I imagine—a month at least. What a life! Another campaign over!   R.

To MRS BROOKE   *Egypt*
                                                 5 April 1915

Dear Mother,

Here we still are: though not for long, perhaps. It's not been a bad time in some ways: but on the days when there's a bit of a sandstorm, life is almost insupportable. I went down with a slight touch of sunstroke a few days ago. Nothing bad, but enough to make me feel pretty miserable, for a little. Patrick Shaw Stewart had it a day or two, before me, and now we're both lying in a quiet hotel bedroom, having moved away from Camp. We shall stay here a few days: to get quite well. We ought to be all right in time for any work. It began with a racking headache, sickness and incessant diarrhoea. Feeding on arrowroot has brought the diarrhoea under a good deal: and my temperature and headache have vanished. So I'm well on the way to recovery. So is Shaw Stewart. A good many of the men have had the same. The glare is awful here.

The first day I was sick—before I got out of camp—was the day when our new G.O.C. in Chief[1]—you'll know who that is—reviewed us. I'd met him once or twice in London. He came to see me after the review and talked for a bit. He offered me a sort of galloper–*aide-de-camp* job on his staff: but I shan't take it. Anyhow, not now, not till this present job's over. Afterwards, if I've had enough of the regimental officer's work, I might like it. But I'm very happy where I am. I'm with quite a good lot of fellows.

---

[1] Sir Ian Hamilton.

I'm sending you a little old small glass bottle I picked up in a bazaar. It's *supposed*, I think, to be an old Egyptian tear-bottle, found in a tomb. But I imagine it's really very recently manufactured. Still it's amusing; and if you clean out the inside with a little warm water, it might look nice, and hold scent.

I was going to write to Alfred to say it was still open to him to come into the R.N.D. when he liked, if he could work the transfer. But I got today a letter from Dent, dated March 12, saying he heard Alfred was off to France that day. I suppose I shall hear if that's so.

The posts are odd. I got a letter from Eddie, March 17 or 18, a Nation, March 8, from you and this from Dent. I think most intermediate letters are somewhere else: waiting to be sent on. They'll catch us up some time.

The pyjamas and handkerchiefs arrived, safe though battered, and the cover much torn; many thanks.

*   *   *

With love
RUPERT

To CATHLEEN NESBITT   *Egypt*
Early in April [*1915*]

Dear child,

I've torn off the heading of this note-paper, so that you shan't know where I am. However, it's not very interesting.

I bought in a bazaar, a real Eastern bazaar, a necklace—or what you will—of amber. It seemed to me pleasant. If ever it gets past the Censor, the Customs, and the thieves, it'll get to you. Smile on it. I doubt if it's worth your wearing. But you may cut it up & turn it to something else. Anyway, there it is: a memorial of one more land my wandering foot has trodden.

Our peaceful existence continues. But it will very soon be over. How long our little corner of the universal war will last, you in England know better than we. But I think nobody knows.

We've been having a pleasant little rest in Egypt, after the exertions of our trip among the islands of Greece. I've seen various things I wanted to see, but had not thought to visit so soon.

We encamped on—it isn't particularizing to say—sand; loose, hot, bloody sand. We ate sand and drank it, and breathed and thought and dreamed it. And above all a fierce torrid sun. After a few days, I and one or two more, rather indignantly, collapsed. Sunstroke is bad. It destroys all the harmonies of the body and of the soul. I had the biggest headache in the world, and a diarrhoea that was part of the cosmic process. Even yet I am but a funnel through which arrowroot is poured. But I lie, in some peace—and much better—on a cool hotel bed. And I think I'll be well for the fighting!

Love

RUPERT

To LASCELLES ABERCROMBIE   *Egypt*
                                              6 April 1915

My dear Lascelles,

The Sun God (he, the Song God) distinguished one of his most dangerous rivals since Marsyas among the X thousand tanned and dirty men blown suddenly on these his special coasts a few days or weeks ago. He unslung his bow. I lie in an hotel, cool at length, with wet cloths on my head and less than nothing in my belly.

*   *   *

I shall be all right in time for the fighting, I hope and believe. (Later) at sea I know now—more certainly every day—what a campaign is. I had a suspicion from Antwerp. It is continual crossing from one place to another, and back, over dreamlike seas: anchoring, or halting, in the oddest places, for nobody knows or quite cares how long; drifting on, at last, to some other, equally unexpected, equally out of the way, equally odd spot: for all the world like a bottle in some corner of the bay at a seaside resort. Somewhere, sometimes, there is fighting. Not for us. In the end, no doubt, our apparently aimless course will drift us through, or anchor us in, a blaze of war, quite suddenly; and as suddenly swirl us out again. Meanwhile—the laziest loitering lotus-day I idled away as a wanderer in the South Seas was a bustle of decision and purpose compared to a campaign.

One just hasn't, though, the time and detachment to write, I find. But I've been collecting a few words, detaching lines from the ambient air, collaring one or two of the golden phrases that a certain wind blows from (will the Censor let me say?) Olympus, across these purple seas. In time, if I'm spared, they'll bloom into a sort of threnody—really a discussion of England—which I have in my head, which has signs of merit.

I wonder if you're an A.S.C. train officer, or a Lowell lecturer, by now. Have your plans matured, at all? Has Eddie pushed you into one of the various R.N.D. transport vacancies created by our removal in this crusade? It would be fun if one could think you were coming out in a future batch—in time to reverse 1453, and celebrate mass in St Sophia. I have little news from England. Posts wait for us all over the place: few have yet found me. I saw a notice of N[ew] N[umbers] 4 in the *Times*: by a laudatory half-wit. He didn't seem to realize that it was 'good-bye'. Perhaps we should have put in a slip to say so; and extracted, even in these times, a few tears, a few shillings.

I may not tell you all I've seen. But your mouth would water. Perhaps Eddie'll tell you: Come and join us.

Is it spring yet with you? For once I almost don't envy the English spring. Almost I have an older one.

Is Wilfrid well? and Mrs W.? My love to them; and to you all.

Ever

RUPERT

To VIOLET ASQUITH *Egypt*
9 April 1915

I'll try to write you a good account of things sometime—when there's anything to write about. Or when, even, I'm just a bit more energetically cree-ative about the various shades and degrees of non-happening through which we loiter. But just now—for these six days—I've been a victim to the sun. He struck me down, all unaware, the day before Sir Ian inspected us. I lay, racked by headache and diarrhoea, under an awning on the sand, while the stokers trudged past. Afterwards, Sir Ian came to see me a moment. A notable meeting: it was generally felt: our greatest poet-soldier and our greatest soldier-poet. We talked blank verse. He looked very worn and white-haired. I thought him a little fearful—not *fearful*, but less than cock-sure—about the job. Later, they took me out of Camp to this hotel, where I've been cool and starving and convalescent. My fellow-sufferer is—Patrick! in the other corner of the room. Not a bad fellow-invalid, when chastened by arrowroot: gay and unchanging and superficially (oh, no doubt really, too!) sympathetic. An appearance of sympathy is what one wants, when sick. Real sympathy is the further call of the hale. I wished you were here: with your experience of internal disease in Egypt—and of my morose invalid manner. Couldn't you have cured—or, certainly, *healed*—me more swiftly? Anyhow, here I am, well up on that difficult slope that leads from arrowroot past chicken broth, by rice puddings, to eggs in milk, and so to eggs, and boiled fish, and finally (they say) chicken and fruit and even real meat. But that is still beyond the next crest. On! on! But while I shall be well, I think, for our first thrust into the fray (unless senility overtakes me), I shall be able to give my Turk, at the utmost a kitten's tap. A diet of arrowroot does not build up violence. I am as weak as a pacifist. The better able to survey and note, maybe. My horror is, just now, that we shall be shut away in some delightful base, till the time comes to be poured in. In we shall go, and see our own bit of fun, and that's all. I hope to God we may be in a position where we can see the various other elements in our motley force doing their little stunts—such as they do before us.

I poked about in a bazaar. And I there found a foolish little bluish stone, like London milk or the white of an uncooked egg. It reminded me of a worser lyric by Keats. I had it sent you—or perhaps the Egyptians, in packing, stole it—in the slight hope that *something* might reach you from me on your birthday (but it won't): and that it might at least say that there I *was*, more tourist still than soldier, and, in my watery amorphous aimlessness, my solitude, my (I thought) almost charming moony pathos, not unlike that blear little stone.

We're a gay enough little party in the Hood. A softened Colonel is well and patient. Charles I like more as I see him more. I didn't realize what awareness and subtlety he concealed under that equine madness. Imagine what an extraordinary, an unprecedented, con-glomeration of sound Oc and I and Denis Browne put up with, when you learn that Patrick with his loud titter, Cleg Kelly with his whinny, and Charles with his great neigh, are all in the same tent. The sound from it frights the Egyptian night, and sends the ghosts of Antony and the gypsy scudding away across the sand.

We had a delicious glimpse of Aubrey and Mary in —— I forgot, I mayn't say! And rode wildly on donkeys through white and black mysterious streets at midnight under a full moon. A *most* odd dream. My attention was divided between a perishable donkey and Immortal Beauty. Both seemed just to evade me. We seemed more than usually incidental.   *   *   *

The *Times* cutting—Eddie sent it to me too—gratified me in my weak state. But it was so badly written, and the fellow thought my *golden star* poem[1] an inverted sonnet! So I couldn't feel his praise highly complimentary. Still, it was a knock for Shakespeare. I've written nothing. I've made two or three faint attempts at an Ode or Threnody: a very serene affair, full of major chords and larger outlooks, like an English lawn at sunset. But I haven't, even loitering on the Aegean, even on our world-forgotten laughing little island, had just the necessary detachment. I suppose it won't be finished. Perhaps if I'm wounded...

I fasten my eyes on the horizon for your hospital ship. Bring out a delicious lot of books. But I fear none of us'll be wounded for a long long time yet.
                                                                Ever

                                                    RUPERT

To EDWARD MARSH   *At sea*
                                                    April [*1915*]
Dear Eddie,

When I had a touch of the sun, in Egypt, I saw a lovely letter of yours to Denis—the only breath of England I've felt. You seemed to have been in very perilous places: far more, certainly, than we.

Patrick & I are both hale & fit again, though notably thinner. However, as everyone has grown very fat on idleness, it's as well. The first few days afloat I was still convalescent. So I could lie in my bunk & read & write in a delicious solitude all day. I actually *did* jot down a line or two. Nothing yet complete (except a song, worthless alone, for Denis to put lovely notes around): but a sonnet or two almost done: & the very respectable & shapely skeleton of an ode-threnody. All of which shall travel to you, if & when they are done.

I saw Sir Ian—or rather, he saw me: lying (did you see Denis' photograph of me?) on a couch of pain. It was very sweet of him. He made a proposal, which, for the time, I didn't accept. It hangs vaguely over my future. It might be fun, after a campaign in my present capacity. But it's really so jolly being with Oc & Denis & Charles & Patrick & Kelly, that it'll have to be very tempting company to persuade me to give it up.

I cannot write you any description of my life. It is entirely featureless. It would need Miss Austen to make anything of it. We

[1] 'The Treasure', *New Numbers*, 4, Dec. 1914.

glide to & fro on an azure sea & forget the war—I must go & censor my platoon's letters.

My long poem is to be about the existence—& non-locality—of England. And it contains the line—

'In Avons of the heart her rivers run.'

Lovely, isn't it?

Freyberg sends his chin-chin. I've no doubt there'd be other messages, if I could find anyone.　　Ever

RUPERT

I do think we're awfully lucky to have our new G.O.C. in C. I hope he'll be very brilliant over it.

To MRS BROOKE　　　　　　　　　　*20 April* [*1915*]

Same address. 4 a.m. On watch

Dear Mother,

Still aboard, and still in the peacefullest surroundings.

We've only got, so far, about 30% of our mail, I judge: and that in little lumps, with gaps. I can judge fairly well by the *Nation* and *Land and Water*, and by the number of periodicals other people get. A little batch of several letters of about March 30 was the last I got. But things March 5–15 are still astray. Two bags of *somebody's* mail has gone overboard in harbour, they say, some weeks ago. I got, by hand, a letter or two from Eddie, and one from Downing Street yesterday. I gather there has been confusion. Ian Hamilton, quite out of his own head, asked me if I'd like to be attached to his staff as a sort of 'galloper' and odd-jobber—'A.D.C.'. He'd tell Eddie and some others he was going to ask me. But I'd made up my mind to see at any rate some of a campaign in my present capacity: and I'm very happy as I am, with several people I like: and it wouldn't be very fair to my company to leave it suddenly at the last moment like this, with a gap it couldn't fill, out here. So we agreed—I. H. and I—that I'd go through this campaign or campaignlet or part of it, and, in the general and unforeseeable re-organization at the end of it, accept his offer, probably, then. He said it would still be open. And there we left it. But I gather that Eddie, thinking I was certain to accept straight off, and being misled by a foolish train of circumstances, jumped to the conclusion I was already transferred: and told you so. The train was this. He told Lady Lytton Sir Ian had asked me. Lady Lytton told Lady Hamilton Sir Ian had put me on his staff. And Lady H. wrote Eddie a note, saying how pleased she was to hear I'd been put—etc.! So Eddie, thinking she'd heard from Sir Ian I *was* already *on*, concluded it was decided, and, I understand, told you so. So I'm afraid he deceived you, into anticipating events by a few months.

However, I gather we're pretty well as safe as if we were all Staff officers, so all's well. There's no further news. I'd like to hear if Alfred is going to France, or elsewhere. If you have any important piece of news, you might repeat it in two or three letters: as the odds are I shall only get one of them.

I think I forgot to tell you that when I was in Cairo, in the Egyptian Army Headquarters Stores, buying a few things, a clergyman in khaki with a flowing black beard came up and spoke to me, and I suddenly recognized Ross,[1] of our house, who is chaplain to the Lancashire division of Territorials in Egypt. Rather a funny meeting.

I see George Peel occasionally. 	Best love

	RUPERT

W. DENIS BROWNE *to* EDWARD MARSH

Off Gallipoli,
The Hood Battalion
Royal Naval Division
Sunday, 25 April [1915]

My dear Eddie,

I wonder how long after you hear the terrible news it will be before you get this. The tragedy was so sudden, so inexplicable, so hopeless; the loss so unspeakable.

Here are the bare facts.

We got to Port Said on Sat. Mar. 27 from Lemnos. So far Rupert had been quite himself. On Monday (29th) he went to Cairo with Oc & Patrick, & stayed for two days, coming back to Port Said on Mar. 31st (Wed.). I went to Cairo that same night, passing Rupert in the train at Ismailia & came back 2 days later on Friday to find him ill with a touch of the sun, a headache & sickness. He slept or dozed outside his tent under an awning all Saturday just as you see him in

---

[1] The Rev. J. E. C. Ross was at School Field, Rugby, with R.B.

a photo I sent you. It was taken that very day. In the morning, about 11 o'clock he was visited by Sir Ian, who apparently asked him to go on his Staff, but he refused. Rupert never told any of us about this, but it seems to be true. I suppose he wouldn't leave his platoon or Freyberg. At 4 in the afternoon he went off in a cab to the Casino Palace Hotel, where he found Patrick who had been laid up with the same thing a day earlier; and they shared a room (no. 17). As he got better he developed a little sore on the right side of his upper lip. It swelled up slightly for about 2 days & then went away. He did not come back to camp before we left Port Said, but he & Patrick came aboard the Grantully Castle the evening before we left (Ap. 9th). We sailed on Sat. April 10th at 6 a.m. We steamed only 4 knots an hour as we were towing a large lighter, which we lost near Cos & wasted a day in recovering: so that it took us 7 days to reach Skyros (via Lemnos) where we anchored on the evening of April 17 (Sat.). Rupert & Patrick got up on the 3rd day of the voyage & R. gradually took up his duties again. He was thinner than I ever remember to have seen him, & weak in proportion; but he picked up as time went on & though he was not up to any great exertion he was well on the way to being quite himself again. He was always cheerful, & perfectly normal at this time, & we all thought he was quite fit.

We anchored in Trebuki Bay (see R's sketch-map) & went ashore from time to time by companies. On Tuesday last (Ap. 20th) he took part in a Divisional Field Day, most of which was confined to a river-bed valley between Mts Paphko & Komaro, with Mt Khokilas (the highest point of the island) at its head. A mile up this valley above the dry river bed is an olive grove of a dozen trees, which I'd noticed two days before for its extraordinary beauty, & here Rupert, Patrick, Charles Lister & I sat while we were resting in the afternoon. He liked the place & spoke of it: and it was here that we buried him.

After a long day from 8 to 4 he came back to the ship rather tired. Our table in the saloon (Rupert, Oc, Patrick, Charles, Cleg & I always sat together) invited a party from the Franconia to dinner, but only Cherry & Kershaw came. Rupert was quiet & talked very little and went to bed early.

Next morning he stayed in bed, feeling seedy I heard. Somehow I did not see him until after dinner that night, when I looked in to ask how he was & to show him the Times cutting of Inge's sermon[1]

[1] Delivered on Easter Sunday 1915 and quoting the sonnet, 'If I should die'.

with the quotation of his sonnet. He said he felt very bad & didn't want the light on. He then said he had seen the cutting (did you send it?) & was sorry that Inge didn't think he was as good as Isaiah. He complained of a swelling on the left side of his upper lip. He was evidently not up to very much, & I left him.

Next morning (Thursday) he was worse. The Battn. Surgeon (McCracken) was not anxious about his lip, but was worried because he had pain in his chest & back. I looked in three times during the day, but he was dozing & I didn't like to disturb him. At midday McCracken got really anxious & sent for the A.D.M.S. Gaskell, the D.A.D.M.S. Casement, & the Brigade S.M.O. Schlesinger (whom I recognized as a Guy's man). They came over about 3 & consulted with McCracken & Goodale (the ship's surgeon & a good bacterio-logist), & the conclusion they arrived at was that he had practically no chance of getting over it: the diagnosis was acute blood-poison-ing. They proposed operating by making an incision in an abscess which had formed on the left side of the neck & was pumping the infected blood from his lip all over the body. But before they could do this, we had the idea of getting him on to a hospital ship. There was a French hospital ship, the Duguay-Trouin, in Skyros, & we asked them to take him in, as anything would have been better than the stuffy cabin he was in, and there were no proper facilities on the Grantully Castle for nursing him. In less than half an hour we had carried him down into a pinnace and taken him straight aboard the Duguay-Trouin. They put him in the best cabin, one of two set back to back on the sun deck aft, on the highest part of the ship. She was originally a naval school at Brest, built in 1878, & was converted in 24 hours into a hospital: everything was very roomy & comfortable, if old-fashioned; but they had every modern appliance & the surgeons did everything they possibly could. He was practically the only patient on the ship & the chief surgeon gave up his whole time to the case, & I believe hardly left him at all. Whether they made the incision in his neck on Thursday night I don't know. Schlesinger said they would probably 'irrigate' the place with antiseptic. Oc & I left him about 6 when we could do nothing more & went to the Franconia, where we sent a wireless message to Admiralty & also one to the G.O.C. in C at Lemnos. We had hoped that he might be able to send either the Sudan or the Cecilia off to Skyros, or, failing that, to send a couple of sisters from the Cecilia in a destroyer. But that would have been no use as Gaskell said it would be impossible to move him again on to another ship: and as a matter of fact all the G.O.C. did was (I believe) to send a message to ask how he was.

Next morning Oc & I went over in a steam pinnace soon after breakfast to see what we could do: and found him very much weaker, but not quite so bad as Schlesinger expected. I stayed on board till 2.30, but there was nothing to be done as he was quite unconscious & they were busy trying all the devices they could think of to do him good & give him ease. Not that he was suffering, for he was barely conscious all Thursday (he just said 'Hallo' when I went to lift him out into the pinnace) & on Friday he was not conscious at all up to the very last & felt no pain whatever. At 2 o'clock the head surgeon told me he was sinking & I went off to the Franconia for the Chaplain for his mother's sake. The chaplain (Failes by name) came back with me & saw him, but he was unconscious so after saying a few prayers he went away. Oc had arrived at 2.30 & I brought Schlesinger from the Royal George. He confirmed the change & told me that it was simply a matter of hours. Oc then went off to see about preliminary arrangements and I sat with Rupert. At 4 o'clock he became weaker & at 4.46 he died.

We had orders to sail next morning at 6 for Gallipoli: and the French ship was off at the same moment for Asia Minor. So Oc & I had to decide at once what to do.

We buried him the same evening in the olive grove I mentioned before—one of the loveliest places on this earth, with grey-green olives round him, one weeping above his head: the ground covered with flowering sage, bluish grey & smelling more delicious than any other flower I know. The path up to it from the sea is narrow & difficult and very stony: it runs by the bed of a dried-up torrent. He was carried up from the boat by his A Company petty officers, led by his platoon-sergeant Saunders: and it was with enormous difficulty that they got the coffin up the narrow way. The journey of a mile took two hours. It was not till 11 that I saw them coming (I had gone up to choose the place & with Freyberg & Charles Lister I turned the sods of his grave: we had some of his platoon to dig). First came one of his men carrying a great white wooden cross with his name painted on it in black: then the firing party, commanded by Patrick; & then the coffin followed by our officers, General Paris, Saunders & one or two others of the Brigade Staff. The Commodore could not be there, nor was Maxwell. Think of it all under a clouded moon, with the three mountains around & behind us, and those divine scents everywhere. We lined his grave with all the flowers we could find & Quilter set a wreath of olive on the coffin. The funeral service was very simply said by the Chaplain and after the Last Post the little lamp-lit procession went once again down the narrow path to the sea.

Freyberg, Oc, I, Charles & Cleg stayed behind & covered the grave with great pieces of white marble which were lying everywhere about. Of the cross at his head you know: it was the large one that headed the procession. On the back of it our Greek interpreter, a man picked up by Oc at Lemnos, wrote, in pencil

ἐνθάδε κεῖται
ὁ δοῦλος τοῦ θεοῦ
ἀνθυπολοχαγὸς τοῦ
Ἀγγλικοῦ Ναυτικοῦ
ἀποθανὼν ὑπὲρ τῆς
ἀπελευθερώσεως τῆς
Κων· πόλεως ἀπὸ
τῶν Τουρκῶν.[1]

It was quite spontaneous, and, don't you think, apt. At his feet was a small wooden cross sent by his platoon.

We could not see the grave again as we sailed from Skyros the next morning at 6 (Sat. Ap. 23rd) [really 24th].

These are some of the bare facts: forgive me for telling them so confusedly & badly. I have had so many interruptions—all day we have been waiting for orders to land on Gallipoli.

I thought you would care to have the facts as they happened. What I can't write about is the irreparable loss that his death is to all of us. That he was taken just the day before we began fighting is in some ways saddest of all. Yet if he had gone from us later we might never have been able to see to his burial. We felt that he would hate to be buried at sea: he actually said in chance talk some time ago that he would like to be buried in a Greek island.

And he lies now in the loveliest of them all in the most heavenly place it can show—he wouldn't wish a better grave, nor, I think, a different burial.

I could speak to you about him better than I can write. It is all so near, so impossible. One can't realize that that spirit that knew and loved all the beautiful things of the world so strongly is cut off from them for ever.

---

[1] Here lies the servant of God, Sub-Lieutenant in the English Navy, who died for the deliverance of Constantinople from the Turks.

He will not miss his immortality. I like to think he went when he had just given his best, when his powers were at their real zenith—& not before.

And yet—the awfulness of it goes on & the blank is there for us all.   W. D. B.

W. DENIS BROWNE *to* EDWARD MARSH

[*April 1915*]

This is our first day under fire; that is, we are lying within 6000 yds of land & one of our cruisers has been bombarding a fort. No Turks are in sight anywhere; but our boats have just come back from a little demonstration close in to the shore & Freyberg has just gone off on a flare-lighting expedition—swimming. We are all anxious about him.

He has been wonderful the last few days. He loved & understood Rupert intuitively in spite of the differences in their temperaments; and last night, when we were making the grave, he was as gentle as a woman, and as strong as a giant.

But they all loved him, Patrick, Charles & Cleg; his men especially.

I can't write you any more just now: I have written fully to his Mother.

We are putting all his things in charge of the purser of this ship: he will send them direct to you for you to do what you think best. I am sure Dudley Ward will do anything to help you. I found one little black notebook & four sheets of notepaper which are all that remains of an ode he was working on. I send a copy of that with this letter. But it must have been mostly in his head, for he spoke of it as being a great new thing he was doing. He quoted once to me the line—(In Avons of the heart her rivers run)—as being one he was delighted with: 'supreme' he said; & a week before his death he gave me a copy of 'The Dance'[1] which he said was not a very good little poem, but rather Elizabethan in feeling & suited to music. He put it—that a bad poem would go to music, while a good one rarely would.

You have everything, to do what you will with it. All Oc & I have done is to sort out things & letters. Several gifts I thought

---

[1] First printed in *The Book of the Homeless*, London, 1916, edited by Edith Wharton and sold for the benefit of Belgian refugees; afterwards included in *Collected Poems*, 1918.

I could identify & marked them in envelopes. One or two things we have kept for the use of his men—a periscope, a compass, some cigarettes and chocolate. It seemed that they would be more use here than if we sent them home.

Johnny Dodge & two others (unknown to you—Gamage & Trimmer) have been snatched away with 150 men to go on trawlers. We don't know where they are.   D.

W. DENIS BROWNE *to* EDWARD MARSH[1]

[*June 1915*]

My dear,

I've gone now too; not too badly I hope. I'm luckier than Rupert, because I've fought. But there's no one to bury me as I buried him, so perhaps he's best off in the long run.

I got a little image from a tomb for you at Cairo: will you ask my mother for it? It is with the rest of my things, packed in a cigarette box.

Dent is looking after my MS music.

Good-bye, my dear, & bless you always for all your goodness to me.

W. D. B.

[1] Written by W.D.B. in anticipation of his death, shortly before he was killed in trench fighting at Gallipoli on 7 June.

INDEX